1 Kings

Reformed Expository Commentary

A Series

Series Editors

Richard D. Phillips
Philip Graham Ryken

Testament Editors

Iain M. Duguid, Old Testament
Daniel M. Doriani, New Testament

1 Kings

PHILIP GRAHAM RYKEN

P&R
PUBLISHING
P.O. BOX 817 • PHILLIPSBURG • NEW JERSEY 08865-0817

Page design by Lakeside Design Plus

Printed in the United States of America

Library of Congress Cataloging-in-Publication Data

Ryken, Philip Graham, 1966-
  1 Kings / Philip Graham Ryken.
      p. cm. -- (Reformed expository commentary)
  Includes bibliographical references and indexes.
  ISBN 978-1-59638-208-4 (cloth)
  1. Bible. O.T. Kings, 1st--Commentaries. I. Title. II. Title: First Kings.
  BS1335.53.R95 2011
  222'.53077--dc22

                        2011012701

To

David Apple, Adam Brice, Pat Canavan, Marion Clark, Andrew Dinardo, Cora Hogue, Paul Jones, Philip Kirkland, Bruce McDowell, Jerry McFarland, Jonny McGreevy, Aaron Messner, Jonathan Olsen, Rick Phillips, Robert Polen, Chris Seah, Bryan Stoudt, Paul Tripp, and Carroll Wynne

– my colleagues and friends –

with genuine admiration for your service to Christ, deep appreciation for your encouragement through prayer, and everlasting gratitude to God for the ministry we have shared at Philadelphia's Tenth Presbyterian Church

CONTENTS

Contents

Series Introduction

In every generation there is a fresh need for the faithful exposition of God's Word in the church. At the same time, the church must constantly do the work of theology: reflecting on the teaching of Scripture, confessing its doctrines of the Christian faith, and applying them to contemporary culture. We believe that these two tasks—the expositional and the theological—are interdependent. Our doctrine must derive from the biblical text, and our understanding of any particular passage of Scripture must arise from the doctrine taught in Scripture as a whole.

We further believe that these interdependent tasks of biblical exposition and theological reflection are best undertaken in the church, and most specifically in the pulpits of the church. This is all the more true since the study of Scripture properly results in doxology and praxis—that is, in praise to God and practical application in the lives of believers. In pursuit of these ends, we are pleased to present the Reformed Expository Commentary as a fresh exposition of Scripture for our generation in the church. We hope and pray that pastors, teachers, Bible study leaders, and many others will find this series to be a faithful, inspiring, and useful resource for the study of God's infallible, inerrant Word.

The Reformed Expository Commentary has four fundamental commitments. First, these commentaries aim to be *biblical*, presenting a comprehensive exposition characterized by careful attention to the details of the text. They are not exegetical commentaries—commenting word by word or even verse by verse—but integrated expositions of whole passages of Scripture. Each commentary will thus present a sequential, systematic treatment of an entire book of the Bible, passage by passage. Second, these commentaries are unashamedly *doctrinal*. We are committed to the Westminster Confession of Faith and catechisms as containing the system of doctrine taught in the Scriptures of the Old and New Testaments. Each volume will teach, promote, and defend the doctrines of the Reformed faith as they are found in the Bible. Third, these commentaries are *redemptive-historical* in their orientation. We believe in the unity of the Bible and its central message of salvation in Christ. We are thus committed to a Christ-centered view of the Old Testament, in which its characters, events, regulations, and institutions are properly understood as pointing us to Christ and his gospel, as well as giving us examples to follow in living by faith. Fourth, these commentaries are *practical*, applying the text of Scripture to contemporary challenges of life—both public and private—with appropriate illustrations.

The contributors to the Reformed Expository Commentary are all pastor-scholars. As pastor, each author will first present his expositions in the pulpit ministry of his church. This means that these commentaries are rooted in the teaching of Scripture to real people in the church. While aiming to be scholarly, these expositions are not academic. Our intent is to be faithful, clear, and helpful to Christians who possess various levels of biblical and theological training—as should be true in any effective pulpit ministry. Inevitably this means that some issues of academic interest will not be covered. Nevertheless, we aim to achieve a responsible level of scholarship, seeking to promote and model this for pastors and other teachers in the church. Significant exegetical and theological difficulties, along with such historical and cultural background as is relevant to the text, will be treated with care.

We strive for a high standard of enduring excellence. This begins with the selection of the authors, all of whom have proved to be outstanding communicators of God's Word. But this pursuit of excellence is also reflected in a disciplined editorial process. Each volume is edited by both a series editor and a testament editor. The testament editors, Iain Duguid for the Old Testament and Daniel Doriani for the New Testament, are accomplished pastors and respected scholars who have taught at the seminary level. Their job is to ensure that each volume is sufficiently conversant with up-to-date scholarship and is faithful and accurate in its exposition of the text. As series editors, we oversee each volume to ensure its overall quality—including excellence of writing, soundness of teaching, and usefulness in application. Working together as an editorial team, along with the publisher, we are devoted to ensuring that these are the best commentaries our gifted authors can provide,

so that the church will be served with trustworthy and exemplary expositions of God's Word.

It is our goal and prayer that the Reformed Expository Commentary will
serve the church by renewing confidence in the clarity and power of Scripture and by upholding the great doctrinal heritage of the Reformed faith.
We hope that pastors who read these commentaries will be encouraged in
their own expository preaching ministry, which we believe to be the best and
most biblical pattern for teaching God's Word in the church. We hope that
lay teachers will find these commentaries among the most useful resources
they rely upon for understanding and presenting the text of the Bible. And
we hope that the devotional quality of these studies of Scripture will instruct
and inspire each Christian who reads them in joyful, obedient discipleship
to Jesus Christ.

May the Lord bless all who read the Reformed Expository Commentary.
We commit these volumes to the Lord Jesus Christ, praying that the Holy
Spirit will use them for the instruction and edification of the church, with
thanksgiving to God the Father for his unceasing faithfulness in building his
church through the ministry of his Word.

Richard D. Phillips
Philip Graham Ryken
Series Editors

PREFACE

David, Solomon, Elijah: the story told in 1 Kings is populated with great heroes of Israel—men of courage and charisma with many frailties and a constant need for grace. This story also has a full share of villains: Adonijah, Shimei, Jeroboam, Ahab. Most of all, though, 1 Kings is the story of Israel's God, who never fails to love his people or to keep them under his kingly care, even when they choose to follow the pathways of folly and idolatry.

Preaching through 1 Kings at Philadelphia's Tenth Presbyterian Church was a huge privilege. Indeed, that privilege seems even more precious now that I have left the congregation I love to follow God's calling to serve as president of Wheaton College.

The sermons on Elijah came first, during my early years at Tenth Church, when I sometimes preached for James Montgomery Boice on Sunday mornings. The sermons on Solomon and his successors came later. Now all this material has been carefully revised with the help of wise comments from good friends. Lois Denier, Cathy Kempf, Glenn McDowell, and Mary Ryken all suggested improvements to the Solomon material (some of which has been published elsewhere). Iain Duguid, Randy Grossman, Rick Phillips, and Jonathan Rockey read the entire manuscript and served me well by correcting my mistakes, strengthening my arguments, asking for more application, and the like.

I am grateful to God for the help of these friends and the joy of serving in Christian community. Special thanks go to Robert Polen for completing the arduous task of entering the final revisions, and to Marilee Melvin for helping me see this book to press. But perhaps my greatest debt of gratitude is owed to everyone who prayed for me as I was studying, meditating, preaching, and finally writing about 1 Kings.

May God the Holy Spirit bless everyone who reads this book with a deeper knowledge of Jesus Christ, who is the best of Israel's kings and the mightiest of all the prophets of God.

Philip Graham Ryken
Wheaton College

1 Kings

THE RISE AND DECLINE OF DAVID'S HOUSE

PART 1

King Solomon:
Money, Sex, and Power

1

KING ME!

1 Kings 1:1–10

*Now Adonijah the son of Haggith exalted himself, saying, "I will
be king." And he prepared for himself chariots and horsemen, and
fifty men to run before him.* (1 Kings 1:5)

*I*n every simple game of checkers there is a thrilling moment
when one of the ordinary playing pieces suddenly becomes
royalty. Having moved and jumped all the way to the far side
of the board, a checker becomes a king. "King me!" commands one of the
players. A second checker is carefully stacked on top of the first checker,
and from then on the new king has the power to move all over the board.

Many people want the game of checkers to become their way of life. Not
content to be ordinary, they want to be the royal center of attention. "King
me!" they say, wanting enough power and money to get the control and buy
the pleasure they want out of life. "King me!" is what the single man is saying
when he gratifies his sexual desire instead of making a selfless commitment
to love a woman for Christ. "King me!" (or "Queen me!" to use a term from
the game of chess) is what the overbearing mother is saying when she makes
her own peace the rule of her household, rather than pursuing the spiritual

5

progress of her children. And "King me!" is what I am saying whenever my own desires become my main concern, even at the expense of others.

The problem with building our own little kingdoms is that we never find our rightful place in the true kingdom of God. This central issue in the Christian life is also the central issue in 1 and 2 Kings. Who will be king? Will we accept the kingship that God has established, or will we always insist on having our own way in life?

OLD KING DAVID

The question of kingship arises right from the beginning of 1 Kings. The books of 1 and 2 Samuel were dominated by the kingship of David. But 1 Kings begins by telling us that "King David was old and advanced in years. And although they covered him with clothes, he could not get warm" (1 Kings 1:1).

For anyone who admires King David, this scene is full of pathos. David was among the greatest of earthly kings—maybe *the* greatest. From boyhood he performed many heroic feats in battle. He killed lions and bears to defend his father's flocks and herds. He slew giants. He conquered kingdoms. He established a fortress for his people in Jerusalem. He sired a royal dynasty, fathering many sons to be the princes of Israel. But now the famous king was old and gray, and for all his former greatness, it was all he could do to stay warm in bed (or should I say deathbed?).

David's feeble decline is a sad reminder of our own frailty. The king was about seventy years old when these events took place (see 2 Sam. 5:4). What happened to him will happen to almost all of us: our hearing will fail; our eyesight will grow dim; our limbs will get weak and brittle. Eventually we will be confined to bed, and maybe we will find it hard to stay warm. How important it is, therefore, to heed this counsel from Scripture: "Remember also your Creator in the days of your youth, before the evil days come and the years draw near of which you will say, 'I have no pleasure in them'" (Eccles. 12:1). If, like David, we give our hearts to God when we are young, we will still remember him when we are old, and he will remember us.

Poor David! As he tried to get warm, his servants tried to help. They put him in warmer pajamas, but the king stayed cold. Then they piled heavy blankets on his royal person, but still he shivered under the covers.

So they proposed a practical remedy—one mentioned in several ancient medical textbooks:[1]

> Therefore his servants said to him, "Let a young woman be sought for my lord the king, and let her wait on the king and be in his service. Let her lie in your arms, that my lord the king may be warm." So they sought for a beautiful young woman throughout all the territory of Israel, and found Abishag the Shunammite, and brought her to the king. The young woman was very beautiful, and she was of service to the king and attended to him, but the king knew her not. (1 Kings 1:2–4)

Abishag's employment as a kind of human hot water bottle raises more questions than it answers. Were David's servants simply trying to keep him warm? If so, then why did they conduct a Miss Israel pageant to find the prettiest young thing in the whole country? Though the situation seems charged with sexuality, we also sense that the king is diminished. This is hardly the David who knew Bathsheba—the David who fathered Solomon and many other sons. Not even a stunning young virgin can warm his blood. On the contrary, his sexual incapacity shows that he has suffered the loss of vitality and virility.

Soon old King David will be dead and buried, which shows one of the inherent limitations of kingship in ancient Israel. All the kings died, throwing the kingship into question for each new generation of the people of God. David was the best of Israel's kings, yet even he went down to the grave, where his body remains to this day. His very mortality meant that he could never be the ultimate king for God's people.

This shows, by way of contrast, the superior kingship that we have in Jesus Christ, who is the true Son of David and the only divine Son of God. Jesus also died, suffering crucifixion for our sins. But on the third day he was raised again to reign forever in kingly majesty. Jesus Christ is the immortal King of all ages (see 1 Tim. 1:16). This is the kingdom we need, ruled by a king who will never die again, but will always live to rule us and defend us. Jesus will never shiver in the cold chill of old age, but will remain at the full blaze of his divine powers for all eternity—our once and forever King.

1. Howard Vos cites Galen, among others; see *1, 2 Kings*, Bible Study Commentary (Grand Rapids: Zondervan, 1989), 34.

I WILL BE KING

As David's kingship came to an end, his royal court was full of intrigue. The courtiers were whispering in the passageways: "Who will be the next king?" This question had been on people's minds for years, much the way that people have long speculated about who would succeed England's Elizabeth II. In fact, there had already been at least two attempts to take the throne away from David: the rebellion of his son Absalom, which led to civil war (2 Sam. 14–18), and the uprising of Sheba the Benjamite (2 Sam. 20). David was able to quell both rebellions, but as he grew older he also grew weaker. Now he could not even get warm in bed, and what one scholar has described as "his shivering impotence" was creating a power vacuum.[2]

As far as God was concerned, David's rightful heir was supposed to be Solomon. Although he was not the oldest son—he was tenth in line—Solomon was the chosen son. God does not always choose the oldest son, as David's own coronation illustrates (1 Sam. 16:10–13). We know from 1 Chronicles 22:9 that the word of the Lord had announced to David that Solomon would be the next king: "Behold, a son shall be born to you who shall be a man of rest. I will give him rest from all his surrounding enemies. For his name shall be Solomon, and I will give peace and quiet to Israel in his days. He shall build a house for my name. He shall be my son, and I will be his father, and I will establish his royal throne in Israel forever" (1 Chron. 22:9–10). By divine calling, Solomon would be Israel's king.

There was another contender for the kingship, however—an alternative candidate to sit on Israel's throne. Most people saw him as the heir apparent. His name was Adonijah, and he seemed to be everything that David used to be but wasn't anymore. The Bible describes him as "a very handsome man, and he was born next after Absalom" (1 Kings 1:6). Humanly speaking, Adonijah had everything going for him. He had all the qualifications that people usually look for. Like his older brother Absalom (an ominous connection, given the civil war that Absalom waged against his father's house; see 2 Sam. 14:25–27), he was easy on the eyes, which counts for a lot in life—more than we sometimes like to admit. As far as kingship was concerned, Adonijah looked the part (at

2. B. O. Long, "A Darkness between Brothers: Solomon and Adonijah," *Journal for the Study of the Old Testament* 19 (1981): 84.

least to people who look at outward appearances, which God doesn't; see 1 Sam. 16:7).

Furthermore, as David's oldest living son, Adonijah was next in line for the throne. He was David's fourth-born son (see 2 Sam. 3:4). The king's oldest son, Amnon, had been killed by his younger brother Absalom, who in turn was put to death. No one knows what happened to Chileab (2 Sam. 3:3), who simply disappears from the story and may perhaps have died in his youth. According to the ancient principle of primogeniture, most people would have said that Adonijah had a legitimate claim to the throne.

So the young man Adonijah decided to seize his chance, declaring his intention to be the king after David. The exact wording of his declaration gives us a window into his soul and maybe into our own souls as well: "Now Adonijah the son of Haggith exalted himself, saying, 'I will be king'" (1 Kings 1:5). Grammatically, the word "I" is in the emphatic position. We can almost imagine Adonijah pointing to himself or even thumping his chest as he said, "I will be king." Furthermore, the form of the verb for exaltation may indicate continuous action,[3] as if to show that Adonijah's self-exaltation was not simply a one-time occurrence; his whole life was all about putting himself forward to be the king.

From the merely human perspective, Adonijah's ambition is thoroughly understandable. After all, who wouldn't want to be the king? Besides, isn't it the natural order of things for a king to show some initiative and seize his crown?

If that is what we think, then we need to remember that this was no ordinary kingdom. The royal house of David was part of God's plan for the salvation of the world. David had received a divine and covenant promise that his dynasty would last forever, that his throne would be established eternally (see 2 Sam. 7:16–17). This was the will of God. It would also be the *work* of God, which meant that rather than making its own choice for a king, Israel was supposed to trust God to provide the man of his choice.

Some commentators interpret David's decline as a constitutional crisis. "The reason for the rivalry among David's sons to be king," they say, "was that the constitutional procedure for determining succession had not been

3. Gene Rice, *Nations under God: A Commentary on the Book of 1 Kings*, International Theological Commentary (Grand Rapids: Eerdmans, 1990), 9.

established."[4] But that was not the real problem. Israel *did* have a policy for the royal succession. The policy was divine appointment: God would anoint his own king in his own good time. As it said in the Law of Moses, "set a King over you whom the LORD your God will choose" (Deut. 17:15). The problem was that men like Adonijah (and also Absalom) would not accept God's choice, but kept exalting themselves. They would not even wait for their father to die (cf. Luke 15:12), but tried to take by force something that was only God's to give.

Have you ever felt the same temptation—the temptation to take what you wanted when you wanted it instead of waiting for what God would give? Little people are tempted to do it by saying, "That's mine!" and grabbing whatever they can get. Bigger kids are tempted to do it by getting angry when they do not get their own way. Some adults are tempted to do it by taking the pleasures of sex without waiting for the gift of marriage. Others are tempted to climb over other people to get the next promotion, or to put themselves forward for ministry without any calling from the church, or to gain ungodly control over their spouses by manipulation or force.

In one way or another, we are all tempted to exalt ourselves. All too often we are like Diotrephes, whom the New Testament describes as someone "who likes to put himself first" (3 John 9). But when we put ourselves on the throne, God is no longer the God of our lives; he is only another one of our servants. Rather than seeking his kingdom, we expect him to advance ours. Sooner or later we will get upset with him for not doing whatever it is that we expect him to do for us. Typically we get angry when we do not get what we want, which makes anger one of the best clues to our own private idolatries. When we are angry at the world or angry with God, it is almost always because we have the wrong person on the throne.

FOR HIS OWN GLORY

To see the shape that self-exaltation takes in our own lives, we need to look more carefully at the way Adonijah crowned himself king. His decision to "king" himself was a decision he made for his own glory and pleasure without ever submitting to the rule of God. We make the same mistake whenever

4. Ibid., 7.

we decide to "king" ourselves: we seek our own honor and pleasure without submitting to the rule of God.

Consider the various ways that Adonijah acted for his own honor. First, "he prepared for himself chariots and horsemen, and fifty men to run before him" (1 Kings 1:5). If you want people to know how important you are, it helps to have your own entourage! So Adonijah gathered his posse, so to speak—an honor guard of palace chariots, with footmen to run ahead and announce his coming. Even before he arrived, people would know that someone important was on the way.

When it comes to being important, image is everything. If you are going to be the king, you have to act like the king, and that includes having people around to treat you like the king. You need to have some followers—people to tell you how great you are. And so, like his brother Absalom before him (another ominous connection), Adonijah grandly employed a retinue of horses and chariots and foot servants (see 2 Sam. 15:1).

Adonijah also made sure to gain the support of some of the most powerful leaders in Israel: "He conferred with Joab the son of Zeruiah and with Abiathar the priest. And they followed Adonijah and helped him" (1 Kings 1:7).

Though their careers ended in disgrace, both of these men were key leaders. Joab was the commander of Israel's army. For many years he had served as David's right-hand man. Joab was the general who helped the king conquer Jerusalem, who suppressed every rebellion against his royal throne, and who protected his life by assassinating his enemies (e.g., 2 Sam. 2:13ff.; 1 Chron. 11:4–6). Unfortunately, Joab had also killed David's son Absalom, which put him out of royal favor and diminished his political influence. Yet perhaps by aligning himself with Adonijah, he could regain his powerful position in the kingdom.

Abiathar the priest was also making a power grab. Like Joab, he was one of the king's old associates, a man who had been with David almost from the beginning (see 1 Sam. 22:20–23). Abiathar was not the high priest, but maybe he wanted to be. In any case, he decided that he would follow Adonijah in his rise to power.

So Adonijah had friends in high places—powerful military and religious leaders who could help him get what he wanted. Knowing the right people is important. If you want to get ahead in life, it helps to be able to say things like, "You know, I was talking to my good friend Joab the other day, and he said . . ." It also helps to have people around who will tell you what you want to hear, affirming your ambitions and praising your purchases without criticizing your faults or correcting your sins.

Adonijah also honored himself by making a public display of his personal wealth and religious commitment: "Adonijah sacrificed sheep, oxen, and fattened cattle by the Serpent's Stone, which is beside En-rogel, and he invited all his brothers, the king's sons, and all the royal officials of Judah" (1 Kings 1:9).

This grand feast, with its long guest list, would accomplish a number of important political purposes. It would enhance Adonijah's reputation for being religious (even though the Serpent's Stone was hardly the proper place to make sacrifices to God!). Throwing a party would also unite people, bringing them together to form a political alliance. Table fellowship was an important sign of solidarity in biblical times. In this case, it virtually amounted to a public coronation ceremony (see 1 Kings 1:11).

Adonijah did all this self-promotion to strengthen his political position. He was hanging out with the right friends, spending time with the popular people, and throwing the biggest parties. At the same time, he was giving many people the impression that he was deeply religious. Yet Adonijah was doing it all for his own honor and glory.

We are tempted to "king" ourselves the same way. We try to impress people with what we have, who we know, or how much we are doing for God. Sometimes we care more about what people think of us than we do about who we really are before God. Thus we surround ourselves with people who will tell us that we are doing the right thing, even (and maybe especially) when we are doing the wrong thing.

How do we do this? We do it by quietly making sure we get most of the credit for the success of a project, or by showing off the electronic gadget we recently purchased, or by letting people know we are wearing the latest fashion, or by giving the impression that we are part of the "in" crowd, or by doing whatever it is that people in our community do to keep score. Maybe we simply fuel our sense of self-importance by gently complaining about our heavy workload, especially the good work we do in Christian ministry. But one way or another, we want people to know how good we are. We may not do it by riding a chariot, hiring fifty servants, and inviting celebrities over for dinner, but we do the same thing in subtler ways. We do it with what we buy, what we say, what we wear, and the general impression we try to leave that we are something more than we really are.

FOOLISH PLEASURE

Not only do we seek our own honor, but we also pursue our own pleasure. Adonijah shows us this as well. It was not simply for his own glory that he crowned himself king; it was also for his own pleasure. The Bible indicates this by telling us that "his father had never at any time displeased him by asking, 'Why have you done thus and so?'" (1 Kings 1:6). This is a terrible indictment of David for his failure in fatherly discipline. It also happens to be one of the most important comments made anywhere in the Bible on the subject of raising children.

The implication is that David should have been holding his sons accountable, and that if only he had done so, Adonijah would not have been living for the glory of a crown that was never his to claim. The Bible further implies that such discipline necessarily would have displeased him, even though it would have been for his own good. But instead, Adonijah was rebellious—spoiled rotten. David had not loved his son wisely, but too well. An excessively indulgent father had produced a self-exalted son. As Paul House wisely comments, "Good looks and a favored status, coupled with parental indulgence, rarely build strong character. Neither do they instill wisdom."[5] Adonijah may well have enjoyed a happy childhood, but his father's lack of discipline eventually led the young man into treason.

These are all principles we can take straight into the Christian home. Fathers and mothers have a responsibility to hold their children accountable for their actions. "Why have you done this?" is a good and often a necessary question to ask. It forces children to explain their actions, and hopefully to examine the underlying motivations of their hearts. This may have the happy result of helping them see how sinful they are, and how much they need a Savior. It may also help them to see the difference between living for their own pleasure and living for God's pleasure, between "kinging" themselves and living for the glory of God.

5. Paul R. House, *1, 2 Kings*, The New American Commentary (Nashville: Broadman & Holman, 1995), 88.

Parents need to know that this kind of accountability often makes children angry. Of course it does! The fallen nature is going to be angry anytime its sins are exposed. But a child's very displeasure may well be a sign that he or she is receiving precisely the discipline that is needed. Of course, the Bible also warns fathers (especially) not to *provoke* their children to anger (see Eph. 6:4), which is often a temptation for fathers. To avoid this, every act of discipline needs to be surrounded with clear and loving communication; repentance and reconciliation may be needed on both sides. But the point in 1 Kings 1:6 is that effective parenting has a way of displeasing children.

If you are a father or a mother, do you love your children enough to displease them? Parents who never displease their children are not doing their job. It is often tempting to make one's day easier by making one's child happier, but to do so in ways that relinquish parental authority. However much peace or popularity this buys when children are young, it will only bring heartache in the end. Matthew Henry wisely said that parents "who honor their sons more than God, as those do who keep them not under good discipline, thereby forfeit the honor they might expect from their sons."[6]

To avoid this disappointment, parents need the wisdom of the Holy Spirit to know how to displease their children only for their children's benefit and for the glory of God, not out of their own frustration. Ask this question: Am I carrying out this discipline because I am good and angry, or because I am thinking clearly and carefully about the training my child needs to make spiritual progress?

Children need to understand this as well. If your parents make you angry sometimes, it is probably because they love you enough to discipline you. If they ask, "Why did you do this?" or "Where have you been?" do not shut them out. Do not decide to do whatever you please. And do not say that it is none of their business. It *is* their business. It is their business because it is your business, and it happens to be their business to help you do your business with God. Otherwise, you will grow up to be like Adonijah, living for your own pleasure, perhaps, but never receiving the blessing of God. If you crown yourself the king, or the queen, eventually your life will turn out to be a royal disappointment!

6. Matthew Henry, *Matthew Henry's Complete Commentary on the Whole Bible*, vol. 2, *Judges to Job* (New York: Fleming Revell, n.d.), n.p.

The True and Rightful King

What should Adonijah have done? One of the best places for anyone to start in life is with the first question of the Westminster Shorter Catechism. Adonijah didn't know that catechism, of course, but he could have learned its first principle from the Law of Moses: "Man's chief end is to glorify God and enjoy him forever." Adonijah had this exactly backward. He was living for his own glory and his own enjoyment rather than for the glory and the pleasure of God. What makes this especially ironic is that the man's very name means "the Lord is Master." Yet Adonijah wanted to be his own master, and thus he never submitted to the rule of God.

To be more specific, he never submitted to the authority of the prophet, the priest, or the king that God had established in Israel. As we have seen, Adonijah conferred with Joab the general and Abiathar the priest. But he never conferred with the three men who had true, God-given spiritual authority in Israel: the prophet, the high priest, and the king. Thus we read in verse 8 that "Zadok the priest and Benaiah the son of Jehoiada and Nathan the prophet and Shimei and Rei and David's mighty men were not with Adonijah." We read further in verse 10 that Adonijah "did not invite Nathan the prophet or Benaiah or the mighty men or Solomon his brother."

The reason this matters is that these men were the rightful leaders of Israel. Many Bible scholars have described this passage as a power struggle between two rival political parties: Judah versus Jerusalem, or the old establishment against the new revolutionaries. But that is to miss the deeper spiritual point. Nathan was Israel's true prophet—a man who even had the courage to stand up against David himself (see 2 Sam. 12:1–15). Zadok was the true high priest—a man directly descended from Aaron, the first high priest in Israel (see 1 Chron. 6:49–53). The other mighty men—like Benaiah, who was the captain of the king's bodyguard (see 2 Sam. 23:20–23), or Solomon, whom God had chosen to be the next king—represented the rightful kingship of David.

So although Adonijah conferred with his supporters, he did not consult the prophet, or the priest, or the king that God had anointed to lead his people. He did not consult them because he knew they would not support him. He had made his own decision to be the king, for his own glory and his own pleasure, without ever submitting to the rule of God, as represented by his prophet, his priest, and his king.

This gives us a practical principle for our own decision making, which is always to submit to the will of God. Am I doing what am I doing because it is what I want to do or because it is what God wants me to do? Happily, in the goodness of God many of the things that God calls us to do *are* the things that we want to do. But whenever there is any conflict, we need to submit to God's authority.

It is characteristic of godly decisions that they are made out in the open, with the help of godly counsel, including from people who are willing to tell us some things we do not want to hear. Submitting to God's will always starts with knowing the Scriptures, which rule some things in and some things out. It also includes listening to the people God has provided for our spiritual guidance: parents, perhaps, or spouses, or teachers, or bosses, or pastors and elders in the church, depending on our situation in life.

This counsel is especially important anytime we are thinking of doing something that we do not want other people to know about. When a child hides something from her parents, or a husband holds secrets from his wife, or a worker misleads her employer, or a church member keeps something from his pastor, this is always a sign of a spiritual problem. This is what Adonijah did. He talked to Joab and Abiathar because he knew they would support him, but he did not talk to Nathan or Zadok, and he certainly never talked to his father David. If we want to hear only from people who will always tell us that we are doing the right thing, we are acting like the rulers of our own lives, and we will end up like Adonijah. The very fact that we do not want certain people to know what we are planning to do may well be the proof that they really do need to know.

Do not seek your own pleasure and glory, but submit to God's will for your life. For Adonijah, this meant consulting with Nathan, Zadok, and David. For us it means submitting to Jesus Christ, who is the true Prophet, the faithful Priest, and the rightful King for the people of God. Every time we see a prophet, a priest, or a king, we can make a connection to Jesus Christ, for the work of these Old Testament leaders pointed to his person and work. Jesus is the Prophet who speaks the Word of God; listen to what he says. Jesus is the Priest who offered himself as a sacrifice; trust in him for the forgiveness of sins. Jesus is the King who rules us and defends us; ask for his protection.

As we consider Christ as King, we can hardly help but notice that his kingship is the antithesis of everything we see in Adonijah. Adonijah announced his own kingship, for his own glory and his own pleasure. But Jesus did exactly the opposite. Unlike proud Adonijah, he did not ride palace chariots or hire footmen to announce his royal majesty. Instead, he rode a lowly donkey, and whatever attendants he had were people who followed him of their own free devotion. Jesus did not come to do his own will, but the will of the Father who sent him, even when this meant going to the cross for our sins. Setting aside his own pleasure, he endured the pains of crucifixion. Then, rather than exalting himself, he waited for God the Father to raise him from the dead and lift him to heaven's high throne (see Phil. 2:6–11).

This is the King we serve: not a king who is in it for himself, but who rules for the good of his people and the glory of God. Now we are called to live the same way: not "kinging" ourselves, but crowning Christ as King, and serving others for Jesus' sake.

2

A Royal Conspiracy

1 Kings 1:11–31

Then Nathan said to Bathsheba the mother of Solomon, "Have you not heard that Adonijah the son of Haggith has become king and David our lord does not know it? Now therefore come, let me give you advice, that you may save your own life and the life of your son Solomon. (1 Kings 1:11–12)

The right to rule as king has been the occasion of many bitter conflicts. Often brother has fought against brother to wear the crown, forcing members of the royal family and citizens of the realm to choose sides.

During the Third Crusade, King Richard I—also known as the Lionheart—waged war against Muslim armies under the command of Saladin. But while Richard was fighting to regain Jerusalem, his brother Prince John was busily trying to crown himself the king of England. Richard hurriedly made a treaty with Saladin and raced home to protect his royal prerogatives. But as he made his way across Europe, the king was captured by Leopold V of Austria and held for a ransom equal to two or three times the amount of his kingdom's annual income.

Everyone in England was forced to choose sides. John offered Leopold half as much money to keep Richard in prison for another couple of years, so he would have time to consolidate his power. Meanwhile, Richard's mother—Eleanor of Aquitane—tried (and eventually succeeded) to raise enough money to have her favorite son rescued and restored to his rightful throne. It was a conflict for the kingdom, which Richard finally won. But while the throne was still in dispute, people had to decide which man they wanted to be king, and how much they would give to support his cause.

We face a similar choice when it comes to the kingdom of God. Will we honor God's true and rightful King, or will we try to seize the crown for ourselves? Which kingdom will we choose? How much will we sacrifice to see it established?

RIVALS FOR THE THRONE

The people of God faced the same choice during the last days of David, when the king was on his deathbed and two of his sons were contesting for the crown. With the question of royal succession on everyone's mind, David's oldest living son, Adonijah, decided to take the throne. "I will be king," he declared (1 Kings 1:5), and then he gathered as many followers as he could—priests and politicians and military leaders. Then Adonijah effectively hosted his own coronation, killing the fatted calf and throwing a huge party not far from Jerusalem. In truth, he did what many of us are tempted to do many times in life: he exalted his own honor, pursued his own pleasure, and grasped for control of his own destiny.

What Adonijah did not do—as the Bible is careful to show—was to let God decide what he was called to do, when and where he was called to do it. This is why Adonijah did not consult with the prophet (Nathan) or the priest (Zadok) that God had anointed over Israel (see 1 Kings 1:8), and why he very conspicuously left his brother Solomon off the guest list for his coronation party (1 Kings 1:10). It also explains why he never asked what his father David wanted him to do, even though his father was the true king of Israel. Consider the audacity of what Adonijah had done: he had named himself the royal heir without having even one word with the king himself!

Adonijah's coup of a party was still in full swing when one man decided to take action: "Nathan said to Bathsheba the mother of Solomon, 'Have you not heard that Adonijah the son of Haggith has become king and David our lord does not know it? Now therefore come, let me give you advice, that you may save your own life and the life of your son Solomon'" (1 Kings 1:11–12).

At this critical moment in the history of the people of God, one man understood exactly what was at stake. Some commentators have accused Nathan of exaggerating when he told Bathsheba that Adonijah had become the king, but this was a true and accurate assessment of what the man was doing: he was exalting himself as king (see 1 Kings 1:5). Nathan also knew what would happen if Adonijah proved to be successful: Bathsheba and Solomon would both be killed, for in ancient times it was customary for a king to put his rivals to death. The whole situation was a royal crisis. By trying to usurp the throne, Adonijah was threatening the royal succession, and with it all the promises that God had made to the house of David. This was more than a power struggle; it was a life-and-death conflict for the kingdom of God. Everyone had to make this destiny-deciding choice: Which king will I serve?

MESSENGERS TO THE KING

Nathan and Bathsheba chose for Solomon, and in choosing for Solomon they were choosing to serve the kingdom of God. We can learn some important lessons from their example, but first we need to hear their story, with all its royal intrigue.

Bathsheba was famous for her beauty, and for David's sin in taking her to sleep with him (see 2 Sam. 11). Bathsheba's first son died, but her second son was Solomon, and when he became the king, she would become the queen mother—a position of power and influence in the ancient world. The faithful prophet Nathan also had a role in those famous events, first rebuking David for his adultery (2 Sam. 12:1–15) and then blessing Solomon as God's beloved son (2 Sam. 12:24–25).

Now it was time for Nathan and Bathsheba to make some history again. After sounding the alarm about Adonijah, Nathan told Bathsheba his clever plan: "Go in at once to King David, and say to him, 'Did you not, my lord the king, swear to your servant, saying, "Solomon your son shall reign after me, and he shall sit on my throne"? Why then is Adonijah king?' Then while you are still speaking with the king, I also will come in after you and confirm your words" (1 Kings 1:13–14).

This was a crafty plan. Nathan was the master strategist, skilled in the art of human persuasion. Bathsheba was the person with the most direct access to the king, so she would go to David first. Together they would act decisively for the kingdom of God.

The coconspirators executed their plan to perfection. First Bathsheba went into the royal bedroom. The Bible tells us that she "went to the king in his chamber (now the king was very old, and Abishag the Shunammite was attending to the king)" (1 Kings 1:15). Their conversation went like this:

> Bathsheba bowed and paid homage to the king, and the king said, "What do you desire?" She said to him, "My lord, you swore to your servant by the LORD your God, saying, 'Solomon your son shall reign after me, and he shall sit on my throne.' And now, behold, Adonijah is king, although you, my lord the king, do not know it. He has sacrificed oxen, fattened cattle, and sheep in abundance, and has invited all the sons of the king, Abiathar the priest, and Joab the commander of the army, but Solomon your servant he has not invited. And now, my lord the king, the eyes of all Israel are on you, to tell them who shall sit on the throne of my lord the king after him. Otherwise it will come to pass, when my lord the king sleeps with his fathers, that I and my son Solomon will be counted offenders." (1 Kings 1:16–21)

Bathsheba approached David deferentially, humbly bowing to give him honor. But she also approached him forthrightly, bluntly telling the king what he needed to hear. She reminded him what he had promised before God, namely, that her son Solomon would succeed him on the throne. Bathsheba also told David some things that he did not know, but needed to know. Earlier we were told that the king did not know Abishag, the beautiful young girl who was brought to keep him warm (1 Kings 1:4). But this was not the only thing that David did not know! He also did not know that his son had crowned himself king. Nor did he know who was and who wasn't on Adonijah's guest list. The king was totally out of touch with what was happening in his own kingdom.

Then Bathsheba challenged David to take action. She appealed to his royal sense of duty. She said the whole nation was looking to him for leadership, waiting for him to declare the next king. Bathsheba also told her husband what was at stake: if David did not take action, then she and her son would surely be killed, for the new king would regard them as traitors to his realm. By failing to invite Solomon to his coronation celebration, Adonijah was declaring that his brother was a dead man.

Like Eleanor of Aquitane, Bathsheba was doing what she could to secure her son's claim to the royal throne. Before she had a chance to finish saying all this, Nathan approached the royal chamber to make his dramatic entrance. He came in right on cue: "While she was still speaking with the king, Nathan the prophet came in. And they told the king, 'Here is Nathan the prophet'" (1 Kings 1:22–23). Like Bathsheba, Nathan entered David's presence with all due respect, for "when he came in before the king, he bowed before the king, with his face to the ground" (1 Kings 1:23). Then, with the king's permission, Nathan said:

> My lord the king, have you said, "Adonijah shall reign after me, and he shall sit on my throne"? For he has gone down this day and has sacrificed oxen, fattened cattle, and sheep in abundance, and has invited all the king's sons, the commanders of the army, and Abiathar the priest. And behold, they are eating and drinking before him, and saying, "Long live King Adonijah!" But me, your servant, and Zadok the priest, and Benaiah the son of Jehoiada, and your servant Solomon he has not invited. Has this thing been brought about by my lord the king and you have not told your servants who should sit on the throne of my lord the king after him? (1 Kings 1:24–27)

Nathan's questions confirmed everything that Bathsheba had been saying about Adonijah. Like Bathsheba, Nathan told David about Adonijah's party, about who was there, and who wasn't. Nathan also added some new information. He made it clear that people were acclaiming Adonijah as king, saying, "Long live King Adonijah!" Frankly, the prophet wanted to know whether any of this had been done under David's royal authority. If so, then why on earth wasn't his prophet informed? If not, then what was David going to do about it? Nathan was challenging David to disavow what Adonijah had done, knowing that a proper succession to the throne could come about only with the king's royal consent. Whereas Bathsheba appealed to David's pity as a husband and father, Nathan appealed to his authority as the king.

It was a brilliant strategy, perfectly executed. With reminders and reprimands, Nathan and Bathsheba motivated David to act. If only one person had come to warn him, perhaps David would have doubted the accuracy of the report he was given. But these messengers came one right after the other, and with two witnesses—the biblical number for establishing any criminal matter in a court of law (Deut. 19:15)—the king was fully persuaded. Now that he knew the truth, he acted accordingly.

HONORING THE KINGDOM'S KING

Some scholars have been critical of Nathan and Bathsheba for being manipulative or even deceptive. Did David *really* swear that Solomon would be the next king, or was Bathsheba trying to pull a fast one on a man who was too old and senile to remember what he had said to whom? Did the people at Adonijah's party *really* say, "Long live King Adonijah!" or was Nathan embellishing his story? Walter Brueggemann accuses the prophet of "crude politics" and calculated manipulation.[1] Richard Nelson says that he tricked David with half-truths, unsubstantiated allegations, and outright lies.[2] He even goes so far as to describe God himself as "an unindicted co-conspirator" in this "sleazy harem intrigue."[3]

We should never be afraid to admit that God often uses sinful human beings to accomplish his sovereign purposes. Yet in this case Nathan and Bathsheba deserve to be defended from any charge of wrongdoing. What they carried out was a holy conspiracy, in which they acted together for the kingdom of God in the most righteous and persuasive way they knew how. From their example, we learn at least three important lessons about keeping our own commitment to the kingdom of God.

First, we learn to honor the kingdom's king. From the beginning of this story, both Nathan and Bathsheba honored the true king of Israel. They honored David as king even though he was old and feeble. When they came into his royal presence, they bowed before him. Rather than acting on his behalf, they respected his right to give his own commands. They continued to honor him right to the end of the story, when "Bathsheba bowed with her face to the ground and paid homage to the king and said, 'May my lord King David live forever!'" (1 Kings 1:31).

1. Walter Brueggemann, *1 & 2 Kings,* Smyth & Helwys Bible Commentary (Macon, GA: Smyth & Helwys, 2000), 20.
2. Richard Nelson, *First and Second Kings,* Interpretation (Louisville: John Knox, 1987), 20.
3. Ibid., 22.

This must have been especially humbling for Bathsheba, because when she entered David's chamber she saw a beautiful young woman with him: Abishag the Shunammite, who had been brought to keep David warm in bed (1 Kings 1:2–3). Even though we know that David and Abishag did not have sexual relations (see 1 Kings 1:4), the young woman's very presence may well have been humiliating for the queen.[4] Yet Bathsheba honored the king—not because he was a perfect man, but simply because he was the king. She honored him for his royal office.

This is one of the ways we know that Nathan and Bathsheba were loyal servants of the true kingdom of God. Unlike Adonijah, who would not even speak to the king, Nathan and Bathsheba gave David the honor that he deserved. They did not do this simply because they were trying to get him to do what they wanted, but also because they recognized him as God's anointed king.

We keep the same commitment whenever we honor Jesus Christ as the true King of the kingdom of God. Whenever we see King David in the Scriptures, we should always have Jesus in mind, because he is the rightful heir to David's throne (Luke 2:4–5). According to the Gospel of Luke, God will give Jesus "the throne of his father David, . . . and of his kingdom there will be no end" (Luke 1:32–33). The apostle Paul said that Jesus is "descended from David" (Rom. 1:3). Jesus himself claimed that he was not only David's son, but also David's Lord (Luke 20:31–44; cf. Ps. 110). And God the Father honored Christ as King by exalting him to the everlasting throne of the universe.

If Jesus sits on David's throne as the ruler of God's kingdom, we should honor him as the King. Jesus is not feeble and frail like old King David, but young and strong forever, full of life and joy. As right as it was for Nathan and Bathsheba to honor David, therefore, Jesus is even more worthy of honor. We honor our King by giving him the homage of our worship—listening to his royal decrees in the preaching of his Word, bowing down before him in prayer, singing his praises with joyful songs, and bringing the tribute of our tithes and offerings. Every time we join in the public worship of God, we enter the throne room of Christ the King to give him the honor that he alone deserves. We also honor the King by pledging our lives to his royal service.

4. Paul R. House, *1, 2 Kings*, The New American Commentary (Nashville: Broadman & Holman, 1995), 91.

Whenever he calls, we will come; wherever he sends, we will go; whatever he commands, we will obey. Jesus is the King, and a king is honored whenever the people of his kingdom do his royal will.

BELIEVING THE KINGDOM'S PROMISE

Being committed to the kingdom also means believing the kingdom's promise—in this case the promise that Solomon would be the next king.

As we have seen, some people doubt whether David really promised his throne to Solomon, or wonder whether Bathsheba was making the whole thing up. After all, they say, whatever conversation the two men had is not recorded anywhere else in Kings. Nevertheless, this *is* what God had promised. In fact, Adonijah may have known this himself. Why else would he invite all his brothers to the feast, except Solomon, if not because he knew or feared that Solomon was the crown prince? We can also take Bathsheba at her word. If not, then what she said to David was blasphemy, for she called his promise an oath that he swore before God (1 Kings 1:17). Yet there is good reason to think that David had indeed promised his throne to Solomon, and that he did so because *God* had called Solomon to be the king.

The prophet Nathan himself made the first promise that David would have a dynasty, when he delivered this message from God: "When your days are fulfilled and you lie down with your fathers, I will raise up your offspring after you, who shall come from your body, and I will establish his kingdom. He shall build a house for my name, and I will establish the throne of his kingdom forever" (2 Sam. 7:12–13). Furthermore, we know from Chronicles that God had indicated which of David's sons would become his heir. According to David, God said: "Behold, a son shall be born to you who shall be a man of rest. I will give him rest from all his surrounding enemies. For his name shall be Solomon, and I will give peace and quiet to Israel in his days. He shall build a house for my name. He shall be my son, and I will be his father, and I will establish his royal throne in Israel forever" (1 Chron. 22:9–10).

So when Bathsheba said that David swore a sacred oath that Solomon would be king, she was not making things up. It was not just "pillow talk," either. Bathsheba was referring to an oath that David made on the basis of a covenant promise. This is fundamental to understanding everything that happens in the first chapter of 1 Kings. Nathan and Bathsheba did what they did because they believed in the kingdom promise of God, which is another reason we know that they were acting righteously. This is not simply "a sordid story of power politics," as some have claimed.[5] On the contrary, their royal conspiracy was a holy conspiracy, a divinely ordained conspiracy, based on the plans and the promises of God.

In this regard, Bathsheba's name seems especially significant, for it means "daughter of the oath."[6] In fact, the second part of her name (*sheba*) has the same verbal root as the word that is used for swearing an oath throughout this chapter (e.g., 1 Kings 1:13). How appropriate! Bathsheba was a daughter of the covenant and therefore she believed the kingdom promise of God, as it was spoken by David the king.

We too have heard the kingdom promises of God. The Bible says that Jesus Christ, the Son of David, has become the King of God's kingdom. As he went around teaching and preaching, Jesus said that the kingdom was near (Luke 10:9), or even that the kingdom had come (Luke 17:21). What Jesus meant by "the kingdom" was the rule and the dominion of God, which he would establish by his death on the cross and resurrection from the dead. The kingdom of Jesus Christ is a kingdom of mercy, forgiveness, and resurrection life. Such a kingdom could be gained only by the offering of a sacrifice for sin and a return from death to eternal life.

Although in many ways the kingdom has come, we are still waiting for all its promises to be totally fulfilled. This is why we pray, "Thy kingdom come." We are looking in faith for the kingdom to come in all its full dominion, and while we wait, we are called to believe the kingdom promises of God.

What do you believe about the kingdom of God? God has promised that his kingdom will grow until all nations repent and believe the gospel (Matt. 24:14). He has promised that his kingdom will be fully established at the second coming of Jesus Christ. He has promised that when his kingdom comes there will be a new heavens and a new earth. He has promised that in his kingdom there will be no more death or dying or pain (Rev. 21:4). He has promised that the citizens of his kingdom will experience the full joy of being at home with Jesus forever (John 14:1–3). And he has promised that his kingdom can never be shaken (Heb. 12:28), but will endure for all eternity.

5. Iain W. Provan, *1 and 2 Kings*, New International Biblical Commentary (Peabody, MA: Hendrickson, 1995), 40.
6. Ibid., 30.

Do you belong to the kingdom of God? If so, then swear ongoing allegiance to Jesus Christ as your King and believe that one day you will see all his kingdom promises come true. Believe this even when the progress of the gospel seems slow, or when things seem to be getting worse instead of better, or when the world seems tired out and broken down, or when you suffer grief and loss and physical pain, or when God seems far away. Even then believe the kingdom promise of the eternal God, taking by faith in Jesus what you cannot see until he comes again.

WORKING FOR THE KINGDOM'S PROGRESS

Everyone who believes the kingdom promise will work for the kingdom's progress, which is a third and final lesson we learn from the example of Nathan, Bathsheba, and also David. When times are hard, people sometimes wonder what one person can do. The prophet Nathan and the queen Bathsheba decided to find out. Though badly outnumbered and running late, they boldly persuaded David to make an official announcement of his private promise that Solomon would be king. They did not wait for some miraculous divine intervention, but acted boldly for the honor of the king.

They were not doing this for themselves alone, but for the kingdom of God. To be sure, what Bathsheba did was also in her own best interest; by supporting her son, she was saving her life (see 1 Kings 1:12). But Nathan and Bathsheba both understood that their own destiny was bound up with the kingdom of the rightful king. So they opposed proud Adonijah, the would-be king who rebelled against the kingdom of God, and spoke instead on behalf of Solomon, interceding for the next king of Israel. In doing so, they were doing kingdom work for the next generation of the people of God.

By the end of this episode, King David had joined their royal conspiracy to do what *he* could do for the kingdom of God. Up to this point David was ignorant of what was really happening to his kingdom and impotent to do anything about it. But as he listened to Nathan and Bathsheba, his blood began to rise. David understood that what Adonijah had done was a direct challenge to his kingly authority. So he rose to the challenge, making one last decision for the glory of the kingdom of God.

To this point the king had spoken barely two words in this chapter (what he says to Bathsheba in verse 16 comprises only two words in Hebrew). But rising in his bed, David summoned Bathsheba back into his royal chamber. It may have been the first royal command he had given in months, but in this climactic moment we can once again sense the man's true and kingly dignity: "King David answered, 'Call Bathsheba to me.' So she came into the king's presence and stood before the king" (1 Kings 1:28). Then David made a sacred vow: "And the king swore, saying, 'As the LORD lives, who has redeemed my soul out of every adversity, as I swore to you by the LORD, the God of Israel, saying, "Solomon your son shall reign after me, and he shall sit on my throne in my place," even so will I do this day'" (1 Kings 1:29–30).

David was joining Nathan and Bathsheba in their kingdom work. He knew who the kingdom's real King was. So he honored the King of all kings, praising the living God for saving him out of many trials. This is the testimony of the same David we know from Samuel and the Psalms—the David who killed lions, slew giants, and conquered kingdoms by the rescuing grace of God. David then repeated the kingdom promise that he had long believed, confirming that what Bathsheba said was true: he had indeed promised before God that Bathsheba's son would be the next king. And he promised immediately to do the kingdom work of putting Solomon on his rightful throne. David had spent an entire lifetime doing kingdom work. Now he vowed that to his dying day, he would act publicly and decisively to advance that kingdom for the coming generation.

What will you do for the kingdom of God? Which side will you take, when people exalt themselves and try to tear down the kingdom of God? Do you see how your own eternal destiny is bound up with what God is doing in the world today? What will you do to make a kingdom difference for the coming generation?

Kingdom work can include any good thing that is done for Christ as King—anything that advances his kingdom, or opposes his proud enemies, or speaks in defense of his kingship. We can do kingdom work in the marketplace. Whenever we make a fair sale, build a solid house, or shine a good shoe—if we do it for Jesus—we are advancing the cause of our King by bearing witness to the values of his kingdom. We can also do kingdom work in the home. Whenever we put beautiful flowers on the table, or pick up our shoes off the floor, or decide to be the first to say, "I'm sorry," we are bearing witness to the kingdom of God. Then we can do kingdom work in society. Whenever we oppose the evil of abortion, or work for the end of child abandonment, or take an active role in what is happening in the lives of people in our neighborhood, this too is kingdom work. We also do kingdom work through the ministry of the church: inviting friends to worship, passing out Bibles, welcoming people with disabilities, supporting workers overseas, laboring in prayer for people doing all kinds of ministry that we ourselves are not called or gifted to do. This is all the more true when we tell people the gospel in words they can hear and understand, which is the most direct way to advance the kingdom of Jesus Christ.

If Jesus Christ is the King, then we should do whatever we can for his kingdom. After all, Jesus himself has done everything that he could do for the kingdom. He has even done what no other king would dare to do: he has offered his own blood to save his people. Given what he has done for us, it is only right for us to do whatever we can for him and for his kingdom. As Matthew Henry said, "Whatever power, interest, or influence, men have— they ought to improve it to the utmost for the preserving and advancing of the kingdom of the Messiah."[7] We should do this not only for our own people, in our own place, at our own time, but also for the coming generation.

---

7. Matthew Henry, *Matthew Henry's Complete Commentary on the Whole Bible*, vol. 2, *Judges to Job* (New York: Fleming Revell, n.d.), n.p.

3

LONG LIVE THE KING!

1 Kings 1:32–53

And the king said to them, "Take with you the servants of your lord and have Solomon my son ride on my own mule, and bring him down to Gihon. And let Zadok the priest and Nathan the prophet there anoint him king over Israel. Then blow the trumpet and say, 'Long live King Solomon!'" (1 Kings 1:33–34)

According to ancient custom, the death of a ruler is greeted with the following words: "The king is dead; long live the king!" This may seem like a contradiction. If the king is dead, then what use is there in wishing him long life? But the point is that the kingdom will endure. Even though one king is dead, another king lives to take his place. The kingship will survive, and therefore people who hope for the continuity of the monarchy say, "The king is dead; long live the king!"

This custom helps to explain what Queen Bathsheba said to King David as she sought to secure the throne for Israel's rightful king. The old king was having trouble getting warm, so everyone thought he was on his deathbed. His oldest son, Adonijah, had gone so far as to proclaim himself the next king (1 Kings 1:5–10). Meanwhile, the prophet Nathan was doing everything he could do to secure the kingship for Solomon, who God had promised would sit on David's throne. Together Nathan and Bathsheba went to inform David what was happening to his kingdom and to persuade him to crown Solomon as king. Once David had promised to do this, "Bathsheba bowed with her face to the ground and paid homage to the king and said, 'May my lord King David live forever!'" (1 Kings 1:31).

Under the circumstances, this may seem like a strange thing to say. The very reason David and Bathsheba were having this conversation was that they both knew that the king *wouldn't* live forever; he was about to die. So why did she say this? Some scholars have wondered whether Bathsheba was speaking ironically, or even taunting the old king. To them her words seem out of place. But Bathsheba's hopes for David's eternal life and everlasting kingdom were *not* misplaced. The king still lives, and so does his dynasty, to the everlasting joy of all the people of God.

INSTRUCTIONS FOR A CORONATION

David may have been dying, but he was not dead yet. As soon as he finished his audience with Bathsheba, he started giving out orders. There was not a moment to lose! In trying to usurp the throne, Adonijah had already announced that he would be king. David knew that it was now or never: if he did not act immediately and decisively to put his son on the throne, God's promise would fail and Solomon would never become king.

So the old king resumed command. He said, "Call to me Zadok the priest, Nathan the prophet, and Benaiah the son of Jehoiada" (1 Kings 1:32). This was a shrewd and godly maneuver. David was calling together the prophet, the priest, and the representative of the king. Adonijah had not consulted any of these men, but David did, and in doing so he united his kingdom under the rule of God, who had appointed them to serve as the rulers of Israel. Then David gave the orders for Solomon's coronation. Here were his royal instructions:

> Take with you the servants of your lord and have Solomon my son ride on my own mule, and bring him down to Gihon. And let Zadok the priest and Nathan the prophet there anoint him king over Israel. Then blow the trumpet and say, "Long live King Solomon!" You shall then come up after him, and he

31

shall come and sit on my throne, for he shall be king in my place. And I have appointed him to be ruler over Israel and over Judah. (1 Kings 1:33–35)

We can tell that the king was used to giving orders, and that he knew exactly what to do. First Solomon would ride on David's own personal mule—the royal mule, which signified his kingship. Riding a mule or donkey was an ancient symbol of royal office. By comparison, seeing Solomon riding a mule would be like seeing the queen of England in her royal carriage, or watching Air Force One take off with the President of the United States onboard.[1] The king was on parade, in all his royal dignity.

Then Solomon would be anointed—the sacred ritual that officially consecrated him as the next king. This was in keeping with the will of God, who had promised that Solomon would rule on David's throne (see 1 Chron. 22:9–10). Anointing was also the custom; Israel's first two kings—Saul and David—had both been anointed with oil (1 Sam. 10:1; 16:1, 13). Now Zadok the priest and Nathan the prophet would pour sacred oil on Solomon's head, divinely designating him as the new king for the people of God.

Next came Solomon's enthronement. Loud trumpets would announce his royal approach to David's throne. With shouts of acclamation, people would proclaim his kingship: "Long live King Solomon!" Then Israel's leaders would follow their new ruler to Israel's throne, where he would sit in the kingly place of David.

This was the right way for King David to announce his immediate successor and for the leaders of Israel to make Solomon their king. David had always called Solomon his beloved son; now he was the first to proclaim him as king. He did it by his royal authority as God's representative. He also did it in broad daylight. Unlike Adonijah, who hosted his own private coronation, Solomon would be paraded through the city streets and crowned at the royal palace—not by his own will, but by godly men acting under the will of God. This was the proper way to conduct a coronation: with a royal mule on kingly parade, with holy oil for sacred anointing, with loud shouts and blaring trumpets, and with the new king seated on his golden throne.

1. Walter Brueggemann, *1 & 2 Kings*, Smyth & Helwys Bible Commentary (Macon, GA: Smyth & Helwys, 2000), 16.

Crown Him!

Once David had given these orders, people had a choice to make. It is the same choice we all face every day: Will we accept the King that God has anointed, submitting to his rule for our lives, or will we put ourselves on the throne, living by the rules of some other kingdom?

First Kings 1 shows what choice people made when David said that Solomon would be king. The people who accepted David's authority as the royal will of God immediately moved to crown Solomon as king. We sense their joy in the marvelous answer that Benaiah the son of Jehoiada gave when King David asked him to assist with Solomon's coronation: "Amen! May the Lord, the God of my lord the king, say so. As the Lord has been with my lord the king, even so may he be with Solomon, and make his throne greater than the throne of my lord King David" (1 Kings 1:36–37).

With a heart full of joy, Benaiah said "Amen!" to the coronation of Solomon, making his choice for the kingdom of God. He honored King David by agreeing with his instructions. He honored King Solomon by affirming his kingship. He also honored God as the Lord of all kings by recognizing his sovereignty over all these events. Benaiah was for the King and for his kingdom.

Benaiah was also a man of prayer, for this is what he was really doing: praying for the kingdom to come. By saying, "May the Lord say so," he was asking God to help David's plans come to fruition. He was asking God to be with Solomon the way he had always been with David, and to expand his kingdom by blessing Solomon even more than he had ever blessed David. Benaiah had the vision to see the glory of the coming kingdom, and he prayed accordingly, asking God to enlarge the greatness of David's dominion. He asked God to do more than he hoped or imagined, and in doing so he honored not only David and Solomon, but also their God.

Yet Benaiah was not the only person who chose the right king. The Bible says further that "Zadok the priest, Nathan the prophet, and Benaiah the son of Jehoiada, and the Cherethites and the Pelethites went down and had Solomon ride on King David's mule and brought him to Gihon. There Zadok the priest took the horn of oil from the tent and anointed Solomon" (1 Kings 1:38–39). These men carefully followed David's royal instructions. The prophet, the priest, and the representative of the king helped Solomon onto the royal mule. They were joined by David's "mighty men" (see 1 Kings 1:8), his own crack troops of Cherethites and Pelethites.[2] Together these men brought him to the holy tent where the priest kept his sacred oil for ritual anointing. Thus they anointed Solomon as king.

Immediately Solomon's kingship received the acclamation that it deserved. The whole kingdom was choosing for David's rightful heir. The priests "blew the trumpet, and all the people said, 'Long live King Solomon!' And all the people went up after him, playing on pipes, and rejoicing with great joy, so that the earth was split by their noise" (1 Kings 1:39–40).

The repetition of the royal refrain "Long live King Solomon!" functions as the climax of 1 Kings 1. What joy it was to see King Solomon take this throne on that happy day! News of his coronation spread through the city like wildfire, and soon everyone was following his parade. Musicians were blowing trumpets. Grown men were cheering and shouting. Women were singing and dancing in the streets. Children were jumping up and down, so excited they hardly knew what to do. The sound of their celebration was almost loud enough to start an earthquake. This is the way to welcome a king: with royal pomp, regal circumstance, and public celebration—something most people would be fortunate to witness once in a lifetime.

Even old King David could feel the joy. The king was still too weak to get up out of bed, but later we are told that "the king's servants came to congratulate our lord King David, saying, 'May your God make the name of Solomon more famous than yours, and make his throne greater than your throne.' And the king bowed himself on the bed. And the king also said, 'Blessed be the LORD, the God of Israel, who has granted someone to sit on my throne this day, my own eyes seeing it'" (1 Kings 1:47–48).

When these servants prayed that Solomon's kingdom would surpass David's, they were not insulting their master, but honoring God's promise to give him a royal dynasty (see 2 Sam. 7:8–16). God would indeed expand his kingdom, and David rejoiced to see the day. Right then and there, while he was still on his bed, he bowed down to worship God and to bless him for the gift of Solomon's kingship. David did not have to be the greatest king, with the most famous kingdom. What he wanted to see was the glory of the

---

2. Iain W. Provan, *1 and 2 Kings*, New International Biblical Commentary (Peabody, MA: Hendrickson, 1995), 29.

kingdom of God. Far from envying his son, therefore, David praised God for the newly anointed king of his future kingdom.

THE CORONATION OF THE CHRIST

Almost every detail of this coronation celebration helps us understand the kingship of Jesus Christ—his anointing, his enthronement, and his everlasting dominion. Most people have never witnessed a real live coronation. In the United States we have never crowned anyone king at all. But proper kings are supposed to be crowned, and in telling us how Solomon was crowned, 1 Kings 1 also helps us understand the coronation of Christ as King.

Jesus of Nazareth was the rightful heir of David's throne. As Matthew tells us in his famous genealogy, Jesus was a lineal descendant of Solomon, and of David, by way of Bathsheba (Matt. 1:6–7). Thus he had a rightful claim to David's throne. When it was time for his kingship to be openly acknowledged, Jesus rode a royal donkey into the kingdom city of Jerusalem (Matt. 21:1–11). It had long been promised that the Christ would ride the foal of a donkey (see Zech. 9:9). So when Jesus rode a donkey on the first Palm Sunday, making his triumphal entry into Jerusalem, it was a public declaration of his royal office. The king was on parade.

King Jesus was also anointed. Indeed, this is the very meaning of the word "Christ," which literally means "the Anointed One." Jesus was anointed, not by a prophet or a priest, but by the Spirit of God. This took place at his baptism in the Jordan River, when the Holy Spirit descended from heaven like a dove and rested on the Son of God (Matt. 3:16; Luke 3:21–22). As Jesus later said, "The Spirit of the Lord is upon me, because he has anointed me" (Luke 4:18; cf. Ps. 89:20; Heb. 1:9).

This shows the superiority of Christ's kingship. The oil that the prophets and the priests used to anoint the Old Testament kings was a sign of the Spirit; it showed that God the Holy Spirit had appointed and equipped a man to serve as king. But Jesus was anointed with the Spirit—not with the sign of the Spirit, but with the third person of the Trinity himself. His kingship was not simply a sign of God's kingly rule, therefore, but the living reality of God's dominion. The divine king was divinely anointed for divine rule.

Eventually, like King Solomon, King Jesus was enthroned, taking his place at the right hand of God on the throne of the universe. But first something strange happened—something that never happened to any other king of any other kingdom: the King with the crown of thorns went to the cross, where he gave his life to save his people.

Most kingdoms do anything and everything they can to protect their king. This is the unspoken premise of the game of chess, for example. When the king falls, the kingdom is lost. Therefore, the king must be protected at all costs. Another notable example comes from the Allied invasion of Normandy on D-day—June 6, 1944. British Prime Minister Winston Churchill desperately wanted to join the expeditionary forces and watch the invasion from the bridge of a battleship in the English Channel. The United States General Dwight David Eisenhower was desperate to stop him, for fear that the Prime Minister might be killed in battle. When it became apparent that Churchill would not be dissuaded, Eisenhower appealed to a higher authority: King George VI. The king went and told Churchill that if it was the Prime Minister's duty to witness the invasion, he could only conclude that it was also his own duty as king to join him on the battleship. At this point Churchill reluctantly agreed to back down, for he knew that he could never expose the king of England to such danger.

King Jesus did exactly the opposite. With royal courage he surrendered his body to be crucified. On the cross he offered a king's ransom: his life for the life of his people. He would die for all the wrong things that we had ever done, completely atoning for all our sins. Jesus would do this as our King. The crown of thorns that was meant to make a mockery of his royal claims actually proclaimed his kingly dignity, even in death.

When Jesus died on the cross, Satan and all the enemies of God could say, "The King is dead!" That is not the end of the story, however, because on the third day God said, "Long live the King!" and Jesus came right up from the grave. Soon he was royally enthroned, as God fulfilled his ancient promise to the house of David. God the Father said to God the Son, "Sit at my right hand" (Ps. 110:1). He "highly exalted" his Son, giving him authority over everything in heaven and earth (see Phil. 2:9–11). What joy there must have been in heaven when the Son of God ascended to his throne! What shouts of triumph! What blasts of trumpets! What songs of praise! The throne of Jesus is greater than the throne of David and Solomon. It is superior to all other dominions, for Jesus sits forever on the throne of heaven as King over all—the royal King that God anointed.

We too may acclaim Jesus as our King. We may do this the way Benaiah did it: saying "Amen" to the kingship of Christ and praying for his kingdom to increase. We do this first by swearing our own allegiance to Christ as King, and by committing ourselves to his service. Then we pray for the kingdom to come. Every time we pray for the gospel to reach our friends and neighbors and for the church to grow around the world, we honor Christ as King. We may also acknowledge the kingship of Christ with our worship, as people did in the streets of Jerusalem. Whether we are men, women, or children, we can all make music for our King, honoring Christ with joyful melodies and loud songs of praise. This is how we serve Christ and his kingdom: by enthroning Jesus in our hearts and saying, "Long the live the King!"

THE PARTY'S OVER

We have seen the choice that most people made: the choice for Solomon as the Lord's anointed king. But what choice did Adonijah make, and what can we learn from it?

At this point in the narrative there is a dramatic scene change, and the Bible takes us back to the feast that Adonijah was hosting right outside Jerusalem. In a crowning moment of self-exaltation, Adonijah had declared himself king (1 Kings 1:5). Then, to gain a wider following, he had thrown a huge banquet for all his friends (1 Kings 1:9–10). It was the biggest, noisiest party that anyone could remember. Adonijah was wining and dining his faithful supporters. While the party was in full swing, the would-be king reveled in his own pretentious glory.

Adonijah's supporters feasted away until everyone was totally stuffed. But as the noise died down, someone heard a sound that caught them all unawares: "Adonijah and all the guests who were with him heard it as they finished feasting. And when Joab heard the sound of the trumpet, he said, 'What does this uproar in the city mean?'" (1 Kings 1:41).

The proper literary term for this kind of situation is *dramatic irony*.[3] Dramatic irony arises whenever the reader knows something that a character in a story does *not* know. In this case, Joab heard the sound of a trumpet, followed by the noise of a crowd. He may not have known what it meant, but

---

3. See Leland Ryken, *How to Read the Bible as Literature* (Grand Rapids: Zondervan, 1984), 55–57.

we do! It was the sound of Solomon's triumph, and therefore the trumpet blast of Adonijah's downfall.

Suddenly a messenger arrived to explain what was happening. While Joab "was still speaking, behold, Jonathan the son of Abiathar the priest came. And Adonijah said, 'Come in, for you are a worthy man and bring good news'" (1 Kings 1:42). This too was ironic, for the news Jonathan brought was not good for Adonijah:

> No, for our lord King David has made Solomon king, and the king has sent with him Zadok the priest, Nathan the prophet, and Benaiah the son of Jehoiada, and the Cherethites and the Pelethites. And they had him ride on the king's mule. And Zadok the priest and Nathan the prophet have anointed him king at Gihon, and they have gone up from there rejoicing, so that the city is in an uproar. This is the noise that you have heard. Solomon sits on the royal throne. (1 Kings 1:43–46)

Poor Adonijah! Everything had been going so well for him, just as he planned. People had even started calling him king. But at the very moment of his apparent triumph, one trumpet blast was all it took to shatter his selfish dreams. For according to Jonathan, it was "a done deal": already the kingship had been securely placed in someone else's hands. David had made Solomon the king. Adonijah's younger brother had been legally anointed by Israel's rightful priest and faithful prophet, with the full support of the king's own royal guard. The new king had ridden the royal mule, to the praise of all the people. Then he had taken his seat on David's throne. Even worse, from Adonijah's perspective, Solomon's enthronement had been done at David's command, with the endorsement of his royal servants (1 Kings 1:47–48).[4] This was the awful truth, as far as Adonijah was concerned: Solomon was king in Israel.

When Adonijah's dinner guests heard what had happened, it was every man for himself. The tide had turned, and they feared that they were dead men: "Then all the guests of Adonijah trembled and rose, and each went his own way" (1 Kings 1:49). It is easy to imagine them quietly sneaking toward the exits and then making a run for it. The party was over. In the

---

4. Notice that as Jonathan delivers this message he insists on referring to "our lord King David" (1 Kings 1:47) rather than acknowledging Adonijah as king.

words of Matthew Henry, the message that Adonijah received "spoiled the sport of his party, dispersed the company, and obliged every man to shift for his own safety."[5]

Sooner or later what happened to Adonijah will happen to anyone who tries to sit on the throne of his own universe. We may become popular for a little while, especially if we throw parties like Adonijah's. We may be able to find people who will call us the king. But eventually our pleasures will turn sour and we will end up all alone, like Adonijah. This has happened to some of the most famous people in the world. Ask Adolf Hitler, who tried to rule the world but died a suicide. Or ask Howard Hughes, who was the richest man in the world but died alone and afraid—a recluse, self-imprisoned in his own home.

Better yet, ask yourself: How well has life worked when you have tried to have it on your own terms, with yourself as the king and everyone else as your servant? Has it been everything you hoped, or has it royally failed to live up to your expectations? And what will happen when you hear the last blast of God's trumpet at the final judgment? Will it bring the good news of your salvation, or will it be the sound of your doom?

ADONIJAH'S CHOICE

Sooner or later, the party will be over. This means that each of us has a choice to make: Do I still claim the right to rule my own life, or am I ready to enthrone Jesus as my King? First Kings 1 ends with Adonijah struggling to make his choice. The royal failure of all his selfish plans had left him in a real predicament. Only that morning he had been having his head sized for a crown; now he was in danger of losing his head altogether! So how would he respond? Would he still insist on calling himself the king, or would he bow before the Lord's anointed?

Adonijah would have been wise to listen to Psalm 2, which describes how the kings of the earth put themselves on the throne and take counsel "against the Lord and against his anointed" (Ps. 2:2). This is exactly what Adonijah had done, of course. But the psalm ends with this advice: "Now therefore, O kings, be wise; be warned, O rulers of the earth. Serve the Lord

5. Matthew Henry, *Matthew Henry's Complete Commentary on the Whole Bible*, vol. 2, *Judges to Job* (New York: Fleming Revell, n.d.), n.p.

with fear, and rejoice with trembling. Kiss the Son, lest he be angry, and you perish in the way" (Ps. 2:10–12). It almost sounds as if the psalmist is speaking directly to Adonijah, because this is exactly what he needed to do if he wanted to save his life: serve the Lord with fear and embrace the kingship of his royal son.

So what did the man do? The Bible says: "Adonijah feared Solomon. So he arose and went and took hold of the horns of the altar" (1 Kings 1:50). The terse phrasing of this verse suggests that Adonijah did all this in rapid succession. If he wanted to save his life, he had to act quickly. There was not a moment to lose! So he ran to the courtyard of the tabernacle and clasped onto the horns of the altar where sacrifices were made for sin. According to the Law of Moses, doing this would save the life of someone who committed involuntary manslaughter (Ex. 21:12–14). That was not the case here, so Adonijah had no legal reason to expect that this would keep him safe, but it was the only thing he could think of—maybe the best way to beg for his life and possibly the only thing that could still save him.

Now Adonijah's fate was in Solomon's hands. Yet rather than claiming vengeance, the new and rightful king showed mercy:

> Then it was told Solomon, "Behold, Adonijah fears King Solomon, for behold, he has laid hold of the horns of the altar, saying, 'Let King Solomon swear to me first that he will not put his servant to death with the sword.'" And Solomon said, "If he will show himself a worthy man, not one of his hairs shall fall to the earth, but if wickedness is found in him, he shall die." So King Solomon sent, and they brought him down from the altar. And he came and paid homage to King Solomon, and Solomon said to him, "Go to your house." (1 Kings 1:51–53)

Oh, how the mighty had fallen! The man who tried to elevate himself was brought low. The man who wanted to be king had to pay homage to his younger brother. The man who tried to give the orders was told to go home. From this point forward Adonijah would be on probation. Solomon let him go only on the condition of good behavior. Now Adonijah had to prove himself to be a worthy man.

Everything we know about Adonijah makes it seem very unlikely that he will be able to meet Solomon's royal condition. In an act of outward submission he has sworn allegiance to the Lord's anointed, but has he truly surrendered the sovereignty of his heart? In verse 51 he is trying to stay in charge by setting the terms under which he will submit to Solomon. Somehow we know that sooner or later Adonijah's false heart will be discovered, and he will die.

For now we are left to put ourselves in the story and consider our own relationship to God's anointed and eternal King: Jesus Christ. The Bible says that Jesus is superior to Solomon (Matt. 12:42), and we see his superiority here. As much as we may admire Solomon for giving Adonijah another chance, we should praise Jesus for giving us more grace. Solomon said that Adonijah's life would be spared if he proved himself worthy, which was certainly fair enough. But Jesus says that he will accept us even when we are *unworthy*, as we all are (see Rom. 5:6–8). Solomon said that if Adonijah sinned he would die. But Jesus, seeing that we had sinned, climbed up onto the altar of sacrifice and died in our place. Now, there's a King for you—a ruler who offers his life for your salvation!

Our King still lives. Eventually David died, and so did Solomon. But Jesus rose from the dead to give everlasting life to David, to Solomon, and to all his royal sons and daughters. There will never be an interruption, an interregnum, or another royal succession in the kingdom of God, because Jesus Christ is the immortal King of all ages (see 1 Tim. 1:17).

Now everyone who belongs to the kingdom of David by choosing for Christ can say, "The King is dead; long live the King!" Long live the King who welcomes the unworthy! Long live the King who died for sinners! Long live the King who rose from the grave! Long live the King who is coming again! God has given us this promise: "Of the increase of his government and of peace there will be no end, on the throne of David and over his kingdom, to establish it and to uphold it with justice and with righteousness from this time forth and forevermore" (Isa. 9:7). Long live the King, and all the loyal subjects of his royal kingdom, who live by faith in the Son of God!

4

DAVID'S LAST WORDS

1 Kings 2:1—11

I am about to go the way of all the earth. Be strong, and show yourself a man, and keep the charge of the LORD your God, walking in his ways and keeping his statutes, his commandments, his rules, and his testimonies, as it is written in the Law of Moses, that you may prosper in all that you do and wherever you turn.
(1 Kings 2:2–3)

A life is a terrible thing to waste. To illustrate this point, John Piper recounts a story his father often told in his days as a fiery Baptist evangelist. It is the story of a man who came to saving faith in Jesus Christ near the end of his earthly existence. Piper writes:

The church had prayed for this man for decades. He was hard and resistant. But this time, for some reason, he showed up when my father was preaching. At the end of the service, during a hymn, to everyone's amazement he came and took my father's hand. They sat down together on the front pew of the church as the people were dismissed. God opened his heart to the Gospel of Christ, and he was saved from his sins and given eternal life. But that did not

stop him from sobbing and saying, as the tears ran down his wrinkled face—
"I've wasted it! I've wasted it!"[1]

By the grace of God, even a life that is almost totally wasted can still be redeemed. As the Scottish theologian Thomas Boston once said, our present existence is only "a short preface to a long eternity."[2] If this is true, then the man's life was not wasted after all; he was only just beginning an eternal life of endless praise. But why wait even a moment longer before starting to serve Jesus? You have only one life to live. Do not waste it by living for yourself when you can use it instead for the glory of God. This was the wisdom that David gave to his son Solomon.

THE WAY OF ALL FLESH

The old king was on his deathbed. In fact, he had been in bed since the opening verse of 1 Kings, when, despite the best efforts of his servants, he simply could not stay warm. Although he had managed to rouse himself long enough to appoint Solomon as his successor, David was still dying. So we are told that his "time to die drew near" (1 Kings 2:1), and later we read: "Then David slept with his fathers and was buried in the city of David. And the time that David reigned over Israel was forty years. He reigned seven years in Hebron and thirty-three years in Jerusalem" (1 Kings 2:10–11).

This was the end of an era. The Scripture says that David served God's purpose in his own generation (Acts 13:36). By the grace of God, he established a capital city that would stand at the center of history and started a dynasty that would save the world. But even King David had to go the way of all flesh, and as he lay dying there were some things he wanted to say before he could die in peace—things that might help his son avoid wasting his life. So David "commanded Solomon his son, saying, 'I am about to go the way of all the earth'" (1 Kings 2:1–2). Then he proceeded to give his last will and testament.

1. John Piper, *Don't Waste Your Life* (Wheaton, IL: Crossway, 2003), 12.
2. Thomas Boston, *Human Nature in Its Fourfold State*, in *The Complete Works of the Late Rev. Thomas Boston of Ettrick*, ed. Samuel M'Millan, 12 vols. (London, 1853; repr., Wheaton, IL: Richard Owen Roberts, 1980), 8:244.

David was fortunate. Some people die so suddenly that they never get the chance to say anything. But most people have some things they want to say before they die. What would you say if you had the chance? We all have to die sometime (unless Jesus comes back to earth first, of course), and one good way to get ready to die is to think ahead to our dying words. What would you say if you knew that you were about to die? What testimony would you give your family and friends? What spiritual legacy would you leave for your children and grandchildren?

SETTLING OLD SCORES

There are two parts to David's farewell discourse. The first part runs from verse 2 to verse 4 and mainly addresses Solomon's soul—the spiritual commitments a king needs to make if he belongs to the kingdom of God. The second part, which runs from verses 5 to 9, addresses the security of Solomon's kingdom—the judgments he needed to make about his friends and enemies if he wanted to hold on to his kingdom.

The two parts of this speech are very different. In the first part David gives general spiritual advice that could apply to almost anyone, but in the second part he gives Solomon specific instructions about how to deal with particular people. The first part of his speech sounds more spiritual; the second part seems much more political. The differences are so obvious that some scholars think they must have come from two different people. In fact, some of them think that what David says in the second part of his speech is vindictive, contradictory, and ungodly.

As always, the best way to answer these objections is to look more carefully at what the Bible actually says. In this case, it may be helpful to start with the hardest part of the passage first (i.e., vv. 5–9). At the end of his long reign over Israel, David still had some outstanding debts to pay, some wrongs to right, and some old scores to settle. Like many other people, when it came time for him to die he still had some unfinished business to take care of—business he failed to handle himself and thus needed to leave for Solomon.

So David told his son that as he took the throne, there were three people he needed to deal with: two enemies and a friend. First, Solomon would have to do something about Joab. David may have been old, but he had not forgotten Joab's sin in assassinating two men in cold blood. So he said:

Moreover, you also know what Joab the son of Zeruiah did to me, how he dealt with the two commanders of the armies of Israel, Abner the son of Ner, and Amasa the son of Jether, whom he killed, avenging in time of peace for blood that had been shed in war, and putting the blood of war on the belt around his waist and on the sandals on his feet. Act therefore according to your wisdom, but do not let his gray head go down to Sheol in peace. (1 Kings 2:5–6)

Joab had long served as the commander of David's armies. He was an effective military leader, but on occasion he used his power in ungodly ways to advance his own personal agenda. Joab had a way of making people disappear, and there was blood on his hands—the blood of Abner and Amasa.

Abner was a leader from the tribe of Benjamin who made a covenant promise to secure David's kingship by making peace with the house of Saul (see 2 Sam. 3:1–21). Yet Joab had a vendetta against Abner (see 2 Sam. 2:18–23) and killed him in cold blood—not during a war, but in peacetime (see 2 Sam. 3:22–30). This murderous act grieved David deeply (see 2 Sam. 3:31–39), and because of Abner's role as a mediator with the house of Saul, it threatened to plunge the nation into civil war.

Amasa met a similar fate. He too had promised to strengthen David's rule—in his case, by bringing the leaders of Judah to help the king put down the rebellion of Sheba (see 2 Sam. 20:1–2, 4). But when Amasa was late for his rendezvous with David, Joab grabbed him by the beard, as if to kiss him, and then ran a sword through his stomach (see 2 Sam. 20:5–10). Joab did not do this under David's orders, but to strengthen his own command of Israel's army (see 2 Sam. 20:23).

Joab was a dangerous man, who sometimes operated as a law unto himself. David had been trying to build alliances with Abner and Amasa—alliances that would strengthen God's kingdom by uniting the tribes of Israel. But Joab saw these men as potential rivals for the top spot in the military, so he put them to death, and in doing so he put his own interests ahead of his king and the kingdom of God.[3]

It is not entirely clear why David failed to deal more decisively with Joab at the time. He criticized and cursed the general (see 2 Sam. 3:28–29), but never brought him to justice. Maybe David thought he lacked the strength to

---

3. See August H. Konkel, *1 & 2 Kings*, NIV Application Commentary (Grand Rapids: Zondervan, 2006), 56–57.

challenge the military, or maybe he knew how useful Joab might be for doing his own dirty work (see 2 Sam. 11:14–18). But when it came time for him to die, he rightly regarded Joab as a potential threat to Solomon, especially since he had sided with Adonijah in his bid for David's throne (1 Kings 1:7). It was up to Solomon to decide exactly what to do, and when to do it, but David advised him not to let the man die of natural causes; instead, Joab should be treated with strict and righteous vengeance.

Barzillai's family should receive just the opposite treatment. "But deal loyally with the sons of Barzillai the Gileadite," David said, "and let them be among those who eat at your table, for with such loyalty they met me when I fled from Absalom your brother" (1 Kings 2:7).

Here David refers to a time of desperate crisis in the history of his kingdom. David's son Absalom had rebelled against his father and plunged Israel into civil war. As a result, David and his loyal servants had to run for their lives. They fled into the wilderness, where they were tired and hungry and thirsty. But Barzillai and some other wealthy men came to the king's rescue. They brought "beds, basins, and earthen vessels, wheat, barley, flour, parched grain, beans and lentils, honey and curds and sheep and cheese" for David and his men to eat (2 Sam. 17:28–29; cf. 19:32). Unlike Joab, Barzillai was kingdom-minded. He sided with the rightful king, even when this called for courage and required costly personal sacrifices to advance his kingdom.

When David eventually returned to Jerusalem, he tried to return the favor by offering Barzillai a permanent place in his royal court (2 Sam. 19:33). But Barzillai was eighty years old by then, so he asked David to receive another member of his household instead (2 Sam. 19:34–40). Now it was up to Solomon to pay David's debt and fulfill David's promise by giving Barzillai's sons a place at his table. This was more than an act of kindness; it was a royal reward for loyal service to the king.

Solomon also had Shimei to deal with—another enemy. David said to his son:

> And there is also with you Shimei the son of Gera, the Benjamite from Bahurim, who cursed me with a grievous curse on the day when I went to Mahanaim. But when he came down to meet me at the Jordan, I swore to him by the LORD, saying, "I will not put you to death with the sword." Now therefore do not hold him guiltless, for you are a wise man. You will know what you

ought to do to him, and you shall bring his gray head down with blood to Sheol. (1 Kings 2:8–9)

Shimei belonged to the house of Saul and therefore held a grudge against David for taking Saul's throne, even after David had become the Lord's anointed king. On one memorable occasion during Absalom's rebellion, Shimei came out to assault David, screaming curses at him, accusing him of murder, and throwing stones at him. But rather than putting Shimei to death, as his servants begged him to do, David trusted God to bless him for being cursed (2 Sam. 6:5–13). Later, when David returned to Jerusalem, Shimei regretted what he had done and begged for mercy, which the king granted by promising not to put him to death "today" (see 2 Sam. 19:18–23).

David kept his promise that day, and afterward, but he still believed that Shimei was guilty of sin and therefore deserved condemnation. Perhaps he rationalized his counsel for Solomon by telling himself that his son was not bound by the oath that he (David) had made to Shimei. So he told his son not to let the man die a natural death, but to send him to an early grave.

ROYAL JUSTICE

These cold-blooded instructions make many readers uncomfortable. Was it right for David to hand out all these death sentences? Some of his last words sound like something out of Mario Puzo's *The Godfather*, in which new Mafia dons secure their power by ruthlessly killing off all their potential rivals. Richard Phillips says that when David "directed Solomon to murder all his rivals and begin his reign with a sword bathed in blood," he "left a legacy [not only] of principle, but also of unbelieving pragmatism; not merely of faith and reliance on God, but also of fleshly self-reliance and worldly use of power."[4]

Perhaps, therefore, this is one of the many places where a great hero from the Bible acts in ways that are less than heroic. This would not be surprising, because the Scriptures of the Old and New Testaments present people the way they really are—not as perfect men and women, but as sinners who desperately need the grace of God. This is for our encouragement, because

4. Richard D. Phillips, *Turning Back the Darkness: The Biblical Pattern of Reformation* (Wheaton, IL: Crossway, 2002), 55.

we know what it is like to want revenge, or to seize our chance to settle an old score. Jesus said that even our hatred is a murderous sin (Matt. 5:21–22), and therefore we need as much of God's mercy as David needed.

A powerful example of setting aside the desire for revenge comes from the Christlike witness of Antoine Rutayisire. When Antoine's family was attacked by Hutu soldiers in the genocidal violence that overwhelmed Rwanda in 1994, it was a matter of life or death that put his faith under fire. Here is how Antoine described what happened, and how he responded:

> "This is our turn," I told myself. Immediately, wild and weird thoughts whirled in my mind at a flashing speed. "Am I going to let them rape my wife, kill my child and all these young women and men in my home under my very eyes without even some attempt to protect them? What type of death are we going to die? Are they going to shoot us or to cut us into pieces?" I shuddered.
>
> Then the idea crossed my mind: "Why don't you grab a stick or any other weapon at hand and go out and fight them? Can't you die like a man?" This was a spontaneous, human reaction. I could recognize my old self surging up, as in the past I would never have tolerated any ill-treatment without some reaction.
>
> I was then deeply convicted in my heart as I remembered all the past efforts I had made to keep my heart pure of anger and bitterness. So I made this short prayer of confession: "Lord, forgive me for thinking of making my own defense and give me grace to obey you even unto death. I ask for your blessing on these people, and if it is your will that we die, have them give time to die praying for them, as You did on the cross." At that very moment, a feeling of deep peace that I had never experienced before flooded through me, and I felt so light inside that a breeze could have swept me off the ground. I had accepted death, and I knew what I would do when the killers came. I was ready to face death with a Christ-like attitude.[5]

Perhaps David would have been wiser to leave vengeance to the Lord, as Antoine Rutayisire did. There is another way to look at the king's instructions, however. Bear in mind that both David and Solomon were anointed to serve as kings in Israel, and that like all other rulers and authorities, they were appointed by God to bear the power of the sword (see Rom. 13:1–4). It was their job to render justice for the people.

5. Antoine Rutayisire, quoted in Anne Coomes, *African Harvest* (London: Monarch, 2002), 187.

Keep this in mind as well: since David was the divinely anointed king, any assault against his royal person was tantamount to an attack against the kingdom of God. This is why David had repeatedly refused to lift his hand against King Saul: he knew that Saul was the Lord's anointed (e.g., 1 Sam. 24:6). Now David himself was the Lord's anointed, and any attack against the king was more than a personal matter: it represented a threat to the kingdom that God had promised to establish.

So the instructions David gave about Joab, Barzillai, and Shimei were kingdom-minded instructions, based on the word of God. Barzillai had served the king well, advancing the cause of his kingdom, and therefore his sons should rightly claim a place at the royal table. But Joab and Shimei had undermined David's kingly plans and cursed his royal dignity. For the peace and security of his kingdom, therefore, King Solomon needed to treat these violent men with strict justice. It was not for his own honor that David gave these instructions. If this had merely been a personal vendetta, he would have done away with Joab and Shimei long ago. But he was doing it now for the good of the kingdom of his beloved son.

This shows how vitally important it is to serve the Lord's anointed king. As David lay dying, the great choice people faced was whether they were for or against the kingdom's true king. The great choice that we face in life is fundamentally the same: will we be for or against Jesus Christ, who is David's royal Son and the King of God's everlasting kingdom?

If we waste our lives by putting our own kingdom ahead of God's kingdom the way that Joab did—or even worse, if we throw rocks at the King as Shimei did, cursing the very name of Jesus Christ—then we deserve his kingly wrath. God is a just and righteous King. His vengeance may not come right away, any more than it came right away for Joab and Shimei. But it will surely come at the final judgment, when everyone who opposes the kingdom of God will perish (see Ps. 2:12; Rev. 19).

Happily, there is life for every loyal servant of God who swears allegiance to Christ as King. Jesus said, "Seek first the kingdom of God and his righteousness, and all these things will be added to you" (Matt. 6:33). If we seek God's kingdom, there will be a place for us at God's royal table, just as there was for the sons of Barzillai. By trusting the King we will receive the gracious gift of eternal life, with many generous rewards for everything we do in the service of his kingdom.

There are really only two kinds of people in the world, who will meet two completely different destinies. What makes the difference is our relationship to Jesus. Some people are servants of the King; others are enemies of his kingdom. What kind of person are you?

What Makes a Man

The rest of 1 Kings 2 explains what Solomon did with David's final instructions, and how he dealt with the men his father told him to reward or punish. But first we need to go back and consider what David said about the spiritual life of Solomon's soul. Of all the commands that the old king gave, these were the dearest to his fatherly heart: "Be strong, and show yourself a man, and keep the charge of the LORD your God, walking in his ways and keeping his statutes, his commandments, his rules, and his testimonies, as it is written in the Law of Moses" (1 Kings 2:2–3; cf. Deut. 31:1–8; Josh. 1:1–9).

David wanted the same thing for Solomon that every father wants for his son: he wanted Solomon to be strong; he wanted him to be a man. But David defined manhood very differently from the way most people define it.

Some people think that a man proves his manhood by showing his physical strength. A real man is a good athlete, or knows how to fight, or has been to battle—he knows how to defend himself and defeat his opponents. David had done all these things in his time. The king was an old warrior, who had killed both man and beast, and who had used his power to conquer a kingdom. But David did not think that physical strength is what would make his son a man.

Some people think that a man proves his manhood by sexual conquest, by proving that he knows what to do with a woman. If this is what makes a man, then David had met this requirement as well, both to his credit and to his shame. But David did not think that being sexually active would make his son a man.

Some people think that a man proves his manhood by having a successful career. A real man's work is well regarded by his colleagues and well rewarded by his employer. He is able to provide for his family; the wealthier he is, the better. If this is what it takes to be a man, then David was a man among men, because he was the wealthiest man in Israel. But the king did not think that getting richer and richer would make his son a man.

Many people think that physical strength, or sexual activity, or professional success, or financial independence will make a man. But if these are the only things we live for, we will waste our lives, because what makes a man is obedience to the Word of God. Manliness is next to godliness. So the way for Solomon to show that he was a man was to keep God's laws and walk in God's ways.

In his famous last words, David used seven different terms to describe the Word of God. He called it a "charge" or a "Law." He referred to God's ways, statutes, commandments, rules, and testimonies. Each of these terms comes from the Word of God itself, specifically from the Law of Moses in the book of Deuteronomy (see Deut. 4:29; 6:1–2; 8:6; 11:1; 29:9). Each term has a slightly different emphasis. Statutes and commandments are general orders from God, like the Ten Commandments. Rules and testimonies govern specific cases, like how much people should pay back for what they steal, or how to offer a particular sacrifice at an annual festival. But David's main point in using all these different terms is that his son should live by every word that comes from the mouth of God.

It is not just this part or that part of the Bible that we should obey, but every last word. There is not one situation Solomon would face in his life as a man or the rule of his kingdom that the Bible does not address. Even when Solomon rewarded his friends and punished his enemies, as David told him to do in the second part of his farewell discourse, this needed to be done according to biblical principles. As one scholar puts it, "The exercise of royal power is not to be arbitrary, for the king is not a law unto himself. It is rather to be in accordance with the Law of Moses."[6]

What was true for Solomon is also true for us: there is not one situation we face in life that the Bible does not address in some practical way. God's Word teaches us how to think, how to speak, and how to live. It tells us what to love and what to hate. It shows us how to glorify God forever. This is why the ministry of the church must be built squarely and unashamedly on the Word of God. As James Boice once said, "we believe the Bible to be the Word of God, the only infallible rule of faith and practice, and it is practical

6. Iain W. Provan, *1 and 2 Kings*, New International Biblical Commentary (Peabody, MA: Hendrickson, 1995), 31.

because we believe the Bible must be the treasure most valued and attended to in the church's life."[7] We read the Word, pray the Word, sing the Word, and preach the Word so that we can believe its saving promises and obey its righteous commands.

When David told Solomon to walk in God's ways, he was telling him to live a biblical lifestyle. The Bible should have "a predominant influence upon our thinking and our manner of life."[8] This is what will make us real men (or real women, as the case may be): basing our lives on the Word of God.

When it comes to godly manliness, God's Word puts everything in proper perspective. The Bible teaches a man to join his physical strength to patience and gentleness, so that rather than striking out in selfish anger, he uses his power to protect the weak. The Bible teaches a man to bring his sexual desire under the control of the Holy Spirit. Rather than satisfying his own lusts, he gives his whole body and his whole heart to one woman for a lifetime, so that God can make a family. In short, the Bible teaches a man to serve God in his daily calling, so that his work brings honor to Jesus Christ instead of to himself, and so that his wealth can advance the kingdom of God rather than being used for his own foolish pleasures. The best and only way to avoid wasting your life is to base everything you do on the Word of God.

LIVING BY THE BOOK

David ended his exhortation about walking God's way by reminding his son of the amazing promises that God had made to his royal house. Why was it so important for Solomon to obey God's Word? David told him it was so "that you may prosper in all that you do and wherever you turn, that the LORD may establish his word that he spoke concerning me, saying, 'If your sons pay close attention to their way, to walk before me in faithfulness with all their heart and with all their soul, you shall not lack a man on the throne of Israel'" (1 Kings 2:3–4).

If Solomon was faithful to God, then he would receive the double blessing of personal prosperity and a perpetual dynasty. According to verse 3, he would prosper in everything he did. This had been David's own experience.

---

7. James Montgomery Boice, "The Sufficiency of the Word of God," The 25th Anniversary Sermon, May 23, 1993, http://www.tenth.org/articles/TheWord.pdf.

8. Marcus A. Brownson, "The Idea for Our Church," *The Presbyterian*, April 1, 1937, 11.

As long as he was careful to do God's will, he was blessed with success in protecting his livestock, defeating his enemies, writing his poetry, growing his family, and founding his dynasty. The Scripture says, "David had success in all his undertakings, for the LORD was with him" (1 Sam. 18:14). It was only when he disobeyed God that David suffered tragic loss through the death of his son, the breakup of his family, and the civil war that threatened to destroy his kingdom.

So David knew what he was talking about: if we want to have God's blessing, we must walk in God's ways. This would be true for Solomon, who was blessed with more wisdom and more wealth than almost anyone else in the history of the world. As long as he was obedient to the Word of God, everything Solomon did was a success. But disobedience would be his downfall, as we will discover.

The same principle holds true today, especially if we define success in biblical terms. People who follow biblical principles will prosper (see Ps. 1:1–3; cf. Matt. 7:24–25). This does not mean that we will never suffer, or that every difficulty we face in life is the direct result of our own personal sin. But it does mean that obedience has God's blessing. We may experience this blessing in our relationships, as the Word of God teaches us how to love. We may experience this blessing in our homes, as the Word of God teaches us how to lead a family. We may experience this blessing in our daily calling, as the Word of God teaches us how to work hard and pursue excellence. But whether we have this kind of success or not, we will certainly be successful spiritually. Obeying God's Word will keep us close to the Holy Spirit; it will help us bring more people to Christ; it will show us more of the glory of God.

For Solomon there would be a unique and added blessing—one with implications for the salvation of the world. Not only would obedience to God bring him personal prosperity, but it would also establish a perpetual dynasty. Solomon was the son of David, to whom God had promised an everlasting kingdom (2 Sam. 7:11–16). This promise was starting to come true, as Solomon took David's throne. But how would his kingdom stay in power? It would not be protected by political alliances, or trade agreements, or military power, or personal vendettas, or anything else that human empires trust for their security. It would be preserved only by faithful obedience to the Word of God.

This promise was clearly conditional: *if* Solomon obeyed, *then* David's throne would be established. The continuity of the dynasty depended on obedience to the Word of God. We find a similar promise in the Psalms: "The LORD swore to David a sure oath from which he will not turn back: 'One of the sons of your body I will set on your throne. If your sons keep my covenant and my testimonies that I shall teach them, their sons also forever shall sit on your throne'" (Ps. 132:11–12). But God made other promises to the house of David that were *not* conditional. God said to David: "Your house and your kingdom shall be made sure forever before me. Your throne shall be established forever" (2 Sam. 7:16).

So which kind of promise did God really give to David? Was it conditional or unconditional? Did the establishment of David's throne depend on Solomon's keeping covenant or not?

These questions are answered for us in the gospel of Jesus Christ, who is the final Son of David. The sad truth about Solomon is that like his father David, he did not give full obedience to the Word of God. Solomon started well, but as we read his tragic story, we will trace his sad decline into idolatry, greed, and immorality. To one degree or another, the same is true of every last king in Israel: they all failed to walk in God's ways and to keep God's commandments.

Except Jesus, that is. Jesus of Nazareth was the only Son of David who did not waste his life, but was royally faithful to God's covenant, keeping all the statutes, rules, commandments, and testimonies that were written in the law of God. This is why God's promises to David were both conditional and unconditional. They were conditional because the king really was required to offer full obedience to the Word of God. They were also unconditional because God knew that one day a King would come and fulfill his command. The dynasty would be established on the basis of the full and perfect obedience of Jesus Christ, and therefore God's absolute promise would not fail. By fulfilling the conditions of the law, Jesus made it possible to receive God's unconditional promise.

FAMOUS LAST WORDS

At the end of his perfect, promise-fulfilling life, Jesus had some famous last words of his own—words that offered forgiveness to his enemies and promised paradise to anyone who trusts in him (see Luke 23:34, 43). Then Jesus finished his saving work by dying on the cross, suffering the violence and death that we deserve for our sins. This was not the end, however, because Jesus rose back from the dead to take his eternal throne.

The apostles testified to these truths whenever they preached the gospel, and on occasion they made a direct connection with (and contrast to) David. Peter confidently preached that David "both died and was buried, and his tomb is with us to this day." But he went on to proclaim a King who is not dead, but alive: "Being therefore a prophet, and knowing that God had sworn with an oath to him that he would set one of his descendants on his throne, he [David] foresaw and spoke about the resurrection of the Christ, that he was not abandoned to Hades, nor did his flesh see corruption. . . . Let all the house of Israel therefore know for certain that God has made [this Jesus] both Lord and Christ" (Acts 2:29–32, 36; cf. 13:36–39).

According to Peter, Jesus refused to waste his life, but as the true and faithful Son of David he gave it up for our salvation. Anyone who repents and believes in him as the risen Christ will be saved. But our salvation does not stop there. Because we are his saved people, Jesus tells us not to waste our lives, but to offer them in full obedience to the Word of God. Here is how Jesus explained it in one of his parables: "Everyone then who hears these words of mine and does them will be like a wise man who built his house on the rock. And the rain fell, and the floods came, and the winds blew and beat on that house, but it did not fall, because it had been founded on the rock" (Matt. 7:24–25).

Is your life founded on the rock of God's Word? The Christmas before he died, my father-in-law gave each of his three daughters a beautiful leather Bible. I thought it was a little strange at the time, because each of them already owned a Bible—more than one, in fact. Each Bible came with a bookmark, on which he printed his picture and wrote what turned out to be some of his last words. "Lisa," he wrote to my wife, "I know no better gift to my child than to share God's Word with her. Love to you, Dad."

Eventually I came to see what my father-in-law was doing: he was giving his last will and testament to his daughters. In doing so, he wanted to give them the best gift he knew, which also happens to be the best gift that David knew. God wants us to have this gift as well—the gift of his Word. If we receive it by faith, the Word of God will make us strong. It will help us become real men and real women. It will keep us from wasting our lives. Indeed, it will save us forever.

5

PUTTING THE KINGDOM FIRST

1 Kings 2:12–46

*The king also said to Shimei, "You know in your own heart all
the harm that you did to David my father. So the LORD will bring
back your harm on your own head. But King Solomon shall be
blessed, and the throne of David shall be established before the
LORD forever." Then the king commanded Benaiah the son of
Jehoiada, and he went out and struck him down, and he died.
So the kingdom was established in the hand of Solomon.*
(1 Kings 2:44–46)

*I*n an article entitled "A New Kind of Urban Christian," Tim Keller
argues that "Christians should be a dynamic counterculture. It
is not enough for Christians to simply live as individuals in the
city. They must live as a particular kind of community. Christians are called
to be an alternate city within every earthly city."

The kind of community Keller has in mind is one in which money, sex,
and power are used for the glory of God—not selfishly, but sacrificially. Here
is how he describes it:

> Regarding sex, the alternate city . . . teaches its members to conform their
> bodily beings to the shape of the gospel—abstinence outside of marriage and

fidelity within. Regarding money, the Christian counterculture encourages a radically generous commitment of time, money, relationships, and living space to social justice and the needs of the poor, the immigrant, and the economically and physically weak. Regarding power, Christian community is visibly committed to power-sharing and relationship-building between races and classes that are alienated outside of the body of Christ.[1]

The Bible has a name for this alternative community: it is called the kingdom of God. One day soon we will see this kingdom in all its glory, at the second coming of Jesus Christ. In the meantime, the struggle to establish his kingdom is fought in every human heart, with each decision we make about our money, our sexuality, and the things in life we want to bring under our control.

The same battle was fought when Solomon established his kingdom in Israel, and if we look carefully at the choices people made either for or against his kingship, we may be able to see ourselves and our own need for a Savior.

ROYAL REVENGE

If the question in 1 Kings 1 was succession (who would be the next king?), the question in chapter 2 is security (will the kingdom stand?).[2] This question gets answered in verse 12, and again in verse 46. Together these two verses form an *inclusio*; they mark the beginning and the end of a section of the Bible and tell us what that section is about. In verse 12 we read that "Solomon sat on the throne of David his father, and his kingdom was firmly established." Verse 46 says the same thing in slightly different words: "So the kingdom was established in the hand of Solomon."

The prophecies were coming true. God had promised to "establish" the kingdom of David's son (2 Sam. 7:12). He said: "I will establish the throne of his kingdom forever" (2 Sam. 7:13). By using the same vocabulary in 1 Kings 2, the Bible is showing us that God is faithful to keep his royal promises to the house of David. The way these promises came true was not by a divine and

1. Tim Keller, "A New Kind of Urban Christian," *Christianity Today* 50, 5 (May 2006): 36.
2. Dale Ralph Davis, *The Wisdom and the Folly: An Exposition of the Book of First Kings* (Fearn, Ross-shire: Christian Focus, 2002), 25–26.

supernatural miracle, but by the swift execution of justice. Solomon established his kingdom by eliminating all his enemies.

We were introduced to these enemies even before we met Solomon. First
Kings began with an attempted coup, in which David's eldest son, Adonijah,
announced that he would be king (1 Kings 1:5). Rather than seeking the
approval of the leaders God had appointed over Israel—David the king,
Zadok the priest, and Nathan the prophet—the would-be king gathered his
own group of loyal supporters. Adonijah's coconspirators included Abiathar
the priest and Joab the general (see 1 Kings 1:7–8).

Once he took the throne, Solomon had to decide what to do with the men
who had plotted against his kingdom. His father had frankly advised him to
crush them. In his last words and final instructions, David told Solomon to
execute vengeance against Joab (1 Kings 2:5–6), and also Shimei, who had
cursed David with a mortal curse (1 Kings 2:8–9). This is more or less what
Solomon did. The rest of 1 Kings 2 recounts how he executed Adonijah
(1 Kings 2:13–25), banished Abiathar (1 Kings 2:26–27), put Joab to death
(1 Kings 2:28–35), and struck down Shimei (1 Kings 2:36–46).

Many commentators are critical of the king for moving down this hit list.
Terence Fretheim calls it "politics as usual, but with more than the usual
complement of ruthlessness."[3] Walter Brueggemann says that Solomon is
guilty of "callous, systematic elimination of all threats."[4] Iain Provan says
that his reasons for putting these men to death were "specious."[5] Others have
compared Solomon's brutal methods to Machiavelli, or to Karl Marx, who
believed that every state was founded on violence.

Maybe there is truth to some of these criticisms, and 1 Kings 2 is mainly
about power politics. Remember, however, that Solomon was the Lord's
anointed king. He had been properly crowned, according to the promise
of God. Therefore, it was necessary for his kingdom to be established.
This was necessary, in fact, for the salvation of the world, because God
had promised that our Messiah would come from the line of David and
Solomon. Furthermore, everyone in Israel owed full allegiance to Solomon
as the rightful king. This was not merely a matter of politics, but a question

---

3. Terence E. Fretheim, *First and Second Kings*, Westminster Bible Companion (Louisville: Westminster
John Knox, 1999), 26.
4. Walter Brueggemann, *1 Kings*, Knox Preaching Guides (Atlanta: John Knox, 1982), 5.
5. Iain W. Provan, *1 and 2 Kings*, New International Biblical Commentary (Peabody, MA: Hendrickson,
1995), 40.

of obedient submission to the kingdom of God. If these men were Solomon's rivals, then they were enemies of the crown that God had placed on Solomon's head.

Thus Adonijah and his henchmen were guilty of the sin of high treason, which has always been rightly regarded as a capital offense. We are not talking here about men who merely disagreed with Solomon's policies, but about men who wanted to take his very throne. The right and proper way for a king to punish such mortal enemies is not by giving them liberty, but by giving them death, or at least exile. As Dale Ralph Davis has written, "The security of the kingdom requires the elimination of its enemies. The kingdom must be preserved from those trying to destroy and undermine it."[6] To disagree with this form of justice is to misunderstand what it means for a king to be the king. As the situation arises, therefore, or as circumstances dictate, Solomon must be wise to follow the counsel of David and establish his kingdom by eliminating his enemies.

ADONIJAH'S FOLLY: SEX AND POWER

Solomon had four enemies to eliminate: Adonijah, Abiathar, Joab, and Shimei. What is important to notice about these men is that they all put their own desire for money, sex, or power ahead of loving obedience to the kingdom of God. Thus the stories of these men give us test cases in temptation.

The first man Solomon had to deal with was Adonijah, who wanted sex and power more than he wanted the kingdom of God. Adonijah's lust for power has been obvious from the beginning of Kings, when he tried to crown himself the king. But at the very moment he was celebrating his own coronation (1 Kings 1:9–10), Adonijah heard that Solomon had become king over Jerusalem (1 Kings 1:39ff.). This made the man fear for his life. Yet Solomon gave him a second chance. If Adonijah proved himself worthy, his life would be spared; but if he turned out to be wicked, he would surely die (1 Kings 1:52).

At first Adonijah honored the new and rightful king. Solomon told him to go home in peace, but the next thing we know, he is back at the palace to make an ungodly request that was based on an unholy desire:

6. Davis, *The Wisdom and the Folly*, 31.

> Then Adonijah the son of Haggith came to Bathsheba the mother of Solomon. And she said, "Do you come peacefully?"
>
> He said, "Peacefully." Then he said, "I have something to say to you."
>
> She said, "Speak."
>
> He said, "You know that the kingdom was mine, and that all Israel fully expected me to reign. However, the kingdom has turned about and become my brother's, for it was his from the LORD. And now I have one request to make of you; do not refuse me."
>
> She said to him, "Speak."
>
> And he said, "Please ask King Solomon—he will not refuse you—to give me Abishag the Shunammite as my wife." (1 Kings 2:13–17)

This may seem like a small request. Adonijah was willing to give up the entire kingdom and even to acknowledge that Solomon's kingship was God's will. All he wanted was Abishag's hand in marriage. But notice what a huge sense of entitlement Adonijah still had. He was angry that life had not met his expectations. "The kingdom was mine," he said, "and you know it!" Even though he acknowledged Solomon's kingship as the Lord's doing, we can sense how bitterly he resented this. Adonijah wanted people to feel sorry for him and give him a consolation prize. Solomon had already shown him mercy by sparing his life. But mercy was not enough for Adonijah. His whole request was based on the premise that he had something more coming to him. He had lost the kingdom— fair enough—but what was in it for him? He demanded some sort of compensation.

How easy it is for us to take the same attitude when the disappointments of life get in the way of our plans for our own kingdoms! We suffer a financial setback, a medical hardship, or a failed relationship. Then, rather than believing that the mercy of Jesus is enough for us, and trusting our King to know what he is doing, we demand something to make up for what we have lost. "I deserve this," we say, and then we take something for ourselves that God does not want us to have—some sinful pleasure, perhaps, or some shiny new product. Rather than letting go of what we want so that we can have what God wants to give us, we find a way to take what we want for ourselves.

What Adonijah wanted to take was Abishag, the beautiful young woman who attended David when he was on his deathbed. Doubtless his desire was partly sexual. After all, Abishag was the best-looking woman in the entire country (see 1 Kings 1:3), and when Adonijah saw her, he wanted her. But he also wanted the power that she represented. Abishag was David's last concubine, and in those days having intercourse with the king's wives was a way to claim the throne. For example, when Absalom tried to take the kingdom away from his father David, he went out on the palace roof to sleep with the king's concubines (2 Sam. 16:21–22). So Adonijah had not abandoned his royal ambitions after all. To possess the harem was to rule the kingdom. It was not just Abishag that he wanted, but the whole kingdom.

We are guilty of the same sin whenever we decide that there is even one thing we will not give up for the kingdom of God. Many people refuse to give up the very thing that Adonijah refused to give up: a sexual relationship, or perhaps a private sexual sin. Understand that when we insist on getting our own satisfaction—however we get it—we are saying "no" to the kingdom of God. We are saying that the mercy of Jesus is not enough for us; we still want to be the king (or the queen, as the case may be). What is the one thing that is keeping you from giving everything for the kingdom of God?

Adonijah wanted Abishag, and he thought he knew how to get her: he would ask Bathsheba to be his go-between. After all, how could Solomon refuse his own mother? "Very well," she said; "I will speak for you to the king" (1 Kings 2:19). So, just as she had gone to King David at Nathan's request (see 1 Kings 1:11–15), the Queen Mother would go to her son at Adonijah's request.

We do not know why Bathsheba agreed to do this. Maybe she went to Solomon as Adonijah's advocate, but just as likely she knew exactly how her son would react.[7] Notice that she never actually indicates whether she agrees with Adonijah or not. In any case, "Bathsheba went to King Solomon to speak to him on behalf of Adonijah. And the king rose to meet her and bowed down to her. Then he sat on his throne and had a seat brought for the king's mother, and she sat on his right" (1 Kings 2:19). Carefully following royal protocol, Solomon treated the Queen Mother with honor and respect. Then Bathsheba proceeded to make her request:

7. Paul R. House, *1, 2 Kings*, The New American Commentary (Nashville: Broadman & Holman, 1995), 100.

"I have one small request to make of you; do not refuse me."

And the king said to her, "Make your request, my mother, for I will not refuse you."

"Let Abishag the Shunammite be given to Adonijah your brother as his wife." (1 Kings 2:20–21)

At this point one scholar wryly remarks, "Unfortunately for Adonijah, Bathsheba does what she promised."[8] For the king responded with explosive anger. He said:

> "And why do you ask Abishag the Shunammite for Adonijah? Ask for him the kingdom also, for he is my older brother, and on his side are Abiathar the priest and Joab the son of Zeruiah." Then King Solomon swore by the LORD, saying, "God do so to me and more also if this word does not cost Adonijah his life! Now therefore as the LORD lives, who has established me and placed me on the throne of David my father, and who has made me a house, as he promised, Adonijah shall be put to death this day." So King Solomon sent Benaiah the son of Jehoiada, and he struck him down, and he died. (1 Kings 2:22–25)

Some people may accuse Solomon of overreacting. After all, Adonijah didn't ask for the whole kingdom; he asked only for Abishag. But Solomon rightly perceived that his older brother's foolish request was really a power play. He also knew that Adonijah had influential allies (Joab and Abiathar) who would support his kingly pretensions. So Solomon swore a solemn oath to put Adonijah to death for high treason. Some scholars have called this death sentence a "self-righteous, self-serving decree."[9] But in swearing this oath, the king properly acknowledges that his kingdom is really God's kingdom, and that therefore it must be defended against all its mortal enemies.

So Adonijah came to a bad end. His sinful request proved that he was not a worthy man. He knew who was supposed to be the king, but he refused to submit to his kingship. He put his own lust for power and pleasure ahead of God's kingdom. He would not give up what he wanted for the glory of God, and so he perished in his sins.

8. Ibid., 99.
9. Walter Brueggemann, *1 & 2 Kings*, Smyth & Helwys Bible Commentary (Macon, GA: Smyth & Helwys, 2000), 34.

JOAB'S FOLLY: POWER AND VIOLENCE

The next two men that Solomon dealt with were Abiathar and Joab—the priest and the general—who put power and violence ahead of the kingdom. Abiathar's story is told very briefly:

> And to Abiathar the priest the king said, "Go to Anathoth, to your estate, for you deserve death. But I will not at this time put you to death, because you carried the ark of the Lord GOD before David my father, and because you shared in all my father's affliction." So Solomon expelled Abiathar from being priest to the LORD, thus fulfilling the word of the LORD that he had spoken concerning the house of Eli in Shiloh. (1 Kings 2:26–27)

Abiathar had backed Adonijah in his failed attempt to seize David's crown. So he too was an opponent of the kingdom of God—an enemy of the Lord's anointed who deserved to be condemned for the capital crime of treason. Yet Solomon did not put Abiathar to death. Because he was a "man of the cloth," and because he had offered sacred service to King David, even through suffering and exile, Solomon spared his life. The priest was expelled rather than executed. Solomon removed him from office and sent him back to his home outside Jerusalem. The Bible says further that this punishment was in fulfillment of the judgment that God had pronounced against the house of Eli (1 Sam. 2:27–36), to which Abiathar belonged (cf. 1 Sam. 14:2–3; 22:20). Apparently this banishment had a corrective effect, because later we will learn that Abiathar was restored to his priesthood (see 1 Kings 4:4).

Things went much worse for Joab, the dangerous old warrior whom David had accused of murder (see 1 Kings 2:5–6). As we saw previously (see chapter 4 of this commentary), in order to advance his own agenda and in direct contradiction to David, Joab viciously killed two men in cold blood: Abner and Amasa (see 2 Sam. 3:1–30; 20:1–23). Joab was among the men who had opposed Solomon's coronation, and when he heard what happened to Adonijah and Abiathar, he knew that he was a dead man: "When the news came to Joab—for Joab had supported Adonijah although he had not supported Absalom—Joab fled to the tent of the LORD and caught hold of the horns of the altar" (1 Kings 2:28).

This was not the first time Joab had received bad news. He was present at Adonijah's party when a messenger announced that Solomon had been crowned as king (see 1 Kings 1:41–48). Now there was more bad news: Solomon was establishing his kingdom by eliminating his enemies. So Joab did what Adonijah had done and ran to the altar outside the tabernacle. The altar was a murderer's last and only sanctuary (see Ex. 21:12–14). There he would be safe, or so he hoped.

Soon the news of what Joab had done reached the royal palace, where Solomon made a swift decision: "And when it was told King Solomon, 'Joab has fled to the tent of the LORD, and behold, he is beside the altar,' Solomon sent Benaiah the son of Jehoiada, saying, 'Go, strike him down'" (1 Kings 2:29). The man who lived by the sword would die by the sword: "So Benaiah came to the tent of the LORD and said to him, 'The king commands, "Come out."' But he said, 'No I will die here'" (1 Kings 2:30).

Joab's refusal created a serious dilemma for Benaiah, who did not want to carry out an execution in the courts of the holy tabernacle. So "Benaiah brought the king word again, saying, 'Thus said Joab, and thus he answered me'" (1 Kings 2:30). In response, the king repeated his orders and made it clear why Joab deserved to die:

> Do as he has said, strike him down and bury him, and thus take away from me and from my father's house the guilt for the blood that Joab shed without cause. The LORD will bring back his bloody deeds on his own head, because, without the knowledge of my father David, he attacked and killed with the sword two men more righteous and better than himself, Abner the son of Ner, commander of the army of Israel, and Amasa the son of Jether, commander of the army of Judah. So shall their blood come back on the head of Joab and on the head of his descendants forever. (1 Kings 2:31–33)

God abhors wrongful violence, and Joab was a violent man. He was guilty of shedding innocent blood, and his bloodguilt for this sin had not yet been paid. It says in Genesis, "Whoever sheds the blood of man, by man shall his blood be shed" (Gen. 9:6). If Solomon did not deal justly with Joab, giving him the punishment that his sins deserved, then he would become guilty himself, for it was his responsibility as king to see that justice was done. Only then could his kingdom be established in peace, as God had promised: "But for David and for his descendants and for his house and for his throne there shall be peace from the LORD forevermore" (1 Kings 2:33).

This time Benaiah did what Solomon said, and executed Joab: "Then Benaiah the son of Jehoiada went up and struck him down and put him to death. And he was buried in his own house in the wilderness. The king put Benaiah the son of Jehoiada over the army in place of Joab, and the king put Zadok the priest in the place of Abiathar" (1 Kings 2:34–35). The Bible seems to imply that Benaiah killed Joab right in the tabernacle. However, he may have done what the Law of Moses required in this situation, which was to drag the criminal away from the altar and put him to death outside the tabernacle (see Ex. 21:14). The altar of God was never intended to protect someone who was guilty of murderous violence.

Do not doubt that judgment will fall on every enemy of the kingdom of God who does not repent. The only way to be safe is to submit to the kingship of Jesus Christ. The Bible says there is no place in the kingdom of God for "the cowardly, the faithless, the detestable, murderers, the sexually immoral, sorcerers, idolaters, and all liars," for they will go to "the lake that burns with fire and sulfur, which is the second death" (Rev. 21:8). Jesus himself said he would "gather out of his kingdom all law-breakers, and throw them into the fiery furnace. In that place there will be weeping and gnashing of teeth. Then the righteous will shine like the sun in the kingdom of their Father. He who has ears, let him hear" (Matt. 13:41–43). Jesus loves to show mercy to anyone who truly repents, but like Solomon, he will render righteous judgment to everyone who insists on remaining his enemy.

In the end, Joab got what he deserved. Joab's unhappy demise reminds us never to excuse our own love for violence. To batter one's spouse, to strike someone in anger, to use hateful and threatening words, even to think murderous thoughts—these are sins against the peace of humanity and the holiness of God. If we do not repent of our violent hearts, but insist on abusing power to get what we want from other people, there is no place for us in the kingdom of God. Going to church will not save us, any more than going to the tabernacle saved Joab. The only thing that can save us is a blood offering to atone for our guilty souls.

Praise God, this is exactly the offering that Jesus made when he was crucified: a blood atonement for all our sins. It is not enough simply to be desperate for mercy, as Joab was; we must also come to God in true repentance for our sins and genuine faith in Jesus Christ. If we hold on to his cross, we will be fully forgiven. As Charles Spurgeon said, in contrasting

Joab's unhappy end with the mercy God has for us in Christ: "the Lord has appointed an altar in the person of his own dear Son, Jesus Christ, where there shall be shelter for the very vilest of sinners if they do but come and lay hold thereon."[10]

Shimei's Folly: Money

The last man to suffer Solomon's wrath was Shimei, who was condemned for putting money ahead of the kingdom of God. We have heard part of his story before. Shimei was the man who threw stones at King David, cursing him and wrongfully accusing him of murder (see 2 Sam. 16:5–13). David had vowed not to kill Shimei, but Solomon was not bound by his father's oath. So in his last words David advised Solomon not to let Shimei live, but to send him to an early grave (1 Kings 2:8–9).

What Solomon decided to do instead was to place Shimei under house arrest: "Then the king sent and summoned Shimei and said to him, 'Build yourself a house in Jerusalem and dwell there, and do not go out from there to any place whatever. For on the day you go out and cross the brook Kidron, know for certain that you shall die. Your blood shall be on your own head'" (1 Kings 2:36–37). This would keep Shimei in Jerusalem—where Solomon could keep an eye on him—and away from his power base with the tribe of Benjamin.

Shimei agreed to Solomon's gracious terms, posturing himself as a faithful servant of the king: "And Shimei said to the king, 'What you say is good; as my lord the king has said, so will your servant do.' So Shimei lived in Jerusalem many days" (1 Kings 2:38). Having given his word, all he had to do was stay in Jerusalem.

But Shimei would not sit still, and eventually he violated the terms of his parole: "But it happened at the end of three years that two of Shimei's servants ran away to Achish, son of Maacah, king of Gath. And when it was told Shimei, 'Behold, your servants are in Gath,' Shimei arose and saddled a donkey and went to Gath to Achish to seek his servants. Shimei went and brought his servants from Gath" (1 Kings 2:39–40). By chasing his runaway slaves all the way to Philistia, Shimei violated the conditions of his house

---

10. Charles Spurgeon, "The Horns of the Altar," in *The Metropolitan Tabernacle Pulpit* (Pasadena, TX: Pilgrim, 1971), 31:114.

arrest. He also broke his promise to the king. He knew it was wrong, but he did it anyway because he wanted to get his property back.

Soon Solomon's spies came to tell him what Shimei had done:

> And when Solomon was told that Shimei had gone from Jerusalem to Gath and returned, the king sent and summoned Shimei and said to him, "Did I not make you swear by the Lord and solemnly warn you, saying, 'Know for certain that on the day you go out and go to any place whatever, you shall die'? And you said to me, 'What you say is good; I will obey.' Why then have you not kept your oath to the Lord and the commandment with which I commanded you?" (1 Kings 2:41–43)

Shimei had no good answer to give; there was nothing he could say in his own defense. He had foolishly disregarded the direct command of his sovereign king, whom he had promised to obey with a solemn oath taken in the presence of God. Therefore Solomon proceeded to pronounce Shimei's doom: "You know in your own heart all the harm that you did to David my father. So the Lord will bring back your harm on your own head. But King Solomon shall be blessed, and the throne of David shall be established before the Lord forever" (1 Kings 2:44–45). Solomon rehearsed Shimei's crimes, both past and present. Then the sentence was quickly executed, as "the king commanded Benaiah the son of Jehoiada, and he went out and struck him down, and he died" (1 Kings 2:46).

So Shimei was destroyed, and Solomon's kingdom was established. But was justice really done? Obviously, it was stupid for Shimei to leave the city of Jerusalem, but was it sinful enough for him to be punished with death?

To answer this question, remember again that Solomon was the Lord's anointed king and that his dominion was the kingdom of God. The root of Shimei's crime was his refusal to put that kingdom first. His own financial prosperity was more important to him than obedience to the kingdom of God. He was like the rich young man that Jesus commanded to sell everything he had and then give his money to the poor (Matt. 19:16–22). That man sadly refused because he loved his money more than he loved the kingdom of God. Shimei made the same ungodly calculation. He wanted to keep all his property for himself. He could not bear to let any of it go, even when that meant disobeying the king and breaking his promise to God.

THE KINGDOM OF CHRIST

Each of the men that Solomon executed had one thing that he refused to give up for the kingdom of God. Adonijah had to have Abishag. Joab wanted his revenge. Shimei would not let go of his servants.

We all face similar temptations. Some of us are like Shimei: our temptation is what money can buy. So we are unwilling to walk away from a lucrative business deal that is not entirely honest. Or we build our careers at the expense of our families. Or we shortchange God by skimping on our tithes and offerings. Other people are like Adonijah: we put sexual gratification ahead of our commitment to the kingdom. Or, like Joab, we are guilty of angry violence.

The question for each of us is: What is the one thing that is keeping me from giving everything to the kingdom of God? It is all or nothing with God, as it is for every self-respecting king. It is the character of a king to demand total allegiance. If we follow God only when he gives us what we want, then we are not treating him like a king at all, but only as a servant. For God to come first for us, he has to come first in everything, including the one thing we really do not want to give up for his kingdom, whatever that one thing may be.

The trouble, of course, is that we often put what we want ahead of what God wants. We build our own kingdoms rather than seeking first the kingdom of God, as Jesus said we should (see Matt. 6:33). This is evident every time we indulge a sinful pleasure, or speak an angry word, or make a selfish purchase. And this is why we need the mercy and forgiveness that God offers us in Jesus, the King who established God's forever kingdom by bleeding on the cross and then rising from the grave. Like Solomon, Jesus established his throne by eliminating all his enemies, only his enemies were the strongest enemies of all: sin, death, and the devil. Jesus defeated these enemies by suffering the deadly punishment that we deserve for our sins (the same punishment, in fact, that Solomon's enemies deserved), so that we would not die, but live.

To accomplish this saving work, Jesus had to put the kingdom first, and so he did. He did not come to do his own will, he said, but the will of his Father in heaven (John 6:38). This included renouncing all the temptations of money, sex, and violence. Jesus could have claimed the wealth of the nations, but chose instead to live in poverty, proving that money was not his master. Nor did Jesus give in to sexual temptation, sinfully gratifying his sexual desire, but lived instead with perfect purity and chastity. He did not seek power through wrongful violence, but patiently suffered the abuse of sinful men, even to the point of death. Jesus put the kingdom first, refusing to let even one single thing get in the way of giving his life for our salvation and doing the work of the kingdom of God.

Now Jesus calls us to join him in putting the kingdom first: first in our minds and hearts, first with our bodies, and first with our bank accounts. It is only when we share our wealth for kingdom work, protect the purity of our sexuality, and give up any claim to rule our own destiny that we are able to stop using money, sex, and power for ourselves, but use them instead for the glory of God and the kingdom of Jesus Christ.

6

SOLOMON'S WISH

1 Kings 3:1—15

And God said to him, "Because you have asked this, and have not
asked for yourself long life or riches or the life of your enemies,
but have asked for yourself understanding to discern what is
right, behold, I now do according to your word. Behold, I give you
a wise and discerning mind, so that none like you has been before
you and none like you shall arise after you." (1 Kings 3:11–12)

*I*f you could wish for anything in the world, what would it be?
Some people wish they had different abilities—more brains,
better looks, stronger skills. Others wish for a change in their
life circumstances. There is something they have that they wish they didn't
have, or something they don't have that they wish they did. What would
your wish be?

The 2005 television reality show *Three Wishes* asked that question in small
towns across America. In each heartwarming episode the producers made
wishes come true, choosing three people to receive the one thing they wanted
more than anything else in life. The application said, "We are looking for
emotional stories of people in need. We want to help deserving people—

people who always help others, but never think of themselves." Then it asked the big question: "If you had one wish in the world and could ask for absolutely anything from the heart, what would it be?"

The television producers said that money was no object, which may explain why the show was canceled after only one season: making wishes come true can get very expensive! But what if your biggest wish really could come true? And what if the person asking what you wanted had infinite resources? This was the opportunity that Almighty God gave to King Solomon: "Ask what I shall give you."

A MAN AFTER DAVID'S HEART

To understand Solomon's wish, we need to know what kind of man he was. Solomon had ascended the throne of his father David—not by his own ambition, but by the sacred anointing of Almighty God (1 Kings 1). After only a short time in power, it was evident that he had the courage to lead. Solomon had established his kingdom by eliminating his enemies (see 1 Kings 2). He was politically savvy, a man of action. But what kind of person was he on the inside, in the spiritual life of his soul?

The Bible describes him as a man after David's own heart: "Solomon loved the LORD, walking in the statutes of David his father" (1 Kings 3:3). This is virtually the highest praise that any person could ever receive. In fact, Solomon is the only man in the entire Bible who is said to have "loved the Lord," in so many words. His heart was full of holy affections for the living God. He adored the divine being, responding to God emotionally. He felt a deep spiritual longing in his soul, a passionate yearning for a closer relationship to God.

Love is more than a feeling, however, and Solomon expressed his love for God in many tangible ways. He often worshiped God, and when he worshiped, he devoutly offered many costly sacrifices: "And the king went to Gibeon to sacrifice there, for that was the great high place. Solomon used to offer a thousand burnt offerings on that altar" (1 Kings 3:4). Imagine the huge expense and extraordinary labor involved in sacrificing a thousand animals on the altar of God! Solomon proved his love for God through sacrifice.

This was a close and personal relationship, for when Solomon made his sacrifices, God appeared to him and spoke with him (see 1 Kings 3:5).

When Solomon in turn spoke to God, he expressed his affection through prayer: "You have shown great and steadfast love to your servant David my father, because he walked before you in faithfulness, in righteousness, and in uprightness of heart toward you. And you have kept for him this great and steadfast love and have given him a son to sit on his throne this day" (1 Kings 3:6).

It is the heart of a lover to praise the beloved. Here Solomon solemnly honors God for what he has done. The king praises God for his dependable love—specifically, the faithful love he has shown in keeping his covenant. He gratefully rehearses what God has done in the history of his family—his tender mercies to David. Then he joyfully celebrates the promises God has kept by putting him on David's throne (see 2 Sam. 7:12).

Solomon's affectionate prayer is a model for our own love life with the living God. Do you love the Lord? Ask the Holy Spirit to stir your heart with holy affections, giving you a longing to be with Jesus. Then show your love in all the practical ways that Solomon showed it. Meet with God often in worship, both publicly and privately. As you worship, make costly personal sacrifices to promote the glory of the God you love. John Piper writes:

> The way of love is both the way of self-denial and the way of ultimate joy. We deny ourselves the fleeting pleasures of sin and luxury and self-absorption in order to seek the kingdom above all things. In doing so we bring the greatest good to others, we magnify the worth of Christ as a treasure chest of joy, and we find our greatest satisfaction.
>
> God is most glorified in us when we are most satisfied in him. And the supremacy of that glory shines most brightly when the satisfaction that we have in him endures in spite of suffering and pain in the mission of love.[1]

As you worship and give, praise God as much as you can for what he has done for your family. Rehearse the ways that God has blessed you by blessing people in past generations. Then celebrate his steadfast love in your own life, rejoicing in the promises he has made and kept for your salvation. When was the last time you told God how much you love him for saving you from an eternity of misery?

1. John Piper, *Let the Nations Be Glad! The Supremacy of God in Missions* (Grand Rapids: Baker, 1993), 12.

In the *Personal Narrative* he wrote to record his spiritual autobiography, Jonathan Edwards often celebrated the love of God with rapturous joy. These words are typical of his religious affections:

> I have sometimes had a sense of the excellent fullness of Christ, and his meekness and suitableness as a Savior; whereby he has appeared to me, far above all, the chief of ten thousands. His blood and atonement have appeared sweet, and his righteousness sweet; which was always accompanied with ardency of spirit; and inward strugglings and breathings, and groanings that cannot be uttered, to be emptied of myself, and swallowed up in Christ.[2]

Jonathan Edwards was a man of singular devotion, and Christians may rarely, if ever, reach the heights of his spiritual passion. But we can all worship, pray, and give out of love for Christ. We can also ask the Holy Spirit to make us better lovers, giving us more love for Jesus.

WARNING SIGNS

As much as he loved the Lord, there are some ominous warning signs that Solomon's love was not wholehearted. The traditional view of 1 Kings is that the king was faithful until the last years of his life. On this interpretation, chapters 1 through 10 give an almost entirely positive view of his kingship, while chapter 11 tells how Solomon turned away from the Lord at the very end. If we study his life more carefully, however, we see early signs of his eventual downfall, especially in his love for money, sex, and power.

The first warning sign in chapter 3 is Solomon's choice of a life partner: "Solomon made a marriage alliance with Pharaoh king of Egypt. He took Pharaoh's daughter and brought her into the city of David until he had finished building his own house and the house of the LORD and the wall around Jerusalem" (1 Kings 3:1).

This union was problematic in several ways. Since we have no reason to think that Pharaoh's daughter had faith in the God of Israel, we can only conclude that Solomon was unequally yoked. This was not an issue of ethnicity, but of spirituality. The Bible fully supports the union of two people from

2. Jonathan Edwards, *Letters and Personal Writings*, ed. George S. Claghorn (New Haven, CT: Yale University Press, 1998).

different ethnic backgrounds, but it condemns the marriage of a believer to an unbeliever (see Ex. 34:15–16; Deut. 7:3–4; 2 Cor. 6:14). It is hardly surprising that marrying outside the faith eventually led Solomon into idolatry (see 1 Kings 11:1–8), that the very king who once was said to "love the Lord" later is said to love "many foreign women" (1 Kings 11:1). His poor example is a warning for Christians not to pursue a romantic relationship with anyone who is not committed to Christ. As Matthew Henry comments, "Unequal matches of the sons of God with the daughters of men have often been of pernicious consequence."[3]

Another problem with this marriage was that it formed an unholy alliance with Egypt, of all places. In those days, a royal marriage was intended to secure a political and military alliance. By marrying Pharaoh's daughter, Solomon was trying to help Israel become a player on the stage of international politics. He was seduced by power as well as by sex. But the Bible takes a dim view of this kind of power play, which was often a temptation for Israel. God wanted his people to trust in him alone for their salvation, rather than trying to find their security by aligning themselves with foreign powers. By becoming Pharaoh's son-in-law, Solomon was turning to Egypt, a nation that was "the antithesis of everything Israelite," a place that in the Bible "bespeaks brutality, exploitation, and bondage, the demeaning of the human spirit, and the suppression of covenantal relations."[4] Going back to Egypt may or may not have been a good political decision, but it certainly was a bad decision spiritually; for although the Bible later gives precious promises for their future salvation (e.g., Isa. 19:19–25; Ezek. 29:13–16), the Egyptians had always been enemies to the people of God. This too is a warning for us—a warning not to try to advance our position by joining spiritual forces with worldly people who are working against the kingdom of God.

There also seems to be a warning sign in the way Solomon worshiped. Verse 1 mentions his great life's work of building a house for God, the temple in Jerusalem. Yet it also mentions that Solomon built a house for himself, and as we will discover, he spent more time and money on his own house than he did on the house that he built for God (compare 1 Kings 6 with the opening

3. Matthew Henry, *Matthew Henry's Complete Commentary on the Whole Bible*, vol. 2, *Judges to Job* (New York: Fleming Revell, n.d.), n.p.

4. Walter Brueggemann, *1 & 2 Kings*, Smyth & Helwys Bible Commentary (Macon, GA: Smyth & Helwys, 2000), 45.

verses of 1 Kings 7). Solomon's heart was tempted away from devotion to God by the love of money.

Added Temptations

There were other temptations as well. Verse 2 explains that until Solomon built his temple, "the people were sacrificing at the high places, however, because no house had yet been built for the name of the Lord" (1 Kings 3:2). Like his people, Solomon "sacrificed and made offerings at the high places. And the king went to Gibeon to sacrifice there, for that was the great high place" (1 Kings 3:3–4). Apparently, the king and his people were worshiping in the name of the one true God. Yet the term "high place" (*bemah*) has extremely negative connotations in the Old Testament, especially throughout 1 and 2 Kings, where all its other uses are pejorative (e.g., 2 Kings 14:4; 15:35). The high places were elevations where people worshiped foreign deities, and before long they became inextricably associated with pagan idolatry. Furthermore, verse 3 seems to present Solomon's worship at the high places as an exception to his love for the Lord: "Solomon loved the Lord, walking in the statutes of David his father, *only* he sacrificed and made offerings at the high places" (1 Kings 3:3). The word "only" (*raq*) is restrictive, indicating that what follows is some sort of exception—in this case, an idolatrous exception to Solomon's love for the Lord.

What shall we make of Solomon's worship at the high places of Israel? Perhaps at this early stage of Israel's history, before the temple was built, it was acceptable for people to worship at such places.[5] After all, where else could they worship? Furthermore, as an indication of God's blessing, when Solomon made his sacrifices at the great high place of Gibeon (where the bronze altar was located; see 2 Chron. 1:5–6), he did have a direct personal encounter there with the living God.

On the other hand, the Lord's appearance at Gibeon says more about his divine grace than about Solomon's obedience. The Law of Moses (which David commended to Solomon in 1 Kings 2:3) explicitly commanded the people of God to destroy the high places of pagan idolatry: "You shall surely destroy all the places where the nations whom you shall dispossess served their gods, on the high mountains and on the hills and under every green tree. . . . You shall not worship the Lord your God in that way" (Deut. 12:2, 4).

---

5. For a full defense of this viewpoint, see August H. Konkel, *1 & 2 Kings*, NIV Application Commentary (Grand Rapids: Zondervan, 2006), 78–80.

Instead of worshiping at the old high places, the people were called to worship God at his chosen place in Jerusalem: "But you shall seek the place that the LORD your God will choose out of all your tribes to put his name and make his habitation there. There you shall go, and there you shall bring your burnt offerings and your sacrifices" (Deut. 12:5–6).

If this is what God commanded, then why was Solomon leading people in the questionable practice of worshiping at the high places? Notice the change that took place, after Solomon met with God at Gibeon: "Then he came to Jerusalem and stood before the ark of the covenant of the LORD, and offered up burnt offerings and peace offerings, and made a feast for all his servants" (1 Kings 3:15). Presumably, this is where the king and his people should have been worshiping all along, at the tent of meeting in Jerusalem. Instead, they started out worshiping at the high places. This is an ominous foreshadowing of their coming apostasy, for both Solomon and his people would later go back to the high places and commit idolatry (see 1 Kings 11:7–8).

So while it is true that Solomon was a king after David's heart, a man who loved the Lord, it is also true that he had a wandering heart that loved money, sex, and power—the very temptations that led to the downfall of Adonijah, Joab, and Shimei in chapter 2. The warning signs of Solomon's tragic downfall are present from the very beginning of his story, which is not just black and white, but colored by shades of gray.

In other words, Solomon was a lot like us. He loved the Lord, as every Christian does. But he also had some other loves in his life—sinful passions that had the power to destroy his spiritual leadership. He did not love the Lord his God with all his heart, soul, and strength (see Deut. 6:5). While there is some truth to the view that Solomon's life started out more positive spiritually, before ending up more negative, the deeper truth is that like every other believer, he was always as much a sinner as he was a saint.

We face the same struggle. In the famous words of Martin Luther, each of us is *simul iustus et peccator*—at the same time both righteous and a sinner. Through faith in Jesus Christ, and on the basis of his perfect life and atoning death, we are perfectly righteous in the sight of God. Yet for as long as we live in this sinful world, we will continue to struggle with remaining sin. This means that the warning signs of our own tragic downfall are present right in our own hearts.

What sinful desires have the power to destroy your life the way money and sex and power divided Solomon's kingdom? We too are tempted by the love of money, the pleasure of sex, and the seduction of power. We face these temptations every time we reach for a credit card, get on the Internet, or start figuring out the best way to get what we want out of other people. Do we recognize how much danger we are in? The sins that go along with money, sex, and power have the capacity to destroy us.

SOLOMON'S WISE REQUEST

To resist temptation and live by the love of God, we need the spiritual wisdom to choose what is right. Wisdom is precisely what Solomon so famously asked for. The king made his wise request in the context of a dream. He was offering a thousand sacrifices at Gibeon, and as he worshiped, "the LORD appeared to Solomon in a dream by night, and God said, 'Ask what I shall give you'" (1 Kings 3:5; cf. 3:15).

God did not place any conditions on the king's request, but simply invited him to ask whatever he wished. This extraordinary and unprecedented invitation was also a serious test, because the way that Solomon responded would reveal the godliness (or ungodliness) of his character. Here is how the king prayed: "And now, O LORD my God, you have made your servant king in place of David my father, although I am but a little child. I do not know how to go out or come in. And your servant is in the midst of your people whom you have chosen, a great people, too many to be numbered or counted for multitude" (1 Kings 3:7–8).

Later, Solomon would become famous for saying, "The fear of the LORD is the beginning of knowledge" (Prov. 1:7). His own request is a perfect example, because the king begins his prayer for wisdom by reverently proclaiming who God is and what God has done. Here is a man who feared the Lord, which for him was the beginning of wisdom. In his prayer, Solomon declares that the Lord is *his* God, the God with whom he has a personal relationship. He acknowledges that the God of David has put him on Israel's throne. He remembers that God has chosen his people, and when he says that they are "too many to be numbered or counted for multitude" (1 Kings 3:8), Solomon echoes the covenant promise God made to Abraham—that his children would be as countless as the stars in the sky, or the sand in the desert (Gen. 22:16–18).

Solomon's wise request in verse 9 was firmly based on a proper knowledge of the greatness of God. His prayer shows us how we should always start to pray about anything: by acknowledging that God is God, that he is our God, that he is at work in our lives, and that he has kept his promises of salvation.

At the same time, Solomon's wise request was also based on a proper knowledge of his own limitations. Like Moses before him (see Ex. 4:10), and like Jeremiah afterwards (see Jer. 1:6), Solomon was somewhat doubtful of his own abilities. When he calls himself "a little child," he does not necessarily mean that he was a youngster. We do not know exactly how old Solomon was at this point, although we do know that he had already fathered a son.[6] By calling himself "a little child," he means that he is inexperienced and thus dependent on God to give him the help he needs. His comment about not knowing "how to come in or go out" is a different way of saying the same thing. This is something a little child would say—a child who still needs permission to go outside, or has trouble opening the door to get back in. Yet the Bible typically uses this expression to refer to military leadership (e.g., Num. 27:16–17; Deut. 31:2–3). Solomon was saying that he did not know how to rule like a king.

Apart from his youthful inexperience, there were some other reasons why Solomon was reluctant to lead. He knew that the people he was called to lead were God's chosen people, and that because they were so precious to God, they deserved the best of royal care. He also knew how numerous they were, which meant that ruling them would be a heavy burden. The task seemed almost overwhelming.

Solomon could do what God was calling him to do only if God helped him do it. So he prayed for wisdom: "Give your servant therefore an understanding mind to govern your people, that I may discern between good and evil, for who is able to govern this your great people?" (1 Kings 3:9; cf. 2 Chron. 1:10). Here Solomon was praying with proper humility. He knew how limited he was, but he also knew how unlimited God was, and so he prayed for divine wisdom. He asked for "an understanding mind," or more literally, "a listening heart."[7]

6. Iain W. Provan, *1 and 2 Kings*, New International Biblical Commentary (Peabody, MA: Hendrickson, 1995), 48.

7. Paul R. House, *1, 2 Kings*, The New American Commentary (Nashville: Broadman & Holman, 1995), 110.

The word for "listening" or "hearing" (*shomea*) implies obedience, because if we are wise, to hear *is* to obey. The word for the "mind" or the "heart" (*leb*) does not refer only to the brain, or to the emotions, but to the whole person: the intellect, the affections, even the will. Solomon was asking that his whole person would be able to discern the will of God.

The king would use this wisdom to govern the great people of God. The kind of wisdom Solomon specifically had in mind was practical wisdom for government. David had counseled him to be wise in dealing with his enemies (1 Kings 2:6, 9), and Solomon had tried to follow his father's counsel. Now he would need the same kind of skill and insight for all the other duties of his kingship. Whether he was ruling his people, or conquering his enemies, or defending the weak and the poor, Solomon would need a discerning mind, and an understanding heart. He did not make this request for his own sake, but for the good of his people and the glory of God. Solomon was making a kingdom-minded prayer request. He did not ask to be wise so that he could become a famous wise man; he asked so that the people of God would be wisely governed.[8]

Solomon's situation was unique: he alone inherited David's throne, so only he could pray exactly this prayer. But his wise request is still an excellent example for us to follow. Unlike Solomon, "I am not a king," writes one commentator, "but shouldn't I pray like one?"[9] Yes, we should pray like Solomon. With all due reverence, we should begin with the character of God and his saving work. In holy humility, we should acknowledge our own limitations, openly admitting how weak we are in honoring our parents, serving our spouse, raising a child, loving a neighbor, leading a ministry, sharing the gospel, or any other single thing that God calls us to do. Then, with all confident faith, we should ask God for the wisdom we need to serve him well in whatever he has called us to do. In ourselves, we are unequal to any of the tasks God has given us to do, but we can ask him to give us a discerning mind and an understanding heart. We should not request this for ourselves, primarily, but for the good of God's people and the sake of his kingdom.

8. Solomon's beautiful prayer in Psalm 72 reveals his heart for God's people and zeal for the honor of God's name.

9. Dale Ralph Davis, *The Wisdom and the Folly: An Exposition of the Book of First Kings* (Fearn, Ross-shire: Christian Focus, 2002), 37.

GOD'S GRACIOUS GIFT

God was pleased to answer Solomon's prayer and grant his wise request:

It pleased the LORD that Solomon had asked this. And God said to him, "Because you have asked this, and have not asked for yourself long life or riches or the life of your enemies, but have asked for yourself understanding to discern what is right, behold, I now do according to your word. Behold, I give you a wise and discerning mind, so that none like you has been before you and none like you shall arise after you." (1 Kings 3:10–12; cf. 2 Chron. 1:11–12)

In saying how pleased he was with Solomon, God said that he was just as pleased with what the king *didn't* request as with what he *did* request. In asking for wisdom, Solomon was refusing to ask for any of the things that most people want out of life. Most people hold on to life so tightly that they would give almost anything to keep the day they have to die from ever coming. But Solomon did not ask God for long life. Most people wish that they had more money and have already made some plans for what they would do with it if they could get their hands on it. But Solomon did not ask God for riches. Most people wish that they could get even with the people who have done them wrong. But Solomon did not ask for revenge against his enemies.

Not that it would have been wrong for Solomon to ask for any of these things. Life is good; money can be useful; it is better to pray for vengeance than to take it into our own hands. Solomon could even have requested these things for the sake of his kingdom. "Long live the king!" he could have prayed. "Give me gold for the walls of your temple, O God." "Take vengeance on the enemies of Israel."

Yet Solomon rightly regarded those earthly goods as inferior to the supreme gift of spiritual wisdom. "Wisdom is better than jewels," he later wrote, "and all that you may desire cannot compare with her" (Prov. 8:11; cf. 16:16). The king knew that the wisdom to know what is right is helpful for every situation. Wisdom helps a young person know which way to go in life. It helps a man love a woman, and a woman love a man. It helps a couple know how to raise a family. Wisdom helps people know how to live, how to work, how to play. It even helps people know how to die, because wise people trust in the Son of God for eternal life. So Solomon wisely asked God for the gift of a discerning heart.

God was so pleased with what Solomon asked that he granted his request. The king became what God promised: the wisest man who ever lived. This gift went beyond Solomon's natural intellectual ability (which must have been exceptional), to endow him with the kind of spiritual insight that can come only from God (see Prov. 2:6). To this day we can learn from the king's wisdom by reading his wise sayings in the book of Proverbs, studying his wise philosophy of life in Ecclesiastes, or hearing his wisdom about love and romance from the Song of Solomon.

After giving Solomon this wisdom, God proceeded to give him even more than he asked or imagined (cf. Eph. 3:20). He said: "I give you also what you have not asked, both riches and honor, so that no other king shall compare with you, all your days. And if you will walk in my ways, keeping my statutes and my commandments, as your father David walked, then I will lengthen your days" (1 Kings 3:13–14).

Solomon thus received the very gifts he had bypassed in his quest for wisdom. God added wealth to Solomon's wisdom, making him the richest man in the world. He gave the king an international reputation for intellectual insight: "King Solomon excelled all the kings of the earth in riches and in wisdom. And the whole earth sought the presence of Solomon to hear his wisdom, which God had put into his mind" (1 Kings 10:23–24). God even said that the king would enjoy a long life, provided that he kept God's covenant the way that David did (cf. 1 Kings 2:1–4).

Although Solomon did not seek the blessings of wealth and fame, they were given to him all the same. The king thus serves as an ideal example of an important principle that Jesus taught his disciples: "Seek first the kingdom of God and his righteousness, and all these things will be added to you" (Matt. 6:33). By far the most important gift that Solomon ever received was wisdom. After all, it takes wisdom to know how to handle all the responsibilities and temptations that come with being rich and famous! If the king had selfishly pursued fame and fortune, God would have not been pleased with his request. But Solomon asked for wisdom, and with the gift of wisdom, God graciously added many other blessings.

WISDOM'S TREASURE

If ever there was a man who could praise God as the fount of every blessing, it was King Solomon. After he awoke from his dream, the king went up to Jerusalem, stood before the ark of the covenant, and presented many offerings to the praise of his God (1 Kings 3:15). This was wise: whenever we receive a gift, we should thank the giver. Since every good and perfect gift comes from God, we live most wisely when our lives are filled with the thankful worship of God.

Solomon never regretted his decision to make wisdom his only wish. Thus he would counsel us to make the same choice. "The beginning of wisdom is this," the king once said: "Get wisdom, and whatever you get, get insight. Prize her highly, and she will exalt you; she will honor you if you embrace her. She will place on your head a graceful garland; she will bestow on you a beautiful crown" (Prov. 4:7–9; cf. Prov. 8:18). This was the story of Solomon's life. He did whatever he could to get wisdom, and then, with the gift of wisdom, came riches and honor. The best counsel that Solomon could give to anyone else was to seek the same superior wisdom that he received—the wisdom that comes only from God.

The way for us to follow Solomon's wise counsel is to study the Scriptures, which are able to make us "wise for salvation through faith in Christ Jesus" (2 Tim. 3:15), and to seek the wisdom of God in the person of Jesus Christ. For as wise as Solomon was, the Bible says that Jesus Christ is infinitely wiser. This explains why, when the Gospel of Matthew speaks of the world-famous wisdom of Solomon, it goes on to say that "something greater than Solomon is here" (Matt. 12:42). That "something greater" is Jesus Christ, the divine Son of God and "wisdom of God" (see 1 Cor. 1:24).

The Bible says that "all the treasures of wisdom and knowledge" are hidden in Jesus Christ (Col. 2:3). His wisdom is more complete and extensive than Solomon's wisdom, because as the divine Son of God, Jesus knows all things. His wisdom is more perfect and permanent than Solomon's wisdom, because as the sinless Savior, Jesus never gave in to sin and its foolish temptations (which was Solomon's downfall, as we will discover—like any other spiritual gift, the king's wisdom was not operative apart from a living and active faith in the one true God). The wisdom of Jesus is more vital and necessary than Solomon's wisdom, because as the everlasting King, Jesus continues to govern everything in earth and heaven.

What may not seem particularly wise is the manner in which Jesus died: by crucifixion. In fact, the Bible frankly admits that the cross of Christ seems like foolishness to the people of this world, who are dying in their sins. What difference could it make for a man to come under God's curse, hang on a tree, and bleed to death? But the Bible also explains that what may seem foolish to us actually is the wisdom of God for our salvation. By his crucifixion, Jesus paid the price for all our sin. However foolish it may seem to some people, the preaching of the cross brings forgiveness and eternal life to everyone who believes in Jesus, who himself has become our wisdom from God (see 1 Cor. 1:18–25, 30).

The wisest thing that we can do in response is to give our lives to Jesus Christ. The supreme wisdom of Jesus Christ is available to us for the asking, wisdom for even the little things of everyday life. It may seem tempting to envy Solomon for the invitation he was given to ask for anything he wanted from God. But God is ready to grant us Solomon's wish and give us "a heart of wisdom" (Ps. 90:12). Jesus told us simply to ask, and it would be given; everyone who asks will receive (Matt. 7:7–8). Do you need wisdom for work, for the future, for a broken relationship, for an obstacle in ministry, or for problems in your family? The Bible gives this promise to anyone who asks in faith: "If any of you lacks wisdom, let him ask God, who gives generously to all without reproach, and it will be given him" (James 1:5).

7

THE WISDOM OF SOLOMON

1 Kings 3:16—28

And all Israel heard of the judgment that the king had rendered,
and they stood in awe of the king, because they perceived that the
wisdom of God was in him to do justice. (1 Kings 3:28)

*T*here is always something deeply satisfying about finding a simple solution to a difficult dilemma. A favorite example is the story of a traveler in a deserted place who came to a fork in the road and had no idea which way to turn. He had been told in advance that there were two men in the region, one of whom always told the truth, and the other of whom was a pathological liar. It so happened that one of these men was waiting at the intersection and offered to give directions. The trouble was that the traveler did not know which man it was: the liar or the truth-teller. So how could he know that he was getting the right directions? What one question could he ask to tell him exactly which way to go?

This difficult dilemma has a simple solution. All the traveler needed to ask was the following question: "If I were to ask the other man for directions, which way would he tell me to go?" Then, once the man answered, the traveler would know that he should take the other road. If he was talking to the liar, the man would be sure to lead him astray. On the other hand, if he was talking to the man who always told the truth, he was sure to get the truth about the other man's lie. Either way, there would be a lie in the directions somewhere, so the traveler would know that he should go the other way.

A more famous example of dilemma-solving comes from the ancient palace of the Phrygian kings in Gordium, where there was an oxcart tied to a post with an intricate knot. According to legend, whoever was able to untie the knot would rule Asia Minor. Never a man to back down from a challenge, and having some considerable interest in ruling Asia Minor himself, Alexander the Great tried to untie the knot when he wintered at Gordium in 333 B.C. Upon discovering that the knot did not have any ends to unravel, Alexander undid the Gordian knot by taking his sword and slicing it in two—a simple solution to a seemingly insoluble dilemma.

A DIFFICULT DILEMMA

A story from the Bible gives the simple solution to an even more difficult dilemma. This particular dilemma could not be solved simply by asking the right question, because even after the right questions had been asked and answered, the dilemma still remained. Nor could it be solved by the stroke of a sword, because the center of the dilemma was not simply a knot, but a baby.

The context for this difficult dilemma and its elegant solution is the extraordinary gift that God had given to King Solomon—the gift of wisdom. Solomon knew that he was unequal to the task of governing the precious, numerous people of God. So he prayed for the gift of an understanding mind that could discern the difference between right and wrong for the people of God. God was pleased with Solomon's request and promised to give him exactly what he asked: "a wise and discerning mind" (1 Kings 3:12). With the gift of surpassing wisdom, God would also grant the king incomparable riches and international fame.

Soon the wisdom of Solomon was put to the test, in the form of a legal dispute over the custody of a child. Like most other matters that made it all the way to the king, this famous judicial case was as difficult as they come. No one else in the entire kingdom could decide what to do. There were no lawyers involved in this case, or other legal representatives—just one woman against another: "two prostitutes came to the king and stood before him" (1 Kings 3:16). The

Bible lets these two women tell their own story, in their own words. The first woman was the plaintiff, and here is the testimony she gave:

> Oh, my lord, this woman and I live in the same house, and I gave birth to a child while she was in the house. Then on the third day after I gave birth, this woman also gave birth. And we were alone. There was no one else with us in the house; only we two were in the house. And this woman's son died in the night, because she lay on him. And she arose at midnight and took my son from beside me, while your servant slept, and laid him at her breast, and laid her dead son at my breast. When I rose in the morning to nurse my child, behold, he was dead. But when I looked at him closely in the morning, behold, he was not the child that I had borne. (1 Kings 3:17–21)

Once heard, this story is never forgotten. The first woman describes a scene of sinful and pitiful squalor. In lurid detail, her testimony takes us inside a whorehouse somewhere in the red-light district around Jerusalem. There were no clients that night, she said, just two lonely hookers and their newborn sons. The following morning she received a horrible shock: the baby at her breast was dead. But a mother always knows her own child, and on closer inspection in the morning light, she discovered that it was not her baby.

Then the woman realized the awful truth. Even though she was not awake at the time, it was obvious what had happened. Sometime during the night the other woman had carelessly rolled over on top of her baby—an awful case of accidental death. Then, with bitter and desperate envy, the grieving woman had switched the babies in the dark, taking the living child to her own breast and handing the other woman a corpse.

At this point the second woman interrupted. She wanted to tell her side of the story, which is how a trial works: the accused always gets the chance to mount a defense. In this case, the defendant did not dispute the first woman's account of the events, but stubbornly insisted that she had the right baby. "No," she said, "the living child is mine, and the dead child is yours." At this point, the trial degenerated into a shouting match. The first woman said, "No, the dead child is yours, and the living child is mine." And so the argument went, back and forth: "Thus they spoke before the king" (1 Kings 3:22).

The whole situation is pitiful, in the sense that everyone in this story deserves our pity. Surely we pity the woman whose son was stolen in the night and who was now desperate to get him back. In her desperation we see every mother's longing for a lost child. Yet we also commiserate with the woman accused of the heinous crime of child-snatching. What a horror it must have been to wake up in the middle of the night, only to discover that she had smothered her son.

Then there is King Solomon, and he too deserves our sympathy. How could he possibly resolve this case? Ordinarily, the testimony of an additional witness would have been required to reach a verdict. According to the Law of Moses, which Solomon was bound to maintain, "a single witness shall not suffice against a person for any crime or for any wrong in connection with any offense that he has committed. Only on the evidence of two witnesses or of three witnesses shall a charge be established" (Deut. 19:15). But in this particular case, there were no other witnesses. The two women had been alone in the night, so it was one woman's word against another's—"she said, she said."

Anyone who has ever tried to resolve a dispute without any witnesses knows how hard it can be to determine exactly what happened. Parents often face this difficulty when trying to adjudicate an argument between two siblings. Teachers have this trouble at school when two students get into a fight. Employers sometimes struggle to resolve a dispute in the workplace. Pastors find it hard to discern the truth about a family conflict or some other broken relationship. There are times when it seems like the only person who really knows the truth is God himself.

SOLOMON'S SIMPLE SOLUTION

In the case of the prostitutes and the two babies, Solomon did not know the truth yet, either. But the king listened carefully to their testimony, and thus he was able to give an accurate summary of the facts in the case: "The one says, 'This is my son that is alive, and your son is dead'; and the other says, 'No; but your son is dead, and my son is the living one'" (1 Kings 3:23). Which woman was telling the truth? This was a serious test of the gift that God had promised. Did Solomon have enough wisdom to discern between good and evil in this case? Could he determine the truth and render a just verdict?

No sooner had the king summarized this royal dilemma than he began to put his simple solution into action. First he said, "Bring me a sword." We can only imagine how startled his servants must have been by this command (to say nothing of the two women). What did Solomon intend to do with this deadly weapon? The sword was brought before the king. Then he gave his deadly command: "Divide the living child in two, and give half to the one and half to the other" (1 Kings 3:24–25).

There was a kind of equity in this legal compromise, but also a horrible cruelty. It was a brutal decree: the bisection of a baby. People must have looked at Solomon with absolute astonishment. This was not wisdom; it was folly! Yet there was a method to the king's apparent madness. For Solomon never intended his command to be executed. Rather, he was staging a trial by ordeal that would reveal each woman's heart.

Immediately Solomon's dreadful decree had its desired effect. The first woman responded with all the passion and compassion of a mother's heart. The Scripture says, "Then the woman whose son was alive said to the king, because her heart yearned for her son, 'Oh, my lord, give her the living child, and by no means put him to death'" (1 Kings 3:26). As soon as the mother heard what Solomon intended to do with his sword, her maternal instincts took over. She had bonded deeply with her newborn son, and she would do anything—anything—to save him. She would even give him up to her enemy, if that would save his life. Tear out her own heart, if you must, but she would save her son. Thus she cried out for the king to spare the child's life.

The first mother made the kind of loving sacrifice that some women make when they put a child up for adoption. Unable to care for children very well themselves, they are willing to suffer the loss of a son or daughter to give the child a better chance in life. Good fathers and mothers make similar sacrifices every day: instead of doing what they want for themselves, they do what is best for their children.

The other woman had a very different response to the threat of Solomon's sword. Callously and heartlessly, she said, "He shall be neither mine nor yours; divide him" (1 Kings 3:26). In the bitterness of her grief, she could only look at the other mother with hateful envy. If she could not have her own son, well, then, no one else would have a son either. With the horrible cruelty of heedless rage, she told the king to go ahead and use his sword; she was willing to take her half of the child.

Now the hearts of both women were revealed, and Solomon knew everything he needed to know to resolve the dilemma, with or without witnesses.

He could tell which woman was the son's mother by her maternal compassion. So he calmly answered both women's pleas for life and death by saying, "Give the living child to the first woman, and by no means put him to death; she is his mother" (1 Kings 3:27).

It was a simple solution to a difficult dilemma. With brilliant insight and wise discernment, Solomon had devised the test that would reveal each woman's heart. As they witnessed the king's wise resolution to this case, the people in the royal throne room must have been astounded. The looks on their faces changed from horror to wonder as they watched the rightful mother reunited with her beloved son. Justice had been done; the king had reached the right verdict. Of course he had! It seemed so simple now: the true mother is the one who will do absolutely anything to save her child. In this way, Solomon spared a child's life and put him back in his mother's arms.

Word of what the king had done spread like wildfire. People were dazzled by the wise and simple way he had solved this difficult dilemma. The story was repeated over and over again all over the city and throughout the surrounding countryside: "And all Israel heard of the judgment that the king had rendered, and they stood in awe of the king, because they perceived that the wisdom of God was in him to do justice" (1 Kings 3:28). If Solomon could settle this case, he had the wisdom for anything. This proved that his prayers had been answered. The king had been given an understanding mind to govern the people, just as he had prayed for (see 1 Kings 3:9). The people recognized his wisdom as nothing less than divine. Thus they honored their king for having the wisdom of God.

WISE JUSTICE

Solomon's verdict was a remarkable confirmation that he had received the holy gift of divine wisdom. It also proved that he was the right man to rule over Israel. In one of his many famous proverbs, Solomon wrote, "The glory of kings is to search things out" (Prov. 25:2). He also said, "A king who sits on the throne of judgment winnows all evil with his eyes" (Prov. 20:8). Solomon's righteous verdict for these two women showed that he was exactly the kind of king his people needed: one who had the insight to search things out and perceive what was evil, to the honor of his name.

There is a question we still need to ask, however: What does this story have to do with us and our need for the gospel of Jesus Christ? All Scripture is beneficial for "training in righteousness" (2 Tim. 3:16). Furthermore, everything in the Bible pertains to the suffering and glory of Jesus Christ (see Luke 24:26–27). So how do we make those life and gospel connections here?

Whenever we consider King Solomon, we need to remember that Jesus described himself as someone "greater than Solomon" (Matt. 12:42). Thus the kingdom of Solomon always points us to the greater kingdom of the Lord Jesus Christ. What is greater about Jesus in this case is his superior wisdom for doing justice. In 1 Kings 3:28 we read of Solomon that "the wisdom of God was in him to do justice." We can apply this statement directly to the person and work of Jesus Christ: the wisdom of God was in him to do justice.

One way to see this connection is to consider the prayer that Solomon offered in Psalm 72, where he asked God for wisdom in judging the people of God:

> Give the king your justice, O God,
>   and your righteousness to the royal son!
> May he judge your people with righteousness,
>   and your poor with justice! . . .
> May he defend the cause of the poor of the people,
>   give deliverance to the children of the needy,
>   and crush the oppressor! (Ps. 72:1–2, 4)

In this prayer Solomon was interceding for himself. As the royal son of God, he needed wisdom for justice. He needed to be able to defend the cause of the poor, just as he had defended a mother from losing her child. He needed to be able to deliver the children of the needy, just as he had saved the mother's son. He needed to crush the oppressor, just as he had exposed the second woman for trying to kidnap someone else's child. Therefore, Solomon prayed for the wise justice to rescue the poor and the needy from their oppressors. He did not give in to the temptation—which often comes to the wealthy and the powerful—to ignore the cries of the oppressed.

Solomon's prayer is also a cry for justice in the everlasting kingdom of God. Like all the other royal psalms, Psalm 72 looks forward to the coming of Christ as the true Son of God. Jesus is the King of all righteousness and the Judge of all justice, who defends the cause of the poor, delivers the children of the needy, and crushes their oppressor. Jesus made this clear from the beginning of his ministry. When he preached his first sermon in Nazareth, he announced that he had come "to proclaim good news to the poor" and "to set at liberty those who are oppressed" (Luke 4:18).

Jesus has promised us justice, and we long for justice to be done. This is a fallen world, where we see so much injustice that sometimes we wonder when or even if everything will be made right. Wrongs go unpunished, including the wrongs done to little children. People get away with dark deeds in the middle of the night. It is hard to know what the truth is. One person says one thing, another person says another, but who is telling the truth? When someone comes with the sword to do justice, he proposes a compromise, the baby gets cut in half, and justice still is not done.

In a world of injustice, we may pray the way that Solomon prayed: "Give the king your justice, O God, and your righteousness to the royal son!" (Ps. 72:1). This prayer is for the wise justice of Jesus Christ. We pray for him to discover what evil has been done and to put things to rights. We want the sinner who has lied and stolen and advocated murder to be found out and brought to justice. We want the innocent child to end up in the arms of the right mother. We want Jesus to do what is just.

Sometimes we see justice done in this life, and sometimes we don't, but justice will be done in the end. The wisdom of God is in Jesus to do justice, and one day he will make everything right. The Bible describes the day of judgment as a day when "God judges the secrets of men by Christ Jesus" (Rom. 2:16). At the final judgment, what happened to the second woman will happen to all the enemies of God. Their sins will be discovered, to their amazement and everlasting dismay, including crimes committed against children in the middle of the night. Jesus Christ will expose the secret motivations of every sinful heart, just as Solomon revealed the hearts of two mothers. Sinful deeds that were never discovered will come out into the clear light of God's eternal day: "For we must all appear before the judgment seat of Christ, so that each one may receive what is due for what he has done in the body, whether good or evil" (2 Cor. 5:10; cf. Matt. 16:27; Rev. 22:12).

People sometimes wonder whether justice will ever be done. In our anger, sometimes we blame God for what is wrong with the world, especially all the terrible evils that seem to go unpunished—the genocides and infanticides of a fallen race. But people are the ones to blame, not God, who is never on the side of injustice. He will make this completely clear on the last of all days, when every wrong will be righted, every terrible evil will be punished, and every unrighteous sinner will be brought to judgment. Jesus is the King, and he will see to it that justice is done.

This will all be to the praise of God and the glory of Jesus Christ. If people held Solomon in awe for reaching the right verdict in one hard case, imagine how much honor Jesus will receive for righting every wrong in the history of the world! At the final judgment, when we see the wise justice of God in Christ, we will stand in awe of our great King. The book of Revelation says that when God executes his final and terrible judgments against sin, his people will cry, "Hallelujah! Salvation and glory and power belong to our God, for his judgments are true and just" (Rev. 19:1–2).

JUST MERCY

Maybe you feel ready to rejoice in the justice of God at the final judgment, but God's justice makes most people feel more than a little uneasy. This is because we know that we ourselves have done many things that we should never have done. Even if we are not guilty of stealing a child, we too have bitterly complained about our losses, envied what other people have, and taken things that did not belong to us. We too have done things in the middle of the night that we hoped no one would ever discover.

What we are desperately hoping to receive, therefore, is not justice, but mercy. However much we want other people to get what we think they deserve, deep down we know that what we need is not what we deserve, but the mercy of God. We catch a glimpse of that mercy in Solomon, whose verdict points us to the merciful wisdom of Jesus Christ.

The story began with two prostitutes appearing before the king. The ugly truth is that both of these women were whores; they sold their bodies for sex. Yet Solomon showed mercy to one of these women by protecting her from injustice.

The mere presence of prostitutes in Israel was an obvious sign of spiritual trouble. In his proverbs Solomon often warned young men to stay away from such women (e.g., Prov. 2:16–19; 5:1–23). This wise counsel was in keeping with the law of God, which explicitly condemned prostitution (see Deut. 23:17; cf. Ex. 20:14). Nevertheless, this very sin was committed in Israel, as it seems to be committed everywhere. We know this because two prostitutes were at the palace, looking for justice.

Remarkably, the king took the time to consider their case. These women, too, were under Solomon's royal authority, so he listened carefully to what they said. Many people would have said that whores and their bastards did not deserve any justice, or mercy, but Solomon treated them as real people who really mattered. How terrible it must have been for the first woman to know the awful truth and not have the witnesses to prove it. Yet for her sake Solomon took the trouble for her to learn the truth.

Then the king did his royal duty. He gave these people true justice, which was a mercy to the woman who received back her son. This is the calling of a righteous king: "He delivers the needy when he calls, the poor and him who has no helper. He has pity on the weak and the needy, and saves the lives of the needy" (Ps. 72:12–13). Thus Solomon had mercy on a baby who was about to lose his mother, and mercy on a woman who would do anything to save her son.

The lives of these people mattered to them as much as your life matters to you. More importantly, every life matters to God—even a life that is enslaved to sin. A reminder of this vital truth came in a dramatic prayer report from a Christian ministry that rescues prostitutes off the streets of Ghana. The women of the Accra Prostitute Rehabilitation Project (a local ministry sponsored by African Enterprise) are loved in the name of Jesus Christ. They are taught practical skills in batik and tie-dye so they can support themselves through honest work. They read the Scriptures together and hear the preaching of the gospel. Most of the women who finish the program praise God for his mercy and become faithful disciples of Jesus Christ.

Newsletters from this ministry are always encouraging, but one report was especially moving. It simply listed the names of the women who were starting the program, with a request for prayer. I saw their names on the page: Victoria Kollie, Esther Sackie, Elizabeth Kpoleh, Roseline Clement, Helena Tokpah, Annie Manbu, and all their sisters. Each woman was lost in sin, but each woman was also a unique creation—a person with a name. These women too were known by God, loved by his people, and freely offered the hope of forgiveness and the promise of eternal life.

This divine mercy is not just for prostitutes and their bastard children. If God has mercy for them, he has mercy for everyone who comes to him in faith. God knows you by name. He also knows whatever it is that you have done wrong. But he still invites you to trust the Savior who is greater than Solomon, whose justice is wise and whose mercy is just.

The prophet Isaiah once made a marvelous prophecy about the royal justice of God's merciful king: "The Spirit of the LORD shall rest upon him, the Spirit of wisdom and understanding. . . . He shall not judge by what his eyes see, or decide disputes by what his ears hear, but with righteousness he shall judge the poor, and decide with equity for the meek of the earth" (Isa. 11:2–4). With all its talk of wisdom and equity and judging disputes, Isaiah's prophecy reminds us of the just and merciful wisdom of King Solomon.

But of course ultimately Isaiah's prophecy is about Jesus Christ, whom the Holy Spirit has given wisdom for justice. As much as people revered King Solomon, we should give greater reverence to Jesus Christ, who is the wisdom of God. Stand in awe, therefore, at the justice he will display at the final judgment, when every wrong will be righted. Tremble at his judgments. God will judge every sin as it deserves. But also stand in awe of God's mercy for poor and needy sinners—the people Jesus knows by name and did everything necessary to save.

Marvel at the wisdom of God in providing such a simple solution for the most difficult dilemma of all—the problem of our sin. How could he maintain his perfect justice while at the same time showing mercy to sinners? How could a just God justify the ungodly, a righteous God take unrighteous people and make them righteous enough for glory? Jesus solved this dilemma by dying on the cross and taking the sword of divine justice in his own side, so that our guilt was paid in blood and we could receive the mercy of God (see Rom. 3:26). The crucifixion is God's simple solution—simple for us, however costly it was for Christ—to the problem of how to atone for sin while at the same time preserving the mercy and justice of God. It is the best of solutions for the worst of problems.

Now we are called to serve our wise King by doing justice and loving mercy, showing other people the same grace that God has shown to us in Jesus Christ. We are agents of God's mercy, so that people will know the grace of our King. No matter how difficult the case, no one is beneath our pity or beyond the mercy of God.

Some years ago now, a young woman experienced God's mercy when she came to the church to confess her sexual sin. It was clear that she was truly sorry for what she had done and had already confessed her sin to the Lord. Yet she was finding it hard to believe that God still loved her. She knew that Jesus had died on the cross to forgive her sins, but she struggled with many despairing thoughts of self-condemnation. Some sort of spiritual breakthrough was badly needed, but it was not clear how. Finally, someone wisely said what turned out to be exactly the thing she needed to hear: "Understand that when God looks at you he does not say, 'There goes that whore'; he says, 'You are my beloved daughter.'"

This is what it means to be under the wise and saving mercy of Christ the King. As far as he is concerned, there are no whores in the family of God, and no bastards . . . only beloved children, whom he has promised to love forever.

8

SOLOMON'S KINGDOM

1 Kings 4:1–21

Judah and Israel were as many as the sand by the sea. They ate and drank and were happy. Solomon ruled over all the kingdoms from the Euphrates to the land of the Philistines and to the border of Egypt. They brought tribute and served Solomon all the days of his life. (1 Kings 4:20–21)

*I*n their best-selling book *Built to Last*, business experts Jim Collins and Jerry Porras analyze the successful habits of visionary companies. By "visionary," they do not simply mean companies that make a lot of money or have been around for a long time. A visionary company, they say, is a premier institution that is widely admired by knowledgeable people, has made an indelible imprint on the world, and has been through multiple generations of chief executives.[1]

King Solomon had similar goals for the organization under his leadership. Solomon was now the third king of Israel, so his kingdom had been through multiple administrations. Solomon knew the promises that God had made

1. James C. Collins and Jerry I. Porras, *Built to Last: Successful Habits of Visionary Companies* (New York: HarperBusiness, 1994), 2.

to David, including the promise of a royal dynasty that would last from age to age. He also knew the promise that God had made to him, that he would become famous for his incomparable wisdom. Here was a kingdom that was destined to make its mark on the world. Solomon was building something to last. More importantly, *God* was building something to last by laying the foundation for a kingdom that would never end.

GETTING ORGANIZED

First Kings 4 tells how Solomon organized his kingdom. Chapter 3 told how Solomon prayed for wisdom and then received it as a gift from God (1 Kings 3:5–12). It also showed how Solomon used that divine wisdom to give people justice in the famous case of the prostitutes and the two babies (1 Kings 3:16–28). The following chapters continue this theme by showing the wisdom of Solomon for construction (1 Kings 5–7), for worship (1 Kings 8), and for commerce (1 Kings 9–10). Chapter 4 fits in with this theme by showing us Solomon's wisdom for administration—the practical organization he needed to govern his people.

The chapter begins with an orderly account of the members of the royal cabinet. Today this information might be presented in the form of an organizational chart, but the Bible simply lists the names of Solomon's staff, with their official duties:

> King Solomon was king over all Israel, and these were his high officials: Azariah the son of Zadok was the priest; Elihoreph and Ahijah the sons of Shisha were secretaries; Jehoshaphat the son of Ahilud was recorder; Benaiah the son of Jehoiada was in command of the army; Zadok and Abiathar were priests; Azariah the son of Nathan was over the officers; Zabud the son of Nathan was priest and king's friend; Ahishar was in charge of the palace; and Adoniram the son of Abda was in charge of the forced labor. (1 Kings 4:1–6)

The names of some of these men are familiar; we have met them before. The support of Nathan, Zadok, and Benaiah was critically important in Solomon's rise to power. It is not surprising to see these men and their sons offer prophetic, priestly, and military leadership for the kingdom. Solomon has put the right men in charge—men who are loyal to his kingship and willing to do kingdom work. What is somewhat surprising to see is that despite his earlier opposition (see 1 Kings 1:7, 19), Abiathar is still a priest and has apparently been restored to the royal court.

The duties of these men cover the full range of kingdom work. There are priests to lead the people in worship—men like Azariah, who by this time had succeeded his father Zadok as the high priest of Israel. There are administrative secretaries (with Egyptian-sounding names)[2] to handle foreign correspondence, as well as court reporters to record Solomon's deeds for posterity. There is a general of the army (Benaiah), a chief of staff (Ahishar), and a friend of the king (Zabud), which in those days was a formal post in the royal court. In short, there is leadership for every branch of government, enabling the king to oversee both foreign and domestic affairs.

Yet one thing in this orderly list seems to strike the wrong note, especially for a nation that had been enslaved to Egypt: Adoniram was in charge of forced labor (1 Kings 4:6). This was something the prophet Samuel had warned about when the people of Israel first clamored for a king. The prophet told them to be careful what they wished, because one day their king would take their children and force them to do his work (see 1 Sam. 8:16–18). Putting someone in charge of forced labor is another warning sign that Solomon is not the perfect king, that tragic flaws in his character will lead to his spiritual downfall. Walter Brueggemann comments:

> On the surface, Solomon's narrative in 1 Kings seems to be a tale of boundless success, prestige, power, and wealth, all the things for which the king did not ask in chapter 3 but that God gave him anyway. If we remember the outcome of the Solomon narrative in chapters 11 and 12 and if we pay attention to the subtle detail of the text, however, we may notice, below the surface success, the rumblings of troublesome things to come.[3]

In addition to the government leaders who served at his royal court in Jerusalem, Solomon appointed provincial governors throughout the whole territory of his dominion, mainly for the purpose of providing food for his royal table. Here is how the Scripture describes them:

2. August H. Konkel, *1 & 2 Kings*, NIV Application Commentary (Grand Rapids: Zondervan, 2006), 95.

3. Walter Brueggemann, *1 & 2 Kings*, Smyth & Helwys Bible Commentary (Macon, GA: Smyth & Helwys, 2000), 71.

Solomon had twelve officers over all Israel, who provided food for the king and his household. Each man had to make provision for one month in the year. These were their names: Ben-hur, in the hill country of Ephraim; Ben-deker, in Makaz, Shaalbim, Beth-shemesh, and Elonbeth-hanan; Ben-hesed, in Arubboth (to him belonged Socoh and all the land of Hepher); Ben-abinadab, in all Naphath-dor (he had Taphath the daughter of Solomon as his wife); Baana the son of Ahilud, in Taanach, Megiddo, and all Beth-shean that is beside Zarethan below Jezreel, and from Beth-shean to Abel-meholah, as far as the other side of Jokmeam; Ben-geber, in Ramoth-gilead (he had the villages of Jair the son of Manasseh, which are in Gilead, and he had the region of Argob, which is in Bashan, sixty great cities with walls and bronze bars); Ahinadab the son of Iddo, in Mahanaim; Ahimaaz, in Naphtali (he had taken Basemath the daughter of Solomon as his wife); Baana the son of Hushai, in Asher and Bealoth; Jehoshaphat the son of Paruah, in Issachar; Shimei the son of Ela, in Benjamin; Geber the son of Uri, in the land of Gilead, the country of Sihon king of the Amorites and of Og king of Bashan. And there was one governor who was over the land. (1 Kings 4:7–19)

There were twelve districts in all, of various shapes and sizes. Based on the town names given, these districts loosely corresponded but did not precisely overlap with the territories Joshua had given the twelve tribes of Israel.[4] Solomon was the king of a large and populous kingdom. From the very beginning, he had been concerned about his ability to rule so many people (see 1 Kings 3:8). Part of the answer was to divide his kingdom into districts, each one under the jurisdiction of a different leader. Solomon was following the same basic advice that Jethro had given to Moses when he was worn out by the heavy burden of leading the Israelites. The answer then was to appoint seventy elders to rule the people of Israel (see Ex. 18). In this case, Solomon appointed twelve officers to rule twelve geographic territories. But in both situations, effective administration required dividing something large into smaller, more manageable units.

However famous they were in their own day, the men in charge of these districts are no longer household names (needless to say, the Ben-hur mentioned in verse 8 was not a star of the silver screen). It is easy for us to overlook

4. Konkel (*1 & 2 Kings*, 97–98) offers a brief and helpful description of each of the twelve provinces. For a more detailed study, consult Yohanan Aharoni, *The Land of the Bible*, rev. ed. (Philadelphia: Westminster, 1979), 309–17.

people like this in the Bible, with all their unfamiliar and unpronounceable names. But the lives of these men mattered to them and to God, which reminds us that we matter too. In the kingdom of God, every person matters. Most of the people in the world have no idea who we are, either, and our names may sound as strange to them as names like Ben-deker and Ahinadab sound to us. But every one of us has a name that is known by God, as well as the ability to serve his kingdom. We should not be discouraged, therefore, if our service to Christ seems insignificant or sometimes gets overlooked by others. God knows the people who belong to him and remembers the work we do for his glory.

The Joy of Order

Admittedly, some scholars doubt whether the work these men did really was for the glory of God, suggesting instead that it was more for the glory of Solomon. After all, their main task was to "stock the commissary for the royal court."[5] The king was "living large," and thus he needed someone to fund his royal appetites. In effect, these men served as the king's Internal Revenue Service. Eventually this form of taxation would become a heavy burden on the people of Israel (see 1 Kings 12:4). Samuel had warned about this, too: the excessive demands that a king would place on his people's best produce (1 Sam. 8:14–15). Brueggemann thus concludes that in presiding over a "vast, imperial economic enterprise," Solomon was preoccupied with taxation ("as governments usually are"), to the neglect of his people and to the eventual destruction of his kingdom.[6]

While there may be some validity to these criticisms, 1 Kings 4 offers a different perspective. It is true that excessive extravagance is sinful, especially when other people have to pay for it. It is also true that some Israelites later complained about the burdens that Solomon placed on them (1 Kings 12). But here in chapter 4 we read that the people "ate and drank and were happy" (1 Kings 4:20). This very positive assessment helps us understand why the Bible gives us so many details about how Solomon organized his kingdom: the people of God find their happiness in the prosperity of the king and his kingdom.

5. Dale Ralph Davis, *The Wisdom and the Folly: An Exposition of the Book of First Kings* (Fearn, Ross-shire: Christian Focus, 2002), 44.

6. Brueggemann, *1 & 2 Kings*, 61, 66.

Here the Holy Spirit is showing that effective administration is a gracious gift that brings joy to the people of God. Our God has a great love for order. This is evident from the way that he made the world, working six days before resting on the seventh, thus establishing a rhythm of work and rest for humanity. God's love for order is evident from the way he put the sun and the moon in the sky to mark out the days and seasons. It is also evident in the little things we see all around us, in the symmetries of every living thing that God has made: the beehive, the spider's web, the organization of the ant colony.

The order of God is also evident in human relationships. We see it in the structure God has established for the home, in which the loving sacrifice of a husband and the loving submission of a wife lay a solid foundation for marriage and family. We see it in his ordering of society, in which governments are given the power of the sword for doing justice. We see it in his instructions for the church, in which all things are to be done "decently and in order" (1 Cor. 14:40). We even see order in the plan of salvation, which is graciously administered by the Father, sacrificially accomplished by the Son, and personally applied by the Holy Spirit. Our God is an orderly God.

God's orderliness is part of his goodness. Of course, there is a kind of order that can be oppressive. The demand for perfect order has a way of stifling creativity and preventing people from flourishing. Sometimes a parent's desire to keep everything in its place can interfere with a child's need to explore the possibilities, for example. We also need to be careful not to overstep our authority in imposing our own sense of organization on other people (like the girl in third grade who always insisted on straightening out my desk). But order is one of God's gracious gifts.

Typically the gift of order comes in the form of a few simple and necessary rules that define the basic structure of our relationships; then within those rules we have extraordinary freedom to decide how to honor God. The Bible gives astonishingly few instructions about marriage, for example, or about organizing a government. Instead, it gives a minimum of basic principles. Then, as we apply these basic principles, we need wisdom to know what kind of order we should bring to every situation in life.

First Kings 4 shows that Solomon had this kind of wisdom. It does this by giving us some of the mundane details of how he got things organized—

details that prove that his kingdom was not some sort of never-never land, but a real place, with real people.[7]

We may not usually think of a bureaucracy as something that brings very much joy, but it did in Solomon's kingdom. His people were happy (1 Kings 4:20)—a rare condition among the nations of men. The organizational wisdom of the king was a blessing for his people, as order always is. This is because we were made with a need for order. Wherever things are in disarray, we may be sure that we are dealing in one way or another with the disorienting effects of sin in a fallen world. But wherever things are well ordered, we catch a glimpse of the goodness of God, because orderliness comes from his common grace. Though far from perfect, the order Solomon brought to his kingdom was a gift from God that gave joy to his people.

The same gift is available to us today, by the work of the Holy Spirit. The New Testament has a name for this gift: it is called "administration" (*kuberneseis*; 1 Cor. 12:28). Most people probably think of administration as one of the less important spiritual gifts. Some people may even think that getting a church better organized will only set up a spiritual bureaucracy. But anyone who has ever been involved with something that was poorly planned and poorly executed knows how important it is to be properly organized. Dale Ralph Davis comments that biblical wisdom

> is not only concerned with moral and accurate judgments but also with efficient and orderly structure that keeps chaos and waste from running life. Some of us deplore having to give attention to administrative and organizational matters, and one can so tightly structure life that one squeezes the breath out of it. Nevertheless, a few moments in a chaotic home or in a workplace lacking clear lines of authority can quickly create a thirst for order.[8]

Almost every form of administration has its weaknesses, but the alternative is to have no administration at all, which is even worse. One is reminded of a well-known witticism about democracy, that of all the forms of government known to humanity, it is the very worst . . . except for all the others.[9] So too with administration: however much we may grumble about bureaucracy, even a bad administration is better than no administration at all. To take a

7. Richard Nelson, *First and Second Kings*, Interpretation (Louisville: John Knox, 1987), 40.
8. Davis, *The Wisdom and the Folly*, 45.
9. Attributed to Sir Winston Churchill.

notable example from American history, the relief efforts in New Orleans after Hurricane Katrina struck in 2005 were a complete fiasco. This was not a failure of compassion, entirely, but also of administration.

Something similar can happen in the church. When a congregation is poorly administered, the souls of its people are placed in spiritual jeopardy. This is why God has given us elders and deacons in the church—an orderly structure for providing spiritual and practical care. This is why it is important for spiritual leaders to organize their time wisely for ministry. This is also why it is important for any congregation, especially a large one, to be well organized for discipleship. Every church needs an effective plan for local and global outreach, as well as people with the gifts to make the plan work.

In and of themselves, these orderly structures will not save anyone's soul. But without them, who will take responsibility for giving spiritual care, or helping people with practical needs, or reaching out to people who need to know Christ? These things do not happen as often or as effectively as they should without proper organization. If we wait for them to happen on their own, they may never happen at all. They require the gift of administration—a spiritual gift we see in Solomon's kingdom and pray for the Holy Spirit to provide in the ministry of the church.

THE COVENANT KINGDOM

The joy of Solomon's kingdom had a deeper source than simply the king's ability to get things organized. By itself, good organization is not able to bring true spiritual joy. It is a necessary but not a sufficient condition for a joyful kingdom. In fact, some of the most repressive governments in history have been all too well organized. One only needs to think of the Nazi railway system and the death trains that always ran on time. There must be a deeper source of blessedness than simply being well organized.

The deep source of joy in the kingdom of Solomon was the faithful promises of God. We see these promises kept in the happy summary that follows the list of Solomon's regional superintendents: "Judah and Israel were as many as the sand by the sea. They ate and drank and were happy. Solomon ruled over all the kingdoms from the Euphrates to the land of the Philistines and to the border of Egypt" (1 Kings 4:20–21).

On the surface of things, these verses simply tell us the size of Solomon's kingdom, in terms of both population and geography. His people were countless in number, like the sand on the seashore. His borders stretched from Egypt to Iraq. But to understand fully the significance of these verses, we need to remember the ancient promises of God. The vocabulary of 1 Kings 4—with all its talk of sand by the seashore and kingdoms from Egypt to the Euphrates—refers directly and explicitly to the covenant promises that God made to Abraham. This is one of the many places where we encounter a recurring theme that ties the Bible together. In his covenant with Abraham, God had promised both land and seed. He would make the descendants of Abraham as numerous as the sand on the seashore, in a large and bountiful country that they could call their very own. Now the promises of the covenant were coming true, to the joy of God's people.

We find God's promises scattered throughout the stories of Abraham in the book of Genesis. God said, "I will make of you a great nation, and I will bless you and make your name great, so that you will be a blessing" (Gen. 12:2). This was the promise that Abraham's people would become a great kingdom. God said, "I will surely bless you, and I will surely multiply your offspring as the stars of heaven and as the sand that is on the seashore" (Gen. 22:17). This was the promise that the people of Abraham's kingdom would be countless in number. God said, "To your offspring I give this land, from the river of Egypt to the great river, the river Euphrates" (Gen. 15:18; cf. Ex. 23:31; Josh. 1:4). This was the promise that Abraham's kingdom would stretch from Egypt to Iraq. Later God said that this kingdom would be "a land flowing with milk and honey" (Ex. 3:8)—a promise of God's provision.

Now God's promises were starting to come true—the covenant promises that he swore to keep. Take a bucket of sand. Count the grains one by one, which would probably take the better part of a week. Then try to estimate how many buckets there are on the seashore. This was the population of Solomon's kingdom, metaphorically speaking. It was more people than he could even count, which is why he begged God for wisdom (1 Kings 3:8). God was keeping the promise of numerous offspring: "Judah and Israel were as many as the sand by the sea" (1 Kings 4:20).

Then take a compass and a surveyor's chain to measure the land where these people lived. The territory that God promised to Abraham was part of the kingdom of Solomon. In the words of one commentator, "The land Moses desired, Joshua conquered, and David subdued now lay in the hands of a man of unsurpassed wisdom."[10] This long-promised land was flowing with milk and honey. The people were living the good life; they "ate and drank and were happy" (1 Kings 4:20).

The deep reason for their joy was that God had been faithful to keep his promises. Solomon's kingdom was more than a good earthly government. It was a covenant kingdom. It was the kingdom that God had always planned to build, based on promises that he could never break because they were sworn by his own perfect and unbreakable word. The people were happy in the prosperity of their king, and in the security of their blessing by the promises of God.

There is a further fulfillment of God's covenant promise at the end of verse 21, where we read that neighboring kingdoms "brought tribute and served Solomon all the days of his life." This too was the fulfillment of an ancient promise. God said that Abraham's name would become great among the nations, and that through him, "all the families of the earth shall be blessed" (Gen. 12:2–3). God told him that he would gain a very great reward (Gen. 15:1) and that he would become "a great and mighty nation" (Gen. 18:18). God said that Abraham's children would "possess the gate of their enemies" (Gen. 22:17); they would have power and influence over their rivals.

Now the wealth and power of the nations was flowing to Solomon, just as God had promised. Kings were coming to bring tribute to his royal treasury. They were swearing fealty to the house of David, promising loyal service to Solomon as Israel's mighty king. Through the reign of Solomon's kingdom, the blessing of Abraham was coming to the nations.

GOOD TO GREAT

Earlier I mentioned a popular business book called *Built to Last*. Author Jim Collins is also well known for another best-seller, in which he tries to explain why some good companies achieve greatness, while others never do. The book is called *Good to Great*, and its title serves as an apt description of

10. Paul R. House, *1, 2 Kings*, The New American Commentary (Nashville: Broadman & Holman, 1995), 116.

the relationship between Solomon's kingdom and the kingdom of the Lord Jesus Christ.[11]

As we consider the kingship of Solomon, the comparison to Christ should never be far from our minds. Jesus claimed to be superior to Solomon—the greater king of a greater kingdom (see Luke 11:31). When we compare Solomon to Christ, we are moving from an earthly dominion to a heavenly kingdom, from a temporary monarchy to an everlasting dynasty, from good to great. As Timothy Dwight wrote in the final stanza of the hymn "I Love Thy Kingdom, Lord," the kingdom of Christ shall receive "the brightest glories earth can yield, and brighter bliss of heav'n."

Everything good in Solomon's kingdom is greatly surpassed in the kingdom of Jesus Christ, which is superior in every way. The kingdom of Christ is better organized. This is the work of God the Holy Spirit, whom Jesus has sent to bring order to the home and to the church, order to our lives and our relationships. This order is not imposed on us from the outside, but comes from the inside out, as the Spirit works within us to produce patience, forgiveness, gentleness, self-control, and the rest of the spiritual virtues that bring harmony to life.

The kingdom of Christ is bigger than Solomon's kingdom, with more people in it, coming from more nations. Jesus said that when he was lifted up, he would draw all people to himself (John 12:32). He said this "to show by what kind of death he was going to die" (John 12:33), namely, by crucifixion. Jesus was lifted up on the cross. There he took the guilt of our sin upon himself, dying in our place, offering his blood to atone for our sin. But Jesus also said this to announce his intention to save the peoples of all nations. In being lifted up, he would draw people to himself. This is exactly what has happened. Down through history, hundreds of millions of people have joined the kingdom of God through faith in Christ and his crucifixion. It is happening right now, as believers in Christ share the gospel with their friends and families, and as missionaries go into the whole world with the gospel. The promise God made to Abraham, which was only partially fulfilled in the days of King Solomon, is coming totally true.

As the gospel is proclaimed in word and deed, more tribute from more nations is coming to Christ. At this very moment, glory and honor and praise

---

11. Jim Collins, *Good to Great: Why Some Companies Make the Leap . . . and Others Don't* (London: Collins, 2001).

are given to him by many people in many places. They are hearing the gospel in words they can understand and responding to God in worship with the heart-language of their souls. This is what David prophesied would happen when his kingdom went from good to great: "All the ends of the earth shall remember and turn to the Lord, and all the families of the nations shall worship before you. For kingship belongs to the Lord, and he rules over the nations" (Ps. 22:27–28). The "kings of the earth will bring their glory" into the kingdom of Christ until finally he receives all the praise that belongs to him (Rev. 21:24). His kingdom will stretch far beyond the borders of Solomon's kingdom, running from north to south and east to west until finally "the earth will be filled with the knowledge of the glory of the Lord as the waters cover the sea" (Hab. 2:14).

How happy we are to belong to this great kingdom! As the people of God, we find our true happiness in the prosperity of our King. The more he is worshiped, the more we rejoice. This is why we love to see spiritual order come to broken lives and damaged relationships. It is why we take such an active interest in the kingdom work that God is doing in our own community and around the world. The work of God's kingdom is the most important work in the world, and our joy is to see it grow.

As we do this kingdom work, we do not depend on our own abilities, least of all in the area of administration. Rather, we depend on the kingdom promise that Jesus will be with us as we do his gospel work in the power of the Holy Spirit. Our desire is for the Lord Jesus Christ to receive as much honor as possible, from as many people as possible, in as many places as possible, for he alone deserves all the glory.

9

THE PEACEABLE KINGDOM

1 Kings 4:22–34

For he had dominion over all the region west of the Euphrates from Tiphsah to Gaza, over all the kings west of the Euphrates. And he had peace on all sides around him. And Judah and Israel lived in safety, from Dan even to Beersheba, every man under his vine and under his fig tree, all the days of Solomon.
(1 Kings 4:24–25)

The nineteenth-century Pennsylvania artist Edward Hicks is remembered chiefly for producing dozens of folk paintings on a single theme. In these familiar images, a small child stands with a placid group of wild and domestic animals: an ox, a wolf, a lion, a leopard, and a lamb. Often the child has one arm wrapped around the lion's neck—a gesture of warm and peaceful intimacy.

Hicks called these imaginative paintings "The Peaceable Kingdom." They were based on a beautiful promise from the prophet Isaiah: "The wolf shall dwell with the lamb, and the leopard shall lie down with the young goat, and the calf and the lion and the fattened calf together; and a little child shall lead them" (Isa. 11:6). Hicks was captivated by this promise of peace on earth. He was looking for the day when people would live in perfect harmony—the day, he said, "when MAN is moved and led by sov'reign grace, to seek that state of everlasting PEACE."[1]

Yet something sad and strange happened to these paintings through the years: they became less and less peaceable. Edward Hicks continued to paint the same theme, but from a different perspective. Rather than looking peaceful and content, his animals began to look tense and uneasy. He placed them farther and farther apart. By the time Hicks produced his last paintings, some of the animals were fighting, tearing at one another with snarling teeth.

The dramatic difference between the first and last paintings reveals a change that was taking place in the artist's soul. Edward Hicks had witnessed so much disunity and disharmony, especially in the church, that gradually he lost confidence in ever seeing peace on earth. The peaceable kingdom was only a dream, not a reality.

THE PROMISE OF THE KINGDOM

The longer we live, the more it seems as if Hicks was right. Here we have no peaceable kingdom. Nations are at war. Churches split. Families fall apart. Children die on the city streets. Sin has created such a disturbance of the peace that it is always difficult and sometimes impossible to live in harmony with God, with nature, with one another, or even with ourselves. With all the horrors we witness in a fallen world and all the troubles we have in our own relationships, how can we still believe there will ever be peace on earth?

We do not believe in "peace on earth" because we have seen earthly peace for ourselves, but only because we have read its promise in the Word of God. When Isaiah prophesied the coming of Christ, he said that "of the increase of his government and of peace there will be no end, on the throne of David and over his kingdom, to establish it and to uphold it with justice and with righteousness from this time forth and forevermore" (Isa. 9:7). Angels made the same promise on the night when Christ was born: "Glory to God in the highest," they said to the Christmas shepherds, "and on earth peace, good will toward men" (Luke 2:14 KJV). A peaceable kingdom is one of the promises

1. Carolyn J. Weekley, *The Kingdoms of Edward Hicks*, Abby Aldrich Rockefeller Folk Art Center Series (New York: Harry N. Abrams, 1999).

of God: a kingdom that will not come in its fullness until the second coming of Jesus Christ.

One good place to catch a glimpse of that kingdom is in the story of King Solomon. In order to help us understand what it will be like to live forever in his glorious presence, God has often described our future blessing in terms of a kingdom—what the Bible calls "the kingdom of our Lord and of his Christ" (Rev. 11:15). For example, Jesus said that it was the Father's good pleasure to give us the kingdom (Luke 12:32). The Scottish preacher Thomas Boston believed that Jesus used this comparison because "the greatest number of earthly good things" come together in a kingdom—a kingdom with peace and prosperity for all its citizens.[2]

King Solomon ruled a peaceable, prosperous kingdom. In 1 Kings 4 he is said explicitly to rule a kingdom that had "peace on all sides" (1 Kings 4:24). This peaceable kingdom is an earthly symbol of spiritual realities. Charles Spurgeon said that "the kingdom of Israel under the sway of Solomon was a fair type of the reign of our Lord Jesus Christ." According to Spurgeon, "The present state of the church may be compared to the reign of David: splendid with victories, but disturbed with battles." Yet "there are better days to come, days in which the kingdom shall be extended and become more manifest; and then the Lord Jesus Christ shall be even more conspicuously seen as the Solomon of the kingdom."[3] Therefore, looking at Solomon's peaceable kingdom is an excellent way for us to see the blessings that God has for us in Jesus Christ (while at the same time recognizing that whatever flaws and limitations we see in Solomon's kingdom show us our need for the superior kingship of Christ).

THE BOUNTY OF THE KING'S TABLE

The closing paragraphs of 1 Kings 4 show us at least four things that Jesus now offers to us as the glorious Solomon of the kingdom of God. First, we see *the bounty of the king's table.* The Bible says that "Solomon's provision for one day was thirty cors of fine flour and sixty cors of meal, ten fat oxen, and

---

2. Thomas Boston, *The Complete Works of the Late Rev. Thomas Boston of Ettrick*, ed. Samuel M'Millan, 12 vols. (London, 1853; repr., Wheaton, IL: Richard Owen Roberts, 1980), 8:318.

3. Charles Spurgeon, "The Dromedaries," in *Metropolitan Tabernacle Pulpit* (Pasadena, TX: Pilgrim, 1972), 25:637.

twenty pasture-fed cattle, a hundred sheep, besides deer, gazelles, roebucks, and fattened fowl" (1 Kings 4:22–23).

These numbers are designed to impress. Earlier we learned how Solomon organized his kingdom into twelve districts to provide food for his royal table, one district per month (1 Kings 4:7–19). Here we are given the king's daily requirements. Every day the bakers in Solomon's kitchens used 180 bushels of the best flour and 360 bushels of meal to bake bread and other pastries. They also put meat on the table: dozens of cattle and oxen, a hundred sheep, animals from the field, birds from the royal aviary. Solomon had a feast every day of the week, provided from the bounty of his kingdom, as tribute from his people.

These provisions were necessary because of the vast contingency attached to the royal palace, or otherwise in the king's employ. According to family tradition, my great-grandmother baked a dozen loaves of bread every day. Given this fact, it is not hard to guess that she had a lot of mouths to feed: sixteen children in all, most of them hardworking farm boys with healthy appetites. Solomon had many more mouths to feed, with estimates ranging from fourteen thousand to as many as thirty-two thousand people.[4]

Then there were all the horses that needed provision. We read that Solomon "had 40,000 stalls of horses for his chariots, and 12,000 horsemen. And those officers supplied provisions for King Solomon, and for all who came to King Solomon's table, each one in his month. They let nothing be lacking. Barley also and straw for the horses and swift steeds they brought to the place where it was required, each according to his duty" (1 Kings 4:26–28; cf. 2 Chron. 9:25). Solomon's stable was as well organized as his table. Every horse for every chariot had all the food and bedding it needed, and every officer in the cavalry took his turn in bringing supplies to Solomon's table.

As we will see by the time we get to the end of Solomon's story, his numerous horses and chariots were cause for spiritual concern. According to the Law of Moses, the king of Israel was never supposed to "acquire many horses for himself" (Deut. 17:16). Horses were a means of military defense. The only defense that Israel really needed was the help of God, but Solomon sought to strengthen his national security by adding more and more horses to his cavalry. It would have been better for him to follow the example of his

4. Paul R. House, *1, 2 Kings*, The New American Commentary (Nashville: Broadman & Holman, 1995), 117.

father David, who said, "Some trust in chariots and some in horses, but we trust in the name of the LORD our God" (Ps. 20:7). For as the psalmist also said, "The king is not saved by his great army; a warrior is not delivered by his great strength. The war horse is a false hope for salvation" (Ps. 33:16–17; cf. Isa. 31:1). Iain Provan thus compares all the king's horses and all the king's chariots to a ticking bomb: in time, trusting in military power would lead to Solomon's downfall.[5] Indeed, the prophet Micah later described Solomon's chariot cities as "the beginning" of Israel's sin (see Mic. 1:13). Rather than resisting the seduction of power, Solomon built a stronger army and then relied on the security it supposedly brought to his kingdom.

Here in chapter 4, however, the emphasis falls on the bounty of the king's table. Solomon's court enjoyed what some people call "the good things in life." Nothing was lacking. Everyone who came to the king's banqueting house (see Song 2:4) had plenty to eat. This abundance extended to the rest of his loyal subjects, every one of whom sat down under his own vine and fig tree (1 Kings 4:25); the people "ate and drank and were happy" (1 Kings 4:20).

Solomon thus enjoyed what every self-respecting monarch must have: a table fit for a king. Kings do not become famous for their frugality. When people go to the palace for dinner they expect a feast, and if the king is unable to provide one, his reputation will suffer. To give just one legendary example, King Arthur never would have been able to gather any brave knights around his celebrated round table unless he was able to give them something good to eat. By definition, royal tables are meant for feasting.

If Jesus Christ is the Solomon of God's kingdom, then what is the bounty of his royal table? The prophets always promised that the Christ would "make for all peoples a feast of rich food, a feast of well-aged wine" (Isa. 25:6). They said this feast would be offered free of cost to every poor and hungry sinner (see Isa. 55:1–2). Then Jesus came into the world and provided miracle bread for his people in the wilderness (e.g., Luke 9:10–17). He did this to show that he had the power to satisfy us—not just to feed our bodies, but also to nourish our souls.

Jesus often compared his kingdom to a great banquet. He said that people would come from east and west to recline at his table (Matt. 8:11). He said that

5. Iain W. Provan, *1 and 2 Kings*, New International Biblical Commentary (Peabody, MA: Hendrickson, 1995), 59.

everyone would be invited: not just the beautiful people and the religious insiders, but the poor and crippled sinners who had never been invited to anything (Luke 14:12–24). Now his royal table is open to anyone who will come.

At the very end of his earthly life Jesus prepared the best of all tables for his disciples—a physical meal that symbolized a spiritual feast. He gave them bread, which signified his body, and wine, representing his blood. This was food for the soul. Then Jesus offered his body and blood on the cross, loving us to death by giving his life for our sins. Now every time we eat his bread and drink his cup we announce his death until he comes again (see 1 Cor. 11:26). When Jesus does come again, we will feast with him forever at "the marriage supper of the Lamb" (Rev. 19:9). The Bible describes salvation in culinary terms because a royal feast is one of the best things in life, and by his kingly grace, God has promised to give us the best of his blessings forever (see Ps. 84:11; Eph. 1:3).

To know Christ as King is to enjoy the best feast that anyone has ever tasted. Perhaps it will be something like the amazing meal that Lisa and I once shared in Newark, New Jersey. It was our twentieth wedding anniversary, and plans were not working out quite as well as I had hoped. We were going to New York City for a few days, and when I was unable to get a good room in Manhattan the first night, we ended up instead at a half-decent hotel at the Newark Airport. (As far as I am aware, Newark has never been a destination of choice for twentieth anniversaries; obviously, I was desperate for accommodations.) But then came dinner, when my wife was finally rewarded for being a good sport. The hotel recommended a place called the Spanish Tavern, and we decided to try it. A free shuttle took us to a 1936 restaurant in an old Hispanic neighborhood of Newark, where we enjoyed rich food and fine wine—one of the best meals ever.

The kingdom of God is like unexpectedly finding a great restaurant on your anniversary. First someone tells you to try Jesus. You are not quite sure what he will be like, but if you are willing to find out, you discover a feast for your soul—the bounty of his royal table.

THE EXTENT OF THE KING'S DOMINION

King Solomon needed so much food for so many people because he had such a large kingdom. Consider *the extent of the king's dominion*: "Solomon

113

ruled over all the kingdoms from the Euphrates to the land of the Philistines and to the border of Egypt. . . . For he had dominion over all the region west of the Euphrates from Tiphsah to Gaza, over all the kings west of the Euphrates" (1 Kings 4:21, 24). Solomon's kingdom was virtually an empire. To the north it went all the way to the Euphrates River, almost to the border of modern-day Turkey. To the south it ran down to Egypt. This was the largest kingdom that Israel ever possessed, right up to the present day. King Solomon controlled a territory equal to or greater than all the territory that David conquered (see 2 Sam. 8:12–13). His empire reached toward the four corners of the earth.

The extent of Solomon's dominion was a direct fulfillment of the covenant promises that God once made to Abraham. At the same time he promised Abraham descendants like the stars in the desert sky, God also promised that the children of Abraham would have a land to call their own: "To your offspring I give this land, from the river of Egypt to the great river, the river Euphrates" (Gen. 15:18). From Egypt to Turkey, God's covenant promise was fulfilled in Solomon's wide dominion.

Solomon's kingdom was also a direct fulfillment of a biblical command. When God first created Adam and Eve, he gave them "dominion" over every living thing (Gen. 1:26). The word that 1 Kings uses to describe Solomon's kingdom is the same word we find in Genesis: the Hebrew word for "dominion" (*radah*). King Solomon thus fulfilled God's original intention for the people made in his image. With God's blessing, and under God's authority, Solomon was taking dominion over part of God's world.

There is an obvious contrast between the kingdom of Solomon and the kingdom of Christ. Whereas Solomon ruled over a limited, carefully defined territory, Jesus reigns as King over the entire universe. As the Creator God, Jesus made the whole universe to begin with (Col. 1:16). Now that he has been raised from the dead and ascended to the right hand of the Father, he claims sovereign dominion over everything in heaven and earth (see Phil. 2:9–11). The Bible says that Jesus must reign until everything is under his feet (see 1 Cor. 15:24–28). Not even one square inch on this entire planet lies outside his royal authority, for all the authority in heaven and earth has been given to him (see Matt. 28:18).

The royal dominion of Jesus Christ is foundational to our own work as servants of the King. The extent of his dominion is what drives our involvement in kingdom work. Rather than surrendering our community to the powers of hell, we claim it as one place where Christ is King, where God is at work in our preaching of his gospel, and where the Holy Spirit empowers us to serve people in need. We take the same approach to global outreach. There are many dark and dangerous places in the world, but in every one of those places Jesus Christ is the rightful King, and therefore we go out into the whole world with an invitation to submit to his royal authority.

As great as it was, the kingdom of Solomon gives us no more than a small glimpse of the greater kingdom of Jesus Christ. God has issued a kingly decree that his royal Son "will have dominion from sea to sea, and from the River to the ends of the earth!" (Ps. 72:8; cf. Zech. 9:10). Therefore, we live and preach the gospel of the kingdom everywhere we go, proclaiming the kingship of Christ in our words and by our deeds. As Charles Spurgeon once said, "The Christian church was designed from the first to be aggressive. It was not intended to remain stationary at any period, but to advance onward until its boundaries became commensurate with those of the world."[6]

THE PEACE OF THE KING'S SUBJECTS

Spurgeon's talk of global expansion might make some people a little nervous. It is important to say, therefore, that the worldwide kingdom of Jesus Christ is a peaceable kingdom. It does not advance by waging military warfare, but by the joyful proclamation of peace with God. Its power is surrendered to the service of love.

Consider, then, *the peace of the king's subjects.* According to 1 Kings, Solomon "had peace on all sides around him. And Judah and Israel lived in safety, from Dan even to Beersheba, every man under his vine and under his fig tree, all the days of Solomon" (1 Kings 4:24–25). This is a remarkable testimony to the peace of Solomon's kingdom. The history of humanity tells the story of many bloody conflicts, especially in Israel, which is still the most hotly contested piece of property on the entire planet. But in Solomon's day, for almost the only time in its history, Israel had peace in every direction. Whereas his father David was constantly at war, Solomon was always at peace; thus we never read about his riding off to battle or winning any

6. Charles Spurgeon, "Metropolitan Tabernacle Statistics," *Sword and Trowel* (April 1865).

famous victories. As God had promised, the son of David ruled a peaceable kingdom: "I will appoint a place for my people Israel and will plant them, so that they may dwell in their own place and be disturbed no more. And violent men shall afflict them no more. . . . I will give you rest from all your enemies" (2 Sam. 7:10–11).

The peace of Solomon's kingdom was both foreign and domestic. Solomon was not at war with the Egyptians, the Syrians, the Philistines, or any of Israel's other neighbors. There was peace on every side. There was also peace within Israel. Since the nation was not at war, people were free to pursue their own prosperity. To use a common biblical metaphor, every man sat "under his vine and under his fig tree" (1 Kings 4:25; cf. Isa. 36:16; Mic. 4:4; Zech. 3:10). In other words, every Israelite had a place to call his own—a place in the shade, with plenty of good things to eat and drink.

This image of the vine and fig tree was George Washington's favorite biblical metaphor. As a victorious general, Washington knew how to win a war, but he also knew how to enjoy his peace. In his letters and other writings he used this image more than forty times, especially when he was sitting under the shade of his own vine and fig tree at his beloved Mount Vernon. The goal of Washington's warfare was to win the happiness of peace for himself and his fellow countrymen. As he wrote to the Marquis de Lafayette not long after the American Revolution, "everyone (under his own vine and fig-tree), shall begin to taste the fruits of freedom."[7]

Washington's hope is the promise of the gospel. Christ has promised peace to all his people, and the kingdom of Solomon helps us see this dimension of his saving work. Like David, Jesus fights to win the victory over all the enemies of his kingdom. He does this mainly through the cross and the empty tomb, where he defeated sin, death, and the devil. But like Solomon, Jesus also reigns over a peaceable kingdom: "he himself is our peace" (Eph. 2:14).

Jesus gives us peace with God, first of all. We are no longer at war with God in the hostility of our sin. On the contrary, "since we have been justified by faith, we have peace with God through our Lord Jesus Christ" (Rom. 5:1), who has made "peace by the blood of his cross" (Col. 1:20). Now we can rest in the peace of knowing that our sins are forgiven. God is for us, not against us, and therefore we are secure in the knowledge of his love.

7. George Washington, letter to the Marquis de Lafayette (June 19, 1788), quoted in Peter A. Lillback, *George Washington's Sacred Fire* (Bryn Mawr, PA: Providence Forum Press, 2006), 317.

Peace with God also gives us peace in this troubled world, where we often experience the kind of personal turmoil and broken relationships that Edward Hicks portrayed in his later paintings. We do not yet live in perfect peace. Nevertheless, we can and do experience peace in troubled times. The peace we have with God gives us peace within. The Bible promises that "the peace of God, which surpasses all understanding, will guard your hearts and your minds in Christ Jesus" (Phil. 4:7; cf. Col. 3:15). When our souls are troubled, God can give us peace, if only we will trust in him.

One day that peace will be made perfect. All our enemies will be defeated forever. There will be no more death or dying. The devil and his demons will be banished for all eternity. Then each of us will have our own vine and fig tree, so to speak. Jesus said there are many rooms in his Father's house, where he has promised to prepare a place for us (John 14:2)—a place in the shade of his everlasting rest. From time to time, we catch a glimpse of God's royal peace already in this life. We sit under the trees beside a quiet lake, with the cool breeze in our face and the sun dancing on the water. Or we get a quiet hour at home with a good book and a warm fire. Sadly, these moments will not last, as we know all too well. But they whisper to us the peace of a heavenly kingdom, where we will sit under the vine of Christ, and under his fig tree.

THE REPUTATION OF THE KING'S WISDOM

Solomon's wide and peaceable dominion, with its bountiful table, helps us see the kingdom of God. But the best part of any good kingdom is the king himself—not just his wealth and power, or the peace and prosperity he brings, but his own royal person. Therefore, 1 Kings 4 ends by reminding us of Solomon's outstanding characteristic, the one supreme and God-given gift that distinguished him from all other kings. Consider, therefore, *the reputation of the king's wisdom.*

God had invited Solomon to ask for anything he pleased. What pleased Solomon to ask was something it pleased God to give: the gift of wisdom (1 Kings 3:4–14). The king had exercised this gift in the famous incident of the prostitutes and the two babies (1 Kings 3:16–28). At the end of chapter 4 the biblical writer joyfully celebrates the wisdom of his king by using the vocabulary for wisdom in almost every verse.

The Bible declares this wisdom in multiple ways. It begins by simply asserting that "God gave Solomon wisdom" (1 Kings 4:29). Then Solomon's wisdom is demonstrated by means of an analogy from nature: "God gave Solomon wisdom and understanding beyond measure, and breadth of mind like the sand on the seashore" (1 Kings 4:29). The king's wisdom was not infinite, of course, because only God is infinitely wise, but Solomon was wise beyond anything that any mere human being could measure. His wisdom was like the sand on the seashore. This analogy reminds us why the king asked for wisdom in the first place: the people he had to govern were too numerous to count (1 Kings 3:8). Yet God gave Solomon wisdom sufficient for his calling—wisdom like the sand on the seashore.

Next the king's wisdom is demonstrated by comparison with other wise men: "Solomon's wisdom surpassed the wisdom of all the people of the east and all the wisdom of Egypt. For he was wiser than all other men, wiser than Ethan the Ezrahite, and Heman, Calcol, and Darda, the sons of Mahol, and his fame was in all the surrounding nations" (1 Kings 4:30–31; cf. 1 Chron. 2:6). Most of these men are long forgotten, but they were nearly as famous in their day as poets like Robert Frost or songwriters like George Gershwin have since become. Ethan and Heman, for example, were poets; they wrote Psalms 88 and 89. Yet by comparison, Solomon was wiser than them all. His world-famous wisdom was superior even to the intellectual giants of Egypt, Persia, and Babylon—the great centers of learning in the ancient world.

Solomon's wisdom is demonstrated as well by the things he wrote and said. The Bible tells us that the king "spoke 3,000 proverbs, and his songs were 1,005" (1 Kings 4:32). Many of these wise sayings and lyrical ballads are preserved in the Scriptures. We find the king's praise songs in Psalms 72 and 127. We read his love songs in the Song of Songs (Song 1:1). We learn his proverbs for daily life from the book of Proverbs, most of which was written by the king himself (see Prov. 1:1). Solomon's literary output is impressive, in both quantity and quality.

The breadth of the king's knowledge was equally impressive. Not only was he skilled in the literary arts, but he also had a scientist's love for the natural world. As Solomon wrote his songs and proverbs, "he spoke of trees, from the cedar that is in Lebanon to the hyssop that grows out of the wall. He spoke also of beasts, and of birds, and of reptiles, and of fish" (1 Kings 4:33). Solomon's knowledge was encyclopedic. He knew about everything from the tallest tree in the forest (the cedar of Lebanon) to the smallest plant growing in the garden wall (the hyssop). The king had a love for botany and biology; he knew both the flora and the fauna of his native Israel. In the words of one commentator, his interests included "what is in the barn and what is in the lake, what graces the skies and what slithers across the kitchen floor."[8]

With a curiosity as wide as the universe, Solomon was interested in everything God made. Not surprisingly, his writings are filled with many analogies based on careful observation of the created world. When he was not making comparisons with eagles in the sky or venomous snakes (see Prov. 23:5, 32), the king was inviting his readers to "go to the ant" (Prov. 6:6) or listen to "the voice of the turtledove" (Song 2:12). Solomon was the renaissance man of the ancient world—a naturalist as well as a songwriter, a philosopher as well as a king.

If we are wise, we will follow his example by finding delight in the world that God has made and learning everything it has to teach us. Gaze at the high constellation in the evening sky. Watch the osprey dive in the mountain lake to claim its prey. Smell the flower that blooms along the path in summertime. Notice the trail of ants crawling from the picnic to the anthill. Do not miss the marvels all around us—the things that God has made, which the Holy Spirit can use to teach us how to live:

> Since God has left the fingerprints of his wisdom everywhere, since there is no place where God does not furnish us with raw materials for godly thinking, Christians should be seized with a rambunctious curiosity to ponder his works, both the majestic and the mundane. The task of wisdom is joyfully to describe and investigate all God's works. We may not be Solomons in insight, but we can gratefully examine the same data.[9]

The king's wisdom is further demonstrated by the people who came to him for counsel: "And people of all nations came to hear the wisdom of Solomon, and from all the kings of the earth, who had heard of his wisdom" (1 Kings 4:34). We will see a famous example of Solomon's international renown in chapter 10, when the Queen of Sheba comes for a visit. But apparently this sort of thing happened all the time. People came to visit this king from all over the

---

8. Dale Ralph Davis, *The Wisdom and the Folly: An Exposition of the Book of First Kings* (Fearn, Ross-shire: Christian Focus, 2002), 49.

9. Ibid., 50.

world. Solomon virtually became an international tourist attraction. By any measure—whether by comparison, by reputation, or simply by the plain assertion of the biblical text—he was the wisest man in the world.

He was not as wise as King Jesus, however (especially in his relationship to money, sex, and power, which Solomon eventually pursued, but Jesus always surrendered for the sake of his Father's kingdom). The kingdom of Solomon is always pointing us to the greater kingdom of Jesus Christ. As we have seen, Jesus sits at a more bountiful table, at which he gives his own body and blood as life for his people. He rules a wider dominion, spanning the globe. He also governs with superior wisdom, for he is greater than Solomon in every way (see Luke 11:31).

The New Testament celebrates the wisdom of Jesus Christ in all the same ways that 1 Kings shows us the wisdom of Solomon. At times our Savior's superior wisdom is simply asserted, such as when the apostle Paul states that Jesus has become for us "our wisdom" (1 Cor. 1:30). On other occasions, his wisdom is demonstrated by way of analogy. So the Bible says, for example, that in Christ are hidden "all the *treasures* of wisdom and knowledge" (Col. 2:3). If Solomon's wisdom was like the sand on the seashore, then the wisdom of Jesus is like sand that has been turned miraculously into diamonds.

We also see the supreme wisdom of Jesus Christ in all the wise things that he said. Like Solomon, Jesus often used memorable metaphors drawn from the created world. He talked about farmers sowing their seed and the wind blowing wherever it pleases, and when he did, he said many wise things about knowing God that will never be forgotten. The royal wisdom of Jesus Christ is shown further by comparison. His wisdom is so superior, the Scripture says, that even his apparent foolishness turns out to be wiser than the wisdom of men (1 Cor. 1:21–25). What some people think is only foolishness—namely, the cross where Jesus died—actually turns out to be God's wise plan for salvation.

Now people from all nations are seeking the wisdom of Jesus Christ. It is happening this very day, as people all over the world worship God in the royal name of Christ the King. I pray that this is happening in your own life as well, that you are coming to trust in Jesus, who is the best and wisest of all kings. Feast on his grace. Serve his wide dominion by doing his kingdom work. Trust his wisdom, believing that he knows what is best. Rest in his peace as you wait for his kingdom to come. His peaceable kingdom is not a dream, but a reality. If you believe, you will see.

10

MATERIALS AND LABOR

1 Kings 5:1—18

And so I intend to build a house for the name of the LORD my God,
as the LORD said to David my father, "Your son, whom I will set on
your throne in your place, shall build the house for my name." Now
therefore command that cedars of Lebanon be cut for me.
(1 Kings 5:5–6a)

On the seventh day of the seventh month in the seventh year of the new millennium (July 7, 2007), officials in Lisbon, Portugal, announced the "New Seven Wonders of the World." More than one hundred million votes selected these man-made structures to replace the Seven Wonders of the Ancient World. The winners included the Taj Mahal, the Roman Colosseum, the Great Wall of China, Petra, Machu Picchu, Chichen Itza, and Christ Redeemer, the statue that towers over Rio de Janeiro.

The contest was not without controversy. The Great Pyramids at Giza were among the original nominees, but Egyptian officials were understandably offended that they were up for a vote at all. In the end, everyone agreed that the Great Pyramids should be honored separately as the only original Wonder that is still standing. Many other famous monuments failed to make the top seven, but some people still think that Stonehenge, or the Hagia Sophia, or the Statue of Liberty deserved a higher ranking.

All of these famous structures show what human beings can do. Each one stands as an enduring tribute to human creativity and ingenuity. Yet as famous as these monuments are, none of them is the most important building ever made. That honor belongs to a building that was not as big as the Colosseum, or as high in the mountains as Machu Picchu, or visible from outer space like the Great Wall of China. It belongs instead to the only building in the world that the living God came down to use for his personal dwelling place: the temple of Solomon in Jerusalem.

This temple was the major public construction project of Solomon's reign as king, one of the great accomplishments that secured his lasting fame. First Kings 5 tells us how Solomon prepared to build a temple for God and, more importantly, why he decided to build it.

Practical details about the materials and labor for an ancient building project may not seem very interesting to some Bible readers. Yet we believe the words of the apostle Paul, who said that "whatever was written in former days was written for our instruction" (Rom. 15:4). Therefore, like everything else in Scripture, the construction of Solomon's temple is for our edification. When we study this passage carefully, and answer some of the objections people have made against it, we can connect the construction of Solomon's temple to the building project that God is doing in us today by the saving work of Jesus Christ and the sanctifying work of the Holy Spirit.

Preparations for Building

The story of Solomon's temple begins with a party of special envoys arriving in Jerusalem: "Now Hiram king of Tyre sent his servants to Solomon when he heard that they had anointed him king in place of his father, for Hiram always loved David" (1 Kings 5:1). This was and is standard protocol for diplomatic relations. When a new leader comes to power, other world leaders send formal greetings to renew the friendly relationship between their two countries.

These well-wishers came from the coastal city of Tyre, which was the capital of the Sidonians, also known as the Phoenicians. As a neighboring kingdom, it was only natural for these neighbors to pay a visit, especially since Hiram was on such friendly terms with King David. In fact, Hiram had graciously provided David with the materials and the labor he needed to build his palace (2 Sam. 5:11).

Now Israel wanted Hiram's help again. In his reply, Solomon told the king of Tyre about his first great project as king of Israel: a house for God (1 Kings 5:2–5). Then Solomon made a specific request: "Now therefore command that cedars of Lebanon be cut for me. And my servants will join your servants, and I will pay you for your servants such wages as you set, for you know that there is no one among us who knows how to cut timber like the Sidonians" (1 Kings 5:6).

Israel's king was proposing a cooperative venture based on a balance of trade. Skilled craftsmen from the kingdom of Tyre would provide some of their world-famous lumber, and in return, Solomon would pay fair wages. The king of Tyre readily agreed to these terms:

> And Hiram sent to Solomon, saying, "I have heard the message that you have sent to me. I am ready to do all you desire in the matter of cedar and cypress timber. My servants shall bring it down to the sea from Lebanon, and I will make it into rafts to go by sea to the place you direct. And I will have them broken up there, and you shall receive it. And you shall meet my wishes by providing food for my household." (1 Kings 5:8–9; cf. 1 Kings 10:11–12)

Some commentators have accused Hiram of changing the terms for this agreement.[1] Rather than allowing any Israelites to come into his country and help with the work, as Solomon had proposed, he insists on shipping the lumber all the way to Israel. But if anything, Hiram was doing even more than Solomon asked. He was willing to supply cypress as well as cedar, and as the leader of a country that excelled at sailing, he was offering to arrange for shipping. The whole transaction is a model of fair business and honest negotiation. Both kings followed through on their commitments, with each man keeping his part of the bargain: "Hiram supplied Solomon with all the timber of cedar and cypress that he desired, while Solomon gave Hiram 20,000 cors of wheat as food for his household, and 20,000 cors of beaten oil. Solomon gave this to Hiram year by year" (1 Kings 5:10–11).

1. See, for example, Iain W. Provan, *1 and 2 Kings*, New International Biblical Commentary (Peabody, MA: Hendrickson, 1995), 63–64.

The Bible treats this commercial exchange as a further example of Solomon's wisdom: "And the LORD gave Solomon wisdom, as he promised him. And there was peace between Hiram and Solomon, and the two of them made a treaty" (1 Kings 5:12). In chapter 3 the king used his God-given gift of wisdom to resolve a life-or-death dispute between two women. In chapter 4 Solomon exercised wisdom in organizing his kingdom, as well as participating in the arts and sciences. The chapter ended by celebrating the king's international reputation for superior wisdom: rulers from many nations came to hear the wisdom of Solomon. Chapter 5 continues this theme by showing Solomon's wisdom for international relations. The king was "wise in statecraft, gaining international agreements, establishing peaceful conditions in the kingdom, laying the groundwork for building activities."[2]

Some have criticized Solomon for making this trade agreement with Hiram. What business did the king of Israel have making a covenant with Gentiles? Perhaps this is another warning sign that he has a wayward heart. Yet the Bible seems to regard the king's treaty with Hiram as an example of royal wisdom, and Dale Ralph Davis points out a more positive way to view Hiram's relationship to Solomon. Here is a king, Davis argues, who shows that all nations will worship the true and living God.[3]

First Hiram came to hear Solomon's wisdom. Then he provided labor and materials for God's temple, which was built to become a house of prayer for all nations (Isa. 56:7). The psalmist said that the cedars of Lebanon were planted and watered by God (Ps. 104:16). The nations and everything they produce, including the cedars of Lebanon (see Ps. 104:16), belong to the Lord. How appropriate, then, for a Gentile king to give cedar trees for the temple. This is a fulfillment of the biblical promise that kings would bear gifts to the temple of God in Jerusalem (Ps. 68:29).

More importantly, Hiram worshiped God with the praise of his own lips. As soon as he received Solomon's message, "he rejoiced greatly and said, 'Blessed be the LORD this day, who has given to David a wise son to be over this great people'" (1 Kings 5:7). With these words, the king of Tyre gave glory to God. He acknowledged the wisdom of God's king in Israel, and thus

2. B. O. Long, *1 Kings, with an Introduction to Historical Literature*, Forms of Old Testament Literature (Grand Rapids: Eerdmans, 1984), 80.
3. Dale Ralph Davis, *The Wisdom and the Folly: An Exposition of the Book of First Kings* (Fearn, Ross-shire: Christian Focus, 2002), 34.

he fulfilled the promise that Solomon made about Israel's king in one of the psalms: "May the kings . . . of the coastlands render him tribute . . . May all kings fall down before him, all nations serve him!" (Ps. 72:10–11). Hiram's worship as a Gentile king thus foreshadows the worship that Jesus Christ is promised to receive from all nations. Rather than seeing Solomon as making a compromise here, we can see him instead as wisely beginning to open the door for other nations to worship the one true God. Now, like Hiram, people from all over the world can offer the tribute of their worship to God.

We may also see Solomon's wisdom for international trade as a model for our relationships. Rather than expecting people to do us favors all the time, Christians should make a point of treating people fairly and generously, especially when we are doing kingdom work. Then our integrity will commend the gospel we preach, and perhaps we will have an opportunity to help lead people to Christ.

A more serious criticism relates to Solomon's workforce. In addition to the helpers that Hiram provided, Solomon needed some workers of his own. So the king "drafted forced labor out of all Israel, and the draft numbered 30,000 men. And he sent them to Lebanon, 10,000 a month in shifts. They would be a month in Lebanon and two months at home. Adoniram was in charge of the draft" (1 Kings 5:13–14). Nor were these men the only workers involved in this massive public project. Solomon had men working with stone as well as lumber—"70,000 burden-bearers and 80,000 stonecutters in the hill country, besides Solomon's 3,300 chief officers who were over the work, who had charge of the people who carried on the work. At the king's command they quarried out great, costly stones in order to lay the foundation of the house with dressed stones" (1 Kings 5:15–17).

In time, the practice of forced labor would bring Solomon under strong criticism (see 1 Kings 12:4). Somehow it seems inappropriate for the king of a nation of former slaves (remember Israel's experience in Egypt) to conscript his citizens! Indeed, some scholars see this as an example of "ambitious, ostentatious religion" acting in collusion with "the forces of economic oppression."[4] Yet the workers who were sent to Lebanon worked only one month out of three, which hardly seems oppressive. Furthermore, 1 Kings 9:22 emphatically states that Solomon did not enslave his own people. Instead,

4. Walter Brueggemann, *1 & 2 Kings*, Smyth & Helwys Bible Commentary (Macon, GA: Smyth & Helwys, 2000), 81.

he conscripted his lumberjacks and stonecutters from among the Canaanites—people whose service now rightfully belonged to the God of Israel (see
1 Kings 9:15–21; cf. Josh. 16:10).[5]

FOR THE GLORY OF THE NAME

First Kings 5 ends with a statement that summarizes the preparations
that Solomon made before building his temple: "So Solomon's builders
and Hiram's builders and the men of Gebal did the cutting and prepared
the timber and the stone to build the house" (1 Kings 5:18). This was the
material that the king used, and these were the men who labored to cut it
down and haul it to Jerusalem.

But why did Solomon decide to build a temple in the first place? The
motivation for this building project is much more important than the lumber
and the stone that went into its construction. It is not just what Solomon did
that matters, but why he did it.

Long before Solomon ever took the throne, his father David had desired
to build a house for God. This was well known. In fact, when Solomon sent
word to Hiram, he said, "You know that David my father could not build a
house for the name of the LORD his God because of the warfare with which
his enemies surrounded him, until the LORD put them under the soles of his
feet" (1 Kings 5:2–3).

To the end of his days, David's only unsatisfied desire and unfulfilled
ambition was to build a house for God. The king had always felt that there
was something wrong about having his own house of cedar while God was
still living in a tent (2 Sam. 7:2). Thus it was in his heart "to build a house
of rest for the ark of the covenant of the LORD and for the footstool of God"
(1 Chron. 28:2; cf. Ps. 132:5). In the hope of building this temple, David purchased a prime piece of real estate (2 Sam. 24:18–25)—a place long associated
with atonement for sin—and began to make plans for construction (1 Chron.
28:11–19). He brought the sacred ark of the holy covenant up to Jerusalem
(2 Sam. 6:1–15). Before his death, he even collected many of the materials
that were needed for construction: wood and stone, gold and silver, iron and
bronze (1 Chron. 22:2–5).

---

5. For a fuller discussion, see I. Mendelsohn, "On Corvee Labor in Ancient Canaan and Israel,"
Bulletin of the American Schools of Oriental Research 167 (1962): 31–35.

Yet God explicitly refused to let David build a temple. Speaking through his prophet Nathan, God said, "I will raise up your offspring after you, who shall come from your body, and I will establish his kingdom. He shall build a house for my name" (2 Sam. 7:12–13). God had a good reason for preventing David from building the temple: "You shall not build a house to my name, because you have shed so much blood before me on the earth" (1 Chron. 22:8; cf. 28:3). Even though David had fought his many battles in the name of the Lord, he was still a man of war, not a man of peace. Thus it was not suitable for him to build God's holy temple.

This helps to put some of our own disappointments into perspective. We all have things that we hope to accomplish in this lifetime. Some of our dreams have not yet become realities, and sometimes we doubt they ever will. Where our ambitions coincide with the will of God, we should continue to pursue them. But sometimes God says "no" to us as he said "no" to David—even for things that are good in themselves and that we want to do for his glory. When this happens, we should follow David's example by accepting God's "no" for an answer. We should also take a long-term view of the kingdom and help other people do the work that God has called them to do, even if it happens to be the work that we were hoping to do. David is a good example, because when he recognized what God was calling Solomon to do, he gave him his royal blessing: "Now, my son, the LORD be with you, so that you may succeed in building the house of the LORD your God" (1 Chron. 22:11).

Some Bible scholars have tried to argue that God did not want a temple at all, and that it was a mistake for Solomon to build one.[6] It certainly is true that God never wanted David to build him a house, but was content instead to dwell in his movable tent, the tabernacle (2 Sam. 7:6–7). It is also true that since God made everything there is, his divine nature does not need a man-made temple at all (see Acts 17:24–25). Nevertheless, it is clear that God called Solomon to build a temple. In doing this work, he had not only the blessing of his father, but also the promise of God, who said to King David: "Behold, a son shall be born to you who shall be a man of rest. . . . I will give peace and quiet to Israel in his days. He shall build a house for my name" (1 Chron. 22:9–10; cf. Deut. 12:5).

6. See Brueggemann, *1 & 2 Kings*, 75, for example.

When the time was right, Solomon embraced his kingdom calling to do kingdom work that fulfilled a kingdom promise. In the providence of God, and for one of the only times in its history, Israel was at peace with all its neighbors. In the absence of warfare, there was a rare opportunity for God's people to complete a building project of this magnitude. When the time came for God to fulfill his promise, Solomon said, "But now the LORD my God has given me rest on every side. There is neither adversary nor misfortune. And so I intend to build a house for the name of the LORD my God, as the LORD said to David my father, 'Your son, whom I will set on your throne in your place, shall build the house for my name'" (1 Kings 5:4–5).

Notice Solomon's motivation. He did not build this temple for political reasons, hoping to unify the twelve tribes of his kingdom. He did not build it for financial reasons, thinking that a project of this magnitude would strengthen Israel's economy. He did not build it for personal reasons, desiring to build something that people would remember, bringing glory to his own name. No, Solomon built this temple for the best of all reasons: he did it for the name of the Lord his God.

Some scholars have pointed out that other ancient kings built similar temples during this general time period: the Sumerians, the Assyrians, the Babylonians, and the Canaanites.[7] In fact, other ancient documents follow a pattern similar to the one we find in 1 Kings. These narratives tell how an ancient king made a decision to build a temple, how he gathered the materials he needed for construction, how his laborers completed their work, and how the temple was dedicated for worship.[8] These ancient documents help confirm the historical authenticity of 1 Kings, but for some people they also raise questions about the uniqueness of Solomon's enterprise. What made his temple different from all the others?

The answer is that Solomon built his temple for the one true God. This temple was for the God of Abraham, Isaac, and Jacob, who had promised to bless all nations through their offspring. It was for the God of his father David, who had sworn that he would make David's royal house an everlasting dynasty. It was for the God who was using Solomon to build his kingdom,

---

7. See V. Hurowitz, *I Have Built You an Exalted House: Temple Building in the Bible in Light of Mesopotamian and Northwest Semitic Writing*, Journal for the Study of the Old Testament 115 (Sheffield: Sheffield Academic Press, 1992).

8. Davis, *The Wisdom and the Folly*, 51.

putting his enemies under his feet and giving him rest on every side. It was for the God who had called him to build a temple and, when it was built, would fill it with his glory (see 1 Kings 8:10–11). There were many other things that Solomon did as king, but this was his first priority and enduring legacy: he built a temple for the name of the Lord his God.

What is the desire of your heart? What is the motivation for the decisions you make about what to do with your time and your money, your body and your soul, your present and your future? The apostle Paul said, "Whatever you do, do all to the glory of God" (1 Cor. 10:31). This becomes the spiritual test for everything in life: Am I doing what I am doing for the glory of God?

Like King Solomon, we are called to serve God's kingdom. Therefore, we make it our ambition to pursue his glory in everything we do. This is our ambition at school: to pursue academic excellence, not for our own achievement, but for the honor of the name of our God. This is our ambition in athletics: to practice hard and compete with good sportsmanship, knowing that this is pleasing to God. This is our ambition at work: to glorify God in the faithful way we use our time, the encouraging way we treat our coworkers, and the honest way we do our business. This is our ambition at home: to treat our family and friends the way a godly person should, even when we are having conflict or under a lot of stress. This is also our ambition in the ministry of the church. As soon as we start to think of Christian service mainly as something that meets our own needs, then we are bound to give up when the going gets tough or get angry when our work goes unappreciated. But if what we do in serving others is really for the name of the Lord, then his grace will help us persevere.

Solomon's motivation for building the temple ought to be the motivation for everything we do in the kingdom of God. When we seek the glory of God, then we are always able to say, "I am doing this in the name of the Lord." This is a good way to test the decisions we make every day about what to eat, buy, watch, wear, and touch. Unless we are able to say—with a straight face and a good conscience—"This is for the glory of God," then it would be better for us to do something else entirely.

THE TRUE TEMPLE

Solomon helps us see how to glorify God, but he also does something more important than simply to set a good example: he points us to Jesus

Christ as the greater Solomon of the kingdom of God. Every time we think about Solomon and the greatness of his kingdom, we should remember what Jesus said in the Gospel of Luke, namely, that he is "greater than Solomon" (Luke 11:31).

One of the ways to see the superior greatness of Jesus Christ here is to consider what he said about the temple of God. Jesus always loved to go to the temple—not the one that Solomon built, but the second temple, which was built after Israel's exile in Babylon. Jesus went there as a young boy and called it "my Father's house" (Luke 2:49). He often visited the temple when he went up to Jerusalem for worship, right up until the last week of his earthly life, when "he was teaching daily in the temple" (Luke 19:47).

One year at Passover, while he was teaching at the temple, Jesus made an extraordinary prophecy. He said, "Destroy this temple, and in three days I will raise it up" (John 2:19). People thought that this was preposterous, of course. It had taken half a century to build the temple. How could anyone possibly tear it down and raise it up again in only three days? The Gospel gives us the answer when it says that Jesus "was speaking about the temple of his body" (John 2:21).

"Temple" is an appropriate word to use for the physical body of Jesus Christ. A temple is a dwelling place for God; it is the place where God lives. Thus Solomon often referred to his temple as "the house of God." But since Jesus Christ is God incarnate—since he is not merely human, but also divine—his physical body *is* a temple. The body of Christ is the true temple; it is the dwelling place of God.

There are many spiritual, theological, and practical connections to make between Solomon's temple and the bodily temple of Jesus Christ. But perhaps the best place to begin is where 1 Kings 5 begins, with the materials for its construction. Solomon's temple was made of cedar and stone, obtained by costly labor. The temple of Christ's body, by contrast, was made of flesh and blood.

Consider how amazing it is that in coming to the world, God the Son would choose a physical body for his dwelling place. This is hardly what we would choose for our dwelling place: a body that would bruise and bleed before it suffered and died. Why not choose instead something more permanent, like a diamond, or more impregnable, like a granite mountain? Better yet, why not come into the world as a kind of Superman, with a body so strong that it could never be nailed to a tree? Yet when Jesus came to dwell with us, he took for his material the weakness of human flesh. The book of Hebrews testifies that when the Son of God came into the world, he said to his Father, "A body you prepared for me" (Heb. 10:5 NIV).

Then Jesus took the temple of his physical body and offered it as a sacrifice for our sin, giving himself for our salvation. Jesus did this for the best of all reasons. He did it to honor the name of the Lord. In doing his kingdom work, he was motivated by his Father's glory. So as he prepared to offer his body for crucifixion, he said to the Father, "Behold, I have come to do your will, O God" (Heb. 10:7), which is another way of saying, "I am doing this in the name of the Lord." Jesus used the temple of his body for the glory of God. In the supremely selfless sacrifice of his death on the cross, he glorified God by saving his people.

THE WONDER OF THE WORLD

Now God is busy working on a new construction project. It is another temple, constructed with even more surprising building material. This temple is not physical, but spiritual, because now God's dwelling place in the world is the church—not as a physical building, but as a living community. Thus the New Testament often uses temple language to describe the church of Jesus Christ. As Paul wrote to the Corinthians, "we are the temple of the living God" (2 Cor. 6:16).

Surely this is the least likely material that anyone has ever used for a major construction project. What could be more difficult to work with than people in the church? We are not beautiful like cedar, but ugly in our sin. We are not solid like stone, but weak and unstable. Nevertheless, God is using us to build a holy temple—a spiritual house in which he lives by his Holy Spirit. "You are God's temple," the Scripture says to the church, and "God's Spirit dwells in you" (1 Cor. 3:16). This is true of us individually: as believers in Christ we are indwelt by the Spirit, and thus we are holy to the Lord.[9] It is also true of us corporately: the church of Jesus Christ is the temple of the living God.

Truly, the church of Jesus Christ is the wonder of the world, the most extraordinary edifice that anyone has ever constructed. The stones in this

9. 1 Cor. 6:19–20.

massive building come from all over the world, as people from all nations come to worship Christ. We are living stones—not stone-cold like ordinary construction materials, but alive with the power of the Holy Spirit (see 1 Peter 2:5). Furthermore, despite the weakness of its materials, this new and living temple is built to last. It is constructed on "a precious corner-stone" (Isa. 28:16; cf. 1 Peter 2:6), Jesus Christ, who is the solid foundation of the church (1 Cor. 3:11). The Bible says that in him "the whole structure, being joined together, grows into a holy temple in the Lord. In him you also are being built together into a dwelling place for God by the Spirit" (Eph. 2:21–22). As living stones, we are the construction materials that God is using to build his spiritual temple.

Knowing what kind of temple God is building puts our own ministry into perspective. It gives us an important question to ask about any service we offer to the Lord, or any ministry we consider as a church: Will this help to build up the spiritual temple that is the people of God and, by doing so, to bring honor to the name of the Lord? When we can answer "yes," we are ready to make wise decisions about the way we live and what we are preparing to do with our future.

The same question can also help us in evaluating the kind of building projects that churches sometimes consider. Some congregations make the mistake of thinking that a building is what makes their church a church, when in fact the church can be the church without any building at all. The real temple is the people of God. Yet Christians can also make a mistake in the opposite direction, forgetting all the ways that God can use physical buildings to accomplish the spiritual purpose of making living stones for his temple. So churches need to ask questions like this: Will this building project or that renovation be useful to the work of the Holy Spirit in building the church? Will it enhance the worship of God? Will it facilitate Christian fellowship? Will it provide a helpful context for evangelism and discipleship?

In themselves, church buildings are neither holy nor unholy. But whereas some buildings can hinder God's kingdom work, others are a spiritual asset for building the temple of the church. Davis writes: "Churches frequently have to be reminded that the kingdom of God is not 'bricks and mortar,' and yet this text shows us that bricks and mortar, or—to be more textual, stone and wood, can testify to the wisdom of God and instruct us not to despise Yahweh's less spectacular, more mundane gifts."[10]

Knowing that God is building a spiritual temple gives us hope for the future. Sometimes living and serving in the church can be discouraging. With all the trouble that Christians have getting along together, and with all the obstacles we face in ministry, we wonder when or even if God will ever finish the work that he is doing in the church. Yet this is typical of most building projects: when the work is only halfway done, it seems so far from completion that it is hard to imagine what it will look like when it is finished, if it ever gets finished at all.

Eric Alexander gave a helpful illustration of this when he preached in London on the 350th anniversary of the Westminster Confession of Faith. At the end of his sermon, Alexander asked: "What is the really important thing that is happening in the world in our generation? What is the most important thing? Where do you need to look in the modern world to see the most significant event from a divine perspective?" He answered by saying, "The most significant thing happening in history is [that] . . . God is building the church of Jesus Christ. The rest of history . . . is simply the scaffolding for the real work."[11]

To illustrate this point, Alexander referred to the building where some of our meetings were held: London's famous Westminster Abbey. He remarked that the last time he had been at the abbey, its stone was black and the whole front of the building was covered with scaffolding. But now he could see that something had been happening behind all that scaffolding. People had been busy cleaning the building, working to bring out its true beauty. So when the scaffolding was finally taken down, the abbey was revealed in the pristine splendor of gleaming white stone.

God is doing something similar with the church. As hard as we are to work with, the Holy Spirit is using our lives as the material to make a spiritual temple. While the scaffolding is still up, it is sometimes hard to see how much work God is really doing. But a day is coming at the end of history when the scaffolding will come down and we will see the wonder of the world: the glory of God in the church of Jesus Christ.

10. Davis, *The Wisdom and the Folly*, 58.
11. Eric Alexander, *To Glorify and Enjoy God* (Edinburgh: Banner of Truth, 1994), 245–46.

11

THIS NEW HOUSE

1 Kings 6:1–13

Concerning this house that you are building, if you will walk in my statutes and obey my rules and keep all my commandments and walk in them, then I will establish my word with you, which I spoke to David your father. And I will dwell among the children of Israel and will not forsake my people Israel. (1 Kings 6:12–13)

*T*rue spiritual vitality depends on the living and working presence of God the Holy Spirit. With the Spirit, a church's ministry of word and deed has the power to bring people to faith in Christ and help them grow in grace. Without the Spirit, nothing that is done in ministry will make any lasting difference for the kingdom of God. It all depends on having the Spirit of Christ in the life of the church. Unless God is in the house, the church will fail.

BREAKING GROUND

We see the vital importance of the Spirit's presence in the story of Solomon's temple. As construction begins, the Bible gives many precise details about the new house that Solomon built for God. But the Bible also makes it clear that the living presence of God is infinitely more important than any building that is raised in his name.

First Kings 5 told how the king wisely arranged for all the materials and labor he needed to build his temple. Then in chapter 6 Solomon breaks ground: "In the four hundred and eightieth year after the people of Israel came out of the land of Egypt, in the fourth year of Solomon's reign over Israel, in the month of Ziv, which is the second month, he began to build the house of the LORD" (1 Kings 6:1).

This verse, with its careful identification of time and place, uses the kind of formal language that people use only when something important is happening. And the temple *was* important. This was a new era for the people of God. Solomon was constructing sacred architecture—a new house for the living God.

From the historical standpoint, the information in this verse is useful for determining when these events took place: probably in 966 B.C., or perhaps as late as 956 B.C. The chronology of this verse also provides a crucial piece of evidence for establishing the date of Israel's exodus from Egypt, which is a long-standing controversy in biblical archaeology. Some scholars argue that the 480 years in 1 Kings 6:1 are a symbolic number, representing 12 generations, each considered as 40 years long (whether they happened to take 40 years or not). This would leave open the possibility that the exodus took place as late as the thirteenth century before Christ. But with all its references to months and years, it seems more natural to read 1 Kings 6:1 as referring literally to 480 years, which would strengthen the case for an early, fifteenth-century date for the exodus.[1]

As important as this verse is for biblical chronology, it is even more important for biblical theology. What Solomon did in building a house for God is directly connected to what God did in bringing his people out of Egypt. First Kings is part of the ongoing history of the one true people of God. As he tells the story of Solomon's temple, the biblical writer looks back to the historic day when his people were released from their bondage by the mighty grace of God. This is similar to the way Abraham Lincoln began his famous Gettysburg Address. When President Lincoln said, "Four score and seven years ago," he was looking back to 1776 as the year the United States

---

1. For a fuller discussion of these issues, see Jack Finegan, *Handbook of Biblical Chronology*, rev. ed. (Peabody, MA: Hendrickson, 1998), 201–6, 225–49.

was founded. But there is something deeper at work in 1 Kings, because Solomon's temple is in direct fulfillment of the promises of God.

Going back to the days of Abraham, God had always promised that he would give his people a land to call their own. During their long bondage in Egypt, the people of God often wondered when that promise would ever come true. But eventually God brought his people out of the land of Egypt, out of the house of bondage. He led them safely through the wilderness, until finally he brought them into the Promised Land.

When Solomon began building a house for God, it was clear that God had fulfilled his long-standing promise of land for his people. Now they were not just saved from Egypt, but also settled in Israel.[2] In their wilderness days, when the Israelites were still wandering, God made his residence at the tabernacle—a portable structure that was appropriate for that stage of Israel's pilgrimage. But now it was time to settle down. Israel had established a permanent place of residence, and therefore God would no longer dwell in a tent, but in a temple.

This temple was part of God's promise. We have already seen how God promised David that his son would build a temple (see 2 Sam. 7:12–13). But the promise of God's dwelling place went all the way back to the days of the prophet Moses. When Moses sang his victory song on the shores of the Red Sea, celebrating God's triumph over the horses and riders of Egypt, he prophesied that God would dwell with his people: "You will bring them in and plant them on your own mountain, the place, O LORD, which you have made for your abode, the sanctuary, O Lord, which your hands have established" (Ex. 15:17). The promise of Moses was fulfilled on the mountain of Zion, where Solomon built a sanctuary for the worship of God.

Moses often referred to this promise in the book of Deuteronomy. There he prophesied a time of rest for God's people, at a place where God's name would dwell and his people would bring their sacrifices (Deut. 12:10–11). From time to time, as Moses gave instructions for Israel's worship, he would mention "the place that the LORD will choose, to make his name dwell there" (Deut. 16:2; cf. 14:23; 16:6, 11; 26:2). He was referring to the city of Jerusalem, but more specifically to the place of worship that God would establish

2. Dale Ralph Davis uses a similar turn of phrase in *The Wisdom and the Folly: An Exposition of the Book of First Kings* (Fearn, Ross-shire: Christian Focus, 2002), 61.

there. These promises were a long time in coming, but they began to see their fulfillment in the second month of Solomon's fourth year.

God makes a similar promise to us today. The most basic promise of his everlasting covenant is that he would come to us and be our God. When God comes to dwell with us—when he comes into our lives by the powerful presence of his Holy Spirit—then we have the best of all blessings, which is God himself living with us. Jesus said, "If anyone loves me, he will keep my word, and my Father will love him, and we will come to him and make our home with him" (John 14:23).

This is the promise of Jesus Christ for anyone who loves him and believes the word of his gospel: the Father, the Son, and the Holy Spirit will come and make their home in your life. They will come with forgiveness for all your sins, help for all your troubles, and comfort in all your sorrows. They will come with strength and grace for every important thing you are called to do in life. They will come and guarantee everlasting joy in the kingdom of God. Will you open the door and welcome God into your life? He is ready and willing to live with you. Jesus says, "If anyone hears my voice and opens the door, I will come in to him and eat with him, and he with me" (Rev. 3:20).

THE HOUSE THAT SOLOMON BUILT

Solomon's temple was to serve as a dwelling place for God, which is why the structure is repeatedly called a "house" (e.g., 1 Kings 6:1). A house is a place where someone lives, so this new house was the dwelling place of God. It was the one place on earth God chose to receive his people's worship and make his presence manifest.

One sign of the temple's importance is the sheer number of details the Bible gives about its construction. The Bible does not provide all the details needed for an exact reconstruction. At most there is enough information for an architectural rendering, not a full set of blueprints. Yet there is sufficient detail "regarding size, quality of materials, and skill of design and workmanship to generate a sense of wonder."[3] From what the Bible says we can easily imagine the simple beauty and stately grandeur of Solomon's temple.

3. Terence E. Fretheim, *First and Second Kings*, Westminster Bible Companion (Louisville: Westminster John Knox, 1999), 40.

There is another reason to look at the temple carefully. Although not all the details of its construction have symbolic or spiritual meaning, many of them do, as we will discover. And since the New Testament describes the church as the temple of God (e.g., Eph. 2:20)—the earthly dwelling place of the Holy Spirit (e.g., Eph. 2:21)—knowing more details about the original temple can help us understand what God is doing in the church.

First Kings 6 tells how Solomon built this house, starting in verses 2 through 10 with its exterior structure. As for size, "the house that King Solomon built for the LORD was sixty cubits long, twenty cubits wide, and thirty cubits high" (1 Kings 6:2). A cubit is the length of a man's arm from elbow to fingertip, or about 18 inches. So the temple was approximately 90 feet long, 30 feet wide, and 45 feet high. It had the same basic proportions as the tabernacle that Moses made in the wilderness, but it was twice as long in every dimension, and therefore quadruple the size (cf. Ex. 26:15ff.). Roughly speaking, the temple was about the size of a church sanctuary that would seat 250 people, but proportionally it was narrow and tall—the height of a four-story building.

Solomon's temple was not very large or impressive by today's standards. But remember that most buildings were smaller in biblical times. Thus the temple would have been bigger and taller than any other building in Jerusalem (except perhaps for the royal palace, once it was completed). Furthermore, since it was perched at virtually the highest point of a mountain, it had a commanding aspect. Still, considered simply from the standpoint of its size, the temple of Solomon was never in the running to be regarded as one of the wonders of the world. Other monuments were bigger or taller or more ornate. But then the building itself was never intended to be the most important thing about the temple. What was really impressive was the God who lived there. The temple was for his glory, not for the pride of the people who built it.

After giving the temple's dimensions, the Bible proceeds to describe its structure: "The vestibule in front of the nave of the house was twenty cubits long, equal to the width of the house, and ten cubits deep in front of the house" (1 Kings 6:3). A "vestibule" is a kind of porch or portico. This was the entrance to the temple. "Nave" is simply another word for the central part of the structure, the main sanctuary. For this part of the temple Solomon made "windows with recessed frames" (1 Kings 6:4)—probably high windows to let in some light. Next to the nave was the "inner sanctuary," or "Most Holy Place" (1 Kings 6:5; cf. 6:16). So there were three main parts to the temple, representing three degrees of holiness: the vestibule, the nave, and the inner sanctuary, which is usually called "the Holy of Holies."

Solomon also built a second structure, which had nearly twice the square footage as the temple proper and surrounded it on three sides: "He also built a structure against the wall of the house, running around the walls of the house, both the nave and the inner sanctuary. And he made side chambers all around" (1 Kings 6:5). This building was part of the temple complex. Presumably its chambers served as storage space for the offerings that people brought to the temple and the scrolls and other sacred items that Israel used in worship. Perhaps these rooms also served as temporary accommodation for priests who were in Jerusalem to do their sacred duty.

This second building may also have served the architectural function of providing support for the main sanctuary, especially given its height. Here is how the Bible describes this three-tiered structure: "The lowest story was five cubits broad, the middle one was six cubits broad, and the third was seven cubits broad. For around the outside of the house he made offsets on the wall in order that the supporting beams should not be inserted into the walls of the house" (1 Kings 6:6). There was a way to enter these side buildings, and also a way to reach the higher floors: "The entrance for the lowest story was on the south side of the house, and one went up by stairs to the middle story, and from the middle story to the third" (1 Kings 6:8).

Notice that the first story was the narrowest (5 cubits), while the third story was the widest (7 cubits). Ordinarily one would expect just the opposite, that a building would be wider at the bottom than at the top. But in this case, part of each story was taken up by what 1 Kings calls "offsets on the wall." In effect, these were buttresses—structural supports that leaned up against the temple. To avoid making any holes in the holy sanctuary, the floors of the side building also rested on these supports. Since the widest support was at the bottom of the temple and took up the most room, the first story of the side building was narrower than the floors above it.[4]

4. For some pictures that are worth a thousand words (or more), see the temple diagrams in Donald J. Wiseman, *1 & 2 Kings: An Introduction and Commentary*, Tyndale Old Testament Commentaries (Leicester: Inter-Varsity, 1993), 103, 107, 108.

The description of the temple exterior ends with a reminder of some of the materials that Solomon used for its construction: "So he built the house and finished it, and he made the ceiling of the house of beams and planks of cedar. He built the structure against the whole house, five cubits high, and it was joined to the house with timbers of cedar" (1 Kings 6:9–10). Solomon covered the ceiling of God's house with cedar that he had obtained from Hiram, king of Tyre (see 1 Kings 5:10–12).

Most of what the Bible tells us about Solomon's construction project would sound relatively familiar to anyone who has ever built a house. But there is one detail here that is utterly astonishing. Visit a building site and you will quickly discover that construction always makes a lot of noise. Yet when Solomon built this new house, "it was with stone prepared at the quarry, so that neither hammer nor axe nor any tool of iron was heard in the house while it was being built" (1 Kings 6:7).

At the end of chapter 5 we learned how Solomon sent more than a hundred thousand workmen into the hills to get the stone he needed for his temple and then haul it up to Jerusalem. These men skillfully shaped each stone with their tools, making sure that it was just the right size and shape to fit into the temple. Then, when it came time to erect the temple, they noiselessly set each stone into its proper place.

There has never been a building project like this before or since. The silence at the building site was a testimony to Solomon's wisdom for building. As it says in one of the proverbs from Solomon's famous book: "Prepare your work outside; get everything ready for yourself in the field, and after that build your house" (Prov. 24:27). But this was more than an example of good planning; it was also a witness to the holiness of God. This was the building site for God's holy temple, the place where Habakkuk would say, "The LORD is in his holy temple; let all the earth keep silence before him" (Hab. 2:20). Thus it was appropriate for Solomon's workmen to build this new house with quiet reverence. They were doing holy work for a holy God.

The preparation of these stones may also remind us of the work that God is doing in our own spiritual lives. The Bible says that when we come to Christ, we are "like living stones" that God is building "as a spiritual house" (1 Peter 2:5). God is not finished with us yet. All through life his Spirit is shaping us in the quarry of sanctification, using suffering and temptation to chip away everything that is still unholy. He uses our quiet times of prayer, with the reading and meditation of Scripture, to construct our character. As we confess our sins and grow in godliness, God is getting us ready to be a perfect fit for his everlasting home.

"If/Then"

Suddenly God interrupted Solomon's building project to make an important announcement: "Concerning this house that you are building, if you will walk in my statutes and obey my rules and keep all my commandments and walk in them, then I will establish my word with you, which I spoke to David your father. And I will dwell among the children of Israel and will not forsake my people Israel" (1 Kings 6:12–13).

Some critical scholars argue that these verses are oddly out of place. They point out that if we were to skip from verse 10 to verse 14 or 15, we could read straight through without any interruption of thought. Verses 11 to 13 are so different in style and content that they must have been added by some later editor.[5] Often this kind of argument is used to discredit the Bible's authenticity and diminish its authority.

In response, it could be pointed out that these verses come at a natural division in the biblical text between the exterior and the interior of the temple. But maybe it is better to admit that this *is* an interruption, while at the same time insisting that God has the right to speak to us whenever he wants. Verse 11 says that "the word of the Lord came to Solomon," so this was a divine interruption. God is like that: he is always intruding on our agenda, getting rid of our plans so that his will may be done.

In this particular case, God's main concern was Solomon's heart. Whereas we tend to focus on the way things appear on the outside, God always looks at the heart (see 1 Sam. 16:7). He wants us to consider what is going on inside us. So this interruption—as intrusive as it may have been—was crucial for Solomon's spiritual health.

God did not tell Solomon to stop what he was doing. He did not disapprove of Solomon's temple. But he wanted to make sure that as he undertook this worthy project, the king did not lose sight of what should have been his top priority. So God interrupted Solomon to remind him to do everything

---

5. Walter Brueggemann, *1 & 2 Kings*, Smyth & Helwys Bible Commentary (Macon, GA: Smyth & Helwys, 2000), 88–89.

in obedience to the will of God. He was saying, "This is what really matters to me: holy obedience. What is in your heart is more important to me than what you do with your hands."

This was especially important for Solomon to remember as he was building this new house. The temple was designed as a place of spiritual transaction, where people did their business with God in prayer, repentance, sacrifice, and praise. But the building where these things took place was not as important as the relationship itself. So God interrupted Solomon to remind him of the supreme importance of personal godliness.

This is an important reality check for everyone, not just for King Solomon. We are often tempted to think that what really matters is what we do. Of course, what we do does matter. But what matters the most is who we are—the obedience of a heart that is surrendered to God. What matters at work is not just getting the job done, but doing it with a sincere desire to honor God. This is also what matters in ministry: not just giving people the impression that we are serving the Lord, but actually serving him, so that with sincerity we are able to say, "Lord, I am doing this out of love for you."

What God said to Solomon when he interrupted him is very similar to what King David said to Solomon when he took the throne. David told his son to "keep the charge of the LORD your God, walking in his ways and keeping his statutes, his commandments, his rules, and his testimonies" (1 Kings 2:3). Now God was basically repeating what David said, in the form of a conditional promise. God made three "if" commands, followed by three "then" promises.

God's "if" statements all have to do with obedience: *if* you will walk in my statutes, *if* you will obey my rules, *if* you keep all my commandments and walk in them. Each of these terms has its own meaning, but here they are used virtually interchangeably. Whether we call them "rules," "statutes," or "commandments," there are some things that God has told us to do in his Word. And whether we call it "walking," "keeping," or "obeying," the point is that God wants us to do what he says.

Here God is referring to the lifestyle he decreed for his people in the Law of Moses. Whether we think of this lifestyle in terms of the Ten Commandments, or the Two Great Commandments (see Matt. 22:37–40), or all the specific case laws that applied those laws to daily life, the basic demand is the same: total obedience to the revealed will of God. God was reminding

Solomon to keep his covenant. The word "walk" makes it clear that faithful obedience was supposed to be the king's whole way of life.

If Solomon was faithful to obey, then God would be faithful to bless. God promised three particular blessings—the "then" promises that go with the "if" commands. They are some of the greatest blessings that God has ever promised to his people.

The first promise was an everlasting dynasty for Solomon on the throne of his father David. "If you . . . keep all my commandments . . . ," God said, "*then* I will establish my word with you, which I spoke to David your father" (1 Kings 6:12). Presumably the word that God had in mind was the promise of an everlasting throne. God had promised David a son who would rule an eternal kingdom: "I will raise up your offspring after you, who shall come from your body, and I will establish his kingdom. He shall build a house for my name, and I will establish the throne of his kingdom forever" (2 Sam. 7:12–13). If Solomon was obedient to this covenant, then his kingdom would never fail.

The second "then" statement promised God's presence: "I will dwell among the children of Israel" (1 Kings 6:13). This was the very reason Solomon was building a temple: so that God would dwell with his people. It was also the deep promise of the covenant. The best gift that God can ever offer is the gift of himself, in all his love and grace. He had made this promise to his people in the time of Moses: "I will make my dwelling among you, and my soul shall not abhor you. And I will walk among you and will be your God, and you shall be my people" (Lev. 26:11–12). Now God was repeating his covenant promise to Solomon. God's presence with his people depended on the faithfulness of their king. If Solomon obeyed, then the whole nation would enjoy the blessed habitation of their God.

The third promise was God's perseverance. Having told Solomon what he would do, God also told him what he would not do: "I . . . will not forsake my people Israel" (1 Kings 6:13). This promise went beyond the second promise and made it more secure. It is one thing to go and live with people; it is another to live with them and never leave. This is something that God had promised his people before (e.g., Deut. 31:6, 8), and now he was promising the same thing again. As long as Solomon obeyed his commandments, God would stay with his people.

143

THE PROMISE KEEPER

The obvious question to ask about these promises is whether Solomon kept God's conditions or not. For as the king went, so went the country. In order for the "then" promises to come true, all the "if" commandments had to be kept. It all depended on the obedience of King Solomon.

Knowing the grammar of verse 12 is crucial to understanding this whole passage. The commands in verse 12 are all given in the second-person singular. When God says "you," he is not speaking to Israel generally, but to Solomon specifically. Covenant obedience is for everyone in Israel, of course, but the "if/then" statements in these verses apply directly to Solomon. The promise of the eternal kingdom, as well as the promise that God would live with his people and never leave, depended on the covenant faithfulness of the king. Now we see why this divine interruption was so important. Israel's destiny did not depend on building the temple. From here on out, everything that happened to the people of God would depend on Solomon's faithfulness in keeping God's command.

So how did Solomon do? Tragically, the king failed to keep God's covenant. We have already seen some early warning signs that Solomon's heart was not fully devoted to the Lord. When we get to chapter 11, we will see that for all his wisdom, he did not end his reign nearly as well as he began. Solomon did not keep the "if" commands that would make all the "then" promises come true. He did not walk in the rules and statutes that forbade the king to marry many wives, to trust in horses and chariots for his national security, or to acquire excessive gold and silver for his personal use (Deut. 17:16–17). Nor did he obey God's commandments about refusing to worship foreign idols.

As a result of Solomon's unfaithfulness, the people of Israel did not receive the full blessing that would have been theirs if the king had kept God's covenant. Solomon's throne did not last forever, and when he died, Israel became a divided kingdom (see 1 Kings 12). Although God lived with his people for a time, eventually his glory departed from the temple. Near the end of Kings we hear him say, "I will cast off this city that I have chosen, Jerusalem, and the house of which I said, My name shall be there" (2 Kings 23:27). So the temple was destroyed and God exiled his people from Jerusalem all the way to Babylon. It was all because of the failure of their king. "If" and "then": 1 Kings 6:11–13 explains most of Israel's subsequent history.

The same "if/then" statements also help explain the gospel of our salvation. As we study the Old Testament, we look in vain for a faithful king who will keep the covenant of God. David and Solomon were two of Israel's best kings, but they both had their fatal flaws. David was a murderer and an adulterer. Solomon married many wives and worshiped many idols. Most of the other kings were even worse, and even the best man among them fell far short of perfect obedience to the law of God. Israel's kings did not walk in God's statutes, obey God's rules, and keep God's commandments. They failed at the "if" commands (as we would have failed, and do fail), and thus they forfeited the "then" promises. The kings of Israel did not secure an everlasting dynasty for David, or enjoy the permanent living presence of God in their community.

Yet all these promises did come true, and God is with his people today, by the power and presence of the Holy Spirit. The promises came true in Jesus Christ, the Son of David and the greater Solomon of the kingdom of God. Jesus walked in God's statutes, fulfilling the whole law of God. He obeyed God's rules, always doing the Father's will. He kept all of God's commandments, loving his Father God with all his heart and loving his neighbor all the way to the cross where he died for our sins. Jesus kept all the "if" commands of the law that open up all the "then" promises of the gospel for everyone who believes in him. Solomon's failure thus points us to the faithfulness of Jesus Christ.

Now we have God's promise that Jesus will sit on David's throne forever, ruling heaven and earth for his Father's glory. We have God's promise that he will live with us and be our God, that Christ will "dwell in [our] hearts through faith" (Eph. 3:17). We also have his promise that he will never leave us or forsake us (see Heb. 13:5). Jesus said, "I am with you always, to the end of the age" (Matt. 28:20). Then he sent his Holy Spirit to be God's guiding and comforting presence in our lives. Jesus is able to make all these promises because he has met all the conditions of our salvation. The law has been kept, the debt has been paid, and now God is with us forever.

Do you believe that you have the living presence of God in your life? After her death, the world was shocked to discover that Mother Teresa—the famous mercy worker of Calcutta—often doubted that God was with her. "Jesus has a very special love for you," she wrote to a friend. But "as for me—The silence and emptiness is so great—that I look and do not see,—Listen and do not hear." Mother Teresa's letters reveal that for almost the last fifty years of her life, with only a brief interruption, she felt no presence of God whatsoever. "I am told God loves me—and yet the reality of darkness & coldness & emptiness is so great that nothing touches my soul." Mother Teresa claimed to have nothing: no faith, "not even the reality of the Presence of God."[6]

There are times when every believer is tempted to doubt the presence of God. What should we do when these doubts start to arise and threaten to overwhelm us? The one thing we should not do is try to work harder for God, thinking that *if* we did a little more for him, *then* we would have the blessing of his presence in our lives. If having the living presence of God depended on our own ability to keep all the "if" commands of the law, then God would have left us long ago. Surely if anyone could find assurance by her own obedience, it would have been Mother Teresa. But as she discovered, knowing the presence of God does not depend on performing even the holiest works of sacrificial obedience. There is no assurance to be found in our own faithfulness.

The only assurance lies in the obedience of Jesus Christ as the perfect King. Because he was faithful, we are forgiven, and even when we fail to keep God's commandments, we are not forsaken. God does not say to us, "*If* you obey, *then* I will bless," but "*Because* Jesus obeyed, therefore I will bless." Jesus lived for us the perfect life, died for us the forgiving death, and rose for us from the grave with resurrection life. Whatever doubts we may have about ourselves, there is no need to doubt what Jesus has done on the cross or promised in the gospel. The living presence of his Holy Spirit will be with all who trust in him.

6. Mother Teresa, *Come Be My Light*, quoted in David Van Biema, "Her Agony," *Time*, September 3, 2007, 36–43.

12

INSIDE SOLOMON'S TEMPLE

1 Kings 6:14–38

*In the fourth year the foundation of the house of the LORD was
laid, in the month of Ziv. And in the eleventh year, in the month
of Bul, which is the eighth month, the house was finished in all its
parts, and according to all its specifications. He was seven years
in building it.* (1 Kings 6:37–38)

*T*he fire that devastated England's Windsor Castle was a costly
disaster. To help pay for the repairs, which cost millions of
pounds, Queen Elizabeth II opened her home to visitors. For
the first time in history, common tourists could pay a small fee for the
unprecedented privilege of walking through Buckingham Palace.

The opening of the palace afforded a rare glimpse of the queen's royal
splendor. To know what people are like, it helps to see where they live, and
for the queen of England, home is where the majesty is. People (like me)
who were fortunate enough to visit Buckingham Palace saw the queen's
royal apartments, with their gilded ornaments and famous masterpieces.
They walked through her stately private gardens. They entered her receiving room to gaze upon her golden throne. To see the royal palace was to
experience the glory of Elizabeth's kingdom.

First Kings gives us a similar experience by taking us on a guided tour of Solomon's temple, the house of God. Sometimes people wonder what God is really like. Since we have never seen him face-to-face, it can be hard to get a clear impression of his true and awesome glory. Visiting the house that Solomon built can help us get to know God better, for when we look at the building carefully, seeing the plan for its structure and the details of its design, we learn the character of the God who made his home there.

HOUSE BEAUTIFUL

First Kings 6 opens with a formal statement introducing the temple and announcing the beginning of its construction. The chapter ends with a similar statement describing its completion: "In the fourth year the foundation of the house of the LORD was laid, in the month of Ziv. And in the eleventh year, in the month of Bul, which is the eighth month, the house was finished in all its parts, and according to all its specifications. He was seven years in building it" (1 Kings 6:37–38).

A Bible scholar would describe this literary technique as *inclusio*: matching language at the beginning and end of a section that serves to bookend the material that comes in between. The first part of the chapter (vv. 2–10) surveyed the temple's exterior structure. Then God interrupted this building project to tell Solomon about all the blessings that would come if he was faithful to keep the commandments of God's covenant (vv. 11–13). The rest of the chapter shows how the temple was finished inside (vv. 14–36)—the interior decorating that makes a house a home. By the end of the chapter we have seen God's house both outside and in.

Since only the priests were allowed to enter the temple itself, most Israelites never would have seen what it looked like. But 1 Kings 6 gives us the inside tour. As we look around, we should ask ourselves this question: What kind of God would live in this kind of house? The answer is that he is a God who loves beauty, who reigns in kingly glory and dwells in matchless holiness. Surprisingly, he is also a God who invites us to come and make our home with him.

The first thing we notice inside Solomon's temple is its natural beauty:

> So Solomon built the house and finished it. He lined the walls of the house on the inside with boards of cedar. From the floor of the house to the walls

of the ceiling, he covered them on the inside with wood, and he covered the floor of the house with boards of cypress. He built twenty cubits of the rear of the house with boards of cedar from the floor to the walls, and he built this within as an inner sanctuary, as the Most Holy Place. The house, that is, the nave in front of the inner sanctuary, was forty cubits long. The cedar within the house was carved in the form of gourds and open flowers. All was cedar; no stone was seen. (1 Kings 6:14–18)

Solomon built his temple with stone quarried from the mountains, but inside everything was covered with cedar—not just the main sanctuary, but also the Holy of Holies. Cedar trees make beautiful wood, so Solomon had purchased a large supply from Hiram, king of Tyre (cf. 1 Kings 5:1–12). Once the main structure was built, Solomon completely paneled its walls with cedar lumber. The floor was also made of wood, in this case cypress, which is sturdier than cedar and more suitable for heavy traffic. As far as we know, the kinds of wood that Solomon used did not have any symbolic significance. But the wood was beautiful, which was reason enough to use it. Solomon wanted this house to be beautiful both inside and out.

The cedar wood inside the temple was beautifully decorated. It was "carved in the form of gourds and open flowers" (1 Kings 6:18), as the fashion then was, for floral decorations were typical in the ancient Near East.[1] Although we do not know the exact design that was used for Solomon's temple, it is easy to imagine the rows of blooming flowers that lined its walls—not for any utilitarian function, but simply for their beauty.

All these directions tell us something important about God. The interior of Solomon's temple was adorned with trees and fruits and flowers from the world that God made, and thus its decor reflected the beauty of creation back to its Creator. God loves beauty; he appreciates artistry and maintains high aesthetic standards: "Splendor and majesty are before him; strength and beauty are in his sanctuary" (Ps. 96:6).

God's love for beauty is evident from the things that he has made. The universe is full of many beautiful splendors, from the starry nebulae in deep space to the yellow aspen on a rocky mountainside. Augustine asked:

1. William G. Dever, "Palaces and Temples in Canaan and Ancient Israel," in *Civilizations of the Ancient Near East*, 4 vols. (New York: Scribners, 1999), 1:608.

What discourse can adequately describe the beauty and utility of creation, which the divine bounty has bestowed upon man to behold and consume? Consider the manifold and varied beauty of sky and earth and sea; the plenteousness of light and its wondrous quality, in the sun, moon and stars in the shadows of the forests; the color and fragrance of flowers; the diversity and multitude of the birds, with their songs and bright colors; the multiform species of living creatures of all kinds, even the smallest of which we behold with the greatest wonder. . . . Consider also the grand spectacle of the sea, robing herself in different colors, like garments; sometimes green, and that in so many different shades; sometimes purple; sometimes blue. . . . Who could give a complete account of all these things?[2]

Not only does God create beauty and love beauty, but he himself is a beautiful God. Whatever beauty we see in the universe finds its source in God's own loveliness. He is "infinitely the most beautiful and excellent," the "foundation and fountain of all beauty," wrote Jonathan Edwards. "All the beauty to be found throughout the whole creation is . . . the reflection of the diffused beams of that being who hath an infinite fullness of brightness and glory."[3]

When Solomon's father dreamed of building a temple, and then going there for worship, it was mainly because he wanted to see this beauty for himself. "One thing have I asked of the LORD," David said: "that I may dwell in the house of the LORD all the days of my life, to gaze upon the beauty of the LORD and to inquire in his temple" (Ps. 27:4). The true beauty of God is not his external appearance, but his inward character. God is beautiful in the love he shows to his children, in the mercy he offers to lost sinners, and in the perfect harmony he displays in all his divine attributes.

We see the beauty of God most clearly of all in the person of his Son Jesus Christ. Not that Jesus was especially beautiful in his physical appearance. In fact, the Bible says just the opposite: "He had no form or majesty that we should look at him, and no beauty that we should desire him" (Isa. 53:2). Yet Jesus Christ is more beautiful than any other person. He is beautiful because of the perfection of his love and the costliness of his sacrifice. For

2. Augustine, *The City of God*, trans. R. W. Dyson (Cambridge: Cambridge University Press, 1998), 22, 24.
3. Jonathan Edwards, *True Virtue* (1765), in *The Works of Jonathan Edwards*, ed. John E. Smith (New Haven, CT: Yale University Press, 1957), 8:550–51.

all its apparent ugliness, his death on the cross was the most beautiful thing that anyone has ever done: one perfect life offered in suffering and pain so that everyone who believes in him would be forgiven.

Now God is doing something beautiful with us. The Holy Spirit is working away at the ugliness of our sin, making us more like Christ, and therefore more and more beautiful all the time. This beauty is not only personal, but also communal, as God constructs his church "into a holy temple in the Lord," and as we are "built together into a dwelling place for God by the Spirit" (Eph. 2:21–22).

If our God is such a beautiful God, then we—of all people—ought to have the highest appreciation for beauty. When Christians settle for low aesthetic standards, we compromise the character of our God. We are called instead to behold the auburn leaf, hear the call of the wild eagle, admire the brushstroke on canvas, listen for the harmonic chord, and then return praise to our Creator. We are called to make beautiful things with our hands, bearing witness to the character of God and his bright plans for the future. We are called to seek the beauty of the city, so people can see in the church a community that cares for the aesthetic needs of the human soul. Will you answer God's call to pursue a divine aesthetic? Care more for the growing beauty of your inner character than for the outward attractions of physical appearance. Cultivate a love for beauty that honors your beautiful God. Take the prayer of Moses and make it your own: "Let the beauty of the Lord our God be upon us" (Ps. 90:17 kjv).

Solid Gold

Solomon's beautiful temple was also golden in its royal splendor. When Howard Carter was asked what he saw with his first glimpse of the treasure in the tomb of King Tutankhamen, the famous archaeologist said, "Wonderful things!" Israel's priests could have said the same thing when they first entered Solomon's temple, for it too was filled with golden treasure:

> The inner sanctuary he prepared in the innermost part of the house, to set there the ark of the covenant of the Lord. The inner sanctuary was twenty cubits long, twenty cubits wide, and twenty cubits high, and he overlaid it with pure gold. He also overlaid an altar of cedar. And Solomon overlaid the inside of the house with pure gold, and he drew chains of gold across, in front of the inner sanctuary, and overlaid it with gold. And he overlaid the whole house

with gold, until all the house was finished. Also the whole altar that belonged
to the inner sanctuary he overlaid with gold. (1 Kings 6:19–22)

There was gold shining everywhere in God's house. This was the main
impression people had when they went inside: the entire interior glittered with
gilded splendor. Gold covered the walls and ceiling of the main sanctuary, as
well as the altar of incense. Gold covered the inner sanctuary. This was the Most
Holy Place in the temple, where Solomon set the sacred ark of the holy covenant,
and where atonement was made for sin (see Lev. 16). The Holy of Holies, as it
was also called, was constructed in the shape of a perfect cube, which was a sign
of orderliness, holiness, and perfection. The entire cube was overlaid with gold
and separated from the rest of the temple by a curtain of golden chains (or a
fabric curtain that was hung on golden rings; see 2 Chron. 3:14). Solomon even
gilded the floors: "The floor of the house he overlaid with gold in the inner and
outer rooms" (1 Kings 6:30). The house of God was golden in its glory.

Some scholars have tried to suggest that all this gold is the "figment of
someone's imagination,"[4] "an exaggeration that probably originated from a
later tradition about the splendor of Solomon's Temple."[5] Yet there is no cred-
ible reason to doubt the historical reliability of the biblical text. Solomon's
temple was covered with gold, as this chapter repeatedly says. It was not just
any gold, either: the Bible explicitly describes it as "pure gold" of the highest
perfection (1 Kings 6:21).

Other scholars have criticized Solomon's gold as an ungodly extravagance.[6] But this was the house of God, who deserves the highest honor. For
him only the best would do. Therefore, Solomon did not spare any expense,
but used the most precious material he could buy. Peter Leithart describes
this costly expenditure as "a significant upgrade from the curtain walls and
dust floor of the tabernacle. The tabernacle was glorious, but Solomon builds
a more glorious house. With the building of the temple, Israel moves from
glory to greater glory."[7]

4. S. J. DeVries, *I Kings*, Word Biblical Commentary (Waco, TX: Word, 1985), 96.

5. G. H. Jones, *1 and 2 Kings*, New Century Bible Commentary, 2 vols. (Grand Rapids: Eerdmans, 1984), 1:169.

6. E.g., Walter Brueggemann, *1 & 2 Kings*, Smyth & Helwys Bible Commentary (Macon, GA: Smyth & Helwys, 2000), 90.

7. Peter Leithart, *1 & 2 Kings*, Brazos Theological Commentary on the Bible (Grand Rapids: Brazos, 2006), 55.

All this gold was appropriate to put in a house built for someone as glorious as God. It is wise to invest our resources in proportion to the relative worth of the object of our expenditure, which in this case was Almighty God. God himself confirmed the wisdom of Solomon's investment when the temple was dedicated and he said, "I have consecrated this house that you have built, by putting my name there forever. My eyes and my heart will be there for all time" (1 Kings 9:3). Gold is the metal of kings. Since God rules over all, it was only right for Solomon to build him a temple of gold, suitable to his royal honor. The famous English poet George Herbert was right to praise King Solomon for his glorious extravagance:

> Lord, with what glory wast thou served of old,
> When Solomon's temple stood and flourished!
>> Where most things were of purest gold;
>> The wood was all embellished.[8]

Admittedly, not even gold is fully worthy of the glory of God. Gold was the best that Solomon had to offer, but because God already owns everything in the universe, nothing on earth could ever approach the true glory of his kingly majesty.

If they had been around in those days, the advertisers at MasterCard could have turned this principle into a commercial. Starting with the 1997 World Series, the company ran an ad campaign with the slogan, "There are some things money can't buy. For everything else, there's MasterCard." The ads listed the purchase price for a series of items (such as hot dogs, baseball hats, and two tickets to a baseball game), followed by something labeled as "priceless" (watching the St. Louis Cardinals win the World Series, for example). Solomon's temple followed a similar logic. Everything inside the temple had its purchase price: the cedar that Solomon bought from Tyre, for example, or the gold he expended from his royal treasury. These were things that money could buy, with or without MasterCard. But what price tag would you place on having God in the house? The golden splendor of Solomon's temple could not even begin to compare with the priceless glory of God.

---

8. George Herbert, "Sion," in *Chapters into Verse: Poetry in English Inspired by the Bible*, vol. 1, *Genesis to Malachi*, ed. Robert Atwan and Laurance Wieder (Oxford: Oxford University Press, 1993), 235.

The deity worshiped at Solomon's temple is a glorious God. He is the King of all kings. Now his royal glory is displayed in Jesus Christ, the greater Solomon of the kingdom of God. Once he made his beautiful sacrifice, offering his body as the sacrifice for our sins, Jesus was raised up again in kingly triumph. God "raised him from the dead and gave him glory" (1 Peter 1:21). Now Jesus reigns supreme as the King of God's kingdom.

If our God is such a glorious King, then we—of all people—ought to give him the royal honor and obedience that he alone deserves. We should bring him gold to proclaim the coming of his kingdom around the world and to build up his spiritual temple in the church. Even though our money is hardly equivalent to his priceless majesty, and even though it belongs to him already, he will graciously receive it as our royal tribute—the gold we offer to our King. Offering such gifts has the additional benefit of helping us grow in godliness, for one of the best ways to master the temptations of money is simply to give it away.

We also have something more precious to offer our King than money: a life surrendered to his service. Our service is not really worthy of his majesty, either, any more than our money is, but it is the best we have to offer, so we should bring it. We should offer Jesus the treasure of our hearts, enthroning him as our King. We should offer him the worship of our mouths, praising him as our glorious God. We should offer him the work of our hands, feeding the poor and healing the wounded because Christ is our King.

Holy, Holy, Holy

God is not just the ruler of the earth, but also the King of heaven. This too was symbolized inside Solomon's temple.

The temple proper was divided into two parts. The outer chamber was called the Holy Place, while the inner chamber at the back was known as the Most Holy Place. The Most Holy Place housed the ark of the covenant, where atonement was made for sin, and which symbolized the footstool of God's throne (see 1 Chron. 28:2; Ps. 132:7–8). This was the place of God's presence, "the very dwelling place of God—insofar as God had an earthly dwelling place."[9] Yet from the book of Hebrews we also know that the Most

9. Iain W. Provan, *1 and 2 Kings*, New International Biblical Commentary (Peabody, MA: Hendrickson, 1995), 67.

Holy Place was meant to serve as an earthly copy of God's heavenly throne room (see Heb. 9:23–24). This explains why Solomon fabricated two angels to stand as guardians of the inner temple:

> In the inner sanctuary he made two cherubim of olivewood, each ten cubits high. Five cubits was the length of one wing of the cherub, and five cubits the length of the other wing of the cherub; it was ten cubits from the tip of one wing to the tip of the other. The other cherub also measured ten cubits; both cherubim had the same measure and the same form. The height of one cherub was ten cubits, and so was that of the other cherub. He put the cherubim in the innermost part of the house. And the wings of the cherubim were spread out so that a wing of one touched the one wall, and a wing of the other cherub touched the other wall; their other wings touched each other in the middle of the house. And he overlaid the cherubim with gold. (1 Kings 6:23–28)

These two magnificent statues dominated the Holy of Holies. Each angelic figure was 15 feet tall, and with a wingspan of equal or greater length, the cherubim completely spanned the inner sanctuary. They were carved from hard olivewood, and plated with gold.

Solomon's golden cherubim remind us again of the beauty of God, and of his kingly majesty. We know from the book of Isaiah and other places that at this very moment there are cherubim in the presence of God (e.g., Isa. 37:16). In effect, these angels are his courtiers, the attendants to his royal throne. The beautiful golden cherubim inside Solomon's temple imitated this heavenly scene, indicating that the temple's inner sanctuary was the throne room of God—a sign of his royal presence and kingly glory. In the words of the psalmist, God sits "enthroned upon the cherubim" (Ps. 80:1).

The cherubim also show us God's holiness. No creature is holier than an angel, for the angels of heaven are perfectly without sin. They are set apart for God's holy service. As the cherubim offer holy worship to God, they reflect so much of his glory that if we could see them now, we would be tempted to worship them. Yet these holy creatures do not claim any worship for themselves. In fact, whenever people have tried to worship any of the angels, they have said, "You must not do that!" (Rev. 19:10; 22:9). Instead, the angels teach us to offer all our praise to God as the one who deserves whatever praise and glory we can give. The angels themselves are pristinely holy, but in worshiping God they show us the supreme greatness of his superior holiness. If such holy creatures give all their worship to God, then he must be even holier.

This comparison reminds me of the first time I met the Reverend William Still, the great Scottish evangelical minister who helped revive the Church of Scotland in the middle of the twentieth century. Two of my favorite preachers (Eric Alexander and Sinclair Ferguson) always spoke about Mr. Still in reverent tones, for he had been one of their fathers in faith and ministry. As much respect as I had for the Rev. Alexander and Dr. Ferguson, I could tell that they had even higher regard for their spiritual mentor. So when I went to study with Mr. Still in Scotland, I knew that I would be in the presence of rare godliness, as proved to be the case.

The cherubim inside Solomon's temple served a similar purpose on an infinitely higher plane. As holy as they are, the cherubim point to a superior holiness. They represent the heavenly angels who worship the infinite holiness of God. By their example, the cherubim call us to "worship the Lord in the splendor of holiness" (Ps. 29:2; cf. 96:9).

Now that we have heard the gospel of the crucifixion and the resurrection, we offer our worship in the name of Jesus Christ, "the Holy One of God" (Mark 1:24). We also hear God's call to a life of Christian holiness that is free from the love of money, free from the lust of the flesh, and free from the pride of self. The holy way to handle our money is to use it all for the glory of God. The holy way to control our sexuality is to keep it within the covenant bonds of matrimony. The holy way to employ our power is to use our authority and influence to serve people in need. We worship a holy Savior, who calls us to be his holy people: "as he who called you is holy, you also be holy in all your conduct" (1 Peter 1:15).

The Gates of Paradise

Solomon's temple was a place of awe-inspiring splendor. Its golden interior was designed to convey a sense of the royal beauty and perfect holiness of God. The biblical description of its construction and decoration is intended to awaken in the heart a longing for God. The Holy Spirit is lifting the veil so we can see by faith into the holy place of God. As marvelous as it was to see the glory of Solomon's architecture, it is infinitely more marvelous to meet the God whose beauty and royalty and holiness his temple proclaimed.

Yet as awesome (and terrifying) as it was for people to go inside Solomon's temple, there were doors that enabled people to enter. The Bible describes the doors that opened into the Holy of Holies: "For the entrance to the inner sanctuary he made doors of olivewood; the lintel and the doorposts were five-sided. He covered the two doors of olivewood with carvings of cherubim, palm trees, and open flowers. He overlaid them with gold and spread gold on the cherubim and on the palm trees" (1 Kings 6:31–32).

Solomon also installed doors at the temple's main entrance: "So also he made for the entrance to the nave doorposts of olivewood, in the form of a square, and two doors of cypress wood. The two leaves of the one door were folding, and the two leaves of the other door were folding. On them he carved cherubim and palm trees and open flowers, and he overlaid them with gold evenly applied on the carved work. He built the inner court with three courses of cut stone and one course of cedar beams" (1 Kings 6:33–36).

These magnificent folding doors gave Solomon and his people limited access to the presence of God. On the one hand, the doors of the temple were there to let people in. There was a way to enter this marvelous building. There was even a way into the inner sanctuary, the Most Holy Place. Praise God for the doors of Solomon's temple, which testify that the infinitely beautiful, royally glorious, perfectly holy God actually desires to have a relationship with his people!

Yet the doors were also there to keep people out. Only the priests were ever allowed to enter the temple at all, and even they could enter only when they were going about their priestly duties. Access to the Holy of Holies was even more tightly restricted. Only one man ever entered the Most Holy Place, and only once a year. On the Day of Atonement, the high priest would enter the inner sanctuary—alone—to make a blood offering for the people's sins (see Lev. 16). Otherwise, the temple was strictly off-limits; its doors were shut to show that people could not come into the presence of God, except by the representation of their priest.

To understand the purpose of having a limited-access temple, it helps to recognize the symbolism of its decorations. Like almost everything else inside the temple, the folding doors to the temple and the inner doors to the Holy of Holies were covered with royal gold. They were also decorated with "carvings of cherubim, palm trees, and open flowers" (1 Kings 6:32, 35). Solomon continued this motif inside: "Around all the walls of the house he carved engraved figures of cherubim and palm trees and open flowers, in the inner and outer rooms" (1 Kings 6:29). Everything was covered with vegetation.

Perhaps the bright angelic figures and fair botanical designs that covered the temple were there simply for the sake of their beauty, which would be reason enough. After all, Solomon believed in art for God's sake. But perhaps these decorations also had a deeper meaning, connected to another place of lush vegetation that was guarded by angels.

The design of Solomon's temple referenced the garden of Eden, which meant that its doors symbolized the very gates of paradise. The garden where our first parents lived contained "every tree that is pleasant to the sight and good for food" (Gen. 2:9). So the trees inside Solomon's temple naturally remind us of our ancestral home, as every tree and flower should. But in this case, there are also angels in the architecture, which establishes a stronger connection with the garden of Eden. When God drove Adam and Eve out of the garden for their sin in eating the forbidden fruit, he placed cherubim somewhere east of Eden "to guard the way to the tree of life" (Gen. 3:24). Whereas formerly the garden of Eden was a place to go and meet with God, now angels barred the way, preventing the man and the woman from reentering paradise.

So when people came to the door of Solomon's temple, and saw the cherubim amid the flowers and trees, they were coming to the gates of paradise. For most people, access to Solomon's virtual garden was still denied; unless they were priests, they would never see the golden wonders inside the temple. Only the High Priest would ever enter the presence of God, who was reigning from his earthly throne in the Holy of Holies. But however limited it may have been, there *was* access. God was opening up the way. The temple was a spiritual portal. The paradise lost could be regained. In fact, the gold inside the temple whispered rumors of an everlasting paradise, where even the streets will be paved with gold (see Rev. 21:21).

That was then; this is now. We are still living somewhere east of Eden, in a fallen and broken world. But God is calling us back home. He wants to have a relationship with us. He wants us to see his royal beauty. He is inviting us into the throne room of his temple, where he is worshiped by holy angels.

The way to enter God's paradise is through faith in Jesus Christ. Jesus said, "I am the door. If anyone enters by me, he will be saved" (John 10:9). Jesus is the door for us because he has already entered *the* Most Holy Place—not the Holy of Holies inside Solomon's temple, which was only a copy of the true reality, but heaven itself. Jesus entered the throne room of heaven as our Priest to present the blood of his own sacrifice on the cross as the once-and-for-all atonement for our sin (see Heb. 9:24–26).

Now, through Jesus, the way is open for us to God. The book of Hebrews says, "Since we have confidence to enter the holy places by the blood of Jesus, by the new and living way that he opened for us through the curtain, that is, through his flesh, and since we have a great priest over the house of God, let us draw near with a true heart in full assurance of faith" (Heb. 10:19–22). Yes, let us draw near to God in his holy temple, through faith in Jesus Christ. He will forgive us; he will receive us; he will save us forever.

There was a time when God lived in Solomon's house, but his long-range plan is for us to come and live in his house, the palace of paradise. I have once been to a palace—Buckingham Palace, the year after the fire at Windsor Castle, when it was opened to the public. Unfortunately, I never saw the queen, in all her royal splendor. But what do I care? Through Jesus I have been invited to the palace of all palaces, the golden paradise of God. When I arrive, the King will be waiting to receive me, in the beauty of his holiness.

13

BETTER HOMES AND GARDENS

1 Kings 7:1—12

Solomon was building his own house thirteen years,
and he finished his entire house. (1 Kings 7:1)

Get the right house, and you can have a great life. This is the premise of the award-winning, feel-good television reality show *Extreme Makeover: Home Edition*. Each week another needy family with a hard-luck story is chosen to receive a brand-new dream house, built in only a week by a team of expert designers and builders. The program has everything people are looking for in a reality show: a vibrant host, high-voltage drama of suffering parents and children with special needs, fast action as the crew races to finish before the deadline, and electric emotion when the family sees its new home for the first time.

The show has also been successful for another reason: it fuels the American dream of owning a beautiful home. "Look at that!" people say when they see the gleaming kitchen appliances, or the Jacuzzi in the master suite, or the racing-car bed in the boys' room. "Wouldn't you love to live in a house like that?" Everyone wants a beautiful home, and even if we do not get to live in the home of our dreams, we still get a vicarious thrill from seeing how "the other half" lives.

We know this is an area of spiritual danger, because the Bible explicitly commands us not to covet our neighbor's house (Ex. 20:17). Why would God tell us this if not because he knows how prone we are to envy the places where other people live? For the followers of Jesus, then, this is an important area for self-examination: Am I living where I live for the glory of God? Am I content with the living space that God has provided for me? Have I brought my longing for better homes and gardens under the kingship of Jesus Christ?

HOME, SWEET HOME

First Kings opens up a biblical perspective on these issues by telling us about Solomon's house—not just the house that he built for God, but also his own home. There are two houses in this story: one for God and one for King Solomon.

The story of how Solomon built this house is tucked inside the longer story of how he built the temple in Jerusalem. Some scholars see this insertion as a digression, yet it seems to come at a natural break in the biblical text. Chapter 5 told how Solomon prepared to build the temple, while chapter 6 told how he actually built it, inside and out. The rest of chapter 7 will tell how Solomon furnished the temple—what he put inside. But the first twelve verses briefly describe the rest of the king's buildings.

There seem to have been five main buildings in the royal complex, although some of the halls the Bible mentions may have been part of larger structures. Three of the buildings had formal titles: the House of the Forest of Lebanon (1 Kings 7:2–5), the Hall of Pillars (1 Kings 7:6), and the Hall of the Throne, or the Hall of Judgment (1 Kings 7:7). Then there was Solomon's own residence, as well as the house he built for his Egyptian wife (1 Kings 7:8).

What are we to make of these buildings? What is their spiritual significance, if any, for the people of God today? It is possible to view these building projects in a positive light. Like anyone else, Solomon needed a place to call home, and since he was the king, it was right and good for him to live in a palace. By its very definition, the place where a king lives is a palace. This is part of the royal dignity that belongs to him by divine right. He is not a private person, but holds a public office. There is a sense, therefore, in which his home belongs to the entire nation. The palace was not simply for Solomon, but also for the kingdom of God.

It is also right and good that Solomon's house was built next to the house of God.[1] The king chose to put his house next door to the temple, bringing his kingship close to God's presence. There are even some ways in which Solomon's house resembled the house of God. People sometimes say that imitation is the sincerest form of flattery. That was certainly true in this case, because in its materials and design, Solomon's palace imitated various features of Solomon's temple. Like the temple, it was made of stone and cedar. In certain respects it had a similar structure, with a porch outside the central hall. The Puritan Matthew Henry thus observed that the court of Solomon's "own house was like that of the temple, so well did he like the model of God's courts that he made his own by it."[2] The close association between the two houses showed that the king was under God's rule, that he was the royal son of God (provided, that is, the king was careful not to get his priorities reversed and think of the temple as his own royal chapel).

Furthermore, Solomon used several of these buildings for official purposes, similar to the way that the grand buildings of government are used in Washington, D.C. This was certainly true of "the Hall of the Throne where he was to pronounce judgment, even the Hall of Judgment. It was finished with cedar from floor to rafters" (1 Kings 7:7). The Bible does not provide this building's dimensions, so it is hard to be sure, but either this hall attached to the House of the Forest of Lebanon or else it stood as a building in its own right. Either way, it was used for rendering judgment, as Solomon had done in the famous case of the prostitutes and the two babies (see 1 Kings 3:16–28). In effect, the Hall of the Throne was Israel's Supreme Court Building.

Giving people justice was one of the king's primary responsibilities. Judging from his prayer in Psalm 72, Solomon took this job seriously. "Give the king your justice, O God," he prayed. "May he judge your people with righteousness, and your poor with justice!" (Ps. 72:1–2). These prayers were answered in the Hall of the Throne, where Solomon administered justice.

1. Peter Leithart develops this argument in *1 & 2 Kings*, Brazos Theological Commentary on the Bible (Grand Rapids: Brazos, 2006), 55, 60, 61.
2. Matthew Henry, *Matthew Henry's Complete Commentary on the Whole Bible*, vol. 2, *Judges to Job* (New York: Fleming Revell, n.d.), n.p.

Perhaps we could even say that this hall was a sign or symbol of the final judgment. Solomon built a temple, which signified the presence of God and opened the way to eternal life. He also built a hall of justice, which signified God's righteousness and prophesied the final judgment. According to Solomon, "a wise king winnows the wicked and drives the wheel over them" (Prov. 20:26), which is a poetical way of saying that he will punish his enemies. So it will be at the final judgment, when Jesus Christ will sit on his throne for justice and wisely declare the eternal destiny of every person who has ever lived. The Hall of the Throne reminds us that one day we will all come to judgment. But Jesus can save us. If we are wise, we will settle our case long before the day of judgment ever comes by claiming the cross as our only defense. If we believe in the crucifixion of Jesus Christ for our sins, we will not be condemned, but have eternal life.

THE DANGER OF DISTRACTION

Part of Solomon's glory was the splendor of his royal palace. Since Solomon was the king, it was virtually his duty to live in such a beautiful house. It was also a blessing from God, who had promised Solomon riches beyond compare (see 1 Kings 3:13). Still, there are some spiritual dangers that typically go with living in palaces. We should take careful note of two temptations that Solomon faced, because they are also temptations for us: distraction and extravagance.

The danger of distraction is evident from the amount of time that it took for Solomon to finish construction: "Solomon was building his own house thirteen years, and he finished his entire house" (1 Kings 7:1). In other words, it took Solomon almost twice as long to build his own house (thirteen years) as it took him to build the house of God (seven years). Admittedly, Solomon took these projects in the right order, making the temple his first and highest priority. Maybe the reason it took him so much longer to build his own house was that it was a lower priority for him, and therefore he took his time. But it seems more likely that it took Solomon longer because his own house was so much bigger.

The Bible calls attention to this contrast in the transition between chapter 6, which ends by saying how long it took King Solomon to build the temple, and chapter 7, which begins by saying how long it took him to build his palace. In the original Hebrew, 1 Kings 7:1 begins with the word "but" or "now," indicating some sort of contrast. A more literal translation goes like this: "He completed the temple . . . He spent seven years building it. But his *own* house Solomon spent thirteen years building."[3] By making this contrast, the Bible may well be raising a concern about Solomon's priorities.

If we are wise, we will raise the same concern about our own priorities. The worship of God and the building of his spiritual temple through the church ought to be our primary goals in life. We were made to glorify God. We glorify him most directly when we gather together with his people and sing his praise. We are also called to invite other people to join us in giving glory to God. This is why we show the love of Christ to our neighbors and share the good news of the gospel around the world. It is so that other people will become part of God's spiritual temple in Jesus Christ.

Yet the cares of life easily distract us from the higher priorities of the kingdom of God. One of the biggest distractions, especially for wealthy Americans, is our living situation. Think of all the trouble we take to find the right place to live, then to pay for it and figure out how to furnish it. Think how much effort it takes to move from one place to another, dragging all our possessions with us. Most Americans take more stuff on the average family vacation than many people in the world own. Think, too, of all the time it takes to fix things around the house, let alone attempt any kind of major home improvement. Then there are all the things we do to keep a household running—all the cleaning and dusting, all the picking up and putting away.

A nice house is not wrong in itself, any more than it was wrong for King Solomon to live in a palace, but we need to be alert to the danger of distraction. Praise God: by the presence of the Holy Spirit, our homes can be places of worship that are used for kingdom work. Yet the more we have, the more trouble it takes. Rather than drawing us closer to God, therefore, and helping us advance his kingdom, our homes threaten to absorb attention that would better be spent in the worship and service of God.

Unless we move in the direction of simplification, which is hard to do while we are living in "the Kingdom of Stuff,"[4] we face the constant danger

3. Iain W. Provan, *1 and 2 Kings*, New International Biblical Commentary (Peabody, MA: Hendrickson, 1995), 69.
4. Mark Buchanan uses this provocative expression in "The Cult of the Next Thing," *Christianity Today*, September 6, 1999, http://www.ctlibrary.com/ct/1999/September6/9ta062.html.

of distraction. Many people think that if only they could get the right house, they would have a great life. But the distractions that come with better homes and gardens are not always good for the soul. In his prophetic book *Gods That Fail*, Vinoth Ramachandra writes:

> The people of the modern West (and the middle class of non-Western cultures) are better fed, better housed, better equipped with health care than those in any previous age in human history. But paradoxically, they also seem to be the most fearful, the most divided, the most superstitious and the most bored generation in human history. All the labor-saving devices of modern technology have only enhanced human stress, and modern life is characterized by restless movement from place to place, from one experience to another, in a frenetic whirl of purposeless activity.[5]

It would be better for us to put a lower priority on a comfortable living situation and a higher priority on the kingdom of God. First Kings takes this perspective in the way it tells the story of Solomon. The major emphasis in chapters 5 through 8 is the house that Solomon built for God. The Bible gives us the full details of the temple's structure and furnishings, plus a lengthy account of its dedication. Solomon's own house took longer to build, but receives much less attention—just twelve verses for five buildings. Even for all its splendor, Solomon's palace receives only brief mention. As far as the Holy Spirit is concerned, this is all it deserves, because Solomon's house was not nearly as important as the house he built for God. By de-emphasizing Solomon's palace, the Bible is keeping things in their proper priority.[6]

What are your priorities? The place where we live is less important than many things. It is less important than what happens inside the place where we live—the way we welcome people into our homes and treat the people we live with every day. Our homes are less important than our relationships with the neighbors who live next door—the love and respect we give them in the name of Jesus Christ. Our homes are less important than the worship we offer in the church, which is the household of faith. The psalmist praised God by saying, "A day in your courts is better than a thousand elsewhere"

5. Vinoth Ramachandra, *Gods That Fail: Modern Idolatry and Christian Mission* (Downers Grove, IL: InterVarsity, 1996), 12–13.

6. Dale Ralph Davis makes this point in *The Wisdom and the Folly: An Exposition of the Book of First Kings* (Fearn, Ross-shire: Christian Focus, 2002), 71–72.

(Ps. 84:10). The places we live are also less important than the construction that God is doing around the world to build his new spiritual temple in Jesus Christ. Do not get distracted. Keep your priorities straight: God's house is more important than your house!

THE DANGER OF EXTRAVAGANCE

As he built his famous palace, Solomon faced a second spiritual danger: extravagance. As we have seen, the king's wealth was a blessing from God, as money always is. But the more financial resources we have, the more important it is—and the more difficult it can be—to use them for the glory of God. With all the treasure he had, Solomon was tempted to be extravagant.

The house the king built was very impressive. There were five buildings in the palace complex, some of them quite large. First the Bible describes a large, multistory building that was used for assemblies, with side chambers for storing treasure (see 1 Kings 10:16–17) and weaponry (see Isa. 22:8):

> He built the House of the Forest of Lebanon. Its length was a hundred cubits and its breadth fifty cubits and its height thirty cubits [roughly 150 feet by 75 feet by 45 feet], and it was built on four rows of cedar pillars, with cedar beams on the pillars. And it was covered with cedar above the chambers that were on the forty-five pillars, fifteen in each row. There were window frames in three rows, and window opposite window in three tiers. All the doorways and windows had square frames, and window was opposite window in three tiers. (1 Kings 7:2–5; cf. 1 Kings 10:16–17; Isa. 22:8)

The House of the Forest of Lebanon must have been very beautiful. There were rows of windows to flood the building with natural light, and so many wooden pillars inside that it almost seemed like Solomon had brought a forest indoors.

Then Solomon "made the Hall of Pillars; its length was fifty cubits, and its breadth thirty cubits. There was a porch in front with pillars, and a canopy in front of them" (1 Kings 7:6). Although it may have been a building in its own right, this colonnade may have served instead as the entranceway to the House of the Forest of Lebanon.

The king also built his own residence, as well as living quarters for his wife. He had not simply one palace, but two: "His own house where he was to dwell, in the other court back of the hall, was of like workmanship. Solomon also made a house like this hall for Pharaoh's daughter whom he had taken in marriage" (1 Kings 7:8). Apparently the queen wanted a place of her own. Given the number of wives that Solomon eventually accumulated (see 1 Kings 11:3), her quarters may also have served as the royal harem.

Eventually Pharaoh's daughter would prove to be a stumbling block for Solomon, tripping him into the sin of idol worship. But the king also faced more immediate temptations with this building project—the temptations that come with living in luxury. Not only were his buildings large, but they were also covered in cedar, which in those days was high-end construction material. There were huge cedar pillars and beams in the House of the Forest of Lebanon (1 Kings 7:2–3). The Hall of Judgment was paneled with cedar from floor to ceiling (1 Kings 7:7). All this beautiful wood had been imported from Tyre at great expense. According to one commentator, the whole project "smacks of affluence and indulgence."[7] Although God had promised to build a house for Solomon (see 2 Sam. 7:11), the king was pretty well determined to do the building himself, rather than trusting God's promise.

Admittedly, 1 Kings does not explicitly criticize Solomon for building such a beautiful palace. Indeed, the tone of this passage seems to be admiring. Yet we do find strong words of warning in the Prophets. Jeremiah pronounced God's woe against any king who says, "I will build myself a great house with spacious upper rooms," or who cuts out windows for his palace and panels the interior with cedar (Jer. 22:14). Then Jeremiah asked a question we could well inquire of Solomon: "Do you think you are a king because you compete in cedar?" (Jer. 22:15). Jeremiah said this with a special concern for social justice. He knew that what made a king was not a palace, but righteousness for the poor and needy. Not that it was wrong for the king to live in a palace, necessarily, but when someone is building a luxury home it is easy to overlook people who do not have a home at all, and could use some help.

As costly as cedar was, Solomon also spent a fortune in stone. His royal palaces "were made of costly stones, cut according to measure, sawed with saws, back and front, even from the foundation to the coping, and from the outside to the great court. The foundation was of costly stones, huge stones,

---

7. Walter Brueggemann, *1 & 2 Kings*, Smyth & Helwys Bible Commentary (Macon, GA: Smyth & Helwys, 2000), 75.

stones of eight and ten cubits. And above were costly stones, cut according to measurement, and cedar. The great court had three courses of cut stone all around, and a course of cedar beams; so had the inner court of the house of the LORD and the vestibule of the house" (1 Kings 7:9–12).

The stones in Solomon's palace were enormous—twelve to fifteen feet across. They were also very expensive. By the time they had been quarried in the hill country and hauled up to the top of Jerusalem's mountain, Solomon had paid a king's ransom in labor costs alone. Virtually every time these stones are mentioned, they are described as "costly." When it came to the king's palace, no expense was spared.

Having a nice home—or wanting a nicer home—is not wrong in itself, but it is an area of spiritual danger, both for Solomon and for us. It is not money that we love as much as the things that money can buy, and one of the things money can buy is luxury, especially today, when so many beautiful things are so readily available. God has given us excellent materials to use for building and renovating our homes. Even Solomon would envy our granite counter-tops, brushed-nickel finishes, and South American hardwoods. These things are all part of the world that God has made, and therefore good in themselves, but they also come at a price. Every time we decide what to buy, or what not to buy, we are making a decision that comes from the heart. So beware of the dangers of self-indulgence!

Americans typically expect to enjoy a rising standard of living. We generally assume that our next home will be nicer than the one we have right now, or else that we will be able to improve the place where we are living by adding a family room or renovating the kitchen. Some people even think that Christians are entitled to a higher standard of living, and that if we trust in God, he will bless us with greater prosperity, like the television preacher who said, "Who would want to get in on something where you're miserable, poor, broke and ugly and you just have to muddle through until you get to heaven? I believe God wants to give us nice things."[8] God does want to give us some nice things, but the nicest thing he wants to give us is himself, and sometimes the other nice things that we want get in the way of our relationship with him.

Like anything good in life, home improvements can be made for the glory of God. We were made for eternity, and as long as we live in a fallen world

8. Joyce Meyer, quoted in David Van Biema and Jeff Chu, "Does God Want You to Be Rich?" *Time*, September 18, 2006, 52.

it is only natural for us to want things to be better than they are. But beware of the dangers of rising expectations and creeping self-indulgence. Unless we are living for the kingdom of God, rather than for our own enjoyment, being upwardly mobile will only be a way of deferring our discontent. We will end up like the housewife in *The Man in the Gray Flannel Suit*, who said to her husband: "I don't know what's the matter with us. Our job is plenty good enough . . . and lots of people would be glad to have a house like this. We shouldn't be so *discontented* all the time."[9] Getting what we want might make us happy for a little while, but soon we go right back to wanting more, getting frustrated with our present situation and dreaming of better homes and gardens.

Every decision we make about our money calls for wisdom, prayer, and discernment. God has not told us exactly how much we ought to spend on our homes (although sometimes it is tempting to wish that he would). He has left this and almost all the other decisions we make about our stewardship to the freedom of our own conscience.

One helpful guideline for giving is the biblical tithe (e.g., Lev. 27:30), which means offering 10 percent of our gross income to the kingdom of God. God is not greedy: if we give him 10 percent, we still have 90 percent left to use for everything else we need. We should not limit ourselves to 10 percent, however, especially those of us who are wealthy, as most Americans are. Nor should we forget that 100 percent of what we own belongs to God; it is *all* to be used for his glory. Even the money we spend on ourselves, so to speak, should be spent with the deliberate intention to honor God.

Another way to test our giving is to compare how much we spend on our own homes to the amount we spend building the house of God through the gospel ministry of the church. Take the amount you spend each month on your mortgage or rent and compare it to how much you give to the kingdom of God. Solomon's temptation was to spend more on his own house than he did for the house of God. Since we face the same temptation, it is good for us to examine our spending. If we believe that building up the church as God's eternal temple is more important than our own earthly dwelling places, this should be evident from the way we spend our money.

9. Sloan Wilson, *The Man in the Gray Flannel Suit* (1955), quoted in Philadelphia's *Inquirer Magazine*, September 20, 1998, 11.

God does not operate strictly on the basis of ratios or percentages; he looks at the heart. But our hearts are directly connected to our bank accounts. What we spend always reflects our true spiritual priorities. We should seek to have confidence before God, therefore, that what we spend also reflects *his* true priorities, which means bringing our comparative expenditures more in line with the values of his kingdom. If we are spending more on ourselves, shortchanging God, we should remember how much it cost the Father to give us the Son, and how much it cost the Son to lay down his life for our sins, and then pray to the Holy Spirit for the grace to give God more and more of what he deserves.

The Lilies of the Field

To help us avoid the dangers of distraction and extravagance, Jesus made a simple and memorable comparison. He was preaching his famous Sermon on the Mount and encouraging people not to worry so much about their own daily needs, but to seek first the kingdom of God. "Consider the lilies of the field," Jesus said, "how they grow: they neither toil nor spin, yet I tell you, even Solomon in all his glory was not arrayed like one of these" (Matt. 6:28–29).

In making this comparison, Jesus assumed that people knew the glories of Solomon's kingdom, including his magnificent palace. King Solomon lived in a dream house full of golden treasure. Yet Jesus was not overly impressed with the king's riches because he knew that even Solomon, for all his glory, could not compare to the simple splendor of a single field lily.

Somehow the lilies of the field manage to avoid the dangers that tempted Solomon, and still tempt us. Lilies are utterly undistracted. To build his house, Solomon had to send thousands of lumberjacks and stonecutters into the hills. When they came back, it took them more than a decade to finish his palace. By contrast, the lilies of the field do not work at all. They neither toil nor spin, but grow effortlessly, basking in the sunshine as they are showered with rain from heaven. Nevertheless, the beauty of the lilies is extravagant—one of the Creator's greatest masterpieces. There is more glory in one single wildflower than in all the palaces of King Solomon.

Jesus wants us to apply this lesson by comparing the field lilies to ourselves. Although it does much less work, the lily of the field is more beautiful than we are. It is also more ephemeral, which is another point of comparison. Flowers do not live nearly as long as we do; they are alive today and gone tomorrow (compare Matt. 6:30 with Ps. 90:10). So here is a plant that does less work than we do, and lives for less time, yet in many ways is more beautiful than we are. God has covered the field lilies with glory.

If God takes such good care of the lilies, then we can trust him to take even better care of us. This is what Jesus wants us to understand. Destined for eternity, we are much more valuable to God than all the lilies of the field. Therefore, we do not need to worry about getting something to eat or having something to wear, let alone finding a better place to live. God knows what we need. He wants us to live for his kingdom, and then let everything else in life fall into place. We spend so much time on our homes, worrying about where we live, and so much money improving them, when what we really need to do is trust God to take care of what we truly need.

We can also trust God that when the time is right, he will give us the biggest home improvement ever—the world's most extreme makeover. The people who get a new home on *Extreme Makeover: Home Edition* are always overwhelmed when they see their new house. The tears flow freely for people who feared they were going to lose everything, and now have a dream home. This tells us something important about the human heart: we all have a deep longing for a place to call home—the place that is just right for us. The show's host takes this longing one step further by choosing a room in each house for a special project, such as the bedroom for a child with special needs. The design of the room reflects the child's interests and accommodates his or her unique needs. In the mansion there is a room that has been prepared exclusively for that particular child.

So it will be on the last of all days, when Jesus comes into his kingdom and takes us home to be with God forever. "In my Father's house are many rooms," Jesus said. "If it were not so, would I have told you that I go to prepare a place for you? And if I go and prepare a place for you, I will come again and will take you to myself, that where I am you may be also" (John 14:2–3). Soon Jesus will come and take us to his Father's house. When we arrive, we will discover (joy of joys!) that he has prepared a place that is perfect for us. So wherever we happen to stay in the meantime, we should remember that we are not home yet, but are on our way to the best home of all.

14

THE FURNITURE IN GOD'S HOUSE

1 Kings 7:13–51

*Thus all the work that King Solomon did on the house of the
LORD was finished. And Solomon brought in the things that
David his father had dedicated, the silver, the gold, and the vessels, and stored them in the treasuries of the house of the LORD.*
(1 Kings 7:51)

Shortly after we moved into our home in Center City, Philadelphia, my father-in-law hitched up a trailer, climbed into his
truck, and drove halfway across the country with a load of beautiful furniture, most of it designed in Scandinavia and made of teak. When
he arrived, for the first time in our married lives suddenly we had a house
full of furniture: beds and dressers, tables and chairs—even the old recliner
where my father-in-law loved to sit and watch football games.

Over the years that furniture has become part of everyday life. Every time
we get out our clothes, or gather around the dinner table, or sit down to watch
a movie, we use the furniture my father-in-law drove from his house to our
house. What belonged to him now belongs to us.

The furniture that Solomon put into the temple at Jerusalem did something similar for the people of God: it became part of their lives. As we saw

in 1 Kings 6, the house that Solomon built for God was an earthly copy of a heavenly reality. As the place where God chose to dwell with his people on earth, the temple was patterned after God's throne room in heaven (see Heb. 9:24). The temple and its furniture thus testified to the glory of God and displayed what kind of grace he had for his people.

God has even more grace for us in his Son, Jesus Christ. We do not have to go to a temple to get this grace, however. Now, instead of making his home at Solomon's temple, God makes his home in us by the presence of the Holy Spirit. Through faith in Christ, we are "a holy temple in the Lord," "a dwelling place for God by the Spirit" (Eph. 2:21–22). The Spirit has fulfilled the promise that the Son made concerning the Father to everyone who loves him: "We will come to him and make our home with him" (John 14:23). Thus the soul of every believer is sacred space, and the place where God now does his interior decorating is in the lives of his people. As we see the furniture in Solomon's temple, therefore, and understand its true spiritual meaning, we also see how God wants to furnish our lives with his grace.

PILLARS OF STRENGTH

The furniture in Solomon's temple was designed and crafted by one of the masters: "King Solomon sent and brought Hiram from Tyre. He was the son of a widow of the tribe of Naphtali, and his father was a man of Tyre, a worker in bronze. And he was full of wisdom, understanding, and skill for making any work in bronze. He came to King Solomon and did all his work" (1 Kings 7:13–14).

The people of Tyre were famous for their skill in working with metal. The most famous of all was Hiram—not Hiram the king, but a different man of the same name. Strangely enough, although Hiram was from Tyre, his mother was Jewish. But the most important thing to know about him is not his ethnic background, or his family connection to the people of God, but his gift for making things with bronze. Hiram was a master craftsman, and his craftsmanship was a God-given talent.

Hiram of Tyre is one of the great artists in the Bible. The language that 1 Kings uses to describe his artistic gift is virtually identical to the language Exodus uses to describe two other famous artisans: Bezalel and Oholiab, who were the leading architects and interior designers for the tabernacle that

Moses built in the wilderness. Bezalel and Oholiab were filled "with the Spirit of God, with ability and intelligence, with knowledge and all craftsmanship, to devise artistic designs, to work in gold, silver, and bronze, in cutting stones for setting, and in carving wood, to work in every craft" (Ex. 31:3–5; cf. 35:30–33). Hiram of Tyre had some of the same God-given skills.

Whenever it was time to build a house for God, first the tabernacle and then later the temple, God gave certain people the gift and calling to produce beautiful works of good art. This reminds us of God's own great love for beauty. It also encourages us to use whatever gifts we have for his glory, especially if we are gifted in any of the arts. Artists are called to work with the stuff of creation to show the glorious truth and the beauty of their Creator.[1] In doing so, they are "acting in the image of One who spoke a world into being and stooped down to form creatures from the dust. They are creaturely creators, shaping the world that the original Creator made."[2]

Hiram fulfilled his God-given calling as an artist by making beautiful things for Solomon's temple in Jerusalem. We do not know enough about the man to be certain whether he had saving faith in the God of Israel. What we do know is that everything Hiram made testified to the goodness of God and can help us understand how the Holy Spirit wants to furnish our souls with his grace.

The first thing Hiram made was a pair of massive pillars: "He cast two pillars of bronze. Eighteen cubits was the height of one pillar, and a line of twelve cubits measured its circumference. It was hollow, and its thickness was four fingers. The second pillar was the same" (1 Kings 7:15; cf. Jer. 52:21). Together these two bronze pillars stood at the entrance to the temple. To translate their size into contemporary units of measure, each pillar was approximately twenty-seven feet tall, eighteen feet around, and several inches thick.

Each pillar was topped with an ornate capital, some seven or eight feet tall. The Bible revels in the beauty of these architectural features:

> He also made two capitals of cast bronze to set on the tops of the pillars. The height of the one capital was five cubits, and the height of the other capital was five cubits. There were lattices of checker work with wreaths of chain work for

1. For more about Bezalel, Oholiab, Christianity, and the arts, see Philip Graham Ryken, *Art for God's Sake* (Phillipsburg, NJ: P&R Publishing, 2006).

2. Andy Crouch, *Culture Making: Recovering Our Creative Calling* (Downers Grove, IL: InterVarsity, 2008), 97.

the capitals on the tops of the pillars, a lattice for the one capital and a lattice for the other capital. Likewise he made pomegranates in two rows around the one latticework to cover the capital that was on the top of the pillar, and he did the same with the other capital. Now the capitals that were on the tops of the pillars in the vestibule were of lily-work, four cubits. The capitals were on the two pillars and also above the rounded projection which was beside the latticework. There were two hundred pomegranates in two rows all around, and so with the other capital. (1 Kings 7:16–20)

We take delight in the beautiful artistry of these capitals, for although it does not give enough detail to produce an exact replica, the Bible does show how intricate they were. The capitals were decorated with rows of fruit and chains of flowers—more echoes from Eden to remind us that the temple was the gateway to paradise.[3] The pomegranates identified the pillars with the priests who served inside the temple, for their garments were fringed with pomegranates (see Ex. 28:31–34). These fruits were symbols of the Promised Land (see Num. 13:23; Deut. 8:8), and also of productivity, for the inside of a pomegranate is packed with large seeds. The lilies were symbols of life, and also of love, for in the Song of Songs, this flower is closely associated with youthful romance (e.g., Song 2:1–2; 6:2–3).

What about the pillars themselves? Although they may have had a structural function in supporting the temple portico, it is more likely that these pillars were freestanding, one on each side of the entrance to the temple. So what was their symbolic meaning for Solomon and their spiritual connection to Jesus Christ and the life of Christian faith?

The meaning of the pillars is explained by their unusual names. Solomon "set up the pillars at the vestibule of the temple. He set up the pillar on the south and called its name Jachin, and he set up the pillar on the north and called its name Boaz. And on the tops of the pillars was lily-work. Thus the work of the pillars was finished" (1 Kings 7:21–22).

The name Jachin means "it is firm," or "he establishes."[4] The same verb is used in the history of Israel to describe the promise that God made to King

3. On the creation symbolism of Solomon's temple, see G. K. Beale, *The Temple and the Church's Mission: A Biblical Theology of the Temple* (Downers Grove, IL: InterVarsity, 2004), 66–86.
4. See Donald J. Wiseman, *1 & 2 Kings: An Introduction and Commentary*, Tyndale Old Testament Commentaries (Leicester: Inter-Varsity, 1993), 114; Paul R. House, *1, 2 Kings*, The New American Commentary (Nashville: Broadman & Holman, 1995), 133.

David and then later fulfilled for his son Solomon—the promise to establish his throne (e.g., 2 Sam. 7:12–13; 1 Kings 2:12, 24). Thus Jachin is closely associated with God's firmly establishing David's throne. To call a pillar by this name is "to encapsulate Yahweh's promise that David's dynasty would be the vehicle through which he would bring his kingdom on earth."[5] To say "Jachin" is really another way of saying, "Thy kingdom come." It is to say, "He will establish" and mean that God will establish his royal throne.

The name Boaz may have had a more personal reference, for the biblical Boaz married Ruth and became the great-grandfather of King David (see Ruth 4:13–22). But the meaning of the name Boaz also has an important signification: it means "it is strong," or "by him he is mighty."[6] Like Jachin, therefore, the name Boaz connotes the strength and stability of a huge pillar, while at the same time testifying that God would establish his kingdom on earth through the royal family of David.

We can take this idea a step further by comparing 1 Kings 7 with one of the royal psalms of David. Psalm 21 begins and ends with "boaz." The key word in both the first and the last verse of the psalm is the same word for "strength" that Solomon used to name his pillar. So it is at least possible—maybe even probable—that Boaz was intended to remind people of this psalm. Something similar happens when someone says, "We the people": a single word or phrase calls to mind a longer statement, in this case the Preamble to the U.S. Constitution. If we want to understand the full meaning of the pillar Boaz, therefore, we need to sing David's psalm: "O LORD, in your *strength* the king rejoices. . . . Be exalted, O LORD, in your *strength*!" (Ps. 21:1, 13).

What is the pillar of your life? The pillars of Solomon's temple were Jachin and Boaz—the strength of God himself, and the stability of the king who sat on his throne. Our pillar is (or ought to be) Jesus Christ, the greater Solomon and the royal Son of David who now rules as the King of God's kingdom. By faith in Christ, the believer's life has become the temple of the Holy Spirit, a dwelling place for the living God. The pillar of that inner temple is Jesus Christ. He is our pillar when everything else in life seems to give way. He is our pillar of strength when we feel weak, the pillar of mercy when we need forgiveness, the pillar of comfort when we suffer loss and grief, and the pillar

5. Dale Ralph Davis, *The Wisdom and the Folly: An Exposition of the Book of First Kings* (Fearn, Ross-shire: Christian Focus, 2002), 74.
6. See Wiseman, *1 & 2 Kings*, 114; House, *1, 2 Kings*, 133.

of hope when we feel as though we have missed our chance in life and do not have much of a future.

When Jesus Christ is the pillar of our souls, then whatever trouble may come, we are able to say, "My flesh and my heart may fail, but God is the strength of my heart and my portion forever" (Ps. 73:26). By God's strength we will persevere through all the troubles of life until the day when Jesus fulfills this promise for us in glory: "I will make him a pillar in the temple of my God" (Rev. 3:12).

THE CLEANSING FONT

The second item that Hiram made for Solomon's temple was an enormous basin:

> Then he made the sea of cast metal. It was round, ten cubits from brim to brim, and five cubits high, and a line of thirty cubits measured its circumference. Under its brim were gourds, for ten cubits, compassing the sea all around. The gourds were in two rows, cast with it when it was cast. It stood on twelve oxen, three facing north, three facing west, three facing south, and three facing east. The sea was set on them, and all their rear parts were inward. Its thickness was a handbreadth, and its brim was made like the brim of a cup, like the flower of a lily. It held two thousand baths. (1 Kings 7:23–26)

This beautiful bronze sea (as it was called) was one of ancient Israel's great technical achievements. Anyone who knows the history of Philadelphia's famous Liberty Bell, which was cast and then recast, knows how hard it is to fabricate a large metal object, especially one with a curved edge. The bronze basin in Solomon's temple was much larger than the Liberty Bell, with a circumference of forty-five feet. It was also designed to hold a huge quantity of water: as much as ten thousand gallons. No wonder people called it "the sea"!

Hiram decorated the sea of bronze with gourds and fashioned its lip in the shape of a lily. He also made a stand for the sea, so that it rested on the backs of twelve metal oxen, three on each side, looking out toward the four points of the compass. Some scholars have worried that the oxen were a sign of Baal worship, but it seems more likely that they stood for the twelve tribes of Israel, and thus did not represent any deity at all.

The bronze basin may have reminded the people of God of their own encounter with the sea. When they made their famous exodus from Egypt, the Israelites walked through the Red Sea on dry land, while Pharaoh's chariots and horsemen were lost at sea (see Ex. 14). We can give a similar testimony, for we too have passed through a symbolical sea. For believers in Christ, baptism is a sacramental deliverance from death—a saving passage through water (see 1 Cor. 10:1–4; 1 Peter 3:20–21).

The water may also have represented the peace of God controlling the chaotic troubles of a fallen world. The sea was a threatening force for people in ancient times, as it still is today, and thus it represented the forces of chaos. We find similar imagery elsewhere in the Bible, where the sea is sometimes regarded as an ominous, threatening force. "Its waters roar and form," wrote the psalmist; "the mountains tremble at its swelling" (Ps. 46:3). Or consider the desperate prayer of Jonah: "You cast me into the deep, into the heart of the seas, and the flood surrounded me; all your waves and your billows passed over me" (Jonah 2:3).

But if our God is Lord of the sea, then he is able to bring its waves under his control: "You rule the raging of the sea; when its waves rise, you still them" (Ps. 89:9). "Mightier than the thunders of many waters, mightier than the waves of the sea, the LORD on high is mighty!" (Ps. 93:4). The mighty power of God was on display at Solomon's temple, where a large volume of water was symbolically stilled. The chaos of the sea was kept in its place by a bronze basin, much the way that God keeps the waters of the sea within boundaries of land.

The same is true for our own troubles in life. No matter how chaotic things may seem, God is still in control and wants to furnish us with inner peace. Rather than getting thrown around by all kinds of turmoil, tossed up and down in an ocean of anxiety, we can trust our Savior to calm the trouble of our worried thoughts. Knowing that Jesus is commander of the winds and the waves, who stilled the storm on the Sea of Galilee (see Luke 8:25), we are able to heed the apostolic command: "let the peace of Christ rule in your hearts" (Col. 3:15).

One further aspect of the sea's symbolism is perhaps the most important of all: the bronze basin was a font for cleansing. According to Exodus 30, God told Moses to make a similar (albeit smaller) basin for the tabernacle in the wilderness—"a basin of bronze, with its stand of bronze, for washing"

(Ex. 30:18). The water in this bronze basin consecrated Aaron and his sons as they performed their priestly duties: "When they go into the tent of meeting, or when they come near the altar to minister, to burn a food offering to the LORD, they shall wash with water, so that they may not die. They shall wash their hands and their feet, so that they may not die. It shall be a statute forever to them, even to him and to his offspring throughout their generations" (Ex. 30:20–21; cf. 40:30–32).

The bronze sea that Solomon built enabled Israel's priests to keep this commandment. So did the ten smaller basins that the king put in his temple: "And he made ten basins of bronze. Each basin held forty baths, each basin measured four cubits, and there was a basin for each of the ten stands. And he set the stands, five on the south side of the house, and five on the north side of the house. And he set the sea at the southeast corner of the house" (1 Kings 7:38–39).

These identical basins were not as large as the great bronze sea, but they each held more than two hundred gallons of water. Solomon set these bronze basins on ten ornate, movable trolleys, as described in the Bible:

He also made the stands of bronze. Each stand was four cubits long, four cubits wide, and three cubits high. This was the construction of the stands: they had panels, and the panels were set in the frames, and on the panels that were set in the frames were lions, oxen, and cherubim. On the frames, both above and below the lions and oxen, there were wreaths of beveled work. Moreover, each stand had four bronze wheels and axles of bronze, and at the four corners were supports for a basin. The supports were cast with wreaths at the side of each. Its opening was within a crown that projected upward one cubit. Its opening was round, as a pedestal is made, a cubit and a half deep. At its opening there were carvings, and its panels were square, not round. And the four wheels were underneath the panels. The axles of the wheels were of one piece with the stands, and the height of a wheel was a cubit and a half. The wheels were made like a chariot wheel; their axles, their rims, their spokes, and their hubs were all cast. There were four supports at the four corners of each stand. The supports were of one piece with the stands. And on the top of the stand there was a round band half a cubit high; and on the top of the stand its stays and its panels were of one piece with it. And on the surfaces of its stays and on its panels, he carved cherubim, lions, and palm trees, according to the space of each, with wreaths all around. After this manner he made the ten stands. All of them were cast alike, of the same measure and the same form. (1 Kings 7:27–37)

The huge quantity of water in all these basins shows that God has a pervasive concern for personal holiness. At the temple, cleanliness really was "next to godliness," because in order to perform their sacred duties, Solomon's priests had to keep themselves ceremonially pure through ritual cleansing. We know from Chronicles that the ten side basins "were to rinse off what was used for the burnt offering, and the sea was for the priests to wash in" (2 Chron. 4:6). So in order to do their kingdom work at the temple of God, both the priests and their sacrifices needed to be washed in water. First they washed themselves (e.g., Lev. 16:4), but they also washed the animals they presented as clean burnt offerings to God.

God's priests still need cleansing today, except that there are two major differences. The first difference is that now *all* God's people are priests. In the days of Solomon only the Levites performed a priestly ministry, but today God has a whole kingdom of priests. Every believer in Jesus Christ has been called into the holy service of God. God is building us into "a spiritual house, to be a holy priesthood, to offer spiritual sacrifices acceptable to God through Jesus Christ" (1 Peter 2:5). Now that atonement has been made for our sins through Christ's sacrifice on the cross, there is no further need for us to offer God any animal sacrifices. But we do offer him the sacrifice of our praise, with a life given for his holy service. Our priestly duty is to proclaim the gospel to the world and to pray for people who need God's saving grace.

In order to offer God service that is truly holy, we must be clean, which brings us to a second major difference between Solomon's temple and the church of Jesus Christ. The cleansing at the temple was only skin deep; it washed the outside of a priest's body. But now that we have become the temple of the Holy Spirit—the place where God dwells—the cleansing takes place right inside us. The various washings that went on at the temple could not "perfect the conscience of the worshiper" (Heb. 9:9). But now the great sea of God's cleansing grace is furnished to our souls. Through faith in Christ, the Holy Spirit makes our hearts clean from sin.

We need this cleansing every day—not just the day we come to Christ, but every day we sin and need to be forgiven. God declares that "the blood of Jesus his Son cleanses us from all sin" (1 John 1:7). We receive this cleansing the very moment that we trust in Christ for our salvation. The blood that Jesus shed on the cross gives us spiritual cleansing from all the guilty stains of our sin. Yet we continue to sin, and therefore we continue to need God's cleansing, not as a matter of our salvation, but as part of the holy work of the Spirit in making us holy for the service of God. God has promised that the blood of Christ will "purify our conscience from dead works to serve the living God" (Heb. 9:14).

When Christians sin, we sometimes start to doubt whether God can still accept our service. But whenever we are tempted by these doubts, we need to remember the furniture God has provided for our souls. As often as we sin, there is cleansing for our forgiveness in the font of God's grace: "If we confess our sins, he is faithful and just to forgive us our sins and to cleanse us from all unrighteousness" (1 John 1:9). Knowing the promise of forgiveness encourages and enables us to obey the Bible's command for our sanctification: "Since we have these promises, beloved, let us cleanse ourselves from every defilement of body and spirit, bringing holiness to completion in the fear of God" (2 Cor. 7:1).

THE WELL-FURNISHED SOUL

The pillars of strength and the sea of cleansing were the biggest objects that Hiram made for Solomon's temple, but he also made many smaller items of equal spiritual importance. In its description of his handiwork, the Bible says that "Hiram also made the pots, the shovels, and the basins" (1 Kings 7:40). Then the Bible offers a summary of his craftsmanship:

> So Hiram finished all the work that he did for King Solomon on the house of the LORD: the two pillars, the two bowls of the capitals that were on the tops of the pillars, and the two latticeworks to cover the two bowls of the capitals that were on the tops of the pillars; and the four hundred pomegranates for the two latticeworks, two rows of pomegranates for each latticework, to cover the two bowls of the capitals that were on the pillars; the ten stands, and the ten basins on the stands; and the one sea, and the twelve oxen underneath the sea. (1 Kings 7:40–44; cf. 2 Chron. 4:11–15)

These temple furnishings were all made of bronze—not a precious metal, but a valuable and functional one. The Bible describes where and how these items were made: "Now the pots, the shovels, and the basins, all these vessels in the house of the LORD, which Hiram made for King Solomon, were of burnished bronze. In the plain of the Jordan the king cast them, in the clay ground between Succoth and Zarethan" (1 Kings 7:45–46; 2 Chron. 4:16–17). The clay was used to make the molds into which the bronze was cast. Thus the furniture for Solomon's temple was made much the same way that man himself was created: out of the ground. Given the large number of sacred articles that Solomon used to furnish his temple, perhaps it is not surprising that they were never weighed: "And Solomon left all the vessels unweighed, because there were so many of them; the weight of the bronze was not ascertained" (1 Kings 7:47; cf. 2 Chron. 4:18).

The pots and shovels mentioned in verses 40 and 45, as well as the dishes and tongs mentioned in verse 49, were patterned after similar utensils that Moses made for the tabernacle in the wilderness (see Ex. 27:3). They were used in connection with offering various sacrifices—for shoveling ashes, spreading incense, carrying hot coals, and sprinkling sacrificial blood, as the high priest did on the Day of Atonement (Lev. 16:11–19). The sacred vessels in Solomon's temple were part of the Old Testament system of sacrifice.

We too are called to a life of sacrifice—not of our animals or our grain, but of our very selves. Jesus Christ has offered himself as the atoning sacrifice for our sins. In joyful response, we now offer everything we are and have back to God. Somewhere in the sacred interior of our souls, we tell Jesus that we are totally available for his service, in whatever way our lives can be used for his glory: giving, praying, singing, teaching, organizing, discipling, or simply showing up and caring for people in need. By the mercy of God, we present ourselves "as a living sacrifice, holy and acceptable to God, which is [our] spiritual worship" (Rom. 12:1).

In addition to this "liturgical equipment," as one commentator calls it,[7]

Solomon made all the vessels that were in the house of the LORD: the golden altar, the golden table for the bread of the Presence, the lampstands of pure gold, five on the south side and five on the north, before the inner sanctuary; the flowers, the lamps, and the tongs, of gold; the cups, snuffers, basins, dishes for incense, and fire pans, of pure gold; and the sockets of gold, for the doors of the innermost part of the house, the Most Holy Place, and for

7. Davis, *The Wisdom and the Folly*, 76.

the doors of the nave of the temple. (1 Kings 7:48–50; cf. 2 Sam. 8:10–12; 2 Chron. 4:19–22)

These items were made of gold, not bronze, to show the relative holiness of their function and their closer proximity to the presence of God. Though some have accused Solomon of "conspicuous consumption" in the fabrication of these sacred objects,[8] it was right and good for him to lavish extravagant care on the temple interior, and to do so at his own personal expense (see 1 Chron. 29:3). Nothing we offer could ever be too good for God, and Solomon was wise to give in proportion to the relative worth of the recipient of his gifts. We too should give our first and our best to God.

The golden altar represented the life of prayer. We know from Exodus 30 that this altar was used in offering incense (Ex. 30:1, 7–8). When a priest burned incense on the golden altar, he was standing directly in front of the ark of the covenant (Ex. 30:6). In effect, he was approaching the mercy seat—the place where God hears and answers prayer. As the incense rose from the altar, it ascended to heaven with his prayers. In the words of King David, referring to the worship of Israel's priests, "Let my prayer be counted as incense before you, and the lifting up of my hands as the evening sacrifice!" (Ps. 141:2; cf. Rev. 5:8; 8:3–4).

God has furnished us with a golden altar for prayer in the power of the Holy Spirit. Jesus said that his temple should be called a house of prayer (see Matt. 21:13). If our souls have become his temple by the indwelling of the Holy Spirit, then our lives should be full of prayer. Every time we receive any blessing from God—even something as simple as a good meal—our prayers of thanksgiving should rise like sacred incense. Every time we see someone in need, our petitions of intercession should be lifted up like the arms of a holy priest. Every time we are feeling anxious or guilty, we should ask God to send his merciful help from heaven. In this way, we make our heart an altar for prayer.

Next to the golden altar was "the golden table for the bread of the Presence" (1 Kings 7:48; cf. Ex. 25:23–30). Every week the priests put twelve loaves of sacred bread on this golden table, presumably to represent the twelve tribes of Israel. The bread was a reminder of God's provision. The same God who

8. Walter Brueggemann, *1 & 2 Kings*, Smyth & Helwys Bible Commentary (Macon, GA: Smyth & Hylwys, 2000), 102.

gave his children manna in the wilderness continued to provide life-giving bread. The bread was also a sign of God's presence, and of his desire to have fellowship with his people. Each week the priests would eat this sacred bread in the presence of the Lord (see Lev. 24:9), sharing table fellowship with their covenant God.[9]

The table of bread is yet another reminder of the way God furnishes our souls with his grace, for God still gives bread to his people. Jesus said that he himself is "the bread of life," the true bread that "comes down from heaven and gives life to the world" (John 6:33, 35). If we have received Jesus by faith, our souls will never go hungry again. In the same way that bread gives us physical life, Jesus gives us spiritual life forever. We are reminded of this every time we eat the daily bread we pray for God to provide (see Matt. 11), or eat the sacramental bread of the Lord's Supper, where Jesus feeds our souls with the bread of his grace.

Finally, every well-furnished home needs light. Thus Solomon's temple was illuminated by the light from ten golden lampstands. The tabernacle in the wilderness had only one lampstand (see Ex. 25:31–40), but the temple was bigger, so Solomon installed five lampstands along each wall, filling the sanctuary with light. Their function was symbolical as well as practical. As Israel's priests entered the holy house of God, the golden lampstands reminded them of the lights that God put in the heavens when he created the world. It also reminded them that God is the true source of all light. "The LORD is my light" (Ps. 27:1), wrote King David, and in his light "we see light" (Ps. 36:9). In other words, God is the light that illuminates every other source of light in the entire universe, whether physical or spiritual.

Now we see the light of God in the person of Jesus Christ. The same Jesus who said that he was the bread of life also said that he was the light of the world (John 8:12). Jesus Christ is the true light who enlightens everyone— the light that has come into this dark world for our salvation (John 1:9). When we put our trust in him, the light of God starts to illuminate every dark corner of our lives. Jesus gives us the light that shows us the truth, uncovers our sin, reveals the right path for us to take in life, and makes us shine for God in a dark world.

9. August H. Konkel, *1 & 2 Kings*, NIV Application Commentary (Grand Rapids: Zondervan, 2006), 145.

Your Heart, Christ's Home

This is the way that God wants to furnish our souls: with stability like mighty pillars, with cleansing grace like a huge font, with prayer like rising incense, with spiritual food like holy bread, and with shining light like a sanctuary full of holy candles.

Is your soul this well furnished? If so, then use the furniture that God has given you, making it part of everyday life. When life seems to be falling apart, and you are not sure how much longer you can stand, remember that Jesus Christ is your pillar of strength. When you are defeated by sin and feeling so unworthy that you doubt there is anything you can do for God, remember that the blood of Christ purifies you from all sin. Use the spiritual furniture that God has given you every day. Go to the sweet altar of prayer. Feed on the bread of God. Live by the light of his Word.

But if God is not living in your soul already, then understand that your soul can be fully furnished today. You do not have to wait for delivery. No one needs to travel across the country to bring it to you. God the Father in heaven will give you all the spiritual furniture you need right now, through faith in Jesus Christ. He will give you his stability, his cleansing, his fellowship in prayer, his food for your soul, and his light for direction in life. Without God, life will always be empty. But when Jesus makes his home in your heart, he will furnish you with everything you need.

15

THE ARK OF THE COVENANT AND THE GLORY

1 Kings 8:1–11

*Then Solomon assembled the elders of Israel and all the heads
of the tribes, the leaders of the fathers' houses of the people of
Israel, before King Solomon in Jerusalem, to bring up the ark of
the covenant of the LORD out of the city of David, which is Zion.*
(1 Kings 8:1)

W ithout question and beyond all doubt, it was the most extraordinary worship service that any of them had ever witnessed.
Indeed, it may have been the most awesome, spine-tingling,
goose-bump-inducing worship that any group of human beings had ever
offered to the living God.

Try to imagine the scene, as described in 2 Chronicles 5. For an entire
week the whole nation of Israel had gathered around the temple of God at
the top of Mount Zion. As the celebration came to its climax, King Solomon
appeared, in all his glory, and with him the leaders of his people. As the
people watched, myriads of priests came streaming out of the temple. These
men had consecrated themselves for the service of God by washing in the

great bronze basin that stood near the Holy Place—the sea of cleansing—and by wearing fine linen. Singers in the Levitical choir and various instrumentalists stood outside the temple with their harps and lyres and cymbals, not to mention 120 trumpets—it was the orchestra of the living God.

On cue, all these musicians burst into praise. With one voice they offered a melody of thanksgiving to God. Their musical text was a famous refrain from King David: "For he is good, for his steadfast love endures forever" (2 Chron. 5:13; cf. Ps. 136). As the people worshiped, glory came down to fill Solomon's temple with holy smoke.

At the center of this liturgical extravaganza was the only thing that could ever be worthy of so much praise: the holy presence of the living God. The ark of the covenant was coming home to the house of God. With the ark, the temple would become what Solomon had built it to become: not just a beautiful building, but the center of his people's worship, the earthly dwelling place for the true and living God.

GOD DESERVES EVERYONE'S PRAISE

The same events are described a little less dramatically in 1 Kings 8. Here we do not read anything about singing psalms or blowing trumpets, but we do read about the sacred ark of God's holy covenant, and therefore we learn about the character of God and what it means to have a relationship with him by faith.

First Kings 7 ends by saying that "all the work that King Solomon did on the house of the LORD was finished. And Solomon brought in the things that David his father had dedicated, the silver, the gold, and the vessels, and stored them in the treasuries of the house of the LORD" (1 Kings 7:51). Of all the furniture that Solomon brought into God's temple, the most important—by far—was the sacred box that represented the very presence of God. It was called the ark of the *covenant* because of its contents: "There was nothing in the ark except the two tablets of stone that Moses put there at Horeb, where the LORD made a covenant with the people of Israel, when they came out of the land of Egypt" (1 Kings 8:9). The same covenant that Moses brought down from the mountain (see Ex. 25:16; 40:20; Deut. 10:1–5)—with all its promises and commands—was still inside the ark. This served as an ongoing reminder of God's love for his people, and of their obligation to keep his

187

holy law. As long as the ark was in Jerusalem, the covenant God was with his covenant people.

To bring the ark into the temple, Solomon first had to go and get it: "Then Solomon assembled the elders of Israel and all the heads of the tribes, the leaders of the father's houses of the people of Israel, before King Solomon in Jerusalem, to bring up the ark of the covenant of the LORD out of the city of David, which is Zion" (1 Kings 8:1).

To understand where the ark was, and why, it helps to know more about its history. The ark of the covenant was made by Bezalel, who was anointed by the Holy Spirit to serve as Israel's master craftsman in the days of Moses (see Ex. 37:1–9). For forty years, the Israelites carried the ark with them in the wilderness as they wandered from place to place. Whenever and wherever they camped, they would put the ark inside the tabernacle, which was the portable dwelling place of God.

When the Israelites finally entered the Promised Land, the ark of the covenant led the way (see Josh. 3:14–17). Eventually they set up the tabernacle in Shiloh, which for many years was the place where Israel held its solemn assemblies for worship (Josh. 18:1). At some point the tabernacle was moved to Gibeon (see 2 Chron. 1:3), while on its return, the ark was housed separately in Kiriath Jearim. However, King David wanted the ark closer to Jerusalem, so he organized a huge procession to bring it to the city by oxcart. This was a memorable trip, because at a certain point when the oxen stumbled, a man named Uzzah reached out to touch the ark and died instantly. When David realized how holy the ark was, and how dangerous it could be, he decided not to take it to Jerusalem after all, but to leave it in the house of Obed-edom. But God blessed Obed-edom, and eventually the king decided to bring the ark all the way up to Jerusalem, with great rejoicing (2 Sam. 6:1–15). Just as the ark had blessed Obed-edom's house, so David wanted the ark to bless his house in Jerusalem.

By the time Solomon built his temple, therefore, the ark of the covenant was already in Jerusalem. It was not up on the Temple Mount, but somewhere lower down the mountain, in a tent that David had pitched for it (see 2 Sam. 6:17; 2 Chron. 1:4). In fact, Solomon offered sacrifices before the ark the night he had his famous dream and received the precious gift of wisdom from God.

Now it was time to bring the ark all the way up the mountain. So King Solomon called a national assembly for worship, from which we learn that our God deserves everyone's praise: "And all the men of Israel assembled to King Solomon at the feast in the month Ethanim, which is the seventh month. And all the elders of Israel came, and the priests took up the ark. And they brought up the ark of the LORD, the tent of meeting, and all the holy vessels that were in the tent; the priests and the Levites brought them up" (1 Kings 8:2–4).

The timing of this festival seems to be significant. Solomon finished building a house for God in the eighth month (1 Kings 6:38). The ark was brought up in the seventh month, which presumably means that the temple was dedicated shortly before it was finished, or else (and this seems more likely) eleven months later, which would give enough time to plan a suitable celebration.[1] Since it took place in the seventh month of the year, the celebration was scheduled to coincide with the Feast of Tabernacles.

The symbolism of this schedule would not have been lost on anyone in Israel, for during the Feast of Tabernacles people lived in tents and other temporary shelters as a way of remembering God's faithfulness to them during the years they wandered through the wilderness. But now that their wandering days were over and they had a more permanent place to live, it was time for God to have a dwelling place too. Although a tabernacle was suitable for the wilderness, it was time for God to come home and live with his people in the land, as he had promised (see Deut. 12:11).

This divine homecoming demanded the presence of everyone in Israel, starting with the king himself. Thus Solomon gathered all the elders of Israel—the men who provided spiritual leadership for the people of God. Then he summoned the leaders of the various tribes in Israel, as well as the fathers of all the households. The priests were also there, and the Levites, carrying the ark and the sacred utensils that were used for worship and sacrifice, in keeping with the law of God (see Num. 4).

Here we observe an important principle of spiritual leadership: certain men are called to lead people in the worship of God. Today this is one of the

1. For a helpful summary of the issues surrounding the date when Solomon dedicated his temple, see Paul R. House, *1, 2 Kings*, The New American Commentary (Nashville: Broadman & Holman, 1995), 137.

responsibilities of elders in the church. The first exercise of their spiritual authority is to fulfill their own chief purpose in life, which is to glorify God and to enjoy him forever. As they worship God, both privately and publicly, the elders inspire other people to worship God as well. When people see men they respect captivated by the gospel of Jesus Christ and moved to joy in the presence of the Holy Spirit, they are drawn to join in the worship of God. Although one sometimes sees churches led largely by women, lacking a strong male presence, a church where men worship God will almost always be full of women and children. This has always been God's plan for the praise of his people.

The same thing happens in the life of a family, where fathers are responsible before God for the worship of their households. As a man listens to the voice of God speaking in Scripture and talks to God in prayer, he sets his heart toward eternity, and by the grace of God, his children will follow. Who is sufficient for these things, yet who can neglect them? Keep family worship simple. Read a short Bible passage after dinner. Sing the first verse of a familiar hymn. Pray as a household at bedtime. Whatever else a man may do in life, he should lead by example in the worship of God.

Israel enjoyed this kind of leadership under Solomon, with wonderful results. According to verse 2, "all the men of Israel" assembled for the worship of God, but verse 5 includes the women and children: "all the congregation of Israel." This was as it should be, for God deserves everyone's praise. He is the Maker of the entire universe and the Lord of all grace. Therefore, everyone should praise him: men and women, young and old, rich and poor, natives and foreigners—there is not one single person who should not give praise to God.

We should praise him too. In the days of Solomon, God was present at the ark of the covenant; now he is present with us in the person of his Son and by the power of his Spirit. Jesus said that anytime as many as two or three people gather in his name, he is right there with us (Matt. 18:20). Therefore, every time we worship we experience something more amazing than the ark of the covenant: the very presence of God!

This is one of the reasons why public worship is such a priority for us: just as Solomon summoned the nation of Israel to the mountaintop, we too have been invited to meet with the living God. Everyone should praise him, answering the summons and obeying the command we are given in the closing verse of the final psalm, "Let everything that has breath praise the LORD!" (Ps. 150:6).

GOD DEMANDS EVERY SACRIFICE

The God who deserves everyone's praise also demands every sacrifice. We see this in the countless offerings people made as the ark ascended the Temple Mount: "And King Solomon and all the congregation of Israel, who had assembled before him, were with him before the ark, sacrificing so many sheep and oxen that they could not be counted or numbered" (1 Kings 8:5).

This is reminiscent of something that happened when David first brought the ark up to Jerusalem: "When those who bore the ark of the LORD had gone six steps, he sacrificed an ox and a fattened animal" (2 Sam. 6:13). It must have been a slow journey: every six steps the priests leading the sacred procession would stop, put down the ark, and make another bloody sacrifice. Solomon did something similar. Whether he did it every six steps or not, he and his people offered so many sacrifices that people lost track of them all. It seems almost strange in a book that does so much counting and numbering (e.g., 1 Kings 8:63), but Solomon made more sacrifices than anyone could count.

These sacrifices were offered with thanksgiving to God, and presumably also as atonement for sin, which was only proper. The people were in the presence of God, signified by the ark of the covenant. In order for unholy people to stand in the presence of a holy God, atonement must be made for their sin. Since there is no forgiveness of sins without the shedding of blood (see Heb. 9:22), this atonement had to be paid in blood, in this case by animals serving as substitutes for the people of God. These animals belonged to God because they were made by him, and in their deaths they glorified their Creator. Only an infinitely worthy deity could ever demand such a costly sacrifice, but demand it he did. So the people reverently and thankfully offered him countless sacrifices, paid in blood.

Animal sacrifices were especially appropriate to make at the ark of the covenant, which contained the tablets of God's law and served as the place where Israel made its annual atonement for sin. Although many offerings were made throughout the year—various sacrifices for sin and many sacrifices of thanksgiving—one offering was the most important of all: the blood sacrifice of atonement that was sprinkled on the ark of the covenant. Every year on the Day of Atonement, the high priest would make an atoning sacrifice for all the sins of God's people (see Lev. 16). This took place during the Feast of Tabernacles, which as we have seen is when Solomon dedicated his temple. On the Day of Atonement, Israel's high priest would take the blood from that sacrifice into the Holy of Holies and sprinkle it on the atonement cover of the ark, also known as the mercy seat (Lev. 16:15–16; cf. Ex. 25:17–22). This made propitiation for God's people. It acknowledged the guilt of their sin, paid the price for their atonement, and turned away the wrath of God.

The Day of Atonement helped prepare God's people for a Savior. The prophets always said that one day a Savior would come to make the perfect sacrifice that God demanded for sin, offering his life as one atonement for many sinners (Isa. 53:3–12). Instead of making countless sacrifices, the Savior would pay for all our sins in a single day (Zech. 3:9). Jesus made this saving sacrifice on the cross. As the Scripture says, "he has appeared once for all at the end of the ages to put away sin by the sacrifice of himself" (Heb. 9:26). This is the gospel of our salvation, in which God provides the sacrifice that God demands. Jesus the Son of God has offered himself as the atonement for our sin.

As far as our salvation is concerned, no further sacrifice is needed. Since God's demand has been fully satisfied through the cross, there is no further sacrifice that we must or even can make for our sins. All that is left to give back to God is the offering of our praise. These sacrifices of our thanksgiving should be like the sacrifices Solomon made for the ark of the covenant: more than anyone can count. If God has the right to demand any sacrifice, then we should sing him countless hymns of praise, offer him countless prayers of thanksgiving, render him countless gifts of money for kingdom work, and serve him with countless deeds of love and mercy.

Robert Coleman tells a story that illustrates the kind of sacrifice God calls us to make in his service. A little boy's sister needed a blood transfusion. She was suffering from the same disease that the boy himself had survived two years earlier. The doctor explained that her only chance of recovery was to receive a blood transfusion from someone else who had conquered the same disease. Since the two children shared the same rare blood type, her brother was the ideal donor.

"Would you give your blood to Mary?" the doctor asked. Johnny hesitated at first, but with his lower lip trembling finally he said, "Sure, for my sister."

Soon the children were wheeled into the hospital room—Mary, pale and thin; Johnny, robust and healthy. Neither one of them spoke, but when their eyes met, Johnny grinned. His smile faded as the nurse inserted the needle into his arm and he watched the blood flow through the tube. When the ordeal was almost over, Johnny's shaky voice broke the silence. "Doctor," he said, "when do I die?"

Only then did the doctor realize why Johnny had hesitated before agreeing to donate his blood: he thought the doctor was asking for all of it! Still, out of love for his sister, he was willing to give it.[2]

Someday God may demand our lifeblood in his service. If he did, he would certainly deserve it. After all, his Son has given his lifeblood for us. Yet, thankfully, most of the sacrifices God asks us to give are much smaller: our love, worship, time, money, comfort, dreams, and desires. We should give Jesus all this and much more, until eventually we lose track of all the sacrifices we have made for the Savior who has given everything to us. Perhaps eventually we will get to the place in life that David Livingstone finally reached. After a life of making costly sacrifices for gospel work, the famous missionary and explorer told an audience at Cambridge University: "I never made a sacrifice. We ought not to talk of 'sacrifice' when we remember the great sacrifice which He made who left His Father's throne on high to give Himself up for us."[3]

God Dwells in Awesome Holiness

The ark of the covenant was designed to show that the God who deserves everyone's praise and demands every sacrifice dwells in awesome holiness. The holiness of the ark was evident from its history. One need only consider the tragic deaths of Nadab, Abihu, and Uzzah (see Lev. 10; 2 Sam. 6:6–7) or the terrible plagues that befell the Philistines when they stole the ark (1 Sam. 5–6) to know that the ark was too dangerous to touch, so closely was it associated with the holiness of God.

2. The story comes from Robert Coleman, *Written in Blood*, as summarized in *750 Engaging Illustrations for Preachers, Teachers, and Writers*, ed. Craig Brian Larson (Grand Rapids: Baker, 2002), 74.

3. David Livingstone, speaking at Cambridge University (December 4, 1857); see John Piper, *Desiring God: Meditations of a Christian Hedonist* (Sisters, OR: Multnomah, 2003), 243.

Appropriately enough, the ark of the covenant was put in a holy place: "Then the priests brought the ark of the covenant of the Lord to its place in the inner sanctuary of the house, in the Most Holy Place, underneath the wings of the cherubim" (1 Kings 8:6). This sacred chamber, also known as the Holy of Holies, was made in the shape of a perfect cube and covered with pure gold (1 Kings 6:19–22). This location showed how holy the ark was: it belonged to the inner sanctum, the very place where God would establish his earthly presence.

The Holy of Holies was the throne room of God—an earthly copy of the place where God rules in heaven (see Heb. 9:24). In effect, the ark was God's throne, or else the footstool for God's throne. One scholar calls it "the transportable throne of Yahweh."[4] In the books of Samuel, for example, the ark of the covenant is described as the place where God is enthroned (1 Sam. 4:4; 2 Sam. 6:2).

To be more specific, the ark of the covenant is the place where God "sits enthroned above the cherubim" (1 Chron. 13:6; cf. Ps. 80:1). Cherubim are holy angels who are constantly employed in the holy worship and sacred service of God. We have encountered them several times before, in the descriptions of the carvings in Solomon's temple (1 Kings 6:23–29, 35). Here we meet them again, resting on top of the ark of the covenant: "For the cherubim spread out their wings over the place of the ark, so that the cherubim overshadowed the ark and its poles. And the poles were so long that the ends of the poles were seen from the Holy Place before the inner sanctuary; but they could not be seen from outside. And they are there to this day" (1 Kings 8:7–8).

It is not entirely clear exactly where these poles were positioned. Possibly they poked against the curtain to the Holy of Holies, or perhaps their tips were barely visible at the edges of the curtain. In any case, the poles added to the sense of mystery surrounding the sacred ark. The priests who served at the temple never saw the ark of the covenant, but they could see the poles that were used to carry it, and thus they knew that the ark was still inside, shrouded in holy mystery.

The cherubim conveyed an even greater sense of God's holiness. Since cherubim serve as the sentinels of God's throne room in heaven, the cherubim

4. Peter Leithart, *1 & 2 Kings*, Brazos Theological Commentary on the Bible (Grand Rapids: Brazos, 2006), 67.

in the temple signified the ark as a place of enthronement. They also testified to God's holiness. Unfallen angels are utterly without sin, and thus they are perfectly holy in all their actions, thoughts, and words. The cherubim constantly bear witness to the holiness of God. The psalmist proclaims that God "sits enthroned upon the cherubim" and then gives this command: "Exalt the LORD our God; worship at his footstool! Holy is he!" (Ps. 99:1, 5).

Whenever we come into the presence of God for worship, we should honor him for his holiness. We should set him apart as the one and only God. We should recognize his supremely perfect being. We should bow before him as the holy, holy, holy God.

If we understand that God is everywhere and that Jesus is with us wherever we go, then everything in life will be suffused with a sense of divine holiness. The same God who is adored by angels and dwells in awesome majesty is also living in us by the Holy Spirit, making our hearts a sacred space. Therefore, anywhere a believer stands is holy ground—even in places of darkness and sin. We carry God's glory with us wherever we go. Furthermore, every conversation we have is a holy opportunity that the Spirit can use to help us bear witness to the gospel of the crucified and risen Christ. This is why the Bible calls every Christian a "saint," which literally means a "holy one" (e.g., Eph. 1:18): we are always near to the presence of a holy God.

GOD DESCENDS IN UNAPPROACHABLE GLORY

This brings us to the most dramatic moment in the story of Solomon and the ark of the covenant: the moment when God descended in unapproachable glory. The whole worship service had been spectacular, with dozens of trumpets blaring, hundreds of priests singing in unison, and thousands of people celebrating the glory of the house of God. But shortly after the priests carried the ark into the temple, they came running back out: "And when the priests came out of the Holy Place, a cloud filled the house of the LORD, so that the priests could not stand to minister because of the cloud, for the glory of the LORD filled the house of the LORD" (1 Kings 8:10–11).

Something similar happened when Moses entered the tabernacle. The moment he finished making a house for God, the glory came down. As we read at the end of Exodus, "Then the cloud covered the tent of meeting, and the glory of the LORD filled the tabernacle. And Moses was not able to enter the tent of meeting because the cloud settled on it, and the glory of the LORD filled the tabernacle" (Ex. 40:34–35).

As it was in the days of Moses, so it was in the days of Solomon: when God first entered the house, his presence was so glorious that the priests could not even stay inside long enough to do their priestly duty! Here we encounter a mysterious irony, or perhaps an ironic mystery. The temple was the one place on earth where people could go and meet with God, through the ministry of a priest. But when the temple was finally open for business, no one could enter because God was too glorious! The true and living God cannot be put in a box, even a box as beautiful as Solomon's temple.

What people saw that day was a *theophany*—a visible manifestation of the invisible God. When God appears to his people in the Old Testament, typically, he does so in the form of a glorious cloud. This was the same cloud that Moses and the children of Israel saw when they traveled through the wilderness, and again when they reached God's holy mountain (Ex. 13:21–22; 16:10; 19:9; 24:15–17). It was the dark and glorious cloud of the presence of God—a physical representation of his divine being.

This cloud was infinitely the most glorious thing at the temple, which for all its golden splendor was made glorious only by the presence of God. Here is how the Puritan Matthew Henry described what Solomon's temple would be without its God: "The temple, though richly beautified, yet while it was without the ark was like a body without a soul, or a candlestick without a candle, or (to speak more properly) a house without an inhabitant. All the cost and pains bestowed on this stately structure are lost if God does not accept them; and, unless he pleases to own it as the place where he will record his name, it is after all but a ruinous heap."[5]

We could say the same thing about the church of Jesus Christ: we are nothing without our God. This is true of church buildings. Is anything more tragic than to see a magnificent house of worship where God is no longer worshiped, where the gospel is no longer preached, and where the Holy Spirit is no longer present in his saving and sanctifying power? The same principle also holds true for the ministries of the church. Unless the Lord is with us, none of the work we do in the church—none of the teaching and preaching, none of the caring and sharing, none of the mercy work or missionary

---

5. Matthew Henry, *Matthew Henry's Complete Commentary on the Whole Bible*, vol. 2, *Judges to Job* (New York: Fleming Revell, n.d.), n.p.

evangelism—will make any difference for the kingdom of God. What would a prayer meeting be without the presence of God to guide people in their prayers? What would a Sunday school class be without the help of the Holy Spirit in teaching and applying the Scriptures? What would mercy ministry be without the living presence of Christ in feeding the hungry or visiting the prisoner?

But when God is in the house, his Word goes out with power and his Spirit changes people's lives from the inside out. What a blessing it was for Israel to see the glory of the Lord filling the temple of the Lord. It was a blessing for the king, because the cloud confirmed that God would indeed condescend to bless the house that Solomon built in his name. It was a blessing for the priests, too, because it showed them the glorious holiness of the God they were called to serve.

It is also a blessing for us, because we too are in the presence of the God of Solomon. He has revealed himself to us, especially in his Word, so that we can perceive his glory. But we will never be able to manage or control God. We will never be able to keep him in one place and say that we know everything there is to know about him. There will always be glorious mysteries about the character of God that go beyond our finite comprehension. The more we encounter him, the more awesome his glory will seem to us.

The first disciples experienced this awesome glory when they went up the mountain with Jesus Christ "and he was transfigured before them, and his clothes became radiant, intensely white, as no one on earth could bleach them" (Mark 9:2–3). The disciples were seeing the glory of God in the person of Jesus Christ. They even saw a majestic cloud, which overshadowed them with the glory of God (Mark 9:7; cf. John 1:14; 2 Peter 1:17). This helped them to know that Jesus Christ is the God of all glory. At the same time, the cloud filled them with holy awe. They knew that they were standing on holy ground, that Jesus was infinitely glorious.

One day we will see the fullness of this glory for ourselves, as Jesus prayed that we would (see John 17:24). We will see Jesus Christ, coming for the nations, descending in the cloud of God's glory (Luke 21:27). We will be ushered into the glorious presence of God. We will enter the holy sanctuary of heaven, which is "filled with smoke from the glory of God and from his power" (Rev. 15:8). But we will not see any temple there, for the temple of that great city "is the Lord God the Almighty and the Lamb" (Rev. 21:22).

This is the God we worship and honor: the God who dwells in awesome holiness and unapproachable glory. This is also the God we are called to serve. The Presbyterian missionary Elizabeth Freeman wrote about this holy service in a letter to one of her nieces. Freeman and her husband John were pioneer missionaries to India. After only seven years of gospel service, they were seized in a Muslim uprising, marched to a nearby parade ground, and shot in cold blood. Earlier Freeman had written these words to live by: "I hope you will be a missionary wherever your lot is cast, and as long as God spares your life; for it makes but little difference after all where we spend these few fleeting years, if they are only spent for the glory of God. Be assured there is nothing else worth living for."[6] No, there is nothing else worth living for except the glory of Solomon's God, whose holy presence is with us wherever we go.

---

6. Quoted in Ruth A. Tucker, *Guardians of the Great Commission: The Story of Women in Modern Missions* (Grand Rapids: Zondervan, 1988), 27.

16

SOLOMON'S BLESSING

1 Kings 8:12–21

Then the king turned around and blessed all the assembly
of Israel, while all the assembly of Israel stood. And he said,
"Blessed be the LORD, the God of Israel, who with his hand has
fulfilled what he promised with his mouth to David my father."
(1 Kings 8:14–15)

How quickly a good biblical word or a true theological phrase can become a Christian cliché. Take the phrase "born again," for example. These words express the deep gospel truth Jesus explained to Nicodemus, that unless we are born from above by the Holy Spirit, we cannot enter the kingdom of God (John 1:3–5). If this is true, then a "born-again Christian" is the only kind of Christian there is. Yet the phrase has become a cliché. In America it often refers to someone who has made a decision for Christ by going forward at an evangelistic crusade, whether or not the individual is committed to a life of Christ-centered discipleship. Good words have lost their full meaning.

There are many other expressions like this, including some that come straight from the Bible. Christians talk about "sharing the good news," or getting "washed in the blood of Jesus," or being "filled with the Spirit," or becoming "brothers and sisters in Christ." The language of these phrases is biblical; their theology is profound. Yet sometimes the phrases themselves are tossed around too casually. The same is true of the word "blessing" in its many popular forms: "God bless you!" "That was such a blessing!" "Count your blessings." Christians say they are blessed with this and blessed with that. Sometimes they even say that they are "blessed to be a blessing."

The frequent use of these and many similar expressions is a mixed blessing (!), to say the least. On the one hand, when they are used properly and reverently, these phrases remind us that God's wonderful grace is at work in our lives. Yet it is possible to talk so flippantly about being blessed that we are not even thinking about God at all, or thanking him for what he has done.

PREAMBLE TO PRAISE

King Solomon was wise not to make this mistake when he dedicated his famous temple in Jerusalem. God had blessed Solomon about as much as any man in history. When that great king numbered his blessings, he could count fabulous riches, a world-class intellect, the promise of everlasting fame . . . and that was only for starters. Solomon also had the blessing of doing something important with his life by building a holy dwelling place for the living God. Solomon knew that everything he owned and did was the gift of God, from whom all blessings flow. So he dedicated his temple with words of blessing.

Remember the context. After seven years of costly labor, Solomon had finished his temple—a magnificent building of white stone decorated inside with glittering gold. But the question still remained: Would God indeed dwell with his people? Would he condescend in glory so his people could meet with him for prayer and sacrifice?

Believing that God would dwell with his people, Solomon built a house in God's name. When the sacred building was finished, holy priests went up the Temple Mount in solemn procession. They were carrying the ark of the covenant, which represented the throne of God and signified the place of his earthly presence. The priests carefully placed the ark in the Holy of Holies. When they were finished, the glory of God came down in a cloud so thick that the priests could not even stay in the temple.

King Solomon recognized this cloud as an appearance of the divine being. God had descended to dwell with his people; this was confirmed by the glory cloud in the temple. In response, Solomon joyfully spoke words that are sometimes printed as lines of poetry: "The LORD has said that he would dwell in thick darkness. I have indeed built you an exalted house, a place for you to dwell in forever" (1 Kings 8:12–13).

Here the king is giving expression to the double mystery of God's immanence *and* transcendence. God is transcendent: he is high and exalted. In fact, he is separated so far from us that he is shrouded in darkness. This imagery appears elsewhere in Scripture. When Moses went up to receive the Ten Commandments, for example, he "drew near to the thick darkness where God was" (Ex. 20:21; cf. Deut. 4:11; 5:22). Similarly, King David said that God "made darkness his covering, his canopy around him" (Ps. 18:11; cf. 97:2). This is one of the great mysteries of the divine being. God is beyond our full comprehension; there are many things about him that we cannot see and do not know. "Truly, you are a God," said the prophet Isaiah, "who hides yourself" (Isa. 45:15). Solomon saw this at the temple, where God appeared in the thick darkness that he had promised.

Yet at the same time, this mysterious God also invites us to know him and be near him. He is immanent as well as transcendent. That is to say, he is a God who wants to be with us. This was Solomon's experience exactly. He knew that God was beyond his reach, that he lived in thick darkness. Yet he also knew that God had called him to build a house on earth that would bring God into close proximity with his people. Solomon brought both of these divine attributes together because he knew that they were both true about God: the nearness and the distance, the closeness and the separation, the immanence and the transcendence. Commenting on the temple, Dale Ralph Davis writes that the cloud "both is Yahweh's glory and covers Yahweh's glory; it both reveals and conceals." Davis says further that this is characteristic of God himself, who "satisfies your need for clarity but not your passion for curiosity."[1]

This is true of our own experience of God (or at least it ought to be). In our relationship with God, we need to recognize both his immanence and his transcendence. God is closer to us than ever in Jesus Christ, who came into the world to be our God. Because he is divine as well as human, Jesus is called Immanuel, which means "God with us" (Matt. 1:23). After he died

---

1. Dale Ralph Davis, *The Wisdom and the Folly: An Exposition of the Book of First Kings* (Fearn, Ross-shire: Christian Focus, 2002), 81, 82.

and rose again, as he ascended into heaven, Jesus promised to be with us always, until the end of the world (Matt. 28:20). Then, to fulfill that promise, Jesus sent us the indwelling presence of the Holy Spirit, who makes our souls a holy temple for the worship and service of God. The triune God is with us—Father, Son, and Holy Spirit.

Yet God remains transcendent in majesty. He is the one and only God, infinite in power and perfect in glory. His ways are above our ways, and his thoughts are higher than our thoughts. We cannot see the fullness of his awesome glory or comprehend the perfection of his eternal attributes. The triune God is far above us.

To know God truly is to know both his immanence and his transcendence. In our intimacy with God, in the times when we sense his close presence and speak with him as a friend to a friend, we should not forget his awesome majesty. He is the God who hides himself in thick darkness. We should not want to have it any other way, but rejoice to stand in awe before the transcendent glory of his divine being. He is God, and we are only his creatures. But when God seems far away, we should not forget the love that the Father always has for us, or the promise that Jesus would never leave us, or the closeness of his ever-present Spirit. The triune God is with us.

King Solomon brought both of these truths together when he dedicated the temple at Jerusalem. God had descended in a mysterious cloud, as he said he would. But this cloud also proved that God was with them to bless them.

BLESSED BE THE LORD

What Solomon said about God's presence in darkness was the preamble to his dedication speech. The king's heart was very full that day. All his hopes had been realized. God had descended to dwell in the exalted house Solomon had built. Now in the rest of his speech the king wanted to thank God for what he had done, so he pronounced the double blessing of a twofold benediction: "Then the king turned around and blessed all the assembly of Israel, while all the assembly of Israel stood. And he said, 'Blessed be the LORD, the God of Israel'" (1 Kings 8:14). Solomon blessed the people by speaking words of blessing to their God.

This famous event from Israel's history is part of the background for worship in the Christian church. Solomon was leading "the assembly of Israel"—

literally, the congregation, or what the New Testament calls a church (e.g., Eph. 3:21). Presumably the king raised his hands in the air, which is an ancient and almost universal gesture of blessing. God's people receive the same kind of blessing today when their pastors raise their hands and pronounce a benediction that is quoted or adapted from a biblical blessing.

The way Solomon blessed his people was by speaking words of blessing back to God. Thus his speech was a double benediction. Verse 14 says that the king blessed the assembly. However, the blessing he gives in verse 15 is not directed to them at all, but to their God: "Blessed be the LORD." In effect, Solomon was blessing the people by blessing their God, and by inviting them to do the same.

When God blesses us, he bestows some gracious gift on us, whether physical or spiritual. But what does it mean for us to bless God? We are not able to give him anything he does not already possess, "for from him and through him and to him are all things" (Rom. 11:36). The only thing we can really offer to God is our worship and praise. For us to bless God, then, is to thank him for all his blessings to us.

Solomon's blessing focused on God's faithfulness. Since this is one of God's familiar attributes, we need to be careful to give it the full respect that it deserves. The other gods of biblical times were hardly known for their faithfulness. "Ancient Near Eastern deities did not receive high grades for fidelity," writes Dale Ralph Davis. "Indeed, even if a pagan deity assured you of blessing, you could not be sure of that assurance, for some other deity might exercise his/her veto power and cancel the benefit thought to be guaranteed. Such is the liability when the world is run by a committee (sometimes called a pantheon)."[2]

We have the same problem with our own deities—the little gods we trust to help us make it through life. We worship pleasure, but our appetites grow and we are never satisfied. We trust in money, but then we find that it cannot buy us love, or even security. We depend on other people, but sooner or later they let us down. Earthly deities are faithless; all our lesser gods will fail. Yet God is faithful from beginning to end. This was Solomon's experience. So as he blessed the Lord, he thanked God for many different aspects of his faithfulness.

2. Ibid., 85.

God was faithful in keeping his promises, specifically to the house of David. Solomon said, "Blessed be the LORD, the God of Israel, who with his hand has fulfilled what he promised with his mouth to David my father" (1 Kings 8:15). God had specifically promised to give David a son who would sit on his throne and build a house for God. Here is how Solomon recounted the history of that promise: "Now it was in the heart of David my father to build a house for the name of the LORD, the God of Israel. But the LORD said to David my father, 'Whereas it was in your heart to build a house for my name, you did well that it was in your heart. Nevertheless, you shall not build the house, but your son who shall be born to you shall build the house for my name'" (1 Kings 8:17–19).

This promise was originally given in 2 Samuel 7, where God said to David, "When your days are fulfilled and you lie down with your fathers, I will raise up your offspring after you, who shall come from your body, and I will establish his kingdom. He shall build a house for my name, and I will establish the throne of his kingdom forever" (2 Sam. 7:12–13). The sequence of these events reminds us how many times we have to wait for God to keep his promises. Many of the promises David received were not fulfilled in his lifetime. Thus the king had to live with disappointment. His dream of building a temple was commendable; the Bible says he did well to have this holy ambition in his heart. Yet God also told David that someone else would do the building. Thus David had to live by faith in God's promise, hoping for what God would do after he died.

Solomon recognized that now the promise had come true. By the grace of God, working through the dramatic events described in 1 Kings 1 and 2, Solomon had ascended to David's throne. Then the new king built a temple, which was also by the grace of God, as described in 1 Kings 5 to 7. The promises God made to David were coming true, as they always do, because God is a faithful God.

For us these promises take on an added dimension in Jesus Christ. God is still building his temple today—a spiritual temple that is dedicated to God by the ministry of Jesus as Solomon's greater Son. This too is a sign of God's faithfulness, as he builds his people into a spiritual house for the praise of his name.

GOD'S GREAT FAITHFULNESS

God is also faithful in other ways. He is faithful in saving his people. Solomon alludes to this when he quotes God as saying: "Since the day that I brought my people Israel out of Egypt" (1 Kings 8:16). This refers to Israel's famous exodus from Egypt, when God led his people through the sea on dry land. The king rehearses these saving events again when he refers to "the covenant of the Lord that he made with our fathers, when he brought them out of the land of Egypt" (1 Kings 8:21). Solomon was putting the temple in its proper historical and theological context, as was appropriate for a dedication ceremony. This building project was only the latest chapter in the long story of Israel's salvation. God had been faithful to save his people, and then to give them a home in the Promised Land.

In keeping his promises, God was being faithful to the honor of his own name. God's "name" really means his reputation. We use a similar expression when we say that someone is "making a name for himself." God's "name" is mentioned many times in these verses. Verse 16 mentions a time when God had not yet associated his sacred divine name with any particular house in any particular city. But verse 18 honors David for wanting to build a house in God's name, and verse 19 promises that his son will actually build it—a house for God's name. Then Solomon built his temple and said: "Now the Lord has fulfilled his promise that he made. For I have risen in the place of David my father, and sit on the throne of Israel, as the Lord promised, and I have built the house for the *name* of the Lord, the God of Israel" (1 Kings 8:20). Solomon did what God promised: he built a house in God's name, which proved that God was faithful in making a name for himself at the temple.

Presbyterians and other Reformed Christians like to quote the first question and answer from the Westminster Shorter Catechism. Question: "What is the chief end of man?" Answer: "Man's chief end is to glorify God, and to enjoy him forever." But not everyone realizes that the chief end of man also happens to be the chief end of God. God's own great purpose is to glorify himself. In doing this God is not selfishly self-centered or sinfully self-absorbed, but simply acknowledging the truth that stands at the epicenter of the universe. God is the Supreme Being, the only one who is infinitely worthy of praise. Furthermore, it is good for everyone to acknowledge this, including us, because when we know the true glory of God we can understand our own place in the universe and get into a proper relationship with our Creator. In the days of Solomon, God helped people do this by putting his glorious name at the temple.

To say that God's name was at the temple was another way of saying that God himself was at the temple, and this was another aspect of his promise-keeping faithfulness. God was faithful in his presence. As long as Solomon obeyed the law, God had promised that he would dwell with his people Israel and never forsake them (see 1 Kings 6:11–13). Once the temple was built as a place for him to dwell (1 Kings 8:13), God kept his promise: he was present at the temple in Jerusalem. To be more specific, he was enthroned between the cherubim on the ark that represented his earthly presence. As Solomon said, "I have provided a place for the ark, in which is the covenant of the LORD that he made with our fathers" (1 Kings 8:21).

The lesson to learn from all of this is that God is always faithful. He is faithful to keep his promises, working out his plan of salvation. He is faithful to be present with his people, bringing honor to the glory of his name. There has never been a promise that God has not kept, or will not keep, when the time comes for its fulfillment.

Have you seen God's faithfulness in your own life the way that Solomon saw it in the kingdom of Israel? Remember everything that God has done for you. He has been faithful to keep all his promises. He has provided for your daily needs. He has forgiven your sins. He is faithfully doing the work of your salvation. God is faithful to call us, justify us, adopt us into his family, and sanctify us. One day soon he will be faithful to glorify us. These are all promises that God has made to us in Christ, and he will be faithful to fulfill them, "for all the promises of God find their Yes in him" (2 Cor. 1:20).

If we are sometimes tempted to think that God has not been faithful, then it must be because we have not been paying careful attention, or else because we have been expecting God to do some things for us that he has never promised to do. He has not promised that we will have financial prosperity, only that he will meet our daily needs. He has not promised us a life free from suffering, only that he will be with us through every trial before he brings us home to glory. He has not promised to tell us the future, only to give us the guidance we need for today. Or perhaps our problem is that we are too impatient to wait for God's timing, in which case we need to wait for him to fulfill his promises when the time is right, which he is always faithful to do.

As we recount how faithful God has been in keeping all his promises, we should be sure to do what Solomon did and bless him for it. The Puritan

Matthew Henry had a fine way of saying this. "What we have the pleasure of," Henry said, "God must have the praise of."[3] We can take this principle and make it personal: "Whatever I have the pleasure of, Lord, I want you to have the praise of. I return to you all the thanksgiving that your faithfulness deserves." Martin Luther liked to say that the whole Christian life was a life of repentance. But the Christian life is also a life of benediction, in which we bless God for all the ways that he is blessing us.

Blessed Be Solomon

There is one aspect of Solomon's blessing that some scholars have roundly criticized. They observe that the king has a lot to say about his own accomplishments, virtually to the point of boasting. Solomon says to the Lord, "I have indeed built you an exalted house" (1 Kings 8:13). Here the king draws attention to the beauty of the temple, calling it "an exalted house"—a phrase that could also be translated as "a lofty abode" or "a princely dwelling." At the same time, he is also calling attention to the fact that he is the one who built this house.

Later in his speech, after blessing God for his promise-keeping faithfulness, Solomon lists more of his accomplishments: "I have risen in the place of David my father, and sit on the throne of Israel, as the Lord promised, and I have built the house for the name of the Lord, the God of Israel. And there I have provided a place for the ark, in which is the covenant of the Lord" (1 Kings 8:20–21). Solomon talks about himself so much that Walter Brueggemann sees the entire speech as self-serving: "While the diction speaks of Yahweh's upholding the promise, in fact the verses congratulate Solomon on his achievement."[4] One is reminded of the Pharisee Jesus told of in his parable about two men at prayer: the man prayed more to himself than to God (Luke 18:9–14).

There are at least two ways to defend Solomon from the accusation of sinful boasting. One is to insist that he is blessing God for making him a blessing to others, and that this is always appropriate. Solomon is not treating the temple he built as an individual achievement, but as something he was

3. Matthew Henry, *Matthew Henry's Complete Commentary on the Whole Bible*, vol. 2, *Judges to Job* (New York: Fleming Revell, n.d.), n.p.
4. Walter Brueggemann, *1 & 2 Kings*, Smyth & Helwys Bible Commentary (Macon, GA: Smyth & Helwys, 2000), 108.

enabled to do by the grace of God. As he dedicates the temple, anything he says about himself is put in the context of God's faithfulness.

Solomon understood the difference between praising ourselves for what we have done and praising God for what he has enabled us to do. The king had just completed a building project that would establish his lasting fame. The whole nation had gathered for the dedication service. How natural it would be for people to credit him for this achievement. But Solomon wanted everyone to know that this was all God's doing. So he started his speech by blessing the Lord. By praising God for this house, he proved that he really did build it "for the name of the LORD" (1 Kings 8:20).

This is a good model for our own thanksgiving. Whenever we give thanks to God, we should start by praising him for the perfections of his own being. We should praise God the way Solomon praised him, blessing him for his faithfulness in keeping all the promises of our salvation. But in addition to praising God for who he is and what he has done, it is also appropriate for us to thank him for what we have done in his name. Anytime we are able to do anything good for the kingdom, God is the one who deserves our thanks and praise. As Matthew Henry said, "Whatever good we do, we must look upon it as the performance of God's promise to us, rather than the performance of our promises to him."[5]

Everything Solomon did in building the temple was a testimony to the faithfulness of his God. The same is true of our own accomplishments, especially in ministry. When people praise us for a job well done—in teaching, perhaps, or in performing some practical deed of mercy—we can honestly admit that what was done was praiseworthy, but we must also insist that God is the one who really deserves the praise. Rather than wanting to receive any notice ourselves, we should give credit where credit is due, blessing God for blessing us: "Bless you, Lord, for what you have done, even through me."

ROYAL DUTY

Another way to defend Solomon from the charge of selfish boasting is to remember his calling. As we listen to Solomon mention his accomplishments, we may be tempted to ask, "Who does this man think he is?" The answer, of course, is that he is the king of God's kingdom, the man chosen

5. Henry, *Judges to Job*, n.p.

by God to lead his people. He is not simply a private individual, therefore, but the Lord's anointed king.

There are reminders of Solomon's kingly office throughout this passage. In verse 16 God says, "Since the day that I brought my people Israel out of Egypt, I chose no city out of all the tribes of Israel in which to build a house, that my name might be there. But I chose David to be over my people Israel" (1 Kings 8:16). Just as God had chosen a people for himself (Israel) and a place for them to live (Jerusalem), so also he chose a king to rule over them (David).[6] David was the king by divine calling and sovereign election. This was part of God's faithfulness: he provided his people with the king of his choice. As God said through the psalmist, "I have made a covenant with my chosen one; I have sworn to David my servant" (Ps. 89:3; cf. 132:11–12).

Now Solomon was the king of God's choice. God had promised David a son who would sit on his throne and build a holy temple. Solomon was that son. He too had a divine calling to royal office. His kingship was God's gracious choice—a sovereign election to a kingdom vocation. Solomon rejoiced to fulfill his calling as king. In blessing God for blessing him, he was celebrating his royal accomplishments.

Some people object to this on the grounds that Solomon was using this occasion to turn the temple to his own personal advantage. "The temple is from Solomon and by Solomon and inevitably for Solomon," Walter Brueggemann complains. "Thus the temple becomes an extravagant arena from which to exhibit and verbalize and insist upon royal claims."[7] Such criticisms help us see what is really happening in this passage and also connect it to the saving message of the gospel. The temple is *not* from Solomon, by Solomon, and for Solomon. On the contrary, it is from God, by God, and for God—just like everything else in the entire universe (see Rom. 11:36). Solomon's speech makes this clear by blessing God for the blessing of his temple.

Yet it is absolutely correct to see a close connection between the temple and the king. Indeed, this is one of the ways that 1 Kings helps us understand the gospel of Jesus Christ. It is the rightful duty of God's rightful king to make a house for the worship of God. When Solomon rejoices in what he has done—or, better, when he rejoices over what God has enabled him to

---

6. Donald J. Wiseman gives a similar outline in *1 & 2 Kings: An Introduction and Commentary*, Tyndale Old Testament Commentaries (Leicester: Inter-Varsity, 1993), 119.

7. Brueggemann, *1 & 2 Kings*, 108.

do—he is celebrating the fulfillment of his kingly duty. The benediction that he pronounces is a royal blessing from beginning to end.

We ourselves receive this blessing in Jesus Christ, who is the greater Solomon of the kingdom of God. Jesus is the true and royal Son of David, chosen to sit on his father's throne. He is also the royal builder of God's eternal temple. In fact, he is the temple himself, because he is God incarnate. That is to say, Jesus Christ is both fully human and fully divine, which means that his own person is the dwelling place of God. This is what the temple was supposed to be: a place that God inhabits. Solomon could only hope that God would dwell in his temple forever (see 1 Kings 8:13), but in Christ that hope has become a reality. Jesus told people, "Destroy this temple, and in three days I will raise it up" (John 2:19). When he said this, Jesus "was speaking about the temple of his body" (John 2:21). What he said was really a prophecy, because three days after his body was killed on the cross, Jesus came back to everlasting life. Then his disciples remembered what he said about tearing down and raising up the temple and they recognized that it referred to the crucifixion and resurrection. Believing in the crucified and risen Christ, they received the blessing of eternal life.

Jesus is the King. Jesus is the temple. Jesus is the one who gives us all the blessings of our faithful God. This is not something to pass off as a mere cliché, but a truth to celebrate. With a heart full of praise, the apostle Paul said, "Blessed be the God and Father of our Lord Jesus Christ, who has blessed us in Christ with every spiritual blessing" (Eph. 1:3). Yes, every blessing of God belongs to us through faith in Jesus Christ. Jesus blesses us with full forgiveness for all our sins, with the righteousness we need to stand before God, with the privileged status of becoming sons and daughters of the Most High God, with the faithful promise of his provision for all our needs, with the living presence of his Holy Spirit, with the total guarantee of eternal life, and with a million other blessings that are his to give.

When we receive these blessings, we should say what Solomon said: "Blessed be the LORD, the God of Israel" (1 Kings 8:15), and also what Paul said: "Blessed be the God and Father of our Lord Jesus Christ" (Eph. 1:3). It is good for us to say, "God bless you!" as long as we really mean it and are not simply throwing around a Christian cliché. But it is also good for us to change the order of those words, to turn our benediction in God's direction, and to say, "Bless *you*, God, for all the blessings that you have given to us."

17

SOLOMON'S DEDICATION

1 Kings 8:22–30

Then Solomon stood before the altar of the LORD in the presence
of all the assembly of Israel and spread out his hands toward
heaven, and said, "O, LORD God of Israel, there is no God like
you, in heaven above or on earth beneath, keeping covenant and
showing steadfast love to your servants who walk before you
with all their heart. . . . But will God indeed dwell on the earth?
Behold, heaven and the highest heaven cannot contain you; how
much less this house that I have built!" (1 Kings 8:22–23, 27)

When the Philadelphia Museum of Art prepared to open its
magnificent Ruth and Raymond G. Perelman Building for
textiles and modern art, it was easy to tell that the dedication
ceremony would be a gala celebration. An enormous velvet ribbon with a
giant red bow was stretched across the entrance. When viewed from the
Benjamin Franklin Parkway, the Perelman Building looked like a gigantic
gift, waiting to be unwrapped.

By all accounts, the dedication lived up to its expectations. All the important local dignitaries were there for the ribbon-cutting, wearing black ties

and formal dinner gowns: board members, politicians, and major donors. Speeches were made, toasts were proposed, and the galleries were opened to the viewing public.

One thing was missing from these festivities, however. The officials who dedicated the Perelman Building neglected to do the most important thing that Solomon did when he built his famous temple in Jerusalem: dedicate the building to God in prayer.

THE KING AT PRAYER

King Solomon's temple was built to be a house of prayer, so it was only appropriate for it to be dedicated with intercession. The prayer the king offered is one of the longest and most important prayers in the whole Bible. With typical wisdom, Solomon gives us a good biblical model for intercession—not just when we are dedicating a church building, but anytime we go to God in prayer.

The dedication ceremony began with a double benediction, as Solomon blessed his people by blessing their God (1 Kings 8:12–21). This was followed by a public prayer: "Then Solomon stood before the altar of the LORD in the presence of all the assembly of Israel and spread out his hands toward heaven" (1 Kings 8:22).

Solomon was standing in the courtyard to the temple (see 2 Chron. 6:13), directly in front of the great bronze altar that was used for making blood sacrifices. This established a proper basis for Solomon's prayer. When sinners approach a holy God, they must come with a sacrifice to atone for their sins. This is one of the reasons why Christians pray "in Jesus' name." By saying this, we are claiming the cross of Christ as the atonement for our sins and the basis for our access to God through prayer.

As he led his people in prayer, King Solomon stood with his arms raised. This is one appropriate posture for prayer, especially when it is offered as a public act of corporate worship. Standing with outstretched arms is a gesture of openness to God. The Puritan Matthew Henry said, "He spread forth his hands, as it were to offer up the prayer from an open enlarged heart and to present it to heaven, and also to receive thence, with both arms, the mercy which he prayed for."[1]

---

1. Matthew Henry, *Matthew Henry's Complete Commentary on the Whole Bible*, vol. 2, *Judges to Job* (New York: Fleming Revell, n.d.), n.p.

The prayer itself, which runs from verse 23 all the way to verse 53, is divided into five main sections. In verses 23 and 24, Solomon offers his opening words of adoration and praise. This is followed in verses 25 and 26 by a petition, in which Solomon asks God to fulfill his royal promises. The third section is introduced with the crucial question that Solomon asks in verse 27: "Will God indeed dwell on earth?" The king's response is really an invocation, in which he invites the presence of God by asking him to hear the prayers his people offer at the temple (1 Kings 8:27–30).

The main body of the prayer—and also its main emphasis, which we will consider in the following chapter of this commentary—is a prayer of confession. What makes it somewhat unusual is that it is a request for *future* forgiveness—what Charles Spurgeon called "the summary of all future prayers offered in the temple."[2] In verses 31 to 51 Solomon mentions seven specific situations of human sin and divine judgment, asking that in each case God would hear his people's cry for mercy and forgive their sins. The king ends his prayer with a final invocation (1 Kings 8:52–53), in which again he asks that God would look on his people with compassion and hear their pleas for mercy.

Solomon's dedicatory prayer is critical for understanding 1 and 2 Kings, in terms of both theology and literary structure. The prayer stands as a climactic moment in Solomon's grand ambition to build a house for God. It identifies the central practical and theological question raised by that building project: Will the God of heaven really dwell with his people on earth? The prayer also anticipates many important events that happen later in these biblical books. The situations Solomon describes in his prayers for future forgiveness are situations that Israel will later face: military defeat, famine, and exile. Thus his prayer serves as a preview of coming destructions.

This prayer is also important for a more practical reason, however: it helps us understand the prayers that Jesus has made for us and that we are called to offer for the church. As we listen to Solomon pray, we should remember that we too have a King who prays for us. Jesus Christ is the greater Solomon who makes royal intercession for our salvation. Then Jesus calls us to pray—not for any man-made temple, but for the church he calls "a holy temple in the Lord" and "a dwelling place for God by the Spirit" (Eph. 2:21, 22). Just

2. Charles H. Spurgeon, "Solomon's Plea," in *The Metropolitan Tabernacle Pulpit* (Pasadena, TX: Pilgrim, 1971), 21:253.

as Solomon dedicated his temple with prayer, we may follow his example by dedicating the work of the church to God in prayer.

Who God Is

The first three parts of Solomon's prayer are his praise, his petition, and his invocation. The king opens his prayer by praising God for who he is: "O Lord, God of Israel, there is no God like you, in heaven above or on earth beneath, keeping covenant and showing steadfast love to your servants who walk before you with all their heart, who have kept with your servant David my father what you declared to him. You spoke with your mouth, and with your hand have fulfilled it this day" (1 Kings 8:23–24).

The king thus began his prayer with God, who is the beginning of everything. He addressed God as the Lord, acknowledging his sovereignty over heaven and earth. He also identified his Lord as the "God of Israel." God is not some abstract or impersonal deity, but someone who has a personal relationship with his people. He is their God, and this is the starting point for everything else in prayer.

To say that the Lord is the God of Israel is not to say that he is merely a tribal deity, as if he were only one among many gods, on a par with the idols of other nations. On the contrary, Solomon praises God for his uniqueness, his incomparability. There is no one else like him. He is the only true deity. No other so-called god even belongs in the same category with God the one and only. There is no other god like him "on earth beneath"—no one else we can trust to satisfy our souls or take care of our physical needs. There is no other god like him "in heaven above"—no other being who deserves our worship. In other words, there is no other god like him at all. He alone is the one true God.

When Solomon prayed this way, he was following an ancient tradition for worship. The prophet Moses said, "Lay it to your heart, that the Lord is God in heaven above and on the earth beneath; there is no other" (Deut. 4:39; cf. Ex. 15:11). The Israelites acknowledged this truth every morning in their daily prayers, when they said, "Hear, O Israel: The Lord our God, the Lord is one" (Deut. 6:4). In making this confession of their faith, they were declaring the incomparability of God. Solomon's father David believed the same doctrine. Thus he prayed, "There is none like you among the gods, O Lord . . . ; you alone are God" (Ps. 86:8, 10).

The one and only Lord God of Israel is a faithful God, and this too was part of Solomon's praise. The king had already declared God's faithfulness in the speech that preceded his prayer (1 Kings 8:15–21). God had faithfully fulfilled his promise to give David a son who would sit on his throne and build a house for God. King Solomon took the faithfulness of God and made it the theme of his praise. One of the things that makes God unique is his steadfast, covenant love—his faithfulness to fulfill all the promises he has vowed to keep.

This incomparable faithfulness was clearly demonstrated in the promises that God made and kept for David (see 2 Sam. 7:12–16). What God said with his mouth, he did with his hand (1 Kings 8:24), establishing a royal dynasty that endures to this day through Jesus Christ, the royal Son of David. No other god has ever promised anyone an eternal kingship, and then delivered on that promise, except God the one and only. He is a promise-keeping God who always keeps his word to his people. God is not just talk. He not only says things, but also does things, and when he does those things, he does what he says. The one true God is totally loyal, absolutely trustworthy, and incomparably faithful.

God keeps his faithful promises because he is also a God of incomparable love. The promises God makes are not arbitrary, but motivated by his affection for his people. As Moses said when he wanted to explain why God made Israel his chosen and treasured possession, "the Lord set his love on you . . . because the Lord loves you" (Deut. 7:7–8). God loves because it is his nature to love. In covenant love, therefore, he kept his commitment to give his people a king.

Solomon's praise should also be our praise, because Israel's experience is also our experience. God is still the Lord of heaven and earth—the ruler of all that is. Nevertheless, he is also *our* God—the one that Jesus called "my Father and your Father," "my God and your God" (John 20:17). So when we come to him in prayer, we address him as "Our Father in heaven," "the Lord our God." Through faith in Jesus Christ, we have a personal relationship with the God of the universe. He is our God, and we are his people.

As we come to our God in prayer, we begin by praising him for the unique attributes of his divine being. We do not do this because we are trying to get on his good side, or to flatter him into giving us what we want, but because it is the absolute truth about the way things are. There is no one else like him; he is the one and only God. So as we pray, we praise him for who he is, acknowledging his faithful, incomparable, promise-keeping love.

God has proved his faithful love to us in Jesus Christ. God kept his promise to provide a Savior by sending his very own Son to die on the cross for our sins and then raising him up from the grave with the power of eternal life. What other god has ever sacrificed his own life to save his people? Only Jesus, whose love never fails. So we praise him as the one and only loving Savior, who is faithful to the very end.

Then we live by the truths that we pray. Since God is a faithful God, we trust him to provide for our needs—even when we are not sure how—knowing that he will follow through. Since he is a loving God, we believe that he cares about us—even when we feel forsaken—knowing that he calls us his own. Since he is a promise-keeping God, we are convinced that he will save us to the very end—even when we are not sure if we can go on—knowing that "he who began a good work in you will bring it to completion at the day of Jesus Christ" (Phil. 1:6).

What God Will Do

Praise to the Lord as the one and only faithful God is the context for everything we ask in prayer. We start by acknowledging God for who he is. Then we ask God to do what he has said, knowing that he is a promise-keeping God.

Solomon followed this logic in his dedicatory prayer. His petitions were based on his praise: "Now therefore, O Lord, God of Israel, keep for your servant David my father what you have promised him, saying, 'You shall not lack a man to sit before me on the throne of Israel, if only your sons pay close attention to their way, to walk before me as you have walked before me.' Now therefore, O God of Israel, let your word be confirmed, which you have spoken to your servant David my father" (1 Kings 8:25–26; cf. 2:4).

People sometimes think of prayer as a way of asking God for things they want. Certainly it is appropriate to tell God what we need. But prayer is also a way of asking God for the things that *God* wants, and the way we know what he wants is by believing his promises, as Solomon did. When the king prayed for the throne of Israel, he was not pursuing his own ambitions, but standing on the promises of God.

God had vowed that one day David would have a son to sit on his royal throne, on the condition of continued obedience. Now King Solomon was praying that God would honor that vow. As a royal son of David, he was counting on God to keep his promise. Looking to the future, he asked God to confirm his word by securing his throne.

If walking with God was the condition of this promise, then implicit in Solomon's kingdom prayer was a request for his own continued faithfulness in walking with God, and also a request that his sons would do the same. Sadly, many of Solomon's sons failed to walk with God. As we will see in the rest of 1 and 2 Kings, their disobedience was Israel's downfall. After Solomon, the kingdom was divided and defeated; the people were carried into exile. Yet eventually Solomon's petitions for the house of David were answered in the person and work of Jesus Christ, who is David's royal Son and the King of the kingdom of God.

Jesus walked with God in all his ways, perfectly obeying the will of his heavenly Father. He walked with God all the way to the cross, where he surrendered his body to crucifixion, dying for our sins. Jesus kept the law of God, and when he came to the end of his life, he prayed that his Father would keep his promise. He said, "Father, into your hands I commit my spirit!" (Luke 23:46). When Jesus said this, he was entrusting his life— body and soul—to his Father's care. He was asking the Father to do what the Father promised that he would do: raise him from the dead and give him an eternal throne. On the third day, God did what he said. His word was confirmed by the bodily resurrection of Jesus Christ and his ascension to the throne of the universe. God kept his promise to Solomon by giving Jesus an everlasting kingdom.

The promises that God kept to his own beloved Son give us every confidence that he will keep his promises to us. Our expectancy in prayer is based on God's fidelity to his promises. We stand on those promises every time we pray—especially when we pray for God's kingdom to come. God has promised that his church will persevere to the very end, that the gates of hell will not prevail against it (Matt. 16:18). So we pray for the church to persevere, even in places where it is under persecution. God has promised that his kingdom will grow from shore to shore until every tribe and nation gives honor and glory to him (e.g., Rev. 7:9). So we pray for God to expand his wide dominion by planting new churches and sending gospel workers to the ends of the earth. God has promised that Jesus will come again (1 Thess. 4:14–17), so we pray for his second coming, asking God that Jesus Christ would be universally acknowledged as the everlasting King.

If we can trust God to keep the big promises of the coming kingdom, then surely we can trust him to keep all the smaller promises he has made to us in Christ, and then pray on that basis. Yet sometimes this is precisely the difficulty: although we believe that God's kingdom will come, we have trouble believing that he will help us resolve a $500 dispute with the insurance company or give us the grace to deal with the irritating person we have to work with every day. Too often we are like the state legislature that spent hours debating a small appropriation for a building repair at the state capitol (everyone seemed to have a different opinion about how to save money on the project), but then passed a multibillion-dollar spending bill without a murmur. Even if we believe that God will work out his saving plan in human history, we still want to control our own kingdom. Rather than trusting God for the little things in life, we quibble with him about how he is managing our affairs.

What we ought to do instead is take a firm stand on the promises of God. He has promised to forgive our sins, provide for our basic needs, and give us something useful to do in the world. So we should pray in faith, asking him to forgive our debts, give us our daily bread, and put us in the right place to use our gifts for his glory. When we pray this way he will surely answer, for we are asking God to do the very things that he has promised to do.

THE BIG QUESTION

Right in the middle of his prayer, Solomon asked a profound theological question. After praising God and praying for him to keep his promises, Solomon posed the most important question he could ask about the temple he had built for God: "Will God indeed dwell on the earth?" (1 Kings 8:27).

Solomon had built a beautiful house for God, but would God really live there?—that was the question. Would the incomparably loving and faithful God dwell in his temple? After all, what would a temple be without its God? We sometimes ask the same question in ministry, as we consider the work of the church: Is God really with us or not? Is he involved in what we are doing, or are we operating without him? Sooner or later, everyone asks the same question at the personal level, especially in times of crisis: Are you really there, Lord, and are you really here, in my situation, or not?

As far as the temple was concerned, King Solomon knew that he could never put God in a box, even a box as big and as beautiful as the temple in Jerusalem. The very idea was absurd. "Behold," said Solomon, "heaven and the highest heaven cannot contain you; how much less this house that I have built!" (1 Kings 8:27).

God is transcendent: he is high above the heavens. How then could he ever be contained on earth? God is immense: his invisible being fills the entire universe. So how could he be held within the four walls of any building? Whatever its precise dimensions, the house that Solomon built did not have nearly enough capacity to contain the God of the universe. God is omnipresent: he is always everywhere all at once. How then could he limit his special presence to one place on earth?

By wrestling with these profound theological questions, Solomon was putting his building project into perspective. We should do the same thing with our own earthly accomplishments, especially in ministry. However noble our service to God may seem, we should remember that even the heavens cannot contain him. Matthew Henry said, "When we have done the most we can for God we must acknowledge the infinite distance and disproportion between us and him, between our services and his perfections."[3] The apostle Paul said it like this, in his famous sermon at Athens, which he preached when he was standing virtually in the shadow of another grand temple, the famous Parthenon: "The God who made the world and everything in it, being Lord of heaven and earth, does not live in temples made by man, nor is he served by human hands, as though he needed anything" (Acts 17:24–25).

One might wonder why this immense, incomparable, infinite God would ever want to have anything to do with us. Nevertheless, Solomon prayed for God to be with his people. After raising the problem of God's presence in verse 27, he proceeded to offer an invocation in verses 28 to 30, inviting the presence of the very God he knew he could not contain.

Solomon spoke to God with earnest humility, identifying himself as God's servant and framing his prayer as a plea for mercy: "Yet have regard to the prayer of your servant and to his plea, O Lord my God, listening

3. Henry, *Judges to Job*, n.p.

to the cry and to the prayer that your servant prays before you this day" (1 Kings 8:28). For all his earthly glory, when Solomon prayed, he styled himself as a humble servant who desperately needed the help of a mighty God. In verse 28 he employed three different words for prayer. The first term—"prayer" (*tepilat*)—is the most general; it refers to any prayer of praise or intercession. A "plea" (*techinat*) is more intense; it is a fervent prayer for help in a time of trouble. Similarly, a "cry" (*rinnah*) is a "ringing cry of joy or sorrow."[4] Solomon's invocation was intense. He was more than just praying: he was crying out and pleading to God.

At the same time, the king also spoke to God with extraordinary intimacy. The incomparable and immense God of heaven and earth also happened to be the Lord *his* God. God is accessible and available. He is someone a person can actually talk to. When we pray, therefore, we may call him *our* God. This is always the best kind of prayer: one in which we recognize *both* who God is *and* who we are in relationship to him. We are people who desperately need our God, and we should pray accordingly, asking the Lord our God to listen to our cry for mercy.

In his invocation—in his prayer inviting God to be present at his temple—Solomon asked God to look and to listen. The king's request was for God to listen "to the cry and to the prayer that your servant prays before you this day, that your eyes may be open night and day toward this house, the place of which you have said, 'My name shall be there'" (1 Kings 8:28; cf. Deut. 12:5).

God had already said that he would make a name for himself at the temple. Even if God was much too immense to be housed at the temple, he could at least put his name there. Thus the temple would be the one place in the whole world that bore the name of the living God. But Solomon wanted something more: he wanted God to keep looking at the temple all the time, always keeping his eyes open to see who was praying there. God *does* keep his eyes open this way. As the psalmist declared, "he who keeps Israel will neither slumber nor sleep" (Ps. 121:4). God is constantly watching over his people, day and night.

God has not only his eyes open, but also his ears. Solomon prayed for this as well. He asked "that you may listen to the prayer that your servant offers

4. Donald J. Wiseman, *1 & 2 Kings: An Introduction and Commentary*, Tyndale Old Testament Commentaries (Leicester: Inter-Varsity, 1993), 120.

toward this place. And listen to the plea of your servant and of your people Israel, when they pray toward this place" (1 Kings 8:29–30). Solomon was asking God to listen to the prayers of his people—both the royal requests of their king and their own personal petitions.

This is the very thing that God desires to do: he loves to listen to his people pray, and for the sake of his name, he loves to answer our prayers. He is not blind and deaf, like the other gods to whom people pray. This is one of the reasons he is so incomparable: he is a looking and listening God, a God who sees and hears. Yes, he is a transcendent God, the high ruler of heaven, but he is also near to us—an immanent God, who hears us when we pray. "Heaven is my throne," God says, "and the earth is my footstool; what is the house that you would build for me, and what is the place of my rest? . . . But this is the one to whom I will look: he who is humble and contrite in spirit" (Isa. 66:1–2).

God's Answer in Christ

Every request that Solomon prayed is answered for us in Jesus Christ. Jesus is the ultimate answer to Solomon's question: Will God indeed dwell on earth? Yes, Jesus is Immanuel, which means "God with us" (Matt. 1:23). God the Son became incarnate in the person of Jesus Christ. He came as a man to live among our fallen race, to die for our sins on the cross, and then to rise again so that we could live with him. In Christ, God has indeed lived on earth.

Jesus is also the ultimate fulfillment of Solomon's example. Just as King Solomon prayed for his people, so King Jesus prays for us as our eternal intercessor (see Rom. 8:34; Heb. 7:25). In the days of Solomon God put his name on the temple. Now he has put his name on us as the living temple of his Holy Spirit (Eph. 2:21–22). As the people of God, we bear the name of Christ in the world. So Jesus prays for us, making royal intercession, asking that our incomparable Father God would turn his heart toward us, opening his eyes and ears to the needs of his church.

These are prayers that God loves to answer. His eyes are open to our needs. His ears are open to our cries. "Call to me," he says, "and I will answer you" (Jer. 33:3; see Ps. 91:15; Jer. 29:12). This is true for the people of God as individual believers. God knows our situation exactly; he is always watching to see what happens to his children. He is also listening to hear our prayers, night and day. He hears the petitions we make from our beds, when we have quiet time to think, and easily get overwhelmed by the troubles of life. He hears the prayers we make throughout the day, in the push and pull of daily life. Night and day, God always hears us when we pray.

The same is true corporately: God always sees the needs of his church and listens to our prayers of praise, petition, and invocation. He hears our prayers for his presence in worship, for the sick, for the lost, for missionaries, and for our own gospel ministry in word and deed. He hears us when we pray, and answers us according to his will, for the purpose of his glory.

When the famous preacher Benjamin Morgan Palmer dedicated the First Presbyterian Church in Columbia, South Carolina, he prayed that God would turn his eyes and ears to that church building as a place that was called by his name. What Palmer said in his sermon of dedication is a suitable prayer for any church on any occasion, including whatever church we may happen to serve:

> As for this building, beautiful as it may be in our eyes . . . the glory we see in it, let it not be the glory of its arches and its timbers . . . not the glory of this chaste pulpit, with its delicate tracery and marble whiteness; not the glory found in the eloquence of the learning of those who, through generations, shall here proclaim the gospel; nor yet the glory traced in the wealth and fashion, refinement and social position of those who throng its courts. But let its glory be The Glory of the Lord Risen Upon It! . . . Let its glory be found in the purity, soundness, and unction of its pastors; in the fidelity and watchfulness of its elders; in the piety and godliness of its members. Let its glory be as a birthplace of souls, where shall always be heard the sobs of awakened penitence and the songs of newborn love. Let its glory be the spirituality of its worship, its fervent prayers, its adorning praise, and the simplicity and truth of its ordinances and sacraments. Let its glory be the communion of saints, who here have fellowship one with another and also with the Father and His Son, Jesus Christ.[5]

---

5. Benjamin Morgan Palmer, quoted in David B. Calhoun, *The Glory of the Lord Risen Upon It: First Presbyterian Church, Columbia, South Carolina, 1795–1995* (Columbia, SC: R. L. Bryan, 1994), v.

18

Solomon's Intercession

1 Kings 8:31–53

*And listen to the plea of your servant and of your people Israel,
when they pray toward this place. And listen in heaven your
dwelling place, and when you hear, forgive.* (1 Kings 8:30)

I am not sure how it ever began, but according to a running gag
in my old high school youth group, the number seven was a
mark of unattainable perfection. No matter how good something was, it could never be "seven good."

The conversation would go something like this: first one of the guys would say that something was "the best"—a sporting event, for example, or maybe a concert or some other social event. Then someone else would say, "Yeah, but was it seven good?" "No, not seven good," the person would have to admit. "Nothing could ever be *seven* good." From time to time, when someone would try to claim that something was, in fact, "seven good," there would be howls of protest. Seven was *always* beyond reach—a standard of perfection beyond what anyone could ever achieve.

There are many notable "sevens" in the Bible, including some that really do reach perfection. In seven days at the beginning of the world, God created everything there is, and then rested from his work. Noah brought seven pairs of clean animals with him on the ark (Gen. 7:2). The blood of a sacrifice was sprinkled seven times to make complete purification (Lev. 16:14, 19). Christ performs seven miraculous signs in the Gospel of John, and there are seven letters to seven churches in the book of Revelation, where seven is also the number of the fullness of the Holy Spirit (Rev. 5:6).

Then there is the prayer that King Solomon offered when he dedicated his famous temple at Jerusalem, which contains seven large petitions for the people of God. According to Jesus, the temple of God should be "a house of prayer" (Luke 19:46). So it was appropriate for Solomon to dedicate his temple with the long prayer that runs from 1 Kings 8:23 to verse 53. The king opened by praising God and asking him to keep the promises he had made to David. Then he invoked God's presence with his people. But the heart of Solomon's prayer consisted of seven petitions of future confession. Knowing how certain his people were to sin, the king anticipated the trouble they would get into and interceded for their forgiveness, even before they sinned. Standing in front of the altar where atonement was made for sin, he asked God to listen to his people's prayers and forgive their many transgressions (1 Kings 8:30).

Solomon's prayer is a model for our own intercession. With apologies to the guys in my old high school youth group, it is a "seven good" prayer. It teaches us how to pray, both for ourselves and for the people of God. It also reminds how Jesus prays for us as our Savior and King. In short, Solomon's prayer is everything that anyone could ever want in a prayer—a sevenfold perfection of intercession. There is a petition for everyone somewhere in this prayer.

First Petition: A Prayer for Justice

Solomon's first petition was a prayer for justice: "If a man sins against his neighbor and is made to take an oath and comes and swears his oath before your altar in this house, then hear in heaven and act and judge your servants, condemning the guilty by bringing his conduct on his own head, and vindicating the righteous by rewarding him according to his righteousness" (1 Kings 8:31–32).

The situation Solomon describes in his first petition is a familiar one. In fact, the king had dealt with this kind of situation himself, most notably in the famous case of the prostitutes and the two babies (1 Kings 3:16–28). Solomon imagines a situation in which one person sins against another person, and thus fails to keep the second great commandment of loving his neighbor (Lev. 19:18; cf. Mark 12:28–31). Such a sin is all too common; it happens every day. But in this case there are no other witnesses, and therefore no other human being knows the truth about what really happened. How will justice ever be done?

Not even Solomon, for all his wisdom, could adjudicate everything. So when it proved impossible to judge between two neighbors, Solomon prayed that God himself would render the verdict and execute the sentence. Although the procedure for this is not fully explained, what Solomon has in mind is some sort of trial by ordeal. We read something similar in the Law of Moses, which says that two parties "shall come before God" (Ex. 22:9), but never actually describes how they are to do so. Apparently the temple priests had some means of determining who was innocent and who was guilty. Possibly this was done by using the Urim and the Thummim—the holy dice, so to speak, that Israel's high priest kept in "the breastpiece of judgment" (see Ex. 28:30). In any case, when people accused of wrongdoing would go to the temple and swear an oath on God's altar, Solomon was asking God to condemn the guilty and reward the righteous.

In making this petition, Solomon was acknowledging that God is a righteous Judge (Ps. 7:11)—"the Judge of all the earth" (Gen. 18:25). Many things are known only to God, who always does what is absolutely right and perfectly just. Therefore, the best and wisest thing for us to do is to leave judgment to the Lord.

One practical way for us to do this is to follow Solomon's example and make God's justice a matter for prayer. We often encounter conflicts where we are grieved by what people are doing, even when it is hard to know who is really telling the truth. We do not have the perfect knowledge to render perfect justice. Instead of getting discouraged or cynical about all the evil in the world, we should pray for justice to be done. We should pray that the guilty will be condemned and the righteous rewarded—if not in this life, then certainly in the life to come. Rather than getting overburdened by a responsibility for justice that we cannot bear, we should call on the justice of God, "who judges impartially according to each one's deeds" (1 Peter 1:17).

SECOND PETITION: A PRAYER FOR RESCUE

Solomon's second petition was a prayer for rescue and return. Again it is clear that the king believed in the utter depravity of the people of God. He prayed, "When your people Israel are defeated before the enemy because they have sinned against you, and if they turn again to you and acknowledge your name and pray and plead with you in this house, then hear in heaven and forgive the sin of your people Israel and bring them again to the land that you gave to their fathers" (1 Kings 8:33–34; cf. Deut. 30:1–10).

Although they were usually victorious, the people of God sometimes suffered defeat in battle. The debacle at Ai was a notable example (see Josh. 7:1–5), as was the loss they suffered at the hands of the Philistines (1 Sam. 4:1–11). In both cases, the Israelites lost the battle because they sinned against God. God had warned his people that if they did not keep his commandments, he would turn against them and allow their enemies to strike them down. According to the justice of God, in the curses he pronounced for breaking his covenant the proper punishment for national rebellion was military defeat (e.g., Lev. 26:17; Deut. 28:25).

Solomon knew that Israel was likely to experience this kind of judgment again. Sooner or later, God's people would be defeated in battle and carried off by some foreign army—a theme to which he will return in his seventh petition. But Solomon also believed in the loving mercy of a forgiving God. So he prayed that when his people were defeated, God would hear their prayers at the temple, forgive their sin, and bring them back to the land that he had promised. Solomon's mention of the temple is crucial. The reason God established the temple as a place to pray for forgiveness was that this was where sacrifices were made for sin.

On the basis of that atonement, the king was praying that there would be a way back home for fallen sinners, as there always is. God is such a loving Father that when we finally come back home after wandering far away in our sin, he will come running to meet us (see Luke 15:20). Jesus Christ is the Good Shepherd who comes looking to find every lost sheep that belongs in his pasture (Luke 15:3–7; cf. John 10:11). When we are lost and far away, the God of mercy will hear our prayer for rescue and return.

THIRD PETITION: A PRAYER FOR PROVISION

The third petition was a prayer for God's provision. Military defeat was not the only punishment that God's people would undergo. Sometimes the land itself would suffer for Israel's sin: "When heaven is shut up and there is no rain because they have sinned against you, if they pray toward this place and acknowledge your name and turn from their sin, when you afflict them, then hear in heaven and forgive the sin of your servants, your people Israel, when you teach them the good way in which they should walk, and grant rain upon your land, which you have given to your people as an inheritance" (1 Kings 8:35–36).

The situation described in these verses comes straight out of Deuteronomy, which shows how important knowing the Scriptures is to the life of prayer. In Deuteronomy God declared that drought was the proper punishment for disobedience. If God's people were careful to obey his commandments—loving him with all their heart, soul, and strength—then God would water their land with rain in its season (Deut. 11:13–14). But if they turned away from the love of God, both the people and their land would come under judgment. God said, "Take care lest your heart be deceived, and you turn aside and serve other gods and worship them; then the anger of the LORD will be kindled against you, and he will shut up the heavens, so that there will be no rain, and the land will yield no fruit, and you will perish quickly off the good land that the LORD is giving you" (Deut. 11:16–17; cf. 28:23–24).

Solomon's prayer was prophetic, for this is exactly what happened in the days of King Ahab, as we read later in 1 Kings. The people turned away from the God of Israel to worship Baal, the storm god of the Canaanites. By the prayers of God's prophet Elijah (see James 5:17), there was no rain on the earth for three long years (1 Kings 17:1). At the end of that time, Elijah went up Mount Carmel to confront the prophets of Baal. There he offered the proper sacrifice for sin, which God accepted with fire (1 Kings 18:36–38). The people turned back to God, lying down with their faces in the dust and shouting, "The LORD, he is God; the LORD, he is God" (1 Kings 18:39). Then Elijah bowed down in prayer; seven times he prayed for God to hear from heaven and send rain to his people. The skies grew black, the clouds opened, and a great rain fell on the earth (1 Kings 18:41–45). God provided for his people again.

All of this was the answer to Solomon's prayers. The king knew how certain his people were to turn away from the worship of God. When they did, he knew exactly what would happen: the land would be afflicted with drought. But Solomon prayed that when they repented, God would forgive their sins and shower them with blessings again. This is the way for us to

227

pray whenever we are in one of the dry times of the spiritual life. We should repent of loving the gods of money, sex, and power, and all the other idols of our age, and then we should pray for God to rain his blessings down on us, refreshing us with the pure water of the Holy Spirit.

FOURTH PETITION: A PRAYER FOR DELIVERANCE

Solomon's fourth petition was similar to the third. As the king anticipated further difficulties his people were likely to face as a result of their sin, he prayed for deliverance from disaster.

Solomon began by listing a comprehensive series of natural disasters: "If there is famine in the land, if there is pestilence or blight or mildew or locust or caterpillar, if their enemy besieges them in the land at their gates, whatever plague, whatever sickness there is" (1 Kings 8:37). Once again, these terrible disasters were all prophesied in Deuteronomy, where God warned his people that the wages of their sin would include famine, pestilence, warfare, and disease (e.g., Deut. 28:38–39, 52, 58–61; 32:23–24). According to prophecy, "the LORD will make the pestilence stick to you until he has consumed you off the land that you are entering to take possession of it. The LORD will strike you with wasting disease and with fever, inflammation and fiery heat, and with drought and with blight and with mildew" (Deut. 28:21–22).

We should not necessarily assume every time we see one of these disasters take place somewhere in the world that God is punishing a nation directly for its sin. Our own nations are not in covenant with God the way that Israel was. Nevertheless, these are some of the biblical judgments against sin, all of which call for prayers of repentance. So Solomon said:

> Whatever prayer, whatever plea is made by any man or by all your people Israel, each knowing the affliction of his own heart and stretching out his hands toward this house, then hear in heaven your dwelling place and forgive and act and render to each whose heart you know, according to all his ways (for you, you only, know the hearts of all the children of mankind), that they may fear you all the days that they live in the land that you gave to our fathers. (1 Kings 8:38–40)

Once again, Solomon is asking God to hear his people when they pray, not just corporately, but also individually. Whenever anyone prays, or when the whole nation prays together—in either case—Solomon is asking God to listen. Solomon asserts that God is uniquely omniscient, that he alone knows the true condition of every person's heart. Then the king aims his prayer squarely at the glory of God. The reason he asks God to forgive his people's sins and to act on their behalf is so that they will fear him all their days—in other words, that they will worship him. The goal of Solomon's fourth petition is the worship of God.

Like the rest of Solomon's prayer, this petition was answered later in the book of Kings. In the days of King Hezekiah, Sennacherib the king of Assyria besieged Jerusalem (2 Kings 18:13–19:13). The situation was desperate, for in those days Assyria had the world's strongest army. In fact, we know from the annals of Assyria that Sennacherib boasted about shutting Israel up "like a bird in a cage."[1] But Hezekiah did what a king ought to do when his nation is in trouble: he went to the holy temple and spread the situation before the Lord in prayer, asking God to save his people (2 Kings 19:14–19). In other words, Hezekiah did exactly what Solomon prayed that people would do: he stretched out his hands toward the house of the Lord.

God answered Hezekiah's prayers, as he always does when his people pray for salvation. That very night the angel of the Lord struck down one hundred eighty-five thousand Assyrian soldiers, forcing King Sennacherib to return home, where he was murdered by his sons as he worshiped the false god Nisroch (2 Kings 19:35–37). History shows how well these prayers actually work, therefore, giving us confidence for our own petitions. Whenever we are afflicted, we may pray for God to deliver us. God knows what is really in our hearts. If our repentance is sincere, he will forgive our sins and deliver us from every disaster.

FIFTH PETITION: A PRAYER FOR OUTSIDERS

For the people who were present at the dedication of the temple, Solomon's fifth petition surely must have been the most surprising. Most of them undoubtedly regarded the temple as a house of worship for the Jews. Yet Solomon also prayed for outsiders:

1. W. S. LaSor, "Sennacherib," in *The International Standard Bible Encyclopedia*, ed. Geoffrey Bromiley et al., 4 vols. (Grand Rapids: Eerdmans, 1988), 4:394.

> Likewise, when a foreigner, who is not of your people Israel, comes from
> a far country for your name's sake (for they shall hear of your great name
> and your mighty hand, and of your outstretched arm), when he comes and
> prays toward this house, hear in heaven your dwelling place and do accord-
> ing to all for which the foreigner calls to you, in order that all the peoples of
> the earth may know your name and fear you, as do your people Israel, and
> that they may know that this house that I have built is called by your name.
> (1 Kings 8:41–43)

As surprising as it may have been to some, this petition was fully in keeping with God's original purpose for the temple. This building was not just for
the Jews; it was always intended to be "a house of prayer for all peoples" (Isa.
56:7; cf. Isa. 2:2–3; Mark 11:17). The temple of Solomon was an international
house of prayer. This is because God has always had a missionary heart for
the nations of the world. Even his sovereign election of the Jews was for the
sake of all peoples. The global reach of his grace went all the way back to
the promise he made to Abraham, that all nations would be blessed through
him (e.g., Gen. 12:1–3).

Solomon prayed that God would fulfill his ancient promise at the temple.
He envisioned foreigners hearing about the God of Israel and then coming
to Jerusalem for worship. Once he built this temple, people would come.
Solomon longed for these outsiders to join the family of God. Thus he asked
God to hear and answer their temple prayers, so that everywhere on earth
people would know the one true God.

Solomon's intercession is one of the great missionary prayers in the history
of redemption, as the king of Israel intercedes for the nations of the world.
Solomon asked God to answer the prayers of people from every tongue and
tribe, so that God in turn would receive their praise. With compassion for
people outside the family of faith, and holy zeal for the glory of God, Solomon wanted his temple to become a mission station for the world.

One of the clearest answers to Solomon's prayer comes in 2 Kings 5, where
a mighty captain in the Syrian army travels to Israel for healing. The warrior's name was Naaman, and when he contracted leprosy, he was desperate
to find a cure. Finally, a little Jewish servant girl mentioned that if he went to
Israel, the prophet of the Lord would surely heal him. Thus Naaman became
the answer to Solomon's prayer: a foreigner from a far country who heard

the name of the Lord, traveled to Israel, received the answer to his prayers, and then gave praise to God, saying, "Behold, I know that there is no God in all the earth but in Israel" (2 Kings 5:15).

We pray for the same thing today: the salvation of the world. We pray that people from all nations would hear about the grace of God, that there is forgiveness for sins through the death and resurrection of Jesus Christ. We pray that they would turn to God in prayer, asking him for the free gift of eternal life. We pray that for the sake of his own glory, God would answer their prayers, and that they in turn would give praise to God for his saving grace. When we pray for the nations, we are standing on God's ancient promise that his grace is for the whole world. At the same time, we are aiming at the highest goal in the universe, which is the glory of God.

SIXTH PETITION: A PRAYER FOR VICTORY

Solomon's sixth petition was a prayer for victory: "If your people go out to battle against their enemy, by whatever way you shall send them, and they pray to the LORD toward the city that you have chosen and the house that I have built for your name, then hear in heaven their prayer and their plea, and maintain their cause" (1 Kings 8:44–45).

Solomon was honest about his people's sin; he knew that often they were their own worst enemy. But he also knew that they had other enemies as well, enemies who would wage war against them. So the king prayed that when his people went out to battle and prayed for the help of their God, he would win them the victory.

There is a notable example of this kind of military situation in 2 Kings 3, where the King of Moab marches against Israel. When he saw what the Moabites were doing, Jehoshaphat the king of Judah asked for the help of his God. Through a miraculous intervention, in which the Moabites mistakenly thought that they saw the blood of the Israelites running red in the water, God answered Jehoshaphat's prayers and delivered his people from their enemies. God loves to defend his people when they pray.

This does not mean that every army that prays to God will win the battle. The kind of warfare Solomon had in mind was a holy war in which God explicitly sent his own people to fight the enemies of his kingdom (see also Deut. 20:1–4). So Solomon's prayer has no direct application to the United

231

States Army, or to the armed forces of any other earthly kingdom. Where it does have direct application is to the church of Jesus Christ in its spiritual warfare with Satan and the powers of his darkness. Today we fight our spiritual battles—battles against temptation, battles for the souls of people who need to know Christ—through prayer. And when we pray, God wins the victory.

SEVENTH PETITION: A PRAYER FOR FORGIVENESS

Solomon's last petition was probably the most important—a prayer for total forgiveness. Once again, the king describes a situation when people will be desperate for the help of their God. In fact, Dale Ralph Davis calls it Solomon's "worst case scenario."[2] Here is how the king began his final petition: "If they sin against you—for there is no one who does not sin—and you are angry with them and give them to an enemy, so that they are carried away captive to the land of the enemy, far off or near" (1 Kings 8:46).

Of course, this is exactly what happened. Solomon's "if" was really more like a "when." By the inspiration of the Holy Spirit, his last petition was a preview of Israel's future history. The people did sin against God, and God was angry with them, and he did give them to an enemy, and they were carried off to captivity. Solomon was praying in advance about the tragic events of 586 B.C., when Jerusalem and its temple were destroyed by the mighty armies of Nebuchadnezzar, and when God's people were carried off to Babylon for seventy long years of exile. Once again, Solomon was "simply praying out of the Pentateuch,"[3] for in the days of Moses, God had warned his people what would happen if they sinned against him: "The LORD will bring a nation against you from far away, from the end of the earth, swooping down like the eagle, a nation whose language you do not understand" (Deut. 28:49; cf. 28:36–37, 64–67; 29:27–28).

Yet Solomon believed in God's grace as much as he believed in God's justice. Thus he prayed for Israel's forgiveness, prophesying the nation's repentance and return:

2. Dale Ralph Davis, *The Wisdom and the Folly: An Exposition of the Book of First Kings* (Fearn, Ross-shire: Christian Focus, 2002), 89.
3. Ibid.

If they turn their heart in the land to which they have been carried captive, and repent and plead with you in the land of their captors, saying, "We have sinned and have acted perversely and wickedly," if they repent with all their mind and with all their heart in the land of their enemies, who carried them captive, and pray to you toward their land, which you gave to their fathers, the city that you have chosen, and the house that I have built for your name, then hear in heaven your dwelling place their prayer and their plea, and maintain their cause and forgive your people who have sinned against you, and all their transgressions that they have committed against you, and grant them compassion in the sight of those who carried them captive, that they may have compassion on them. (1 Kings 8:47–50; cf. Deut. 30:1–10)

King Solomon believed in the merciful compassion of a rescuing God—a God who listens when his people pray. Even when we fall into sin and wander far away from God, he will still hear our prayers, and when we pray, he will forgive.

Prayers like this rescued Israel from captivity. When the prophet Daniel was exiled to Babylon, he opened his windows toward Jerusalem, turned his heart toward the temple, and prayed to the living God (Dan. 6:10; cf. Neh. 1:4–11; Jonah 2:4). The book of Daniel records his prayer of confession, which sounds like something straight out of Solomon. Daniel confessed that Israel had acted wickedly in sinning against God (Dan. 9:3–15). He asked God to have mercy on his people, to forgive their sins and restore his holy temple in Jerusalem (Dan. 9:16–19). This was exactly the kind of prayer that King Solomon asked God to hear and answer. Thus Daniel's prayer turned out to be part of the answer to Solomon's prayer: a prayer of confession asking for the forgiveness of a merciful God. God answered both of their prayers by forgiving his people's sins and bringing them back home from Babylon.

Solomon knew that such prayers would be answered because he knew the character of God. Why would God ever answer the prayers of a rebellious people? Because "they are your people," Solomon said, "and your heritage, which you brought out of Egypt, from the midst of the iron furnace" (1 Kings 8:51). Solomon appealed to God's covenant loyalty—his long-standing, long-suffering commitment to save the people that he rescued from Egypt. Out of all the nations on earth, God had chosen this people to be his treasured possession (Deut. 7:6).

Since God had a vested interest in their salvation, Solomon prayed that he would continue to hear and answer their prayers: "Let your eyes be open to the plea of your servant and to the plea of your people Israel, giving ear to them whenever they call to you. For you separated them from among all the peoples of the earth to be your heritage, as you declared through Moses your servant, when you brought our fathers out of Egypt, O Lord GOD" (1 Kings 8:52–53; cf. Ex. 19:5; Lev. 26:40–45). This was Solomon's prayer, and as we will see when we get to 1 Kings 9:3, God would indeed answer.

As the church of Jesus Christ, we are able to make the same strong claim that God will hear our prayers. We belong to God's chosen race and treasured people (see 1 Peter 2:9). Therefore, when we lift our hands to the living temple—to Jesus himself—God will hear and answer our prayers. He will answer our prayers on the basis of the atoning sacrifice that Jesus made for our sins—not at the temple, but on the cross.

PRAYING LIKE SOLOMON

Solomon's seven petitions cover almost everything that anyone could ever need, even in all the desperate troubles of a fallen world. Solomon prayed for deliverance from danger, provision for daily needs, and victory over fierce enemies. He prayed that even in the worst-case scenario, God would bring his people back home. He prayed this for people who were far away from God, even for people who had never known God at all. Most of all, Solomon prayed for our biggest need, which is the forgiveness of our sins against a holy God.

Everyone needs this prayer. We know this from the way that Solomon includes every one of us. At the beginning of his final petition, the king made one little editorial comment that condemns the entire human race: "for there is no one who does not sin" (1 Kings 8:46). This had been the logical premise of Solomon's prayer from the very beginning. In his wisdom, the king knew people well enough to know that everyone is a sinner, including anyone who belongs to the people of God. So he prayed a sinner's prayer for the forgiveness of a merciful God.

We make Solomon's prayer our own by confessing our own personal and individual sin against God, admitting that *we* are guilty of what Solomon called "wicked" and "perverse" transgression (see 1 Kings 8:47). We pray this way when we see what a disaster our lives have become, often because of our own rebellion against the will of God. How many of our wounds are self-inflicted by sin! We need God to heal us, forgive us, and deliver us. We may pray for God to do all this even if we are spiritual outsiders who have never prayed to him before. We can still pray for God's help when we are far away from him, in captivity to sin. All we need to do is turn to Jesus Christ—the living temple who offered his own body as the atonement for our sin. When the worst-case scenario becomes the story of our lives, there is still a way back home to God for anyone who truly repents and believes in Christ.

We also make Solomon's prayer our own by offering these petitions for one another. When he made these petitions, Solomon was not praying for himself, but for all the people of God. This is a corporate prayer, and we too are called to pray for God's people. We pray that justice will be done in the church, so that any dispute will be fairly judged, and that the persecuted church will receive its reward on the last day. We pray that God will provide for his people's needs and rescue them from every danger, including natural disasters. We pray for victory over our enemies: sin, death, and all the temptations of the devil. We pray for all the people and nations that are outside the church, asking God to bring them in and make them a part of his family. We pray for all the wayward sinners who have wandered away from the church, asking God to bring them home from their spiritual exile. These are the prayers we offer for all the people of God.

As we pray, we know that Jesus is praying for us. As we have seen throughout 1 Kings, Jesus Christ is the greater Solomon of the kingdom of God. So when we see Solomon at his prayers, we should remember that we too have a King who knows our weakness and is always praying for us (Heb. 4:15; 7:25). Jesus ever lives to intercede for people who are oppressed and need justice, for people in spiritual danger who need deliverance, for suffering people who need survival. Jesus prays for God to protect us from our enemy, the evil one (John 17:15). Most of all, he prays for people who sin and need a Savior. This is the best "sinner's prayer" of all: the one Jesus prays for us, asking God to take the blood from his cross and use it to cover all our sin.

How do we know that God will answer our prayers and forgive all our sins? We know this because the Bible says that God is merciful to every penitent sinner. The apostle Peter learned this the time he asked Jesus how many times he had to forgive his brother. "As many as seven times?" Peter asked (Matt. 18:21). Obviously, Peter was exaggerating. How could anyone possibly forgive somebody *seven* times for the same offense? Peter would have fit right in with my old high school youth group. He knew that seven was too much, that it was beyond the limit of forgiveness.

But Jesus said, "I do not say to you seven times, but seventy times seven" (Matt. 18:22). Jesus said this because he knew the infinite grace of God, who is willing to forgive and forgive and forgive. By faith in that infinite grace Solomon made seven petitions for the forgiveness of God. By the same faith we can use these same petitions again and again, all through life, asking God to hear from heaven and forgive our sins for Jesus' sake. His grace is greater than all our sin. It is, in fact, a "seven good" grace from a "seven good" God who has given us a "seven good" Savior.

19

SOLOMON'S BENEDICTION

1 Kings 8:54—66

Now as Solomon finished offering all this prayer and plea to the
LORD, he arose from before the altar of the LORD, where he had
knelt with hands outstretched toward heaven. And he stood and
blessed all the assembly of Israel with a loud voice.
(1 Kings 8:54–55)

or every festival there must be a feast. What would a wedding be without a reception, or Thanksgiving without turkey and stuffing, or a Little League championship without a pizza party? Good food and drink are essential to any grand celebration.

One year our family traveled to Phoenix for a medical convention at which my father-in-law was to be honored as the outgoing president. On the first evening hundreds of doctors and their families loaded onto buses and went downtown for an open-air fiesta. Each guest was given a colorful sombrero, and when the buses pulled up to the plaza, a live band was playing music for salsa dancing. Everyone was ready to party.

We piled off the buses and rushed to the buffet tables, hungry for the good Mexican food we had been promised. Yet within half an hour the tables were empty and word began to spread that there was no more food. Soon the guests were climbing back on the buses and demanding to be taken back to the hotel, where they could get something to eat. Just before the buses drove away, a delivery truck pulled up with a stack of pizzas. The hosts desperately pleaded for everyone to stay, but it was too little, too late: the party was over.

There is no fiesta without a feast. If this is true, then there was only one appropriate way for Solomon's temple prayer to end. The king was dedicating the most important building in the history of the world—the one place on earth where God promised to meet with his people. As soon as the building was furnished, the presence of God descended in a bright cloud of luminous glory. Then Solomon dedicated the temple through prayer, and as he came to the end of his petitions, it was time for a feast.

SECOND BLESSING

To see how the people feasted, and why, we first need to hear the benediction that Solomon gave—a blessing that was also a prayer. The Bible says that "as Solomon finished offering all this prayer and plea to the LORD, he arose from before the altar of the LORD, where he had knelt with hands outstretched toward heaven. And he stood and blessed all the assembly of Israel with a loud voice" (1 Kings 8:54–55).

The king began his prayer standing up (1 Kings 8:22), but at some point he started kneeling, so that when he was finished praying he needed to stand back up again. Perhaps Solomon had wanted to give honor to God by kneeling in his presence. Maybe the burden of his seven long petitions for Israel's forgiveness had forced him to his knees.[1] In any case, he went from standing to kneeling to standing again.

Solomon's prayer ended the way it began, with a benediction. Before he started to pray, the king stood up and blessed the Israelites by blessing their God: "Blessed be the LORD, the God of Israel" (1 Kings 8:15). He ended his prayer with a similar blessing. Bible scholars call this an *inclusio*—a literary form that ends the same way it began in order to mark off a complete unit of text. Solomon blessed his people from beginning to end, pronouncing a benediction both before and after his prayer.

---

1. Richard Nelson, *First and Second Kings*, Interpretation (Louisville: John Knox, 1987), 55.

In the dismissal, Solomon blessed God for his faithfulness: "Blessed be the LORD who has given rest to his people Israel, according to all that he promised. Not one word has failed of all his good promise, which he spoke by Moses his servant" (1 Kings 8:56).

The faithfulness of God in keeping his promises is a familiar Old Testament theme. At the end of Joshua's battles, when the Israelites vanquished their enemies in the Promised Land, the Scripture says that "not one word of all the good promises that the LORD had made to the house of Israel had failed; all came to pass" (Josh. 21:45). King Solomon said something similar before his prayer of dedication, when he declared that God had "fulfilled what he promised with his mouth to David my father" (1 Kings 8:15). Whether we think of his promises to Moses or his promises to David, the God of Israel is a promise-keeping God.

God made many promises to his people, but the one Solomon had in mind was the promise that he would give "rest to his people" (1 Kings 8:56)—rest from warfare with their enemies (see Ex. 33:14). Here is what God promised through Moses:

> But when you go over the Jordan and live in the land that the LORD your God is giving you to inherit, and when he gives you rest from all your enemies around, so that you live in safety, then to the place that the LORD your God will choose, to make his name dwell there, there you shall bring all that I command you: your burnt offerings and your sacrifices. (Deut. 12:10–11)

These promises were fulfilled at Solomon's temple in Jerusalem. Once the people were living in safety and security, at rest from all their enemies, they gathered at the place God chose as the dwelling place for his name, the house for worship and sacrifice. This all happened because with God a promise made is a promise kept.

The promises God kept for Israel give us confidence that he will also keep the promises he has made to us. We too are the recipients of the promises of God, specifically the promises he has made in Christ. "For no matter how many promises God has made," the Scripture says, "they are 'Yes' in Christ" (2 Cor. 1:20 NIV).

In Christ we have the promise of rest, for Jesus said, "Come to me, all who labor and are heavy laden, and I will give you rest" (Matt. 11:28). In

Christ we have the promise of victory over the enemies of sin, death, and the devil: "For he must reign until he has put all his enemies under his feet" (1 Cor. 15:25). In Christ we have the promise of a place to worship, for his very body is the temple of the living God (see John 2:19–22). So for anyone who is weary and needs rest, for anyone who feels defeated by sin and needs victory over temptation, for anyone who is facing death and needs deliverance, for anyone whose heart longs to find a Savior who is worthy of worship, God has a promise he will keep in Jesus Christ.

If we find ourselves wondering whether God's promises will come true— or whether they will come true for us—we need only to wait for them to be fulfilled. We wait in faith for the land that God has promised to us, the land of heaven. There we will find rest from all our weariness, victory over all our sin, deliverance on the other side of death, and a home where we can worship God forever. These and all the other promises that God has made to us in Christ will come true, as we will see . . . if we believe.

THE GOD WE NEED

As he blessed God for keeping his promises, Solomon also prayed for God to bless his people. What started out as a benediction turned into a petition. According to Donald Wiseman, "the 'Blessing of Solomon' is not strictly a blessing but a prayer for the continuing close relationship between God and his people."[2] In the words of Dale Ralph Davis, it is a "prayer-blessing"[3]—a prayer for the blessings we need from God.

Most people have strong opinions about the blessings they want from God. We have a long list of things we want God to do for us, and we are quick to let him know when he doesn't deliver. We want God to ratify our plans, satisfy our desires, and gratify our pleasures. As Christian Smith discovered in his landmark study of teenage religion, many Americans view God as a "cosmic butler," always ready to wait on us hand and foot.[4] No doubt this explains why we are often disappointed with God: he does not give us the service we expect.

2. Donald J. Wiseman, *1 & 2 Kings: An Introduction and Commentary*, Tyndale Old Testament Commentaries (Leicester: Inter-Varsity, 1993), 123.
3. Dale Ralph Davis, *The Wisdom and the Folly: An Exposition of the Book of First Kings* (Fearn, Ross-shire: Christian Focus, 2002), 92.
4. See Christian Smith and Melinda Lundquist Denton, *Soul Searching: The Religious and Spiritual Lives of American Teenagers* (Oxford: Oxford University Press, 2005).

The problem is not that we want too much from God, but that we want too many of the wrong things and not nearly enough of the best that God has to give. When he asked one student what God was like, Christian Smith was informed that God was good. So he asked a follow-up question: "What good has God done in your life?" The answer was, "Well, I have a house, parents, I have the Internet, I have a phone, I have cable." If that is all we need in life, then we do not need God at all; we just need a well-paying job. But Solomon was wise enough to ask God for the things we really need, and his prayer list in 1 Kings 8:57–60 helps us set the agenda for our own intercession.

Consider which of Solomon's petitions you need the most, or that you need to pray the most for your family or your church.

Solomon asked for God's *abiding presence*: "The LORD our God be with us, as he was with our fathers. May he not leave us or forsake us" (1 Kings 8:57). More than all the other blessings that God has to give, we need God himself in the living presence of his grace. All the great spiritual leaders in the Bible understood this. We see it in Moses, who was promised that the God of the burning bush would go with him wherever he went (Ex. 3:12). We see it in Joshua, who was told that God would never leave him or forsake him (Josh. 1:9; cf. Deut. 31:6–8). We see it in the psalmist, who said, "The LORD will not forsake his people" (Ps. 94:14; cf. Heb. 13:5). In all of life's decisions and difficulties, we need God to be with us to help us through. As Matthew Henry said, the presence of God "is all in all to the happiness of a church and nation and of every particular person."[5] So for the sake of our own joy, we pray for God's abiding presence.

King Solomon had a specific reason for asking God to be with his people. He wanted them to be holy. So he prayed for God's *sanctifying Spirit*: "that he may incline our hearts to him, to walk in all his ways and to keep his commandments, his statutes, and his rules, which he commanded our fathers" (1 Kings 8:58; cf. Ps. 119:36).

This prayer shows deep insight into the spiritual need of fallen human beings. The sad truth is that because of sin, our hearts are *not* inclined to walk in God's ways, to say nothing of keeping his commandments. Have you ever wondered why it is so easy to sin, and so hard to be holy? It is because our sinful hearts lean away from God, not toward him. In the words of Matthew

5. Matthew Henry, *Matthew Henry's Complete Commentary on the Whole Bible*, vol. 2, *Judges to Job* (New York: Fleming Revell, n.d.), n.p.

Henry, "Our hearts are naturally averse to our duty, and apt to decline from God."[6] Therefore, we need a powerful work of God's Spirit to turn our hearts back in his direction. As Henry also said, "it is his grace that inclines them, grace that must be obtained by prayer." So we pray for the sanctifying Spirit to make our hearts want what God wants. Only then will we walk in God's ways and keep God's commandments.

Next Solomon prayed for God's *listening ear*. More specifically, he asked God to listen to his people when they made any of the seven petitions he had just prayed: "Let these words of mine, with which I have pleaded before the LORD, be near to the LORD our God day and night, and may he maintain the cause of his servant and the cause of his people Israel" (1 Kings 8:59). Solomon was asking God to let his prayer of dedication stand for all time, so that when his people prayed for justice, or forgiveness, or protection, or deliverance—whatever they asked in faith, at any time of day or night—God would hear their prayers and answer with power.

Then King Solomon prayed for God's *universal glory*, asking "that all the peoples of the earth may know that the LORD is God; there is no other" (1 Kings 8:60; cf. Deut. 4:35; Isa. 45:5). This prayer was based on the belief that there is only one God. The people of God declared this every morning in their daily confession: "Hear, O Israel: The LORD our God, the LORD is one" (Deut. 6:4). If this is true—that God is unique, that he is the one and only God—then it should be acknowledged everywhere. Thus Solomon prayed for God's glory among the nations, that he would be known to be God by all people in all places.

When the king prayed for the universal glory of God, he was praying that God would fulfill his mission to the world. God's own glorious purpose is to receive the praise of all peoples, filling the whole earth with his glory. This puts our own missionary work, with all its joys and discouragements, into perspective. As Christopher Wright explains in his book *The Mission of God*, our own "efforts to make God known must be set within the prior framework of God's own will to be known. We are seeking to accomplish what God himself wills to happen." This is reassuring, Wright says, because "we know that behind all our fumbling efforts and inadequate communication stands the supreme will of the living God, reaching out in loving self-revelation, incred-

6. Ibid.

ibly willing to open blind eyes and reveal his glory through the treasures of the gospel delivered in the clay pots of his witnesses."[7]

This is the God we need: not a deity who does what we want him to do, as if we were the center of the universe, but a God who exists for his own glory. We need this God every day. In verse 59 Solomon asks for God's help "as each day requires." So this is a daily prayer for the daily needs of the people of God. Every day we need God to be with us through all the trials and triumphs of life. Every day we need him to incline our hearts in his direction; otherwise, we will wander away. Every day we need him to hear our prayers and answer them for the sake of his glory in the world. These are the recommended daily requirements of the Christian life: the abiding presence, the sanctifying Spirit, and the listening ear of the God who alone deserves all the glory.

The Obedience That God Requires

How should we respond to God's loving presence and transforming grace? When we know the God who is with us all the way, who turns our heart in the right direction, and who answers all our prayers with glory, what is the right way to respond? At the end of Solomon's dedication, we see the obedience that God requires, the sacrifice that God demands, and the praise that God deserves.

First we see *the obedience God requires*. At the end of his benediction, Solomon gave what one scholar calls his "dedication exhortation."[8] Because there is only one true God—a gracious and life-changing God who listens when his people pray—"let your heart therefore be wholly true to the LORD our God, walking in his statutes and keeping his commandments, as at this day" (1 Kings 8:61).

If God has inclined our hearts to him by the power of the Holy Spirit, then our hearts should be true. Here is a call to radical holiness—the full obedience that God requires from every believer. This obedience is not just for Old Testament believers living under the law, but also for New Testament believers saved by the gospel of Jesus Christ. When Jesus commissioned his disciples to go into all the world and preach the gospel, he told them to

7. Christopher J. H. Wright, *The Mission of God: Unlocking the Bible's Grand Narrative* (Downers Grove, IL: InterVarsity, 2006), 129–30.

8. August H. Konkel, *1 & 2 Kings*, NIV Application Commentary (Grand Rapids: Zondervan, 2006), 176.

teach people to obey everything that he commanded (Matt. 28:18–20). Jesus therefore gives us the same basic command that Solomon gave to Israel. We do not obey in order to be saved; we obey because we have been saved.

So let your heart be true to the commands of Christ. Practice gospel holiness. Put God first in everything. Honor the Lord's Day with worship, rest, and mercy. Give generously to gospel work. Promote and preserve sexual purity. Do not covet what you do not have, or grow bitter over what God has taken away. Do not be double-minded, sometimes obeying God, but often pursuing sinful passions. Let your heart be wholly true to the Lord your God.

Notice where this kind of obedience begins: according to Solomon, it starts inside, with a heart that is committed to keeping God's command. Then it works its way out in the way we actually live. What we need, therefore, is the change of heart that only the Holy Spirit can bring as he inclines us in God's direction.

To say the same thing in another way, we can keep the commands of verse 61 only if God answers the prayer of verse 59 and turns our hearts toward him. This is a prayer that God loves to answer; therefore, we should not be afraid to pursue gospel holiness, even in the areas of temptation where we face the fiercest struggle. God is able and willing to incline our hearts to full obedience. All we need to do is pray, and then obey.

THE SACRIFICE THAT GOD DEMANDS

There is also *the sacrifice that God demands*. This brings us to the unforgettable ending to the dedication of the temple. Solomon finished the benediction at the end of his dedicatory prayer; then "the king, and all Israel with him, offered sacrifice before the LORD. Solomon offered as peace offerings to the LORD 22,000 oxen and 120,000 sheep. So the king and all the people of Israel dedicated the house of the LORD" (1 Kings 8:62–63). Thus the temple was dedicated with sacrifice as well as prayer.

What is amazing here is the sheer number of sacrifices that were offered. Earlier we were told that when the ark of the covenant was first brought up to the temple, Solomon sacrificed countless sheep and oxen (1 Kings 8:5). More sacrifices were offered after the dedication, so many that not even the great bronze altar in the temple courtyard was large enough to handle all of them. To make room for all the sacrifices, Solomon ended up sanctifying the whole courtyard as a place of sacrifice: "The same day the king consecrated the middle of the court that was before the house of the LORD, for there he offered the burnt offering and the grain offering and the fat pieces of the peace offerings, because the bronze altar that was before the LORD was too small to receive the burnt offering and the grain offering and the fat pieces of the peace offerings" (1 Kings 8:64; cf. 9:25).

In all, Solomon sacrificed more than 140,000 sheep and oxen. The number is so large that some scholars have claimed that it must be an exaggeration. Impossible, they say; the number is "utterly fantastic."[9] Yet when we consider that these were the sacrifices of an entire nation, offered by twelve tribes over a period of seven days, there is no legitimate reason to question the accuracy of the biblical text. We do better to stand in awe of these sacrifices than to doubt them, and to consider what sacrifice God demands of us.

Strictly speaking, these were not sacrifices of atonement that did away with the guilt of sin. Within the sacrificial system, there were several kinds of sacrifices, as described in the opening chapters of Leviticus.[10] Two such sacrifices are mentioned in 1 Kings 8:64, where it is said that Solomon consecrated the courtyard with a burnt offering (*'olah*) and a grain offering (*minhah*), as well as peace offerings. But the sacrifices that people offered to dedicate the temple were peace offerings, also known as fellowship offerings (1 Kings 8:63–64; cf. Lev. 3:1–17; 7:11–38).

The biblical term for these offerings (*shelamim*) came from the Hebrew word for "peace" (*shalom*). These sacrifices showed that God was at peace with his people, and they did so in a remarkable way. The fat parts of the sacrifice were burned as an offering unto God, but the meat was given to the priests and the people. In other words, this was an offering that God shared in communion with his people. Part of the sacrifice was for him, and part of it was for them. The fellowship offering was a covenant meal for people who were so much at peace with God that they could sit down and share a meal with him. What better way to dedicate the temple as a place to meet with

9. S. J. DeVries, *1 Kings*, Word Biblical Commentaries (Waco, TX: Word, 1985), 127.
10. For a helpful survey of the various sacrifices, see Tremper Longman III, *Immanuel in Our Place: Seeing Christ in Israel's Worship*, The Gospel According to the Old Testament (Phillipsburg, NJ: P&R Publishing, 2001), 75–115.

God than to sit down at the house of the Lord and share a feast with him? As the people feasted, they rejoiced in the presence of their God.

We experience this joy more completely and more intensely in Jesus Christ. In his very person, Jesus Christ *is* the living temple of the living God. His physical body is the house of the Lord, the place where humanity meets deity. The way Jesus dedicated the holy temple of his body—the way he consecrated that sacred space—was by offering *himself* as the sacrifice to make peace with God. We have peace with God by the blood of his cross (see Col. 1:20). Jesus Christ is the peace offering who brings us into fellowship with a holy God. We feast upon his grace, as signified in the sacred meal of Holy Communion.

Now we joyfully respond to the peace-making grace of Jesus Christ with sacrifices of our own. We do not sacrifice animals, like the Israelites did, but we do give him the first and the best of everything we have, dedicating ourselves for his service.

What sacrifices is God calling us to make for his kingdom? Truth be told, we would rather not make any sacrifices at all. Instead we prefer the approach taken in a magazine advertisement that promised "worship without sacrifice." The ad was for a cosmetic described as a "moisturizing long lasting bronzing powder." In other words, the product would make a woman look like she had a tan without spending any time in the sun: worship without sacrifice.

As far as the Bible is concerned, there is no worship without sacrifice. There would be no worship at all unless Jesus had made the ultimate sacrifice of his broken body and crucified blood. But even the worship we offer God in response demands sacrifice: the sacrifice of our time and money, our dreams and ambitions, our thoughts and words and actions. There is no worship without sacrifice.

A simple story helps to illustrate this principle. The story comes from a youth group canoe trip that my youngest sister took when she was in junior high. The first night out, she was distressed to discover that despite all warnings and preparations to the contrary, her sleeping bag was soaking wet. It was a miserable and sleepless night. But the next night my sister's youth director made a noble sacrifice: he traded his warm, dry sleeping bag for her cold soggy one. After the trip was over, my sister responded with a small sacrifice of her own: a pan of homemade brownies.

In a similar, yet infinitely costlier way, Jesus Christ made his bed in the misery of our sin, so that he could offer us the comfort of his righteousness. Now we respond with little sacrifices of our own. What we give could never measure up to the cost of his supreme sacrifice, any more than my sister's homemade brownies were a fair trade for even one night in a cold, wet sleeping bag. But whatever we give to God—whatever time or money or service—is nothing less than God demands.

THE PRAISE THAT GOD DESERVES

Finally, we respond to God with *the praise that he deserves*. Here is how the Bible summarizes Solomon's weeklong celebration, as well as what happened afterward:

> So Solomon held the feast at that time, and all Israel with him, a great assembly, from Lebo-hamath to the Brook of Egypt, before the LORD our God, seven days. On the eighth day he sent the people away, and they blessed the king and went to their homes joyful and glad of heart for all the goodness that the LORD had shown to David his servant and to Israel his people. (1 Kings 8:65–66)

The geographic references in these verses may be unfamiliar to most Bible readers today, but they indicate that the whole nation of Israel celebrated this feast. Lebo-hamath and the Brook of Egypt were the extreme boundaries of Solomon's kingdom. Everyone from north to south was in attendance. To put this in an American frame of reference, it would be like saying that everyone from Alaska down to the Everglades went to Washington, DC.

All these people were doing the same thing. They were united in their praise to God and his anointed king. In addition to blessing the Lord, the people also blessed their king. So at the same time they rejoiced in God and his holy temple, they also rejoiced in Solomon and his royal kingship. They blessed the king for the honor he gave to God in building a holy temple for worship. Solomon was the joy of his people.

We have a similar yet greater joy in the kingdom of Jesus Christ. The praise we offer to God is centered on our King, Jesus Christ, both on his glory as the Son of God and on his salvation through the cross and the empty tomb. This joyful worship is not just for Sundays in church, but for every day of the week and every place we go. Just as the Israelites went home praising their God and their king, we too are called to take the joy of Jesus with us everywhere we go.

Are you offering God the praise that he deserves? Louie Giglio has defined worship simply as "our response to what we value most." So another way to ask the question is this: Does your response to God demonstrate that he is what you value most in life?

Giglio observes that worship is the one thing we all do. It is "what we're all about on any given day." We are always saying, "This person, this thing, this experience (this whatever) is what matters most to me . . . it's the thing I put first in my life." This "thing" will differ from person to person. It might be a relationship or an ambition. It might be our friends or our status or our stuff. It might be some form of pleasure. But whatever we call it, "everybody has an altar. And every altar has a throne." According to Giglio, it is easy to identify what is on the throne for us:

> You simply follow the trail of your time, your affection, your energy, your money, and your loyalty. At the end of that trail you'll find a throne; and whatever, or whomever, is on that throne is what's of highest value to you. On that throne is what you worship. Sure, not too many of us walk around saying, "I worship my stuff. I worship my X-Box. I worship this pleasure. I worship her. I worship my body. I worship me!" But the trail never lies. We may say we value this thing or that thing more than any other, but the volume of our actions speaks louder than our words.[11]

When Solomon and his people dedicated the temple, they had the volume turned all the way up. With every blessing they pronounced and every animal they sacrificed, they declared the glory of their God. They kept the volume up all the way home as they praised their king and his kingdom.

How do you go home from worship in the house of the Lord? Do you go rejoicing in Christ and his kingdom, offering him the obedience he requires and the sacrifice he demands? Or does your attention quickly turn to the things you really worship: the relationships, the pleasures, and the entertainments that claim your higher allegiance? Whatever you choose to worship, make sure it is worthy of a feast, as only Jesus is.

---

11. Louie Giglio, "Wired for a Life of Worship, Part 1," as posted on blog.worship.com (March 16, 2007).

20

SOLOMON'S CHOICE

1 Kings 9:1–28

And as for you, if you will walk before me, as David your
father walked, with integrity of heart and uprightness, doing
according to all that I have commanded you, and keeping my
statutes and my rules, then I will establish your royal throne
over Israel forever, as I promised David your father, saying,
"You shall not lack a man on the throne of Israel."
(1 Kings 9:4–5)

here are only two roads to go by—only two paths to follow in life—and every person must choose which one to take. This is the premise of Robert Frost's famous poem "The Road Not Taken." "Two roads diverged in a yellow wood," Frost writes, and immediately the poet knows he will have to make a choice. Because he is only one traveler, he cannot travel both roads. Nor is he likely to pass this way again. So he makes his fateful choice: "I took the one less traveled by," the poet recalls, "and that has made all the difference."[1]

---

1. Robert Frost, "The Road Not Taken," in *Mountain Interval* (New York: Henry Holt, 1921).

Jesus said something similar about roads and pathways: "The way is easy that leads to destruction, and those who enter by it are many." But "the way is hard that leads to life, and those who find it are few" (Matt. 7:13–14). According to Jesus, everyone must choose which path to follow, and taking the less traveled road makes all the difference between eternal life and everlasting destruction.

Some Christians seem to think that this is a choice we make only once in life, when we first decide to follow Christ. But in fact we face this choice every day, at every moment. Will I choose God's way or my own way, his kingdom or my kingdom, his sovereign plan or my personal agenda? Which path will I take in how I handle my work, what I do with my free time, and how I treat the people I live with? Which way will I go, and which road will I leave untaken? Where in life am I facing the choice between God's way and the wrong way?

ONE WAY OR ANOTHER

The choice came to King Solomon at the apex of achievement: "As soon as Solomon had finished building the house of the LORD and the king's house and all that Solomon desired to build, the LORD appeared to Solomon a second time, as he had appeared to him at Gibeon" (1 Kings 9:1–2).

When Solomon first ascended to Israel's throne, God appeared to him at Gibeon and gave him the opportunity of a lifetime (1 Kings 3:1–15). The king could ask for anything he wanted, and God would give it to him. Wisely, Solomon chose wisdom.

Now it was time for the king to choose again, and then to keep on choosing. God appeared to Solomon in another dream, offering him another choice. The first lesson we learn from this dramatic encounter is very simple: *everyone has a choice to make in life, either for God or against him, and the choice we make will end either in blessing or in disaster.*

One road to take is the way of obedience that leads to blessing. God said to Solomon:

And as for you, if you will walk before me, as David your father walked, with integrity of heart and uprightness, doing according to all that I have commanded you, and keeping my statutes and my rules, then I will establish your royal throne over Israel forever, as I promised David your father, saying, "You shall not lack a man on the throne of Israel" (1 Kings 9:4–5).

These verses are presented in the form of an "if/then" construction. There are certain conditions that Solomon has to meet. *If* he chooses the right road—if he decides to walk with God like his father David—*then* he will experience God's blessing. David set the spiritual standard for all the kings who followed after him. Not that he was perfect, of course. But David was a man after God's own heart (1 Sam. 13:14), a man of spiritual integrity who ruled with righteousness. If Solomon chose to follow in those footsteps, he would be going down the right path in life.

The instructions God gave to Solomon are nearly identical to the ones Solomon himself gave to Israel back in 1 Kings 8:61, when he said, "Let your heart be wholly true to the Lord our God, walking in his statutes and keeping his commandments." What God requires is nothing less than full obedience to his revealed will. This is a matter of the heart, not just outward obedience. What God wanted from Solomon—what he wants from everyone—is a heart for godliness. If Solomon met this condition, the reward for walking with God would be nothing less than an eternal kingdom. God would keep his promise to David (see 2 Sam. 7:12–13) by establishing the royal dynasty of an everlasting throne.

The same principle also applies to us: if we follow God in the way of obedience, we will have his blessing. Obedience itself will be a blessing, as we experience the joy of walking with God. Virtue really is its own reward. But obedience also leads to many other blessings. If we work the way God tells us to work, we will have something to share with others (Eph. 4:28). If we love the way God tells us to love, we will be able to make strong relationships that last a lifetime. If we feed the hungry, help the sick, and visit people in prison, we will enter into our Father's happiness (Matt. 25:31–40). These and many other blessings will be ours if we take the road less traveled.

There is another way to go in life, however—the way of disobedience that leads to destruction. Here is how God posed the choice to King Solomon:

But if you turn aside from following me, you or your children, and do not keep my commandments and my statutes that I have set before you, but go and serve other gods and worship them, then I will cut off Israel from the land that I have given them, and the house that I have consecrated for my name I will cast out of my sight, and Israel will become a proverb and a byword among all peoples. And this house will become a heap of ruins. (1 Kings 9:6–8; cf. Lev. 26:27–33; Deut. 28:36–37)

Once again, the grammatical construction is conditional. *If* Solomon goes down the road of disobedience, *then* certain things will happen, all of them disastrous. This sober warning has a gracious purpose. God wants Solomon to know the wages of his sin. And not just Solomon, either: his children are included—the royal sons of Israel. The language shifts from the singular to the plural in order to include not only the king, but also his country. If the people choose the wrong road, they will suffer virtually the worst consequences that any of them could imagine, including the loss of everything they hold dear. They will be cut off from the land that God promised and the temple that Solomon built. They will lose their title to the Promised Land and their membership in the house of God. In the words of one commentator, "The temple is no sooner built than we hear of its inevitable end; the empire is no sooner created than we hear of its inevitable destruction."[2]

Maybe even worse, the people of God will become a laughingstock to other nations. People will treat Israel with reproach and disrespect. "If you don't watch out," pagan mothers will say to their children, "you'll end up like the Israelites!" Like Sodom and Gomorrah, Israel will become an example of divine judgment, a permanent object lesson of what happens when people turn away from God (see Deut. 29:23; Jer. 24:19).

All of this will happen if Solomon and the people of Israel turn away to worship other gods. The Bible goes on to prophesy what people will say when they see Israel at the bitter end of their long road to idolatry:

Everyone passing by it will be astonished and will hiss, and they will say, "Why has the LORD done thus to this land and to this house?" Then they will say, "Because they abandoned the LORD their God, who brought their fathers out of the land of Egypt and laid hold on other gods and worshiped them and served them. Therefore the LORD has brought all this disaster on them." (1 Kings 9:8–9; cf. Deut. 29:22–28; Lamentations 2:15–17)

2. Iain W. Provan, *1 and 2 Kings*, New International Biblical Commentary (Peabody, MA: Hendrickson, 1995), 83.

When this happens, the Israelites will have only themselves to blame. The disaster that strikes will be the Lord's doing, as disaster always is. After all, God is sovereign over everything that happens. Yet it will still be Israel's fault. God will abandon them because they have abandoned God. What started out simply as Solomon's foolish choice will become a national disaster. Then the whole world will know that the king and his country have sinned by worshiping idols.

This is a gracious warning to us about where our own idols will lead. Choose the wrong road in life, and it will end in such disaster that even people outside the church will know that we have taken a wrong turn. However attractive other gods may seem to us—money and material possessions, sex and physical pleasure, power and interpersonal control—they will lead to our own destruction. The road to a life of deception begins with one little lie. The road to bankruptcy begins with one unwise expenditure. The road to addiction begins with one foolish indulgence. But before long our sins will be exposed, we will suffer the consequences of our wrong choices, people will see what has become of us, and if we do not repent, we will perish, for "broad is the way, that leadeth to destruction" (Matt. 7:13 KJV).

SOLOMON'S PAST SUCCESS

Here is a second lesson to learn from Solomon's choice: *everyone has a choice to make in life, and this choice is always before us, even if we have made the right choice before.* God is not a choice that we make only once at the beginning of the Christian life, but every time we choose anything at all. We still have a choice to make, even if we have made the right choice before.

King Solomon is the perfect example. Up to this point in his life, he had made almost all the right choices. The Bible says that "at the end of twenty years," Solomon "had built the two houses, the house of the LORD and the king's house" (1 Kings 9:10). He had chosen to follow God's plan for kingship, not seizing the throne, but trusting God to exalt him. As a result of that choice, and by the sovereign purpose of God, he had become the king of Israel. Right at the beginning of his kingship, Solomon chose to ask God for wisdom rather than wealth. As a result of that choice, and by God's unmerited grace, he was granted riches and fame as well as a superior intellect. Later Solomon chose to build a house for God. As a result of that choice, and by divine consecration, the temple he built was filled with the glory of God.

Solomon was a total success, a man who accomplished everything he wanted in life and received all kinds of accolades. He was the kind of man who was the captain of his football team, married the homecoming queen, turned a small business into a major corporation, was elected to public office, and (by the way) won a Nobel Prize for the poetry he wrote in his spare time. To this day, people still talk about "Solomon in all his glory" (Matt. 6:29).

Solomon was also a spiritual success. The Lord blessed him for everything he accomplished. He even honored the king as a man of prayer. The prayer Solomon offered when he dedicated the temple went from his mouth to God's ear. So God said to Solomon, "I have heard your prayer and your plea, which you have made before me. I have consecrated this house that you have built, by putting my name there forever. My eyes and my heart will be there for all time" (1 Kings 9:3). God would do what Solomon asked. He would put his name on the temple, and then his eyes and his heart would turn there to answer prayer. Solomon's intercession would stand for all time, giving Israel direct access to the throne of grace in every time of need or trouble.

Here was a king who did more for God than almost anyone else in the history of the world. But for all his past success, Solomon still had to choose for God every day, and every moment of every day. He could not simply presume upon his divinely anointed kingship. He could not rely on the choice he made for wisdom at the beginning of his ministry. He could not depend on one perfect prayer offered in a single moment of sincere devotion. He could not find spiritual safety in what he did for God in the past, even if that included building the most magnificent temple in the world.

Solomon still had to choose. If he continued to walk with God—if he led his family in the worship of God, if he ruled with righteousness, if he practiced personal holiness—then he would receive all the blessings that God has promised for obedience. But if he turned away from God and started heading down the road to idolatry, he would fall under judgment.

We face the same choice—the choice of daily obedience. What we did for God yesterday will not answer the demand he places on us today. No matter how well we began the Christian life, no matter how faithfully we answered God's call to service, no matter how earnestly we turned to God in prayer, no matter what we have accomplished in ministry, the choice is still before us today and every day for the rest of our lives.

This is not to deny the doctrine of divine election, of course. Our choice for God is based on the choice that he made for us before the foundation of the world (see Eph. 1:3–12). Once we truly come to Christ, we will never lose our salvation. But the way we work out our salvation (see Phil. 2:12), the way we make our calling and election sure (see 2 Peter 1:10), the way we are kept secure for salvation (1 Peter 1:5), and the way we glorify God is by following him today, not by trusting in something we did for God yesterday, or the day before that.

There is no place for coasting in the Christian life. The only way to grow spiritually is to keep choosing for God now, even if we have chosen for him before. We choose for God by reading his Word and going to him in prayer for everything we need. We choose for God by studying hard in school and following his plan for our calling and career. We choose for God by being content with what we have and not grasping for more. We also choose for God by saying "No!" to sin and "Yes!" to holiness, by saying, "I'm sorry," "I forgive you," and "I love you." We choose for God by putting him first in everything we do, including any area of life where we know what he wants us to do, but are having trouble doing it.

SOLOMON'S FUTURE ACCOMPLISHMENTS

The choice we make for or against God is more important than anything else we accomplish in life. This is a third lesson we learn from the choice that God put before Solomon, and from the way the king responded: *what matters the most in life—no matter what else we achieve—is choosing the right spiritual road.*

Once again, Solomon is the perfect (or rather, imperfect) example. In addition to mentioning his past achievements, 1 Kings 9 also lists his future accomplishments in commerce, politics, and military defense. Over the course of his reign, Solomon did all the things that kings hope to do. But no matter what else he accomplished in life, the most important thing he did was to make his daily choice for or against God.

Consider a few of Solomon's many notable accomplishments. The man was a success at international trade:

At the end of twenty years, in which Solomon had built the two houses, the house of the LORD and the king's house, and Hiram king of Tyre had supplied Solomon with cedar and cypress timber and gold, as much as he desired, King Solomon gave to Hiram twenty cities in the land of Galilee. But when Hiram came from Tyre to see the cities that Solomon had given him, they did not please him. Therefore, he said, "What kind of cities are these that you have given me, my brother?" So they are called the land of Cabul to this day. Hiram had sent to the king 120 talents of gold. (1 Kings 9:10–14)

These verses describe the continuation of an old alliance between Tyre and Israel. King Hiram was far from pleased with the deal that Solomon gave him, but apparently he was not in a position to do too much about it, because he ended up sending Solomon a huge quantity of gold (about four tons). So Solomon added to his fabulous wealth, as God had promised (see 1 Kings 3:13), and he did so at Hiram's expense.

Solomon was also a success at completing huge building projects. The king had a passion for building, and in addition to the temple and the palace, his massive labor force constructed extensive military fortifications:

And this is the account of the forced labor that King Solomon drafted to build the house of the LORD and his own house and the Millo and the wall of Jerusalem and Hazor and Megiddo and Gezer (Pharaoh king of Egypt had gone up and captured Gezer and burned it with fire, and had killed the Canaanites who lived in the city, and had given it as dowry to his daughter, Solomon's wife; so Solomon rebuilt Gezer) and Lower Beth-horon and Baalath and Tamar in the wilderness, in the land of Judah, and all the store cities that Solomon had, and the cities for his chariots, and the cities for his horsemen, and whatever Solomon desired to build in Jerusalem, in Lebanon, and in all the land of his dominion. (1 Kings 9:15–19)

Solomon built cities, walls, and palaces along the road that leads from Mesopotamia down to Egypt, as the Bible testifies, and as we can confirm from the archaeological record.[3] The king was able to build whatever he wanted to build.

3. See Dale Ralph Davis, *The Wisdom and the Folly: An Exposition of the Book of First Kings* (Fearn, Ross-shire: Christian Focus, 2002), 98; Donald J. Wiseman, *1 & 2 Kings: An Introduction and Commentary*, Tyndale Old Testament Commentaries (Leicester: Inter-Varsity, 1993), 126–27.

In addition to all his wealth and military might, Solomon also had power over his people. Thousands of his workers came from other nations: "All the people who were left of the Amorites, the Hittites, the Perizzites, the Hivites, and the Jebusites, who were not of the people of Israel—their descendants who were left after them in the land, whom the people of Israel were unable to devote to destruction—these Solomon drafted to be slaves, and so they are to this day" (1 Kings 9:20–21). Other workers were Israelites, who did not labor as slaves, but as servants of the king: "But of the people of Israel Solomon made no slaves. They were the soldiers, they were his officials, his commanders, his captains, his chariot commanders and his horsemen. These were the chief officers who were over Solomon's work: 550 who had charge of the people who carried on the work" (1 Kings 9:22–23).

Solomon also had a beautiful wife, who was well cared for, with a palace to call her own: "Pharaoh's daughter went up from the city of David to her own house that Solomon had built for her" (1 Kings 9:24). Solomon also built her "the Millo," which may have been a beautiful terrace.[4]

There is more. The king also had a royal navy, which enabled him to form lucrative shipping partnerships that gained him even more gold: "King Solomon built a fleet of ships at Ezion-geber, which is near Eloth on the shore of the Red Sea, in the land of Edom. And Hiram sent with the fleet his servants, seamen who were familiar with the sea, together with the servants of Solomon. And they went to Ophir and brought from there gold, 420 talents, and they brought it to King Solomon" (1 Kings 9:26–28).

In short, Solomon had everything that a king could ever want out of life: money, property, possessions, servants, and beautiful women. It was his kingdom, and he was living in it, with more of everything than anyone else in the world. Yet every day he still had to make his spiritual choice. No matter how successful he was—no matter how much money he had, or how much power over other people—Solomon still had to choose for God, or else against him. Would he thank God for all his money, and then put it to use for kingdom work? Would he exercise his power to serve the poor and protect the weak? Would he grow proud of what he had accomplished, or would he give all the glory to God?

4. R. D. Patterson and H. J. Austel, "1 and 2 Kings," in *Expositor's Bible Commentary* (Grand Rapids: Zondervan, 1988), 4:97.

The more we have of what this world has to offer, the easier it is to think that we are on the right track, even when we are wandering down the road to idolatry. What really counts in life is not academic success, or athletic accomplishments, or a bigger bank account, or reaching the top of our profession, or taking pride in our family, but the spiritual choice we make in our hearts for God, or else against him.

This truth is a warning for people who are highly successful (at least in the way the world defines success). We can get everything we want out of life, but we still end up losing, if we choose our own road instead of God's road. Dale Ralph Davis says it well: "One may be enjoying a thoroughly successful kingly (or financial or professional or ministerial) career and yet end in utter ruin unless one takes obedience to the first commandment as his very highest calling."[5] In other words, unless we put God first in everything, we are heading for our own destruction. Our love for earthly possessions will fill us with greed; our desire for sexual pleasure will lead us into foolhardy relationships; our lust for personal prominence will cause us to trample on the needs of others. If that is the way we are heading in life, then we are bound for failure. We had better go another direction and turn down the road not taken—the road of faith in Jesus Christ! As the Scripture says, "Take care, brothers, lest there be in any of you an evil, unbelieving heart, leading you to fall away from the living God" (Heb. 3:12).

This truth is also a comfort in every failure. No matter how badly things have gone, maybe even as the result of our own sin, we still have a chance to choose for God, especially if we know the Savior who made all the right choices when he lived and suffered and died for us. We choose for God by fully repenting of all the wrong things we have done. We choose for God by trusting that he knows what he is doing, even when it may not seem that way to us. We choose him by believing he will provide whatever we truly need. We choose him by persevering through the darkest trial, knowing that as long as we walk with him, he will stay with us to the end of the road.

WHAT JESUS CHOSE

Will you make the right choice in life? Will you choose the broad and easy path that leads to destruction, or will you choose the narrow road that for

5. Davis, *The Wisdom and the Folly*, 101.

most people is "the road not taken"? It does not matter what we have done for God, or how successful we are in life; the real question is whether we will choose for God today, tomorrow, and every day for the rest of our lives.

To see what is at stake in this choice, we need only consider what happened to King Solomon. Some scholars are thoroughly critical of what Solomon does in this chapter. They point to the way he takes advantage of Hiram, to his use of forced labor, to his marrying foreign wives, to his trading away parcels of the Promised Land, and to his growing military as signs of his coming apostasy.[6]

There may well be some validity to these criticisms. Yet at the same time Solomon is commended for his piety. The Scripture says, "Three times a year Solomon used to offer up burnt offerings and peace offerings on the altar that he built to the LORD, making offerings with it before the LORD. So he finished the house" (1 Kings 9:25). Undoubtedly this verse refers to Passover, Pentecost, and Tabernacles as the three festivals Solomon celebrated every year in Jerusalem. These were the high holy days when the king fulfilled his religious obligations.

Maybe this was only for show—a public display of civil religion, as some political candidates have been known to make around election time. But the fact remains that Solomon made the proper sacrifices at the proper time. He chose for God at the temple, fulfilling all righteousness.

The trouble is that Solomon did not finish nearly as well as he started, as we will discover when we get to chapter 11 and read about his spiritual bankruptcy. The "if" at the beginning of 1 Kings 9:6 turned out to be a "when." Solomon did not stay on the right road, but chose to turn in another direction. So even as the Bible records the splendors of the Solomonic age, it is setting the stage to show how even the greatest earthly glories are lost when people stop choosing the one true God.

How can we avoid Solomon's folly and keep choosing for God? It would be nice to think that we will make the right choice in life, and keep on making it, but this will take more than good intentions. Not everyone does make the right choice in life. Indeed, not everyone can. In fact, there is a sense in which no one can at all.

6. See, for example, Walter Brueggemann, *1 & 2 Kings*, Smyth & Helwys Bible Commentary (Macon, GA: Smyth & Helwys, 2000), 128; J. Gray, *1 and 2 Kings: A Commentary*, Old Testament Library, 2nd ed. (Philadelphia: Westminster, 1970), 223–24.

This was the lesson that Israel learned in the last days of Joshua, and afterward. The choice that God gave to Solomon is very similar to the choice that Joshua gave the people of Israel just before he died. That day Joshua challenged the people to choose which God they would serve. They chose wisely, saying, "We will serve the LORD, for he is our God" (Josh. 24:18).

It was a promising beginning. But Joshua believed in the doctrine of sin, and thus he responded with a reality check: "You are not able to serve the LORD, for he is a holy God" (Josh. 24:19). Joshua was saying that sinful people are incapable of making all the right choices in life. So even if we begin with the best of intentions, without the grace of God we still end up on the road to destruction.

Joshua's warning turned out to be the story of Solomon's life. It also happens to be the story of our own lives: not always choosing for God, but often going the wrong direction, even to our own destruction.

Praise God that we have a Savior who always made the right choice in life, following the road less traveled all the way to the cross. Jesus had to make the same choice that we have to make. There were always two roads before him, forcing him to choose for or against the will of God. He had to make the choice when he was a little boy and needed to learn obedience. He had to make it again when he was attacked by the devil in the wilderness, facing all the temptations of hell. He had to make it when he was with his Father in the garden, wondering if there might be some alternative to crucifixion.

Jesus chose for God. He chose for God every moment of every day, even when it cost him his life. Because he is the only person who ever did choose for God—all the time, every time—he was able to make perfect atonement for our sins. Now Jesus is able to bring us all the way down the road to salvation. He himself is the road to God, the way to eternal life. If we trust in him, his right choices count for us, even when we make the wrong choice. And when the choice comes to us again, as it does every day, and we are struggling hard to choose for God, Jesus is there to keep us on the road less traveled—the road that leads to life.

21

SOLOMON AND THE
QUEEN OF SHEBA

1 Kings 10:1—13

Now when the queen of Sheba heard of the fame of Solomon
concerning the name of the LORD, she came to test him with
hard questions. (1 Kings 10:1)

*I*t remains one of the most famous journeys in history, a dramatic encounter between East and West. In the year 1271, young Marco Polo accompanied his father and uncle as they left Venice, followed the Silk Road to China, and eventually arrived at the palace of Kublai Khan, head of the Mongol Empire.

Marco stayed for more than a decade, traveling throughout the Orient on diplomatic missions for the great Khan. When he finally returned to Italy, he wrote the book that immortalized his journey: *The Travels of Marco Polo*. Marco had many sensational stories to tell about the places he went and the people he met along the way, yet some people doubted whether these tales were really true. Almost no one from Europe had ever traveled as far as China, and of course they had no way of knowing the truth about things they had never seen.

According to one tradition, Marco Polo gave a public demonstration to convince people that his stories were true. He invited the leaders of Venice to dinner. To receive his guests, he wore the simple costume of a Chinese peasant. But once everyone had arrived, he opened his pockets to reveal hundreds of rubies and other jewels. He knew that people would not believe in a faraway kingdom until they saw its treasure for themselves.

The queen of Sheba had a similar perspective. She too had heard the glories of a distant kingdom, yet she had trouble believing that everything she heard was true. So she decided to see for herself, traveling across the Middle East to visit Jerusalem, a journey that led to one of the most famous diplomatic encounters in the history of international relations. For us this is much more than simply a matter of historical interest; it is something with profound spiritual implications, because according to Jesus, Solomon and the queen of Sheba can teach us the way to eternal life.

SEE FOR YOURSELF

Solomon and the queen of Sheba are a study in contrasts: Arab meets Israelite; a curious woman visits a wise and wealthy man. Their encounter was full of diplomatic intrigue. Although state visits are more common today, it was somewhat unusual in those days for a reigning monarch to make such a journey in person. Typically someone like the queen of Sheba would have sent emissaries to Solomon's court. Instead, she traveled more than a thousand miles through the desert to meet Israel's king in person.

King Solomon is more famous today, of course, but the queen of Sheba was an important person in her own right. There was greatness about her—a greatness magnificently expressed in Handel's triumphant "Arrival of the Queen of Sheba," from his oratorio *Solomon*. As a reigning monarch, the queen had a large entourage. She was also worth a fortune. The Bible says that she "came to Jerusalem with a very great retinue, with camels bearing spices and very much gold and precious stones" (1 Kings 10:2). Later in the story we will hear about all the gold, spices, and precious stones that she offered Solomon as gifts—especially the spices (1 Kings 10:10). The queen of Sheba, who ruled a kingdom in what is now the country of Yemen, was one of the most powerful and influential women in the world.

Yet the true source of the woman's greatness was her intellectual curiosity. It was not simply what she owned that made her important, but also what she wanted to know: "Now when the queen of Sheba heard of the fame of Solomon concerning the name of the LORD, she came to test him with hard questions. . . . And when she came to Solomon, she told him all that was on her mind" (1 Kings 10:1–2).

Solomon's reputation was well deserved, for he had been granted the gift of unsurpassed wisdom. By the blessing of God, when Solomon became king of Israel he was given "wisdom and understanding beyond measure, and breadth of mind like the sand on the seashore" (1 Kings 4:29). People from all over the world wanted to hear what King Solomon had to say about almost everything.

The queen of Sheba was curious about Solomon. She had heard about the king's legendary wisdom and she wanted to see for herself. Frankly, she did not quite believe the reports she had received (see 1 Kings 10:7). She was a skeptic of the healthiest kind: although she did not believe everything she heard, she was always open to believing the truth. So the queen tested Solomon's knowledge, perhaps by posing the kind of riddles mentioned in Proverbs 1:6, or else by describing difficult problems and then seeing how he would resolve them. According to Bible scholars, "such tests of practical sagacity and poetic susceptibility were part of the diplomatic encounters of the day."[1]

The queen of Sheba asked Solomon the hardest questions she knew because she wanted to know things for herself. The woman had the kind of curiosity we later see in Marcella, one of the early church mothers. Marcella was a close friend of the great Bible scholar Jerome, who praised her passion to know what the Bible actually said. According to Jerome, Marcella never came to any Bible study or worship service "without asking something about Scripture, nor did she immediately accept my explanation as satisfactory, but she proposed questions from the opposite viewpoint, not for the sake of being contentious, but so that by asking, she might learn." Jerome went on to say "that whatever in us was gathered by long study and by lengthy meditation . . . this she tasted, this she learned, this she possessed."[2]

---

1. J. Gray, *1 and 2 Kings*, Old Testament Library, 2nd ed. (Philadelphia: Westminster, 1970), 241.
2. Jerome, "Epistle 127," quoted in Christopher A. Hall, *Reading Scriptures with the Church Fathers* (Downers Grove, IL: InterVarsity, 1998), 44.

The same could be said of the queen of Sheba: she asked in order to understand. Therefore, by the time Solomon was finished answering all her questions, she was able to testify that she knew the truth. She said to the king, "The report was true that I heard in my own land of your words and of your wisdom, but I did not believe the reports until I came and my own eyes had seen it" (1 Kings 10:6–7).

Sooner or later, anyone who follows the queen's example will learn the truth about Jesus, just as she learned the truth about Solomon. If we are wise, we will be curious enough to get good, honest answers to all the ultimate questions: Why is there something rather than nothing? Is there a God? If there is, then what is the meaning of my existence? God is not intimidated by such hard and testing questions, nor is he unable to answer them. But we must come with the right kind of skepticism—not the kind that refuses to believe anything at all, but the kind that is committed to believe only what is really true.

The Bible says that Jesus Christ is the King of all kings (e.g., Rev. 19:16). Will you come and see for yourself that what he says is really true? The queen of Sheba traveled a thousand miles to find out if Solomon was everything that people said he was. What are you willing to do to find out the truth about Jesus? If anything, the reports about him are even more remarkable. It is said that he is the Son of God and the Savior of the world. According to the good news of his gospel, Jesus died on the cross to pay for the sins of everyone who believes in him and rose from the dead to give eternal life. If this is true, it is the most important thing that has ever happened. If we are not sure whether it is true or not, we should at least be curious enough to find out!

Many skeptical men and women have come to God with all the hard riddles of life, and to their joy they have discovered for themselves that Jesus "is the true God and eternal life" (1 John 5:20). There are many good examples of such discoveries in the Bible. Think of Job, who had pages and pages of spiritual questions, until finally he met God for himself. Then Job had to admit, "I had heard of you by the hearing of the ear, but now my eye sees you; therefore I despise myself, and repent in dust and ashes" (Job 42:5–6). Or consider Thomas, the doubting disciple, who at first refused to believe that Jesus had come back from the grave. Thomas said that he would not believe until he could see the very wounds that Jesus had received when he was nailed to the cross. Yet as skeptical as he was, Thomas was still open to the truth; so when he saw Jesus for himself, he was ready to say, "My Lord and my God!" (John 20:28).

There are also many good examples of spiritual discovery in the history of the church. A notable example from recent times is Lee Strobel, the award-winning journalist who wrote *The Case for Christ*. Strobel had always assumed that "God was merely a product of wishful thinking, of ancient mythology, of primitive superstition."[3] He had also assumed that all the available evidence showed that Jesus was merely an ordinary human being. Then, to his dismay, Strobel's wife became a Christian. The change in her life was so extraordinary that he decided to launch an all-out investigation into the facts surrounding Christianity. Setting aside his former prejudices, he took a fresh look at the evidence. He read books, asked questions, interviewed experts, studied history, explored archaeology, and, most importantly, studied the Bible verse by verse. By the time he was finished, Strobel had to admit the unthinkable: Jesus Christ is the Savior God.

Anyone who is willing to take a serious look at Jesus will discover that he is everything advertised and more. The best way to take a good look at Jesus is to read what the Bible says about him, especially in the Gospels of Matthew, Mark, Luke, and John. These books were written "so that you may believe that Jesus is the Christ, the Son of God, and that by believing you may have life in his name" (John 20:31; cf. Luke 1:4). The biblical Gospels offer eyewitness accounts of people who not only heard about Jesus, but also saw him and touched him (see 1 John 1:1–2). So read them to see the life of Jesus—the things he said and did. Study his death—the suffering he endured in dying on the cross, as well as everything the Bible says about the meaning of his crucifixion. Consider also his resurrection—his triumphant return from the grave.

To read the Gospels is to hear news of a faraway kingdom. It is also to see Jesus; you will see that he is the Christ, the living Son of God, the only Savior from sin. Anyone who trusts in him will be ready to give the same testimony about Jesus that the queen of Sheba gave about Solomon: "I did not believe the reports until I came and my own eyes had seen it. And behold, the half was not told me" (1 Kings 10:7).

---

3. Lee Strobel, *The Case for Christ* (Grand Rapids: Zondervan, 1998).

Honor the King's Breathtaking Wisdom

The queen of Sheba is a wonderful example to follow in coming to trust in Christ. She moved from unbelief (or disbelief) to faith in the kingdom of God. At the same time, she also shows us how to respond to the king of that kingdom. Keep in mind that Solomon is a "type" of Christ. In other words, Solomon reveals the pattern of the salvation that God later provided for us in Christ. Therefore, in the story of Solomon and the queen of Sheba we see how to respond to Jesus: by honoring his breathtaking wisdom, worshiping his royal majesty, and offering him golden treasure.

If wisdom is what the queen of Sheba was seeking, wisdom is exactly what she found. First she tested Solomon's intellectual, theological, and philosophical acumen. Whatever she asked, the king was able to answer: "And Solomon answered all her questions; there was nothing hidden from the king that he could not explain to her" (1 Kings 10:3). Questions that were hard for others were easy for Solomon. With his divine gift of wisdom, he knew all the answers. Here is how the poet Robert Browning described the king's response to the queen: "She proves him with hard questions: before she has reached the middle / He smiling supplies the end, straight solves them riddle by riddle."[4]

We can still see Solomon's wisdom today by contemplating his famous Proverbs, reading his love letters in the Song of Solomon, or studying his philosophy in the book of Ecclesiastes. The queen of Sheba witnessed Solomon's wisdom worked out in the government of his kingdom—its architecture, cuisine, fashion, worship, and administration. After making her state visit to the king's elegant court, after seeing his stylish palace and dining at his sumptuous table, she was left totally speechless: "And when the queen of Sheba had seen all the wisdom of Solomon, the house that he had built, the food of his table, the seating of his officials, and the attendance of his servants, their clothing, his cupbearers, and his burnt offerings that he offered at the house of the LORD, there was no more breath in her" (1 Kings 10:4–5).

The queen of Sheba was overwhelmed by what she saw. As great as she was, she recognized that she was in the presence of someone superior. Solo-

---

4. Robert Browning, "Solomon and Balkis," in *Chapters into Verse: Poetry in English Inspired by the Bible*, vol. 1, *Genesis to Malachi*, ed. Robert Atwan and Laurance Wieder (Oxford: Oxford University Press, 1993), 240.

mon took her breath away. He was a much wiser king than she had ever imagined. At first she did not quite believe the reports she had heard about him, but now she realized that they hardly did him justice. "And behold," she said, gasping for air, "the half was not told me. Your wisdom and prosperity surpass the report that I heard" (1 Kings 10:7). Thus the queen of Sheba honored the breathtaking wisdom of King Solomon.

She was so impressed that she could not help but envy Solomon's loyal subjects: "Happy are your men! Happy are your servants, who continually stand before you and hear your wisdom!" (1 Kings 10:8). The queen of Sheba recognized that Solomon's wisdom was not simply for his own benefit, but for the blessing of his people, who found their greatest joy in the service of their worthy king.

We should give even more honor to and find even more joy in Jesus Christ, for as wise as Solomon was, he did not know even half of what Jesus knows. Talk about breathtaking! The Bible says that in Jesus "are hidden all the treasures of wisdom and knowledge" (Col. 2:3). There is nothing to be known that Christ does not already know. He is absolutely omniscient; his wisdom is infinite; he is "the only wise God" (1 Tim. 1:17 KJV).

As the Creator God (see Col. 1:16), Jesus Christ knows everything there is to know about creation, from the smallest subatomic particle that has yet to be detected by science to the biggest black hole in outer space. Jesus has total knowledge of the physical universe. Consider his breathtaking wisdom in putting the earth exactly where it is, close enough to the sun to give us light and heat, but not so close that we are burning up. Or consider his complete comprehension of every living creature. To give just one example, I once had the privilege to see the bull elephant at the Night Safari in Singapore—a huge animal in the moonlight, with a full set of enormous tusks. As the Son of God, Jesus made that magnificent animal. He knows everything about its life history, from its enormous toenails to the folds of skin on its giant ears.

But that is not all. Consider the breathtaking wisdom that Jesus demonstrated in everything he ever taught. Think of his enigmatic parables, pregnant with meaning, like the Good Samaritan or the Prodigal Son. Think of his provocative teaching in the Sermon on the Mount, or his wise words about the future in the Olivet Discourse. Think of what Jesus said about hatred really amounting to murder, for example, or about doing unto others what we would have them do unto us, or about the absolute difference between serving God and serving money. Every word he ever spoke is full of divine wisdom.

Then consider what Jesus did for our salvation—the wisdom of his saving work. Seeing that we are unable to save ourselves, he wisely came to do everything that had to be done to save us: living the perfect life that we could never live, offering his own life as an infinitely precious sacrifice for our sins, rising again to give eternal life to everyone who trusts in him. Then, instead of leaving us to find our own way back to God, Jesus wisely sent us the Holy Spirit to give us new spiritual life.

Consider as well the wisdom that Jesus has displayed in the church. Just as the queen of Sheba admired the beauty of Solomon's temple, the food of Solomon's table, and the clothing of Solomon's servants (1 Kings 10:4–5), we too may admire the beauty of the temple God is building by his Spirit, the sacramental food we eat at the royal table of the Lord's Supper, and the robes of righteousness he gives to all his servants. The physical realities of the kingdom of Solomon point us toward the spiritual realities of the kingdom of God.

Jesus is wiser than Solomon in every way. His wisdom in creation and redemption ought to be enough to take our breath away. How happy we should be to serve this all-wise King, and to hear his words of wisdom! We honor his wisdom by praising him for everything we see in creation. We honor his wisdom by listening to what he says, and then doing it. We honor his wisdom by trusting his plan of salvation, fully believing in the cross and the empty tomb.

We also honor the wisdom of God by trusting what he is doing in our lives right now. Sometimes it is easy to think that God could or should be doing a little better than he is at managing our affairs. When we consider our family situation, or our work situation, or our financial situation, it can be tempting to think that we know some wiser way for him to run our lives. This too is breathtaking—breathtaking in its arrogance. If Jesus Christ is the all-wise God of creation and salvation, then we honor his wisdom by fully trusting his plan for our lives. How much happier we are when we learn to believe in the wisdom of our King without doubting, complaining, or second-guessing his will.

WORSHIP THE KING'S ROYAL MAJESTY

As soon as the queen of Sheba recovered her breath, she had something to say. Here was her response of praise: "Blessed be the LORD your God, who has delighted in you and set you on the throne of Israel! Because the LORD loved Israel forever, he has made you king, that you may execute justice and righteousness" (1 Kings 10:9).

Thus the queen of Sheba worshiped the king's royal majesty. With high praise, she rejoiced in the ruler of God's kingdom, and in that rejoicing, she worshiped the royal majesty of God himself—the King of all kings. The queen recognized that Solomon was God's gift to his people—a gift of his everlasting love. By setting Solomon on the throne, God was establishing justice and righteousness in Israel. God did this because he loved his people, and also because he loved Solomon. Solomon was the king of God's delight, as well as the proof of God's love for his people.

By her good example, the queen of Sheba draws us into deep mysteries of the worship of God. Whatever she said about Solomon is something we can say even more emphatically about Jesus Christ as the King of God's everlasting kingdom. As much as God delighted in Solomon, he delights even more in his eternal Son. As we often hear the Father say in the Gospels, he is "well pleased" with his Son (e.g., Matt. 3:17; 17:5). He is so well pleased, in fact, that he has given Jesus the everlasting throne of the universe (Eph. 1:20–22). God has done this because he loves us and because he wants to establish his justice and righteousness on the earth. He has given us Christ to be our King, to rule us and defend us. So we worship his Royal Majesty, saying, "Blessed be the Lord your God, who has delighted in you and set you on the throne of heaven!" In saying this, we worship both the Father and the Son who is the proof of our Father's love.

What makes the queen's worship especially significant is that she came from Sheba, which was outside the covenant community. She did not belong to the family of Israel, but came from the Arabian Peninsula, probably somewhere near the modern-day country of Yemen.[5] This fact gives wider importance to her worship. The queen of Sheba was one of the very first Gentiles to worship the King of God's kingdom, as typified in King Solomon.

This made Sheba one of the first fulfillments of the ancient prophecies that God would bless all nations with his saving grace (e.g., Gen. 12:3; 17:4–6; 22:18). The promises of God were coming true for the nations. The queen's ethnicity also made her the answer to Solomon's prayers. In Psalm 72, as

---

5. Donald J. Wiseman, *1 & 2 Kings: An Introduction and Commentary*, Tyndale Old Testament Commentaries (Leicester: Inter-Varsity, 1993), 129.

he made his petitions for God to bless his royal kingdom, King Solomon explicitly asked that desert tribes would bow down before him, that kings would fall at his feet, that all nations would call him blessed (Ps. 72:9, 11, 17). Later, in his prayer of dedication for the temple, Solomon prayed "that all the peoples of the earth may know that the Lord is God" (1 Kings 8:60). With the arrival of the queen of Sheba, his prayers were coming true.

We see an even bigger answer to Solomon's prayers in the worldwide worship of Jesus Christ. When Christ was born, wise men came from the east, announcing that they had come to worship his Majesty, the King (Matt. 2:1–2). They too were royalty, and like the queen of Sheba, they symbolized the nations that would come to Christ. As the King of all kings, Jesus now deserves and receives the worship and the praise of all nations. He is not the King of the Jews only, but also of the Arabs, the Asians, the Africans, and the Americans. Jesus Christ is the Savior of the world.

This is why the queen of Sheba is so significant, and why her journey to Jerusalem is one of the most important state visits in the history of the world. Her royal highness is a gospel sign pointing us to the global worship of Jesus Christ. Already in the Old Testament we see God working his plan for all nations and all peoples to worship him. The international fame of Solomon anticipates the attractive power of Jesus Christ and the worldwide scope of his kingdom. When we worship Jesus in his royal majesty—whoever we are and wherever we are from—we fulfill God's purpose for the world.

GIVE THE KING YOUR GOLDEN TREASURE

One final thing we can do for our King is to give him our golden treasure. The queen of Sheba did something more than simply feel faint in the presence of Solomon's superior wisdom, or speak to him words of praise; she also did something tangible: "Then she gave the king 120 talents of gold, and a very great quantity of spices and precious stones. Never again came such an abundance of spices as these that the queen of Sheba gave to King Solomon" (1 Kings 10:10).

Nor was Sheba the only one, for "the fleet of Hiram, which brought gold from Ophir, brought from Ophir a very great amount of almug wood and precious stones. And the king made of the almug wood supports for the house of the Lord and for the king's house, also lyres and harps for the singers. No such almug wood has come or been seen to this day" (1 Kings 10:11–12; cf. Ps. 45:9).

This too was the answer to Solomon's prayers. It was not simply the worship of nations that he desired, but also the gift of their tribute. So he prayed, "May the kings of Tarshish and of the coastlands render him tribute" (Ps. 72:10); "may gold of Sheba be given to him!" (Ps. 72:15). In answer to these prayers, the king of Tyre and the queen of Sheba came with all kinds of precious gems, beautiful woods for building the temple and making musical instruments, valuable spices from the famous Arabian markets, and a large treasury of gold, fit for a king. Solomon's treasuries were already full of gold, of course, but he was such a mighty king that he was worthy of even more tribute.

Once again, these extravagant gifts remind us what the prophets said about the Savior—prophecies about the coming of the Christ. Isaiah said:

Nations shall come to your light,
    and kings to the brightness of your rising. . . .
A multitude of camels shall cover you,
    the young camels of Midian and Ephah;
    all those from Sheba shall come.
They shall bring gold and frankincense,
    and shall bring good news, the praises of the LORD. (Isa. 60:3, 6)

This was one of many specific promises fulfilled in the birth of Jesus Christ. The wise men from the east came to do something more than simply worship the newborn King. They also brought gifts of frankincense and gold (Matt. 2:11)—the wealth of kings that God had promised would come on camels from the east. This was the promise of the nations, that they would bring their treasure to the King.

Jesus Christ is worthy of all our golden treasure, and everything else that we can offer him. Not that we could ever add to his bank account, of course, as if he needed anything from us (see Rom. 11:35–36). Who has ever given anything to God? Whatever we have is from him and through him. But whatever we have is also *for* him, and therefore he is worthy of our wealth. So we bring him our golden treasure, giving money to the King for the work of his kingdom. We support the ministry of his word, the worship of his church, and the proclamation of his grace to the nations. We do this because Jesus

Christ is royally worthy to receive our tribute, and because the work of his glorious kingdom is the best investment we can possibly make.

RECEIVE THE KING'S ROYAL BLESSING

All this talk of golden treasure may lead some people to think that it is very costly to be a Christian. People probably said the same thing about the queen of Sheba. After all, she gave Solomon large gifts from her own personal fortune. But in the end, this proved to be for her own benefit, because in return she received a royal blessing.

This was already true at the time of her visit: "King Solomon gave to the queen of Sheba all that she desired, whatever she asked besides what was given her by the bounty of King Solomon. So she turned and went back to her own land with her servants" (1 Kings 10:13). Solomon gave the queen everything she wanted—not just his wisdom, but also his wealth. He sent her home with the bountiful blessing of his kingdom.

An even greater blessing still awaits her, on the last of all days, when Jesus Christ will come into his everlasting kingdom. Then the queen of Sheba will receive the blessing of eternal life. We know this because Jesus explicitly stated that she would be present at the final judgment, standing with the righteous. Jesus said this to the people of his own generation who wanted him to give them some sort of sign to prove that he was the Christ. They wondered whether it was worthwhile to follow Jesus. He told them, "The queen of the South will rise up at the judgment with the men of this generation and condemn them, for she came from the ends of the earth to hear the wisdom of Solomon, and behold, something greater than Solomon is here" (Luke 11:31).

There is a comparison here, and also a warning. King Jesus is greater than King Solomon—infinitely greater. Just as Solomon gave the queen of Sheba everything she desired, so Jesus has promised to give us whatever we ask in faith. But of course Jesus has much more to give. In his perfect wisdom, and out of his infinite wealth, he is able to give us every blessing in heaven! Therefore, we should come to Jesus the way that the queen of Sheba went to Solomon. We should say of Jesus what Sheba said when she met Solomon: "Blessed be the LORD!" (1 Kings 10:9). Even old King Solomon was worthy of some recognition. The queen of Sheba proved it by traveling a thousand miles to honor his wisdom and give him her gold. If Solomon was worthy to receive all of that, then Jesus is worthy of even more—more honor, more worship, more treasure.

If we do not give Jesus as much as he deserves, then the queen of Sheba will condemn us at the final judgment. Really, what else could she do? She gave full honor to Solomon, who was not even half the king that Jesus is. So how could she do anything but condemn someone who refuses to honor the wisdom of Jesus Christ, or worship his majesty, or give him the gold that he deserves? "If I honored Solomon," she will say, "you should have worshiped Jesus."

We will see the queen of Sheba at the final judgment. What will she say about us then? And what will Jesus say? We will see him too, as the Judge of all mankind. Anyone who refuses to acknowledge Christ as King will be condemned. But anyone who seeks Jesus sincerely and honors him royally will receive all his blessings forever—whatever we rightly and truly desire.

22

SIC TRANSIT GLORIA MUNDI

1 Kings 10:14–29

Thus King Solomon excelled all the kings of the earth in riches and in wisdom. And the whole earth sought the presence of Solomon to hear his wisdom, which God had put into his mind. Every one of them brought his present, articles of silver and gold, garments, myrrh, spices, horses, and mules, so much year by year.
(1 Kings 10:23–25)

The year was 1859. The town was Titusville, Pennsylvania, where a prospector named Edwin Drake was looking for oil. In those days petroleum was skimmed from places where it seeped through the ground—a process that could produce only a few barrels a day. But Edwin Drake had the wild idea that there might be some way to pump oil out of the ground. So he built a newfangled contraption to test his theory—an iron pipe driven by a steam engine, drilling into the bedrock. "Drake's Folly" they called it . . . until the day he struck black gold and started pumping out twenty-five barrels of oil a day.

Thus began the "liquid gold rush." Soon Titusville was overrun with people looking to make a fortune—businessmen, entrepreneurs, and fools who lost their money almost as fast as they gained it. In the words of one eyewitness, "Almost everybody you meet has been suddenly enriched or suddenly ruined (perhaps both within a short space of time)." Drake himself lost everything he had and wandered the streets in an old tattered coat. A farmer named "Coal-Oil Johnnie" used proceeds from his oil rights to cover his shirtfront with diamonds, but in three years he too was bankrupt, having thrown away half a million dollars.

The man who rose and fell most quickly must have been Henry Rouse. When Rouse finally saw oil gushing from his well, he lit a cigar to celebrate. Unfortunately, a spark from his cigar set the oil on fire. Rouse was caught in the flames and fatally burned. Somehow he managed to drag himself to the edge of the inferno and throw his wallet to safety. The wallet was saved, but Rouse himself never lived to see any of the profits.[1]

A famous Latin expression describes Titusville well: *sic transit gloria mundi*, which means "thus passes the glory of the world." The treasures of this life are always short-lived. So whenever we see prosperity, it is wise for us to say, "*sic transit gloria mundi*." Whatever fame or fortune we may experience, it will soon pass away. Just ask King Solomon.

NATIONAL TREASURE

The second half of 1 Kings 10 describes the golden age of Solomon's empire, which stands as the high-water mark of kingship in Israel before the coming of Christ. The key word in this passage is "gold," which is mentioned no fewer than ten times. The Bible wants to impress us with the splendid glories of Solomon's golden kingdom. But we also need to keep this all in its proper biblical context, remembering how quickly earthly glory will pass away, and how easy it is for gold to become our god.

One way to measure Solomon's glory is to weigh all his gold, which is what people still do with gold today. The Bible says that "the weight of gold that came to Solomon in one year was 666 talents of gold" (1 Kings 10:14). Whether this was Solomon's annual income or whether it was only the tax revenue he received in one record-setting year, 666

1. These stories are told in Marvin Olasky, *The American Leadership Tradition* (Wheaton, IL: Crossway, 2000), 127. See also Deborah Lynn Black's article "Titusville, PA," as posted on American *Profile*.com.

talents of gold is a staggering fortune. It amounts to hundreds of millions of dollars in today's economy—maybe as much as a billion. But that is not all. We also need to include Solomon's international trade and count all the gold that "came from the explorers and from the business of the merchants, and from all the kings of the west and from the governors of the land" (1 Kings 10:15).

We do not know exactly how much gold this was, but we can make a fair estimate by visiting the king's summer palace: "Solomon made 200 large shields of beaten gold; 600 shekels of gold went into each shield. And he made 300 shields of beaten gold; three minas of gold went into each shield. And the king put them in the House of the Forest of Lebanon" (1 Kings 10:16–17). Today we would make it into solid bars, but the gold in Solomon's treasury was fashioned into ceremonial shields. Each shield was worth a small fortune, and Solomon had hundreds of them, both large and small.

It is sometimes said that these figures must be an exaggeration, but there is no reason to doubt them. The Bible carefully records the exact details, as we would expect in the official records of a royal court, especially for something as valuable as gold. Furthermore, the amounts of gold registered are in line with contemporary records from other places, such as the royal house of Egypt, or the temples of Mesopotamia.[2]

The fact is that Solomon owned an enormous amount of gold—so much that by comparison silver was worth almost nothing: "All King Solomon's drinking vessels were of gold. . . . None were of silver; silver was not considered as anything in the days of Solomon" (1 Kings 10:21). In those days Jerusalem really was "Jerusalem the Golden." There was such an overabundance of gold that it led to the devaluation of silver. A similar comment is made in verse 27: "And the king made silver as common in Jerusalem as stone, and he made cedar as plentiful as the sycamore of the Shephelah." In Handel's oratorio based on the life of Solomon, the king celebrates his prosperity with a song:

Gold now is common on our happy shore,
And cedars frequent are as sycamore.

2. A. R. Millard, "Solomon's Gold," *Vox Evangelica* 12 (1981): 13–17; "Does the Bible Exaggerate King Solomon's Golden Wealth?" *Biblical Archaeology Review* 15, 3 (1989): 20ff.

All, all conspires to bless my days;
Fair plenty does her treasures raise,
And o'er the fruitful plains her countless gifts displays.

People sometimes say, "All that glitters is not gold." When it comes to Solomon, however, we can say just the opposite: "not all that glitters is gold." For Solomon owned many other precious treasures of opulent beauty. Consider his throne:

> The king also made a great ivory throne and overlaid it with the finest gold. The throne had six steps, and at the back of the throne was a calf's head, and on each side of the seat were armrests and two lions standing beside the armrests, while twelve lions stood there, one on each end of a step on the six steps. The like of it was never made in any kingdom. (1 Kings 10:18–20)

Every king needs a throne to serve as a symbol of his royal supremacy, but the seat of Solomon's kingdom was the envy of emperors. Made of ivory and overlaid with gold, his throne was truly unique: there was nothing else like it anywhere in the world. The lions on Solomon's throne were emblems of the tribe of Judah (see Gen. 49:9–10), and thus they served as royal symbols of the king's God-given power.

Solomon was also successful at business: "For the king had a fleet of ships of Tarshish at sea with the fleet of Hiram. Once every three years the fleet of ships of Tarshish used to come bringing gold, silver, ivory, apes, and peacocks" (1 Kings 10:22). Solomon owned a fleet of large seagoing vessels that could sail to Tarshish and back. They returned from their travels full of precious metals and rare specimens of exotic animals, in keeping with the king's passion for zoology.

All these treasures, both animal and mineral, kept flowing into Jerusalem. Solomon's kingdom became a major center for international trade. With all the revenues and exchanges, to say nothing of the taxes and tariffs, the king's global business accumulated an enormous fortune.

THE GOLDEN AGE

This all sounds very impressive, but how does the Bible evaluate the glory days of Solomon's empire? What are we to make of all his gold? What can the king's riches teach us about the spiritual implications of wealth and our own relationship to the good things of this life?

We need to recognize that gold is good in itself. So are apes, peacocks, silver, and even ivory, depending on how it is obtained. These are beautiful things created by God for the enjoyment of his people. Gold is especially beautiful, which is one of the reasons why it is universally acknowledged as a valuable treasure. In keeping with this reputation, the Bible often puts gold in a positive light. There are hundreds of references to gold in the Scriptures of the Old and New Testaments, and many of them recognize its durable splendor.

The place to start is at the very beginning, when gold was created by God as one of earth's essential elements. In describing the beautiful rivers that flowed through the garden of Eden, the book of Genesis says they "flowed around the whole land of Havilah, where there is gold. And the gold of that land is good" (Gen. 2:11–12). Gold is part of the good world that God created. It is a gift of his common grace and a reason for his praise. Haggai 2:8 says: "The gold is mine, declares the LORD of hosts."

The goodness of gold explains why we see such a large quantity of it in the houses that were built for the worship of God. When Moses made his tabernacle in the wilderness, according to the instructions God gave him on Mount Sinai, everything in the holy places was covered with gold. The same was true at Solomon's temple in Jerusalem, with its gilded interior. These sacred spaces show that gold is a suitable element for expressing the majesty of God.

Some of the great heroes of biblical faith counted gold among their prized possessions, including Abraham (Gen. 13:2), Joseph (Gen. 41:42), and Mordecai (Esth. 8:15). There are also biblical images that trade on gold's beauty and durability. Gold is a suitable ornament for a bride to wear on her wedding day (e.g., Ps. 45:9, 13). The refining of gold, which burns away impurity, is a symbol of the sanctifying work of the Holy Spirit (e.g., Job 23:10; Mal. 3:3). Gold is even described as a good material to use in building on the spiritual foundation of Jesus Christ (1 Cor. 3:12).

In keeping with these biblical images of adornment and refinement, the gold from Solomon's glory days is presented in a positive light. Gold is the metal of kings, and thus Solomon's gold was a sign of his royal majesty. This is evident from the way the Bible describes his wealth and wisdom: "Thus King

Solomon excelled all the kings of the earth in riches and in wisdom. And the whole earth sought the presence of Solomon to hear his wisdom, which God had put into his mind. Every one of them brought his present, articles of silver and gold, garments, myrrh, spices, horses, and mules, so much year by year" (1 Kings 10:23–25). This summary praises the glories of Solomon's kingdom, putting his wealth and wisdom in the category of excellence. It is to Solomon's praise that the world sought his wisdom, and also that people brought him their precious treasures.

Remember as well that this golden age was God's answer to Solomon's prayers. In Psalm 72 the king asked for the wealth of nations—not for himself alone, but for the sake of God's kingdom. The king's gold was an answer to prayer, therefore, and also the fulfillment of a promise. Back at the beginning of his reign, when Solomon honored God by asking for wisdom, God promised him the added blessing of incomparable riches: "I give you also what you have not asked, both riches and honor, so that no other king shall compare with you, all your days" (1 Kings 3:13). So this is what we are to make of Solomon's gold: it was the answer to his royal prayers and the fulfillment of a divine promise, to the glory of the kingdom of God.

We can say something similar about the riches that God has given to us. God has fulfilled his promise to take care of us. He has answered our prayers to provide everything we need. In fact, he has done much more than that. Many Christians in the West are much wealthier than Solomon. We may not have as much gold, but we eat a greater variety of fresh food, wear more comfortable clothes, sit in more functional furniture, listen to a better selection of music, and use much faster transportation. Life is good, and we should praise God for all his blessings, which are more than we deserve and much, much more than most people in the world have ever had. Praise God for the glories of our own golden age!

THIS PASSING SPLENDOR

Yet for all its glory, we always need to remember that earthly gold is only a passing splendor. No matter how costly it is, from an eternal perspective gold is extremely limited in value. Therefore, we should be careful not to be overly impressed with the glories of Solomon's kingdom, let alone our own earthly treasures. Soon Solomon's glory days would be over. Already he was reaching the point of diminishing returns. How many golden shields can a king really use, anyway?

To keep things in their proper perspective, we need to hear the other side of what the Bible says about gold. While openly acknowledging its splendor, the Bible also mentions some spiritual things that are much more valuable. Gold is not as precious as wisdom, for example. As Solomon said himself, in one of his famous proverbs, "How much better to get wisdom than gold!" (Prov. 16:16; cf. 3:14). Or listen to the words of Job, who said of wisdom:

> It cannot be bought for gold,
>   and silver cannot be weighed as its price.
> It cannot be valued in the gold of Ophir,
>   in precious onyx or sapphire.
> Gold and glass cannot equal it,
>   nor can it be exchanged for jewels of fine gold. (Job 28:15–17)

Gold is also much less valuable than the Word of God, which is the source of all true wisdom. King David said that the law of God is more desirable than gold, "even much fine gold" (Ps. 19:10; cf. 119:127). Similarly, the apostle Peter presented faith in Christ as something "more precious than gold" (1 Peter 1:7). As valuable as it is, gold cannot compare with the priceless treasure of knowing and doing the will of God or believing the gospel of Jesus Christ—his death and resurrection for our salvation. All these things are in the Scriptures, where we find our soul's true and priceless treasure: Jesus Christ. All the gold in the world is not worth even a single ounce of the saving truth that leads to eternal life in him.

If Jesus Christ is the treasure of treasures, then the poorest sinner who has a Bible to read and believes its saving message is wealthier than the richest man in the world. This is because gold cannot satisfy the soul. British Prime Minister Tony Blair was right when he said, "We enjoy a thousand material advantages over any previous generation, and yet we suffer a depth of insecurity and spiritual doubt they never knew."[3] Although there are many things

---

3. William Shawcross, *Queen and Country: The Fifty-Year Reign of Elizabeth II* (New York: Simon and Schuster, 2002), 226.

280

that money can buy, the precious things of God are not for sale. Whatever else it may be able to do for us, our earthly gold cannot comfort us, forgive us, or save us. As the prophet Ezekiel said of people under divine judgment, "silver and gold are not able to deliver them in the day of the wrath of the Lord" (Ezek. 7:19; cf. Zeph. 1:18).

The limitations of wealth are important to understand, because many people do put their confidence in earthly treasures. Despite many biblical warnings against the mortal danger of false worship, they bow down to their silver and their gold. This was a problem already in the days of Moses. There was gold in the tabernacle, to be sure, but there was also gold in the sacred cow that Aaron made for the people to worship. And there was gold in many of the other idols that people worshiped in ancient times. "Their idols are silver and gold," the psalmist said (Ps. 115:4; cf. Ex. 20:23).

We face the same temptation—not to bow down to golden idols, perhaps, but to worship things that money can buy. Some people covet golden jewelry; they feel better when they can flash a little "bling-bling." Other people find their significance in their homes and automobiles—the big-ticket items. Some people enjoy the buzz they get from having the latest technology or from wearing something new.

At the right price, at the right time, and for the right reason, any of these purchases may be legitimate. But whether we use gold coins or a golden credit card, the danger is that we will try to find our comfort and security in something we can buy. Clement of Alexandria wisely said that wealth, when not properly governed, becomes

a stronghold of evil. Many who cast their eyes on it will never reach the kingdom of heaven, for they are sick for the things of the world, and live proudly in luxury. But those who are in earnest about salvation must settle this beforehand in their mind: all we possess is given to us for the sake of self-sufficiency, and one may attain that with only a few things.[4]

One practical way to resist our own golden temptations is to make the kinds of comparisons that the Bible makes, reminding ourselves that earthly treasure is not worth nearly as much as the Holy Scriptures, or the spiritual wisdom they bring. "I love my new furniture," we might say—or perhaps,

4. Clement of Alexandria, "True Wealth," re:generation Quarterly 4, 4 (Winter 1998): 15.

"I would love to have new furniture"—"but that should not be as precious to me as the time I can spend today reading the Word of the living God." "I sure wish I had one of *those*," we might admit when we see some flashy new product in the catalog or on the computer screen, "but why should I waste my time wanting one of those when I know that one day Jesus will take me to heaven?"

Unless we are making these kinds of comparisons all the time, we will be in constant danger of turning earthly gold into an ungodly idol, and we will forget that the best way to spend our money is to invest it in people and ministries that spread the gospel. So remember that the treasures of this world are not the glories of the kingdom of God. Do not trust the gold of earthly gain to satisfy your soul. Job was on the right track when he said, "If I have made gold my trust or called fine gold my confidence, if I have rejoiced because my wealth was abundant . . . I would have been false to God above" (Job 31:24–25, 28).

Remember this as well: you will lose all your gold when you die. You may well lose it sooner than that, as many people do. But even if you amass a large fortune, and manage to hold on to it until you are old and gray, you will still have to leave it all behind when you die. Charles Spurgeon told the story of a shipowner who was asked about the state of his soul. "Soul?" the man replied, incredulously. "I have no time to take care of my soul. I have enough to do just taking care of my ships." But as Spurgeon pointed out, the man was not too busy to die, which he did only a week later.[5] Thus passes the glory of the world; *sic transit gloria mundi*.

Is there a better example of this truth than King Solomon? How quickly his glory passed away! In 1 Kings 14 we read how "Shishak king of Egypt came up against Jerusalem. He took away the treasures of the house of the LORD and the treasures of the king's house. He took away everything. He also took away all the shields of gold that Solomon had made" (1 Kings 14:25–26). Thus the very gold that made Solomon's kingdom so glorious eventually ended up in Egypt.

But of course Solomon was dead by then anyway. He had already left all his earthly treasure behind, as everyone always does. Thus passes the glory of the world, as Solomon knew it would. In Ecclesiastes the king lamented hav-

---

5. Spurgeon's story is recounted by Richard D. Phillips in *Turning Your World Upside Down: Kingdom Priorities in the Parables of Jesus* (Phillipsburg, NJ: P&R Publishing, 2003), 102.

ing to leave everything "to the man who will come after me, and who knows whether he will be wise or a fool?" (Eccl. 2:18). As it happened, Solomon's worst fears were realized: he left his treasures to his fool of a son Rehoboam, who proceeded to lose them all. *Sic transit gloria mundi!*

If we say this about Solomon, we should also be prepared to say it about ourselves and our own golden treasures, for they too will pass away.

FOOL'S GOLD AND OTHER TEMPTATIONS

The glories of gold, with all their fleeting splendor, call us to be wise in the way we live. Some people think that what they own is the most important thing in life: whoever gets the most gold wins. But the most important thing in life is to glorify God, which we do or fail to do independent of our income level or our tax bracket.

This is where Solomon's story takes such a tragic turn. As wise as he was, at least for most of his reign, somewhere along the way Solomon started making some deadly spiritual compromises. He stopped choosing to follow God with his whole heart every day, and started living for his own glory, seeking his own security and pursuing his own pleasure.

This should not surprise us. It is hard for rich people to enter the kingdom of God—virtually impossible, in fact. Jesus said, "It is easier for a camel to go through the eye of a needle than for a rich person to enter the kingdom of God" (Matt. 19:24). This is something that only God can do by the supernatural power of his Spirit. It takes the work of the Holy Spirit to strip away all confidence in ourselves and enable us to put all our trust in the grace of God instead. So it is not surprising that someone as wealthy as Solomon failed to be fully obedient to the law of God, any more than it would be surprising for rich people like us to get caught up in all the temptations of the good life.

Gold is one of the most dangerous temptations in the world. As Augustine once said, "The love of possessions is a sort of a trap, which entangles the soul and prevents it flying to God."[6] King Solomon would have done well to heed the warnings that Moses gave in the book of Deuteronomy, and so would we: "Take care lest you forget the LORD your God . . . , lest, when you have eaten and are full and have built good houses and live in them, and

---

6. Jill Haak Adels, ed., *The Wisdom of the Saints: An Anthology* (Oxford: Oxford University Press, 1989), 164.

when . . . your silver and your gold is multiplied . . . , then . . . you forget the LORD your God, who brought you out of the land of Egypt, out of the house of slavery" (Deut. 8:11–14). How easy it is for rich people to forget the God of their salvation! The more we have, the easier it is to think that we have everything we need without God.

The way King Solomon kept accumulating more and more gold is a sign that he was giving in to this danger. The Law of Moses explicitly told the king of Israel not to do this, not to "acquire for himself excessive silver and gold" (Deut. 17:17). Maybe it is hard to decide exactly how much gold is too much, but for Solomon it was probably somewhere between his first and his five hundredth golden shield. The desire to hoard was starting to take control of his heart.

What about our own hearts? Have we learned to say "enough is enough," or do we continue to think of more and more things that we would like to own? Clement of Alexandria said:

> God has given to us, I know well, the liberty of using things—but only so far as necessary; and he has determined that our use of them should be shared. . . . How much wiser to spend money on human beings, than on jewels and gold! . . . In the end it is not the one who keeps, but the one who gives away, who is rich; and it is giving away, not possession, which renders a man happy.[7]

King Solomon also faced another serious temptation, which was to put his trust in military power. The chapter thus ends with a further warning sign of spiritual danger:

> And Solomon gathered together chariots and horsemen. He had 1,400 chariots and 12,000 horsemen, whom he stationed in the chariot cities and with the king in Jerusalem. . . . And Solomon's import of horses was from Egypt and Kue, and the king's traders received them from Kue at a price. A chariot could be imported from Egypt for 600 shekels of silver and a horse for 150, and so through the king's traders they were exported to all the kings of the Hittites and the kings of Syria. (1 Kings 10:26, 28–29)

To put it bluntly, King Solomon had become an arms dealer for the Middle East. As the middleman between the Egyptians and the Syrians—importing

---

7. Clement of Alexandria, "True Wealth," 15.

284

and exporting chariots, buying low and selling high—Solomon turned a large profit. Yet in the long run this proved to be very foolish. In later days the Syrians and the Egyptians both attacked the Israelites (e.g., 1 Kings 14:25–26; 20:1–43; 2 Kings 5:1–2). Thus the king was supplying his enemies with the weapons for Israel's own destruction!

What Solomon did was also in direct violation of the Law of Moses, which said that the king "must not acquire many horses for himself or cause the people to return to Egypt in order to acquire many horses, since the LORD has said to you, 'You shall never return that way again'" (Deut. 17:16). By trading with Egypt for horses and chariots, Solomon was going to the very place that he was forbidden to go.

By the time we get to chapter 11, Solomon will be spiritually bankrupt. But the warning signs of his eventual downfall are obvious already in chapter 10: his misguided quest for more and more gold, as well as his misplaced confidence in earthly power.

That was Solomon, but what about us? What are the warning signs that we are headed toward our own downfall? Maybe it is the endless quest for more, as if getting something that we do not have right now would really satisfy our souls. Maybe it is the confidence we place in our money to secure our future, or in our skills to guarantee our success. It would be easy to excuse ourselves by saying that everyone else is doing it. Solomon could say the same thing. He was the king, after all, and kings are supposed to get more gold to buy more chariots, are they not?

Before we make excuses for investing in the wrong kind of treasure, we should listen to the warning of the apostle John: "The world is passing away along with its desires, but whoever does the will of God abides forever" (1 John 2:17). This was John's way of saying *sic transit gloria mundi*. This world is passing away, along with everything in it. So do not be overly impressed by earthly gold. Do not make the wrong spiritual choices that will ruin your soul. And do not miss the real glory that is waiting for everyone who trusts in Jesus alone for salvation.

GLORY DAYS

One day there will be another golden kingdom. In fact, Solomon's gold held the promise of this more glorious kingdom. It was for this reason, perhaps more than any other, that God gave Solomon so much gold: he did it to prepare us for the golden kingdom of God. When Jesus preached the kingdom of God, he assumed that people had some idea what a kingdom was, and he used Solomon's kingdom as an example. The kingdom of Solomon was the kingdom *par excellence*—"Solomon in all his glory," Jesus called it (Matt. 6:29).

Yet for all its glory, Solomon's gold gives us only a glimpse of the greater glories of the kingdom of Jesus Christ. When we get to the book of Revelation, where the Bible opens a window on eternity, we see many glittering splendors. As it was at the creation, so it will be in the consummation: the gold of paradise is good. The crowns of the saints are made of gold (e.g., Rev. 4:4). So are the streets of heaven (Rev. 21:21). In fact, the whole heavenly city is described as a golden metropolis—a city of pure gold (Rev. 21:18).

The point of these comparisons is not to tell us what building materials God will use in the New Jerusalem, but to give us a sense of the permanence and grandeur of that blessed place. The golden kingdom of Solomon is only a glimmer of the glories that God has for us in Jesus Christ. His heavenly kingdom will be glorious, like pure gold, and it will last forever—a golden age that will never end. As John Newton wrote at the end of his hymn "Glorious Things of Thee Are Spoken," in contrasting earthly possessions with heavenly glory:

> Fading is the worldling's pleasure,
> All his boasted pomp and show;
> Solid joys and lasting treasure
> None but Zion's children know.

None of the children in the heavenly Zion ever says *sic transit gloria mundi*. Instead, they say *sic durat gloria Dei*: "thus endures the glory of God." Here, then, is the place to store our treasure: not in a kingdom that is passing away, but in a golden age that will never end.

23

A REAL TRAGEDY

1 Kings 11:1–8

For when Solomon was old his wives turned away his heart after other gods, and his heart was not wholly true to the LORD his God, as was the heart of David his father. (1 Kings 11:4)

ost Bible stories are comedies—not in the popular sense that they are funny (although there is more humor in the Bible than many people realize), but in the literary sense that they have a happy ending. Noah and his family pass through the deep waters of a great flood, but they see the rainbow on the other side. Joseph gets sold into slavery, but rises to greatness and saves a nation from famine. And so on. The Bible is full of happy endings. The happiest story of all, of course, is the gospel, in which Jesus rises again after dying, and then comes to us with the promise that our own story will have a happy ending too: eternal life through faith in him.

Not every story has a happy ending, however. Some Bible stories are tragedies—not simply in the popular sense that they are sad, but in the more technical sense that we use the word "tragedy" in world literature. Shakespeare wrote several famous tragedies—great plays like *King Lear*, *Othello*, and *Romeo and Juliet*. Long before Shakespeare, there were the ancient Greek tragedians: Aeschylus, Sophocles, and Euripides. From the dramas that these men wrote, we learn that a tragedy is a "story of exceptional calamity," moving from prosperity to catastrophe, "in which a protagonist of high degree and greatness of spirit makes a choice and as a result inevitably falls into a state of suffering, sometimes attaining perception."[1] To put this definition in simpler terms, a tragedy is a story in which a great man who makes the wrong choice falls into bitter disgrace and (sometimes) learns from his mistakes.

One of the saddest tragedies in the Bible is the story of King Solomon. Solomon was one of the greatest kings the world has ever seen. Yet at the end of his life he made one of the most foolish choices that anyone has ever made, with disastrous consequences for himself and his kingdom. O Solomon! Where did you go so wrong, and how can we learn to avoid making the same mistakes that you made?

SOLOMON'S GREATNESS

A real tragedy is always the story of some great person. According to the conventions of world literature, tragedy focuses on "the tragic protagonist, a person of high social standing, usually a king or ruler. The high position of a tragic hero at the beginning of the story goes beyond his or her belonging to the social elite; this exalted figure is understood to be representative of general humanity. Ordinarily a tragic hero possesses something that we can call greatness of spirit."[2]

Solomon meets this qualification for a tragic hero, and then some, for he was one of the greatest men who ever lived. To begin with, Solomon came from noble birth. As the son of David, he was heir to the world's most famous dynasty. He had a high position: he was the king of Israel.

Furthermore, almost everything that Solomon ever did was a total success. His rise to power was celebrated by his entire nation. Any and all rivals to his throne were quickly subdued. Solomon had a powerful army of horses and chariots, which he never even needed to use in battle, because his kingdom was always at peace. Under the blessing of God, in Solomon's days the kingdom of Israel grew to its widest expanse.

1. Leland Ryken, *How to Read the Bible as Literature* (Grand Rapids: Zondervan, 1984), 83–84.
2. Ibid.

King Solomon was also a famous builder. His golden temple in Jerusalem was one of the wonders of the ancient world. To his everlasting praise, Solomon built the earthly dwelling place for the living God. He also built a large palace for himself, with its Hall of Pillars, Hall of the Throne, and House of the Forest of Lebanon. Solomon was extraordinarily wealthy, as anyone could tell from the buildings he constructed. His kingdom was full of silver and gold, to say nothing of priceless jewels and other precious treasures. Traders and investors came to Israel from all over the world. Everything that Solomon touched turned to gold. The Bible says he had riches beyond compare (1 Kings 3:13)—a glorious kingdom!

In addition, the king was famous for his skills and abilities. Solomon was an accomplished naturalist, with a comprehensive knowledge of plants and animals. He was a learned scholar, whose philosophical writings still give timeless insight into man's place in the universe. He was a brilliant poet, whose lyrical love songs burn with romantic passion. Above all, Solomon was a man of wisdom, for this was the unique gift that distinguished him from all others, the gift that he received from God. Solomon was the wisest man in the world—maybe the wisest man in history (apart from the Son of God, of course). People came from all over the world to hear what Solomon had to say, and when they heard his wisdom for themselves, sometimes it took their breath away (see 1 Kings 10:5).

Solomon was such a good king that rather than envying his success, people rejoiced in the glory of his kingdom. His own citizens "blessed the king and went to their homes joyful and glad of heart for all the goodness that the LORD had shown to David his servant and to Israel his people" (1 Kings 8:66). Similarly, the queen of Sheba blessed God for the happiness of Solomon's kingdom.

Then, in addition to everything else, Solomon was a man of prayer. His personal piety is demonstrated in the magnificent prayer he gave at the dedication of the temple (1 Kings 8:22–53). Solomon's dedicatory prayer is one of the best prayers in the entire Bible, a model for thanksgiving, confession, intercession, and praise. Part of Solomon's greatness was his godliness.

King Solomon was a very great man, but we have not yet mentioned the greatest thing about him, which is that his kingdom reveals the pattern for the kingdom of the Lord Jesus Christ. Solomon occupies a central place in biblical theology, the history of redemption. He stands in the line of kings leading up to the kingship of Christ. The glory of his kingdom thus shows the glory of Jesus Christ as the greater Solomon of the kingdom of God.

Very simply, Solomon was one of the greatest men who ever lived. Anyone who ever heard the wisdom of his counsel or watched him lead his people in prayer would never have expected his kingship to end in tragedy. "Anyone but Solomon," they would have said. "He is the *last* person that I could ever imagine falling into serious sin. He is one of the best and wisest men in the world."

Maybe some people would say something similar about us, as they have said it about many Christians who have fallen tragically into sin, including many Christians. We ought to be one of the best people they know. We have made a lifetime commitment to Jesus Christ and we are active in the worship of the church. God has given us spiritual gifts that we are using to serve other people. For some of our friends and neighbors and family members, we are the living, breathing definition of a Christian.

Yet how easy it would be for the story of our lives to turn into a real tragedy! Consider wisely: what sin or sins are you tempted to commit, or have committed, that can only lead to exceptional calamity? If it happened to King Solomon, as wise and as great as he was, it can happen to anyone. "Therefore," the Bible says, "let anyone who thinks that he stands take heed lest he fall" (1 Cor. 10:12).

SOLOMON'S FOLLY

To avoid making the same mistake that Solomon made, it is important to understand the precise nature of his tragic choice. In tragedy, the hero always has a choice to make, and it is making the wrong choice that leads to all the trouble. One literary critic writes:

> Usually the tragic action begins with the protagonist facing a dilemma. He is drawn in two or more directions and must make a moral choice. This means that a tragic hero is always responsible for his downfall, since he has made the tragic choice. Usually the tragic hero is also deserving of his catastrophe, with his fall stemming from some frailty of character.[3]

3. Leland Ryken, *The Literature of the Bible* (Grand Rapids: Zondervan, 1980), 95.

The word Aristotle used for this tragic flaw was *hamartia*, which also happens to be one of the main New Testament words for sin—a missing of the mark. Aristotle described it as "some great error or frailty," a "defect which is painful or destructive."[4]

So what was Solomon's destructive defect? Ironically, at first he made the right choice, not the wrong choice. When Solomon first rose to power, God gave him the choice of a lifetime: whatever the king asked, God would give. Wisely, Solomon chose wisdom, and as a result, God promised him a lifetime of blessing.

But choosing for godliness is not the kind of choice that we make only once in life and then everything else falls into place automatically. This is something people usually misunderstand about Solomon. They assume that once he chose wisdom, his success was guaranteed. Sadly, many people have the same misunderstanding about making a decision for Jesus Christ. They assume that once they have given their lives to Christ, or prayed "the sinner's prayer," they do not need to choose for godliness ever again. But as Solomon said himself, every follower of God is called to keep following God. In Proverbs he wrote:

My son, do not lose sight of these—
   keep sound wisdom and discretion,
and they will be life for your soul
   and adornment for your neck.
Then you will walk on your way securely,
   and your foot will not stumble. (Prov. 3:21–23)

In reality, the choice for or against the kingdom of God comes to us every day, in every choice we make. God made this clear to Solomon on multiple occasions. Immediately after granting his gift of wisdom, God said to Solomon, "If you will walk in my ways, . . . I will lengthen your days" (1 Kings 3:14). Long life was contingent upon faithful obedience. God said virtually the same thing to Solomon after he built the temple (1 Kings 6:11–13), and then again after he prayed his dedicatory prayer (1 Kings 9:1–9). It was only as Solomon walked with God that he would experience God's blessing. This was the choice that he had to make every day of his life for as long as he lived.

4. Ryken, *How to Read the Bible as Literature*, 83–84.

It is also the same choice that *we* have to make. A Christian is not someone who chooses for Christ once, but someone who chooses for Christ and then lives out that choice every day for the rest of his or her life. Our ongoing access to divine wisdom is dependent on a living, vital faith relationship to the Son of God. In our relationships, in the expenditure of our time and money, in the use of our bodies, in the little frustrations that happen every day—in all of the complexities of life—will we choose for God or against him?

Solomon's choice was tragic, and thus his life became a sad commentary on one of his own warnings: "Cease to hear instruction, my son, and you will stray from the words of knowledge" (Prov. 19:27). According to 1 Kings 11, eventually the king committed many disgraceful sins that were offensive to the holiness of God and led directly to the downfall of his kingdom. Solomon was not faithful in marriage, but "loved many foreign women, along with the daughter of Pharaoh: Moabite, Ammonite, Edomite, Sidonian, and Hittite women" (1 Kings 11:1). How many women did he "love"? At least a thousand, which was a thousand times too many! The king was living so large that even his sin was supersized: "He had 700 wives, princesses, and 300 concubines" (1 Kings 11:3; cf. 1 Chron. 3:1–9).

In those days it was customary for kings to take many wives, but Solomon took more than most. He was called to be a one-woman man, just as Christian husbands today are called to give all their affection to the one woman that God has called them to love by sacrifice (see Eph. 5:25–31). In a godly marriage, there is room for only one main emotional connection, one overriding passion, one sexual bond. Instead, Solomon foolishly squandered his affections on women he was forbidden to touch. Obviously, he could not truly love these women in any meaningful sense of the word "love." When the Bible says that he "clung to these [women] in love" (1 Kings 11:2), the connotation is frankly sexual. This was a foolish sin of marital infidelity.

Solomon was guilty of more than sexual sin, however. The mention of "princesses" is a clear indication that many of these marriages represented political alliances. By marrying the daughters of foreign kings, Solomon was practicing politics, lusting after power as well as sex. These women came from the very nations that God told Israel to drive out of the Promised Land. Yet Solomon foolishly joined forces with them through covenant matrimony.

Even worse, the king began to worship their gods. This was something that God had warned about from the very beginning. "You shall not intermarry with them," he said, "giving your daughters to their sons or taking their daughters for your sons, for they would turn away your sons from following me, to serve other gods. Then the anger of the LORD would be kindled against you, and he would destroy you quickly" (Deut. 7:3–4; cf. Ex. 34:15–16). Foolishly, Solomon failed to heed this warning. The issue with these foreign wives was not their ethnicity (the Bible fully endorses multiethnic marriages), but their religion. The women whom Solomon married did not believe in the one true God, but came "from the nations concerning which the LORD had said to the people of Israel, 'You shall not enter into marriage with them, neither shall they with you, for surely they will turn away your heart after their gods'" (1 Kings 11:2).

It was bad enough for Solomon to marry these women, breaking the seventh commandment by committing adultery. But he also began to worship their idols, thereby breaking both the first and the second commandments, which forbid the worship of other gods. Solomon's polygamy turned him into a polytheist. He "went after Ashtoreth the goddess of the Sidonians, and after Milcom the abomination of the Ammonites" (1 Kings 11:5). Ashtoreth was the sex goddess of the Canaanites. Milcom is less familiar, although some scholars identify him with Molech, who was worshiped with child sacrifices (e.g., Jer. 32:35). Nevertheless, "Solomon built a high place for Chemosh the abomination of Moab, and for Molech the abomination of the Ammonites, on the mountain east of Jerusalem. And so he did for all his foreign wives, who made offerings and sacrificed to their gods" (1 Kings 11:7–8). The mountain east of Jerusalem is the Mount of Olives, which stands directly opposite the Temple Mount. Thus Solomon practiced the grotesque and damnable rites of pagan worship within plain sight of God's holy temple.

What Solomon did was wicked. The Bible says that he "did what was evil in the sight of the LORD and did not wholly follow the LORD, as David his father had done" (1 Kings 11:6). What Solomon did was not only wicked, but also foolish. It was foolish to lust after sex and power, foolish to have a thousand wives, and foolish to worship their gods. These things were foolish because they violated the commandments of God, and also because doing them did not make very much sense to begin with. "In the ancient world," notes Paul House, "polytheists tended to worship the gods of nations who had conquered their armies or at least the gods of countries more powerful than their own. Ironically, Solomon worships the gods of people he has conquered and already controls. What could he possibly gain from such activity?"[5]

Solomon's wicked folly is very familiar, because the sins that he committed are equally common today. We are living in a sex-crazed society, where the seductions of sin are always on display. Longing for intimacy, young people in the church are often tempted to do what Solomon did and have a relationship with someone who does not believe in the God of the Bible. Rather than worshiping the only true God, people worship many false gods: money and pleasure, work and leisure, self and sexuality. Other people say that all religions are essentially the same, that Buddha and Muhammad deserve as much honor as Jesus does. Sometimes this is even true in the church, where people claim to worship Jesus, but also follow other gods or engage in practices drawn from other religions.

Solomon seems like just the king for these postmodern times. His sins are still very much with us, which means that we ourselves may be in danger of a tragic downfall. Unless we learn from his mistakes, we might fall to sexual temptation, or end up marrying an unbeliever, or get involved in false religion, just like he did.

Lesson 1: The Little Choices We Make

Typically a tragic hero will learn from his mistakes. His story does not simply end in destruction, but leads to some profound recognition of what went wrong. The hero comes to a place of perception, where he sees the tragic choice that led to his tragic failure. He may even come to the point of repentance.

First Kings does not directly tell us what Solomon learned from his mistakes. For this we need the book of Ecclesiastes, where the king explains how he learned to "fear God and keep his commandments" (Eccl. 12:13). Yet we can learn the same lessons by studying 1 Kings and looking carefully at what went wrong. An elder from Philadelphia's Tenth Presbyterian Church used to summarize Solomon's life by saying this: "Why make your own mistakes, when you can learn from mine?" Though Solomon's vaunted wisdom failed him, he may yet become a source of wisdom for us.

5. Paul R. House, *1, 2 Kings*, The New American Commentary (Nashville: Broadman & Holman, 1995), 167.

We learn at least two important lessons from the tragedy of King Solomon. The first is that *we start falling into sin long before we ever fall into disgrace*. So if we wish to avoid our own tragic downfall, we need to fight against every little sin by the power of the Holy Spirit.

Notice the contrast or even contradiction between the way Solomon's story began and the way it ended. When Solomon first rose to power and chose wisdom over wealth, the Bible tells us that he "loved the Lord" (1 Kings 3:3). The word used here for "love" (*ahab*) is the same word that is used at the end of the story to describe the king's relationship to foreign women (see 1 Kings 11:1). An absolute change has taken place in Solomon's affections. The man who once loved God ended up loving many pagan wives. As Richard Phillips writes in his analysis of the "deformation" of Old Testament Israel, King Solomon "took foreign wives, the loveliest daughters of Egypt and Moab, Ammon and Sidonia, and in so doing took their gods into his heart."[6]

How did this change take place? It did not happen overnight. Solomon did not wake up one day and suddenly decide to stop loving God and start loving someone else. No, the spiritual change happened little by little, as it always does. "A small difference in trajectory," comments Mark Dever, "can make a big difference in destination. . . . Sin often begins with what may feel like a minor concession—maybe an allowance for this shortcoming or a brief indulgence for that desire. But that simple change of trajectory can set you on a course to a deadly destination."[7]

All the way through Solomon's story we can see warning signs of an impending tragedy. The king was headed on the wrong spiritual trajectory. It all began when he made an alliance with Egypt, of all places, by marrying Pharaoh's daughter (1 Kings 3:1). This was one seed of his destruction: marrying outside the faith. On occasion, Solomon would also go to worship at one of the high places of the Canaanites (1 Kings 3:3–4)—a further warning sign of impending idolatry.

Then there were the royal commands that Solomon broke. God specifically told the kings of Israel not to build up a cavalry or accumulate excessive amounts of silver and gold (Deut. 17:14–17). But Solomon purchased tens of thousands of horses and chariots, including many from Egypt, which

6. Richard D. Phillips, *Turning Back the Darkness: The Biblical Pattern of Reformation* (Wheaton, IL: Crossway, 2002), 58.

7. Mark Dever, *The Message of the Old Testament: Promises Made* (Wheaton, IL: Crossway, 2006), 293.

God had expressly forbidden (1 Kings 4:26; 10:28–29; cf. Deut. 17:16). The king also gathered vast treasuries of silver and gold (1 Kings 10:14–25). The glories of Solomon's kingdom became the downfall of his soul. Little by little, he was making the wrong spiritual choices, until finally when he "was old his wives turned away his heart after other gods, and his heart was not wholly true to the LORD his God, as was the heart of David his father" (1 Kings 11:4).

Some people are surprised that Solomon came to such a bad end, but the details in his story clearly foreshadow his downfall. Solomon's life was like a tower of blocks. With each tragic and sinful choice, he was pulling another block out of the structure of his existence. For a long time his life still seemed solid, at least from the outside. But the king was getting weaker and weaker, until finally he collapsed in a heap of ungodly sins.

It was not just at the end that Solomon made the wrong choice, but all the way along. His story thus gives us "a picture of gradual acquiescence with evil. The writer of the tragedy of Solomon does not present the tragedy as an isolated act of the will. He is interested not in the moment of sensuality and materialism and idolatry, but in the lifelong habit of weakness for women, love of splendor, and idolatry."[8] This was the direction that Solomon's life was heading. He never explicitly decided to stop loving God. Yet the more he loved other things, the less he loved God, until one day he was not living for God or loving him at all.

Solomon started falling into sin long before he ever fell into disgrace. There were a lot of little decisions that led up to his big disaster, as there always are. What choices are you making, and where will they lead in the end? The consequences of Solomon's tragic choice were totally disastrous. They ended up dividing and destroying an entire nation. Yet they seemed like such small sins at the beginning: a little more luxury, a brief flirtation with an exotic romance, a new style of worship. Whoever expected that they would lead Solomon into immorality and idolatry?

Our own sins may seem equally small, and even easier to justify. "Maybe I didn't need to buy that," we might say, "but it really wasn't all that expensive." "These pictures do not actually show enough skin to count as pornography." "I know I'm getting emotionally attached, but it's appropriate to have a good

8. Ryken, *The Literature of the Bible*, 100.

working relationship with my coworker." "I don't care if he's not a Christian; he's a nice person and besides, maybe I'll get a chance to share the gospel." Before we know it, we get pulled into self-indulgent spending, or a habit of sexual sin, or an adulterous affair, or a match that was never made in heaven. Long before most people ever fall into disgrace, they sow the seeds of their own destruction by making lots of little spiritual compromises.

Learn from Solomon's mistake! Resist every little sin as if your life depended on it. The Puritans sometimes compared little sins to baby snakes wriggling out of the nest: they are tiny, but deadly, and if they are not put to death when they hatch, they will grow into huge serpents. So whenever we see even the littlest sin that could turn our lives into a tragedy, we should fight against it with all the power of the Holy Spirit. Read the Bible that the Spirit has given to help us grow in grace, taking careful note of what it says about your predominant temptations. Receive the sacraments that the Spirit uses to strengthen our faith and holiness. Pray for the Spirit to increase your desire for God and wither your appetite for iniquity. The Scripture says that "if by the Spirit you put to death the deeds of the body, you will live" (Rom. 8:13).

Then we should ask God to give us the grace to make the right choices with our money, our relationships, and everything else in life. Even if it is only a small decision, making the right decision will keep us from falling into spiritual decline. If we are young, we are wise to choose the path that God wants us to take in life and then stay on it. If we are old and have already chosen that path, we should not turn away from it the way that Solomon did in his later years. Choose for Jesus and then keep choosing for him all the way to the end of life.

Lesson 2: Sin Is Where the Heart Is

Here is a second lesson that we can learn from Solomon's mistake: *even the greatest spiritual gifts will not keep us from sin if our hearts turn away from God.*

This lesson helps us understand the mystery of Solomon's tragedy. People always ask: How could such a wise man be so foolish? If God truly gave Solomon the gift of wisdom, then why wasn't he wise enough to avoid falling into disgrace?

The answer is that the gifts of God never operate independently or automatically, but always according to the affection of our hearts. In biblical usage, the heart is "the willing, loving, thinking centre of the person."[9] The heart is the control center of our lives, and thus the use of our gifts is governed by the condition of our heart.[10] Our talents can be useful for building the kingdom of God, but only to the extent that our hearts are committed to the glory of God. When our hearts turn away from God, even the gifts that he has given will be used against him. This is a sober warning for anyone who is strongly gifted, because the more gifted we are, the more damage we are likely to do when our hearts turn away from the God of grace. So it was that when Solomon's heart turned away from God, even his wisdom turned into folly.

At the beginning of his reign, Solomon's heart was in the right place. The reason he asked God for wisdom was that he had a heart for God's people: he wanted to rule them well. When he prayed for "an understanding mind," more literally he requested an understanding *heart* (1 Kings 3:9; cf. 10:24). Having a heart for God is the essence of what it means to be a believer. Solomon started out with that holy affection; the living God was his first and truest love. This is evident from the way he governed his people, built the temple, and prayed to the living God. King Solomon kept the first and greatest commandment: "You shall love the LORD your God with all your heart" (Deut. 6:5).

The tragedy is that Solomon's heart ended up in the wrong place. He lost his first love. Chapter 11 emphasizes this by diagnosing his downfall as heart failure. In verse 1 we read that the king "loved many foreign women." Solomon was guilty of sinful affections, of loving the wrong things in life. In verse 2, when God explains what is wrong with taking pagan brides, he says, "they will turn away your heart after their gods" (1 Kings 11:2; cf. Deut. 17:17). This is exactly what happened: "His wives turned away his heart" (1 Kings 11:3). Or again: "When Solomon was old his wives turned away his heart after other gods, and his heart was not wholly true to the LORD his God" (1 Kings 11:4).

9. Dale Ralph Davis, *The Wisdom and the Folly: An Exposition of the Book of First Kings* (Fearn, Ross-shire: Christian Focus, 2002), 114.

10. Paul David Tripp often uses this analogy in his preaching ministry at Tenth Presbyterian Church and elsewhere.

The vocabulary used to describe the change in Solomon's affections is intensive. The Bible says that he "clung" to his wives. Typically the Bible uses the Hebrew verb for clinging (*dbq*) to describe the way someone holds on to God by faith (e.g., Deut. 30:20). But in Solomon's case the same verb is used to describe the holding of an ungodly affection that led to the great sin of worshiping other gods. The Bible says it over and over again: Solomon's story became a tragedy because his heart loved other things more than the living God. He did love God, to a certain extent, but he had a deeply divided heart that also loved too many women and worshiped too many gods.

When our hearts turn away from God, our spiritual gifts will not prevent us from falling into grievous sin. Solomon's wisdom did not keep him holy; nor did the temple he built keep him from idolatry. The Bible says that Solomon ended up doing "what was evil in the sight of the Lord" (1 Kings 11:6). The same man who was wise enough to build a house for God was so foolish that he ended up building high places for the worship of pagan deities. There is no telling what a man will do when his heart turns away from the Lord!

Learn from Solomon's mistake and apply this lesson to your own life: spiritual gifts will not keep us from sin if we have a heart that is turning away from God. Mastering theology, serving the poor, giving to Christian work, teaching the church—none of these gifts will protect us from spiritual failure if we love the world or love ourselves more than we love God. Solomon was one of the most gifted men who ever lived. If his wisdom could not save him, then how will our own gifts ever save us?

There is no telling what we might do if our hearts turn away from God. Apart from the grace of God and the work of his Spirit, we could very well end up doing something evil that tears down everything we have built, as Solomon did. People always seem surprised when well-known Christians fall into sin. Perhaps this is because they have been looking at their gifts rather than their hearts. But the heart is the most important thing of all.

Here are some good questions to ask for self-examination: What is my heart condition? What is the greatest object of my affections? Honestly, am I growing ever more deeply in love with Jesus, or is my heart turning away toward tragedy, as Solomon's did? The Bible warns us not to rely on our gifts to make us faithful, but to keep ourselves "in the love of God, waiting for the mercy of our Lord Jesus Christ that leads to eternal life" (Jude 21). By his grace, God himself will guard us from sin, for he has promised "to keep you from falling and to present you before his glorious presence without fault and with great joy" (Jude 24 NIV).

WHATEVER HAPPENED TO OLD KING SOLOMON?

People often wonder what happened to Solomon in the end. Did he ever repent of his sins? Will we see him in heaven? Was he saved?

This is always the most important question for anyone. Nothing is more important in life than where we will end up for eternity, whether in heaven or hell. A person may commit many harmful sins, as Solomon did, yet still end up in heaven by the grace of God through faith in Jesus Christ. All is well for the soul that ends well.

We have good reason to be hopeful about Solomon's salvation. One reason to be hopeful is that God had promised David that although his son would be disciplined, he would not be forsaken: "I will be to him a father, and he shall be to me a son. When he commits iniquity, I will discipline him with the rod of men, with the stripes of the sons of men, but my steadfast love will not depart from him, as I took it from Saul, whom I put away from before you" (2 Sam. 7:14–15). If the book of Ecclesiastes is any indication, the king learned from his mistakes and came back into a right relationship with God. Furthermore, based on what we know from the Gospels, Jesus regarded Solomon as having a vital place in the history of salvation. One can almost imagine Solomon singing George Beverly Shea's famous hymn as a confession of his own faith:

> I'd rather have Jesus than silver or gold;
> I'd rather be His than have riches untold;
> I'd rather have Jesus than houses or lands;
> I'd rather be led by His nail-pierced hand
> Than to be the king of a vast domain,
> Or be held in sin's dread sway;
> I'd rather have Jesus than anything
> This world affords today.

Whether Solomon was saved or not, we can be absolutely sure of our own salvation. Even after all our wrong affections—after all the times that our own hearts have wandered away from the God we love—our salvation is still secure. This is because we are not saved by our own love for God; rather, we are saved by his love for us in Christ. This is the good news of the gospel: the way we get to heaven is not by loving God enough to make him want to let us in, but by Jesus, loving us enough to die on the cross for our sins. Jesus Christ is the greater Solomon of our salvation, whose heart never turned away from God, but kept on loving him to the very end, and will keep on loving us until we get to glory.

God has mercy for us, even after all the tragic choices that we have made and all the wrong affections that have led us away from him. If we are wise, we will repent from the heart for all the wrong things we have done. We will ask the Holy Spirit to write some new chapters in the story of our lives—better chapters than 1 Kings 11! By the love of Jesus, the story that the Spirit writes will turn out better than we ever imagined.

Jesus is a new kind of hero, one who steps into our tragic story to take our place. We are the people with the tragic and sinful flaw. We are the ones who deserve to suffer the consequences for our sin. Yet Jesus has stepped in to suffer the wrath of God in our place. This is why he came into the world: to enter into our tragic situation and rescue us from our downfall. This is also why Jesus died on the cross: to bear the full punishment that we deserve for our sin.

By dying in our place, Jesus turns our tragedy into a comedy—a story with a happy ending. God is angry with us because of our sin. We deserve to fall under his righteous judgment. But God has saved us from his own wrath by sending his Son to be our Savior.

24

THE FALL OF THE HOUSE OF DAVID

1 Kings 11:9–25

Therefore the LORD said to Solomon, "Since this has been your practice and you have not kept my covenant and my statutes that I have commanded you, I will surely tear the kingdom from you and will give it to your servant. Yet for the sake of David your father I will not do it in your days, but I will tear it out of the hand of your son." (1 Kings 11:11–12)

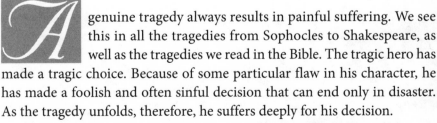genuine tragedy always results in painful suffering. We see this in all the tragedies from Sophocles to Shakespeare, as well as the tragedies we read in the Bible. The tragic hero has made a tragic choice. Because of some particular flaw in his character, he has made a foolish and often sinful decision that can end only in disaster. As the tragedy unfolds, therefore, he suffers deeply for his decision.

We see tragic suffering in *King Lear*, one of William Shakespeare's famous tragedies. The play begins with the old king dividing his kingdom among three daughters. Two of them flatter their father, hoping to gain a bigger share of the inheritance. But when their sister Cordelia refuses to play their selfish game, King Lear flies into a rage. Dividing the inheritance equally between

Cordelia's undeserving sisters, the king banishes her from his kingdom. By the time Lear realizes his mistake and recognizes that he has rejected the only daughter who truly loves him, it is too late. The play ends with Lear in anguish, holding his daughter's corpse in his arms and saying, "I might have saved her; now she's gone for ever! Cordelia, Cordelia!"[1]

Yet even this deep sorrow cannot compare with the suffering we see in the tragedy of Solomon the Wise. Solomon too had made his fateful choice. He had chosen to marry foreign women and to worship their many gods. The result of his tragic decision was painful suffering for himself, his family, and his kingdom.

The Bible tells the story of Solomon's tragedy so that we can avoid making the same mistakes he made. The choices of sin are always tragic, and we are tempted to make them every day. If we are wise, therefore, we will let the Holy Spirit use Solomon's example to teach us our own need for God's saving grace.

THE RIGHTEOUS ANGER OF GOD

The first thing we learn from Solomon's tragic suffering is that God is angry because of our sin, and rightly so. The Bible says this very plainly: "And the LORD was angry with Solomon, because his heart had turned away from the LORD" (1 Kings 11:9). It was not simply the sin that made God angry, as if somehow the sin could be separated from the sinner; it was the man who committed this sin who became the personal object of divine wrath. The Lord was angry with Solomon. His response confronts us with a biblical truth that most people would rather not talk about, even if they happen to believe it, which most people do not. That biblical truth is the wrath of God.

These are immoral times, when people want the freedom to do whatever they want to do, whenever and with whomever they want to do it; or perhaps it would be more accurate to say that these are *amoral* times, when people do not give much thought to doing what is right at all. This is especially true in America, where people generally like to think that what they do is nobody's business but their own. People often take offense when they are challenged

1. William Shakespeare, *King Lear*, act 5, scene 3.

in some particular area of personal morality. "What's *your* problem?" they say. "It's no big deal." Then they proceed to justify their vulgar words, or premarital sex, or dishonest practice of business—whatever sins they are tempted to commit.

People certainly do not want anyone to bring God into the discussion. They talk about the separation of church and state, but often what they mean is the separation of God from daily life. What business does God have telling us what to do, anyway? If people believe in God at all, they like to think of him as a kind of cosmic Santa Claus who is there to do nice things for people, but not to disapprove of what we are doing.

The God who put Solomon on the throne of Israel reveals himself as a God of wrath as well as mercy. The anger of God is not an irrational emotion, but a righteous rejection of sin. To say that God is "angry" is not to say that he is guilty of an irate and reckless rage. His wrath is not a character flaw. Nor is it an unworthy divine attribute, a blemish on God's otherwise perfect reputation. On the contrary, the wrath of God is one of his holy perfections. To say that God is "angry" is to express in human terms his absolute opposition to ungodliness, uncontaminated by all the things that usually make our anger sinful. Leon Morris thus defines the wrath of God as his "personal divine revulsion to evil."[2] Similarly, John Stott says that wrath is God's "continued, settled antagonism, aroused only by evil, and expressed in its condemnation."[3] Elsewhere, Stott defines the wrath of God as his "righteous reaction to evil, his implacable hostility to it, his refusal to condone it, and his judgment upon it."[4] God is perfectly righteous and pristinely holy. How then could he respond to sin with anything except a pure intention to destroy it?

The truth is that God had good reason to be angry with Solomon. The Bible tells us exactly why the king fell under divine judgment. It was "because his heart had turned away from the LORD, the God of Israel, who had appeared to him twice and had commanded him concerning this thing, that he should not go after other gods. But he did not keep what the LORD commanded" (1 Kings 11:9–10).

2. Leon Morris, *The Cross in the New Testament* (Grand Rapids: Eerdmans, 1965), 190–91.
3. John Stott, *The Cross of Christ* (Downers Grove, IL: InterVarsity, 1986), 106.
4. John Stott, "God's Judgment," in *Believing and Obeying Jesus Christ: The Urbana 1979 Compendium*, ed. John W. Alexander (Downers Grove, IL: InterVarsity, 1980), 48.

Notice all the ways that Solomon had offended God's holiness. To begin with, the king's heart had turned away from the love of God. Although formerly he had openly professed his affection for God, in his later days Solomon fell out of love. God is supremely amiable: because of his solitary deity and his absolute divine perfection, he is uniquely and infinitely worthy of all our affection. The only true God deserves all our love. Yet Solomon had forsaken this supreme affection, and because God holds us responsible for what our hearts choose to love, he was angry with Solomon. He was angry with a holy jealousy, which is the righteous prerogative of any lover who has an exclusive claim on his beloved's affection.

Solomon had forsaken his first love despite the fact that God had appeared to him on two separate occasions to bless him and to tell him the way that he should live. Very few people have ever had the rare and extraordinary privilege of meeting God face-to-face. This happened to Solomon not once but *twice*, at the beginning of his reign (1 Kings 3:5ff.) and then again when he built his famous temple (1 Kings 9:1ff.). Nevertheless, Solomon turned away from God. His spiritual experiences did not keep him from sin any more than his spiritual gifts did. Therefore, God was angry with Solomon for rejecting their relationship.

Solomon had also committed the greatest of all sins, which further helps to explain why God was so angry with him. Solomon was guilty of "going after other gods." There is only one true and living God, who was and is and is to come—the Father, the Son, and the Holy Spirit. Yet Solomon had decided to worship false gods who cannot save. There is no greater sin than this: to dishonor God by worshiping anyone or anything else.

God was also angry with Solomon because "he did not keep what the Lord commanded" (1 Kings 11:10; cf. 2:4; 8:25; 9:4–9). Solomon broke the first commandment by having other gods before God. He broke the second commandment by making idolatrous images. This sin dishonored his father David, and therefore it violated the fifth commandment. It included adultery, and thus it broke the seventh commandment. This is what happens when people turn away from God: by the time they are finished, they break every commandment in the Book. It is not enough to know the commandments, although that is a good place to start. God demands that we *do* the commandments, and if we do not, then he is right to be angry.

For all these reasons, God was angry with Solomon, and rightly so. His wrath was fully in keeping with his divine character, and with the words that he had spoken to his people: "You shall not go after other gods, the gods of the peoples who are around you, for the LORD your God in your midst is a jealous God, lest the anger of the LORD your God be kindled against you" (Deut. 6:14–15).

If God is holy, then he must be utterly opposed to sin, including our own sin. This is devastating for us because we are guilty of the same sins as Solomon. Our hearts have often turned away from the love of God. Even if we say that we truly love him, we also have to admit that our spiritual affections often grow cold. God has come to us not just once or twice, but repeatedly. Every time we hear his Word, he comes to us again, offering us his grace and showing us his love. Yet we insist on sinning against him. Of all the sins we love to commit, our greatest sin is going after other gods—the selfish and foolish pleasures of a fallen world. In doing this, we end up breaking God's commandments. In our greed, we break the command not to covet; in our lust, we break the command not to commit sexual sin; in our ambition, we break the command to honor the rights of others, given their position in life. Who can honestly claim to have kept all of God's commandments, or to have loved him with a pure and perfect love? But if we do not love and obey God, then apart from the grace of Jesus Christ, he is angry with us for our sin, and justly so.

Stephen Lungu came to the painful realization of God's anger against his sin at an evangelistic tent meeting in Highfield, Rhodesia. Lungu had gone to the rally hell-bent on destruction. He and other members of a street gang called the Black Shadows were armed with explosives. They had decided to kill as many Christians as they could.

When the gang members arrived at the meeting slightly ahead of schedule, they decided to go in for a few minutes and listen to the evangelist. Soon Lungu was captivated by what he was hearing. "Many of you are in grave danger," the preacher said. "All of you have sinned. You have cheated. You have lied. You have harmed people." Stephen Lungu felt like the preacher's finger was pointing straight at him. How did this man know what he had done? He thought that someone must have told the preacher all about him, because these were exactly the sins that he himself had committed. Lungu started ducking every time the preacher pointed, hoping to avoid his accusatory finger. But the evangelist kept telling him what everyone needs to hear: God knows all about our sin and will judge us for it.[5]

The Consequences of Solomon's Sin

The anger of God has real consequences, both in this life and in the life to come. If God is angry with people for their sin, then he will certainly punish them for it. This is part of sin's tragedy: it leads to judgment. Because of God's perfect justice, sinners are liable to suffer the consequences of their sin.

We see this clearly in the tragedy of King Solomon. In earlier days, God spoke to Solomon using the word "if" (e.g., 1 Kings 9:4): *if* Solomon walked with God in holy obedience, *then* God would establish his throne. Otherwise, his kingdom would be lost. The blessings of his dynasty were conditional on keeping the commandments.

When God spoke to Solomon this time, however, he started with the word "since": "Since this has been your practice and you have not kept my covenant and my statutes that I have commanded you, I will surely tear the kingdom from you and will give it to your servant" (1 Kings 11:11). Unfortunately, it had become Solomon's regular practice *not* to keep the commandments of God. Since the condition of the covenant had not been kept, certain consequences were sure to follow. Solomon's kingdom would be ripped out of his hands—the tragic downfall of the house of David.

Although Solomon would not lose his kingdom immediately, the difficulties he started to face sounded the alarm for a coming catastrophe. Solomon's kingdom had always been at peace, but now he started to have enemies. Where formerly there was peace on every side (see 1 Kings 5:4), now there seemed to be enemies on every side.

First Kings 11 tells the story of two of these "adversaries" (1 Kings 11:14, 23). One of them came from Edom, in the south: "And the LORD raised up an adversary against Solomon, Hadad the Edomite. He was of the royal house in Edom" (1 Kings 11:14). Ever since the days of Jacob and Esau, there had been bad blood between the Israelites and the Edomites.

5. Stephen Lungu, with Anne Coomes, *Out of the Black Shadows* (Grand Rapids: Monarch, 2001), 78–80.

The Edomites were the descendants of Esau, while the Israelites came from Jacob, the younger brother who stole Esau's blessing and birthright (see Gen. 25:29–34; 27:1–45).

In Solomon's day, there had been some recent history between these two tribes: "For when David was in Edom, and Joab the commander of the army went up to bury the slain, he struck down every male in Edom (for Joab and all Israel remained there six months, until he had cut off every male in Edom)" (1 Kings 11:15–16). Needless to say, Israel's conquest did not endear them to the Edomites. Elsewhere we read that David's men killed almost twenty thousand men, before subjecting the rest of them to slavery (2 Sam. 8:13–14; cf. 1 Chron. 8:12–13). The few Edomites who somehow managed to survive were not favorably disposed to the house of David.

This was especially true for the only member of Edom's royal family who escaped with his life: "Hadad fled to Egypt, together with certain Edomites of his father's servants, Hadad still being a little child" (1 Kings 11:17). The Bible then tells how Hadad and his men

> set out from Midian and came to Paran and took men with them from Paran and came to Egypt, to Pharaoh king of Egypt, who gave him a house and assigned him an allowance of food and gave him land. And Hadad found great favor in the sight of Pharaoh, so that he gave him in marriage the sister of his own wife, the sister of Tahpenes the queen. And the sister of Tahpenes bore him Genubath his son, whom Tahpenes weaned in Pharaoh's house. And Genubath was in Pharaoh's house among the sons of Pharaoh. (1 Kings 11:18–20)

Living in Egypt, Hadad not only survived, but also thrived. He was welcomed as a prominent member of Pharaoh's royal court. He was blessed with a nice house and good food to eat. He claimed the hand of Pharaoh's sister-in-law in marriage. His son was raised as one of the princes of Egypt.

Yet for all the blessings he experienced in Egypt, Hadad never forgot what Israel had done to the Edomites. He named his son "Genubath," which means "to steal" (from the Hebrew verb *ganab*), possibly to serve as a constant reminder of the kingdom that had been taken away from him. He bided his time in Egypt—a bitter victim nursing a hateful grudge while he gathered his power and waited for the day of his revenge.

Hadad's story finds a contemporary parallel in the character of Inigo Montoya, from the 1987 film *The Princess Bride*. When Montoya was a young boy, he witnessed his father's murder at the hands of a man with six fingers. Dedicating his life to avenging his father's death, he trained to become the world's greatest swordfighter, and when he was old enough, he traveled the world in search of his father's killer. During all this time he kept rehearsing the famous lines that he would finally utter when he came face-to-face with his enemy and put him to death: "Hello! My name is Inigo Montoya! You killed my father; prepare to die!"

Like Inigo Montoya, Hadad was waiting for revenge, and when the chance finally came, he seized it: "But when Hadad heard in Egypt that David slept with his fathers and that Joab the commander of the army was dead, Hadad said to Pharaoh, 'Let me depart, that I may go to my own country.' But Pharaoh said to him, 'What have you lacked with me that you are now seeking to go to your own country?' And he said to him, 'Only let me depart'" (1 Kings 11:21–22). So Hadad persuaded Pharaoh to let him go, and from that time on, the Edomites began to harass Solomon on his southern borders, chipping away at his empire.

Why does the Bible take the trouble to tell us this story, which at first may seem somewhat tangential to the story of King Solomon? To be sure, Hadad's revenge is one of the tragic consequences of Solomon's sin. From this time forward, the opposition of the Edomites would cause trouble for Israel. The story also shows how futile it was for Israel to make an alliance with Egypt. During the same time period that Pharaoh was selling chariots to Solomon (see 1 Kings 10:28–29) and offering the hand of his daughter in marriage (see 1 Kings 3:1), he was harboring Israel's enemies. All this is true. But why does the Bible tell this story in so much detail?

To answer this question, it is important to notice how similar Hadad's story sounds to the story of Israel in Egypt. A nation sojourns in Egypt, where it is given bread to eat and a place to live, and where some of its sons become princes. At the end of this sojourn, the leader of that nation asks Pharaoh to let his people go—a request he initially refuses, before eventually granting. Does any of this sound familiar?

The story of Hadad follows the main plotlines of the exodus, in which Moses and the children of Israel escaped from Egypt and returned to the Promised Land. Except that everything in Hadad's story is backward. The nation coming out of Egypt is not Israel, but Edom. This turnabout is God's doing—not for Israel's benefit, but this time to Israel's detriment. The Bible plainly states that the Lord raised up Hadad as an adversary against Solomon (1 Kings 11:14). The broader point is that this is what happens when our hearts turn away from the Lord: his hand goes against us, and we suffer the consequences for our sin.

The story of Rezon makes a similar point. If Hadad was harassing Solomon to the south, then Rezon was raiding him from the north:

> God also raised up as an adversary to him, Rezon the son of Eliada, who had fled from his master Hadadezer king of Zobah. And he gathered men about him and became leader of a marauding band, after the killing by David. And they went to Damascus and lived there and made him king in Damascus. He was an adversary of Israel all the days of Solomon, doing harm as Hadad did. And he loathed Israel and reigned over Syria. (1 Kings 11:23–25)

This story has political relevance as up-to-date as the evening news. Israel and Syria are still fighting over the same territory today—such as the Golan Heights. We see this conflict throughout 1 and 2 Kings, in which the Syrians attack the Israelites again and again. Therefore, this episode has literary significance: it sets the stage for some of the stories that follow.

But this story also has spiritual significance in its own right. Rezon and his band of rebels were waging guerrilla warfare. In former times, this had been the role that David had occupied. In the days before his royal dynasty, when Saul was still the king of Israel, David had been the leader of a marauding band (e.g., 1 Sam. 27:8ff.). But now everything is backward. The house of David is not *on* the attack, but *under* attack. The roles are reversed. Solomon is playing Saul to Rezon's David, which is a clear sign that his dynasty has fallen under the judgment of God.

THE CONSEQUENCES OF OUR OWN SIN

This is what happens when our hearts turn away from the Lord: because of God's justice, we are liable to suffer the tragic consequences of our sin. At one level, the stories of Rezon and Hadad are about the politics of war. But at a more fundamental level, they are about sin and judgment. Political and military conflict is never outside the sovereignty of God. In this particular case, the Bible tells us that God was raising up adversaries against Solomon because the king had committed the great sin of worshiping other gods. His sufferings were deserved; they were the tragic consequence of his own tragic choice.

God still operates the same way today. As a righteous Judge, he often brings sinners to judgment. Admittedly, we do not always know the purposes of God. Why does he allow this nation to triumph or those people to suffer? Yet by the sovereign justice of God, people often suffer the consequences of their sins. Self-destructive choices lead to destruction, not simply because this is the way the universe works, but because the universe is governed by a just and righteous God. People who sin are liable to suffer his divine judgment.

For anyone who belongs to God through faith in Christ, these judgments are never punitive, only corrective. In his fatherly love and discipline, God will use whatever consequences we suffer for our sins to do his good work in our lives (see Heb. 12:3–11). Nevertheless, the judgments of God are a serious matter for self-examination. The moral choices we make have real consequences. What we do with our money, the way we handle sex, the exercise of power—we are responsible before God for each and every decision we make. Could it be that some of our present sufferings are the tragic result of our own sin? If so, then God is correcting us with justice.

We should consider the sinful choices that we are making in life: the growing resentment over a personal disagreement, perhaps, or the little compromises with sexual sin. Maybe we are tempted to use angry words, or to pursue foolish pleasures. Where will these sins lead in the end? What tragic consequences will result?

There is also the reality of the final judgment to consider. We will all stand before God to be judged for everything we have ever done. All the righteous judgments we see in the Bible—including what Solomon suffered at the hands of Hadad and Rezon—are intended to remind us of the last of all judgments, when Jesus Christ will come again to open and shut the gates of heaven and hell.

For many people, the coming of Christ will be a tragedy to end all trag- edies. As a result of their own deliberate choice to follow other gods, they will fall under judgment and suffer God's wrath forever.

How Tragedy Becomes Comedy

Is there any hope for us to receive mercy? There is always hope in Jesus, even through the darkest hour. We find such hope here in this passage, as we do everywhere in the Bible. It is true that God is angry with us because of our sin and that we deserve to fall under his righteous judgment. But this is also true: God has saved us from judgment by sending his Son to be our Savior. We are objects of wrath who nonetheless have received mercy (see Eph. 2:1–7), because Christ has taken all of God's anger against our sin on the cross.

At the same time that we see God acting in justice against Solomon for his sin, we also see him acting in mercy to save his people. Even as we witness the downfall of the house of David, we know that this cannot be the end of his royal line. For according to the promises of God, Solomon was a beloved son who would not be lost forever. "When he commits iniquity," God said, "I will discipline him with the rod of men, with the stripes of the sons of men, but my steadfast love will not depart from him" (2 Sam. 7:14–15). Whatever judgment Solomon suffered would be corrective, not destructive, for the love of God would never leave him. God also promised that David's house, David's kingdom, and David's throne would last forever (2 Sam. 7:16).

God never goes back on his promise. Therefore, in Solomon's later years, when the king tragically turned away from the Lord and suffered for his sins, God still preserved a remnant of his dynasty—enough to keep his promises. Although God would indeed take Solomon's kingdom away, his justice was tempered with the mercy of his steadfast love: "Yet for the sake of David your father I will not do it in your days, but I will tear it out of the hand of your son" (1 Kings 11:12).

There was some mercy in this for Solomon. The full weight of divine judgment would be deferred, which is more than he deserved. Solomon's kingdom would not be lost until after the old king died.

There is far greater mercy, however, in what God promised next: "I will not tear away all the kingdom, but I will give one tribe to your son, for the sake of

David my servant and for the sake of Jerusalem that I have chosen" (1 Kings 11:13). Even in his wrath, God remembered mercy, as he always does. He remembered the promises that he had made to his anointed king and to his chosen people, represented here by the city of Jerusalem. God remembered that he had promised his people an everlasting kingdom, ruled by David's son. For the sake of those promises he would protect the royal tribe of Judah. He would preserve the royal lineage, so that in the fullness of time, a Savior-King from the house of David would rise to God's eternal throne.

Here is a promise for us to possess—a promise that finds its fulfillment in the house and line of David. If God had not preserved a tribe for David in the days after King Solomon, then none of the promises of salvation would ever come true. But God protected a remnant of the kingdom, preparing the way for our salvation. This is part of the story of Jesus Christ, as we know from the royal genealogies in the Gospels. Jesus of Nazareth was the son of Solomon (see Matt. 1:6–7), and therefore the rightful heir to David's throne.

Jesus is the royal Savior who alone can rescue us from the wrath that we deserve. He does this specifically through the cross where he was crucified. Some people say that the painful death of Jesus Christ was a tragic mistake, but strictly speaking, "tragic" is exactly the wrong word to use in describing our Savior's death. The hero in a tragedy is the victim of his own tragic mistakes, his own sinful flaws. Yet Jesus Christ is perfectly flawless. He never committed even the tiniest little sin. Whatever suffering he endured was not deserved, therefore, but undeserved, and thus it could not be tragic in the proper sense of the word.

What then was the cause of the painful death that Jesus died? It was not caused by his sin, but by our own. This makes Jesus a new kind of hero, one who steps into our tragic story to take our place. We are the people with the tragic and sinful flaw. We are the ones who deserve to suffer the consequences for our sin. Yet Jesus has stepped in to suffer the wrath of God in our place. This is why the Gospels feel almost like tragedies: they lead to the cross, where Jesus suffered the full and painful punishment that we deserve for our sin. These sufferings did not result from any flaw in his character, however, but from a perfection: his infinite love for fallen sinners.

By dying in our place, Jesus turns our tragedy into a comedy—a story with a happy ending. God is angry with us because of our sin. We deserve to fall under his righteous judgment. But God has saved us from his own wrath by sending his Son to enter our tragic situation and rescue us from eternal downfall.

The story of Stephen Lungu ends with this kind of rescue. Earlier I described how Lungu went to an evangelistic meeting armed with explosives and ready to use them. Listening to the preacher, he came to the sudden and painful realization that God was angry with his sin. Yet the evangelist did not stop with the wrath of God; he also preached the compassion of Christ. "Suddenly I began to understand what Christianity was all about," Lungu later wrote. Jesus

> had suffered in all the ways that I knew so well. Poverty, oppression, hunger, thirst, loneliness. I had known all of these, and so had he. But the amazing thing was, he had not needed to know such suffering—but he had accepted it in his love for me. He had come to earth for my sake, to pay the price for my sins. My wages were death, but Jesus paid the price for me.[6]

Yes, this *is* what Christianity is all about. The tragedy of our sin has fallen on Jesus Christ. Although we are as guilty as Solomon in our misuse of money, sex, and power, there is forgiveness for us through the cross. Therefore, we are saved from the wrath of God to live happily ever after.

6. Ibid., 81.

PART 2

Divided Kingdom: The Wages of Sin

25

Two Nations, under God

1 Kings 11:26–43

And he said to Jeroboam, "Take for yourself ten pieces, for thus says the LORD, the God of Israel, 'Behold, I am about to tear the kingdom from the hand of Solomon and will give you ten tribes (but he shall have one tribe, for the sake of my servant David and for the sake of Jerusalem, the city that I have chosen out of all the tribes of Israel).'" (1 Kings 11:31–32)

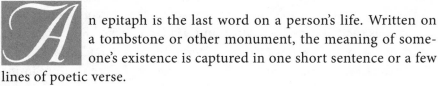n epitaph is the last word on a person's life. Written on a tombstone or other monument, the meaning of someone's existence is captured in one short sentence or a few lines of poetic verse.

Some epitaphs remind us of our own mortality, like the famous Latin inscription that reads *Hodie mihi, cras tibi* ("Today for me, tomorrow for thee"). Other epitaphs remind us of the debt that we owe to soldiers who died fighting for our freedom, like the inscription from John Maxwell Edmonds that appears on the World War II Kohima Monument: "When you go home, tell them of us, and say, *For your tomorrows these gave their today.*"

317

Then there are the epitaphs that testify to the saving, sanctifying grace of Jesus Christ. David Livingstone was a pioneer missionary to inland Africa. His tomb in London's Westminster Abbey reads, "For thirty years his life was spent in an unwearied effort to evangelize." Ruth Bell Graham's epitaph says less about her work, and more about the help of the Holy Spirit. She borrowed it from a highway road sign: "End of Construction: Thank You for Your Patience."

One day death will come for each of us, as it comes for everyone. If death does not come today, it will come on some tomorrow. When it comes, what will people write on *your* tombstone? What will they say when your time on earth is done?

The Prophecy of the Divided Kingdom

First Kings 11 gives us the last word on King Solomon, at least for this part of the Bible, bringing us to the end of his famous kingship. After forty years on Israel's throne, Solomon's life ended the same way that anyone's life ends. He died and was buried, leaving behind his earthly splendor. What epitaph should we write for this great man, who began so well in life, yet made such a tragic mistake?

Chapter 11 tells the story of Solomon's heart failure, how he sinned against God by loving pagan wives and worshiping foreign idols. This terrible sin led to many tragic consequences, both for the king and for his kingdom. In the words of one commentator, "Solomon and Israel have risen to great heights only to fall into idolatry, division, decay, and, ultimately, exile."[1]

The disintegration of Solomon's empire came at the hand of his enemies—adversaries that God raised against him. Hadad attacked Solomon from Edom in the south (1 Kings 11:14–22). Rezon the Syrian raided Israel from the north (1 Kings 11:23–25). But the worst enemy of all came from inside Solomon's own kingdom.

This fearsome enemy was a member of the royal court: "Jeroboam the son of Nebat, an Ephraimite of Zeredah, a servant of Solomon, whose mother's name was Zeruah, a widow, also lifted up his hand against the king" (1 Kings 11:26). This too was the will of God, for Jeroboam had been given the direct prophecy

1. Paul R. House, *1, 2 Kings*, The New American Commentary (Nashville: Broadman & Holman, 1995), 165.

of a future kingdom, which the Bible identifies as "the reason why he lifted up his hand against the king" (1 Kings 11:27). The prophecy came sometime before the end of Solomon's reign, when the king had "built the Millo," which may have been a terrace, and "closed up the breach of the city of David his father" (1 Kings 11:27; cf. 9:24).

From what we know about Jeroboam, it is not surprising that he rose to power. The Bible says, "The man Jeroboam was very able, and when Solomon saw that the young man was industrious he gave him charge over all the forced labor of the house of Joseph" (1 Kings 11:28). The word 1 Kings uses to describe his ability (*gibbor*) is the same word that the book of Ruth uses to describe noble Boaz (Ruth 2:1). Jeroboam was a man of real stature. He was a gifted leader, a man of wealth and influence. We might also compare him to Joseph, who always rose to the top of any organization. Jeroboam was such a hard worker, and did such excellent work, that despite his youth and inexperience he was quickly promoted to management. Solomon put Jeroboam in charge of his workforce among the northern tribes.[2]

All in all, the man sounds like the person described in one of Solomon's own proverbs: "Do you see a man skillful in his work? He will stand before kings" (Prov. 22:29). The irony is that in promoting Jeroboam, Solomon was elevating the very man who would eventually divide his kingdom.

The division of Solomon's kingdom was the will of God, as we know from the strange and dramatic prophecy that changed Jeroboam's life: "And at that time, when Jeroboam went out of Jerusalem, the prophet Ahijah the Shilonite found him on the road. Now Ahijah had dressed himself in a new garment, and the two of them were alone in the open country. Then Ahijah laid hold of the new garment that was on him, and tore it into twelve pieces" (1 Kings 11:29–30).

Ahijah is one of the lesser-known prophets in the Bible—even less well known than most of the so-called minor prophets. The ministry of the prophets will become increasingly important in Israel from this point forward. The books of 1 and 2 Kings are mainly about Israel's kings, of course, but when the kings wandered away from God, the Holy Spirit raised up godly prophets to speak the truth in Israel. Prophetic ministry compensated for

---

2. In all likelihood, this was not slave labor. For a careful explanation of the difference between *sebel* (1 Kings 11:28) and *mas* (1 Kings 5:13–14), see Iain W. Provan, *1 and 2 Kings*, New International Biblical Commentary (Peabody, MA: Hendrickson, 1995), 97–98.

the failure of ungodly kings; so with the decline of the kingdom, there was a corresponding rise in prophecy.

The prophet Ahijah came from Shiloh, which is where the famous prophet Samuel had served in the days before David brought the tabernacle up to Jerusalem. Ahijah suddenly and unexpectedly appeared to Jeroboam as he was leaving the city. Then he did something that must have seemed very strange: he took his brand-new robe and tore it into twelve pieces.

The prophets had a way of doing this sort of thing—performance prophecy, one might call it. First they would perform some unusual act, such as burying a linen belt and then digging it up again, for example, or buying a brand-new clay pot and then smashing it into a thousand pieces (see Jer. 13:1–11; 19:1–15). Each prophetic act was an object lesson, a sign of spiritual truth that foretold the future. To explain what it all meant, the prophet would follow his performance by making a public statement—a clear promise from God that always came true. The sign had a meaning, and thus the prophetic act was interpreted by the prophetic word.

In this case, Ahijah's prophecy would change the course of history. The prophet took ten of the twelve pieces that he tore from his coat and said to Jeroboam, "Take for yourself ten pieces, for thus says the Lord, the God of Israel, 'Behold, I am about to tear the kingdom from the hand of Solomon and will give you ten tribes'" (1 Kings 11:31).

The torn cloak was a sign of God's judgment: Solomon's kingdom would be torn apart. Something similar happened to King Saul when he had his tragic downfall. The prophet Samuel told Saul that God had rejected him as king. When the prophet turned to leave, Saul desperately grabbed his cloak, tearing its hem. Samuel interpreted the tear as a sign of God's judgment. He said to King Saul, "The Lord has torn the kingdom of Israel from you this day" (1 Sam. 15:28; cf. 24:1–7).

What Ahijah did with his cloak had a similar meaning: God was tearing away Solomon's kingdom. This meaning is reinforced by the vocabulary of the passage. The Hebrew word for "cloak" (*salma*) is based on the same three consonants as the name Solomon (*shlomoh*)—almost as if the king himself would be divided. According to Ahijah, Solomon's kingdom would be torn into twelve little pieces. This number is significant because each piece represented one of the twelve tribes of Israel, going back to the original twelve sons of Jacob.

What Ahijah foretold was a monumental event in biblical history. Up to this point, the twelve tribes of Israel had always been united—even when they were slaves in Egypt. But from this point forward, the kingdom would be divided, north and south. The ten northern tribes would be taken away from Solomon and given to Jeroboam, and thus they would leave the house of David. This was an act of divine judgment, in which Jeroboam served as the agent of God's justice. God said to him, "I will take the kingdom out of his son's hand and will give it to you, ten tribes. . . . I will take you, and you shall reign over all that your soul desires, and you shall be king over Israel" (1 Kings 11:35, 37).

In the long run, this division turned out to be especially disastrous for the ten tribes in the north, usually referred to as "Israel" (the southern tribes were often called "Judah"). The northern kings did not come from the line of David and did not walk in God's ways. Eventually those ten tribes would be carried off by the Assyrians and lost forever—the famous "lost tribes of Israel."

If the divided kingdom was so disastrous, then why did God allow it to happen? It was all because of Israel's idolatry—the sin that Solomon started by worshiping other gods. Ahijah said as much to Jeroboam. In his prophecy, he not only told what God was going to do, but also explained why God was going to do it. It was "because they have forsaken me and worshiped Ashtoreth the goddess of the Sidonians, Chemosh the god of Moab, and Milcom the god of the Ammonites, and they have not walked in my ways, doing what is right in my sight and keeping my statutes and my rules, as David his father did" (1 Kings 11:33).

See where sin leads. When Solomon first started to commit little sins of luxury and sexual immorality, he never dreamed that he would fall into public disgrace, or that God would divide his kingdom. But these were the direct and deadly consequences of the choices he made to commit the sins he loved to commit. Sometimes even a small change in our affections can lead us into serious sin, with painful consequences that will last well into the future. In this case, the sins of Solomon became the sins of his people. One man's divided heart ended up dividing a whole kingdom.[3]

3. Iain Provan, ibid., 94, employs a similar turn of phrase.

What will the consequences of our own sin be, if we do not repent? Where will our sinful desires lead us, if we do not stop craving money, sex, power, and all the other ungodly affections of a divided heart?

When Solomon heard about Ahijah's prophecy, he did everything he could to stop it from ever coming true. Just as Saul had once tried to kill David, Solomon tried to assassinate Jeroboam, but by then it was too late: "Solomon sought therefore to kill Jeroboam. But Jeroboam arose and fled into Egypt, to Shishak king of Egypt, and was in Egypt until the death of Solomon" (1 Kings 11:40). God had spoken: the kingdom would be divided. So Jeroboam waited for the day when he would rule over Israel.

LESSONS TO LEARN

There are several spiritual lessons that we can learn from Ahijah's prophecy and from the long-term consequences of Solomon's tragic fall into sin. They are lessons about the way God works in the world. There is also one great promise in this passage—the promise of grace from God that will triumph over sin and judgment.

The first lesson to learn is that *God is the ruler of all nations.* Whenever we see one leader raised up and another ruler cast down, we should know that God is exercising his sovereign authority over kings and kingdoms.

It would be possible to look at 1 Kings 11 primarily at the human level and to analyze it purely in political terms. Indeed, this is the approach that some scholars have taken with the books of 1 and 2 Kings generally.[4] They see the division between Israel in the north and Judah in the south as a tribal conflict. Jeroboam's rise to power was the combined result of his own natural ability, the failed policies of King Solomon, and the inevitable differences between people who lived in different places.

Humanly speaking, a good argument can be made for each of these factors, but the most important factor is divine. Jeroboam rose to power because God raised him up as an adversary against Solomon. The ten tribes of the northern kingdom were given to him by the hand of God (1 Kings 11:31, 35), who did this to punish his people for their great sin of worshiping other gods (1 Kings 11:33). God was in control of all these events. The division of the kingdom was

---

4. A notable example is Walter Brueggemann, *1 & 2 Kings*, Smyth & Helwys Bible Commentary (Macon, GA: Smyth & Helwys, 2000).

an act of his divine judgment. Even after the kingdom was divided, he remained the ruler of both the north and the south as two nations, under God.

What was true for Israel in the days of the divided kingdom is true for us today: God is the ruler of all nations. What happens around the world has its historical causes and political factors, to be sure. But everything that happens is still under the sovereign authority of Almighty God. Like Jeroboam, the rulers of nations rise to power only by the permission of God's will. As the Scripture says, "there is no authority except from God, and those that exist have been instituted by God" (Rom. 13:1). National catastrophes are also under God's control. In the words of the prophet Amos, "Does disaster come to a city, unless the Lord has done it?" (Amos 3:6). Whatever happens is under God's control, not outside of it.

We should remember the sovereignty of God whenever there is trouble in the world, or we are worried that there will be. We should remember it when there are political elections and we do not know the result in advance. We should remember it when we see wild fluctuations in the financial markets, or armed conflicts in distant countries, or shifts of power from one nation to another, or all the smaller problems we face at home. God is still on his throne, ruling over the affairs of all nations.

This does not mean that we always understand God's purposes, why sometimes he seems to bless the undeserving, or to allow the righteous to suffer. But even if we cannot explain why God has done what he has done, we may still believe that he has done it. When the world seems out of control, do not doubt or despair, but remember that God is the ruler of all nations!

Another lesson to learn from this passage is that *all of us are obligated to follow God, whether we decide to follow him or not.* We see this in the command that God gave to Jeroboam, which was very similar to the command he once gave to Solomon: "And if you will listen to all that I command you, and will walk in my ways, and do what is right in my eyes by keeping my statutes and my commandments, as David my servant did, I will be with you and will build you a sure house, as I built for David, and I will give Israel to you" (1 Kings 11:38; cf. 3:14; 6:12–13; 9:4–7).

What may seem somewhat surprising about this command is that Jeroboam was not the legitimate heir to Israel's throne. He did not belong to the house and line of David. Yet God offered him the blessings of David nonetheless. He promised to be with Jeroboam and to establish his kingdom.

Notice, however, that these blessings were contingent on Jeroboam's obedience. If he wanted to rule over David's kingdom, Jeroboam had to keep the law of God. This meant obeying God's commandments and walking in God's ways. It meant following David's example as a man after God's own heart. It was only as Jeroboam did these things that he would experience the full blessing of God in ruling over Israel. The promise God gave him was conditional on obedience.

If Jeroboam had obeyed God the way he was told, there would have been *two* nations that followed God, not just one: Israel in the north and Judah in the south. Yet Jeroboam had little interest in serving God. He decided to serve his own interests instead, and soon he became the king of false worship. If David served as the royal standard for kingship in Israel, then Jeroboam was constantly held up as a negative example: the king who decided not to follow God (e.g., 1 Kings 16:7, 26).

Yet Jeroboam was still obligated to follow God—this is the point. Even though he decided that he did not want anything to do with God, he was still accountable to God for what he did and what he failed to do. Jeroboam was called to listen to what God said and to do what was right in God's sight. He would be judged by that standard. Whether he decided to honor God or not, he was still responsible for his behavior.

The same is true for every human being on the face of the earth. If God is truly God, then his law is the rule for every person's life. We are called to walk in his ways and keep his commandments. This means loving God more than anything else and loving other people as much as we love ourselves. It means not swearing, not stealing, and not committing sexual sin. More positively, loving God means worshiping God, honoring our parents, and telling the truth. God will hold us responsible for everything we do and everything we fail to do. Even if we decide not to have anything to do with God at all, he will still judge us according to his law. Whoever we are—whether we are atheists, agnostics, or believers—we are all accountable to God.

GOD'S REMNANT

The good news is that there is also one great promise in this passage, a promise of grace that triumphs over judgment. This is something we often see in the Old Testament. The passages that threaten the most severe judgment also contain some of the clearest promises of saving mercy—like bright stars shining through the blackest night.

First Kings 11 is one of the saddest passages in the entire Bible. The divided kingdom was a complete catastrophe. The painful consequences of that divinely ordained division lasted for centuries. Eventually the northern tribes were scattered among the nations and lost forever. But God had not forgotten his promises. He never does! Therefore, even as he was judging his people for their sins, he was also working for their salvation.

There are reminders of God's saving grace throughout this passage. Almost every other verse in Ahijah's prophecy contains a promise of God's faithfulness to the house of David. The first reminder comes in verse 32, which stands as a kind of parenthesis. Yes, it is true that Jeroboam will get ten tribes, but that still leaves two tribes left over. So God promised Solomon to "have one tribe, for the sake of my servant David and for the sake of Jerusalem, the city that I have chosen out of all the tribes of Israel."

Ten tribes plus one tribe may seem like it adds up to only eleven, but the Bible seems to assume we understand that Solomon still rules the royal tribe of Judah, which was based in and around Jerusalem. The additional tribe that belonged to him was Benjamin (see 1 Kings 12:21). Alternatively, the tribe in view here is Judah, with Benjamin left unstated because it was too small and insignificant to mention. In any case, even in the divided kingdom, the descendants of Solomon would have a tribe to call their own. Judah plus Benjamin plus the ten tribes of Jeroboam equals the twelve tribes of Israel.

There is another gracious promise in verse 34: "Nevertheless, I will not take the whole kingdom out of his hand, but I will make him ruler all the days of his life, for the sake of David my servant whom I chose, who kept my commandments and my statutes." Verse 32 promised that God would not take the whole kingdom away from Solomon, but would leave him one little tribe. According to the promise of verse 34, even this act of judgment would not happen right away. Solomon would remain in power until the day of his death. It was only after his lifetime that his kingdom would be divided. Even though everything appeared to be going well for Solomon, in fact the king was under judgment. Similarly, we should not judge a church by its apparent success but by its biblical faithfulness, for a congregation may be headed for divine judgment at the very time it seems to be meeting with outward success.

Notice why God showed Solomon this favor: he did it for David's sake, for the chosen king who kept his commandments. Not that David had earned anything from God, of course. No one can ever claim anything from God on the basis of merit. Like everyone else, King David was a sinner saved by grace. What distinguished him, though, were the promises that God had made to him—the famous kingdom promises in 2 Samuel 7, where God promised David the forever throne of an everlasting kingdom. Later, when God said that he would spare Solomon "for David's sake," it was a shorthand way of referring to the kingdom promise he had made to David.

The next promise of grace is even more reassuring: "Yet to his son I will give one tribe, that David my servant may always have a lamp before me in Jerusalem, the city where I have chosen to put my name" (1 Kings 11:36). God had already said that Solomon would get to keep one tribe. Here that promise is extended out into the future. Even after Solomon's sin—the divided heart that divided a kingdom—God would not forsake the promise he had made to David. The flame in David's lamp would never be extinguished.

In biblical times, the lamp was a symbol of life. To die was to have one's lamp put out (e.g., Job 18:5–6; Prov. 20:20); to live was to keep shining, like the light on a lampstand (e.g., 2 Sam. 21:17). When God said that David would always have a lamp shining before him, he meant that David's kingship would endure forever.

The promise in verse 39 is similar: "I will afflict the offspring of David because of this, but not forever." Judgment would last for a night, but mercy would come in the morning. David's kingdom would rise again.

This reassurance was in keeping with the promises God made to David in 2 Samuel 7. There God said that if and when David's son was disobedient, "I will discipline him with the rod of men, . . . but my steadfast love will not depart from him" (2 Sam. 7:14–15). Whatever punishment Solomon endured as the result of his sin was not God's final judgment, therefore, but only God's fatherly discipline. It was a corrective judgment to preserve his people, not destroy them. This is an important principle to understand about the way God works in the world. Sometimes God brings his own people under discipline, but when he does, it is only temporary, never permanent. God graciously puts us under discipline in order to accomplish his good purpose in our lives. According to Hebrews 12:6, this discipline is a sign of God's loving concern for the life of his beloved children.

These were the promises that God made to David and then repeated to Solomon. At the time he divided the kingdom in justice, God promised to preserve the kingdom by grace. Two tribes would endure: Judah and Benjamin. By the grace of God, a remnant would survive. Out of that remnant, when the time was right, a true and righteous king would come again from the tribe of Judah. His royal lamp would shine in Jerusalem.

All these promises find their fulfillment in Jesus Christ, the greater Solomon of the kingdom of God. The reason God said that David's son would have a tribe—and the reason he kept saying this over and over again—was that he had a plan for our salvation that depended on the house of David. One day he would send a Savior to be the King of his people forever. In order to keep that promise, God had to preserve the tribe of David until the coming of Jesus Christ, the Son of David. He is the light of the world (John 8:12), whose lamp still burns in the house of God (see Rev. 1:12–13).

What hope these promises must have given to the people who first heard them. It is important to remember when the books of 1 and 2 Kings were written: not during the days of King Solomon, but long afterward, when the people of God were exiles in Babylon. For them, the divided kingdom was not a fact of history, but a painful reality. They were living in the sixth century before Christ, long after God had handed ten tribes over to Jeroboam. By then the northern tribes, who had been carried off into captivity centuries before, were gone forever.

Now the southern tribes were in captivity too. The book of 2 Kings ends with Judah carried off into Babylon. In the days of that long exile, God's people must have often wondered whether they would ever be saved. There are times when we wonder the same thing. When circumstances are difficult, it is tempting to think that everything we have or had is lost, that there is not much left for us in life. Our only true hope at such times is in the promises of God, which is exactly why God kept repeating these promises, especially the promise of salvation through the royal line of David. God wanted his people to know that he had not forgotten what he had promised: a lamp for David in the kingdom of God.

When the time was right, the King would come. God would work his plan of salvation all the way to the cross, then beyond the cross to the empty tomb, and beyond that to the throne of heaven, where Jesus rules the nations in kingly majesty. God has provided safety from his judgment in Jesus Christ, who is the true Son of David, the light of the world.

If God was still at work in the last days of King Solomon, even after his tragic downfall, he is still at work in our own lives as well. Sooner or later, people will disappoint us, including some of the people we count on the most in life. People in Israel were disappointed with Solomon, especially when they had to suffer the tragic consequences for his sin. But God was still faithful to his promises of salvation.

God will keep his promises to us as well. At times we may feel that the church is weak, or think that we are outnumbered, or worry that we are accomplishing little in the world. People felt the same way after Solomon. But God was still faithful to his promises. He will keep his promises to us as well. Jesus has promised that his church will not perish, but prevail against the powers of hell (Matt. 16:18). So believe the promise: God's remnant will be preserved; his tribe will increase. God will do everything for us that he has promised. He will provide for our needs; he will forgive our sins; he will deliver us from danger; and when our work on earth is done, he will bring us home safe to God.

THE LAST WORD ON SOLOMON

The story of Solomon's life ends with these words: "Now the rest of the acts of Solomon, and all that he did, and his wisdom, are they not written in the Book of the Acts of Solomon? And the time that Solomon reigned in Jerusalem over all Israel was forty years. And Solomon slept with his fathers and was buried in the city of David his father. And Rehoboam his son reigned in his place" (1 Kings 11:41–43).

These lines are not very memorable, as epitaphs go. In closing the record on Solomon's life, this summary refers to other official documents, which have long since disappeared. The biblical record simply reminds us of the king's long reign. Solomon ruled for forty years, a full generation, as long as his father David. When his work on earth was done, his soul returned to God, while his body was buried in Jerusalem, where he slept with his fathers. The royal line continued, as Solomon's son Rehoboam ruled in his place. But the glory days were over, as we will soon see.

As we come to the end of Solomon's life, how should we evaluate his kingship? What epitaph should we write on his tombstone?

There are many good lines to choose from Solomon's own writings. If we consider the way he began, by asking God for the wisdom to rule over Israel, we might choose Proverbs 1:7: "The fear of the LORD is the beginning of knowledge." If we look at the way the king lived, especially in his later days, we choose this verse instead: "Eat and drink and find enjoyment . . . under the sun" (Eccl. 5:18). But Solomon learned how empty it is to live without God, so maybe we should choose this verse instead: "Vanity of vanities! All is vanity" (Eccl. 1:2). Or we might look at the way the king died, and quote his famous words from Ecclesiastes 3:20: "All are from the dust, and to dust all return." If we are hopeful about Solomon's salvation, as I believe we should be, then we could draw an epitaph from the love song he wrote for his Savior: "He brought me to the banqueting house, and his banner over me was love" (Song 2:4).

Whatever epitaph we write for Solomon, the fact that he needs an epitaph at all is a reminder of his limitations. Praise God that we know the greater Solomon of a greater kingdom, who still has grace for us. We know Jesus Christ—the King without an epitaph for his tombstone. No one wrote an inscription for his grave. They did not even have time to prepare his body for burial, let alone carve his name into stone. Besides, what epitaph would you write for a man who would come back to life on the third day? "Back soon"? "See you on Sunday"? Maybe the words of the angels would suffice: "He is not here, but has risen" (Luke 24:6).

Praise God for Jesus Christ, the risen King, the true and righteous Solomon of our salvation! By the power of his resurrection, we will be able to serve God to the end of our days, and afterward to offer our Savior an eternity of praise.

26

A HOUSE DIVIDED

1 Kings 12:1–24

And when all Israel saw that the king did not listen to them, the people answered the king, "What portion do we have in David? We have no inheritance in the son of Jesse. To your tents, O Israel! Look now to your own house, David." So Israel went to their tents. But Rehoboam reigned over the people of Israel who lived in the cities of Judah. (1 Kings 12:16–17)

here are two kinds of people in the world: the people who use other people, and the people who get used. This is the thesis of Ken Ivy's book *Pimpology: The 48 Laws of the Game.* To use Ivy's vulgar categories, everyone is either a pimp or a whore—not just on the streets of the ghetto, but at home, in the business world, and everywhere else in life. He writes:

You are either the kind of person who will have people working for you, bringing you the money, or you are the kind of person who will work for someone else, hand over your hard-earned dough, and let someone tell you what to do. This reality may be offensive to some, but it's real, and if you open your eyes to what is truly going on in this world, you will see that everyone falls into one category or the other.[1]

According to this philosophy of life, there are only the two alternatives: serving or being served. Given the title of his book, it is not hard guess which category the author has chosen. He is a taker, not a giver. "To be valued," Ivy says, "the key is not to give, but to receive—the more, the better. You don't want to 'earn' your price, you want to 'cost' it."[2]

Ken Ivy has taken the devil's part of the bargain, but he is basically right about the choice that everyone faces in life. To serve or to be served?—that is the question. We see the question posed repeatedly in 1 Kings 12, as Rehoboam takes the throne and Jeroboam challenges his kingship.

JEROBOAM'S CHALLENGE

King Rehoboam was the son of Solomon, the grandson of David, and therefore the rightful heir to Israel's throne. First Kings 11 ends by stating that the kingdom continued, with Rehoboam reigning in Solomon's place. Chapter 12 tells us that the king's first move was to travel "to Shechem, for all Israel had come to Shechem to make him king" (1 Kings 12:1). Shechem was a city of historical significance. It was the first city that Abraham visited in the Promised Land (Gen. 12:6)—the place where Joseph's bones were buried (Josh. 24:32), where Joshua renewed God's covenant with Israel (Josh. 24:1), and where Abimelech was crowned as king (Judg. 9:6). Shechem was also a city of political significance. Located some forty miles north of Jerusalem, it was in the heart of the northern territories.

Rehoboam went to Shechem hoping to consolidate his power. Already he had broad support in his native Jerusalem, but in order to govern the entire kingdom, he would need a wider consensus among the other tribes of Israel. So Rehoboam traveled to Shechem for his would-be coronation.

There the king was immediately challenged by Jeroboam. According to the prophet Ahijah, Jeroboam was destined to rule the ten tribes of the northern kingdom. This was the will of God, who was acting in judgment against

1. Ken Ivy, with Karen Hunter, *Pimpology: The 48 Laws of the Game* (New York: Simon Spotlight Entertainment, 2007), 1.
2. Ibid., 7.

Solomon and against his people for their great sin in worshiping other gods. As the story unfolds, we see how God's will was accomplished, and how his word came true.

For years Jeroboam had stayed in Egypt, waiting for Solomon to die. But now that Rehoboam was taking the throne, it was time for Jeroboam to come home and issue a direct challenge to his authority:

> And as soon as Jeroboam the son of Nebat heard of it (for he was still in Egypt, where he had fled from King Solomon), then Jeroboam returned from Egypt. And they sent and called him, and Jeroboam and all the assembly of Israel came and said to Rehoboam, "Your father made our yoke heavy. Now therefore lighten the hard service of your father and his heavy yoke on us, and we will serve you." (1 Kings 12:2–4)

This sounds like the first round of negotiations for a union contract. Jeroboam came with a large delegation and a long list of demands. Speaking on behalf of the northern tribes, he wanted better working conditions: higher pay, lower taxes, more vacation time. The concessions he demanded sound almost like something out of Exodus where the Israelites tried to get better terms from Pharaoh (e.g., Ex. 5). Indeed, some commentators have seen Jeroboam as a second Moses, delivering God's people from the bondage of slavery.[3] Only this time Solomon is the ruler who is regarded as the oppressor, not Pharaoh—a sure sign that there is trouble in Israel!

Scholars have debated whether or not Jeroboam's complaints about Solomon's heavy yoke were justified. Bible scholars who believe that Jeroboam was painting an accurate picture of working conditions under Solomon point to the many building projects that were completed during his reign over Israel. They take Jeroboam's words at face value: Solomon was a harsh and oppressive king.

Other scholars suspect that Jeroboam's complaints are partly political propaganda. Although 1 Kings describes Solomon's building projects, and the people who built them, it never says that his rule was oppressive or that he held his own people in bondage. Furthermore, we should consider the source. Jeroboam is making a power play here, and thus trying to provoke a

3. For example, see Iain W. Provan, *1 and 2 Kings*, New International Biblical Commentary (Peabody, MA: Hendrickson, 1995), 104.

conflict, so of course he criticizes the old regime. Besides, when are laborers ever completely satisfied with their workload or their pay scale?

Whether or not he was telling the truth about Solomon, one thing is for sure: Jeroboam had no intention of submitting to the rule of God's anointed king. Rather than offering full allegiance to Rehoboam as the son of David, he insisted on setting his own terms for any service he would offer to the king. Jeroboam was not asking, but demanding: if and only if Rehoboam would lighten the yoke, then and only then would he do kingdom work. Any obedience he offered was conditional on the king's giving in to his demands.

Jeroboam approached Rehoboam the same way many people approach God: with a long list of demands. We say we are willing to serve him, but only on the condition that he will offer us better terms. We do not fully surrender to his sovereign will, but insist on dictating how hard or how easy our service will be. We say, "I will do this for you, Lord, but not that." Or we say, "I will do that for you, Lord, as long as you will do this for me." But of course this is really a way of saying that we do not want God to be king at all. We would rather be the kings and queens of our own little kingdoms.

REHOBOAM'S CHOICE

The choice that Rehoboam faced was simple: to go easy or to go hard, to stay the course, maintaining the status quo, or to give the northern tribes change they could believe in. The king was not entirely sure what he should do, so he asked for a little more time to think about it. "He said to them, 'Go away for three days, then come again to me.' So the people went away" (1 Kings 12:5).

To help him make his decision, Rehoboam summoned two sets of advisers. The advice they gave him was so completely contradictory that it clarified his choice. It also clarifies the basic choice we all have to make in all our relationships with other people, whether to serve or to be served.

First, "King Rehoboam took counsel with the old men, who had stood before Solomon his father while he was yet alive." He asked them the obvious question: "How do you advise me to answer this people?" (1 Kings 12:6).

Even before these men offer their advice, we can anticipate that it will be well worth hearing, because these men were the elders of Israel. Rehoboam was about forty-one years old at the time (see 1 Kings 14:21), but these men

333

were even older, which gave them every opportunity to learn from experience. Older people are not always wiser, of course, but often they are, and the relative age of these men commands our respect, as it should have commanded the respect of Rehoboam. As Solomon said in one of his famous proverbs, "gray hair is a crown of glory; it is gained in a righteous life" (Prov. 16:31). Therefore, it is wise for us to listen to our elders. That was especially true in this case because these men had served under Solomon, who was the wisest of all earthly kings.

So even before these elders offered any counsel, there should have been a strong presumption in their favor. Here is the advice they gave to Rehoboam: "If you will be a servant to this people today and serve them, and speak good words to them when you answer them, then they will be your servants forever" (1 Kings 12:7). With all their experience in politics, these old men knew that even kings require the consent of the governed. If Rehoboam spoke kindly to Jeroboam and the other challengers, answering them with gentle diplomacy, he would win them over. The elders also understood that the person who rules the most people is called to serve the most people. Thus they advised Rehoboam to make himself the servant of Israel. In the words of Richard Phillips, "The old men counseled a course of godly humility, servant leadership, and moderation in his exercise of power."[4]

This was sound advice, based on the biblical principle of servant-leadership. The king is the ruler and defender of his people. He is called by God to protect them from danger and provide for their needs. It is his responsibility to ensure that the citizens of his realm are well cared for, that they have the full opportunity to thrive in business, in culture, and in the life of the family. To that end, the king labors with all his might to give his people what they need to flourish.

We need the same kind of leadership today in the home, in the church, and in public life. Husbands and fathers are good servant-leaders when they pray for their wives, as well as care for the emotional and physical needs of their children. Pastors and elders are good servant-leaders when they bless the people in their churches with words of spiritual encouragement. Employers are good servant-leaders when they look after the total welfare of their employees, rather than simply looking at the bottom line. Servant-leaders

4. Richard D. Phillips, *Turning Back the Darkness: The Biblical Pattern of Reformation* (Wheaton, IL: Crossway, 2002), 68.

devote every possible energy to blessing the people they are called to serve, even to the point of sacrificing their own safety and prosperity. This is true greatness in the kingdom of God, for as Jesus said, "whoever would be great among you must be your servant" (Matt. 20:26). For the followers of Christ, the opportunity to lead is always a greater opportunity to serve.

Unfortunately, this was not the approach that Rehoboam wanted to take, or the advice that he decided to follow. Not wanting to serve, but rather to be served, he "abandoned the counsel that the old men gave him and took counsel with the young men who had grown up with him and stood before him" (1 Kings 12:8).

These young men were Rehoboam's contemporaries, the buddies he had grown up with, men who by now were in their late 30s and early 40s. To see how closely the new king identified with these men, we need only notice the pronoun he uses when he addresses them in verse 9: "What do you advise that *we* answer this people who have said to me, 'Lighten the yoke that your father put on us'?" This was the same question that Rehoboam asked in verse 6, only there he had addressed the old men as "you." Here he uses the pronoun "we." Even before he makes his decision, we sense that Rehoboam will do whatever his friends tell him to do. Never once does he turn to prayer or seek guidance from the word of God.

There is always a strong temptation to do what our friends tell us to do rather than to do what God says is right. This temptation is especially strong for young people. As sociologists have often observed, many teenagers are influenced more by their peers than by their parents. This can be very dangerous, because in addition to lacking the life experience that leads to wisdom, many young people live for selfish pleasure. Young people should be careful, therefore, not to follow their friends in using bad language, abusing their bodies, or looking at sexually explicit material. They should listen more to their parents than to their friends, especially if they are not believers. As Solomon once said, "Whoever walks with the wise becomes wise, but the companion of fools will suffer harm" (Prov. 13:20).

The danger here is not just for teenagers, however. Even later in life, it is tempting to disregard the counsel of people who are older than we are, assuming that they are out of touch and out of date. Young adults are wise to listen to older Christians, especially in matters of love and romance. Young parents are wise to listen to fathers and mothers whose children have grown up to serve the Lord. Young pastors are wise to consult seasoned, godly elders in the church. At every stage of life, the Lord provides someone to give us good counsel—usually someone who is older and wiser than we are.

The advice that Rehoboam received from his friends was exactly the opposite of the advice that he received from his elders. His friends said:

> Thus shall you speak to this people who said to you, "Your father made our yoke heavy, but you lighten it for us," thus shall you say to them, "My little finger is thicker than my father's thighs. And now, whereas my father laid on you a heavy yoke, I will add to your yoke. My father disciplined you with whips, but I will discipline you with scorpions." (1 Kings 12:10–11)

These men were arrogant hard-liners. With harsh words, they urged Rehoboam to give the northern tribes even harsher labor. In calling for harder working conditions, their response sounds almost like the answer that Pharaoh gave to Moses and Aaron the first time they asked him to let God's people go (see Ex. 5). The language they used to say this was crude, rude, and abusive—an obvious sign of spiritual immaturity. When they talked about Rehoboam's "little finger," they actually said "little one," referring to a different part of his anatomy altogether.[5] A "scorpion" was a kind of whip—not just an ordinary lash, but a stinging, "nail-barbed scourge."[6] Basically, they were telling Rehoboam to act like a bully, boasting that he was a bigger man than his father and then beating Jeroboam into submission.

Whether we see it in the church, at home, or in public life, this kind of leadership is always utterly disastrous. There is a kind of man who always demands that people do what he wants them to do. If necessary, he will use verbal and even physical abuse to get them to do it. There are pastors and elders who lord it over their congregations, husbands and fathers who are tyrants in their own homes, dictators and despots who rule by iron force. Usually these bullies are trying desperately to hide their deep personal insecurity. They are not resting in the grace that God has for them, or content with who they are in Christ. Otherwise, they would have the love and the courage to lead by service and sacrifice.

5. See Provan, *1 and 2 Kings*, 107.
6. Donald J. Wiseman, *1 & 2 Kings: An Introduction and Commentary*, Tyndale Old Testament Commentaries (Leicester: Inter-Varsity, 1993), 141.

Anyone in a position of spiritual leadership has a choice to make, either to follow the advice of Solomon's wise men or to listen to the foolish counsel of Rehoboam's peer group. Which kind of leader will we choose to be: a servant or a tyrant?

The irony is that until leaders learn to serve others instead of themselves, they will never enjoy the respect they crave. Yet sadly this is the course that Rehoboam decided to follow. Instead of listening to his people and giving them a gracious response, he repeated the bad advice of his friends almost verbatim:

> So Jeroboam and all the people came to Rehoboam the third day, as the king said, "Come to me again the third day." And the king answered the people harshly, and forsaking the counsel that the old men had given him, he spoke to them according to the counsel of the young men, saying, "My father made your yoke heavy, but I will add to your yoke. My father disciplined you with whips, but I will discipline you with scorpions." (1 Kings 12:12–14)

Jeroboam's Choice

Rehoboam's choice was wrong in itself, and it caused problems that lasted for centuries. Nevertheless, God still used it to accomplish his purpose for his people. Here again we encounter the great mystery of God's sovereignty and man's responsibility (or even, in this case, God's sovereignty and man's stupidity). Rehoboam was fully responsible for the decision he made to make things worse instead of better. Yet even this was part of God's plan, as the Bible makes clear: "So the king did not listen to the people, for it was a turn of affairs brought about by the LORD that he might fulfill his word, which the LORD spoke by Ahijah the Shilonite to Jeroboam the son of Nebat" (1 Kings 12:15; cf. 11:29–31).

God had said that Jeroboam would rule ten of the twelve tribes of Israel. Now, through the reckless choice of Rehoboam, God's promise would come true. This turn of events was brought about by the deliberate will of Almighty God, in accordance with his perfect word. As Spurgeon explained it, "God had nothing to do with the sin or the folly, but in some way which we can never explain, in a mysterious way in which we are to believe without hesitation, God was in it all."[7]

7. C. H. Spurgeon, "This Thing Is from Me," in *Metropolitan Tabernacle Pulpit* (Pasadena, TX: Pilgrim, 1976), 42:363.

Therefore, at the same time we learn all the practical lessons these men have to teach us, mainly by negative example, we also need to be careful not to miss the larger lesson of the sovereignty of God. In spite of all the mistakes we make, his promises always come true.

In this particular case, God's promise came true through the decision that Jeroboam made. He too had a choice to make. It was essentially the same choice that Rehoboam faced, and that everyone faces, either to serve or to be served. Would Jeroboam and all the northern tribes serve Israel's true and rightful king, or would they go their own direction? Once they heard what Rehoboam had to say to them, their minds were made up: "And when all Israel saw that the king did not listen to them, the people answered the king, 'What portion do we have in David? We have no inheritance in the son of Jesse. To your tents, O Israel! Look now to your own house, David.' So Israel went to their tents" (1 Kings 12:16).

"To your tents, O Israel!" was an ancient battle cry. It was a way of saying, "Every man for himself!" or perhaps, "Every tribe for itself!" Back in chapter 8, when the Israelites celebrated Solomon's temple with a feast, they all went home rejoicing, with words of praise for their king (1 Kings 8:66). This time they went home rebelling, with words of contempt for the king they refused to honor.

In political terms, this was an act of secession. The northern tribes were seceding from their union with the southern tribes over the issue of slavery. From now on, Israel in the north and Judah in the south would be a house divided. But Jeroboam and his tribes were also rebelling against the plan of salvation. God had promised a Savior-King to come from the house and the line of David. From that perspective, Jeroboam's words to Rehoboam are chilling: "What portion do we have in David?" "We have no inheritance in the son of Jesse." "Look now to your own house, David."

With these words, Jeroboam and the northern tribes rejected the house of David, and with it, they rejected the way of salvation. One angry, impulsive response caused a permanent division. Paul House calls it an "incredibly poor decision" that "tears down in a few days what David and Solomon labored eighty years to build."[8] To be sure, there were still some people in the northern kingdom of Israel who worshiped the God of Israel. We will

8. Paul R. House, *1, 2 Kings*, The New American Commentary (Nashville: Broadman & Holman, 1995), 182.

meet some of them later in 1 and 2 Kings. But as a nation, they were rebelling against God's true king. Rather than walking the narrow path of salvation with the royal tribe of Judah, the ten tribes of Israel were heading down the broad highway to destruction.

Jeroboam's rebellion against Rehoboam is reminiscent of the opening words of Psalm 2: "Why do the nations rage and the peoples plot in vain? The kings of the earth set themselves, and the rulers take counsel together, against the LORD and against his anointed, saying, 'Let us burst their bonds apart and cast away their cords from us'" (Ps. 2:1–3). This is what Jeroboam did: he took counsel against the Lord's anointed. If only he had heeded the warning from the end of the psalm: "Now therefore, O kings, be wise; be warned, O rulers of the earth. Serve the LORD with fear, and rejoice with trembling. Kiss the Son, lest he be angry, and you perish in the way, for his wrath is quickly kindled" (Ps. 2:10–12).

The words that Jeroboam used in rejecting the son of Solomon sound similar to what the people of Israel said when they were rejecting the Son of God, calling for Christ to be crucified. When Pilate asked if they really wanted him to crucify their king, they said, "We have no king but Caesar" (John 19:15). They also said, "His blood be on us and on our children!" (Matt. 27:25). Later some of them came to faith in Christ. But many of them never did, and they were lost forever.

Understand what is at stake in the decision we make for or against Jesus Christ. To serve God's true and eternal King is to enter the way to everlasting life. Through faith in Christ, we will enter paradise. But to reject the kingship of Christ is to fall under the judgment of God. If we go our own way in life—if we insist on having the upper hand over other people, refusing to give up our foolish and selfish pleasures, always breaking God's commandments and never submitting to his will for our lives—then we will never enter the kingdom of God. Unless we repent, we will be lost forever.

REHOBOAM'S REPRIEVE

Both Rehoboam and Jeroboam made the wrong decision, choosing to be served rather than to serve. With Jeroboam's rebellion, the choice came to Rehoboam again. The same thing happens to all of us. The opportunity to choose for or against God does not come only once in life, but every day, with every decision we make. What we think about, talk about, look at, work on, play with, spend on—these are all kingdom decisions, and they all have to be made every day.

In this case, King Rehoboam was not going to let the northern tribes go without a fight. He already "reigned over the people of Israel who lived in the cities of Judah" (1 Kings 12:17), but he wanted to rule the whole kingdom. So as soon as he heard Jeroboam's rebellious reply, he started to take action: "Then King Rehoboam sent Adoram, who was taskmaster over the forced labor, and all Israel stoned him to death with stones" (1 Kings 12:18). So much for diplomacy! Sending the slave driver to serve as his envoy was hardly the best way for Rehoboam to conciliate his adversaries. Not surprisingly, Adoram's mission proved to be fatal; rather than respecting the king's representative, the northern tribes put him to death.

Recognizing that his own life was now in mortal danger, Rehoboam "hurried to mount his chariot to flee to Jerusalem" (1 Kings 12:18). From that point forward he would be the king of a diminished kingdom. The year was 930 B.C., and as the Bible records, "Israel has been in rebellion against the house of David to this day. And when all Israel heard that Jeroboam had returned, they sent and called him to the assembly and made him king over all Israel. There was none that followed the house of David but the tribe of Judah only" (1 Kings 12:18–20).

Rebohoam could see that his kingship was failing, but he did not give up without a fight. Once diplomacy failed, he resorted to the use of military force. Maybe he could unite the divided house through bloody conquest. So the king mustered his troops: "When Rehoboam came to Jerusalem, he assembled all the house of Judah and the tribe of Benjamin, 180,000 chosen warriors, to fight against the house of Israel, to restore the kingdom to Rehoboam the son of Solomon" (1 Kings 12:21). Not content to rule only one tribe, he wanted to rule them all. Thus the stage was set for all-out civil war.

It was just then that God intervened in mercy. The divided kingdom was an act of God's justice. Nevertheless, God would not allow his kingdom to be destroyed. So God summoned Shemaiah, the man of God (which is to say, a prophet), and gave him this word: "Say to Rehoboam the son of Solomon, king of Judah, and to all the house of Judah and Benjamin, and to the rest of the people, 'Thus says the LORD, You shall not go up or fight against your relatives the people of Israel. Every man return to his home, for this thing is from me'" (1 Kings 12:23–24).

Speaking with divine authority, Shemaiah told the southern tribes that they should not go to war against their brothers. The tragedy of the divided kingdom was the will of God. This thing was from him. It was his judgment against his people for the sin of Solomon in worshiping other gods. Therefore, the tribes of Judah and Benjamin should let the other tribes go. Instead of going to war, they should go back home.

Remarkably, Rehoboam and his men did not fight against the will of God, but "listened to the word of the LORD and went home again, according to the word of the LORD" (1 Kings 12:24). This is a mighty testimony to the power of God's Word, as spoken by God's prophet. Though desperate for revenge, Rehoboam and his entire army submitted to the will of God. "Here is one Shemaiah," said Charles Spurgeon in his sermon on this verse:

> Some of you never heard of him before, perhaps you will never hear of him again; he appears once in this history, and then he vanishes; he comes, and he goes,—only fancy this one man constraining to peace a hundred and eighty thousand chosen men, warriors ready to fight against the house of Israel, by giving to them in very plain, unpolished words, the simple command of God.[9]

The word of God has the power to change the course of history. It also has the power to change a man's life—even a man who has been choosing to live for himself rather than to serve the kingdom of God. Given everything that has happened in this chapter so far, we would hardly expect Rehoboam to listen to what God says. Yet when the man of God told him not to go to war, he listened and obeyed.

The surprise ending to Rehoboam's story is a reminder that God does not give up on us, even when we go our own way in life. We still have an opportunity to hear what God says, and then obey it. Even after all the foolish mistakes we have made, we may yet find wisdom. God is still speaking to us through the Scriptures, calling us to follow Christ as our King. He is inviting us to make the right choice in life, and to keep making it. Choose for service,

9. Spurgeon, "This Thing Is from Me," 42:361–62.

not selfishness. Choose for the true King, not your own kingdom. Choose for God's Word, not your own will in life.

A BETTER CHOICE

As you make your choice, remember the words of Jesus: "You know that those who are considered rulers of the Gentiles lord it over them, and their great ones exercise authority over them" (Mark 10:42). Although Jesus was talking about the Gentiles when he said this, he might just as well have been talking about Jeroboam and Rehoboam—great ones who wanted to lord it over others. Jesus calls his disciples to live a different way. "It shall not be so among you," he said. "But whoever would be great among you must be your servant, and whoever would be first among you must be slave of all" (Mark 10:43–44).

Jesus not only said this, but also did it. He is a completely different kind of king—one who came "not to be served but to serve, and to give his life as a ransom for many" (Mark 10:45). Jesus kept serving all the way to the cross, where he offered his life for our sins. Now his life and death are the pattern for our service in the kingdom of God. Jesus calls us to live the way he lived, and to lead the way he led.

Some people say that there are two kinds of people in the world: people who use other people, and people who get used. But God is not a pimp, and therefore we do not live by that kind of "pimpology." The two kinds of people in the world are the people who serve and the people who demand to be served. Which kind of person are you?

It was easy to tell what kind of person Daniel Parmenter was: a servant-leader. One Valentine's Day he was sitting in an ocean science class at Northern Illinois University, next to his girlfriend, Lauren. When a gunman entered the lecture hall and began emptying his shotgun, Parmenter began praying out loud for God's help and mercy. Quickly he pulled his girlfriend to the floor and covered her body with his massive, six-foot five-inch frame. She was badly injured, but survived the attack. Parmenter did not. His head and his back were riddled with the bullets he took to save Lauren's life.

What Daniel Parmenter did was not surprising, because he had become a servant long before he ever became a hero. His friends and family described him as the kind of boy who helped rescue a smaller child from a tree, who stuck up for a friend when he was being bullied at school, who offered to switch positions for the good of his football team, who called his mom and his sister on Valentine's Day to tell them that he loved them.[10]

Most people never get the chance to be a hero, but everyone gets opportunities to be a servant every day. What will you do with the opportunities God is giving to you? You do not have to be a hero, just a servant, for the sake of the King who died serving you.

10. The details of Daniel Parmenter's life and death were retold by Russell Working in "He Was Trying to Protect Her," *Chicago Tribune*, February 20, 2008.

27

GODS THAT FAIL

1 Kings 12:25—13:10

So the king took counsel and made two calves of gold. And he said to the people, "You have gone up to Jerusalem long enough. Behold your gods, O Israel, who brought you up out of the land of Egypt." And he set one in Bethel, and the other he put in Dan. Then this thing became a sin, for the people went as far as Dan to be before one. (1 Kings 12:28–30)

n the spring of 2005, *Business Week* ran a cover story on one of America's biggest businesses: the evangelical church. Theologian Sam Storms took the article as an opportunity to raise a concern about the "mini-gospel" of the "megachurch." Storms made it clear that he had no objection to churches' getting better organized, serving better coffee, or replacing wooden pews with theater seating. But he *was* concerned about the disappearance of the Word of God. "What bothers me," he wrote, "is the consistent and somewhat humanistic message of human potential, personal fulfillment, and hope for prosperity, together with an obsession for self-esteem, that is proclaimed from pulpits that rarely hear the echo of solid exegesis or communication of the content of Holy Scripture."

Storms proceeded to observe that "this soul-shrinking 'gospel' serves only to distract people from what makes the biblical gospel good news: the majestic, mind-blowing beauty of a transcendently holy God who graciously condescends in the person of his Son to absorb in himself the punishment we all so richly and eternally deserved." He concluded that what is missing from many churches is "the breathtaking splendor and heart-thumping glory of the revelation of God in the face of Jesus Christ."[1]

That same spring Dr. Storms also wrote "An Appeal to All Pastors," in which he lamented the deplorable neglect of biblical teaching in the American church. As he traveled across the country, he would ask people about the strengths and weaknesses of their churches. Here was the typical response:

> Well, we've got a great youth program. And there's plenty of parking space. . . . But honestly, it doesn't seem like our pastor spends much time in the Word. He'll read a passage here and there, but he never goes very deep into its meaning. I get the feeling he doesn't think it's very relevant to our lives today. He shows some interesting video clips from recent movies and he's up to date on political events. But Scripture doesn't play a huge rule in our services. I've even stopped bringing my Bible to church. I never seem to need it.[2]

Neglecting the Word of God to do our own thing is as old as the Old Testament. One of the clearest places to see it is in the story of King Jeroboam, who had his own way of worshiping God. When we see how Jeroboam wandered away from the word of God, and why, we may also see the sinful tendencies in our own hearts.

Jeroboam's New Jerusalem

Jeroboam was the king of Israel—the man who took the ten northern tribes away from Judah and Benjamin in the south. By the will of God, the kingdom was divided. Mercifully, this transpired without a civil war, but Jeroboam still thought that he needed stronger defenses, so he "built Shechem in the hill country of Ephraim and lived there. And he went out from there and built Penuel" (1 Kings 12:25).

1. Sam Storms, "The Mega Church and the Mini Gospel," Enjoying God Ministries (June 8, 2005).
2. Sam Storms, "An Appeal to All Pastors," Enjoying God Ministries (April 23, 2005).

Shechem was the capital of the northern kingdom. Jeroboam wanted this city to replace Jerusalem in the hearts of his people. In the past, God's people had always gone up to worship in Jerusalem, the place of pilgrimage. This worried King Jeroboam because he thought it would weaken people's allegiance to the northern kingdom. If he wanted to capture their hearts, he had to control their worship. So he said: "Now the kingdom will turn back to the house of David. If this people go up to offer sacrifices in the temple of the Lord at Jerusalem, then the heart of this people will turn again to their lord, to Rehoboam king of Judah, and they will kill me and return to Rehoboam king of Judah" (1 Kings 12:26–27).

These words show how insecure Jeroboam was. He had become the king of his people by popular acclaim. Yet he was still worried that after a few trips back to Jerusalem, people would decide they wanted Rehoboam to be king after all, and they would kill him. So Jeroboam divided the people of God—not just geographically, but also spiritually. From this point on, there would be two nations with two religions.

We should see this for what it really was: a lack of faith in God's word. God had promised Jeroboam a kingdom (1 Kings 11:31, 35), and thus the king did not need to be afraid of losing it. Yet the promise was not enough for Jeroboam. He felt he needed more security than the word of God could provide, so he built great cities to protect himself.

This can be a temptation for all of us. God has promised to provide for all our needs, but when finances are tight, it can still be tempting to worry about what we need. God has promised to accept us simply for trusting in what Jesus has done for us in his life and death and resurrection, but it can still be tempting for us to think that there is something more we have to do before God will be pleased with us. Will we take God at his word, or will we keep struggling anxiously for what he has promised to give?

Jeroboam's New Gods

It is instructive to see what happened to Jeroboam when he stopped trusting the word of God. His disbelief led him into disobedience—in particular, the sin of false worship.

The way the Bible describes the king's decision to commit this sin is very revealing: "Jeroboam said in his heart" (1 Kings 12:26). Jeroboam did not seek the will of God through prayer; he simply followed his own personal inclinations. In this respect, Jeroboam sounds a lot like the young nurse that Robert Bellah quoted in his book *Habits of the Heart*. Her name was Sheila, and here is how she described her religion: "I believe in God. I'm not a religious fanatic. I can't remember the last time I went to church. My faith has carried me a long way. It's Sheilaism. Just my own little voice."[3]

The trouble with listening to our own little voice is that our sinful heart desires to lead us into sin. John Calvin aptly described the human heart as "a perpetual factory of idols."[4] If we listen to our hearts rather than to the Word of God, we will end up worshiping anything and everything except the one true God, which is exactly what happened with Jeroboam:

So the king took counsel and made two calves of gold. And he said to the people, "You have gone up to Jerusalem long enough. Behold your gods, O Israel, who brought you up out of the land of Egypt." And he set one in Bethel, and the other he put in Dan. Then this thing became a sin, for the people went as far as Dan to be before one. (1 Kings 12:28–30)

For anyone who knows the Bible and its theology, what Jeroboam said and did sets off major alarms. Jerusalem was God's chosen city, but Jeroboam rejected it. He had already taken the northern tribes away from the son of David; now he was taking them away from the worship of God. There is only one true and living God, who alone deserves to be worshiped, but Jeroboam talked about "gods" in the plural. God had told his people not to make for themselves any carved images, or any likenesses of living creatures. He told them not to bow down to them or serve them. This was the second of his Ten Commandments (see Ex. 20:4–5; Deut. 5:8–9). But Jeroboam was setting up golden idols, even praising them for their saving power.

If his shocking words sound familiar, it is because they are almost a direct quotation from one of the darkest days in Israel's history. Back in Exodus, when the people of God were waiting for Moses to come down the mountain, the prophet's brother Aaron made a golden calf. When he presented it to the people, Aaron said, "These are your gods, O Israel, who brought you up out

3. Robert Bellah, *Habits of the Heart* (Berkeley, CA: University of California Press, 1985), 232–33.
4. John Calvin, *Institutes of the Christian Religion*, ed. John T. McNeill, trans. Ford Lewis Battles, 2 vols., Library of Christian Classics 20–21 (Philadelphia: Westminster, 1960), 1.11.8.

of the land of Egypt!" (Ex. 32:4). Now history was repeating itself. This was the second coming of Aaron's sin, only this time it was twice as bad, because Jeroboam made two unholy cows, not just one.

Today some people might try to justify what Jeroboam did by appealing to an alternative tradition. In the same way that secular Bible scholars argue that we should listen to false Gospels like Judas and Thomas, they would advocate going back to Aaron and recovering the liberating calf worship that had been "suppressed" by Moses and the religious elite.

The truth is that Jeroboam was guilty of the gross sin of pagan idolatry, of making for himself "other gods and metal images" (1 Kings 14:9). There were many bull gods in Egypt, where the king had been living during the last years of Solomon. There were also bull gods among the Canaanite deities—gods and goddesses of fertility. Now the Israelites were worshiping them too, confusing the worship of God with man-made idols. There was a golden calf in the south at Bethel, where Jacob had once seen his vision of a ladder with angels going back and forth from heaven (see Gen. 28:10–22). Another golden calf was set up in the north at Dan, where false worship had been practiced since the time of the judges (see Judg. 18:30–31). Idolatry had been institutionalized, and forever afterward, the golden shrines of these bovine deities would live in infamy.

Worshiping these idols may seem very primitive, but the heart of Jeroboam's sin is still with us. Today we are often told that there is more than one god, or even that we can worship Jesus Christ through more than one religion. We may claim not to worship any golden cows, yet we spend hours basking in the warm glow of the computer terminal and the television screen, which constantly tell us to love the world and rarely if ever tell us to love Jesus or serve the kingdom of God. Which would be easier for most of us: to go a whole week without prayer or without using visual technology?

People still use the same arguments that Jeroboam used to justify idolatry. There is an appeal to religious diversity: if one God is good, why not worship more than one? There is an appeal to chronology: out with the old, in with the new. There is an appeal to convenience. Why go all the way to Jerusalem, Jeroboam said, when you can worship much closer to home instead, in places like Bethel and Dan? So also today we are told that worship services should be shorter, with less preaching and prayer. The church should schedule its ministry to leave more time free for secular activities on Sunday.

Jeroboam's approach to worship would also be at home with today's politicians. The historian Edward Gibbon said that in the last days of Rome, "all religions were regarded by the people as equally *true*, by the philosophers as equally *false*, and by the politicians as equally *useful*." This was Jeroboam's view exactly. He was mainly interested in religion as a means of gaining political and economic control. Setting up temples in Bethel and Dan was a power play and a money grab. By using religion in the service of the state, he was keeping people and their tourist shekels away from Jerusalem.

This too is a temptation, and not just for politicians who are trying to use God to get more votes. In his comments on this passage, Dale Ralph Davis says, "If you cannot trust God, you will use religion."[5] This is a temptation for all of us: to employ religion for our own purposes. Some people use religion for personal fulfillment, as a way of feeling better about themselves. Others try to use religious practices as a way of getting to heaven—by doing good works, for example, or observing the sacraments. Still others think of religion as a means to financial prosperity.

These are only some of the things that people do with religion. But God will not be used. His grace cannot be bought or sold. His Word is not a political tool, a self-help program, or a means of personal fulfillment. Rather than using religion, God simply wants us to believe what he has said. To be specific, he wants us to believe the message of the gospel, trusting Jesus for salvation. Then, by his grace, through the power of the Holy Spirit, we will be able to live a life that is pleasing to him—not for our own purposes, but for his glory.

Jeroboam's New Religion

The golden calves were bad enough, but Jeroboam did not stop there. There were other sins produced in the idol factory of his heart. Chapter 12 thus ends with a description of the rest of his liturgical innovations—the false worship he offered to his false gods:

> He also made temples on high places and appointed priests from among all the people, who were not of the Levites. And Jeroboam appointed a feast on

5. Dale Ralph Davis, *The Wisdom and the Folly: An Exposition of the Book of First Kings* (Fearn, Ross-shire: Christian Focus, 2002), 140.

the fifteenth day of the eighth month like the feast that was in Judah, and he offered sacrifices on the altar. So he did in Bethel, sacrificing to the calves that he made. And he placed in Bethel the priests of the high places that he had made. He went up to the altar that he had made in Bethel on the fifteenth day in the eighth month, in the month that he had devised from his own heart. And he instituted a feast for the people of Israel and went up to the altar to make offerings. (1 Kings 12:31–33)

By the time that he was done, there was hardly any biblical regulation for worship that Jeroboam did not violate. This is what happens when we follow our own hearts instead of the Word of God: we will do whatever we please, rather than what is pleasing to God.

What pleased Jeroboam was to build his own temples. Rather than honoring the temple in Jerusalem, which was the earthly house of the living God, Jeroboam erected his own houses of worship—not just at Bethel and Dan, but all over the country. The king also appointed his own priests. Instead of following the Levitical line (see Deut. 18:1–5), he ordained men from the other tribes of Israel. Jeroboam followed his own liturgical calendar. Rather than observing the biblical festivals, like the Feast of Tabernacles, he started his own feast in his own month.[6]

Jeroboam did things his way rather than God's way. He even claimed the prerogatives of the priesthood, presiding as priest over Israel, making ungodly sacrifices on his unholy altar. Thus Jeroboam worshiped his own gods, at his own times, during his own festivals, at his own temples, in his own cities, with his own priests. As the Bible describes what the man did, it repeatedly uses the Hebrew word for "made" (*asah*). Jeroboam made this, and he made that, and by the time he was finished, he had a man-made religion.[7]

A theologian would call what Jeroboam did a violation of the "regulative principle" for worship. God has the right to determine how he wants to be honored. To that end, he has given us clear instructions about how to worship him. He has taught us how to pray and what kinds of sacrifices to bring. He has instituted the appropriate sacraments for public worship. But rather

6. According to Numbers 29:12, the Feast of Tabernacles was to be celebrated on the fifteenth day of the seventh month, not the fifteenth day of the eighth month, as Jeroboam dictated.

7. Davis, *The Wisdom and the Folly*, 144.

than following the regulations that God has given in his Word, Jeroboam decided to invent his own way to worship. For him, worship was not a divine gift, but a human invention.

Jeroboam's idolatry reminds us how important it is to avoid the temptation to invent new religious rituals, but instead to follow the simple, biblical rhythms of worship: singing and prayer, offerings and testimonies, the ministry of Word and sacrament, with the confession of our faith. More importantly, what Jeroboam did is a reminder to trust in Christ alone for our salvation. Understand that when Jeroboam rejected Jerusalem, he was rejecting the atoning sacrifices that were made there for sinners. The temple was the one and only place that God had appointed for the forgiveness of sins. Once Jeroboam rejected the worship of Jerusalem, it did not matter what else he did: he would never be saved, because he had abandoned the only true way of getting right with God. His own gods would fail, and his sins would never be forgiven. This is why Sam Storms' warning about the "minigospel" of some "megachurches" is apropos. The purpose of the church, like God's purpose for Jeroboam's Israel, is to glorify God and to proclaim the forgiveness of sins. No congregation can long succeed if its spiritual mission is abandoned.

Today the one place where any and every sin can be forgiven is the cross of Jesus Christ. The word of that cross may be "folly to those who are perishing, but to us who are being saved it is the power of God" (1 Cor. 1:18). Do not imagine that any man-made religion can save. Do not abandon the only place where anyone can find forgiveness. Believe in Jesus, and by the power of the cross where he was crucified, your sins will be fully forgiven.

THE HAND OF JUDGMENT

When people reject the Word of God to do their own thing, as Jeroboam did, they are bound by the power of that Word nonetheless. Jeroboam was in deliberate violation of God's word. God had told the king to keep all his commandments and to walk in all his ways; then God would build him a dynasty like the house of David (1 Kings 11:38). Jeroboam responded to this clear command by stubbornly disobeying God's direct orders. He willfully followed the counsel of his own sinful heart, which was diametrically opposed to the will of God. Nevertheless, he could not escape the power of the very word that he rejected. If the king obeyed God's word, he would be blessed; but if he disobeyed that word, he would be condemned, and there was nothing his false gods could do to save him.

The power of God's word was revealed by the prophet who suddenly and unexpectedly came to confront Jeroboam: "And behold, a man of God came out of Judah by the word of the LORD to Bethel" (1 Kings 13:1). We are told that this man of God came from Judah, the tribe of David. But to Jeroboam it must have seemed as if he came out of nowhere, because he caught the king in the very act of idolatry, at the scene of his religious crime:

> Jeroboam was standing by the altar to make offerings. And the man cried against the altar by the word of the LORD and said, "O altar, altar, thus says the LORD: 'Behold, a son shall be born to the house of David, Josiah by name, and he shall sacrifice on you the priests of the high places who make offerings on you, and human bones shall be burned on you.'" And he gave a sign the same day, saying, "This is the sign that the LORD has spoken: 'Behold, the altar shall be torn down, and the ashes that are on it shall be poured out.'" (1 Kings 13:1–3)

Even when people go their own way to worship their own gods and invent their own religions, God still speaks. Here he pronounces a terrible prophecy of judgment against Jeroboam. At the very moment that the king was dedicating the shrine of Bethel with a sacrifice, God told him that his ungodly altar would be desecrated and his unholy priests destroyed. But even that was not the worst of it. These devastating acts of judgment would be carried out by a king from the house of David, which meant that Jeroboam's dynasty would not endure. The man of God thus prophesied the fall of the house of Jeroboam.

The words of this reforming prophet were very bold. He prophesied directly to the altar—a dramatic form of address known as "apostrophe." He also named some names, making a predictive prophecy. The king who would bring judgment against the house of Jeroboam would be named Josiah. Like all the other prophecies of God, these words came true. The Bible later recounts the reformation that took place in Israel during the days of Josiah:

> The altar at Bethel, the high place erected by Jeroboam the son of Nebat, who made Israel to sin, that altar with the high place he pulled down and burned, reducing it to dust. He also burned the Asherah. And as Josiah turned, he

saw the tombs there on the mount. And he sent and took the bones out of the tombs and burned them on the altar and defiled it, according to the word of the LORD that the man of God proclaimed, who had predicted these things. (2 Kings 23:15–16)

Eventually, the prophecy came true. It was completely and comprehensively fulfilled, down to the last detail. This happened despite the fact that Jeroboam did everything he could to prevent it: "And when the king heard the saying of the man of God, which he cried against the altar at Bethel, Jeroboam stretched out his hand from the altar, saying, 'Seize him'" (1 Kings 13:4).

This is what ungodly governments always do when they are challenged by someone speaking the true word of God. They try to stop the church by the use of force. We see this today in China, North Korea, Saudi Arabia, and many other places around the world where Christians are in chains and it is forbidden to preach the gospel. But trying to stop the word of God always fails. The apostle Paul wrote about this when he was imprisoned in Rome. "I am suffering," he said, "bound with chains as a criminal. But the word of God is not bound!" (2 Tim. 2:9).

King Jeroboam learned the same lesson firsthand (!), for "his hand, which he stretched out against him, dried up, so that he could not draw it back to himself. The altar also was torn down, and the ashes poured out from the altar, according to the sign that the man of God had given by the word of the LORD" (1 Kings 13:4–5). So the prophecy came true. By a direct miracle, or by some providential cataclysm, Jeroboam's altar was torn in two. The ashes poured out, as the prophet had predicted—a clear and immediate sign that God had spoken the truth in judgment. Jeroboam's gods had failed, as false gods always do.

Of greater concern to the king was the shriveling of his hand—an act of judgment against his own body. The same hand that Jeroboam had lifted against the house of Solomon (1 Kings 11:26), and that had grasped the northern kingdom as a gift from God (1 Kings 11:31), was now useless and paralyzed. Donald Wiseman wonders whether this may have been "a muscular spasm or nervous rigidity at the shock of identifying his victim as a prophet." Others have attributed Jeroboam's malady to a sudden blocking of the main artery or to a cerebral embolism.[8] Whatever it was, this act of judgment proved the power of the word of God.

---

8. Some of the medical options are briefly mentioned in Donald J. Wiseman, *1 & 2 Kings: An Introduction and Commentary*, Tyndale Old Testament Commentaries (Leicester: Inter-Varsity, 1993), 146.

The word of God is more powerful than mighty kings and all the enemies of the kingdom of God. It is more powerful than the fallen worshipers who serve the failed gods of false religions. As the Scripture says, "The word of God is living and active, sharper than any two-edged sword, piercing to the division of soul and of spirit, of joints and of marrow, and discerning the thoughts and intentions of the heart. And no creature is hidden from his sight, but all are naked and exposed to the eyes of him to whom we must give account" (Heb. 4:12–13).

JEROBOAM'S RESPONSE, AND OURS

Jeroboam's heart had been exposed by the word of God. At first he had refused to listen to God's word at all. He had gone his own way instead, worshiping idols of his own invention. But then he was rebuked by the word that he had rejected. Mercifully, God was giving him another opportunity to obey. So how should Jeroboam respond? And how should we respond when the Bible rebukes us for all the idols that we are tempted to worship, and when we begin to fear the judgment of God?

The king's first response seems almost righteous. Jeroboam cried for help, asking to be delivered: "And the king said to the man of God, 'Entreat now the favor of the LORD your God, and pray for me, that my hand may be restored to me.' And the man of God entreated the LORD, and the king's hand was restored to him and became as it was before" (1 Kings 13:6).

Rather than getting angry with the man of God, Jeroboam asked for help, which seems commendable. Notice as well the basis for his request: he did not plead his own merit, but asked for the favor of the Lord—a mercy he knew he did not deserve. Best of all, by the grace of God, the prophet's prayers were answered. His intercession as a true man of God had the power to heal.

Yet Jeroboam's request was only *partly* commendable. He did not pray to God himself, but depended on someone else to do it for him—a middleman. This is because Jeroboam did not have a personal relationship with God. When he talked about the Lord, it was "the Lord your God," not "the Lord my God." He never repented of his sin, but only wanted relief from its consequences—a dangerous temptation.

The king's heart still was not in the right place. Any doubt about his true intentions was dispelled by what he said next: "Come home with me, and refresh yourself, and I will give you a reward" (1 Kings 13:7). Jeroboam was still thinking of religion as something he could manipulate for his own purposes, something he could buy and sell. In effect, he was trying to bribe God's prophet. By purchasing the man's loyalty, perhaps he could gain the power of his miraculous prayers.

In the same way that he attempted to prevent his people from going to Jerusalem, therefore, Jeroboam tried to keep the man of God from returning to Judah. Yet the man of God was not for sale:

> And the man of God said to the king, "If you give me half your house, I will not go in with you. And I will not eat bread or drink water in this place, for so was it commanded me by the word of the LORD, saying, 'You shall neither eat bread nor drink water nor return by the way that you came.'" So he went another way and did not return by the way that he came to Bethel. (1 Kings 13:8–10)

The man of God remained faithful, but to the very end Jeroboam was trying to work the religious system, hoping to get something from God, when he should have repented instead. It is sad to see what became of King Jeroboam. In answer to prayer his body was healed, but for the neglect of repentance his soul was never saved.

What will we do when the Word of God rebukes us? Will we continue to go our own way, or will we turn and be saved?

In the fall of 1547, a member of England's royal court was sitting under the proclamation of the Word of God. The preacher's name was Hugh Latimer, the famous Reformer. The listener's name was John Bradford, and he was starting to feel very uncomfortable. Like a reforming prophet, Latimer was preaching on integrity—especially the need for honesty and integrity in financial dealings. As he listened to the man of God, Bradford began to be convicted of his sin. In his work as a paymaster in the army, he had colluded with Sir John Harrington to defraud the crown. Now he realized that he had a choice to make. Would he reject the rebuke of the Word of God, or would he repent of his sin and make restitution?

One of Bradford's biographers tells us what he decided: "Master Latimer . . . did earnestly speak of restitution to be made of things falsely gotten. This did so strike him to the heart that he could never be quiet till by the advice of the same Master Latimer a restitution was made."[9] That restitution was very costly. It exposed Bradford to public shame. It also made him some enemies in high places, men who did not want their own crimes to be exposed. But John Bradford did what was right. When the Word of God rebuked him, he did not keep going his own way, but made a full repentance.

The Word of God calls us away from idolatry to repentance, faith, and the glory of God. Make whatever repentance is needed. Do not reject God's Word. Do not try to work religion to personal advantage. Do not go your own way, but listen to the true Word of God.

9. J. C. Ryle, *Five English Reformers* (Edinburgh: Banner of Truth, 1960), 122.

28

The Man of God from Judah

1 Kings 13:11—34

And as they sat at the table, the word of the LORD came to the prophet who had brought him back. And he cried to the man of God who came from Judah, "Thus says the LORD, 'Because you have disobeyed the word of the LORD and have not kept the command that the LORD your God commanded you . . .'"
(1 Kings 13:20–21)

*I*t is one of the strangest stories in the Bible. A brave prophet obeys the command of the Lord, then turns right around and disobeys the very same command. Another old prophet tells a tricky lie, only later to tell the truth. A ferocious lion kills a prophet but refuses to eat him, tamely waiting for the man to be buried instead. At the end of the story, a man asks to be buried with the bones of a man he destroyed with a lie.

It is not the kind of story that finds its way into children's story Bibles, or that most pastors ever preach. The problem is not so much that the story is too bizarre, but that it raises too many questions that are hard to answer, including fundamental questions of fairness. The story is also troubling because it is hard to tell who the "good guys" are (if indeed there are any). Even the "men of God" who tell the truth turn out to be liars and lawbreakers.

Yet maybe this is where we can begin to see the connection to our own experience. Is it really surprising to see spiritual failure in the lives of religious leaders? We see this all the time, and sometimes it makes us wonder: if our teachers and preachers are also guilty of sin, what hope is there for God's work in the world? According to 1 Kings 13, our only hope is the true word of God and his saving power to raise the dead.

A STRANGE COMMAND

The way to understand any strange story is to read it carefully. This story begins at the altar in Bethel, where wicked King Jeroboam was offering ungodly sacrifices to pagan idols of his own invention. Suddenly the man of God from Judah—an otherwise unidentified and unknown prophet—walked up and bravely condemned the altar with a curse. Jeroboam tried to seize the man, but instantly his hand was paralyzed—a crippling curse that was reversed only when the prophet prayed for the king and God answered with healing power.

Afterward, Jeroboam tried to persuade the man from Judah to stay in Bethel, where he could serve the northern kingdom of Israel. But the man of God refused. He knew that this was not his calling, and a man should never allow himself to be distracted from what God has called him to do. In this case, God had given him very specific instructions: "You shall neither eat bread nor drink water nor return by the way that you came" (1 Kings 13:9).

Why did God give these strange instructions? Maybe this was to show that the royal tribe of Judah should not have any fellowship with the northern kingdom and its sinful worship. Or perhaps God gave this strict command not to socialize because he knew that Jeroboam would try to get the prophet to stay with him in Bethel. Whatever the reason, this was a clear command from God, and the man of God obeyed it. Apparently, he was the kind of person who says, "God said it; I believe it; that settles it!" Refusing to accept the king's invitation, he "went another way and did not return by the way that he came to Bethel" (1 Kings 13:10).

The prophet's obedience is a good example for every man or woman of God. If we are servants of God, we are called to do whatever he commands, as carefully as we can. Full obedience is especially necessary for anyone who speaks the word of God. As E. M. Bounds wisely said, "It is not great talents or great learning or great preachers that God needs, but men great in holiness, great in faith, great in love, great in fidelity, great for God—men always preaching by holy sermons in the pulpit, by holy lives out of it. These can mould a generation for God."[1]

Here the very best example is our Savior himself, Jesus Christ. He too was faced with the temptation to turn aside from his calling for food and drink. When he was alone in the wilderness, Jesus was invited to dine with the devil rather than to live by the bread of his Father's pleasure (Luke 4:2–4). Jesus resisted this and every other temptation. He lived by the word he preached, so that when it came time for him to die on the cross, he could make perfect atonement for all our sin.

A Renewed Temptation

Unfortunately, the man of God from Judah did not persevere the way that Jesus did. At first he resisted the temptation to eat and drink in Bethel. But the temptation came again, as temptation does. Sometimes temptation comes the same way it came to the man from Judah: immediately after speaking the word of God, and even after resisting temptation. Just because he was brave enough to prophesy against King Jeroboam did not mean that this prophet did not need the power of God to give him victory over temptation. We have the same desperate need. The reason Jesus taught us to pray for God to deliver us from the evil one (Matt. 6:13), and to pray this every day (Matt. 6:11), is that we are always vulnerable to another spiritual attack.

This time the temptation came from another prophet, of all people. We are not given the man's name, but simply told that he lived in Bethel, and that his sons had told him all about what had happened earlier that day at the altar: "Now an old prophet lived in Bethel. And his sons came and told him all that the man of God had done that day in Bethel. They also told to their father the words that he had spoken to the king" (1 Kings 13:11). Immediately the old prophet sprang into action:

> And their father said to them, "Which way did he go?" And his sons showed him the way that the man of God who came from Judah had gone. And he said

1. E. M. Bounds, *Power through Prayer* (London: Marshall Brothers, 1907), 13–14.

to his sons, "Saddle the donkey for me." So they saddled the donkey for him and he mounted it. And he went after the man of God and found him sitting under an oak. And he said to him, "Are you the man of God who came from Judah?" And he said, "I am." (1 Kings 13:12–14)

We do not know why the prophet of Bethel was so eager to catch the man from Judah before he left town, but for whatever reason, the old prophet gave him the invitation on which the story turns: "Come home with me and eat bread" (1 Kings 13:15). Apparently this was a deliberate temptation. Presumably the old prophet's sons had told him that the man from Judah was not permitted to eat or drink in the northern kingdom. Maybe he simply wanted to meet the man who had the courage to stand up to King Jeroboam. Yet for reasons that are never fully explained, the prophet of Bethel invited the man from Judah to do the very thing that he was forbidden to do.

In response, the man of God from Judah gave exactly the response that we would expect a godly man to give. He said to the old prophet, "I may not return with you, or go in with you, neither will I eat bread nor drink water with you in this place, for it was said to me by the word of the LORD, 'You shall neither eat bread nor drink water there, nor return by the way that you came'" (1 Kings 13:16–17). Notice how the man of God resisted this temptation. He did it the same way that Jesus resisted all his temptations: by repeating the word of God (Luke 4:4, 8, 12). This is one of the reasons it is so important for us to know our Bibles: so we can take our stand against temptation.

This time the old prophet of Bethel simply would not take "no" for an answer. At this point he did something very wicked. He told the man of God from Judah that he had received fresh revelation—a new word from God. "I also am a prophet as you are," he said, "and an angel spoke to me by the word of the LORD, saying, 'Bring him back with you into your house that he may eat bread and drink water'" (1 Kings 13:18).

Some people would be very impressed by this kind of claim. If someone says he has received a word of knowledge, who are we to disagree? Should we not expect fresh light to break forth from the Spirit of God? Are we not commanded to obey his word, whatever it says, and whenever it is spoken? This is the way some preachers gain control over their congregations, and some Christians try to manipulate other people. "God told me to do this," they say, or, worse, "God told me to tell you to do this."

In this particular case, the prophet of Bethel was lying. We know this because the Bible tells us so: "But he lied to him" (1 Kings 13:18). Yet even without this privileged information, the man from Judah should have known better than to listen to what the other prophet said, even for a moment. What the old prophet said directly contradicted the command that God had already given. This is one way to know for sure that a prophecy is false: when it contradicts a clear command from God, who never goes back on his word.

Notice as well that the old prophet based his claim on a message from an angel, which never should have impressed a man who received his instructions directly from God himself. One is reminded of the warning that the apostle Paul gave to the Galatians: "But even if we or an angel from heaven should preach to you a gospel contrary to the one we preached to you, let him be accursed" (Gal. 1:8).

The old prophet's invitation was a seductive temptation, based on a spurious revelation. But do not feel sorry for the man of God from Judah. Do not imagine that he was treated unfairly, that he was the helpless victim of a lie he could never detect. On the contrary, the man of God should have believed the word of God. Here we encounter a rule for Christian scholarship, as well as Christian ministry and practice: no new word of God, or insight from God's Word, can contradict the same word of God we have already received.

Now the man of God had a decision to make. What would he do this time: stay in Bethel or go home to Judah? Just because we resist a temptation once does not mean that we will resist it when it comes again. The man from Judah had rejected Jeroboam, but this temptation was subtler and therefore stronger. Now a false prophet was pressuring him to believe that sin itself was God's will for his life.

We experience the same struggle. The temptation to commit sins like anger, greed, lust, and gossip does not come just once, but again and again. Often it comes from people who try to tell us that sin is the right thing to do. Even the very worst sins of violence and perversion have been justified by appealing to the will of God. But just because somebody *says* that something is God's will does not mean that it *is* God's will. We are called only to obey the will of God given in the Word of God.

This is where the man of God failed. Rather than doing what he was told to do, "he went back with him and ate bread in his house and drank water"

(1 Kings 13:19). If only he had been wise enough to obey what the law said about listening to false prophets (see Deut. 13:1–3), or to follow the advice that John later gave in his first epistle: "Beloved, do not believe every spirit, but test the spirits to see whether they are from God, for many false prophets have gone out into the world" (1 John 4:1; cf. Rev. 2:2). The issue here is not simply disobedience, but failure to discern false prophecy. Purported revelation always stands under the judgment of prior revelation. By not testing the spirit of the false prophet, the man of God fell for a lie. Be careful not to make the same mistake! When people say, "The Lord said this," or "God told me that," make sure that the only thing you believe is the true Word of God, and that the only thing you do is the true will of God.

A Severe Judgment

At this point in the story, we cannot help but feel a little disappointed. Maybe the prophet of Bethel was a liar, but we expected more from the man of Judah, especially given the way that he stood up to King Jeroboam. He really should have known better than to disobey the word of God. But even the best of men are only men at best, so sometimes we see sin in the lives of spiritual leaders. That is certainly true in this story, where we meet two prophets who are both disobedient to the will of God (unless, as some have argued, the prophet of Bethel was sent to test the man of God from Judah; the Bible is silent on this point).

Not only are we disappointed with these men, but we are also worried for them—worried that trouble will come as the result of their sin. And trouble did come, through a terrible prophecy of divine judgment. Strangely enough, this prophecy came through the prophet of Bethel, who had proved to be a false prophet. Nevertheless, "as they sat at the table, the word of the LORD came to the prophet who had brought him back" (1 Kings 13:20).

This time the word he spoke really did come from God. If this seems strange, we should remember that the word of God always comes through sinful men. Even the Gospels were written by fallen disciples. The same thing happens every Sunday, as God's true Word is preached by sinful men to sinful people.

The word that came to the old prophet was an ominous portent of doom. He cried out against the man of God from Judah: "Thus says the LORD,

'Because you have disobeyed the word of the LORD and have not kept the command that the LORD your God commanded you, but have come back and have eaten bread and drunk water in the place of which he said to you, "Eat no bread and drink no water," your body shall not come to the tomb of your fathers'" (1 Kings 13:21–22).

This was not a declaration of final judgment, damning the man to perdition, yet it was a prophecy of dishonor. The man of God would not make it back to Judah alive. He would die away from home, suffering the further disgrace of not being buried with his own people.

These words all came true, as the words of God always do. So it came to pass that "after he had eaten bread and drunk, he saddled the donkey for the prophet whom he had brought back. And as he went away a lion met him on the road and killed him" (1 Kings 13:23–24). So the servant of God died for his disobedience.

What happened next was at least a wonder, if not a miracle. The prophet's body "was thrown in the road, and the donkey stood beside it; the lion also stood beside the body. And behold, men passed by and saw the body thrown in the road and the lion standing by the body" (1 Kings 13:24–25). For some strange reason, the lion seemed to have lost his appetite. He did not devour his victim, as lions generally do. Nor did he show any culinary interest in the tasty donkey that was standing nearby. No, this lion was "on Yahweh's leash."[2]

When people saw this strange sight, naturally they wanted to tell everyone about it. This was part of God's providential plan for getting word back to Bethel, because the eyewitnesses "came and told it in the city where the old prophet lived" (1 Kings 13:25). When the old prophet heard what people were saying in the city streets, he realized immediately what had happened: "It is the man of God who disobeyed the word of the LORD; therefore the LORD has given him to the lion, which has torn him and killed him, according to the word that the LORD spoke to him" (1 Kings 13:26).

It may sound a little disingenuous for this prophet to accuse the other man of disobedience when he was the one who led him astray in the first place. Nevertheless, what the old prophet said was true. The dead man was indeed

---

2. Dale Ralph Davis, *The Wisdom and the Folly: An Exposition of the Book of First Kings* (Fearn, Ross-shire: Christian Focus, 2002), 156.

the man of God, who had disobeyed the word of God and who had been given to the lion as a result. This all took place according to the word of the Lord, in fulfillment of divine prophecy. Now it was "clear that God's law stands over everyone—that even prophets must obey it, or face judgment."[3]

A Tender Burial

This may seem like it should be the end of the story. The man who sinned had suffered lethal consequences, in fulfillment of the word of God. If this were simply a cautionary tale, the lesson would be complete: do not disobey the call or the command of God, or else you will surely perish. What more needs to be said?

This is not the end of the story, however. God's lion was still standing guard over the dead man's body, marking the spot, waiting patiently for the last act in this biblical drama. It was time for the old prophet to go and investigate: "And he said to his sons, 'Saddle the donkey for me.' And they saddled it. And he went and found his body thrown in the road, and the donkey and the lion standing beside the body. The lion had not eaten the body or torn the donkey" (1 Kings 13:27–28).

As the old man looked at the body of the fallen prophet, he was moved with compassion. These men were spiritual brothers. For all their failings, including their betrayals, they both served as prophets of the living God. The old prophet of Bethel knew it was his duty to give his brother a decent burial. So "the prophet took up the body of the man of God and laid it on the donkey and brought it back to the city to mourn and to bury him. And he laid the body in his own grave. And they mourned over him, saying, 'Alas, my brother!'" (1 Kings 13:29–30).

It was a sad funeral. These men shed tears of human sorrow for the loss of life, and tears of family grief for a brother in ministry. For the old prophet, they must also have been tears of personal remorse, because he knew that his deception had destroyed a servant of God. The only thing to do now was to dignify this death with the honor of a decent burial. By God's own will and prophecy, the man of God from Judah was not buried with his fathers, but at least he was laid to rest by his spiritual brothers.

---

3. Iain W. Provan, *1 and 2 Kings*, New International Biblical Commentary (Peabody, MA: Hendrickson, 1995), 115.

Afterward, the old prophet of Bethel made a touching request. He said to his sons, "When I die, bury me in the grave in which the man of God is buried; lay my bones beside his bones. For the saying that he called out by the word of the Lord against the altar in Bethel and against all the houses of the high places that are in the cities of Samaria shall surely come to pass" (1 Kings 13:31–32).

The old prophet was speaking the truth this time. Though the man from Judah had died for his disobedience, his prophecy would still come true. Judgment was coming against King Jeroboam and all the false worship he had instituted in Israel. When judgment came, and Bethel was destroyed, its graves would be desecrated. The man of God from Judah had been very explicit about this in his prophecy (see 1 Kings 13:2). When the high place was torn down, human bones would be burned on its altar—the bones of the people who had worshiped Jeroboam's golden calf.

The old prophet of Bethel believed this prophecy and wanted to make sure that it would never happen to him. He wanted to rest in peace, with the hope of eternal life. Therefore, he asked to be buried right next to the man of God from Judah, in the very same tomb. He was hoping to find safety with the bones of a true prophet.

The Tale of Two Kingdoms

Before we see what this story means for us today, it is important to see what it meant to its original hearers. For them, these true historical events served as a kind of living parable: the tale of two kingdoms. After the death of Solomon, the kingdom was divided between Israel and Judah, between ten tribes in the north and two tribes in the south. First Kings 13 tells the spiritual story of these two kingdoms, helping us understand this whole period in Israel's history.

There are two prophets in the story, one from each kingdom. Notice that they are not identified by name, but according to their geography, which gives them symbolic significance.[4] One prophet is called "the man of God from Judah," the southern kingdom. The other old prophet lives in Bethel, which was a major worship center in Israel, the northern kingdom.

4. Peter Leithart, *1 & 2 Kings*, Brazos Theological Commentary on the Bible (Grand Rapids: Brazos, 2006), 99, 101.

The actions of these two prophets represent the history of their two nations. The man of God came from Judah to rebuke Jeroboam the king of Israel for his ungodly worship. In the same way, the kingdom of Judah was a witness to Israel. Judah was the tribe of David, the true and rightful king. Judah's capital city was Jerusalem, which was the home of God's true temple, the proper place of atonement for sin. Judah thus stood as a witness to Israel of the true way of salvation, and also as a rebuke to Israel for its false worship.

For its part, Israel often enticed Judah to sin, which is exactly what the prophet of Bethel did. In the same way that the old prophet tempted the man of God by deceiving him, the kingdom of Israel would tempt Judah to practice false religion. In the end, both prophets turned out to be sinners, and so did both kingdoms. The two nations never reunited, but their people were brothers to the death, just like the prophets in this story— spiritual brothers who both stood under the word they proclaimed and were called to obey.

The Old Testament people of God could see themselves in this story. Here is how one commentator summarizes the living parable of 1 Kings 13:

> The individuals mirror their kingdoms, and their tragedy portends the tragic destiny awaiting Israel and Judah. Israel has become unfaithful. Judah can speak the word that Israel needs to hear; but if Judah, too, following Israel's lead, compromises its worship (as history shows it will do), then both are doomed to overcome their separation only in death. Judah will be buried in an alien land, and Israel will be saved only so far as it is joined to Judah.[5]

Like many parables, this story was intended to serve as a warning. To the people of Judah, it said, "Do not be deceived! Israel's worship is false, and if you turn away from God's calling, you will perish." To the people of Israel, the story said, "Listen to the saving word of God that comes through the tribe of Judah."

Sadly, Israel refused to heed God's warning. This is clear from the epilogue: "After this thing Jeroboam did not turn from his evil way, but made priests for the high places again from among all the people. Any who would, he ordained to be priests of the high places. And this thing became sin to the

5. Jerome T. Walsh, "The Contexts of 1 Kings xiii," *Vetus Testamentum* 39 (1989): 368.

house of Jeroboam, so as to cut it off and to destroy it from the face of the earth" (1 Kings 13:33–34).

The words "after this thing" indicate that these events—both the prophecy that the man of God spoke against the altar and the lion attack that later killed him—should have served as a warning to King Jeroboam. He had received the words of the prophet. He had suffered the judgment of God in his own withered hand. He had heard about the prophet's strange death on the road back to Judah. Jeroboam heard words of judgment that were attested by miracles of power. Yet in spite of all the warnings he received, he never abandoned the high places of false worship.

In fact, Jeroboam went from bad to worse. He did not follow God's way, but went his own way. The original Hebrew highlights the difference by using a play on words: Jeroboam did not turn back to God, but turned to his own evil way (1 Kings 13:33). To say the same thing another way, he did not repent of his sin, but returned to it. He appointed false priests all over Israel, giving ministerial credentials to men without any calling from God or qualifications to serve.

For these sins—and for many others—the house of Jeroboam would be cut off from the face of the earth. If the man of God was killed by the lion of God's justice, how could an evil king ever expect to escape the coming judgment?

LET GOD BE TRUE

These things were written for the people of God as a warning against false worship, as a call to repentance, and as a testimony to the truth of God's saving word. Judah and Israel were headed for spiritual failure, but God was giving both kingdoms a merciful opportunity to repent. There was still hope for them, if only they would heed the warning signs of judgment and believe the word of God.

If there is one thing we can count on in this story, it is the truth of God's word. The entire episode is an illustration of something the apostle Paul once said: "Let God be true, but every man a liar" (Rom. 3:4 KJV). In other words, even if everyone else fails to tell the truth, God will still be true to his word.

This is exactly what happens in 1 Kings 13. In one way or another, every man proves false to the word of God. Dale Ralph Davis describes how each man responded to God's word. The word of God was Jeroboam's mercy, Davis says, yet he despised it by continuing the worship of false gods. For the man of God from Judah, the word of God was his safety, yet he abandoned it by staying to eat and drink in Bethel. For the old prophet of Bethel, the word of God was his profession, yet he abused it by claiming that his lie was the truth of God.[6]

Every one of these men was false, but the word of God was still true, even when it came from the lips of a known liar. This chapter is full of the word of God—of God speaking to people, saying and commanding and prophesying things, giving people his word. In each and every case, his word comes true. The altar of Bethel would be destroyed. The man from Judah would never go home to his fathers. Jeroboam's dynasty would end.

Never doubt the Word of God, which is true in every historical fact it claims, every theological principle it espouses, every final judgment it threatens, and every hopeful promise it offers to us in Jesus Christ. In a culture of lies, the truth of God will stand. Even when spiritual leaders fail, or prove false, like the men in this story, the Word of God still does its saving work. Do not use the falsehood of men as an excuse for not believing or obeying the Bible. Do not reject God's Word, as Jeroboam did, or leave it behind, as the man from Judah did. Do not claim that your word is really God's word, as the old prophet of Bethel did. Simply believe what God has said in the Bible, and you will rest in the peace of eternal life. Even when everyone else turns out to be false, God is infinitely and eternally true.

We need to know this, and believe it, because only the Word of God has the power to save us beyond the grave. The old prophet of Bethel was grasping for this when he made plans for his funeral. He knew his own failings. He knew that what the man from Judah said about the coming judgment was true. So he asked to be buried with the bones of that true prophet, as if perhaps lying in the same tomb could save him from the coming fires of judgment.

As I considered this man's dying wish, it reminded me of an experience in my own life. Shortly after the death of James Montgomery Boice, the well-known minister who preceded me as senior minister of Philadelphia's Tenth Presbyterian Church, I went to the family home for prayer. One of Dr.

---

6. Davis, *The Wisdom and the Folly*, 151–57.

Boice's daughters asked if I wanted to see the place where his body was resting. It had been a peaceful death—praise God!—and the family was sitting quietly in the bedroom.

I could see right away that there was no life in Dr. Boice's body, that his soul had returned to its Maker. I could also tell there was nothing more that he could do for anyone's salvation. How futile it would be to think that the death of any mortal man could give life to anyone else! Dr. Boice was a man of God who spoke the Word of God. As a preacher, he was my brother. But what good would it do to make the request that the prophet of Bethel made when he asked to be buried in his brother's tomb? What eternal good would it do for anyone to be buried in anyone else's tomb? Despite the fascination that some people have with the relics of departed saints, there is no intrinsic power in anyone's old bones.

Well, as it turns out, there is one exception. Once there was a perfect Prophet, who always did what God said, who was never false and always said what was true, even unto death. When that holy man of God died—the Man of God from Bethlehem, the Son of God from heaven—he was also buried. He did not stay in the grave, however; by the word of God, his body rose again.

If we believe the Word of God, then we will ask to be buried in that man's tomb. We will pray to enter his grave, and then rise beyond it to eternal life. The Bible says that everyone who believes in Jesus Christ has been buried with him into death, so that just as he was raised from the dead, we too may live again (see Rom. 6:3–11; cf. Col. 3:3–4). God has the power to make dead bones live. Therefore, everyone who is buried with Christ, spiritually speaking, will also rise with Christ from the grave and live forever. This is the true Word of God!

29

A SICKNESS UNTO DEATH

1 Kings 14:1–20

Then Jeroboam's wife arose and departed and came to Tirzah.
And as she came to the threshold of the house, the child died. And
all Israel buried him and mourned for him, according to the word
of the LORD, which he spoke by his servant Ahijah the prophet.
(1 Kings 14:17–18)

*T*oday they would put the child in the hospital. The nurses would come and go at all hours of the day and night, checking vital signs and adjusting equipment before hurrying off to the next patient. The parents would sit anxiously by the bedside, listening to the whoosh of the ventilator, arranging the stuffed animals and the get-well cards, waiting desperately for some doctor to come and give them test results.

Things were different in biblical times. There were no hospitals, heart monitors, or surgical procedures. Yet the great fear that clutched at the throat of every mother and father was the same: the fear of losing a beloved child.

When the deadly fear of death comes—as it comes to everyone eventually in one form or another—we face a spiritual choice that reveals the true condition of our soul. Are we ready to face the great matters of life and death?

Either we will trust in God with a genuine and humble faith, submitting to his sovereignty over life and death, or else we will desperately grasp for anything to give us more control—some medical procedure or superstition that might give us the hope of survival. We may even use religion to try to manipulate God into giving us what we want; many people who say they do not believe in God nevertheless pray for bedside miracles.

ABIJAH'S ILLNESS

First Kings 14 tells the story of one child's illness and one family's struggle with life and death—a spiritual struggle that began with a physical illness: "At that time Abijah the son of Jeroboam fell sick" (1 Kings 14:1).

This situation was a real crisis. It was a medical crisis, because in the ancient world there was no such thing as a routine illness. Almost any sickness could end in death. It was also a political crisis. Jeroboam was the king of Israel, so Abijah was the crown prince—the rightful heir to his father's throne. It was not just the boy's life that was in danger, therefore, but the royal dynasty.

In addition, and in ways that Jeroboam did not yet fully understand, this was also a spiritual crisis. From what we know already, it seems doubtful that the king will be ready for this challenge. Remember that Jeroboam was the king of the northern kingdom. After the death of Solomon, the kingdom of Israel was torn in two. Solomon's son Rehoboam managed to hold on to a remnant: the two southern tribes of Judah and Benjamin, usually referred to as the kingdom of Judah. But by the will of God, Jeroboam tore away the ten northern tribes, commonly known as Israel.

Jeroboam was a wicked king. In chapter 13 he presumed to stand in the place of the high priest and offer sacrifices to the Most High God. When a man of God came to prophesy against him for this sacrilege, Jeroboam stretched out his hand to seize the prophet. God withered the king's hand in judgment. Although his hand was subsequently restored, Jeroboam did not cease his wicked ways. In direct violation of the law of God, he set up his own system of worship. The chapter thus ends with a summary of his sins and a dreadful prophecy of divine judgment: "Jeroboam did not turn from his evil way, but made priests for the high places again from among all the people. Any who would, he ordained to be priests of the high places. And this thing became sin to the house of Jeroboam, so as to cut it off and to destroy it from the face of the earth" (1 Kings 13:33–34).

This prophecy began to come true in chapter 14, on the sickbed of Jeroboam's princely son. The child's illness was a gracious opportunity for the king to turn back to God. Every illness is a reminder that we live in a fallen world, that our bodies are weak and that one day we will die. Therefore, every illness is an opportunity to grow in faith. The same can be said of every trial we face. What problems are we facing in life, and what does God want us to learn about trusting in him?

JEROBOAM'S DECEPTION

Rather than praying for mercy and trusting in the Lord, Jeroboam tried to work the religious system. Refusing to submit to the sovereignty of his Creator, he tried to manipulate God into giving him what he wanted.

Jeroboam did this by way of a crafty deception. He said to his wife, the Egyptian princess: "Arise, and disguise yourself, that it not be known that you are the wife of Jeroboam, and go to Shiloh. Behold, Ahijah the prophet is there, who said of me that I should be king over this people. Take with you ten loaves, some cakes, and a jar of honey, and go to him. He will tell you what shall happen to the child" (1 Kings 14:2–3).

These words are very revealing, telling us more about the king's spiritual condition than he cared to admit. They tell us that deep down, Jeroboam actually believed in the one true God. Even though he rejected God, when things got desperate he knew which God he had rejected! We know this because when the king was in trouble, he did not turn to one of his own priests. Instead, he went for help to the only prophet he knew who had the power to speak for God, the one who had promised him a kingdom.

This shows us something important about people who do not have a saving relationship with Jesus Christ. Whether people admit it or not, everyone believes in God, including atheists. The Bible says that God's eternal power is evident to everyone, and that even people who refuse to honor him know that he is really there (see Rom. 1:18–21). For some people, this becomes obvious when they get desperate for a cure, or have some other problem in life, and end up turning for help to a Christian friend—someone who seems to have direct access to God.

In our witness for Christ, we should make it our goal to be a go-to person for spiritual assistance. People outside the church may not be ready to consider the claims of Christ. But if we constantly love them with the truth, they will know how much we care about them and remember what we say about spiritual things. By the grace of God, when the time is right we will get an opportunity to give them the good news of salvation.

Jeroboam's words also reveal that his view of God was diminished and distorted. On the one hand, he still believed in the God of the prophet Ahijah. On the other hand, he doubted God's power to know all things. Otherwise, why would he even attempt a disguise? Jeroboam doubted the omniscience of an all-knowing God. Somehow he believed that God's prophet would never catch on to his deception. This would enable him to get a good word from the Lord—not the bad news that he deserved, but the good news he was hoping to get about his son's recovery.

This is what many people want from God: not the truth they need to hear, but the immediate help they wish they deserved but really don't. As one commentator explains it, "Jeroboam wants the help of the word in the emergencies of life but not the rule of the word over the course of life."[1] To avoid making the same mistake, we need to ask ourselves what we are hearing from God: the truth we need, or only the message we want to hear? If we want the true word of the all-knowing God, we have to accept the bad news about our sin as well as the good news about the grace of God.

The king's words also reveal a guilty conscience. When the prophet Ahijah first promised Jeroboam a kingdom, he told him to follow in the footsteps of King David by keeping the commandments of God (1 Kings 11:39). But Jeroboam had done exactly the opposite: he had followed his own path in life, breaking God's law. This probably explains why he felt as if he needed to mask his true intentions. Given the way that he was running his kingdom, it would never do for him to appear before Ahijah in person. If he did, the prophet was sure to condemn him, and then what hope would there be for his son? Much better, then, for him to send his wife incognito, in the hope that she would go unrecognized.

Jeroboam's fear that God was not on his side was an obvious sign of a guilty conscience. Deep down he knew that all he deserved was judgment,

---

1. Dale Ralph Davis, *The Wisdom and the Folly: An Exposition of the Book of First Kings* (Fearn, Ross-shire: Christian Focus, 2002), 162.

and that the only way he could get a favorable result was by pretending to be someone else.

Deep down, all of us know that we do not measure up to God's perfect standard, either. We have done many things that we should not have done and failed to do many things that we should have done. Desperate for God to accept us, or to give us what we want, we often pretend to be something we are not. We disguise ourselves, concealing our wicked intentions, hoping against hope that God will never find out. Wishing that there might be good news for us, even if it is not the truth, we pretend to be someone other than who we really are, even when we go to church.

AHIJAH'S GREETING

The only person Jeroboam really fooled was himself. Yet his wife dutifully did as she was told, practicing deception: "She arose and went to Shiloh and came to the house of Ahijah" (1 Kings 14:4). The woman went in disguise, wearing a peasant costume to conceal her identity as the royal queen. She went bearing gifts—not extravagant items that might blow her cover, but the kind of fresh produce and baked goods that a farmer's wife might bring. She went hoping to be told her fortune.

At this point the Bible tells us something about the prophet that would seem to put him at a further disadvantage: "Now Ahijah could not see, for his eyes were dim because of his age" (1 Kings 14:4). The old prophet was visually impaired. Like Isaac, who unwittingly gave his blessing to the unintended son, Ahijah suffered from failing eyesight. How would he ever be able to see through Mrs. Jeroboam's disguise?

Yet Ahijah was the true prophet of God. Therefore, his apparent disability did not matter in the least. Our physical limitations do not limit the Holy Spirit's ability to use us to do God's work. Though this man was blind, yet he could see. He did not need physical eyesight, but only the revelation of the Holy Spirit, who would tell him everything he needed to know: "And the LORD said to Ahijah, 'Behold, the wife of Jeroboam is coming to inquire of you concerning her son, for he is sick. Thus and thus shall you say to her'" (1 Kings 14:5).

This sets up one of the most dramatic discovery scenes in the Bible. Jeroboam's wife came to the doorstep, totally disguised, ready to trick the old prophet and manipulate the word of God. She had traveled all the way to Shiloh without anyone recognizing her, but how could she fool a prophet who knew the future? By divine revelation, Ahijah knew exactly who she was and why she was there. No sooner did he hear her footstep than he exposed her secret: "When she came, she pretended to be another woman. But when Ahijah heard the sound of her feet, as she came in at the door, he said, 'Come in, wife of Jeroboam. Why do you pretend to be another? For I am charged with unbearable news for you'" (1 Kings 14:5–6).

Abraham Lincoln said, "You can fool all of the people some of the time, and some of the people all of the time, but you cannot fool all of the people all of the time," or words to that effect. That famous statement has a theological corollary: you can never fool God, and if you think you can, you are only fooling yourself! God knows absolutely every detail of our existence, down to the number of hairs on our heads (Matt. 10:30). Why would we ever think, therefore, that we could fool him?

When it comes to God, honesty is always the best policy. The Bible says, "Whoever conceals his transgressions will not prosper, but he who confesses and forsakes them will obtain mercy" (Prov. 28:13). There are many good examples of this in the Psalms—honest and open confessions of private sin. God knows "the secrets of the heart" (Ps. 44:21). Therefore, we should never pretend to be holier, or more religious, or more dedicated to God than we really are.

A prayer letter I once received from a high school student preparing to go on a summer mission trip showed the kind of honesty we need to have with God, and with one another. Here is how the student asked his friends and family to pray for him: "We are working with a lot of kids this year, and kids become very annoying very quickly. Please pray that we can love them, teach them, and not yell at them. I am a chronic procrastinator. I am also the laziest person I know. Please pray that I would be able to work hard. I don't love people. They annoy me. They aren't perfect. Please pray that I would accept this and love them for who they are."

These are the prayer requests of a person who is honest about sin and the need for spiritual help. They challenge us to stop pretending, to take the mask off—at least before God—long enough to confess our sins.

It is only when we are honest with God about the bad news of sin that we can hear the good news he has for us in Jesus, that God will accept us by faith. Everyone who believes in Jesus Christ stands before God in perfection. God covers us or clothes us with the very righteousness of Jesus, the perfect Son of God (see 1 Cor. 1:30). This is not a false disguise, but a gift of grace that enables us to become a new person who is fully accepted by God. Rather than trying to trick ourselves, trick other people, and trick God into thinking that we are something we are not, it is better for us to come to God as we are, and then ask him to change us into something we could never become, except by the grace of Jesus. If we know we are not the person we ought to be, we should not pretend to be someone else, but ask God to make us the person he wants us to be.

GOD'S INDICTMENT

The greeting Ahijah gave to Jeroboam's wife when she walked in the door must have been the surprise of her life. What the prophet said next was even more shocking. Not only did he see through her useless disguise, but he also pronounced God's judgment against her husband's kingdom. Ahijah had terrible news for Jeroboam, a message from "the LORD, the God of Israel" (1 Kings 14:7).

This message came in two parts: an indictment documenting the sins of Jeroboam, and a sentence of judgment pronounced by God the great Judge. From these words we learn what happens to people who practice deception, who treat religion as a way of getting what they want, who turn to God only as a last resort, and who even then do not really trust him. Such people always come to a bad end.

To put things in legal terms, verses 7 to 9 form the indictment. Here Ahijah reminds Jeroboam how greatly blessed he was and tells him how far short he came from meeting God's standard of righteousness:

Because I exalted you from among the people and made you leader over my people Israel and tore the kingdom away from the house of David and gave it to you, and yet you have not been like my servant David, who kept my commandments and followed me with all his heart, doing only that which was right in my eyes, but you have done evil above all who were before you and have gone and made for yourself other gods and metal images, provoking me to anger, and have cast me behind your back. (1 Kings 14:7–9)

King Jeroboam had been greatly blessed. God had given him a kingdom, exalting him over ten of the twelve tribes of David. God had also given him a clear pattern to follow in ruling that kingdom: the example of David, who kept God's commandments for kingship. God had even promised Jeroboam a dynasty like David's, provided that he continued to obey (see 1 Kings 11:38).

Yet all these blessings were wasted on Jeroboam, because he sinned against God. Rather than doing what was right and good, he did what was sinful and evil. In fact, Ahijah says that his behavior was worse than anyone who had gone before him. His particular sin was idolatry—not just worshiping other gods, but actually making them. Perhaps the worst condemnation comes at the end of verse 9, in the phrase that describes Jeroboam's general attitude toward God: he cast God behind his back, or as people would say it today, he turned his back on God.

What is our own attitude toward God? Are we dealing with him openly and honestly, or have we turned our back on him?

Before giving an answer, we should consider all the blessings that God has brought into our lives—not a kingdom, perhaps, but many blessings nonetheless. We have life and strength with God's generous provision for our daily needs, as well as our gifts and talents, whatever they happen to be. Maybe there are times when we wish God had given us something he has given to someone else, but rather than thinking about what we lack, it is good for us to remember everything we have been given.

Then we should consider the royal pattern that God has set for us in the person of his Son, Jesus Christ, the true and everlasting King over the house of David. Consider the kindness of Christ, the humility of Christ, and the life of his self-sacrificing love. Consider as well the promise that God has given us of eternal life in his Son.

Now, are we living up to everything that God has given us, or should we be indicted for turning our back on him? We turn our backs on God when we worship other gods, like money, sex, and power. We do it when we neglect to thank God for his many blessings, but complain instead about all the troubles of life. We do it when we fail to feed upon his Word, or speak with him in prayer, but turn to him only as a last resort. In these and a thousand other ways, we turn our backs on God.

God's Sentence

Sin is a serious matter, as Jeroboam discovered. In every trial there must be a verdict. So what judgment did God render against the king for his many sins?

The sentence was death for Jeroboam and the rest of his household, as God spoke one of the most dreadful prophecies in the Bible—a judgment of absolute doom: "Therefore behold, I will bring harm upon the house of Jeroboam and will cut off from Jeroboam every male, both bond and free in Israel, and will burn up the house of Jeroboam, as a man burns up dung until it is all gone. Anyone belonging to Jeroboam who dies in the city the dogs shall eat, and anyone who dies in the open country the birds of the heavens shall eat, for the LORD has spoken it" (1 Kings 14:10–11).

In truth, this is a vulgar prophecy. The venerable King James Version frankly and accurately translates the Hebrew expression for "every male" as "him that pisseth against the wall." The house of Jeroboam will be treated like so much excrement. His sons will not receive the honor of a decent burial, but die like dogs in the city streets. The end of Jeroboam's dynasty thus serves as a preview of the final judgment, which will bring dishonor and destruction to every enemy of God.

Ahijah goes on to prophesy what will happen in the days following Jeroboam's kingdom: "Moreover, the LORD will raise up for himself a king over Israel who shall cut off the house of Jeroboam today" (1 Kings 14:14). The word "today" does not refer to the day the prophecy was given, but to the day it would be fulfilled.[2] As we read in verses 19 and 20, when Jeroboam died he was succeeded by his son: "Now the rest of the acts of Jeroboam, how he warred and how he reigned, behold, they are written in the Book of the Chronicles of the Kings of Israel. And the time that Jeroboam reigned was twenty-two years. And he slept with his fathers, and Nadab his son reigned in his place" (1 Kings 14:19–20). But Nadab's reign was short-lived. After only two years as king, he was struck down in cold blood, together

2. Terence E. Fretheim, *First and Second Kings*, Westminster Bible Companion (Louisville: Westminster John Knox, 1999), 85.

with everyone else in the house of Jeroboam. Thus the prophecy came true (1 Kings 15:28–30).

Ahijah's next prophecy looked even further into the future, beyond Jeroboam, to the end of the northern kingdom. As the direct result of their disobedience, the ten tribes of Israel would be removed from the Promised Land altogether:

> And henceforth, the LORD will strike Israel as a reed is shaken in the water, and root up Israel out of this good land that he gave to their fathers and scatter them beyond the Euphrates, because they have made their Asherim, provoking the LORD to anger. And he will give Israel up because of the sins of Jeroboam, which he sinned and made Israel to sin. (1 Kings 14:14–16)

These themes come up again and again in the biblical books of 1 and 2 Kings, with each generation repeating the sins of Jeroboam: goddess worship and idolatry. Because of their disregard for the holiness of God, eventually the people would suffer his righteous wrath. In the year 722 B.C., the northern tribes would be carried off to exile in Assyria, never to return again (see 2 Kings 17:21–23). But the seeds of their destruction were sown two hundred years earlier. Jeroboam's reign was the beginning of their end.

LIFE AFTER DEATH

At its widest angle, Ahijah's prophecy takes in centuries of sin and judgment. But the prophet also focuses on one particular individual: a little boy on his sickbed, whose parents were hoping desperately for a cure. This is where we all must return in the end: to our own individual situation. The dying prince reminds us of our own plight, for all of us are mortal, and each of us must appear before God for judgment. The question is not if we will die, but when, and whether we are ready to meet our Maker when we do. Where do we stand with life and death and the judgment of God?

The prophet Ahijah had a word from the Lord for Prince Abijah. This is what his mother had come to find out in the first place: whether her boy would live or die. The prophet said to her: "Arise therefore, go to your house. When your feet enter the city, the child shall die. And all Israel shall mourn for him and bury him, for he only of Jeroboam shall come to the grave, because in him there is found something pleasing to the Lord, the God of Israel, in the house of Jeroboam" (1 Kings 14:12–13).

At the beginning of this story Abijah seemed like the unfortunate one. He was on his sickbed, after all, and there was a chance he would never recover. The prophecy that he would die seems even more unfortunate, but in fact Abijah turns out to be the fortunate one. He is the only person in his family whose life was pleasing to the Lord. This prophecy does not tell us exactly why God was pleased with Abijah, but from what the Bible does say we know that the child had put his trust in God. We know this because elsewhere the Bible says that without faith it is *impossible* to please God (Heb. 11:6). So if there was anything that pleased God about Abijah, it must have come from his faith. The boy would still die, of course, but at least his death would be properly mourned and his body would receive a decent burial. Abijah's early yet dignified death actually was the proof that he was under the grace of God. The literal meaning of the boy's name came true, both in his life and in his death: "The Lord is my father."

Abijah's story reminds us that there is a fate worse than death. When Jesus heard that his friend Lazarus had fallen ill, he assured his disciples that the man did not have a "sickness unto death" (John 11:4 kjv). This was a strange saying, because Lazarus did in fact die. But he did not stay dead! As a sign of the resurrection power of God, Lazarus was raised from the grave. So when Jesus said that Lazarus did not have a sickness unto death, he meant that his sickness would not lead to eternal and spiritual death; it was not the deadly sickness of unforgiven sin. By the mercy of God, therefore, Lazarus would not die but live, not just on the day that Jesus brought him back from the grave, but for all eternity.

Whether we are healthy or sick, whether we live or die, the most important thing is to have the saving cure for sin, without which we will surely fall under the everlasting judgment of God. That saving cure is the forgiveness of our sins and the promise of eternal life through the death and resurrection of Jesus Christ.

Ahijah's prophecy shows that little Abijah had been cured of sin. His life was pleasing to the Lord, so although he died, his sickness was not unto spiritual death. Do not be surprised by his illness, thinking that the righteous do not suffer or die, even in their youth. God often calls his children to suffer, and sooner or later, he will call us home to himself. Abijah was the one person in his family who was ready to die, for he had put his trust in God. Blessed is the person who is as ready to die as he was!

It is sad to say, but his mother's case seems much less hopeful. Everything happened to her exactly the way it was prophesied: "Jeroboam's wife arose and departed and came to Tirzah. And as she came to the threshold of the house, the child died. And all Israel buried him and mourned for him, according to the word of the LORD, which he spoke by his servant Ahijah the prophet" (1 Kings 14:17–18).

Once again, her footstep at the door was a portent of doom. The moment she set foot in her house, her son breathed his last. This was a sure sign that Ahijah's word was true, that all his pronouncements of judgment were the very prophecies of God. If this first and most immediate prophecy came true, then the rest of the prophecies were sure to follow. Judgment was at hand. Yet as far as we know, Jeroboam's wife never repented. Although she returned home, she never returned to God.

In spite of all the judgments that come true in Scripture, many people still doubt that God will ever punish their sins. They have heard of the final judgment, perhaps, and after that, an eternal hell, but they do not believe a word of it, or else they hope somehow to hide their sins from God.

This is a huge mistake. Søren Kierkegaard warned about this in one of his major writings. The Danish philosopher is well known for an 1849 treatise entitled *The Sickness unto Death*, in which he wrote about spiritual death and the despair of sin. But earlier Kierkegaard wrote about the folly of thinking that we can hide our sin from God and thus avoid facing his judgment. He compared life to a masquerade ball, at which all the partygoers wear fancy costumes. But we will not be able to stay in disguise forever. "Do you not know," Kierkegaard wrote, "that there comes a midnight hour when everyone has to throw off his mask? Do you think you can slip away a little before midnight in order to avoid this? Or are you not terrified by it?"[3]

Kierkegaard was warning that eventually our masks will come off and our sins will be exposed before God. Rather than waiting until the final judgment, we had better be honest with God now, while there is still time for us to receive his mercy in Christ.

---

3. Søren Kierkegaard, *Either/Or*, trans. Walter Lowrie (New York: Doubleday, 1959), 2:146.

One woman who received this mercy was a visitor to Charles Spurgeon's famous Metropolitan Tabernacle in London.[4] Recently a man from Newington had been converted under Spurgeon's preaching and started to attend church there regularly. This was over his wife's strong objections. Yet she was curious to know exactly what her husband had been hearing in church. One Sunday evening in July of 1864 she decided to go and hear Dr. Spurgeon. Not wanting to be recognized, she wore a thick veil with a heavy shawl and sat at the back of the upper gallery. Having waited for her husband to leave home before her, she arrived a little late and was just entering the church when she heard Spurgeon announce his text: "Come in, thou wife of Jeroboam; why feignest thou thyself to be another? for I am sent to thee with heavy tidings" (1 Kings 14:6 KJV).

Needless to say, Spurgeon had the woman's full attention! In fact, she later claimed that the famous minister had pointed directly at her when he read the text. Later in the service, when Spurgeon told his congregation that God will "search you out, and unmask your true character, disguise yourself as you may," the woman knew that this was true. She heard the gospel, confessed her sins, and believed in Christ, thus receiving the saving cure that comes through the cross and the empty tomb. Jesus offers the same healing cure to everyone. If you receive him, he will save you from the sickness that leads to everlasting death.

4. This story is recounted in Davis, *The Wisdom and the Folly*, 161.

30

Like Father, Like Son

1 Kings 14:21—15:8

*And Judah did what was evil in the sight of the Lord, and they
provoked him to jealousy with their sins that they committed,
more than all that their fathers had done. (1 Kings 14:22)*

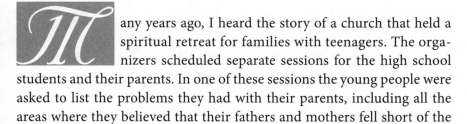any years ago, I heard the story of a church that held a
spiritual retreat for families with teenagers. The orga-
nizers scheduled separate sessions for the high school
students and their parents. In one of these sessions the young people were
asked to list the problems they had with their parents, including all the
areas where they believed that their fathers and mothers fell short of the
glory of God.

Soon the chalkboard was covered with complaints. Anyone who has ever
been a teenager (or lived with one) will have a good idea what they wrote
down: "My parents never treat me with respect." "They don't give me the
freedom to make my own decisions." "They get angry about things that
aren't important." "Instead of trusting me, they're always checking up on me."
"They never listen!" And so on. By the time they were done, the teenagers
had a long list of areas where their parents needed to change. It must have
felt good to see it there in black and white.

Then the parents were invited in to see what their sons and daughters had written—their youth group manifesto. Everyone sat quietly as the leader read through the list. Naturally the teenagers were curious to see how their parents would react. What they didn't know was that there was a chalkboard behind the chalkboard with the list of complaints their parents had written. When the time was right, the discussion leader pushed the top chalkboard to one side, revealing what the parents had written. Their list had been even longer, at first, but in the end they had decided to erase everything and write only a single sentence. "The trouble with our teenagers," they wrote, "is that they are so much like us."

This is the sad truth of family life in a fallen world. We would prefer to think that other people are the problem, when in fact we are part of the problem, too. One of the places we see this most clearly is the family, where the sins of fathers and mothers become the sins of their sons and daughters.

There are many examples of this sad legacy in the Bible, including the story of Rehoboam and Abijam. Their relationship shows how the sins of the father become the sins of the son, and also how God can intervene in a family to bring the hope of redemption.

The Sins of the Father

Rehoboam was the king of Judah, the southern kingdom. His father Solomon had ruled all twelve tribes of Israel, but after Solomon died, the ten northern tribes were torn away from his dominion and given to King Jeroboam. Thus Rehoboam had only two tribes to claim as his own: Judah and Benjamin.

From this point on, the story line of Kings switches back and forth between these two kingdoms: Israel in the north and Judah in the south. We see the action unfold in two places at once, like a movie that keeps switching scenes between the hero who is stuck in prison and the friends who are coming to rescue him. Chapters 13 and 14 are mainly about King Jeroboam in the north, but then the story returns to the southern kingdom: "Now Rehoboam the son of Solomon reigned in Judah. Rehoboam was forty-one years old when he began to reign, and he reigned seventeen years in Jerusalem, the city that the LORD had chosen out of all the tribes of Israel, to put his name there. His mother's name was Naamah the Ammonite" (1 Kings 14:21).

The great blessing of Rehoboam's life was to sit on David's throne, ruling as king in Jerusalem. Many things could be said about his seventeen years of kingship, but the Bible has only one, highly selective interest. The Bible is not very interested in what the kings of Judah and Israel built, or the size of their economies, or other details of their political history. The Bible's main interest is their faithfulness to God. Even when other subjects are discussed—the battles and the building projects—the Bible's primary concern is always personal godliness.

The most important thing to know about anyone is whether or not that person has a heart for God. We may accomplish many things in life. We may also fail to accomplish many things. But the most important thing about us—the one thing that will make a difference for all eternity—is whether we have a saving relationship with the living God. This is the great question of existence that everyone has to settle: Have I given my life to Jesus Christ, the Son of God?

From the spiritual standpoint, Rehoboam's kingship was a huge disappointment. Back in chapter 12 we saw how he disregarded his elders and divided a kingdom. Here in chapter 14 we see his sin of false worship—a spiritual failure that led to the loss of his peace and prosperity. This was not Rehoboam's sin alone, but also the sin of his people: "And Judah did what was evil in the sight of the LORD, and they provoked him to jealousy with their sins that they committed, more than all that their fathers had done. For they also built for themselves high places and pillars and Asherim on every high hill and under every green tree, and there were also male cult prostitutes in the land" (1 Kings 14:22–24).

As went the king, so went the kingdom. By rejecting the true worship of God, Rehoboam led the people of Judah into all kinds of ungodliness. They did what was evil in God's sight. In fact, they were even more sinful than their fathers, which is saying something, given their history of grumbling, complaining, and idolatry.

There was hardly any form of false worship that Rehoboam failed to practice. His people practiced their religion at "high places." These were altars to pagan deities, often located on hilltops or other elevations. They set up "pillars" to the gods—sacred standing stones that were forbidden by the Law of Moses (see Deut. 16:22). They also set up "Asherim," which were wooden representations of the female deity. According to Deuteronomy, all these

385

idols were supposed to be destroyed: "You shall tear down their altars and dash in pieces their pillars and burn their Asherim with fire. You shall chop down the carved images of their gods and destroy their name out of that place. You shall not worship the LORD your God in that way" (Deut. 12:3–4). Yet the shrines of these gods and goddesses dotted the Judean countryside. People were worshiping "on every high hill and under every green tree" (1 Kings 14:23).

Even worse, their religious practices included flagrant sexual sin. This was typical of Canaanite religion, in which worshipers sought to be united to various deities by having sexual relations with temple prostitutes, both male and female. This too was in direct violation of the Law of Moses, which explicitly forbade the sons and daughters of Israel from becoming cult prostitutes (Deut. 23:17). But Rehoboam's people wanted to do whatever they pleased. Therefore, they "did according to all the abominations of the nations that the LORD drove out before the people of Israel" (1 Kings 14:24).

An abomination is anything hateful to God, any odious sin that rebels against his holiness. The practice of pagan religion, the worship of false gods, the indulgence of sexual immorality—the Bible calls all these sins abominable.

This shows the radical difference between contemporary culture and biblical Christianity. Many people believe that sexuality is simply a matter of personal preference and private pleasure without any spiritual significance. "What business does God have in my bedroom?" But the Bible treats sexuality as a God-given gift with God-given instructions. One of these instructions is that sexual intercourse is a spiritually binding act that honors God only when it is shared between a man and a woman who have made a love covenant for life. Sexual promiscuity of any kind is contrary to the holiness of God.

The Bible also takes a different perspective on worship. Many people believe that it does not matter which god people serve, as long as they are sincere. In fact, the more gods and goddesses the better! This attitude was reflected in a 2008 ad campaign for the Unitarian Universalist Association. The slogan read, "My God is better than your God!" This was a way of saying that religious truth claims are childish, that people who say they worship the only true God are guilty of a kind of spiritual one-upmanship. Ironically, the ad went on to practice exactly what it preached against, because it claimed that universalism, in which all gods are created equal, is better than any exclusive form of religion. In other words, "Our *gods* are better than your God!"

The real question, however, is whether any god is really a god at all. The God of the Bible confronts our culture by claiming to be the one and only true God of the entire universe. He makes this claim on every page of the Old and New Testaments, as he does here in his jealous demand that he alone is worthy of Judah's worship. By worshiping other gods—the very gods they were supposed to eliminate from the Promised Land—his people provoked him to holy jealousy (1 Kings 14:22).

Jealousy has a bad reputation, but it has its proper place in protecting what a person loves. Some relationships are meant to be exclusive, such as the sexual relationship between a husband and wife. A husband ought to be protective of his wife's affections, and vice versa. If a man is unfaithful to his wife, she has the right to be jealous; this is a virtue, not a vice.

The same is true when it comes to God's love relationship with the particular people he has chosen out of all the world to be his very own. God promises to be everything that we could ever want or need. Therefore, he rightly demands our total affection. "For him to be jealous of this exclusive relationship," writes Paul House, "is no character flaw. Instead it magnifies God's righteousness, concern, and covenant loyalty."[1]

Our God is a jealous God, who rightly demands our total allegiance and absolute affection. So beware the sins of Rehoboam! If we turn to the worship of other gods—if we make our own pleasure the highest goal in life, if we love our money, if we gratify sexual desire in sinful ways, if we proudly hold a grudge, or if we commit spiritual adultery in any other way—we provoke the righteous jealousy of a holy God.

VISITING THE INIQUITY OF THE FATHER

In considering the sins of Rehoboam, it is hard not to think of the dire judgment that Paul pronounced in Romans:

Although they knew God, they did not honor him as God or give thanks to him, but they became futile in their thinking, and their foolish hearts were

1. Paul R. House, *1, 2 Kings*, The New American Commentary (Nashville: Broadman & Holman, 1995), 194.

darkened. Claiming to be wise, they became fools, and exchanged the glory of the immortal God for images. . . . Therefore God gave them up in the lusts of their hearts to impurity, to the dishonoring of their bodies among themselves, because they exchanged the truth about God for a lie. (Rom. 1:21–25)

This is exactly what happened to the people of Judah. Although they knew God, they did not worship him as God, and therefore God gave them over to foolish and destructive lusts. In the end, Rehoboam lost the peace and prosperity of his kingdom.

He lost his prosperity to the Egyptians, of all people: "In the fifth year of King Rehoboam, Shishak king of Egypt came up against Jerusalem. He took away the treasures of the house of the LORD and the treasures of the king's house. He took away everything. He also took away all the shields of gold that Solomon had made" (1 Kings 14:25–26; cf. 7:51; 10:14–22).

Egypt's attack had military and political significance. Shishak was a Libyan potentate who seized control of Egypt and sought to expand its influence. To that end, he sent his powerful army north across the Negev and into Judah—an invasion attested in the Egyptian records at Karnak.[2]

More importantly, these events had spiritual significance. To see this, it helps to remember the glories of Solomon. When that famous king was at the height of his powers, his treasury was the envy of emperors. Now his gold was all but gone, paid as tribute to prevent Shishak from ravaging Jerusalem. If we were to ask Solomon to comment, he might well quote this wise proverb: "Cast but a glance at riches, and they are gone, for they will surely sprout wings and fly off to the sky like an eagle" (Prov. 23:5 NIV). The wealth of Rehoboam's kingdom—both from his own royal palace and from the holy temple of God—flew away to the Land of the Nile. In a reversal of the exodus, the spoils returned to Egypt.

Even after the splendor was gone, however, Rehoboam desperately tried to keep up appearances. The golden age was over; Solomon's golden shields were lost forever. But "King Rehoboam made in their place shields of bronze, and committed them to the hands of the officers of the guard, who kept the door of the king's house. And as often as the king went into the house of the LORD, the guard carried them and brought them back to the guardroom"

2. Kenneth A. Kitchen, *The Third Intermediate Period in Egypt (1100–600 B.C.)* (London: Aris & Phillips, 1972), 292–94.

(1 Kings 14:27–28). How the mighty had fallen! Rehoboam's royal court still followed the old rituals, but now Judah was off the gold standard. The officers of the king's guard carried bronze instead—what Matthew Henry called "an emblem of the diminution of his glory."[3]

The devaluation of Judah's currency was a portent of the coming judgment, a clear and early sign of the wrath of God. Unless the people repented, all their glory would pass away. Eventually an enemy would come and carry off everything, including the people themselves.

Rehoboam lost his peace as well as his prosperity. The story of his kingship ends with these words: "And there was war between Rehoboam and Jeroboam continually. And Rehoboam slept with his fathers and was buried with his fathers in the city of David. His mother's name was Naamah the Ammonite. And Abijam his son reigned in his place" (1 Kings 14:30–31). To the end of his days, there was civil war between north and south. The divided kingdom of Judah and Israel was locked in a never-ending struggle, like the stalemate between the Israelis and the Palestinians today. Whereas Solomon ruled a peaceable kingdom, his son was always at war.

Much more could be said about Rehoboam. There is always more that could be said. The Bible itself tells us that its history is highly selective: "Now the rest of the acts of Rehoboam and all that he did, are they not written in the Book of the Chronicles of the Kings of Judah?" (1 Kings 14:29). The Bible does not tell us everything, but what it does tell is enough to learn the spiritual lessons that God wants us to learn. As it says in an old versification of Psalm 78:

> Let children thus learn / from history's light
> To hope in our God / and walk in his sight,
> The God of their fathers / to fear and obey,
> And ne'er like their fathers / to turn from his way.[4]

What happened to Rehoboam is not an isolated incident. In telling this story, the Bible is showing us where our own sin will lead us: to worship false gods instead of the true God is to lose our peace and our prosperity.

---

3. Matthew Henry, *Matthew Henry's Complete Commentary on the Whole Bible*, vol. 2, *Judges to Job* (New York: Fleming Revell, n.d.), n.p.

4. From *The Psalter* (1912).

Idolatry always impoverishes. We worship other gods because we think they will add something to us. For example, we think that money will enable us to have more possessions, and that this will make us happy. Yet the more possessions we have, the more trouble it takes to look after them, and the less time we have to do things that really satisfy, like worship God and serve other people.

Furthermore, we will eventually lose all our possessions anyway. Jesus said, "Do not lay up for yourselves treasures on earth, where moth and rust destroy and where thieves break in and steal" (Matt. 6:19). This is exactly what happened to Rehoboam: an Egyptian thief came to steal his gold. But instead of learning his lesson and turning his back on earthly treasure, the king said, "The show must go on!" and made shields of bronze. We face the same temptation. Even when the gods of money fail us, we hold on to them more tightly than ever. We see this every time there is an economic recession. Rather than letting God loosen our grip on earthly treasure, we desperately cling to what we have the way the king's guards protected their bronze more carefully than their gold.

False gods also take away our peace. In fact, this is one of the best ways to figure out which gods we truly worship. When we get into an angry conflict, it is almost always because our idols are threatened. As James said in his practical epistle: "What causes quarrels and what causes fights among you? Is it not this, that your passions are at war within you? . . . You covet and cannot obtain, so you fight and quarrel" (James 4:1–2).

In other words, our irritability is an index to our idolatry. When we get into a conflict, we need to ask ourselves: "What is my real issue here? Why is this making me so upset?" When there are angry words in the house, do not keep pointing out what is wrong with others, but consider what might be wrong with you. When there is conflict in the church, rather than simply assuming that we are acting from noble principles, we should consider whether petty resentments are keeping us from seeing things clearly. False gods rob us of our peace as well as our prosperity.

Just Like His Father

Rehoboam's tragedy was to pass these sins on to the next generation—a legacy of depravity. Chapter 15 begins with Abijam taking his father's throne:

"Now in the eighteenth year of King Jeroboam the son of Nebat, Abijam began to reign over Judah. He reigned for three years in Jerusalem. His mother's name was Maacah the daughter of Abishalom" (1 Kings 15:1–2).

The first and most important question to ask about this new king is not what nations he conquered, or buildings he constructed, or gold he added to his treasury, but whether he followed after God. Unfortunately, this was a case of "like father, like son." Abijam "walked in all the sins that his father did before him, and his heart was not wholly true to the Lord his God, as the heart of David his father" (1 Kings 15:3).

Children are always like their parents, including in ways they wish they were nothing like them at all. Children often say, "I swear I will never do that to *my* children." I think of the daughter who gave her father a withering look and said, "Please tell me that I'm adopted!" Yet whether we are adopted or not, our lives are connected in ways we cannot control and may not fully understand. As one woman said, "Mirror, mirror on the wall; I am my mother after all!"

Although children sometimes fail to admire their parents, they never fail to imitate them. One way that children are certain to follow their parents is in the commission of sin, which has an intergenerational influence. Sin takes a somewhat different shape in each person's life, of course, but we all share the same fallen nature. The more time we spend with people, the more we are influenced by their depravity. Children are the most heavily influenced people of all. They do not always learn what we are trying to teach them, but somehow they always seem to pick up our sins.

This is why it is critically important for parents to pursue personal godliness. Whatever else we may leave for our children, not just the children in our own homes but also children who grow up in the church as the family of God, we are passing on to them a spiritual legacy. The kind of person I am is the kind of person my children may become. Therefore, it is not just for my own sake that I need a stronger relationship with Christ; it is also for the sake of the rising generation.

According to Chronicles, there are at least a few things that Abijam did right, such as defeating Jeroboam in battle by standing on the promises of God (see 2 Chron. 13). Yet the portrait in 1 Kings 14 is much less flattering. Here we read that Abijam committed *all* the sins of Rehoboam. Some have seen these two accounts as contradictory, but I think Dale Ralph Davis is right when he says that "the writers of Chronicles and Kings are making two different points. Chronicles implies Abijah was reasonably orthodox when compared with Jeroboam; Kings says he is covenantally defective when compared to David."[5] Abijam may have been much better than the worst king of the northern kingdom, but he fell far short of the best king of Israel.

First Kings proves this point by showing us what was in Abijam's heart. Although he did some things well, "his heart was not wholly true to the LORD his God, as the heart of David his father" (1 Kings 15:3). God always sees the heart. What matters the most to him is not outward actions, but inward affections. Whatever sins Abijam committed were the fruit of his own false heart, and not simply the result of his father's bad example. The new king suffered from a coronary condition: the diseased depravity of a divided heart.

Abijam's bad example reminds us how vitally important it is for children to examine their own hearts. How easy it is to blame our parents for what is wrong in our own lives! If only my mother had done this, or my father hadn't done that, then it would be so much easier for me to do what God wants me to do. God knows the wounds we have suffered, and the weakness we have as a result, but he would also have us consider the spiritual condition of our own hearts. Am I totally devoted to the Lord, or am I caught between two loves?

Many Christians want so many things the world seems to offer that their love for Christ is only halfhearted. What are some of the signs of a divided heart? We have a divided heart when we sing praises to God on Sunday, but rarely think about him the rest of the week. We have a divided heart when we give some money to Christian work, but claim the rest for ourselves rather than saving and spending everything for the glory of God. We have a divided heart when we talk about spiritual things with other Christians, but never share our faith with anyone outside the church. We have a divided heart when we keep sinning the same old sins, and perhaps confessing them from time to time, but never with any serious intention of turning away from them forever.

THE HOPE OF A SAVIOR

The consequences of a divided heart are always disastrous. So it is not surprising that Abijam faced what his father faced—the fierce conflict of civil war:

5. Dale Ralph Davis, *The Wisdom and the Folly: An Exposition of the Book of First Kings* (Fearn, Ross-shire: Christian Focus, 2002), 173.

"Now there was war between Rehoboam and Jeroboam all the days of his life. The rest of the acts of Abijam and all that he did, are they not written in the Book of the Chronicles of the Kings of Judah? And there was war between Abijam and Jeroboam. And Abijam slept with his fathers, and they buried him in the city of David. And Asa his son reigned in his place" (1 Kings 15:6–8).

All of this may seem rather discouraging: one bad king giving birth to another bad king. We wonder when the cycle of sin will ever be broken. If the sins of the fathers are visited on the children (as the second commandment says they are; see Ex. 20:5), how can any family ever escape the legacy of depravity?

What every family needs is the direct intervention of the grace of God. The story of Abijam gives unmerited divine grace as the explanation for why his house was not destroyed altogether. This man hardly deserved to sit on the throne of God's earthly kingdom. "Nevertheless," the Bible says, "for David's sake the LORD his God gave him a lamp in Jerusalem, setting up his son after him, and establishing Jerusalem, because David did what was right in the eyes of the LORD and did not turn aside from anything that he commanded him all the days of his life, except in the matter of Uriah the Hittite" (1 Kings 15:4–5). God preserved the royal line of Abijam, but he did not do this for Abijam's sake. He did it for the sake of his father David.

Abijam's family was saved in the name of a righteous king. Not that David was perfect, of course. First Kings explicitly mentions one very large exception to his godliness: his adultery with Bathsheba, leading to his murder of Uriah. But the Bible is showing us a basic principle of salvation, namely, that people can be saved by a righteous king. To be more specific, we can be saved by the promise God made to King David, that his son would become the everlasting king (see 2 Sam. 7:12–16). When the Bible said that Abijam had "a lamp in Jerusalem," this was an image of kingship that meant that he was established as the promised king. In effect, David's lamp would not be extinguished (cf. 1 Kings 11:36; 2 Kings 8:19).

The grace that God showed to Abijam points us to the saving work of Jesus Christ. Like Abijam, we are saved by God's promise to David—the promise that God has fulfilled in Jesus Christ, the Son of David and the Son of God. By his sinless life and sacrificial death, King Jesus has offered perfect righteousness to God. In Christ, the sins of the fathers and sons, and the sins of the mothers and daughters, are all forgiven.

Now, by the life of his resurrection from the grave, Jesus gives us the power to grow in godliness. God intervenes in our lives and families. We are not simply stuck in our sins, doomed to repeat them again and again, generation after generation, but we can also see the Holy Spirit bring new life and righteousness to us and to our children. We are not doomed to decline, but by faith in Jesus Christ, we can rise in righteousness. Some of *our* sins may well become *their* sins, but by the grace of God, our repentance can also become their repentance, and our sanctification may lead to their sanctification. By his infinite grace in Jesus, God has intervened to save the family of fallen humanity. As we trust in him, and as we pray for his grace, he will intervene in our lives.

When God does intervene, his grace often extends to other members of the family. The difference it makes when God intervenes can be illustrated by the contrast between two American men who both lived in the eighteenth century: Max Jukes and Jonathan Edwards. Max Jukes was a hard-drinking hunter who lived in the woods and, as far as anyone knows, had little or no interest in God. Neither Jukes nor the girl that he married was a believer in Jesus Christ. When a sociologist later researched local records to determine what became of their family, he discovered that out of more than a thousand descendants, half a dozen were murderers, seventy-six were convicted criminals, a hundred were drunkards, more than three hundred died as paupers, and as many as half the women were prostitutes.

By contrast, consider the legacy of Jonathan Edwards, who put his trust in Jesus Christ, married a godly woman, and saw God graciously intervene in the life of his family. By the end of the following century, Edwards's descendants included thirteen college presidents, sixty-five college professors, more than a hundred lawyers and judges, sixty physicians, seventy-five military officers, sixty authors, eighty public officials, including three senators, and, perhaps most importantly, a hundred pastors and missionaries.[6]

Admittedly, most families are neither as ungodly as the family of Max Jukes nor as successful as the family of Jonathan Edwards. Yet their families illustrate the difference it makes when God intervenes and we experience his grace through faith in Jesus Christ. It makes all the difference in the world, not just for us, but also for our children.

---

6. Research on the Jukes family was first done by sociologist Richard Dugdale in 1874. The results are summarized by Leonard Ravenhill and compared with the Edwards family in *America Is Too Young to Die* (Minneapolis: Bethany, 1979), 112.

31

A KING AFTER DAVID'S HEART

1 Kings 15:9–24

And Asa did what was right in the eyes of the LORD, as David
his father had done. He put away the male cult prostitutes out
of the land and removed all the idols that his fathers had made.
(1 Kings 15:11–12)

*T*he last thing anyone expected from Edward VI was a reformation of religion. Edward took the throne of England when
he was only nine years old. The boy's father, Henry VIII, had
broken with the pope in Rome, but this was more for personal and political reasons than out of any sincere desire to follow a biblical pattern for the
church. Henry's failure to obey the Scriptures is especially evident from his
disastrous family life: he had six wives, and was faithful to none of them.

It was against expectation, then, that his son Edward VI advanced the Reformation in England. During Edward's short reign as king, an English Bible
was placed in every parish church. So that people could hear and understand
the Word of God, sermons were to be preached in English every Sunday, by
order of the king. For priests who did not know how to preach, the church
provided a *Book of Homilies*, which included a sermon that began with the
basic doctrine of the Reformation: "The first entry unto God, good Christian

people, is through faith: whereby we be justified before God." Laypeople were allowed to join their priests in receiving the full sacrament of the Lord's Supper (both the bread and the cup). People were discouraged from praying to the saints, and images of Mary were removed from the church, lest they become objects of worship.[1]

As a result of these and many other reforms, by 1553 the English Reformation was complete. Since Edward was so young, these reforms were partly due to the influence of Thomas Cranmer and other advisers. But they also represented the convictions of Edward's own heart. When the boy died at the tender age of 15, his dying prayer was that the Lord God would defend his realm from false worship and maintain true religion in England. From a line of unworthy rulers, God had raised up a king after his own heart.

RELIGIOUS REFORMATION

Edward's example is a strong encouragement to anyone from a questionable background. We are not crippled by the past. The Holy Spirit can intervene to do a powerful work of grace in our lives and our families. What is weak can be made strong. What is wounded can be healed. What is lost can be saved. Even if no one else in our family has ever been faithful to God, we can do something to serve his kingdom—maybe more than anyone before us. The future is full of spiritual possibilities.

A notable example of God's intervening grace comes from the story of King Asa, who belonged to the house of David: "In the twentieth year of Jeroboam king of Israel, Asa began to reign over Judah, and he reigned forty-one years in Jerusalem. His mother's name was Maacah the daughter of Abishalom" (1 Kings 15:9–10).

Humanly speaking, there was little reason to expect that Asa would be faithful to God. His grandfather, King Rehoboam, was a fool in the biblical sense that he refused to follow God. In his folly, Rehoboam divided a kingdom and led his people into idolatry. Asa's father Abijam was little better. He was a double-hearted man who walked in all the sins of Rehoboam.

---

1. The religious reforms of Edward VI are summarized in Nigel Heard, *Edward VI and Mary: A Mid-Tudor Crisis?*, Access to History (London: Hodder and Stoughton, 1990), 66–80, and W. J. Sheils, *The English Reformation, 1530–1570*, Seminar Studies in History (London: Longman, 1989), 31–50.

When Asa took the throne, therefore, his subjects probably expected that it would be another case of "like father, like son." Whether a man's character is shaped by nature or nurture, Asa was an unlikely candidate for godliness. His birth seems to have been the result of an incestuous relationship,[2] for Maacah was both Abijam's mother and the woman who gave birth to Abijam's son (see 1 Kings 15:2, 9–10). According to Old Testament law, this was a sin against God, an abomination that was punishable by death (see Lev. 18:7, 29; 20:11).

It would be easy to think that Asa would never amount to anything. Sometimes we are tempted to think the same way about ourselves, or about our children—that given our past, anything we do for God will be very limited. Yet Asa turned out to be one of the few good kings of Judah. According to Kings, "Asa did what was right in the eyes of the LORD, as David his father had done. He put away the male cult prostitutes out of the land and removed all the idols that his fathers had made" (1 Kings 15:11–12).

In other words, Asa was a spiritual success in exactly the areas where his father and grandfather had failed. Rehoboam had introduced many pagan practices into Judah's worship: goddess worship, ritual prostitution, and the like. Rehoboam's son Abijam repeated the sins of his father. But Asa was a reformer. Like his great-grandfather David, he had a heart for the worship of the one true God. Therefore, Asa put an end to the worship of false deities and the depraved practices of Canaanite religion. Asa brought spiritual reformation to the people of God.

The only explanation for this surprising turn of events is the grace of God. God did not abandon this family to their sins, but raised a generation that was faithful to him.

This gives us hope for the gracious work of God in our own lives and families. Humanly speaking, we may not seem very promising. Sometimes we fear that we are doomed to repeat the sins of our fathers and mothers, or that our children may not have the heart for God that they need to make a difference in the world for Christ. But the God of Asa is a God of gracious intervention who has the power to bring new spiritual life. He is the God of the empty tomb, who raised Jesus from the grave. Now the rising power of Christ is available to everyone who believes: the power to heal, the power to save, the power to transform.

2. See Iain W. Provan, *1 and 2 Kings*, New International Biblical Commentary (Peabody, MA: Hendrickson, 1995), 126.

Knowing God's saving power encourages us to pray for grace, both for ourselves and for our children. We pray for hearts totally devoted to worship God alone. At a time when most people say that many gods are really the same god, we hold on to the biblical truth that there is only one God, in three persons: the loving Father, the saving Son, and the sanctifying Spirit. Even if we cannot eliminate every form of false religion, at least we can bear witness to the one true God.

We also pray for an end to idolatry, so that like Asa, we can tear down anything that would lead us away from the love of God. What is standing in the way of complete obedience to God, either for us or for our children? Whether it is a craving for some pleasure, or the love of an earthly possession, or the selfish demand to have life work out the way we want it, we are all tempted to love something other than God. But God is in the business of idol removal. He has the power to break down the gods our families have worshiped, freeing us to offer our lives in service to him.

A good example of this kind of freedom comes from the life of Mary Bosanquet. Mary came from a wealthy English family. She was born in a beautiful house and grew up wearing fine clothing and sparkling jewels. When she was still a young woman, Mary gave her heart to Jesus. Her father was so incensed that he disinherited her. But by the grace of God, the bondage of greed had now been broken in Mary's life. She took what little she had and moved into a two-room house with borrowed furniture. It is said that Mary's story inspired Henry Lyte to write this famous hymn:

> Jesus, I my cross have taken, all to leave and follow Thee.
> Destitute, despised, forsaken, Thou from hence my all shall be.
> Perish every fond ambition, all I've sought or hoped or known.
> Yet how rich is my condition! God and Heaven are still mine own.[3]

COSTLY DISCIPLESHIP

Leaving every idol behind to worship Jesus can be very costly. Jesus spoke plainly about this with his disciples: "If anyone comes to me and does not hate his own father and mother and wife and children and brothers

---

3. This story is recounted in Robert K. Brown and Mark R. Norton, eds., *The One Year Great Songs of Faith* (Wheaton, IL: Tyndale, 1995), 44.

and sisters, yes, and even his own life, he cannot be my disciple. Whoever does not bear his own cross and come after me cannot be my disciple" (Luke 14:26–27). Then Jesus went on to say, "Any one of you who does not renounce all that he has cannot be my disciple" (Luke 14:33).

We must count the cost of total discipleship. King Asa not only counted that cost, but also paid its price. His decision to follow God shows us the cost of discipleship in two areas: personal relationships and financial stewardship.

Part of the price that Asa paid was in his family relationships, for in addition to tearing down pagan idols, "he also removed Maacah his mother from being queen mother because she had made an abominable image for Asherah. And Asa cut down her image and burned it at the brook Kidron" (1 Kings 15:13).

The queen mother had a prominent cultural and political role in ancient society. In many cases, her power was second only to that of the king. As the leading figure in the royal harem, she held spiritual influence over both the royal household and the surrounding public.[4] In this particular case, the queen mother was leading people in the worship of pagan deities. Asa's mother Maacah had erected an image to Asherah—the vulgar Canaanite sex goddess who consorted with the storm god Baal.

Asa must have been under tremendous personal and public pressure to let this sin go unpunished. Doubtless his mother would be highly offended at a direct attack on her ungodly religion. How could the king do such a thing to his own mother? Yet Asa honored God by tearing down her idol and burning it to ashes.

We need to be careful how we follow Asa's example. When some people come to faith in Christ, they are so excited about what God has done that immediately they start setting people straight, especially within their own families. Often they are so obnoxious that it takes a long time to undo the damage. Nobody likes a spiritual know-it-all. Rather than telling people everything that is wrong with their religion, therefore, sometimes it is better to start loving them with the love of Jesus and then to wait for the Holy Spirit to give us the opportunity to share our faith.

Recognize Asa's unique position. He was the king, and therefore he had the God-given responsibility to establish Judah's religion. Before we destroy

4. August H. Konkel, *1 & 2 Kings*, NIV Application Commentary (Grand Rapids: Zondervan, 2006), 268.

anyone's property, or command people to stop worshiping false gods, we had better make sure that God has given us the spiritual authority to do so. Children rarely have this kind of authority over their parents; Asa was an exception because God had made him the king.

Yet as long as we heed these cautions, we should follow Asa's example in putting our commitment to God ahead of personal relationships, not letting family and friends get in the way of our commitment to Christ. There will be times when our love for Jesus will cost us something in our closest relationships. We may be called to serve Christ in a far country, over the objections of our parents or children. We may have to refuse to endorse someone's sexual lifestyle. We may need to decline to participate in a worship practice that is dishonoring to Christ. We may end up facing ridicule at school or at work because of what we do or decide not to do out of loyalty to Christ.

The cost is different for every Christian, and some of the hard choices we face may be matters of personal conscience. But the principle is the same for every disciple: Jesus always comes first, even at the cost of a relationship.

A dramatic example of costly discipleship comes from the life of Donald Smarto, who formerly served as the director of the Institute for Prison Ministries at the Billy Graham Center in Wheaton, Illinois. When Smarto gave his life to Christ, this set him at odds with his family, which was heavily involved in organized crime. In the 1980s his two older brothers were accused of committing the largest bank robbery in U.S. history. Although Smarto did not know the details of what they had done, he was subpoenaed to testify at their public trial. He was asked if his brothers had ever offered him a large sum of money to pay for medical bills. Smarto answered truthfully: they had offered him $50,000. As a result of this testimony, the rest of his family vowed that they would never speak to him again. To show that he was dead to them, they sent him a package returning every gift that he had ever given to them.

In his spiritual autobiography, Smarto writes, "I still love each of my family members deeply, and fervently hope that they will be saved. . . . Many times in the years that followed, I've asked myself if given the same set of circumstances, I would testify again. The answer would be yes." Then Smarto explains why:

> When I entered a personal relationship with Jesus, I had no idea what the ramifications were. I wouldn't have wanted to know that it could lead to sepa-

ration from my own family. . . . I think now I understand better the meaning of taking up your cross. I had always wanted the cross to be something more manageable, something that I was willing to take on. In my own life, the cross has proven to be precisely what I did not want, often what would hurt the most.[5]

In addition to the cost of taking up our cross, there is another price we pay to follow Jesus—the price we pay in our financial stewardship. As one part of our commitment to Christ, we give regular tithes and special offerings to the work of his kingdom. Here again, Asa sets a good example: "he brought into the house of the LORD the sacred gifts of his father and his own sacred gifts, silver, and gold, and vessels" (1 Kings 15:15).

Remember that Asa's grandfather Rehoboam had suffered the loss of great treasure. In judgment for his idolatrous sins, God had sent Shishak from Egypt to plunder the treasuries of Jerusalem (see 1 Kings 14:25–26). But King Asa took the gold of his father Abijam and brought it back into the temple for the public worship of God. Then he added his own costly gifts of silver and gold. By offering his treasure to the Lord, Asa was able to restore the temple's tarnished image.

Giving money may not be the most important way to serve God, but its spiritual significance should not be underestimated, either. Of course it is possible to give money to God without ever giving one's heart. In fact, this is one of the reasons why the church needed to be reformed at the time of Edward VI. Many people were still giving money to the church in order to get something from God, like a shorter time in purgatory, for example. Some people give money to God for similar reasons today: they like to think that they are doing something for God, and that in return God will do something for them. Such giving does not have God's blessing because God cannot be bribed.

When they are given for the right reason, however, costly gifts to kingdom work are a clear sign of healthy discipleship. Making financial sacrifices to support the preaching of the gospel is one of the best ways to knock down the idol of materialism. It also shows that we understand and appreciate what God has done for us in Jesus Christ. We do not give to get something from God, but because he has given everything to us—not just our money, but the

5. Donald Smarto, *Pursued: A True Story of Crime, Faith and Family* (Downers Grove, IL: InterVarsity, 1990), 196.

401

salvation of our souls through the death and resurrection of Jesus. Giving money to God is an act of our worship, a way of indicating that we are giving our whole selves to God. For these and many other reasons, costly giving is one of the leading indicators of true Christian discipleship.

Whenever we give, we are following in the footsteps of King Asa. More importantly, we are giving thanks to King Jesus, who gave his life for us. As we grow in our love for him, we are called to make more and more costly sacrifices to share the good news of his grace.

Earlier I mentioned the story of Mary Bosanquet, who gave up her inherited wealth to follow Jesus. Even in her poverty, Mary continued to make costly sacrifices for kingdom work. "Give all you can," she heard John Wesley say in one of his sermons, and that is exactly what Mary did. She opened her home to people in need, becoming one of the first deaconesses in the Methodist church. Later, when God provided a larger home for her to live in, she converted it into a school, an orphanage, a hospital, and a halfway house, all in one.[6] Mary's life shows us the cost of Christian discipleship: do not stop giving, but keep offering up more and more for Jesus.

Spiritual Compromise

The Bible commends King Asa for paying the price to bring reformation to the people of God. Yet we should not imagine that Asa was the perfect king. The Bible frankly admits several of his failings, and when we see them, they may well remind us of some of our own spiritual struggles.

Although it is true that Asa ended idolatry, he did not insist that everyone should go to Jerusalem for public worship, as God had commanded. Instead, it says in verse 14 that "the high places were not taken away." When the Holy Spirit came, he would enable people to worship God everywhere in spirit and truth (see John 4:23–24). But until that time, the temple at Jerusalem was set apart as the one place on earth that God had established for right and proper worship. Asa's failure to take down the other high places left his reformation incomplete. Even if people served God at those places, instead of serving idols, they were not worshiping God at the place that was pleasing to him. Asa was not totally true in worship.

6. For more details of Bosanquet's life and ministry, see W. B. Daniel, *The Illustrated History of Methodism in Great Britain, America, and Australia* (New York: Methodist Book Concern, 1884), 292–95.

The king also failed to honor God fully in his political relationships. We see this in the great conflict of his kingship—his ongoing civil war with the northern kingdom. According to verse 16 and also verse 32, "there was war between Asa and Baasha king of Israel all their days." This was not surprising. Rehoboam and Jeroboam had divided the kingdom between ten tribes in the north (Israel) and two tribes in the south (Judah), setting their descendants at war and making the glory of Solomon's peaceable kingdom little more than a distant memory.

Baasha, who became the king of Israel after Jeroboam (see 1 Kings 15:33ff.), posed a dire threat to Asa and the southern kingdom. He "went up against Judah and built Ramah, that he might permit no one to go out or come in to Asa king of Judah" (1 Kings 15:17). In effect, Baasha was building a blockade. Ramah was only a few miles north of Jerusalem, so by building a city there, Baasha was preventing goods and supplies from flowing into Jerusalem.

From the political perspective, Asa's way of dealing with this threat must have seemed wise. Since Israel was bigger than Judah, it was only natural for Asa to think that he needed some allies. So he shrewdly negotiated a deal with the Syrians:

> Then Asa took all the silver and the gold that were left in the treasuries of the house of the Lord and the treasures of the king's house and gave them into the hands of his servants. And King Asa sent them to Ben-hadad the son of Tabrimmon, the son of Hezion, king of Syria, who lived in Damascus, saying, "Let there be a covenant between me and you, as there was between my father and your father. Behold, I am sending to you a present of silver and gold. Go, break your covenant with Baasha king of Israel, that he may withdraw from me." (1 Kings 15:18–19)

Many people would approve of what Asa did. "All's fair in love and war," they would say. In this case, Asa used his political acumen to find a diplomatic solution to a military threat. Admittedly, this was very expensive. To come up with all the cash he needed to solidify this strategic alliance, Asa ended up "plundering his own treasury."[7] But at least his strategy worked. Ben-hadad took the money and "listened to King Asa and sent the commanders of his armies against the cities of Israel and conquered Ijon,

---

7. Peter Leithart, *1 & 2 Kings*, Brazos Theological Commentary on the Bible (Grand Rapids: Brazos, 2006), 115.

403

Dan, Abel-beth-maacah, and all Chinneroth, with all the land of Naphtali" (1 Kings 15:20).

Soon Syria's attacks on the northern kingdom had their desired effect, for "when Baasha heard of it, he stopped building Ramah, and he lived in Tirzah" (1 Kings 15:21). Baasha's retreat had the further benefit of allowing Judah to take building materials from Ramah and use them to build up their own cities: "Then King Asa made a proclamation to all Judah, none was exempt, and they carried away the stones of Ramah and its timber, with which Baasha had been building, and with them King Asa built Geba of Benjamin and Mizpah" (1 Kings 15:22). Now Judah was stronger than ever—a triumph of international diplomacy.

Or was it? In order to buy the favor of the Syrians, Asa had plundered silver and gold from the house of his God. Then he used this stolen treasure to persuade the king of Syria to break covenant with Israel. So instead of trusting the Lord for protection, Asa had resorted to bribery, theft, and deception. It was all because he acted out of fear for his enemies rather than faith in his God.

This is a temptation for all of us. When the pressure is on, and trouble comes, it is easy to turn to our own resources rather than to trust entirely in the grace of God. Rather than praying for God to provide for our needs, we are tempted to find some sneaky way to steal from someone else—from the government, from our employer, or even from our own family. Rather than asking God to help us do our own best work, we are tempted to cheat in school. Rather than trusting God with our reputation, we are tempted to make ourselves look better than we really are. Like Asa, we do things our way rather than God's way.

The consequences of spiritual compromise are always disastrous, as they were for Asa. Rather than receiving tribute from Gentile kings, like his father Solomon, Asa ended up giving his own treasure away to the Syrians. The king of Syria proceeded to attack Israel and claim part of its territory for himself (see 1 Kings 15:20), which meant—very ironically—that Asa ended up funding the hostile takeover of part of the Promised Land.

This all took place because Asa trusted his own resources rather than believing in the promises of God. According to Chronicles, when Asa made his foolish bargain with the Syrians, a prophet came to condemn him for relying on the king of Syria rather than the King of kings (2 Chron. 16:7).

"For the eyes of the LORD run to and fro throughout the whole earth," the prophet said, "to give strong support to those whose heart is blameless toward him. You have done foolishly in this, for from now on you will have wars" (2 Chron. 16:9). And so he did. From this time forward, the Syrians were a constant threat to Asa and his kingdom.

ASA'S END

The book of Kings ends its account of Asa's kingship with the following summary:

> Now the rest of all the acts of Asa, all his might, and all that he did, and the cities that he built, are they not written in the Book of the Chronicles of the Kings of Judah? But in his old age he was diseased in his feet. And Asa slept with his fathers and was buried with his fathers in the city of David his father, and Jehoshaphat his son reigned in his place. (1 Kings 15:23–24)

After the king's death, we are left to evaluate his life. Usually we see things in black and white, but this is hard to do with Asa. The king had a long and prosperous reign, during which—against all expectation—he brought reformation to Judah's worship. He made a costly commitment to God, sacrificing his own peace and prosperity to advance the kingdom.

Yet Asa was also guilty of tragic spiritual compromise. This is "why we find the Bible so disturbing," writes Dale Ralph Davis, because "it tells us that success is no authentication of fidelity. Circumstantial success and covenantal failure can exist side-by-side."[8] Was Asa a hero or a villain, a saint or a sinner? It is impossible to put him in only one category. He wanted to follow God, and sometimes he did, but he also made spiritual compromises that went against everything his heavenly kingdom stood for. In other words, Asa was a lot like us: called to be a saint, but still struggling as a sinner.

So how shall we evaluate this man's life? One way is to say that Asa shows us our need for a more perfect king to be our Savior. As the story ends, we are still waiting for a king to bring full and final reformation to the people of God. Asa was an early reformer. Later there will be even better kings,

---

8. Dale Ralph Davis, *The Wisdom and the Folly: An Exposition of the Book of First Kings* (Fearn, Ross-shire: Christian Focus, 2002), 177.

like Joash, who repaired the temple (2 Kings 12), and Hezekiah, who finally removed the high places (see 2 Kings 18:4). But even those kings had their flaws. The only perfect King is Jesus Christ. He alone has the power to break down all our sinful idolatries, help us pay the price of costly discipleship, and protect us from every soul-destroying compromise. Like the rest of Israel's kings, Asa teaches us to put our trust in Christ.

There is another way to evaluate the man's life, however, and that is to point out that even for all his failures, Asa was accepted by God to the end of his life. Verse 11 compares him favorably with King David—the royal standard for righteousness. Asa was a king after David's heart, which is really another way of saying that he was a man after God's own heart. Verse 14 gives him this high commendation: "Nevertheless, the heart of Asa was wholly true to the LORD all his days."

What hope this verse gives to anyone who wants to live for God but continues to struggle with remaining sin! Asa was accepted by God, which is a clear testimony that sinners are saved by grace. Although the king was far from perfect, God regarded his heart as true. Recognizing that Asa's faith was sincere, that his desire to serve was genuine, God accepted him as he was—not on the basis of perfect merit, but by his own forgiving grace.

This is the only hope that anyone has. Our salvation does not depend on our service for God, but on his grace in accepting us as we are, through the perfect kingship and atoning death of Jesus Christ. A true heart is a heart that trusts in the forgiveness that God offers to us in Jesus Christ. We cannot deny our sin. Nevertheless, our Savior can give us hearts that are true to him all our days, so that afterward, when we are laid to rest, we will be gathered to Asa and all our other spiritual fathers in the eternal city of David's Son.

32

THE SINS OF THE FATHERS

1 Kings 15:25—16:7

Nadab the son of Jeroboam began to reign over Israel in the second year of Asa king of Judah, and he reigned over Israel two years. He did what was evil in the sight of the LORD and walked in the way of his father, and in his sin which he made Israel to sin.
(1 Kings 15:25–26)

eople do not read about the Ten Commandments as often as they used to, but if they did, they might be terrified to hear what these commandments say. When I talk about terror, I am not referring to the voice of God, which thundered from the mountain. Nor am I referring to the difficulty we have in keeping God's law in all its perfection, which is terrifying, too. I refer instead to the dreadful judgment God pronounced against anyone who breaks the second commandment by worshiping idols. "You shall not bow down to them or serve them," he said, "for I the LORD your God am a jealous God, visiting the iniquity of the fathers on the children to the third and the fourth generation of those who hate me" (Ex. 20:5).

Some scholars have seen this warning simply as a description of the way things run in the family. Because children always imitate their parents, the sins of the fathers become the sins of their children. But others see the commandment as containing a divine curse: when God judges us for our sins, the consequences last for generations, especially when generation after generation is filled with hatred for God.

We see this curse worked out in the lives of the kings who followed Jeroboam on the throne of Israel. The sins of the fathers became the sins of the sons. As we witness this intergenerational idolatry, the story of these kings stands as a warning to us. We too are living at a time when people worship money, sex, power, and many other selfish gods. Though the United States of America and other modern nations are not in covenant with God the way that Israel was, we still stand under the judgment of God. Like James Dobson, we may wonder "how a God of justice can bless and preserve a nation in which murder is its centerpiece and sexual immorality its pastime. History teaches that the Holy One of Israel cannot and will not withhold judgment from those who flaunt the moral code of the universe. I don't know how or when His wrath will befall those who wallow in evil, but Scripture assures us that it will come."[1]

Maybe God's wrath has come already, as we suffer warfare, terrorism, storms, floods, hunger, economic hardship, and moral confusion. What will it take for God to bring us back to him? Will we listen to the word of judgment he speaks to us today? The sad story of Jeroboam's descendants calls us all to repentance.

Living in Sin instead of Righteousness

Most people find it hard to keep track of all the kings of Israel. What makes it doubly difficult is that after Solomon the kingdom was divided in two, with ten tribes in the north and two tribes in the south. So there are two sets of kings to remember: the kings of Israel in the north and Judah in the south. Yet there is one simple rule to help us remember which kings were bad and which kings were good: all the kings of the northern kingdom rebelled against the righteous worship of God. Not one of them was good; all of them walked in the sins of Jeroboam, from here to the end of Kings.

Reading about these rulers proves the apostle Paul's sad description of life without Christ. He said that such people are "without hope and without God

---

1. James Dobson, *Family News from Dr. James Dobson*, January 1998, 9.

in the world" (Eph. 2:12 NIV). The northern kings show us what happens to a person, a family, or a society that turns its back on God. Their bad example invites us to choose whether we want to live with Christ or without him.

So consider Nadab and Baasha, and notice two things about the way they lived. First, *they lived in sin instead of living for righteousness*. Thus the Bible says, "Nadab the son of Jeroboam began to reign over Israel in the second year of Asa king of Judah, and he reigned over Israel two years. He did what was evil in the sight of the LORD and walked in the way of his father, and in his sin which he made Israel to sin" (1 Kings 15:25–26).

By way of reminder, Nadab's father was Jeroboam, the first king of the northern kingdom. After the death of Solomon, the Lord took ten tribes away from the house of David and gave them to Jeroboam, with the promise that if he walked in God's ways, he would have God's blessing (1 Kings 11:28–38). But Jeroboam chose to walk his own way instead, by setting up golden calves and practicing pagan idolatry (1 Kings 12:25–33). Now Nadab was following in Jeroboam's footsteps—like father, like son. His evil ways led other people into sin.

What the Bible says about the next king is virtually identical: "In the third year of Asa king of Judah, Baasha the son of Ahijah began to reign over all Israel at Tirzah, and he reigned twenty-four years. He did what was evil in the sight of the LORD and walked in the way of Jeroboam and in his sin which he made Israel to sin" (1 Kings 15:33–34). It was the same old, same old. Baasha committed the same sins as Nadab, walking down the same road to perdition.

This is the way things usually go in a fallen world, where the sins of the fathers become the sins of the sons. One generation passes, another rises, but people still commit the same old sins. We see this in the city. Generation after generation, the business district is characterized by greedy idolatry, with little concern for the poor and broken streets of the city. Ethnic neighborhoods are charged with racial animosity. Even when the population changes, the prejudice remains. We see the same thing in the home, where evil patterns of sexual sin and domestic violence last for generations, or where subtler sins like pride and laziness seem to run in the family.

Everywhere we look, we see people living in sin rather than righteousness, and we wonder how or when or if the cycle will ever be broken. Maybe we see the same thing when we look in the mirror. No matter how much we want to be part of the solution, we are still part of the problem. Have our actions been righteous? Have our words been wholesome? Have our thoughts been full of humility and love?

LIVING BY POWER INSTEAD OF PROMISES

Notice something else about the way these kings lived: *they lived by power instead of promises*—their own power rather than the promises of God.

In former days, the true kings of Israel were appointed by the will and purpose of God. They took the throne by the royal promise that God made to King David (2 Sam. 7:1–17). We saw an example of this back in 1 Kings 1, when Adonijah tried to make himself the king. He found himself rejected in favor of Solomon, who did not rule by his own power, but patiently waited for God to fulfill his promise to put him on the throne. Solomon was just like his father David, who refused to harm King Saul, but believed that the God who anointed him could also be trusted to put him on the throne. We see the same pattern in the life of Jesus Christ, who humbled himself unto death and then waited for his Father to keep his promise to raise him from the dead and exalt him to the right hand of God (see Phil. 2:5–11). The true king takes the throne by the promise of God.

Not so with Nadab and Baasha. Nadab ruled for only a couple of years before Baasha struck him down. It happened while he was on the attack: "Baasha the son of Ahijah, of the house of Issachar, conspired against him. And Baasha struck him down at Gibbethon, which belonged to the Philistines, for Nadab and all Israel were laying siege to Gibbethon. So Baasha killed him in the third year of Asa king of Judah and reigned in his place" (1 Kings 15:27–28). In short, Nadab was assassinated.

Baasha did not stop there, but "as soon as he was king, he killed all the house of Jeroboam. He left to the house of Jeroboam not one that breathed, until he had destroyed it" (1 Kings 15:29). This was common practice in those days. When a rival claimed the throne, he murdered every member of the old king's family. When a man is not living by the promises of God, he has to do whatever he can to gain control, even if it means going on a bloody rampage. Rather than waiting for God to lift him up, he has to pull himself up by the laces of his own war boots.

Baasha lived by his own power rather than the promises of God. As a result, he spent the rest of his kingship locked in an endless military power struggle with the southern kingdom: "And there was war between Asa and Baasha king of Israel all their days" (1 Kings 15:32). Rather than depending on God to protect a kingdom that was rightfully his, Baasha had to fight with all his might to keep his throne.

This is what happens when we live by our own power rather than God's promises. Without God's help, it is up to us to hold on to what we have, so we have to fight to keep it. This leads to conflict in every human relationship: sibling rivalry, wrongful divorce, bitter infighting in the church, gang violence in the city, ruthless takeovers in business, war between nations. With every conflict, we wonder when or how or if the cycle will ever be broken.

If we are honest, we have to admit that we are often tempted to live the same way: by our own power instead of God's promise. We worry about our life and health rather than trusting God's promise to ordain the number of our days. We strive for recognition, trying to make sure that people notice who we are and what we have done, rather than trusting God's promise to lift us up. We get anxious about our job situation instead of trusting God's promise to provide. We insist on having our own way at home, rather than sacrificing for others and then giving space for God to work. Even in ministry we serve God by our own ability, rather than coming to God with our weakness and asking him to keep his promise to use our feeble efforts for his glory.

This is not to say, of course, that we should never go to the doctor, or look hard for a job, or prepare well to serve God in ministry. But there is a world of spiritual difference between doing everything in our own strength and resting on the perfect promises of God. In his little pamphlet *Directions for Renewing Our Covenant with God*, John Wesley wrote, "Christ has many services to be done. Some are easy, others are difficult. Some bring honor, others bring reproach. Some are suitable to our natural inclinations and temporal interests, others are contrary to both. Yet the power to do all these things is given to us in Christ, who strengthens us."[2] This is the promise of God: "I can do all things through him who strengthens me" (Phil. 4:13).

---

2. John Wesley, *Directions for Renewing Our Covenant with God*, 2nd ed. (London: J. Paramore, 1781).

THE WORD OF JUDGMENT

Nadab and Baasha did not live by the power of God's promise, but by the strength of their own ambitions. They gave little thought to what God might say about their wicked ways, their ungodly worship, or their murderous violence. Many people operate the same way today. Most of the time they ignore God completely. If they think about him at all, it is only to doubt his Word or to deny that he has any influence on the world today.

Sometimes we are tempted to have the same doubts, especially when we see how much evil there is in this broken world. Where is God when fathers abandon their children and people get shot in the street? Sometimes it is tempting to doubt that justice will ever be done and to think instead that sin will continue from father to son forever.

The Bible answers these doubts in the story of Nadab and Baasha. These evil men had rejected God to go their own sinful way, but God still had something to say to them: a word of judgment that showed that they were still under his authority. This is important to remember whenever evil seems to triumph. Do not be discouraged. God still has something to say. Because he is sovereign, writes Dale Ralph Davis, "no moment in history, however given to evil, will find him in absentia."[3] God is not on the side of evil, but always speaks against it in righteous anger. His word still rules; his will continues to dictate; sin will come to judgment.

This was certainly true for Nadab with respect to his sin. The king's assassination was not a random act of violence, but the fulfillment of God's judgment. After telling how the house of Jeroboam was put to the sword, the Bible makes an important comment. It says that the death of Nadab was "according to the word of the LORD that he spoke by his servant Ahijah the Shilonite. It was for the sins of Jeroboam that he sinned and that he made Israel to sin, and because of the anger to which he provoked the LORD, the God of Israel" (1 Kings 15:29–30).

In his younger days, Ahijah had promised Jeroboam a kingdom (1 Kings 11:28–38). But when he was old and blind, Ahijah prophesied the death of Jeroboam's son (1 Kings 14:4–16). More specifically, the prophet said that every member of his dynasty would die by the sword, with their bodies left

3. Dale Ralph Davis, *The Wisdom and the Folly: An Exposition of the Book of First Kings* (Fearn, Ross-shire: Christian Focus, 2002), 179.

for scavengers (1 Kings 14:10–11). These prophecies all came true when Baasha assassinated Nadab and the rest of the royal family. After he died, the king's epitaph read: "Now the rest of the acts of Nadab and all that he did, are they not written in the Book of the Chronicles of the Kings of Israel?" (1 Kings 15:31). There is no indication that Nadab ever turned to God in repentance and faith, and so he fell under the judgment of his father's sin.

Not that Baasha was any more righteous than Nadab. The sovereign God often uses evil men to accomplish his righteous purpose, as he did in the case of Baasha. God is not the author of evil, so evil men still have to answer for their wickedness. "This is basic biblical theology," writes Dale Ralph Davis: "Yahweh uses evil men to punish other evil men and later judges the evil instruments he used for their own evil." Thus it is possible to "inflict God's judgment and in so doing incur God's judgment."[4] So after Baasha assassinated Nadab, God sent him a message of judgment:

> And the word of the LORD came to Jehu the son of Hanani against Baasha, saying, "Since I exalted you out of the dust and made you leader over my people Israel, and you have walked in the way of Jeroboam and have made my people Israel to sin, provoking me to anger with their sins, behold, I will utterly sweep away Baasha and his house, and I will make your house like the house of Jeroboam son of Nebat. Anyone belonging to Baasha who dies in the city the dogs shall eat, and anyone of his who dies in the field the birds of the heavens shall eat." (1 Kings 16:1–4)

After this terrible prophecy, the Bible proceeds immediately to give Baasha's obituary, without any obvious hope of salvation: "Now the rest of the acts of Baasha and what he did, and his might, are they not written in the Book of the Chronicles of the Kings of Israel? And Baasha slept with his fathers and was buried at Tirzah, and Elah his son reigned in his place" (1 Kings 16:5–6).

Thus Baasha's family came to a bad end, as the sins of the father were visited on his sons, who would not even receive the honor of a decent burial. In case there is any doubt as to why his family was punished this way, the Bible gives two reasons for the justice of God. Why was it that "the word of the LORD came by the prophet Jehu the son of Hanani against Baasha and

4. Ibid., 180, 185.

413

his house"? It was "both because of all the evil that he did in the sight of the LORD, provoking him to anger with the work of his hands, in being like the house of Jeroboam, and also because he destroyed it" (1 Kings 16:7). God held Baasha responsible for his sin, judging him both for his pagan idolatry and for his murderous violence. Dust he was, and to the dust he returned, swept away by the wrath of God.

THE FINAL JUDGMENT

What makes this especially sad is that things did not have to end this way. The prophet said that God had allowed Baasha to serve as king, raising him up from the dust of earth to the throne of his people. Whatever place we have in this world is a gift from God, and Baasha's place was the throne of Israel. God had done great things for him, giving him every opportunity to offer useful service to the kingdom. Yet Baasha took the sinful way of power rather than the righteous way of believing the promises of God. He chose to be an idolater rather than a worshiper, "a murderer, not a reformer."[5]

What will we do with the privileges and opportunities that God has given to us? Will we continue in sin, or turn to righteousness? Will we live by our own power or by the promises of God? And how will we respond when God speaks a word of judgment?

Responding to the word of God's judgment is as necessary today as it was for Nadab and Baasha. God still has something to say. He has a word of judgment that he speaks to the world—not by the prophet Jehu, but in the pages of Scripture and the preaching of his pastors. In righteous anger, God will bring an end to evil. The Bible says that even now his wrath "is revealed from heaven against all ungodliness and unrighteousness of men" (Rom. 1:18). The Bible calls Jesus Christ the Judge of the living and the dead (2 Tim. 4:1). It says that "we will all stand before the judgment seat of God" (Rom. 14:10), and that when Jesus comes again in glory, he will make an everlasting separation between those who belong to his kingdom and those who "go away into eternal punishment" (Matt. 25:46). Therefore, Jesus gives us this warning: "Do not fear those who kill the body but cannot kill the soul. Rather fear him who can destroy both soul and body in hell" (Matt. 10:28).

5. Paul R. House, *1, 2 Kings*, The New American Commentary (Nashville: Broadman & Holman, 1995), 200.

This is the word of judgment that God still speaks today. Most people would rather not hear it. Sometimes it is tempting not to preach it. Billy Graham faced this temptation early in his ministry as an evangelist, when he knew his audience would include Henry Luce, the famous publisher of *Time* and *Life* magazines. Billy said:

> I had already announced from the pulpit that I would be preaching on judgment and hell. The temptation came very strongly to me that maybe I should switch to another subject. Mr. Luce was a New York sophisticate. It seemed to me to be the least likely way to win his favor. Then, the Lord laid Jeremiah 1:17 on my heart. "Speak unto them all that I command thee: be not dismayed at their faces, lest I confound thee before them." It was as if he was saying to me, "If you pull your punches, I'll confound you. I'll make you look like a fool in front of men!"[6]

So Billy Graham continued to preach the word of God's judgment, as well as repentance for sin, faith in Christ for forgiveness, and eternal life through the cross and the empty tomb. We preach the same message today, starting with judgment. This is the message that all of us need to hear, whether we want to hear it or not.

In his commentary on 1 Kings, Matthew Henry said that God spoke judgment against Baasha for two very good reasons. First, he did it to turn Baasha away from his sin. As Henry stated it: "God threatens, that he may not strike, as one that desires not the death of sinners." When Jehu came to speak God's word of judgment, Baasha had a choice to make. Would he listen and repent (as King Jehoshaphat later did when he received a message from the very same prophet; see 2 Chron. 19), or would he ignore God and perish?

God gives us the same choice today. If we are wise, we will make a better choice than Baasha. God says, "I have no pleasure in the death of the wicked, but that the wicked turn from his way and live" (Ezek. 33:11). He also says that he "desires all people to be saved and to come to the knowledge of the truth" (1 Tim. 2:4). To that end, God warns us about the coming judgment. But he also says that whoever believes in his Son will not perish, but have everlasting life (John 3:16). This is one reason why God speaks a word of judgment: so we will see our sin clearly enough to repent and put our faith in Jesus.

6. *Billy Graham: God's Ambassador* (Minneapolis: Billy Graham Evangelistic Association, 1999), 58.

According to Matthew Henry, there is a second reason why God spoke against Baasha, and why he speaks against sin today. He does it so that when disaster strikes, as it surely will, everyone will know that it is the judgment of God. God could have simply judged the house of Baasha without ever announcing that this was his intention. But in that case no one would ever know for sure why the sons of Baasha died the way they did. God sent his prophet, Henry said, so people would know "that the destruction when it did come, whoever might be instruments of it, was the act of God's justice and the punishment of sin."[7]

Everyone will know the same thing at the final judgment. Then we will see God bring every wicked deed to justice—not just the sins of Nadab and Baasha and other evil men, but all the sins of ordinary sinners. On that dread day, we will know *why* God is visiting the sins of the fathers upon the sons. We will know this because he has spoken his word of judgment to the world, announcing that there is a heaven and there is a hell, and that what makes the difference is faith in Jesus Christ. People often want to criticize God for doing this or not doing that, but rather than criticizing his word of judgment, it is better for us simply to repent.

The German evangelist Wilhelm Busch was walking through the city of Essen one day when he met two miners standing on the pavement. One of the workmen said, "This is Pastor Busch! A nice fellow!" When Busch thanked him for this compliment, the man said, "Yes, a nice fellow, but he's crazy!" Naturally, the pastor wanted to know why the man thought he was crazy, so he asked for an explanation. The man said, "Pastor Busch! A nice fellow! Only, he never stops talking about Jesus."

As far as Busch was concerned, this was the best compliment of all. "My friend," he replied, "I'm not crazy. A hundred years from now, you will be in eternity. The only thing that will matter then will be whether or not you have known Jesus. That is what determines whether you will be in heaven or hell. Tell me, do you know Jesus?"[8]

What answer would you give to the pastor's question? Do you know Jesus or not? And what difference will it make a hundred years from now? It would

7. Matthew Henry, *Matthew Henry's Complete Commentary on the Whole Bible*, vol. 2, *Judges to Job* (New York: Fleming Revell, n.d.), n.p.

8. Wilhelm Busch, *Jesus Our Destiny*, trans. Doris Orrett Huser, 8th ed. (Basil, Switzerland: Brunnen Publishing, 2005), 10.

be nice to say that the miner listened to what Busch was saying and started to get serious about the state of his soul, but he didn't. No, he laughed it off as another one of the pastor's crazy questions. "You see," he said to his friend, "there he goes again!"

Maybe Wilhelm Busch *was* crazy. Maybe he was crazy to think that sin will come to judgment. Maybe he was crazy to believe in the pains of hell and the promise of heaven. Maybe he was crazy to say that Jesus died on the cross for sinners and that knowing Jesus makes an eternal difference. Maybe the man's gospel was crazy from beginning to end.

Then again, maybe Wilhelm Busch wasn't crazy at all, but spoke the truth of God. In that case, we would be crazy not to listen, crazy not to repent of our sins, and crazy not to ask Jesus to save us to live on through all the centuries of eternity.

33

THREE BAD KINGS

1 Kings 16:8–28

Omri did what was evil in the sight of the LORD, and did more evil than all who were before him. For he walked in all the way of Jeroboam the son of Nebat, and in the sins that he made Israel to sin, provoking the LORD, the God of Israel, to anger by their idols.
(1 Kings 16:25–26)

*I*n his book *The People of the Lie*, psychologist M. Scott Peck tells the story of Charlene, who came to him for counsel. In talking about religion, Charlene explained why she refused to consider Christianity. "There's no room for *me* in that," she said. "That would be my death! . . . I don't want to live for God. I will not. I want to live for . . . my own sake."[1]

In saying this, Charlene was assuming that living for God is less rewarding and less interesting than living for oneself. This is a common assumption. Rather than practicing self-denial, people pursue self-gratification. They go to godless parties. They satisfy their sexual curiosity. They get as much

---

1. M. Scott Peck, *The People of the Lie: The Hope for Healing Human Evil* (New York: Simon and Schuster, 1983), 168.

money to buy as many things as they can. As soon as they start to get bored with one thing, they move on to something else. Money, sex, power—sin always seems to offer something new.

By contrast, the life of Christian faith seems rather boring to many people. You go to church every week. You try to be nice to people. You have a long list of things that you still want to do but know you shouldn't, so usually you don't, and you spend most of your time with people who don't do those things either. Life may be good, but it isn't very exciting. This is the way many people view Christianity: more boring than the alternative.

One way to test these assumptions is to look at the life history of people who wanted to do something more interesting than to follow God. We meet some people like that in 1 Kings 16. Their names were Elah, Zimri, and Omri—three bad kings of the northern kingdom who followed Nadab and Baasha in repeating the sins of Jeroboam. Each man's story gives us an opportunity to consider what kind of life we want to live—whether it is more compelling and satisfying to live with God or without him.

THE DANGER OF STRONG DRINK

The next king after Baasha was Elah, whom the Bible introduces with the standard formula: "In the twenty-sixth year of Asa king of Judah, Elah the son of Baasha began to reign over Israel in Tirzah, and he reigned two years" (1 Kings 16:8). Then Elah was cut down by one of his rivals: "His servant Zimri, commander of half his chariots, conspired against him. When he was at Tirzah, drinking himself drunk in the house of Arza, who was over the household in Tirzah, Zimri came in and struck him down and killed him, in the twenty-seventh year of Asa king of Judah, and reigned in his place" (1 Kings 16:9–10).

What happened next is all too predictable. Just as Baasha destroyed the house of Nadab, so Zimri destroyed the house of Elah. In an act of Mafia-style violence, the commander eliminated any possibility of revenge by killing every member of Elah's family: "When he [Zimri] began to reign, as soon as he had seated himself on his throne, he struck down all the house of Baasha. He did not leave him a single male of his relatives or his friends" (1 Kings 16:11).

This was an evil deed by an evil man. Not content to eliminate Elah's family members, Zimri also killed the king's friends. This was wicked; nevertheless,

419

it was the fulfillment of a prophecy—another proof that God's word always comes true. Elah was the son of Baasha, and God had pronounced judgment against Baasha and his sons for worshiping other gods and leading people into the sin of idolatry: "Thus Zimri destroyed all the house of Baasha, according to the word of the LORD, which he spoke against Baasha by Jehu the prophet, for all the sins of Baasha and the sins of Elah his son, which they sinned and which they made Israel to sin, provoking the LORD God of Israel to anger with their idols" (1 Kings 16:12–13). The sins of the father were visited on his son, vindicating the word of God.

The Bible describes Elah's assassination as a conspiracy. Obviously, Zimri was the ringleader. Possibly Arza was in on the plot as well, since he was the one carousing with Elah when he died. Yet Elah was far from an innocent victim. It is apparent from verse 15 that his army was in Philistia at the time, laying its ongoing siege against the city of Gibbethon (see 1 Kings 15:27), trying to recapture land that Israel had won in the days of King David. This question arises: why wasn't Elah with his troops, leading them into battle? Instead, the king was in his cups.

This is partly a cautionary tale about the dangers of drinking. Elah died one of the most ignoble deaths in the Bible. Rather than dying on the field of battle, giving his blood to defend his country, his life ended in a drunken stupor. People probably said that Elah "really knew how to party," but today his dishonorable demise is a strong warning against the dangers of strong drink. The manner of Elah's death also gives us an opportunity to consider what the Bible says about alcohol.

To begin with, the Bible does not prohibit alcohol, but celebrates its proper use as a blessing from God. The fermentation of the fruit of the vine is nearly as old as the human race, going back at least as far as the time of Noah (see Gen. 10:20–21). In biblical times, the beverage of choice was wine (not grape juice), especially where water was hard to come by. The Bible praises wine as part of the earth's richness (Gen. 27:28), a gift from God (Hos. 2:8), something to drink "with a merry heart" (Eccl. 9:7). The absence of wine was a covenant curse (Deut. 28:39, 51), which implies that its abundance is a covenant blessing. Wine is such a blessing that the first miracle Jesus performed was wine for a wedding (John 2:1–11). At the end of his life, wine was one of the basic elements in the Last Supper that Jesus celebrated with his disciples. Wine is also a symbol of eternal glory. When the prophets foretold the new heavens and the new earth, they said that "in that day the mountains shall drip sweet wine" (Joel 3:18), and "the LORD of hosts will make for all peoples . . . a feast of well-aged wine" (Isa. 25:6). So from here to eternity, wine is a gift from God, a blessing of both the old and the new creation.

More needs to be said, however, because the Bible also warns against any and every abuse of alcohol. In the Old Testament, strong wine is not simply a sign of God's blessing, but also of his coming wrath (e.g., Jer. 25:15). In keeping with this imagery, the Bible condemns intoxication. There is joy in feasting "for strength," the Bible says, but "not for drunkenness" (Eccl. 10:17). "Wine is a mocker, strong drink a brawler, and whoever is led astray by it is not wise" (Prov. 20:1). Indeed, whoever is led astray by wine or strong drink will suffer a wide range of damaging physical and spiritual consequences, as the Proverbs also explain (Prov. 23:29–35).

In the New Testament, drunkenness is almost always included in the lists of ungodly behaviors that belong to the sinful nature (e.g., 1 Cor. 5:11; Gal. 5:21; 1 Peter 4:3). This is such an important spiritual issue that the apostle Paul draws a direct contrast between getting drunk and being filled with the Holy Spirit: "Do not get drunk with wine, for that is debauchery, but be filled with the Spirit" (Eph. 5:18). From what Ephesians goes on to say, it is evident that getting drunk gets in the way of singing God's praise, hearing God's Word, and loving God's people (see Eph. 5:19–21). Although we have freedom in the use of alcohol, its abuse quenches the Spirit.

All these warnings are especially important today, when the alcohol content of many drinks is much higher than in biblical times. Nor do these warnings apply only to alcohol: what people shoot, smoke, sniff, and snort can be every bit as foolish as what they drink. Any drug can lead to immorality, intoxication, and life-dominating dependence.

At this point, some Christians want a list of rules or guidelines to govern their relationship with alcohol. Yet the Bible does not address every situation in life directly, and this is one of the many areas where we have to exercise godly discernment, not just keep a list of rules. Nevertheless, there are some broad principles to remember, one or two prohibitions to obey, and some practical suggestions to follow.

The broad principles are to honor God in every choice we make and to love our neighbors as ourselves. So rather than simply asking, "Is this permissible?" we need to ask more important questions like, "Is this beneficial?" As far as absolute prohibitions are concerned, believers in Christ are forbidden to get drunk. We are also forbidden to look down on brothers and sisters who as a matter of conscience make different but God-honoring choices than we do about the use of alcohol.

Beyond these simple principles and prohibitions, there are also some practical suggestions it is wise to follow. If the Bible says not to get drunk, then we need to stop well before our judgment is impaired. We also need to be careful not to compromise our witness for Christ by making poor decisions about when and where and how much to drink. This means avoiding parties and other social situations where there is so much drinking that there is no real opportunity for the Holy Spirit to work.

If this is an area where we tend to err on the side of caution, we need to watch out for a judgmental spirit toward our brothers and sisters in Christ. On the other hand, if we enjoy celebrating our Christian liberties, we must not let our liberty turn into license. To that end, we need to make sure that any wine gladdening our hearts (Ps. 104:15) is a holy and God-centered pleasure, something that is received with true thanksgiving (1 Tim. 4:4). If alcohol has a controlling influence on us—or if people who love us say that it does—then we need to seek immediate spiritual help, as well as whatever medical help may be needed for dealing with our addiction. If other people think we have a problem, and we still do not think so, then this is a clear sign that our judgment is already impaired, especially if we are drinking often and alone.

In determining the proper use of alcohol, our perfect example is Jesus Christ, who was known to raise a glass with his disciples, but never lost the control of the Holy Spirit. As surprising as it may seem to some people, Jesus had a reputation for knowing how to have a good time (Luke 7:34). Yet he never allowed his enjoyment of the fruit of the vine to get in the way of serving other people or doing the work of God's kingdom. If we are wise, we will follow his example with joyful sobriety. If we find that we are unable to follow his example, then we need to seek the spiritual care of the church and. even more, to know the forgiveness and deliverance that God has for us in Jesus.

THE SIN OF SUICIDE

When last we met Zimri, life seemed to be going rather well for him. His conspiracy having worked to perfection, he was free to sit on Israel's throne. But unfortunately for Zimri, his kingship did not last very long: "In the twenty-seventh year of Asa king of Judah, Zimri reigned seven days in Tirzah" (1 Kings 16:15). This is not a typographical error. Zimri was overthrown only one week after he took the throne—the shortest reign in Israel's history. This reminds us how quickly things fall apart when we exalt ourselves rather than waiting patiently for God to put us where he wants us. Zimri's pride went before his fall. Those who live by the sword often die by the sword. So it was for Zimri—a violent man who came to a violent end.

Here is how the Bible tells the story of Zimri's end: "Now the troops were encamped against Gibbethon, which belonged to the Philistines, and the troops who were encamped heard it said, 'Zimri has conspired, and he has killed the king'" (1 Kings 16:15–16). As the news of the coup d'etat quickly spread, one man seized his chance for greatness. Zimri may have been crafty enough to plot an assassination, but he did not have the support of the military. So while he was busy sending Elah to an early grave, "all Israel made Omri, the commander of the army, king over Israel that day in the camp" (1 Kings 16:16). As far as Omri was concerned, one good coup deserves another. So he "went up from Gibbethon, and all Israel with him, and they besieged Tirzah" (1 Kings 16:17).

This set the stage for a dramatic scene at the palace of the northern kingdom. For "when Zimri saw that the city was taken, he went into the citadel of the king's house and burned the king's house over him with fire and died, because of his sins that he committed, doing evil in the sight of the LORD, walking in the way of Jeroboam, and for his sin which he committed, making Israel to sin" (1 Kings 16:18–19).

This too was an act of God's judgment. At the human level Zimri took his own life. But under the mighty will of a sovereign God, his death was also an act of divine judgment. Zimri was on the throne for only a single week, yet seven days were enough for him to follow in the footsteps of Jeroboam and sin against God. So the word of God ruled against him, and Zimri died in his sins.

How the mighty had fallen! One day Zimri was on top of the world. Enthroned by his own ambitions, he had taken what he wanted out of life. But just a few days later he died in absolute despair, going in one short week from murder to suicide.

Zimri's death is reminiscent of a dramatic scene near the climax of J. R. R. Tolkien's epic trilogy *The Lord of the Rings*. Lord Denethor, who serves as the Steward of Gondor, fears that his city will fall to its enemies and get burned to the ground. Despairing of all hope, he orders his servants to build a funeral pyre. Before anyone can stop him, he sets a torch to the bonfire and leaps into the flames, where he dies a fiery death. The bystanders turn away in horror, aghast at what Denethor has done.[2]

The death of Zimri was also a horror, but rather than simply turning away, we should see it as an opportunity to consider what we want out of life. Zimri had everything he wanted. He was the king of his universe. But since he went against God, his position was never secure. Sadly, his story is not unique. Many people spend their whole lives trying to reach the top, but never truly seeking after God. In the end, any success they have will prove to be fleeting. They will have to leave everything behind, as Zimri did, and like him they may well die in despair. Are we living for what lasts, or will it all turn to ashes?

Zimri's fiery death also gives us an opportunity to consider what the Bible teaches about suicide. Suicide is always a cause for great sadness, but what people often wonder is whether it is an unforgivable sin. It *is* a sin, of course, as every murder is. To commit suicide is to declare lordship over one's own life. It is to claim the right to number one's days—a right that belongs only to God. It is to betray the love of family and friends. It is to refuse to serve the kingdom of God. In short, suicide is a sin of self-murder.

We need to know this so that we recognize what is at stake whenever we or others are tempted to commit suicide. It is not a sin to be tempted to commit suicide (or to commit any other sin, for that matter). Sooner or later, nearly everyone entertains at least fleeting thoughts of ending their earthly existence, including some of the people we meet in the Bible. "What would happen if . . ." we wonder. But for some people, suicidal thoughts become a preoccupation. We should recognize these thoughts for what they are: a temptation that comes from hell itself. God does not want us to die, but to live, and to know the power of his grace to help us through all the troubles of life. While there is life, there is always hope in Jesus. So if we are ever tempted to take our own lives, we should fight that temptation with everything we

2. J. R. R. Tolkien, *The Return of the King* (New York: Ballantine, 1965), 155–59.

have. We should not fight it alone, however. Instead, we should talk about our struggle with a trusted friend or spiritual leader—someone who can care for us with the life-preserving love of God. The hope of Jesus can be found in the help of the church.

Granted that suicide is a sin, we still need to ask whether or not it is a forgivable sin. Some people think that it is not. After all, how can someone who dies in sin be saved? And how can people be forgiven for a sin when they do not have the chance to repent afterward?

The simple answer is that there is forgiveness for every sin through the cross of Jesus Christ. This is clear from everything else the Bible says about sin and forgiveness. The Bible assures us that there is forgiveness for big sins as well as all the little sins we commit every day. The blood of the Son of God is powerful enough to pay for any and every sin, including suicide. Furthermore, there is as much forgiveness for the sins we commit at the end of life as there is for the sins we commit at the beginning. The cross covers all our sins: past, present, and future— even the dying sin of suicide. This forgiveness is not only for sins we have explicitly confessed, but also for ones we leave unconfessed until the day we die. Otherwise, the cross would not be enough to save us; our salvation would always partly depend on our own ongoing repentance. We could never be sure of our salvation, because our souls would always hang in the balance, and if we died with even one unconfessed sin, we would be damned.

Praise God that there is forgiveness for all our sins in Jesus! Whatever reason we can come up with for doubting that suicide can be forgiven would really be a reason for doubting that any sin can be forgiven. There will always be some sins that seem too big or too late to be forgiven. There will always be some sins that we have never fully confessed. This is exactly why we need Jesus to save us. We have sinned ourselves beyond any possibility of our own redemption. Not even our repentance is perfect enough to save us. But Jesus offers us perfect salvation. All we need to do is ask him to forgive all our sins through the cross—not just the sins we have already committed, but all the sins we will commit from now until the day we die.

Having said that the sin of suicide can be forgiven in Christ, and having acknowledged that the temptation to commit suicide is not a sin in itself,

425

it remains a dreadful sin for us even to contemplate. Suicide is the most foolish long-term solution to short-term problems. It is an act of unbelief, a squandering of the stewardship of our precious lives, and a source of grievous wounds to loved ones left behind. May God preserve us from this sin!

The Epitome of Evil

There is one more king for us to consider, and he was the worst king of all. If Elah was a drunkard, and Zimri a murderer, then Omri was the epitome of evil. The fact that he followed Zimri in such rapid succession is an obvious sign that things were falling apart. Down in Judah, everything was peaceful, as wise King Asa continued to reign, decade after decade. But up in Israel there was a rapid succession of rulers.

Another sign of disarray is that the divided kingdom almost divided again. After Zimri died, "the people of Israel were divided into two parts. Half of the people followed Tibni the son of Ginath, to make him king, and half followed Omri" (1 Kings 16:21). The civil war between these rival factions lasted for several years, but Omri would not be denied his prize, and in the end "the people who followed Omri overcame the people who followed Tibni the son of Ginath. So Tibni died, and Omri became king. In the thirty-first year of Asa king of Judah, Omri began to reign over Israel, and he reigned for twelve years; six years he reigned in Tirzah" (1 Kings 16:22–23).

Humanly speaking, Omri was a great man. He was such a strong leader that he was anointed the next king by popular demand. After a time of political and military instability, he was able to unify his kingdom and establish relative peace with the southern kingdom. Omri was a political success.

Once he had consolidated his power, Omri launched a successful campaign to build a new capital city: "He bought the hill of Samaria from Shemer for two talents of silver, and he fortified the hill and called the name of the city that he built Samaria, after the name of Shemer, the owner of the hill" (1 Kings 16:24). Samaria was a city to rival the capital that David built—another "city on a hill" that was purchased from a private property owner (2 Sam. 24:18ff.). Situated in a strategic location, and commanding a wide view of the surrounding country, Samaria remained the grand capital of the northern kingdom until it was attacked by the Assyrians in 722 B.C.

Omri was a famous king—a man who made his mark on history. This is confirmed by documents from ancient Assyria, which refer to Israel as "the land of Omri."[3] His dynasty lasted for three generations.

Yet for all his earthly accomplishments, Omri was a spiritual failure. This is why the Bible says precious little about his success and a good deal more about his sin: "Omri did what was evil in the sight of the LORD, and did more evil than all who were before him. For he walked in all the way of Jeroboam the son of Nebat, and in the sins that he made Israel to sin, provoking the LORD, the God of Israel, to anger by their idols" (1 Kings 16:25–26).

The Bible has nothing good to say about Omri at all. He was even worse than Jeroboam, if such a thing were possible. In fact, to this point in history, he was the worst king that Israel ever had. This is the ways things often go in a fallen world, both personally and internationally. The northern kings were still following in the footsteps of Jeroboam, whose evil influence lasted for generations. Choices have consequences, and when it comes to sin and righteousness, things do not simply stay as they are. Apart from the grace of God, they generally go from bad to worse. We see this in the moral degeneration of our own times. The human race is incapable of its own moral improvement, as the twentieth century demonstrated so convincingly and comprehensively.

What should concern us more than the trends of history, though, is our own spiritual condition. What will our own lives or our families look like a generation from now if God does not intervene? Whatever else we may accomplish, God will look to see whether we have a heart for him. Earthly accomplishments have their place in life, and even the Bible acknowledges that Omri was a great builder. But God is most concerned with character and the direction of a person's heart. Dale Ralph Davis comments that here the biblical author "is not saying he is ignorant of Omri's achievements—he is saying they don't matter." Then Davis asks this question: "Do the passions that drive your living and doing only elicit a yawn from heaven?"[4]

---

3. See J. A. Montgomery and H. S. Gehman, *A Critical and Exegetical Commentary on the Book of Kings*, International Critical Commentary (1951; repr., Edinburgh: T&T Clark, 1986), 284–85.

4. Dale Ralph Davis, *The Wisdom and the Folly: An Exposition of the Book of First Kings* (Fearn, Ross-shire: Christian Focus, 2002), 193.

427

STOP THE BOREDOM!

To ask the same question a different way, are you living for anything that really matters? People who have a passion usually believe that their passion is the most important thing in the world. Some people are driven by their work, which is so consuming that it starts taking over their time for rest. Some people have a passion for a sport or hobby, anything from skydiving to needlepoint. Others have a passion for television or electronic entertainment. Some people have a passion for their own pleasure, whatever pleasure happens to be available at the moment. Then there are people who have the same passions as the kings in this chapter: a passion for drugs and alcohol, for power, or for building a reputation.

Every person has a different passion. Usually we depend on that passion to make life interesting. We hope that whatever we enjoy will save us from the boredom of our existence. So people give more and more of themselves over to their passions, until finally their lives are dominated by listening to a certain kind of music, or playing endless rounds of golf, or whatever it is that drives their living and their doing.

The reality is that living for anything other than the love of Jesus and the glory of God will leave us totally empty. Living for ourselves turns out to be more boring than living for God and loving other people. The Bible shows this in the tedious repetition of the kings of Israel. Each king takes the throne. Each king reigns for a little while, some longer than others. Then each king dies. After a while, the repetition becomes mind-numbing: "Now the rest of the acts of Elah and all that he did, are they not written in the Book of the Chronicles of the Kings of Israel?" (1 Kings 16:14). Whatever else Elah may have done, it was nothing praiseworthy or important enough to go in the Bible, nothing that advanced the kingdom or promoted the glory of God.

The Bible says almost exactly the same thing about Zimri: "Now the rest of the acts of Zimri, and the conspiracy that he made, are they not written in the Book of the Chronicles of the Kings of Israel?" (1 Kings 16:20). The same with Omri: "Now the rest of the acts of Omri that he did, and the might that he showed, are they not written in the Book of the Chronicles of the Kings of Israel? And Omri slept with his fathers and was buried in Samaria, and Ahab his son reigned in his place" (1 Kings 16:27–28). Each king enters and exits the same way. He took the throne, he sinned, he died.

Some people complain about all this boring repetition. Peter Leithart describes the way they feel when they read this part of Kings. It is "a school-child's nightmare," he says, "the kind of chronicle that evokes lifelong loathing of history. A king rises, a king reigns, a king sins, a king dies. His son rises, his son reigns, his son sins, and his son dies. Meaningless and confusing dates for indistinguishable kings, all told in a colorless and repetitive prose."[5]

But maybe this is part of the point. The stories of these bad kings show us the monotony of idolatry. "They are the records," writes Dale Ralph Davis, "of sinful men who simply repeat the sins and evil of those before them. Sin is never creative but merely imitative. . . . Goodness has an originality inherent in it which evil hasn't got. Evil can distort and ruin and corrupt and do re-runs, but it can't be original, nor even scintillating. Evil carries a built-in yawn."[6]

If we waste our lives worshiping idols, we will never escape the boredom. The trivial pursuit of money, sex, and power will turn out to be tedious. We see this principle at work in contemporary culture, where we have a greater variety of entertainment than anyone in history, yet we are more dissatisfied than ever. We see the effects perhaps most clearly in the lives of young people who just say "whatever" to life, but we also see it in the lives of old people who do not have anything left to live for at all.

The people who live the most interesting lives are the ones who live for God and not themselves. We see this in the stories of the Old Testament. The people who lived for God, including good and godly kings, had great adventures. They traveled to far countries. They were rescued from grave dangers. They witnessed miracles. They slew giants. They built kingdoms. Together they found life in God's word, joy in God's worship, and meaning in living for him.

We see the same thing in the life of Jesus Christ, which was anything but boring. Jesus was always having conversations with people about things that really mattered: not just the latest news, weather, and sports, but the kingdom of God and the life to come. He was always making a difference in people's lives by helping them and healing them. This is the passion that drove all his living and doing: to glorify God by serving others rather than serving

5. Peter Leithart, *1 & 2 Kings*, Brazos Theological Commentary on the Bible (Grand Rapids: Brazos, 2006), 110.

6. Davis, *The Wisdom and the Folly*, 181.

himself. Jesus pursued this passion all the way to the cross, where he gave his life for our sins before rising in joyful triumph.

What will you do with your life? What passion will drive your living and doing? Do not lead an ordinary life that never has any eternal significance. Instead, do more for God than ever before, and then discover what an adventure it is to live for him. Here are some ways to serve the Lord, none of them boring:

- Defeat the devil by fighting against the sin that is dragging you down.
- Do not give up on the trouble in your family, but pray it through and see what God will do.
- Make the daring and difficult choice about work or school—the choice that will grow your faith.
- Start a relationship with someone who needs a friend.
- Get involved with ministry to the poor.
- Talk about your faith with one friend who needs to hear the gospel, and then watch the Spirit work.
- Open your heart to God's Word and let it do its life-changing work in your soul.
- Get on the front lines of what God is doing in the world through prayer.
- Offer yourself to God for missionary work and see where he sends you.

But whatever you do, for heaven's sake, do something interesting for God instead of something boring for yourself!

PART 3

Prophet Elijah: The Power of Prayer

34

A MAN LIKE US

1 Kings 16:29—17:6

Now Elijah the Tishbite, of Tishbe in Gilead, said to Ahab, "As the
LORD the God of Israel lives, before whom I stand, there shall be
neither dew nor rain these years, except by my word."
(1 Kings 17:1)

lijah was a man like us. This is the startling conclusion that the
apostle James reached about the life and ministry of the great
prophet Elijah: "The prayer of a righteous person has great power
as it is working. Elijah was a man with a nature like ours, and he prayed fervently that it might not rain, and for three years and six months it did not rain
on the earth" (James 5:16–17).

This is an audacious interpretation of the life of Elijah and the significance
of his ministry for the church. "Elijah was a man just like us," the New International Version says. This statement is hard to swallow, because anyone
who knows anything about Elijah knows that he was hardly anything like
us at all.

Elijah endured the great agricultural calamity of his times: he lived through
a famine that lasted for three and a half years. Elijah staged the great religious
showdown of his times: he faced the prophets of Baal at Mount Carmel and

called down fire from heaven. Elijah executed the great judicial sentence of his times: he struck down 450 false prophets at the Kishon River. Elijah performed the great athletic feat of his times: he ran seventeen miles from Carmel down to Jezreel, ahead of a horse and chariots. He gave food to the hungry; he brought the dead back to life; he spoke with God on the mountain; he did not die, but was taken up into heaven in a whirlwind and a chariot of fire. *This* was a man *just* like us?

Nevertheless, the Scripture says that Elijah "was a man with a nature like ours." Paul and Barnabas used the same Greek word (*homoiopathes*) in Lystra, where the townspeople tried to worship them as gods (see Acts 14:15). The apostles rightly insisted that they too were only mortal men. The same was true of Elijah. He was a real person, who put on his sandals one foot at a time. He was a human being with human passions and human needs like anyone else. This means that—great prophet though he was—Elijah's life of faith, obedience, and prayer is not out of reach. He is a suitable example for us of godliness.

An Evil Day

How was Elijah like us? First, because he lived in an evil day, when Ahab was king over Israel. The seven kings of Israel who followed David and Solomon were a sorry lot. Jeroboam set up idols. Nadab was an evildoer. Baasha was a murderer. Elah was a drunkard. Zimri was really bad: he murdered Elah. Omri was even worse: he "did more evil than all who were before him" (1 Kings 16:25). But Ahab was the worst of all, which was no small accomplishment: "In the thirty-eighth year of Asa king of Judah, Ahab the son of Omri began to reign over Israel, and Ahab the son of Omri reigned over Israel in Samaria twenty-two years. And Ahab the son of Omri did evil in the sight of the LORD, more than all who were before him. . . . Ahab did more to provoke the LORD, the God of Israel, to anger than all the kings of Israel who were before him" (1 Kings 16:29–30, 33).

How bad was Ahab? So bad that he considered the sins of his fathers to be little more than trivialities. Even a man as wicked as Omri may have been touched from time to time with some feeling of remorse or shame for his wicked deeds. But not Ahab. If someone had gone to him and said, "Listen, what you are doing is wrong," he would have said, "What's your problem?"

Sin was nothing to Ahab. His conscience was inoculated against remorse; it was seared and cauterized against sorrow for sin. The sins of his fathers seemed inconsequential to him. His life thus stands as a warning to parents to live by the grace of God, lest their children give their hearts to evil, like the sons of the kings of Israel.

How bad was Ahab? So bad that he married a wicked woman: "And as if it had been a light thing for him to walk in the sins of Jeroboam the son of Nebat, he took for his wife Jezebel the daughter of Ethbaal king of the Sidonians" (1 Kings 16:31). Wicked queen Jezebel was the evil woman behind the evil man. Jezebel and Ahab deserved each other—the Bonnie and Clyde of the Old Testament. Ahab was a schemer. It is easy to tell what he was really up to from the way Scripture describes his marriage: Jezebel was "the daughter of Ethbaal king of the Sidonians" (1 Kings 16:31). Thus, to marry her was a political move that established an alliance between Ahab and Ethbaal, between Israel and Sidon. Sadly, it also established an alliance between Israel and the false god Baal. Even the king's name indicated his idolatry: Ethbaal. Yet as events would prove, Ahab's little scheme failed. His covenant with an earthly king could not save his life in battle. In trying to save his life, he lost it. This is a warning to those who make their own plans rather than following the Lord's leading: a life lived on its own terms will end in failure and destruction.

How bad was Ahab? So bad that it was not enough for him to marry a Baal-worshiper; he also wanted to *become* a Baal-worshiper: Ahab "went and served Baal and worshiped him. He erected an altar for Baal in the house of Baal, which he built in Samaria. And Ahab made an Asherah" (1 Kings 16:32–33). Baal and Asherah were the god of rain and the goddess of fortune. King Ahab built an altar and a sacred pole for this unholy couple so that his subjects could join him in his apostasy. Perhaps they also enjoyed the temple prostitution that made Baal and Asherah worship so popular in ancient Canaan.

How bad was Ahab? Evil in the king soon begets evil in the kingdom: "In his days Hiel of Bethel built Jericho. He laid its foundation at the cost of Abiram his firstborn, and set up its gates at the cost of his youngest son Segub, according to the word of the LORD, which he spoke by Joshua the son of Nun" (1 Kings 16:34; cf. Josh. 6:26). This news clipping from Elijah's times gives the message of 1 Kings in a nutshell: sin has devastating consequences, just as the prophets foretold. The incident also shows that Ahab ruled over an immoral kingdom. Since the days of Joshua, no one had dared to defy God's curse against Jericho (see Josh. 6:26). But Hiel deliberately rebuilt the city, which shows how bad things became under Ahab's rule. The king's subjects deliberately did things God commanded them not to do, including sacrificing their children for their own pleasure. When the Scripture says that Hiel of Bethel rebuilt Jericho "at the cost of" his sons, it is not clear whether this meant that he performed a literal child sacrifice (as the Canaanites sometimes did; cf. 2 Kings 3:26) or that God visited his house with judgment. Either way, Hiel recklessly put his own ambitions ahead of his family, with deadly consequences.

All of this ought to sound familiar, because we also live in the kind of times Elijah lived in. This is a day when children consider the sins of their parents a trivial matter. It is a day of casual sex, recreational drugs, gratuitous violence, and the slaughter of unborn children. This is a day when secular and spiritual leaders trust in their own schemes rather than God's instructions for the health of the nation and the growth of the church. This is a day when people bow down before the idols of money, power, beauty, sex, and self. James was right: Elijah was a man like us; he lived in an evil day.

The God Who Is There

Elijah was also a man like us because he knew the same God that we know. Chapter 17 opens with the prophet testifying, "As the Lord the God of Israel lives" (1 Kings 17:1). Each word is significant. The "Lord"—this means Yahweh, or Jehovah, the name above every name, the special name for God given to Moses at the burning bush. This Lord was Elijah's God, for the prophet's very name means "My God is the Lord." The "God of Israel"— this means the God who has made a covenant with his people, the God who really is the God of Israel, even if Ahab was trying to forget about him. The Lord, the God of Israel, "lives." This is where the emphasis falls, on the fact that the God of Israel is a *living* Lord.

Elijah's opening address is a stinging rebuke to Ahab and the false god he worshiped. Ahab's lifestyle was a denial that God lives. When Ahab considered sin trivial, and when he trusted in his own schemes and set up pagan idols to worship, he really was denying the existence of a living God. "God is dead," his actions declared. But by the judgment he would bring, God would prove to Ahab that he is the living God.

What Elijah said is also a stinging rebuke to Ahab's false god. Baal is *not* a god who lives. Even people who believed in Baal could not consider him a living god. According to the principles of their own theology, Baal was alive during the rainy season—a crucial time of year in an arid climate—but dead during the dry season. He was "all wet," we might say, which means that he was a weak god to serve in a dry climate. When Elijah stood before Ahab in a parched wilderness and spoke of the living God, he was rebuking Baal, the so-called rain god. Elijah's living God is Lord of both the dry season and the rainy season.

The same God is alive today. Rain or shine, God is God. Therefore, those who serve him really are like Elijah: we serve a living God. This is all the more true for us than it was for Elijah because God has now revealed himself in Jesus Christ. By bringing Jesus back to life and raising him up from the dead, God won the victory over death and proved that he was and is and will be the living God forever.

The living God keeps his word. Certainly he kept his word of judgment to Israel: "As the LORD the God of Israel lives, before whom I stand, there shall be neither dew nor rain these years, except by my word" (1 Kings 17:1). The drought in Elijah's day was not simply a random natural disaster, but a specific punishment on God's people for their sin. According to God's law (see Deut. 11:16–17), drought was the proper punishment for pagan idolatry. The Israelites trusted in the god of rain; therefore, the true and living God decreed that no rain would fall on them—a specific curse that directly addressed Baal's claim to be the rainmaker. Even the dew would dry up. And God kept his word about this: in chapter 18 poor King Ahab himself will be found wandering in the wilderness, looking for grass for his donkeys.

The judgments of Scripture are not idle threats. If God says he will bring down the proud, punish sin, and reserve fires of judgment for everyone who rebels against him, we should take him at his word. God keeps his word of judgment.

God also keeps his word of promise, as he did for Elijah: "Then the word of the LORD came to him, 'Depart from here and turn eastward and hide yourself by the brook Cherith, which is east of the Jordan. You shall drink from the brook, and I have commanded the ravens to feed you there.' So he went and did according to the word of the LORD. He went and lived by the brook Cherith that is east of the Jordan. And the ravens brought him bread and meat in the morning, and bread and meat in the evening, and he drank from the brook" (1 Kings 17:2–6).

God said Elijah would drink from the brook, and he did. God said ravens would feed Elijah, and they did.[1] Do not doubt that the promises of Scripture are trustworthy sayings. If God says he will exalt the humble, forgive sins for Jesus' sake, and prepare a heaven of joy for everyone who trusts in him, then believe it! He is a God who keeps his word of promise.

The living, speaking God cares for his people. When the dew dried up and the rain clouds disappeared, Elijah did not shrivel up and blow away. Even in an evil day, God protects those who belong to him.

Notice the extravagance of God's care for Elijah. God provided for Elijah not only by extraordinary means, but also with extraordinary abundance. It would have been enough for God to give Elijah enough to live on. All the prophet needed was a little bread and a little water once a day. But God gave Elijah as much water as he cared to drink, with bread *and* meat, twice a day.

Elijah's food was a kind of aftertaste of the meals that God provided for his children in the wilderness. After God brought the Israelites out of Egypt, he gave them manna in the morning and quail in the evening. The people of God ate bread once a day and meat once a day. But Elijah was given a double portion of daily bread and daily meat. To put this in contemporary terms, he had pancakes and bacon for breakfast *and* an all-beef patty on a bun for dinner. God was showing double honor to Elijah his prophet—a generous provision, especially for a man who to this point had preached only one short sermon!

Elijah Prays

What James said is true: Elijah was a man like us. He trusted in the living, speaking, caring God during an evil day.

Since Elijah was a man like us, we are called to become men and women like him. Elijah's strategy for living for God in an evil day can be summarized

1. There may be a parallel here to what happens later in the chapter: ravens were ceremonially unclean, yet God used them to provide for his prophet, just as he would use a Gentile woman to care for his daily needs (see 1 Kings 17:8–9).

in three simple words: pray, obey, stay. First, Elijah prayed. To live for God in an evil day is to become a person of prayer. In 1 Kings 17 it seems as if God is doing all the talking, through Elijah, to Ahab. But the book of James offers this profound interpretation of the ministry of Elijah: "He prayed fervently that it might not rain, and for three years and six months it did not rain on the earth" (James 5:17). The expression James uses in Greek appears to be carried over from Hebrew. To translate more literally, "with prayer, he prayed," or "praying, he prayed." Thus Elijah is held up as an example for us—not as a preacher, a prophet, a miracle worker, or an athlete, although he was all these things—but as a man of prayer.

James indicates that the judgment God announced to Ahab, through Elijah, was first prompted by the prayers of Elijah. So before God talked to Ahab, Elijah talked to God. Before the prophet came to the palace gates in Samaria, he was in his prayer closet in Gilead. Before he was on his feet before the king of Israel, he was on his knees before the King of kings.

Elijah had been on his knees for quite some time. Careful study of the Scriptures reveals how long Elijah had been in prayer. The famine ended in the third year (1 Kings 18:1), but James says that Elijah prayed earnestly and it did not rain for three *and a half* years. Jesus said the same thing when he preached in Nazareth: "in Israel in the days of Elijah, when the heavens were shut up three years and six months, and a great famine came over all the land" (Luke 4:25). By doing a little simple arithmetic, we can deduce that Elijah had been in prayer for at least six months before he went to speak with Ahab.

No wonder God chose Elijah to be his messenger! When God needed a herald to go and speak divine judgment to Ahab, Elijah was his man. The prophet was an intimate friend of God. He had proved by his prayers that he was zealous and dependable, that he was concerned for the Lord's work, and that he understood God's purpose for his people. The call to serve God often begins with a burden to pray for the Lord's work for some particular person, particular problem, or particular place. As we pray, we begin to discern God's calling.

Little wonder as well that this hillbilly from Gilead was so bold when he turned up at the gates of Ahab's palace. Elijah was not swayed by public opinion. He was not dismayed by the sophistication of Ahab's courtiers. He was not intimidated by the wicked queen who put the prophets of the Lord to death. As he stood in the presence of the king, Elijah was far more conscious that he was standing in the presence of the King of kings. The prophet had such courage because he knew that he was now *standing* before the God who lives just as he had so often *knelt* before the God who lives. Because Elijah lived his life *coram Deo*—in the conscious presence of God—he was not frightened to stand before an evil, ungodly king. The fear of God had driven out Elijah's fear of man, and thus he had the kind of spiritual boldness that is given only to those who linger in the presence of the living God.

Was it right for Elijah to pray the way he prayed? Was it permissible for him to invite privation and suffering upon his own neighbors? Was it loving for him to intercede for the land of milk and honey to be turned into a parched and sterile wilderness?

Yes, it was good and right for Elijah to pray for drought in Israel. His prayer came directly from the Word of God: "Take care lest your heart be deceived, and you turn aside and serve other gods and worship them; then the anger of the LORD will be kindled against you, and he will shut up the heavens, so that there will be no rain, and the land will yield no fruit, and you will perish quickly off the good land that the LORD is giving you" (Deut. 11:16–17).

Elijah was a careful student of the Word of God. He was also jealous for the glory of God. He knew that he lived in an evil day, and thus he lived in the expectation that the judgment of God would be revealed against his people. Furthermore, he discerned that the prevailing sin of his day was idolatry, so he knew precisely what kind of judgment to expect: famine. Elijah was not afraid to pray for judgment, because he knew that spiritual apostasy is a far worse disaster for a nation than physical calamity, and that moral delinquency is a greater tragedy for the people of God than material suffering. The prophet had a proper sense of what would bring glory to God, and he knew what his own people must suffer before they would turn back to God. A. W. Pink asks:

> Why was it Elijah prayed "that it might not rain"? Not because he was impervious to human suffering, not because he took a fiendish delight in witnessing the misery of his neighbours, but because he put *the glory of God* before everything else, even before his own natural feelings . . . Elijah was "very jealous

for the Lord God of hosts," 1 Kings 19:10, and longed to see His great Name vindicated and His backslidden people restored. Thus it was the glory of God and true love for Israel which actuated his petition.[2]

Would any of us dare to pray such a prayer today, asking God to act in judgment so that his people's hearts would turn back to him? If not, it is not because such prayers are no longer possible. The Scripture says Elijah was a man like us. If we do not pray such prayers, it may be because we are no longer men and women like Elijah. Since we live in an evil day, our prayers are as necessary as ever, and since we serve a living God, our prayers can be as effective as Elijah's prayers.

May the Lord make us people of prayer, so that we may pray the way Elijah prayed: *righteously*, so that our prayers are undiluted by disobedience and unhindered by unconfessed sin; *powerfully*, so that we prevail against the tide of idolatry; *effectively*, so that we discern the very things that God intends to do in our day; and *earnestly*, so that our hearts grow strong through our persistence in prayer.

Elijah Obeys and Stays

To live for God in an evil day is to obey as well as to pray: The Scripture says that Elijah "went and did according to the word of the Lord" (1 Kings 17:5). It sounds simple, but sometimes the simple things are the hard things in the Christian life. All the Lord wanted from Elijah was simple obedience to his revealed will, which is what he wants from any of us.

Christians often struggle to know the Lord's calling for their lives, but those who walk with God find that he leads them where they need to go, when they need to go there. Following God is something like walking up a staircase in the dark. We may not be able to see everything that lies ahead, but if we keep climbing—step by step—we will reach out with our unsteady feet and find a firm place to stand, all the way to the top.

Elijah found his way to the top. Notice that God did not tell the prophet to go to Cherith until *after* he had delivered his message to Ahab: "And the word of the Lord came to him" (1 Kings 17:2). Elijah went the whole way down from Gilead to Ahab, not having the slightest clue what God wanted

2. A. W. Pink, *The Life of Elijah*, rev. ed. (Edinburgh: Banner of Truth, 1963), 27.

him to do next. He simply declared the judgment of God to Ahab, and then waited for the call of God to lead him forward.

Elijah's call came right on time. God told Elijah where to go, just when he needed to go there. God's first words must have come as a great relief: "Leave here." Well, Elijah was no fool. He was not going to hang around Ahab's palace a moment longer than necessary, especially if Jezebel happened to be around! But then came a command that was not so easy to obey: "Depart from here and turn eastward and hide yourself by the brook Cherith, which is east of the Jordan" (1 Kings 17:3). This was hardly the pension plan for retired prophets for which Elijah had been hoping! Nor did God give him the meal plan he expected: "You shall drink from the brook, and I have commanded the ravens to feed you there" (1 Kings 17:4). "Drink from the brook? But it's not going to rain for years!" Elijah might have thought. "Fed by the ravens? But they are just birds!" he might have objected.

Yet whatever objections Elijah may have had, the Scripture simply says that "he went and did according to the word of the LORD" (1 Kings 17:5). Elijah did not make the simple things any harder than they needed to be. He simply obeyed the word that God revealed, as every believer should.

True obedience has staying power. It needs to, because living for God in an evil day takes more than one act of obedience. More often it requires a long obedience in the same direction. Once Elijah arrived in the place of God's provision, he had to stay there, and so he did: He "went and lived by the brook Cherith that is east of the Jordan" (1 Kings 17:5).

The Bible does not reveal how hard it was for Elijah to stay at Cherith, but it could not have been easy. The prophet was hiding from Jezebel to keep out of danger. He was hidden from the people of Israel so that there would be a famine of the word of God as well as a famine of grain. It may well have been a trial for a man of speech and action like Elijah to be quiet and still. Yet all the Bible reveals is that Elijah stayed right where God put him.

Elijah stayed put because he knew that God would stay with him. In what was Elijah trusting when he stayed at Cherith? Was he trusting in the brook and the ravens? Elijah was not trusting in the brook, but in the God who made the brook. He did not put his confidence in ravens, but in the God who sent the ravens. He had learned to trust not in the outward circumstances of his provision, but in the God who provides.

Notice how all of Elijah's actions correspond to the attributes of the God he served. Elijah was the kind of man he was because God is the kind of God he is. Because God is a living God, Elijah was able to pray to him. Because God always keeps his word, Elijah had a word to obey. Because God cares for his people, Elijah could stay where he was and depend on God's provision. He was a praying, obeying, staying prophet because the God he served is a living, word-keeping, caring God.

God always stays with his people. He will care for us, too, even if he has to use ravens to do it. In a sermon called "Elijah by the Brook," Al Martin tells of a cold, snowy winter night in a German village when a boy and his mother were in desperate straits. They had run out of food. The fire was out, and there was nothing left to burn to keep their cottage warm. So the mother was shocked, as they prayed, to hear her son walk across the room and fling the cottage door wide open to the cold night air.

"My son, why are you opening the door on such a cold night?" she cried out.

"It's for the ravens, Mother," the little boy simply replied. He knew the story of Elijah by the brook. He remembered how God had provided for his prophet and trusted that God would send his ravens, snow or no snow.

It so happened that the burgomaster was walking about that snowy night to see that all was well in the village. He was amazed to see an open door at the tiny home, so he went to investigate. He met the woman at the door and asked what was the matter. When she explained that she and her son were waiting for God to send his ravens, the burgomaster replied, "I will be your raven, both now and ever."[3]

The poor mother and child were just like Elijah. Although they lived in an evil day, they knew the same God that Elijah knew. As they prayed for his provision, they discovered the same thing that we will discover as we trust in him: he is a living God, who always keeps his word and always cares for his people.

3. Quoted in a sermon by Albert N. Martin, from F. B. Meyer, *Elijah: And the Secret of His Power* (Fort Washington, PA: Christian Literature Crusade, 1954), 25–26.

35

DAILY BREAD, SAVING GRACE

1 Kings 17:7–16

*"For thus says the LORD, the God of Israel, 'The jar of flour shall
not be spent, and the jug of oil shall not be empty, until the day
that the LORD sends rain upon the earth.'" And she went and
did as Elijah said. And she and he and her household ate for
many days. (1 Kings 17:14–15)*

hen Elijah lived in the Cherith Ravine, he seemed to be trusting
God about as much as a man can. The prophet was stretched
to the very limits of his faith. Surely it was enough for the man
to live alone in the wilderness, to slurp water from a brook, and to eat from
the beaks of ravens! Yet God called Elijah to tighten his belt and take one
more step of obedience: "after a while the brook dried up, because there was
no rain in the land" (1 Kings 17:7).

What a severe test of faith this must have been, even for a man of prayer
like Elijah! A brook does not dry up overnight. It dies a slow death, dwin-
dling away day by day. Although the Cherith had been only a brook in the
first place, at least a brook is something. But after a time the brook became
a stream, the stream became a creek, and the creek became a trickle. Finally,
one morning, there was nothing at all.

GIVE US THIS DAY OUR DAILY BREAD

A man's faith might well dwindle away in the time it takes a brook to become a dry riverbed. Yet Elijah's faith did not wither. Instead, the prophet learned this simple lesson all over again: God gives daily bread to his servants. Just when Elijah was at the end of his brook, "then the word of the LORD came to him, 'Arise, go to Zarephath, which belongs to Sidon, and dwell there. Behold, I have commanded a widow there to feed you'" (1 Kings 17:8–9).

"God must be joking!" the prophet may well have thought. It was one thing to be fed by birds, but another thing entirely to go to Sidon, of all places. We learn as much as we want to know about Sidon in 1 Kings 16:31, where the Scripture says that Ahab "took for his wife Jezebel the daughter of Ethbaal king of the Sidonians." Sidon was Jezebel's stomping grounds; Zarephath was on Baal's home turf. The town contained all the brazen idolatry, unholy sacrifices, and temple prostitution that went along with Baal worship. Thus God was commanding Elijah to go down into the cesspool of sin, and not just to go there, but also to "dwell there" (1 Kings 17:9).

"So [the prophet] arose and went to Zarephath" (1 Kings 17:10). As the baseball player Yogi Berra famously said, this is like "déjà vu all over again." All God wanted from Elijah when he went to Cherith was simple obedience. He wanted him to stay and obey. Once again, this is all God wants from Elijah as he goes to Zarephath. Faithful service to God often requires obedience to the same instructions over and over again.

When Elijah arrived at the town gates of Zarephath, things did not look terribly promising. There was no more rain in Sidon than there was in Israel. Apparently, God was teaching the Baal-worshipers in Sidon a little theology. He was showing the Sidonians that he (and not Baal) is the God who sends rain.

When Elijah "came to the gate of the city, behold, a widow was there gathering sticks" (1 Kings 17:10). She was just a poor woman with a few sticks. Elijah hardly seems to have had the courage to ask her for a meal. "Bring me a little water in a vessel, that I may drink," he said at first (1 Kings 17:10). And then he got a little bolder: "And as she was going to bring it, he called to her and said, 'Bring me a morsel of bread in your hand'" (1 Kings 17:11). Elijah was not asking for much: just a little water and a morsel of bread. But even

445

this was too much for the woman to give: "And she said, 'As the LORD your God lives, I have nothing baked, only a handful of flour in a jar and a little oil in a jug. And now I am gathering a couple of sticks that I may go in and prepare it for myself and my son, that we may eat it and die'" (1 Kings 17:12). Needless to say, it was not the best time for an out-of-town guest to show up! The widow had barely enough on hand to make a muffin, let alone a loaf of bread. Not that she was inhospitable, but she was down to her last meal.

Yet Elijah trusted in the word of God. Even though the widow barely had two sticks to rub together, Elijah ordered his meal: "Do not fear; go and do as you have said. But first make me a little cake of it and bring it to me, and afterward make something for yourself and your son" (1 Kings 17:13). In giving this command, Elijah was trusting the promise of God to provide daily bread. Although the widow was scraping the bottom of the barrel, Elijah knew that God's resources cannot be exhausted: "For thus says the LORD the God of Israel, 'The jar of flour shall not be spent, and the jug of oil shall not be empty, until the day that the Lord sends rain upon the earth'" (1 Kings 17:14). Back at Cherith Elijah trusted not in brook or bird, but in the God of brooks and ravens. Now in Zarephath, Elijah is trusting not in flour or oil, but in the God of field and orchard.

Elijah's trust was well placed, for the God of Elijah keeps his word: "And she went and did as Elijah said. And she and he and her household ate for many days. The jar of flour was not spent, neither did the jug of oil become empty, according to the word of the LORD that he spoke by Elijah" (1 Kings 17:15–16). There were no leftovers, no loaves to freeze in ziplock bags and save for another day. This was *daily bread* demanding *daily faith* in the providence of God. Every day that Elijah stayed in Zarephath, the widow went to her barrel of flour and her jar of oil and had just enough to make bread for one more day.

The Dutch Christian Corrie ten Boom had a similar experience in the German concentration camp at Ravensbrook. Corrie and her sister Betsie were captured by the Nazis for hiding Jews during World War II. Betsie became ill during their long imprisonment. Here is how Corrie describes giving her sister life-preserving vitamins:

> Another strange thing was happening. The bottle was continuing to produce drops. It scarcely seemed possible, so small a bottle, so many doses a day. Now, in addition to Betsie, a dozen others on our pier were taking it.

My instinct was always to hoard it—Betsie was growing so very weak! But the others were ill as well. It was hard to say no to eyes that burned with fever, hands that shook with chill. I tried to save it for the very weakest—but even these soon numbered fifteen, twenty, twenty-five. . . .

And still, every time I tilted the little bottle, a drop appeared at the tip of the glass stopper. It just couldn't be! I held it up to the light, trying to see how much was left, but the dark brown glass was too thick to see through.

"There was a woman in the Bible," Betsie said, "whose oil jar was never empty." She turned to it in the Book of Kings, the story of the poor widow of Zarephath. . . .

It was one thing to believe that such things were possible thousands of years ago, another to have it happen now, to us, this very day. And yet it happened this day, and the next, and the next, until an awed little group of spectators stood around watching the drops fall onto the daily rations of bread.

Many nights I lay awake in the shower of straw dust from the mattress above, trying to fathom the marvel of supply lavished upon us. "Maybe," I whispered to Betsie, "only a molecule or two really gets through that little pinhole—and then in the air it expands!"

I heard her soft laughter in the dark. "Don't try too hard to explain it, Corrie. Just accept it as a surprise from a Father who loves you."

Then Corrie writes about the day that another prisoner brought some treasure back to the barracks: a piece of newspaper, a slice of bread, and a small sack of vitamins! "Back at the bunk I took the bottle from the straw. 'We'll finish the drops first,' I decided. But that night, no matter how long I held it upside down, or how hard I shook it, not another drop appeared."[1]

Corrie ten Boom was encountering the same God that Elijah knew. Ravensbrook turned out to be aptly named, for there the ten Booms experienced the same providential care that Elijah received at his "raven's brook," and afterward. Elijah had enough to drink from the Brook Cherith—every day—until he licked the very last drop from the riverbed. Then the Lord sent him to the widow's home in Zarephath, where he had enough to eat—every day—until the day rain fell on the earth again.

This is the same God we serve today—the God who gives his servants daily bread. The Lord provides what we need every day. He gives us more than enough to survive and thrive. Therefore, we can offer the same testimony

1. Corrie ten Boom, *The Hiding Place* (New York: Bantam, 1971), 202–3.

as the psalmist: "Oh, fear the LORD, you his saints, for those who fear him have no lack!" (Ps. 34:9).

GRACE FOR THE HELPLESS

The God who provides daily bread also gives saving grace. This is the most basic and important lesson in all of Scripture, namely, that salvation is from the Lord. Elijah's encounter with the widow of Zarephath teaches that God's saving grace is for at least five kinds of people.

First, saving grace is *for the weak and helpless*. The widow of Zarephath had once been a woman of means, for there was an upper room in her house (1 Kings 17:19). In those days, to have a second story was to possess at least some of the finer things in life. But the widow had fallen on hard times. She was weak and helpless, living as she did without the protection of a husband in a culture where unattached women were vulnerable to abuse. Her son, too, was weak and helpless. He lived without the security of a father or a model of manliness in the home. Finally, the day came when the mother and son were down to their last few twigs, their last fistful of flour, and their last few drops of oil. How weak and helpless they were!

Yet God's saving grace is *for* the weak and helpless. The story of the widow and her son demonstrates the truth of Deuteronomy 10:17: "For the LORD your God is God of gods and Lord of lords, the great, the mighty, and the awesome God, who is not partial and takes no bribe." If God shows no partiality, then we do not have to "be somebody" to catch his attention. If he accepts no bribes, then we do not have to be wealthy to receive his grace. God does not favor the rich and famous. On the contrary, "he executes justice for the fatherless and the widow, and loves the sojourner, giving him food and clothing" (Deut. 10:18). What a beautiful promise! God defends the cause of the fatherless, like the fatherless boy in Zarephath, and protects the plight of the widow, like the boy's husbandless mother. God gave these needy people his saving grace, serving as the only father and husband they would ever need.

Not that we must become widows or orphans, of course, to receive God's saving grace. The point is that God's grace is for *everyone*. If his saving favor is for the weakest and the most helpless, then it is available to us as well. Not even orphans and widows have an exclusive claim on the blessing of God. His saving grace is for everyone, from the least to the greatest.

GRACE FOR OUTSIDERS

God's saving grace is also *for those who are outside his family.* The widow of Zarephath seems to have been a good person. When Elijah asked for a drink, she politely gave it to him (1 Kings 17:11). She minded her p's and q's in following the ancient custom that obliged women to draw water for men.

The widow also acknowledged the existence of God. The first thing she said to Elijah was "As the LORD your God lives" (1 Kings 17:12). This may simply have been a manner of speaking. People sometimes say "So help me God" or "God bless you" without meaning anything of the kind. Yet it seems likely that this detail has been set down in Scripture for our instruction. Although the widow lived in Baal's hometown, she confessed that the God of Elijah is a living God.

The living God is not yet her God, however. Here the widow's precise wording seems important: "As the LORD *your* God lives" (1 Kings 17:12). The living God may be Elijah's God, but he is not yet *her* God. Thus she refers to him in the second rather than the first person. The widow has not yet trusted in God for herself, making a personal appropriation of the grace of God by faith. She is still outside the family of God, and she knows it.

Many individuals remain outside the family of God. They may be nice people. They may try to live good and moral lives, minding their moral p's and q's. They may even believe that there is a God. Yet they are still outside his family. It is not enough to believe that there is a God; if we are to be saved, he must become *our* God. Unless and until Jesus Christ becomes the Lord of our lives, we remain outside the family of God.

A simple illustration may help to convey this truth. When I walk past the bank on the corner, I may believe that there is money in the bank's safe. I may even believe this by a sort of faith. Not having been in the vault to see the money, I nevertheless believe that there is money in the bank. But this means little or nothing to me unless I have made a deposit. Money in the bank is of no value to me unless it is my own money.

Something similar holds true until I put my trust in Jesus Christ. I may believe that there is a God who has the power to give eternal life, but this means nothing to me unless I have made my own deposit on that salvation. The death of Jesus is of no value to me unless I believe that he died on the cross for my personal sins. Similarly, the resurrection of

Jesus Christ is of no value to me until I trust that he was raised from the dead to claim the victory over my death. Until we trust in Jesus Christ for ourselves, we are still outside the family of God; we have not yet received God's saving grace.

Anyone who is outside the family of God should not despair, however. The grace of God is for those who are still outside his family. The living God sent Elijah to the widow of Zarephath so that she might be brought into the family of God. In the same way, the living God sends out word today to invite everyone to become his child. Anyone who leaves sin behind and comes to Christ for grace will be saved.

SOVEREIGN GRACE

God's grace is *for those whom God chooses*. Saving grace is sovereign grace; God's grace is God's choice. To put this in theological terms, the grace of God is a matter of divine election.

Of all the widows at all the town gates gathering all the sticks in the whole Middle East, was there a more unlikely prospect to receive God's grace than the widow of Zarephath? She lived on Jezebel's plantation. What could she have known about the God of Israel? What chance in a million could she have to hear the good news about the living God?

The answer to this question is recorded in the Gospel of Luke. Jesus had been preaching to his friends and neighbors in his hometown of Nazareth. Although they all spoke well of him, they saw in him nothing more than the son of a carpenter. This was his response to their unbelief:

> Truly, I say to you, no prophet is acceptable in his hometown. But in truth, I tell you, there were many widows in Israel in the days of Elijah, when the heavens were shut up three years and six months, and a great famine came over all the land, and Elijah was sent to none of them but only to Zarephath, in the land of Sidon, to a woman who was a widow. (Luke 4:24–26)

Here we learn that Elijah's visit to Zarephath was a reproach to Israel for their lack of faith. We also learn that the good news of salvation in Jesus Christ is for Gentiles in Sidonia as well as for Jews in Israel. The gospel is for every people from every nation in the world.

But Jesus also teaches that saving grace is a matter of divine election. It was God's will and purpose to save the widow of Zarephath. He sent Elijah so that she might receive saving grace. Of all the widows to whom God's prophet might have been sent, she alone was chosen. Furthermore, she was chosen even before she put her personal trust in God. This is the mystery of the sovereignty of God's saving grace.

God is always sovereign in salvation. He chose his children before the foundation of the world, predestinating us "for adoption through Jesus Christ, according to the purpose of his will" (Eph. 1:4–5). We never would have heard of the good news of grace unless God had sent his word to us. When we heard the gospel, we would not have believed it unless God had given us the gift of faith. In short, we never would have been saved unless God had given us his saving grace. From beginning to end, salvation is the work of God, which is why it is called "grace."

GRACE FOR THE DYING

God's saving grace is also *for those who are about to die*. When Elijah arrived in Zarephath, the widow was about to die. "I have nothing baked," she said, "only a handful of flour in a jar and a little oil in a jug. And now I am gathering a couple of sticks that I may go in and prepare it for myself and my son, that we may eat it and die" (1 Kings 17:12). The widow's words have a ring of resignation about them; she speaks with a sense of inevitability. She and her son have been wasting away for weeks. Now they will gather, bake, eat, and die. Just a handful of flour and a drop of oil stand between them and eternity. If God's prophet had arrived only a week later, they would have been corpses. Elijah came just in time, which is really to say that God's saving grace came just in time. When the widow and her son were about to die, the Lord delivered them.

When will we die? No one can say for sure. We may not expect to die soon, but perhaps nothing more than a clogged artery or the front of a bus stands between us and eternity. Early in 1995 tenor Richard Versalle stood on a ladder at the Metropolitan Opera in New York. He was performing the opening scene of *The Makropulos Case* and singing this line: "You can only live so long." Never have truer words been sung, for before Versalle finished singing he suffered a heart attack and fell to the stage, dead.[2]

Since we are all mortal, it is comforting to know that God's saving grace is for those who are about to die. This comfort is not just for those who are about to die a physical death, but especially for those who are about to die a spiritual and eternal death. We receive this saving grace in Jesus Christ, who became a man, died on the cross, and was raised again to pay the penalty for sin and to claim victory over death. This is God's grace for us: "For while we were still weak, at the right time Christ died for the ungodly. For one will scarcely die for a righteous person—though perhaps for a good person one would dare even to die—but God shows his love for us in that while we were still sinners, Christ died for us" (Rom. 5:6–8).

God's sovereign saving grace is for anyone and everyone. It is for the weak and the helpless, for those outside the family of God, and for those about to die. God's grace is for all of us, whoever we are.

SAVED BY GRACE THROUGH FAITH

God's saving grace is *only for those who come to God in faith*, however. The weak, the outsiders, and the dying must trust in God for salvation. This is what the widow of Zarephath did: she came to God in saving faith. She rested on God's sovereign grace and trusted in him for her salvation. Even in her desperation, she trusted the word of God.

Elijah first came to the widow of Zarephath with comfort and assurance, but his further instructions were an extreme test of her faith: "Elijah said to her, 'Do not fear. Go and do as you have said. But first make me a little cake of it and bring it to me, and afterward make something for yourself and your son'" (1 Kings 17:13).

"How about tomorrow, Lord?" the widow might have suggested. "Your prophet looks healthy enough to me. Surely he could make it through the night. Why don't I just make a little something for myself right now, and then I can worry about tomorrow when it comes?!" This is what the widow might have said. But the Scripture reports that instead "she went and did as Elijah said" (1 Kings 17:15). This is real faith! If we were down to our last

2. *Time*, January 15, 1995.

452

meal, would we give the main course to our pastor? This woman gave her first and her best for the Lord's work. She took the step of faith that the Lord required, *first* feeding the Lord's prophet and *then* making something for herself and her son.

The widow could do this only if she trusted God to provide. When she staked her life on God's promise, God did not disappoint her. Her faith was secure in his salvation. This is the consistent pattern of God's sovereign and saving grace: it always comes to those who trust in God.

When the widow of Zarephath received Elijah, in effect she was receiving Jesus Christ by faith. Jesus said to his disciples, "Whoever receives you receives me. . . . The one who receives a prophet because he is a prophet will receive a prophet's reward" (Matt. 10:40-41). This was how the widow of Zarephath received Elijah. She received him as a prophet sent from God, and to receive Elijah in this way was tantamount to receiving Jesus Christ.

Jesus said that the proper recompense for receiving a prophet is a "prophet's reward." What is a "prophet's reward"? It is the reward that a prophet himself deserves from God. In this case, we have seen how God rewarded Elijah with daily bread and saving grace. When the widow received Elijah as God's prophet, she received the same bread and the same grace: the prophet's reward. The same reward is available to everyone who receives Jesus by faith. Anyone who trusts in Jesus Christ will receive daily bread and saving grace.

36

LOOK, YOUR SON IS ALIVE!

1 Kings 17:17–24

And the LORD listened to the voice of Elijah. And the life of the child came into him again, and he revived. And Elijah took the child and brought him down from the upper chamber into the house and delivered him to his mother. And Elijah said, "See, your son lives." (1 Kings 17:22–23)

*T*he movie star Marilyn Monroe was once asked if she believed in God. She answered, "I just believe in everything—a little bit."[1] With apologies to America's fifth president, and his policy of opposition to European interference, this is the new Monroe Doctrine. It is the theological principle that as long as we believe in everything, everything will be all right. The more gods the merrier: a little of this and a little of that, but not too much of any one deity in particular.

The Monroe Doctrine has become the basic religious principle of American culture. People do not want to be intolerant, so they believe a little bit of everything. A majority of Americans believe in God, the Bible, Jesus, the

---

1. Marilyn Monroe, as quoted in James H. Smylie, "Church Growth and Decline in Historical Perspective," *American Presbyterians* 73, 3 (Fall 1995): 1.

power of positive thinking, the basic goodness of humanity, luck, alien life-forms, and checking their horoscopes every day. The only way to believe all these things at the same time is to adhere to the Monroe Doctrine: believe everything a little bit.

THE GOD OF ELIJAH

Elijah was up against a similar worldview in his times. The prophet lived in a nation that had ceased to believe that the Lord is the one and only living God. People had forgotten that there is no God but God. They no longer said *soli Deo gloria*, "to God alone be the glory." Instead, they believed in everything a little bit. They were mixing a little Baal worship and a little goddess worship with their worship of the Lord God of Israel.

This is one of the reasons why 1 Kings 17 continues to be relevant for the church today. It speaks to the religious pluralism of present times just as it spoke to the religious pluralism of Elijah's day. The whole thrust of Elijah's ministry was to refute the Monroe Doctrine. The burden of the prophet's teaching was to demonstrate that there is only one God—the God of Abraham, Isaac, and Jacob, the Lord God of the Bible.

Elijah has already taught us almost everything we need to know about the one true God. First Kings 17 is like God 101: a short course in the attributes and work of Almighty God. This chapter reveals the *character* of God. It teaches that God hates sin, judges sinners justly, keeps his promises, has mercy on the needy, loves the widow and the fatherless, and adopts foreigners into his own family. God is holy and just, loving and merciful. This is who God is.

This chapter also teaches what God does, revealing three of his great works: creation, providence, and redemption. First Kings 17 reveals God's work of *creation*, first of all. The Lord, the God of Israel, is the one who sends the rain in its season, or causes drought to fall upon the land. He is the Lord of creation. He rules and governs the elements of the natural world that he made and sustains.

First Kings 17 also demonstrates God's work of *providence*. Day by day, God provided everything Elijah needed. He gave him a safe place to live in the Cherith Ravine, with bread and meat to eat, twice a day. Then God provided everything the widow of Zarephath needed, along with her son and

Elijah. The jar of flour was not used up and the jug of oil did not run dry because God gave them their daily bread.

Then this chapter reveals God's work of *redemption*. As we turn to the last section of 1 Kings, God brings the widow's son from death to life and the widow herself from disbelief to saving faith. God demonstrates that he is the Lord of life and the God of the resurrection.

Creation, providence, redemption—1 Kings 17 introduces three great works of God. Together they comprise a proof for the Godness of God. They show that God is really God, with a capital G. Only God can make the world, provide daily bread, and bring the dead back to life. What was announced in the first verse of the chapter is true: "The Lord the God of Israel lives," and soon the whole nation of Israel will know it (see 1 Kings 18:39).

The last eight verses of 1 Kings 17 thus form the climax of Elijah's argument for the Godness of God. The case has been building, but it reaches its pinnacle when Elijah carries a boy down from the roof and says, "Look, your son is alive!" (1 Kings 17:23 NIV). The resurrection of the widow's son gives the strongest proof of the deity of God. It clinches the argument, so that by the time we get to the end of 1 Kings 17, we have been fully introduced to God, the one and only.

From Death to Life

God is the main character of this chapter; he is the hero, or protagonist. Thus the lessons to be learned from 1 Kings 17 are not about Elijah, primarily. They are drawn from his life, of course, but they are really about the living God.

There is something to learn about God's relationship with his people from each character in this story. To begin with, the widow's son passes from death to life. The Bible does not comment on the boy's spiritual condition. It is not certain whether he had come to trust in the Lord God of Israel, although certainly he had seen ample evidence of God's provision. We do not know if Elijah's God had become his God. We only know that sometime after the prophet came to his house, the boy became ill: "After this the son of the woman, the mistress of the house, became ill. And his illness was so severe that there was no breath left in him" (1 Kings 17:17). It is apparent from these words that this boy was actually dead—not nearly dead, or mostly dead, but actually dead. As the Coroner sang in *The Wizard of Oz,* he was "undeniably and reliably dead!" Both his mother and his pastor testify to his death in Holy Scripture, and it is not until *after* Elijah prays that the boy's life returns to him (1 Kings 17:22).

The sickness and death of this child remind us of the frailty of human existence. Every one of us is subject to sickness and death, and we run the whole race of our lives knowing that death is waiting for us at the finish line. All men are mortal. Every day people hear news of the death of a friend or family member. At any moment, a precious memory may cause us to grieve afresh for the loss of a loved one. We always live life under the shadow of death, for sin has entered the world, and with sin, death (see Rom. 5:12).

This story is not about death, however; it is about the power of God *over* death. What is perhaps surprising is that it is a story from the Old Testament. We know about the power of God over death from the New Testament. We know that his divine, life-giving power was demonstrated once and for all in the resurrection of Jesus Christ from the dead. We know that although Jesus was dead and buried, "he was raised on the third day in accordance with the Scriptures" (1 Cor. 15:4).

We know all this from the New Testament, but here in 1 Kings 17 we see the power of God over death already in the *Old* Testament. It is almost as if God could not contain himself, as if he could not hold back his power over death, or his compassion for the grieving, or his joy in bringing the dead back to life. God interrupted and overturned death by giving life to this boy, as if to say, "See, I am the God of resurrection!"

The raising of the widow's son in Zarephath was one of the Old Testament events that pointed the people of God forward to Jesus Christ. This miracle anticipated the resurrection power of God that was fully revealed in Jesus. In the Gospels, God revealed his power over death by raising the son of the widow of Nain, Lazarus, and finally Jesus himself. Furthermore, this miracle pointed toward the power of the resurrection of Jesus Christ in the life of every believer. Everyone has been born in sin and is subject to death because of sin. But everyone who knows God and has faith in Jesus Christ has crossed over from death to spiritual life: "And you were dead in the trespasses and sins in which you once walked, following the course of this world. . . . But God, being rich in mercy, because of the great love with which he loved us, even when we were dead in our trespasses, made us alive together with Christ" (Eph. 2:1–5).

This new life in Christ is eternal. Believers in Christ will die a physical death—as the widow's son did—but we will not die a permanent death. The body of the believer that dies will be raised again to everlasting life.

Anyone who has not yet trusted in Jesus Christ is still dead in transgressions and sins. Such a person is spiritually dead already and will enter into eternal death. Yet the God of heaven and earth—who alone has power over death—offers eternal life. We will not receive this life by putting our trust in the Monroe Doctrine, believing a little of this and a little of that. We must give our whole selves over to the God who raised Jesus from the dead. Only then will we pass from death to life.

FROM DISBELIEF TO FAITH

God's resurrection power also did something in the life of the widow, bringing her from disbelief to faith. The woman's spiritual condition was one of "*dis*belief" rather than "*un*belief." An unbeliever is someone who has not yet put his or her faith in God. The widow was not an unbeliever in this sense. She had received the miraculous grace of God. Even though she was down to her last meal, and even though she was an alien to the family of God, God sent his prophet to save her from starvation. The widow had enough faith in God to trust his word and to give Elijah the main course of her last meal, trusting that God would provide her daily bread.

Yet the troubles of life had made a disbeliever out of the widow. In particular, she was in disbelief about the goodness of God. She knew something of God's grace; she had learned to trust him for her daily bread. However, she did not have the spiritual resources to cope with the death of her son. She was filled not only with grief, but also with resentment. When he died she found that she had little faith, or none at all. She had faith enough for the good times, but not the bad times—for life, but not for death. This is easy to understand, for this poor woman lost everything when she lost her son. She lost her closest companion, her only family member, and almost all security for her old age. In the words of A. W. Pink, "In him all her affections were centered, and with his death all her hopes were destroyed."[2]

2. A. W. Pink, *The Life of Elijah*, rev. ed. (Edinburgh: Banner of Truth, 1963), 79.

The widow's suffering was similar to the kind of suffering depicted in a painting put on display in 1995 at the Pittsburgh City-County Building: *The Marcus Pieta* by James Douglas Adams. The painting depicts a single woman holding her son in one arm. He is wearing a team jacket, baggy pants, and Velcro sneakers. He has been shot dead. The woman's other arm is extended, palm outstretched, pleading for mercy, perhaps. Like the widow of Zarephath, she is in disbelief.

It all happened so suddenly! Just when life seemed to be working out, just when she had been delivered from starvation, just when the burdens of being a single parent were lifted, her son was taken from her. Things had gone from bad, to good, to worse. It all seemed so unfair!

It is easy to pity this woman. Many women and men have had similar experiences often. Believers are delivered by the grace of God from some trouble in life, only to be overwhelmed when trouble strikes again. Sometimes the fact of the first deliverance almost seems to make the new trouble *more* difficult to endure. Many Christians feel as if they have already learned all the lessons they care to learn from suffering. When suffering comes again, it is easy to wonder how much more we can take. We do not lose our faith, perhaps, but we are in disbelief about the goodness of God.

Notice one further detail in the widow's lament. Because she is in disbelief she lashes out against Elijah: "What have you against me, O man of God?" (1 Kings 17:18). Elijah has worn out his welcome. The widow does not like God's message, so she blames God's messenger. Although her complaint is really with God, Elijah is his representative on the scene, so she directs her anger at him, as people often do in times of trial.

What the widow says to God's prophet reveals that she has some consciousness of sin, and of God's determination to punish it. The woman says to Elijah, "You have come to me to bring my sin to remembrance and to cause the death of my son!" (1 Kings 17:18; cf. Luke 5:8). When the woman speaks of sin brought "to remembrance," she is referring to the remembrance of God.[3] It is as if the arrival of a man of God at her house has drawn her sin to God's attention, which in turn has brought her under God's judgment.

This faulty theology betrays a guilty conscience. The woman's real problem is not that God has suddenly noticed her sin, but that she herself has

---

3. This form (hiphil) of the Hebrew verb for remembering (*zur*) always implies God as the subject.

459

finally noticed it. Suffering has convicted her of sin. In all likelihood, Elijah had taught the widow and her son from the Scriptures, perhaps leading them in devotions after their daily meal. He may well have explained how he had prayed down the drought that was punishing God's people for their sins. He may have quoted this Scripture to them concerning God's true prophet: "And whoever will not listen to my words that he shall speak in my name, I myself will require it of him" (Deut. 18:19). Or perhaps Elijah lived a life of such singular godliness that having him in her home had induced the proper fear of God. In any case, the widow had learned God's requirements for holy living, and she recognized that she was falling short of God's standard.

Having seen the power of God, now the woman was frightened by it. She knew that there was a connection between sin and death, that human mortality springs from total depravity. The widow had a guilty conscience, and thus she saw the death of her son as God's punishment for her sins.

At this point the widow started to do the kinds of things that people often do when they have a guilty conscience. She should have repented for her sins and asked God to forgive her. Instead, she shifted the blame from herself to Elijah and tried to get as far away from God as possible. "Why did you come here?" "Why have you done this?" "Why have you brought me to God's attention?"

What rescued the widow from these foolish complaints and transformed her heart was a personal encounter with the resurrection power of God, through the ministry of his prophet. Here we may draw a contrast between Hiel of Bethel, whose disobedience cost him the life of his sons (see 1 Kings 16:34), and the widow of Zarephath, who went to God's prophet with her trouble and found deliverance. When Elijah placed her son back in her arms alive, the woman said: "Now I know that you are a man of God, and that the word of the LORD in your mouth is truth" (1 Kings 17:24). Now the widow knows! Now she believes! Now she trusts! It was not until the woman held her living, breathing son in her arms that she came to a firm conviction of the truth of God.

The widow of Zarephath shows how faith in the living God is grounded in the factuality of the resurrection. Belief in the resurrection of the body is not just for super-Christians; it is the foundation for true faith. Resurrection is the proof of the promise of God. It is on the basis of the raising of her son that the widow of Zarephath was able to give her testimony: "Now I know that you are a man of God, and that the word of the Lord in your mouth is truth" (1 Kings 17:24).

Another Day, Another Miracle

Something similar but even greater happened during the earthly ministry of Jesus Christ. On one occasion Jesus went to the town of Nain, and "as he drew near to the gate of the town, behold, a man who had died was being carried out, the only son of his mother, and she was a widow, and a considerable crowd from the town was with her" (Luke 7:11–12).

The connections between the widow of Zarephath and the widow of Nain are unmistakable.[4] They are both widows, they have both lost their only sons, and they are both grief-stricken. Then they both witnessed the same miracle, as their sons were returned to them by the life-giving power of God. These two miracles both had the same result: when people saw what God had done, they believed in him. When the people of Nain saw the power of God over death, they put their faith in Jesus Christ: "Fear seized them all, and they glorified God, saying, 'A great prophet has arisen among us!' and 'God has visited his people!'" (Luke 17:16). The life-giving power of God confirms the Word of God and brings people to faith in Jesus Christ.

Believing Thomas learned the same thing when he saw the risen Christ. Thomas had maintained that he would not put his faith in Christ unless he could see him with his own eyes and touch him with his own hands. So when Jesus appeared to Thomas, he showed him his resurrection body: "Then he said to Thomas, 'Put your finger here, and see my hands; and put out your hand, and place it in my side. Do not disbelieve, but believe.' Thomas answered him, 'My Lord and my God!'" (John 20:27–28). A personal encounter with the resurrection power of God made a believer out of Thomas. He was brought from disbelief to faith in the risen Christ.

For some years I attended a Bible study for a diverse group of pastors who preached at churches in Center City Philadelphia. The study confirmed the Monroe Doctrine: given the variety of our theological and denominational backgrounds, the pastors in the group believed everything a little bit. One year, in the week before Easter Sunday, I was reminded of the necessity of

---

4. Luke highlights these connections by using vocabulary from the Greek translation of the Old Testament (i.e., the Septuagint).

the resurrection for true Christian faith. With the approach of Easter, there was a palpable sense of uneasiness in the study. Several pastors lamented the "Here-we-go-again" feeling that they have at Eastertime, especially on the Saturday night before Easter Sunday. After I left the Bible study, I was able to put my finger on the source of their discomfort: they were trying to work up the faith to believe in the resurrection of Jesus Christ, but they were not sure how they could do it again this year.

Believing in the resurrection of Jesus Christ is not an annual event; for the believer in Christ it is a daily reality. Believing in the resurrection of Jesus Christ is not the last step in the Christian pilgrimage, but the very first step. Christian faith does not begin at the cross (although that is where our sins were paid for); Christian faith begins at the empty tomb.

Anyone who has not yet come to absolute certainty about the bodily resurrection of Jesus Christ is not yet a Christian. The Bible says that Jesus was raised from the dead. Anyone who believes this has eternal life. We do not need to fear that God will judge us for our sins, or to think that our painful circumstances in life prove that God is angry with us, as the widow of Zarephath believed. On the contrary, the resurrection of Jesus from the dead proves that God is and always will be for us, not against us.

FROM DOUBTING QUESTIONS TO FAITHFUL PRAYER

Elijah had faith in the resurrection power of God. Yet he still had a few questions for God. Everything seemed to be going well for him. He was getting one square meal a day, while living in a nice loft in Zarephath. But then his landlady came to him with a dead body and a charge of homicide. With her dead son in her arms, she accused Elijah of fatal pastoral malpractice: "What have you against me, O man of God? You have come to me to bring my sin to remembrance and to cause the death of my son!" (1 Kings 17:18). Elijah had a congregation of only two to begin with. Now one of his parishioners was dead and the other was attacking his ministry, which is the way pastoral ministry goes, sometimes.

Elijah did not defend his ministry, but showed remarkable restraint in the face of opposition. He did not explain why the woman's accusations were unjust. He did not blame her for her sins. He did not give a lecture about why bad things happen to good people.

Instead, the prophet gave her the kind of soft answer that turns away wrath (see Prov. 15:1). "Give me your son," Elijah said (1 Kings 17:19). The prophet's grace under pressure is a powerful testimony to the quality of his spiritual life. Elijah was as godly in private as he was in public. In time, his faith would be strong enough to turn a whole nation back to God (see 1 Kings 18), and to obey God again after a season of doubt and despair (see 1 Kings 19). In his portrait of Elijah, F. B. Meyer observes:

> We need more of this practical godliness. Many deceive themselves. They go to fervid meetings, and profess that they have placed all upon the altar; they speak as if they were indeed filled with the Holy Ghost. But when they return to their homes, the least friction, or interference with their plans, or mistake on the part of others, or angry outburst, arouses a sudden and violent mani-festation of temper.[5]

What was Elijah's secret? He took his problems to the Lord: "And he said to her, 'Give me your son.' And he took him from her arms and carried him up into the upper chamber where he lodged, and laid him on his own bed. And he cried to the LORD" (1 Kings 17:19–20).

Earlier, when the prophet had prayed for God to withhold rain from Israel, his petition was based on the promise of God. This time Elijah did not have a particular promise to rely on, only a life-or-death problem. So he did what any believer should do: when he had trouble in ministry, he went to be alone with his Lord. In the privacy of his chamber, Elijah did not hesitate to bring all his problems, questions, and doubts before the Lord in prayer: "O LORD my God, have you brought calamity even upon the widow with whom I sojourn, by killing her son?" (1 Kings 17:20). These words come in the form of a question, which shows that Elijah did not understand the Lord's pur-poses any more than the widow did. This is often the case with God's minis-ters: they do not have all the answers. Yet Elijah revealed his godliness in his taking his questions, concerns, doubts, and anxieties to God in prayer.

Once he had poured out his heart to God, Elijah prayed in faith. Remem-ber the testimony of the apostle James, who considered Elijah a prime exam-ple of how "the prayer of a righteous person has great power as it is working"

5. F. B. Meyer, *Elijah: And the Secret of His Power* (Fort Washington, PA: Christian Literature Crusade, 1992), 54.

(James 5:16). Here again, Elijah is schooling us in the power of prayer. Without limiting God in any way, he told his troubles to the Lord and asked him to intervene with saving power.

In his exposition of this passage, A. W. Pink drew no fewer than seven spiritual lessons from Elijah's prayer:

> First, Elijah's retiring to his own private chamber, that he might be alone with God. Second, his fervency: he "cried unto the Lord"—no mere lip-service was this. Third, his reliance upon his own personal interest in the Lord, avowing his covenant relationship: "O Lord, my God." Fourth, his encouraging himself in God's attributes: here, the Divine sovereignty and supremacy—"hast Thou also brought evil upon the widow." Fifth, his earnestness and importunity: evidenced by his "stretching himself upon the child" no less than three times. Sixth, his appeal to God's tender mercy: "the *widow* with whom I sojourn." Finally, the definiteness of his petition: "Let this child's soul come into him again."[6]

These are all valuable lessons. But perhaps the most outstanding virtue of Elijah's prayer is that he prayed in faith. Bear in mind that the prophet was praying for something he had *never* experienced before. In fact, this is the first resuscitation recorded in all of Scripture. In all likelihood, therefore, it is the first return from death in the history of the human race. Elijah had no miraculous example upon which to base his prayer. Yet because he knew the power of God, the great prophet prayed with resurrection faith.

Even Elijah's posture for prayer demonstrated his faith. According to the Levitical laws, it was unlawful and impure for a holy man to touch a corpse (see Lev. 22:4). Yet Elijah "stretched himself upon the child three times and cried to the LORD, 'O LORD my God, let this child's life come into him again'" (1 Kings 17:21). It was not the prophet's touch itself that raised the boy; only God has the power to give life. But Elijah's touch was an act of faith, faith that God could make the unclean clean and the dead to live again: "And the LORD listened to the voice of Elijah. And the life of the child came into him again, and he revived. And Elijah took the child and brought him down from the upper chamber into the house and delivered him to his mother. And Elijah said, 'See, your son lives'" (1 Kings 17:22–23). Thus it was by faith that the widow received her son back from the dead (see Heb. 11:35).

6. Pink, *The Life of Elijah*, 90–91.

Anyone who believes in the resurrection can pray with the faith of Elijah. Remember that Elijah is a man just like us. Remember, too, that God has raised Jesus Christ from the grave with the power of everlasting life. On the basis of that saving resurrection we should be bold in asking God for the vision to pray for spiritual blessings beyond anything we have ever experienced before. Pray for the things that are not with the confidence that God may yet cause them to be. Pray for spiritual blessings to be poured out on the church and the world that could come only from a God who has the power to bring the dead back to life.

37

THE REAL TROUBLEMAKER

1 Kings 18:1–18

So Obadiah went to meet Ahab, and told him. And Ahab went to meet Elijah. When Ahab saw Elijah, Ahab said to him, "Is it you, you troubler of Israel?" And he answered, "I have not troubled Israel, but you have, and your father's house, because you have abandoned the commandments of the LORD and followed the Baals." (1 Kings 18:16–18)

It was a long, hot, dry, dusty summer:

The surface of the earth crusted, a thin hard crust, and as the sky became pale, so the earth became pale, pink in the red country and white in the gray country. In the water-cut gullies the earth dusted down in dry little streams. Gophers and ant lions started small avalanches. And as the sharp sun struck day after day, the leaves of the young corn became less stiff and erect; they bent in a curve at first, and then, as the central ribs of strength grew weak, each leaf tilted downward. Then it was June, and the sun shone more fiercely. The brown lines on the corn leaves widened and moved in on the central ribs. The weeds frayed and edged back toward their roots. The air was thin and the sky more pale; and every day the earth paled.[1]

---

1. John Steinbeck, *The Grapes of Wrath* (New York: Viking, 1967), 1–2.

Thus John Steinbeck described a severe drought in his novel *The Grapes of Wrath*, set in the 1930s, when the Great Plains became the American Dust Bowl.

One survivor described the dust storms of those days:

> We could see it coming in my part of western Iowa. At first there was a yellow haze across the horizon, and then as the dust climbed in the hot sky, it became orange and finally brown, and the sun was dimmed. In the first minutes we stood in mute groups just watching, and then windows were slammed shut despite the 100° heat, and the women pushed strips of rags around frames and sills in a pathetic effort to keep the monster at bay. It never worked. The dust found the crevices and loose joints and piled up in the corners and drifted through the air. Sometimes you could hear it on the roof.[2]

There was a long, hot, dry, dusty season in the days of Elijah, only it lasted for three years. "After many days," the Scripture says (1 Kings 18:1), emphasizing the day-in, day-out dreariness of drought. For more than three years there had been no rain in the land, nor any dew (see 1 Kings 17:1). "Now the famine was severe in Samaria" (1 Kings 18:2). F. B. Meyer imagines it like this:

> The music of the brooklets was still. No green pastures carpeted the hills or vales. There was neither blossom on the fig-tree nor fruit in the vines; and the labour of the olive failed. The ground was chapt and barren.... And, probably, the roads in the neighbourhood of the villages and towns were dotted by the stiffened corpses of the abject poor, who had succumbed to the severity of their privations.[3]

This deadly drought forms an intermission between two mighty acts of God. At the end of chapter 17 God raised the dead. Later in chapter 18 God will send fire and rain from heaven. But for now Israel suffers a long intermission, which slows the story down and shows how badly the drought was affecting the land. There was no escape from the judgment of God. Even the king of Israel was out foraging for his animals (1 Kings 18:5), for a high position is no protection in the day of divine judgment!

2. Hugh Sidey, *Time*, June 10, 1996, 50.
3. F. B. Meyer, *Elijah: And the Secret of His Power* (Fort Washington, PA: Christian Literature Crusade, 1992), 61.

The people of Israel had put their trust in Baal, the god of rain, but Baal could not help them now. The God of Israel, the living Lord and only God, had shut the rain up in heaven, and thus there was a desperate famine in the land.

THE SECULAR SAINT

Chapter 18 opens with a dispute about who was to blame for the trouble in this society. Why had this drought happened? Who was responsible? Would the real troublemaker please stand up?

Some have identified Obadiah (who is probably not the author of the book of Obadiah) as one of the troublemakers. In his portrait of Elijah, F. B. Meyer draws a sharp contrast between Elijah and Obadiah.[4] He argues that by serving as Ahab's chamberlain Obadiah had made a compromise with the world. He had chosen a secular career over a sacred calling, politics over the pastorate. Meyer believes that it was wrong for Obadiah to serve wicked King Ahab. He points out that Obadiah usually calls that abominable Ahab his "lord" (1 Kings 18:10, 11, 14), which may suggest that he has divided his loyalties between two masters (cf. Matt. 6:24).

Meyer observes further that Obadiah lacked courage. He was afraid to go tell Ahab that Elijah had appeared. "How have I sinned," Obadiah asks Elijah, "that you would give your servant into the hand of Ahab, to kill me?" (1 Kings 18:9; cf. 1 Kings 17:18). This is the kind of pragmatic question someone asks when he has been in politics too long. Obadiah was trying to save his own skin. If he were truly a man of God, he would have taken his stand and been dismissed by Ahab long ago. Meyer thus gives him this epitaph: "though a good man, there was evidently a great lack of moral strength, of backbone, of vigorous life, in his character."[5]

So was Obadiah worldly, cowardly, and ungodly? No, Obadiah was not the real troublemaker. Though he had a secular calling, there is evidence that he was a secular saint; although he was in the world, he was not entirely of the world (cf. John 17:14–16; 2 Cor. 10:3). True, Obadiah was not as courageous as Elijah. Yet he was a believer in the God of Israel, and there are ways in which he serves as a godly example for Christians who have difficult, secular jobs.

4. Ibid., 63–71.
5. Ibid., 63.

To begin with, Obadiah held an important political post. He "was over the household" (1 Kings 18:3). In other words, he was Ahab's chief of staff. But notice the character the man showed as he occupied this secular post: he "feared the LORD greatly" (1 Kings 18:3). Obadiah was not a nominal believer, or a marginal church attender. He was godly, devout, and committed to the Lord, and thus the rest of his actions need to be interpreted on that basis.

How does a strong believer remain faithful to God in the secular marketplace? Obadiah faced strong temptation to compromise. Obadiah's boss was *not* a believer. On the contrary, King Ahab was an evil man. He was hostile to biblical faith and God-honoring discipleship. One can almost imagine Obadiah going to his weekly Bible study and saying, "I'd like to ask for prayer about my work situation, and especially for my boss, who doesn't know the Lord in a personal way."

Yet Obadiah did not use Ahab's wickedness as an excuse to do second-rate work. Instead, he was loyal to his employer. Since Obadiah was placed in charge of the palace, he must have been one of Ahab's most trusted advisers. So in the midst of a national crisis, Ahab turned to Obadiah for help. "And Ahab said to Obadiah, 'Go through the land to all the springs of water and to all the valleys. Perhaps we may find grass and save the horses and mules alive, and not lose some of the animals.' So they divided the land between them to pass through it. Ahab went in one direction by himself, and Obadiah went in another direction by himself" (1 Kings 18:5–6). Obadiah was a faithful servant to his master and a loyal subject to his king, not because Ahab was a righteous man, but because he knew the king's authority was ordained by God (cf. Rom. 13:1).

Every Christian should do the same kind of work on a secular job: first-rate, respectful, loyal work. Obadiah is an example of what Paul meant when he exhorted working people:

> Slaves, obey in everything those who are your earthly masters, not by way of eye-service, as people-pleasers, but with sincerity of heart, fearing the Lord. Whatever you do, work heartily, as for the Lord and not for men, knowing that from the Lord you will receive the inheritance as your reward. You are serving the Lord Christ. (Col. 3:22–24).

Obadiah's faithfulness to Ahab did not prevent him from being faithful to God. When he called Ahab "lord," it was out of respect, still recognizing that God was his ultimate master. He treated Elijah with the same respect, also calling him "lord" (1 Kings 18:7). As long as Ahab did not ask him to do anything that violated his commitment to God, Obadiah was completely loyal. He may have been quiet about his spiritual allegiance, but when push finally came to shove, he obeyed God rather than men (cf. Acts 5:29). He did not let his allegiance to the king of Israel usurp his allegiance to the King of kings.

Obadiah's Courage

The proof of Obadiah's piety came when Jezebel persecuted the prophets of God. Jezebel was Ahab's First Lady—a woman that William Still aptly described as "a striding woman, a feminine tycoon, a harridan, termagant, virago."[6]

Jezebel started by bringing strange gods into the king's house (1 Kings 16:31–33). This was bad enough, but then the queen persecuted the people of God. So what did Obadiah do when the boss's wife went on the warpath and he was tempted to compromise his faith? "When Jezebel cut off the prophets of the Lord, Obadiah took a hundred prophets and hid them by fifties in a cave and fed them with bread and water" (1 Kings 18:4). Obadiah was no coward. He took a stand for God, doing something that only a devout believer would do. At great risk to his career and personal safety, Obadiah shrewdly used his political influence to protect a whole seminary of prophets.

Christians are called to show the same courage when confronted with moral dilemmas in their work. A colleague may ask for help covering a mistake with a white lie. A boss may pressure his employees to cut corners for a client. A company may even have well-established policies that are fundamentally dishonest. The Christian's obligation to God in such situations is very simple: obey God rather than men. If we are tempted to do something unethical at work, very likely the Holy Spirit will give us an uneasy conscience about it. If we are still not sure whether something is right or wrong, we should search the Scriptures and seek the counsel of Christian friends. But once we know what is right to do, we are called to do the right thing and then trust that God will be glorified through our integrity.

6. William Still, *Elijah* (Gilcomston South Aberdeen Church, 1990), 25.

Obadiah did the right thing. He took a hundred prophets and hid them in caves, probably near Mount Carmel, where there are hundreds of caverns. There is a lesson in this action about the variety of the providence of God. There were one hundred and one prophets in Israel that God protected, but he did not save them all in the same way. God used miraculous means to save Elijah (remember the widow of Zarephath, for example), but he used ordinary means to save the other hundred prophets. On occasion God used ravens to bring meat and bread to Elijah. Such provision was extraordinary, miraculous. But when the rest of the prophets went hungry, God used his servant Obadiah to supply them with food and water. Although God is capable of providing for our needs with a miraculous providence, his usual procedure is to provide through ordinary means.

This is a much-needed lesson for any church that is clamoring for signs and wonders. The late John Wimber, founder of the Vineyard churches, exemplified this thirst for the miraculous. When Wimber first became a believer, he started to read about the miracles in Scripture and could not figure out why he did not see more of them happening in his local church. He went to his pastor and said, "When are you going to do all the stuff?" His pastor said, "What stuff?" Wimber replied, "You know *the stuff*, like walking on water, healing the sick, and raising the dead?"[7]

God can do "the stuff," and sometimes he does. He did "the stuff" for Elijah. He even raised the dead for him. It is easy to imagine how this would be marketed in the contemporary church. Elijah's handlers would sell bookmarks printed with "The Prayer of Zarephath" and publish copies of the *Cherith Cookbook*, with a hundred and one ways to cook bread and meat. Elijah would become a faith healer, raising the dead on cable TV. After his show they would run infomercials for the Elijah Diet. Understand, however, that God did not do "the stuff" for the other hundred prophets. Not the miraculous stuff, anyway. God provided for his other servants in a mundane and unspectacular way. Yet this provision was equally providential. The prophets in the cave had as much reason to praise God when they saw Obadiah coming as Elijah did when he saw the ravens.

One can almost imagine a prophet hiding in Obadiah's cave, listening to some of Elijah's sermons, deciding that true believers are fed only by

7. John Wimber, from an interview in the 1990s.

ravens, and then going off to find his own brook. Such a prophet would have gone hungry because he would have been stepping outside God's ordinary providence.

Do not yearn for the extraordinary provision of God, but trust in his ordinary providence. Do not "expect a miracle." If 1 Kings 18 is any indication, the chances are at least a hundred to one that God will provide for us in some ordinary way. This is an encouragement whenever we wait for God's provision. God will provide. All the legwork we have done during a job search will finally pay off. A friend from church will tell us about the apartment we have been looking for. A health problem will be solved by conventional medicine. Many times the Lord will use the faithfulness of believers like Obadiah to provide what we need.

Obadiah proved himself faithful to God, and to Elijah. True, he was sometimes fearful. In particular, Obadiah worried that Ahab would kill him when he told him that he had found Elijah (see 1 Kings 18:9, 12, 14). Elijah was forcing Obadiah to declare his ultimate allegiance, and Obadiah was struggling with the implications this would have for his relationship to the king and, indeed, for his very life. His fears were not altogether unreasonable. Obadiah had seen firsthand Ahab's relentless pursuit of Elijah: "As the LORD your God lives, there is no nation or kingdom where my lord has not sent to seek you. And when they would say, 'He is not here,' he would take an oath of the kingdom or nation, that they had not found you. And now you say, 'Go, tell your lord, "Behold, Elijah is here"'" (1 Kings 18:10–11).

Who wouldn't be afraid? As Ahab's chief of staff, Obadiah knew full well what kind of temper his boss had and how angry he was with Elijah. He was also familiar with Ahab's usual methods for dealing with political opponents. When Obadiah said, "How have I sinned, that you would give your servant into the hand of Ahab, to kill me?" (1 Kings 18:9), he was really saying, "You must be joking, Elijah! You don't know Ahab like I know Ahab. When he finds out that I've been talking to you, he'll kill me."

Obadiah's next objection betrayed a lack of trust in God's sovereign care: "And as soon as I have gone from you, the Spirit of the LORD will carry you I know not where. And so, when I come and tell Ahab and he cannot find you, he will kill me, although I your servant have feared the LORD from my youth" (1 Kings 18:12). Obadiah was worried that Elijah would disappear again before Ahab could find him, in which case the king would be angrier with Obadiah than ever. Indeed, Obadiah feared that he would become a dead man: "Has it not been told my lord what I did when Jezebel killed the prophets of the LORD, how I hid a hundred men of the LORD's prophets by fifties in a cave and fed them with bread and water? And now you say, 'Go, tell your lord, "Behold, Elijah is here"'; and he will kill me" (1 Kings 18:13–14).

Nevertheless, in spite of all his fears, Obadiah obeyed the Lord. This is the important thing, that in the end he was faithful to the Lord: "So Obadiah went to meet Ahab, and told him" (1 Kings 18:16). Obadiah had enough courage to do what the Lord commanded him to do, even when he was afraid to do it. This is the measure of our own courage as well: Are we willing and able to do the hard things God calls us to do, in spite of all our fears? And are we willing to declare publicly our commitment to Christ? We do not know how Ahab responded to Obadiah for bringing him news of Elijah's whereabouts, but perhaps this is part of the point. Regardless of how Ahab responded, it was Obadiah's duty—as it is our duty—simply to obey God's command.

THE PERSECUTED PROPHET

Elijah had even more courage than Obadiah—the kind that comes from having a living relationship with the living God. Elijah was not the real troublemaker, any more than Obadiah was. When the Lord told Elijah to go to King Ahab, the prophet did what he always did and obeyed the Lord: "After many days the word of the LORD came to Elijah, in the third year, saying, 'Go, show yourself to Ahab, and I will send rain upon the earth.' So Elijah went to show himself to Ahab" (1 Kings 18:1–2). When the Lord said, "Go," Elijah did not ask, "How far?"; he just went.

The fact that Elijah is not a troublemaker is evident from his strong response to Obadiah's fears: "As the LORD of hosts lives, before whom I stand, I will surely show myself to him today" (1 Kings 18:15). Elijah knew his God. Even though he lived in a culture that said "God is dead," Elijah had not lost his theological bearings. He knew that he served the living God, and therefore he had determined to keep on serving that God by doing exactly what God told him to do.

Elijah was no troublemaker, but Ahab thought that he was. The king thought that God's prophet had been making trouble for Israel, so he tried to pin the blame for the drought on Elijah. Finally, the king and the prophet had their long-awaited, much-anticipated, widely publicized meeting: "When Ahab saw Elijah, Ahab said to him, 'Is it you, you troubler of Israel?'" (1 Kings 18:17)—more literally, "the one who has brought a curse upon Israel."

The Bible does not explain why Obadiah and Ahab had such trouble recognizing Elijah. Earlier, when Obadiah "was on the way, behold, Elijah met him. And Obadiah recognized him and fell on his face and said, 'Is it you, my lord Elijah?'" (1 Kings 18:7). Perhaps Elijah had a wild look about him after all his time in the wilderness, or had disguised himself in some way. Or maybe Ahab had been looking for Elijah so long that he could hardly believe his eyes when he found him. After all, the king had organized an international manhunt for Elijah, with an "all points" bulletin for his arrest. As Obadiah explained, "there is no nation or kingdom where my lord has not sent to seek you. And when they would say, 'He is not here,' he would take an oath of the kingdom or nation, that they had not found you" (1 Kings 18:10). Ahab wanted to make sure that none of the surrounding nations granted Elijah asylum. The prophet was Israel's Most Wanted.

This vendetta was enacted because Ahab held Elijah personally responsible for the famine in the land: "Is it you, you troubler of Israel?" (1 Kings 18:17). Ahab gave Elijah no friendly salutation and greeted him with no kindly respect. Instead he accused him of treason. Ahab's accusation is a sober warning about what happens to God's people in days of judgment. First the world will shut its ears to God's Word. Then it will point an accusatory finger at God's people. When trouble comes, the people of this world do not turn back to God, but turn against him and his people. Sometimes God's enemies will stop at nothing to kill God's people (cf. John 16:2). So Jezebel attacked the prophets of God. With a hit list that included every seminary student in the country, she was killing off the prophets of the Lord (1 Kings 18:4, 13).

And so it ever is. The religious leaders of Israel said essentially the same thing about the apostle Paul that Ahab said about Elijah. They hauled him up for trial before Felix and said, "For we have found this man a plague, one who stirs up riots among all the Jews throughout the world" (Acts 24:5; cf. Acts 16:20–17:6). The peaceful work of preaching the gospel is a threat to the fortresses of evil. The values of the kingdom of heaven are such a total reversal of the values of the kingdom of this world that faithful servants of God always seem like troublemakers in the eyes of the world.

The same thing happened in the early church. In his *Life of Claudius*, Suetonius speaks of "disturbances" breaking out in Rome at the instigation of one "Chrestus," which indicates that trouble was being caused in the name of Christ.[8] In the time of Tacitus, church members were wrongfully charged with practicing incest and cannibalism as part of public worship because of their love for "brothers and sisters" and their eating and drinking "the body and blood of Christ." Under Nero, the Christians were blamed for the burning of Rome and summarily executed. For the next several hundred years Christianity was a capital offense in the Roman Empire. As Tertullian wryly observed, "If the Tiber rises too high or the Nile too low, the cry is 'The Christians to the lion.'"[9] "Let us not forget why the Christians were killed," wrote Francis Schaffer. "They were not killed because they worshiped Jesus. . . . Nobody cared who worshiped whom so long as the worshiper did not disrupt the unity of the state, centered in the formal worship of Caesar. The reason the Christians were killed was because they were rebels."[10]

The same thing happened during the Protestant Reformation in Europe. When Martin Luther started preaching justification by grace alone through faith alone, the pope called him a "pestiferous virus."[11] In fact, John Calvin wrote his *Institutes* to defend the Reformation against those who said that Protestant Christians were lawless troublemakers.[12]

The world thought that Jesus was a troublemaker, too. Indeed, no one had ever caused more trouble than Jesus! When he was brought to trial before Pilate, his accusers said, "We found this man misleading our nation. . . . He stirs up the people, teaching throughout all Judea, from Galilee even to this place" (Luke 23:2, 5). The preaching of the gospel draws some men and women to God in faith and repentance, but at the same time it makes other men and women hostile to God and his messengers. The coming of Jesus

---

8. Ralph Martin Novak, *Christianity and the Roman Empire: Background Texts* (Harrisburg, PA: Trinity Press International, 2001), 20.

9. Henry Chadwick, *The Early Church*, The Pelican History of the Church, vol. 1 (London: Penguin, 1967), 21–29.

10. Francis Schaffer, *How Shall We Then Live? The Rise and Decline of Western Thought and Culture* (Wheaton, IL: Crossway, 2005), 24.

11. Pope Leo X, *Exsurge Domine*, 1520, in Roland H. Bainton, *Here I Stand: A Life of Martin Luther* (New York: Abingdon, 1950), 147.

12. See John Calvin's "Prefatory Address to King Francis I of France," in Calvin, *Institutes of the Christian Religion*, ed. John T. McNeill, trans. Ford Lewis Battles, 2 vols., Library of Christian Classics 20–21 (Philadelphia: Westminster, 1960), 1:9–31.

Christ into the world had and continues to have this double effect. For those who accept it, the rule of Christ brings peace; for those who oppose it, the rule of Christ seems to bring nothing but trouble.

These examples remind us not to be surprised when the world attacks the church of Jesus Christ. Most Western Christians do not think about religious persecution as often as we should. The fact is that the church is facing more severe persecution right now than at any other time in its history. The "Annual Statistical Table on Global Mission" estimates that there have been as many as two hundred thousand Christian martyrs every year since 1970.[13] However accurate these numbers may be, they serve as a reminder that North America is not at the center of what God is doing in the world. Christians in places like China, East Africa, the Middle East, and South America are suffering and dying for their faith in Jesus Christ at the hands of communists, fascists, Muslims, and Hindus.

Now the first rumblings of religious persecution have begun to be heard in America. The media often treats evangelical Christians as scapegoats for social problems. As American society continues to unravel, this attitude may lead to economic reprisals, to legal threat, and ultimately to physical violence.

One example of this hostility was the rash of church burnings in the mid-1990s, especially in the South. Many of these cases of arson seemed racially motivated, since most of the churches burned to the ground were owned by either black or multiracial congregations. But church burnings are a form of religious persecution as well as racial hatred. It is no accident that churches are being attacked, because it is the church that poses the severest threat to bigotry. In the eyes of God's enemies, churches that practice racial reconciliation are troublemakers.

The hatred of the world should neither discourage nor frighten us. By the grace of God believers can be bold like Elijah, fearless in the face of an evil king. Jesus offers this encouragement: "If the world hates you, know that it has hated me before it hated you. If you were of the world, the world would love you as its own; but because you are not of the world, but I chose you out of the world, therefore the world hates you" (John 15:18–19).

13. David B. Barrett, "Annual Statistical Table on Global Mission: 1996," *International Bulletin of Mission Research*, January 1996, 24–25.

THE REAL TROUBLEMAKER

Neither Obadiah nor Elijah was the real troublemaker in Israel. No, the real troublemaker was King Ahab. Ahab tried to serve all the trouble on Elijah, but here was Elijah's return of serve: "And he answered, 'I have not troubled Israel, but you have, and your father's house, because you have abandoned the commandments of the LORD and followed the Baals'" (1 Kings 18:18).

This is the climax of the first confrontation between Ahab and Elijah. Their encounter is like the scene at the end of a mystery novel when the identity of the killer is revealed. Elijah points the finger at Ahab: "I have not troubled Israel, but you have, and your father's house, because you have abandoned the commandments of the LORD and followed the Baals" (1 Kings 18:18). The king is the one who has brought severe famine to the land. The word Elijah uses for "trouble" is the same word used in Joshua 7:25 to describe the military defeat that Israel suffered because Achan stole the plunder that belonged to God. It is always the people who live in rebellion against God who bring the trouble of God's judgment against a nation.

Elijah accused Ahab of two kinds of sins: omission and commission. A sin of omission is something we did not do that we should have done. It is an area of life where we have failed to follow God. A sin of commission, on the other hand, is something we did that we should not have done. It is a transgression, an area of life where we have deliberately overstepped God's boundary.

Ahab had been sinning both ways. He had "abandoned the command-ments of the LORD" (1 Kings 18:18). These were sins of omission. Ahab was not doing what he was supposed to be doing. Plus, he had "followed the Baals" (1 Kings 18:18). This kind of false worship was a transgres-sion, a sin of commission. Ahab was doing what he was not supposed to be doing.

Ahab's actions reveal that he was in bad spiritual shape. The king ought to have been repenting of his sins and crying to God for mercy. For the sake of his people, he ought to have been praying for God to turn away his wrath. Instead, he was trying to persevere through divine judgment in his own strength, going through the land to look for grass for his livestock

(1 Kings 18:5–6). According to A. W. Pink, "there is not a single syllable here about *God!* not a word about the awful *sins* which had called down His displeasure upon the land! Fountains, brooks and grass were all that occupied Ahab's thoughts—*relief* from the Divine affliction was all he cared about."[14]

Ahab's main concern was his animals. Horses were desperately important to Ahab because he believed that they were essential to national security. The records of Shalmaneser III of Assyria indicate that Ahab provided some two thousand chariots when the Syrian coalition battled Assyria at Qarqar.[15] Observe the contrast between Obadiah, who was protecting the Lord's prophets, and Ahab, who was mainly concerned about saving his (horse) hides! Divine judgment had made Ahab more selfish. He valued his own horses more highly than he valued other people, doubtless because their military superiority gave him a sense of physical safety. This attitude is something the Bible explicitly warns against. According to the psalmist, "the war horse is a false hope for salvation" (Ps. 33:17)—a warning that the United States and other military powers would be wise to apply to their armaments.

Ahab may be contrasted with David, a king after God's own heart. David also fell under divine judgment, but "he saw the angel who was striking the people, and said, 'Behold, I have sinned, and I have done wickedly. But these sheep, what have they done? Please let your hand be against me and against my father's house'" (2 Sam. 24:17). David was a true king and spiritual leader. He accepted responsibility for his sin, recognizing that he himself was the troublemaker. Ahab was no such king. He abdicated his spiritual responsibility and thus he was the real troublemaker, the one who abandoned the Lord and followed after Baal.

It is not hard to know which example to follow. If we are honest with ourselves, and with God, we will see that we are often the cause of our own spiritual difficulties. If so, then our situation will not get resolved by blaming other people, but only by confessing our own sin. Nor is it hard to see what kind of king we truly need. Jesus displayed the best spiritual leadership of all when he took our sins upon himself at the cross. "Let your hand be against me," he said to his Father. Although Jesus was no troublemaker, he invited

---

14. A. W. Pink, *The Life of Elijah*, rev. ed. (Edinburgh: Banner of Truth, 1963), 97.

15. James B. Pritchard, *Ancient Near Eastern Texts* (Princeton, NJ: Princeton University Press, 1955), 279.

trouble upon himself in order to save his people. Sooner or later, most people do what Ahab did and look for someone to blame for their troubles. Jesus did just the opposite. Though blameless himself, he nevertheless took the blame for our sin in order to save us.

Sadly, Ahab never did accept responsibility for Israel's drought. More trouble would follow. But soon the grace of God would come to bring the long, hot, dry summer to an end. What God said to Elijah at the beginning of the passage is full of promise: "Go, show yourself to Ahab, and I will send rain upon the earth" (1 Kings 18:1).

38

No God but God

1 Kings 18:19–29

And Elijah came near to all the people and said, "How long will
you go limping between two different opinions? If the LORD is
God, follow him; but if Baal, then follow him. . . . And you call
upon the name of your god, and I will call upon the name of the
LORD, and the God who answers by fire, he is God."
(1 Kings 18:21, 24)

E lijah was going up the mountain to meet Almighty God. He had
been waiting a long time, through three hot summers in Samaria, Cherith, and Zarephath. Finally, Elijah was going up the
mountain to see the Godness of God revealed in the fire on the mountain.

The prophet would not go up the mountain alone. Wicked King Ahab
would be there, with all his lackeys. Four hundred fifty prophets of Baal
would be there, plus four hundred prophets of Asherah, if they could drag
themselves away from their feasting at Jezebel's table. All the people of Israel
would be there, too, from every corner of the kingdom. They would all be
there, high on top of Mount Carmel, looking out over Palestine from the
Mediterranean Sea in the west to the Jordan River in the east, from Mount

Hermon in the north to the vale of Jezreel in the south. All the plains and mountains of Israel would be spread out like a tablecloth before them.

The Silence of Doubt

As one imagines the spectacle of all the prophets, livestock, wood, altars, shouting, dancing, and body piercing on the mountain, it would be easy to miss the silence. In fact, there were two great silences on Mount Carmel—two silences before the thunderbolt. The first was the silence of doubt. It was the embarrassed silence of a people who did not know which God they wanted to serve.

The prophet Elijah had thrown down the gauntlet, issuing his challenge to Ahab. When the king went out to meet Elijah, he accused him of being a troublemaker, of offending Baal so that the rain would not fall on Israel. But Elijah knew who the real troublemaker was. So he turned Ahab's words against him: "I have not troubled Israel, but you have, and your father's house, because you have abandoned the commandments of the Lord and followed the Baals. Now therefore send and gather all Israel to me at Mount Carmel, and the 450 prophets of Baal and the 400 prophets of Asherah, who eat at Jezebel's table" (1 Kings 18:18–19).

To prove his point, Elijah proposed one of the great religious debates, showdowns, and heavyweight bouts of all time. It was Baal against the Lord God of Israel, winner take all. The stakes were high. The religious destiny of God's people was hanging in the balance. In one corner was Baal, the storm god of the Canaanites, with all his backers: twenty-two score and ten prophets on the government's payroll. In the other corner stood the Lord God of heaven and earth, with his only prophet, Elijah.

A good fight always draws a big crowd, so when Ahab sent his promoters throughout his kingdom (see 1 Kings 18:20), it was easy to gather the whole nation for the rumble at Carmel. When they had all taken their places, "Elijah came near to all the people and said, 'How long will you go limping between two different opinions? If the Lord is God, follow him; but if Baal, then follow him'" (1 Kings 18:21).

Silence. "And the people did not answer him a word" (1 Kings 18:21). The silence was embarrassing, like the awkward pause when someone has said something so offensive and so shocking that no one quite knows what to say.

481

Yet the silence spoke volumes. It meant the people of Israel did not know where they had placed their ultimate allegiance. They did not know which God they trusted. On the one hand, their attraction to Baal was so strong that they could not stand up and pledge allegiance to the living God. On the other hand, they had been raised in the traditions of the Torah and could not quite bring themselves to deny the existence of the Lord God of Israel.

To say it another way, the people of Israel wanted to hedge their bets. They wanted to have their Baal and their Yahweh, too. They were firm adherents of the "Monroe Doctrine" that we mentioned back in chapter 36—named for the actress Marilyn Monroe, who thought that people should believe everything a little bit. Thus, like many people in our culture, they wanted to believe that there are many roads to one God. They wanted to believe whatever they liked, even if some of their beliefs contradicted others. If one god is good, they thought, then two are better, and three are better still. According to this pluralistic perspective, people can never believe in too many religions or put their trust in too many gods.

Something like the Monroe Doctrine was the fundamental religious idea of Elijah's day. The people of Israel liked to believe in everything a little bit. They liked to believe in the Lord God of Abraham, Isaac, and Jacob . . . a little bit. They liked to believe in Baal . . . a little bit. They liked to believe in Asherah . . . a little bit. So when Elijah confronted them on the mountain and forced them to declare their ultimate allegiance, they had nothing to say for themselves.

LIMPING ALONG

Elijah accused the people of Israel of limping between two opinions, using the word one would use for someone who is lame. The Israelites were limping along, tottering from side to side, hobbling through life. It was as if they had a racing sandal on one foot and a ski boot on the other. They had one foot on the path of obedience and one foot down in the ditch of bondage to Baal. So Elijah wanted to know just one thing: how long would they waver between two opinions?

I learned the futility of wavering between two opinions early in my baseball career. I was taking batting practice my first spring of Little League, and I was afraid. The high school kid who pitched batting practice was throwing sidearm, inside and *hard*. So instead of keeping both of my feet in the batter's box, I started stepping toward foul territory, way out past third base. Coaches call this "stepping in the bucket," when a batter steps so far away from home plate that he is not able to hit the ball. I was wavering between two opinions: I wanted to hit the ball and I also wanted to get out of the way. But anyone who wants to hit a baseball has to be single-minded about it, stepping right toward the pitcher's mound and driving the ball.

The people of Israel had one foot in the bucket. They were stepping toward foul territory, wavering between two opinions. They had divided hearts. They wanted to worship the Lord God of Israel and still enjoy a little casual Baal worship on the side.

We, too, live in a culture that limps between multiple opinions. A monument to our religious pluralism was built on the campus of Vanderbilt University in 1993, when the Divinity School dedicated its new All Faith Chapel to Hindus, Jews, Catholics, Protestants, Muslims, the Baha'i, and the Orthodox Christian Fellowship. The architecture of the All Faith Chapel is devoid of any explicitly religious symbolism. It is an empty shell of a building. But the chapel does have a cupboard for every religion. Although permanent religious symbols are not incorporated into the chapel's design, storage cabinets are available to hold the accoutrements that each tradition uses in worship. If you are Jewish, you can get a Star of David and a menorah out of the cupboard; Christians have access to a cross and some Bibles; Muslims can put out some prayer rugs; and so forth. One might almost say that Vanderbilt students come out of the closet every time they worship.

The All Faith Chapel was built for a culture that does not entirely know what it believes, or for one that wants to believe in everything a little bit. At the dedication ceremony Vanderbilt University chaplain Beverly Asbury said, "This place is for all faiths. Its dedication consists of many acts and of one. There is diversity in our unity, and there is unity in our diversity as we dedicate this space and add to its light, each in the way of a distinctive tradition."[1]

Christians sometimes lead the same kind of lives. Rather than letting God be everything for us, we make space for a little lust, a little self-indulgence, a little materialism, and so we limp along through life, not walking

1. *First Things*, November 1993, 54.

steadily for Christ. We are like the people Woody Allen mocked for taking "God" and "Carpet" with equal seriousness. By "Carpet," Allen meant the middle-class home "with its decorations, color combinations, furniture, appliances, and sound systems"—"a place where one feels secure and in control." But as Os Guinness points out, "Any god who will share his throne with carpet has little to do with the God of the Bible—despite sharing the same name."[2]

When faced with such spiritual confusion in his day, Elijah demanded that people make up their minds. He made the same demand that Moses made when he came down from the mountain, saw the people of God worshiping a golden calf, and said, "Who is on the LORD's side? let him come unto me" (Ex. 32:26 KJV). Joshua made the same demand after the death of Moses, when he said to the children of Israel, "Choose this day whom you will serve" (Josh. 24:15). The same demand comes to every man, woman, and child in every generation: *How long will you waver between two opinions?* If the Lord is God, then follow him.

We cannot hedge our bets. We cannot straddle the fence. We cannot take a wait-and-see attitude about following God. The God of Elijah is exclusive. He allows no rivals. He will not share his glory with any other god. To believe in God is to follow him with our whole lives. But we cannot do this if we are still on the fence, trying to decide if God is God or not. If we are still on the fence, then we are not following God and may not even know him in a saving way at all. If we are not with God, we are against him (Matt. 12:30). The Bible teaches that we are separated from God by our sin and that the only way we can be delivered from eternal judgment is to trust in Jesus Christ, believing that his death on the cross and his resurrection from the grave deliver us from our sins.

With God it is all or nothing. He wants our whole heart, mind, soul, and strength. Jesus said, "No one can serve two masters" (Matt. 6:24). The Puritans used to put it this way: "You cannot serve God by halves." So, we need to ask ourselves, have I given my whole self to God, or am I still dragging around the ski boot of love for this world? If the Lord is God, then we are called to follow him with both feet, making him first in worship, first in work, first in leisure, and first in the life of the home.

2. Os Guinness and Jonn Seel, eds., *No God but God* (Chicago: Moody, 1992), 40.

Here is one simple way to test whether we are limping between two opinions. The true believer is not silent. When the waverer is asked about spiritual things, he or she is not quite sure what to say, like the Israelites at Carmel. But when a Christian is asked about spiritual things, he or she is able to give a bold testimony of faith in Christ.

John Mortimer—a barrister and man-about-town in London—once conducted a series of candid interviews with prominent leaders in the English church. One of the men Mortimer interviewed was Robert Runcie, then the Archbishop of Canterbury, the head of the Anglican church. Mortimer asked Runcie the same simple question Elijah asked Israel: "Do you believe in God?" There was an awkward silence, the silence of doubt. "Well," Runcie replied, "sort of, in a manner of speaking, depending upon what you mean by 'God.'"[3] On this occasion at least, Runcie was a waverer. He was tottering between two opinions, and thus he was not ready to give a strong testimony of faith in Christ.

If Elijah could have spoken with the archbishop, he may well have said to him what he is saying to us: "How long will you go limping between two different opinions? If the Lord is God, follow him; but if Baal, then follow him. And if you do follow God, speak up for him!" When a spiritual topic comes up in a conversation with a neighbor, or when a coworker asks an important question about life, we should be ready to give a clear answer that testifies to the grace and truth of God.

REFUTATION AND DEMONSTRATION

We have seen the silence of doubt. Before we consider the second silence on the mountainside, we should consider Elijah's method of evangelism. What was his strategy for doing apologetics? How did he defend his faith in the living God? God has not called us to the top of Mount Carmel, but there is something to be learned from Elijah's two-part strategy: disproof and then proof.[4] First, the disproof of the false god, and then the proof of the true God—the refutation of Baal before the demonstration of the God of Israel.

Elijah began his disproof with a display of good sportsmanship, in which he gave his opponents every advantage. Taking on all comers, the prophet

3. Oscar Handlin, "The Unmarked Way," *The American Scholar*, Summer 1996, 350.
4. Guinness and Seel, *No God but God*, 15.

485

was badly outnumbered: "Then Elijah said to the people, 'I, even I only, am left a prophet of the LORD, but Baal's prophets are 450 men'" (1 Kings 18:22). If there were bookmakers on Mount Carmel, they were getting 450-to-1 odds against Elijah. Nevertheless, God's man Elijah offered the prophets of Baal the home-bull advantage: "'Let two bulls be given to us, and let them choose one bull for themselves and cut it in pieces and lay it on the wood, but put no fire to it. And I will prepare the other bull and lay it on the wood and put no fire to it. And you call upon the name of your god, and I will call upon the name of the LORD, and the God who answers by fire, he is God.' And all the people answered, 'It is well spoken'" (1 Kings 18:23–24). This was good sportsmanship. Just in case one bull proved to be preferable for sacrificing, Elijah let his opponents choose first.

Then Elijah let the prophets of Baal go first: "Then Elijah said to the prophets of Baal, 'Choose for yourselves one bull and prepare it first, for you are many, and call upon the name of your god, but put no fire to it'" (1 Kings 18:25). Remember, this was a sudden-death competition: whoever succeeded in bringing down fire just once would win the contest immediately. Elijah had said, "The God who answers by fire, he is God" (1 Kings 18:24). So if Baal had answered with fire, Elijah would have never even had the chance to try his bull. He would have been a dead man first.

Furthermore, this entire contest played to Baal's supposed strengths as a deity of nature. Baal was the god of the sun, so warmth and heat were his areas of special expertise. Baal was the god of the storm, so fire was right up his alley. Surely the god of thunder could manage at least one lightning bolt to ignite his bull!

All of this shows Elijah's absolute confidence in God, which is a good model for confident evangelism. Christians tend to be very defensive. We have our own schools, magazines, TV programs, radio shows, and books. We hunker down in our own little communities because we feel threatened by a culture that is hostile to biblical faith, and when we do go out into the world, we keep it pretty quiet.

By contrast, Elijah went up on the mountain and confronted his culture. He was not afraid of the number of those who opposed him, or intimidated by the strength of their arguments. Elijah went out in broad daylight and let his opponents make the strongest possible case for their religious beliefs. He was not afraid to do this because he knew that ultimately they would fail. He knew

486

that Baal was nothing, and that even if Baal had 450 prophets, 450 times 0 is still 0. From the beginning, Elijah knew that it was no contest, that any attempt to prove Baal would actually end up destroying Baal's credibility.

This is precisely what happened, of course. Despite the fact that his prophets did everything they could to call down fire, to the point of injuring themselves, Baal never answered: "And [the prophets of Baal] took the bull that was given them, and they prepared it and called upon the name of Baal from morning until noon, saying, 'O Baal, answer us!' But there was no voice, and no one answered. And they limped around the altar that they had made" (1 Kings 18:26). Baal was a total failure. Once his prophets of Baal had made their case, Elijah was scathing in his sarcasm. James A. Montgomery describes "Elijah's satire in a nut-shell" as "the raciest comment ever made on Pagan mythology."[5] Here is how the Bible records it: "And at noon Elijah mocked them, saying, 'Cry aloud, for he is a god. Either he is musing, or he is relieving himself, or he is on a journey, or perhaps he is asleep and must be awakened'" (1 Kings 18:27).

Perhaps Baal was thinking deep thoughts. Perhaps he was "busy," as in "Mr. Baal is in a meeting right now." Actually, the word for "busy" is a euphemism. To put it more graphically and more literally, Elijah was saying that perhaps Baal had gone to use the men's room. The prophet also wondered whether perhaps Baal had fallen asleep or taken a journey. Maybe he was taking a siesta, or a road trip. Or maybe he was on vacation. After all, according to Canaanite mythology, Baal made an annual journey to the underworld.

This was all part of Elijah's refutation, his disproof of Baal. The prophet was cutting Baal down to size, diminishing his stature, reducing him to human terms. To do this, he imagined Baal engaging in the activities of human beings, with all their physical limitations. Elijah gave him no respect, because he refused to grant that Baal was really a god at all.

Something similar happens at the end of *The Wizard of Oz*. When Dorothy and her friends reach the Emerald City, they hear the voice of THE GREAT AND TERRIBLE OZ. At first they are afraid of him, but then Dorothy's little dog Toto pulls back the curtain and the great wizard is revealed to be a little old man with a megaphone. The wizard is exposed as a huckster and a cheat.

When Elijah pulled back the curtain, he exposed Baal as a fraud and a huckster, too. Elijah's mockery may not seem very sportsmanlike, yet it was

5. James A. Montgomery, *The Book of Kings*, ed. Henry S. Gehman, International Critical Commentary (Edinburgh: T&T Clark, 1951), 302.

right and good for Elijah to mock Baal. Elijah's mockery was holy sarcasm. The prophet's overriding motivation was to demonstrate the glory of God, and in order to do this, he needed to show that God has no rivals. Elijah had to disprove Baal before he could prove God. He had to show that no other god can stand in the ring with the God of Israel. There is no God but God. Compared to the Lord God Almighty, any other deity is a total joke.

Consider the absolute contrast between Baal and the God of Elijah. In comparison to busy, sleepy Baal, the majesty of the Lord God Almighty shines forth with full force and perfect beauty. The Lord God Almighty is always living and active. He is never lost in his thoughts, because he knows all things instantly and completely. He does not have bodily functions; he is spirit and does not have a body. He never takes a vacation; he sustains all things at all times by his power. The God of Elijah is never sleepy and never takes a nap: "He who keeps you will not slumber. Behold, he who keeps Israel will neither slumber nor sleep" (Ps. 121:3–4).

There is no need to limp between two opinions. The Lord, he *is* God, and there is no other. He and he alone is never absent, never distracted, never asleep. Therefore, we can trust him to watch over us and care for us in every spiritual confrontation or difficult situation we face. He is always living and active and able to save.

THE SILENCE OF THE NO GOD

One of the best things about the living God is that he hears and answers prayer. Our study of Elijah began in the book of James, who said: "The prayer of a righteous person has great power as it is working. Elijah was a man with a nature like ours, and he prayed fervently that it might not rain, and for three years and six months it did not rain on the earth. Then he prayed again, and heaven gave rain, and the earth bore its fruit" (James 5:16–18). As the apostle James examined the ministry of the prophet Elijah, one thing leaped out at him. The distinguishing characteristic or telltale mark of Elijah's ministry was prayer.

What does 1 Kings 18 teach us about prayer? In fact, prayer is the key to the whole chapter. At the outset, Elijah said, "You call upon the name of your god, and I will call upon the name of the LORD, and the God who answers by fire, he is God" (1 Kings 18:24). So the showdown on Mount Carmel was all about which God was able to answer prayer. The whole contest was to be settled on the basis of answered prayer as the proof of deity.

What about Baal? Could he answer prayer? Not a chance! The second silence on the mountain was the silence of a god who did not and could not answer prayer, a god who is no god at all.

There was a moment of silence the first time Baal's prophets prayed. They were making a lot of noise, but "there was no voice, and no one answered" (1 Kings 18:26). The prophets of Baal did not like the sound of that silence, because they knew what it meant. They could hear that their prayers were not being answered, so they erupted into a desperate frenzy of dancing and shouting: "And at noon Elijah mocked them, saying, 'Cry aloud, for he is a god. Either he is musing, or he is relieving himself, or he is on a journey, or perhaps he is asleep and must be awakened.' And they cried aloud and cut themselves after their custom with swords and lances, until the blood gushed out upon them" (1 Kings 18:27–28). But as darkness drew near a hush fell over Carmel: "And as midday passed, they raved on until the time of the offering of the oblation, but there was no voice. No one answered; no one paid attention" (1 Kings 18:29). Three times the Scripture says it (such repetition is the biblical way of adding exclamation marks): Baal did not respond. He did not answer. He did not even pay attention. This is because Baal was an absolute nothing, a triple zero. Over against the holy, holy, holy God of Elijah, Baal was nothing, nothing, nothing. Thus the rumble at Carmel was a mismatch from the very beginning. The Lord God turned out to be an infinity-weight, but Baal was lighter than the lightest lightweight: he weighed nothing at all.

The second great silence on the mountain proved the absolute futility of Baal worship, once and for all. Mr. Baal was losing the bullfight. His prophets could not be faulted for a lack of commitment, but there is more to true religion than having an intense religious experience. The only thing that really matters is worshiping the right God. In this case, the Scripture was confirmed:

> The idols of the nations are silver and gold,
>   the work of human hands.
> They have mouths, but do not speak;
>   they have eyes, but do not see;
> they have ears, but do not hear,
>   nor is there any breath in their mouths. (Ps. 135:15–17)

Baal was one of the silent gods that the psalmist criticized—a god who cannot speak or answer.

Take all the false gods of this world—all the idols and religious impostors—none of them can answer prayer.

Some people worship success, selling their souls to climb the corporate ladder. They might receive awards, promotions, and bonuses. But there is one thing a career cannot do: it cannot answer prayer.

Some people worship pleasure, pampering themselves with rich foods, exciting sporting events, and the latest music. They live with as much luxury as they can afford and as much sexuality as they can get away with. But there is one thing that food and concerts and travel and pornography cannot do: they cannot answer prayer.

Some people worship the state, putting confidence in political solutions. Government may offer some stability and security. It may even offer a welfare check. But there is at least one thing that government cannot do: answer prayer.

Some people worship personal beauty, giving priority to their outward appearance. As "churches empty, health clubs flourish; as traditional fervor wanes, attention to the body waxes."[6] The beautiful may receive attention from those they seek to attract. But there is one thing that cosmetics and accessories cannot accomplish: they cannot answer prayer.

Some people worship control, seeking to gain security in life by bringing order to some small corner of the universe. They might make an idol out of peace and quiet, or a tidy home, or a coin collection. But there is one thing a clean house and shiny coins cannot do: they cannot answer prayer.

All these things can become gods. We may bow down before them, giving them our money, time, and loyalty. We may offer them our affection. They may well cause us to waver between two opinions. But they are not true gods because they cannot answer prayer. This means they will disappoint us when we need them most. When we are lonely, they cannot hear us. When we are sick, they cannot heal us. When we are dying, they cannot save us.

Worst of all, when we repent, false gods cannot forgive us. Understand that what the people of Israel were really praying for was atonement for their sins. The reason they sacrificed bulls on the mountain was to seek forgive-

6. Nancy Brewka Clark, "Faith in the Flesh: An Essay on Secular Society's Preoccupation with Life [Somewhat] Eternal," *Lynn Magazine*, October 1985, 18.

ness. It was not simply any old prayer that they wanted answered, but prayer for forgiveness. The worship service at Mount Carmel featured prayer for atonement, for salvation, through the acceptance of a sacrifice for sin. Yet false gods cannot answer such prayers. They cannot accept atonement for sin, and thus they cannot forgive.

The true God *can* answer prayer. He can accept atonement for sin and forgive all our sins. He is the God who speaks and is not silent. The ultimate proof came when Jesus Christ was raised from the dead. The accounts of his crucifixion close by reporting that "Jesus, calling out with a loud voice, said, 'Father, into your hands I commit my spirit!' And having said this he breathed his last" (Luke 23:46). Imagine what would have happened if Jesus had offered his final prayer to Baal or to any other false god. Silence. No one would have responded; no one would have answered; no one would have paid attention. No other god could have heard his final words from the cross or answered his dying prayer by accepting the sacrifice that he made for our sins. No other god could have raised him from the dead for our salvation.

Praise God, therefore, that Jesus prayed to the God who *is* God! He prayed in faith to the living God, the Lord God of Israel. The God of Elijah and the Father of our Lord Jesus Christ heard that prayer and answered it by raising Jesus from the dead. There is only one God. There is no God but God—the God who answers prayer to accomplish our salvation.

39

THE LORD, HE IS GOD

1 Kings 18:30—40

Then the fire of the LORD fell and consumed the burnt offering
and the wood and the stones and the dust, and licked up the water
that was in the trench. And when all the people saw it, they fell on
their faces and said, "The LORD, he is God; the LORD, he is God."
(1 Kings 18:38–39)

Mr. Baal was losing the bullfight. The silence on the mountain proved that he was not God at all. Because he was deaf and dumb, his prophets were running into pyrotechnical difficulties. But then it was God's turn. It was time for the God who really is God to hear and to answer with a thunderbolt.

THE PREPARATION

Elijah prepared for his proof with an invitation: "Then Elijah said to all the people, 'Come near to me.' And all the people came near to him. And he repaired the altar of the LORD that had been thrown down" (1 Kings 18:30). Like a father gathering his children, the prophet invited God's people to come back to God. As the children of Israel crowded around to see what he would do, Elijah gathered the stones of the broken altar and rebuilt it. This action gives a clear indication of Israel's spiritual condition. The altar needed to be rebuilt because it was in ruins. The place of worship was in a shambles because the hearts of the people were in a shambles, too, spiritually speaking.

Elijah rebuilt the altar properly (see Ex. 20:25–26; Lev. 1:6–8). He "took twelve stones, according to the number of the tribes of the sons of Jacob, to whom the word of the LORD came, saying, 'Israel shall be your name,' and with the stones he built an altar in the name of the LORD. And he made a trench about the altar, as great as would contain two seahs of seed" (1 Kings 18:31–32). Twelve stones for twelve tribes reminded the people that all Israel belonged to God by covenant promise. They also symbolized the reunification of a nation that had been divided since the death of King Solomon. Elijah was gathering the tribes of Israel together at the altar of God. He was calling them back to the faith of their fathers, back to their national covenant, and back to the biblical practice of worship. He did not rebuild the altar in the name of a false god but "in the name of the LORD" (1 Kings 18:32). The Lord's prophet rebuilt the Lord's altar for the Lord's people in the Lord's name.

THE PRAYER

Then Elijah prayed. Notice the simplicity of Elijah's prayer. The prophets of Baal had been praying all day, shouting at their god to get out of bed. But when the prophet Elijah stepped forward, he simply prayed:

O LORD, God of Abraham, Isaac, and Israel, let it be known this day that you are God in Israel, and that I am your servant, and that I have done all these things at your word. Answer me, O LORD, answer me, that this people may know that you, O LORD, are God, and that you have turned their hearts back. (1 Kings 18:36–37)

That is all. After six hours of prayer to Baal, Elijah prayed for less than a minute.

The power of Elijah's prayer did not depend on its length, its eloquence, or its volume. A prophet has to pray long and loud only if his god is hard of hearing. But Elijah's God hears and answers. The power of his prayer did not lie in the prayer itself, but in the God to whom he prayed. Thus Elijah prayed the way that Jesus later taught his disciples to pray: "And when you pray, do not heap up empty phrases as the Gentiles do, for they think that they will be heard for their many words. Do not be like them, for your Father knows what you need before you ask him" (Matt. 6:7–8).

Elijah's preparations and prayer stand in complete contrast to the worship of Baal. The people at Mount Carmel must have been very impressed with the way they led worship. The prophets of Baal were spectacular. Forget religious broadcasting: these guys could have done the choreography for the Grammy Awards! They worshiped long, calling "upon the name of Baal from morning until noon" (1 Kings 18:26)—six hours altogether. They worshiped loud: "O Baal, answer us!" they shouted. Felix Mendelssohn's oratorio *Elijah* captures the volume of their worship when the chorus sings "O Baal, answer us!" with a rushing cascade of sound. Their worship was vigorous, as they danced "around the altar that they had made." Their worship was costly: "And they cried aloud and cut themselves after their custom with swords and lances, until the blood gushed out upon them" (1 Kings 18:28).

This was hardly a boring worship service. All the singing, dancing, slashing, and shouting must have been very exciting. "How was the service at Carmel?" someone might have asked. "It was awesome. It went on for hours. There was this huge worship team up on the mountain. Blood everywhere. Four hundred and fifty prophets singing 'Come on, Baal, Light My Fire'!" But God judges by the heart, and what seems impressive from the outside is often empty on the inside.

Religious frenzy is not necessarily a sign of spiritual life. That was especially true in this case because the prophets of Baal were not worshiping the living God the way he demands to be worshiped. God did not command long services or loud prayers. He certainly did not demand his worshipers to wound themselves. This practice could have come only from the devil, for there is no masochism in biblical worship. In fact, God expressly forbade his people to pierce their bodies: "You shall not make any cuts on your body for the dead or tattoo yourselves: I am the LORD" (Lev. 19:28); "You are the sons of the LORD your God. You shall not cut yourselves or make any baldness on your foreheads for the dead" (Deut. 14:1). God's people belong to him in body as well as in soul. He wants our bodies to be beautiful for worship.

We are reminded by the blood flowing from the prophets of Baal that false gods are harsh taskmasters. Idols abuse their worshipers. Today many people believe that it does not matter who or what we worship, as long as we believe in something. But the Bible teaches that it *does* matter who or what we worship because false gods always harm their followers. If we worship worldly success, we will pay for it with spiritual failure. If we worship comfort, we will pay for it with spiritual unrest. If we worship sex, we will pay for it with broken relationships. If we worship risky adventure, we may pay for it with a broken body. False gods always exact their price. Satan wants a piece of our bodies as well as our souls.

We are also warned by the prophets of Baal that to worship God properly is to worship him in spirit and in truth (see John 4:24). Paul reminded the Corinthians that God is not a God of confusion but of peace (1 Cor. 14:33). Elijah worshiped the true God in the simple, biblical way. He offered a proper sacrifice on a proper altar built with the proper number of stones. He did not whip himself into a frenzy or wound himself.

Furthermore, Elijah offered his sacrifice at the proper time of day. The prophets of Baal worshiped right up until the time for the evening sacrifice. But Elijah offered his sacrifice for atonement at the proper time, "the time of the offering of the oblation" (1 Kings 18:36). This small detail shows the difference between false worship and true worship. The prophets of Baal worshiped any way they pleased, but Elijah worshiped the way God pleased. He not only worshiped the right God, but also worshiped him the right way.

Theologians sometimes call the principle that governed Elijah's worship the "regulative principle." The Westminster Confession of Faith (20.1) expresses this principle as follows: "[T]he acceptable way of worshiping the true God is instituted by Himself, and so limited by His own revealed will, that He may not be worshiped according to the imaginations and devices of men, or the suggestions of Satan, under any visible representation, or any other way not prescribed in the holy Scripture."

Christians sometimes disagree about how this regulative principle ought to be applied, but the principle itself is valid. Because God is the one who receives our worship, he has the right to determine what kind of worship we must offer. The New Testament describes corporate worship through prayer, the reading and preaching of the Word of God, the sacraments of baptism and the Lord's Supper, singing, the confession of our faith, and the giving of offerings. We may be creative in the way we do these things, but we are not to worship God in ways that he did not intend. Elijah was accepted by God because he worshiped in the way that was acceptable to God.

THE PROOF

After the prayer came the proof. Remember that Elijah had a two-part strategy for evangelism. When it came to apologetics, or to defending his faith, Elijah had a one-two punch. First, he disproved the false god, which was accomplished in the silence on the mountain. Second, he proved the true God. The refutation of Baal came before the demonstration of the Lord God.

In the previous chapter of this commentary we noticed that Elijah gave his spiritual opponents every advantage. He also gave himself a serious handicap:

> And he put the wood in order and cut the bull in pieces and laid it on the wood. And he said, "Fill four jars with water and pour it on the burnt offering and on the wood." And he said, "Do it a second time." And they did it a second time. And he said, "Do it a third time." And they did it a third time. And the water ran around the altar and filled the trench also with water. (1 Kings 18:33–35)

This was all part of Elijah's master plan. The prophet was savvy enough to know that whenever God performs a miracle, there are doubters. So he made it as clear as possible that only God could start this fire. Elijah made sure that everyone could see how soggy his altar was. Perhaps he sent his helpers to the Kishon River, which flows just at the base of Mount Carmel. Everyone would have watched Elijah's helpers run down the mountain and then labor to walk back up, with the water sloshing over the sides of their jars. Then everyone would have watched them douse the altar. Water was running all over the pieces of the bull, dripping all over the wood and the stones, filling the great trenches Elijah had dug around the altar. Three times they filled the jars and poured them out again.

Only God could light this sacrifice. The pyrotechnics needed to light the bull were far beyond Elijah's capabilities. It takes more than a spark to light soggy wood. Only God could consume the sacrifice on the altar. And so he did, for with God all things are possible: "Then the fire of the LORD fell and consumed the burnt offering and the wood and the stones and the dust, and licked up the water that was in the trench" (1 Kings 18:38). No bull. No wood. No stones. No soil. No water. Nothing was left. This was not merely a fire, but a mighty conflagration. The fire of the Lord God Almighty came down from heaven and consumed *everything*.

The fire that came from heaven proved the Godness of the Lord God of Israel. The Lord, the God of Elijah, is a burning and consuming fire (see Deut. 4:24). He is the God who sent fire and brimstone upon Sodom and Gomorrah (Gen. 19:24), who appeared to Moses in the burning bush (Ex. 3), who led the children of Israel with a fiery pillar by night (Ex. 13:21), who consumed the burnt offering on Aaron's altar (Lev. 9:24), who destroyed Nadab and Abihu with flames when they offered unauthorized fire (Lev. 10:1–2), and who sent fire from heaven when Solomon dedicated the temple (2 Chron. 7:1). He is the same God who defeated Baal on Mount Carmel with fire from the mountain, accepting Elijah's sacrifice for the atonement of Israel's sin.

We are thus reminded that God is his own proof. Only God can prove his own existence. Elijah helped to disprove Baal, but he did not really prove God at all. God proved himself!

The same thing is true whenever we share the good news about Jesus Christ. We may sometimes disprove the false gods of this world. If we tug long enough at the loose ends of any non-Christian worldview, it will begin to unravel from its own contradictions. But we cannot prove God to an unbeliever. When we speak to people about our faith in Jesus Christ, we can offer many persuasive arguments in defense of biblical truth. We can talk about the mountains and the stars and how the whole universe gives abundant evidence of intelligent design. We can talk about the reliability of the Bible and how the science of archaeology confirms the truth of biblical history. We can talk about the historical evidence for Jesus Christ and how the four Gospels give independent testimonies of his life, death, and resurrection. We can give many persuasive and convincing arguments for the truth of Christianity. But only God can prove himself.

Believing in God—not just believing in some vague divine being, but believing in the God of the Bible—is a spiritual matter. Only God can change an unbeliever's mind and heart. Sinners must be transformed by the fire of the Holy Spirit before they will come to Jesus Christ for salvation from sin. This is really what Elijah prayed for on Mount Carmel: he prayed that God would turn the hearts of Israel back to God (1 Kings 18:37). The fire from heaven was not simply a sign of God's power, but an act of spiritual grace that brought regeneration to the people of God.

The brilliant seventeenth-century French mathematician and philosopher Blaise Pascal wrote an account of his conversion to Christianity. A servant discovered it after Pascal's death, concealed in the lining of the man's coat. Pascal wrote:

> In the year of Grace, 1654,
> On Monday, 23rd November, Feast of St. Clement . . .
> From about half past ten in the evening
> until about half past twelve
> > FIRE
> God of Abraham, God of Isaac, God of Jacob
> not of the philosophers and scholars.
> Certitude. Certitude. Feeling. Joy. Peace.
> God of Jesus Christ.[1]

God did for Pascal what scholars and philosophers were unable to do: he proved himself by giving Pascal the fire of the Holy Spirit. Our job is to do what Elijah did. We are to identify the idols of our culture and confront people with the choice between the one true God and every false God. Then we pray, because only the fire of the Holy Spirit can change a sinner's mind and heart. It is ours to speak and to pray but God's to convert.

More Proof

The Chinese Christian Watchman Nee offers a fascinating account of the way God once proved himself in his book *Sit, Walk, Stand*.[2] Sometime before the outbreak of World War II, Watchman Nee led an evangelistic mission to an island south of the Chinese mainland. Six of the evangelists were

1. Pascal, quoted in Donald W. McCullough, *The Trivialization of God* (Colorado Springs: NavPress, 1995), 77.
2. For a fuller account of these events, see Watchman Nee, *Sit, Walk, Stand* (Fort Washington, PA: Christian Literature Crusade, 1957), 57–64.

veteran missionaries, but they also brought with them young brother Wu. After days of vigorous preaching without any apparent success, Wu was so frustrated that he asked, "Why is it that none of you will believe?"

The people answered, "We have a god—one god—Ta-wang, and he has never failed us."

"How do you know that you can trust him?" asked Wu.

The people explained: "We have held his festival procession every January for 286 years. The chosen day is revealed by divination beforehand, and every year without fail his day is a perfect one without rain or cloud."

"And when is the procession this year?" asked Wu.

"It is fixed for January 11 at eight in the morning."

"Then," announced Wu audaciously, "I promise you that it will certainly rain on the eleventh."

They cried out, "That is enough! No more preaching! If there is rain on the eleventh, then your God is God."

Then Wu went to tell the other missionaries what he had done. He had laid down a challenge like the challenge Elijah gave to Israel: "And you call upon the name of your god, and I will call upon the name of the LORD, and the God who answers by fire, he is God" (1 Kings 18:24). Wu's challenge may have been impetuous, it may have been reckless, it may have made the other evangelists more than a little nervous, but by the time the other missionaries heard what their brother had said, it was too late to do anything about it. Just as in Elijah's day, the news quickly spread throughout the land.

What would the Christians do? They did not doubt that Ta-wang was capable of providing fair weather. Either through demonic influence or through the ability of the local fishermen to predict the weather, it had not rained on the festival day for nearly three centuries. Yet they began to pray, trusting that the God of Elijah was with them. They did not pray desperately, but confidently, resting in the finished work of Jesus Christ and in his power over sin and death.

Here is how Watchman Nee describes the events of January 11:

I was awakened by the direct rays of the sun through the single window of our attic. "This isn't rain!" I said. It was already past seven o'clock. I got up, knelt down and prayed. "Lord," I said, "please send the rain!" . . . I walked downstairs before God in silence. We sat down to breakfast—eight of us together, including our host—all very quiet. There was no cloud in the sky, but we knew God was committed. As we bowed to say grace before the food

I said, "I think the time is up. Rain must come now. We can bring it to the Lord's remembrance."

Even before the evangelists pronounced the "Amen" at the end of their prayer, they could hear a few drops of rain pitter-patter on the tiles. As they ate their rice, the drops became a steady shower. As they began to have seconds, they asked God for a heavier downpour, and the rain came down in buckets. By the time they had finished breakfast, the streets were flooded and the bottom three steps of the house were covered with water.

Later the missionaries heard what had happened in the village. As the rain began, some of the younger men began to say: "There is God; there is no more Ta-wang! He is kept in by the rain." But Ta-wang was a portable idol, so the older men carried him out on a litter to begin the festival procession. As soon as they brought their god outside, the downpour increased. The men who were bearing the litter slipped and fell, whereupon Ta-wang tumbled from his chair, breaking his jaw and his left arm. But he could still be repaired, so they patched him together and brought him outside again, until the rain came down so hard that they could not see and the mud grew so thick that they could not walk. God proved himself, defeating Ta-wang as easily as he defeated Baal.

Yet another story of God's power over nature and triumph over idolatry comes from the missionary work of W. J. Davis among the Bantu peoples of South Africa. During the late 1840s a severe drought caused the soil to dry up and cattle to perish. Fears of famine caused the tribal chief to engage the services of professional rainmakers. When their efforts proved unsuccessful, the rainmakers blamed their failure on the presence of the missionaries. Davis acted quickly to protect his family. Riding into the chief's village, he interrupted the proceedings and announced that the witchcraft of the rainmakers and the sins of the people were the real culprits. Like a latter-day Elijah he gave his opponents a challenge: "Come to chapel next Sabbath, and we will pray to God, who made the heavens and the earth, to give us rain, and we will see who is the true God, and who are His true servants, and your best friends."

After the chief accepted this challenge, Davis and the other missionaries spent the following day in fasting and prayer. When Sunday came, there was not a cloud in the sky. But as Davis and the congregation knelt in prayer, "big rain drops began to patter on the zinc roof of the chapel. . . . The whole region was so saturated with water that the river nearly became so swollen that the chief and his mother could not cross it that night, and hence had to remain at the mission station till the next day."[3]

God proves himself when his people pray. He does not always prove himself in miraculous ways, of course, but he does prove himself. If God has not yet proved himself to us or to some of the people we love, then we should pray for the consuming fire of the Holy Spirit. The God of Elijah loves to hear and to answer the prayers we offer for hearts to turn back to him.

THE PROSTRATION

After the proof came the prostration. "Prostration" means falling down flat on one's face, like taking cover from gunfire or getting knocked over by a bus. This is exactly what happened to the Israelites when the fire came down from heaven: "And when all the people saw it, they fell on their faces and said, 'The LORD, he is God; the LORD, he is God'" (1 Kings 18:39).

This was real worship—not the worship of yelling and shouting, of slashing and bloodletting, but the worship of total prostration before the awesome majesty of God. Truly, this was worship in spirit and in truth. It was worship in spirit because the posture of prostration demonstrates absolute reverence in the presence of God. When the Lord reveals himself in the fire on the mountain, the only appropriate response is to fall flat on one's face.

It was also worship in truth, because the words that were coming from the people's mouths were absolutely true. At the beginning of the confrontation between Baal and the Lord, the people of Israel did not know what to say. Back when they were wavering between two opinions we heard the silence of their doubt (see 1 Kings 18:21). But now they had found their tongues: "The LORD, he is God; the LORD, he is God." No false god could ever be worshiped like this! The worship of the people of Israel was no longer man-centered like Baal worship; now they were totally absorbed in the Godness of God.

It must have been wonderful to be on Mount Carmel, to lie in the dust shouting, "The LORD, he is God" over and over again: "The LORD, he is God; the LORD, he *is* God." We should have such worship. We *can* have such

3. The story of W. J. Davis is recounted in the *International Bulletin of Missionary Research* (October 2001): 153–54.

worship. We do not need to see the fire on the mountain to experience the Godness of God in our worship. If there is little passion in our worship, it is not because we do not have enough dancing and shouting and frenzy. If there is little awe in our worship, it is not because we do not have swords and spears and blood. It is because we do not have a due sense of the weightiness, the holiness, and the majesty of Almighty God.

Annie Dillard has written about the sense of awe, even danger, that we ought to have when we come to worship the Lord God:

> On the whole, I do not find Christians, outside the catacombs, sufficiently sensible of the conditions. Does anyone have the foggiest idea what sort of power we so blithely invoke? Or, as I suspect, does no one believe a word of it? The churches are children playing on the floor with their chemistry sets, mixing up a batch of TNT to kill a Sunday morning. It is madness to wear ladies' straw hats and velvet hats to church; we should all be wearing crash helmets. Ushers should issue life preservers and signal flares; they should lash us to our pews. For the sleeping god may wake some day and take offense, or the waking god may draw us out to where we can never return.[4]

We have lost a sense of the weightiness of the majesty of God, not only in our worship, but in our whole lives. The problem does not lie with God; it lies with us. We are too much like the prophets of Baal. We mistake the external forms of worship for the reality of the presence of Almighty God. At the same time, we are too much like the people of Israel. We limp between two opinions, worshiping with divided affections. With one foot we step into the house of the Lord, but we have left one foot somewhere out in the streets of the city.

If we want to recapture a sense of the awesomeness of God, we need to do what the people of Israel did after they got up and dusted themselves off. They did not remain prostrate for long, for Elijah compelled them to put an end to their wavering: "And Elijah said to them, 'Seize the prophets of Baal; let not one of them escape.' And they seized them. And Elijah brought them down to the brook Kishon and slaughtered them there" (1 Kings 18:40).

This was in fulfillment of the commandment of God (see Deut. 13:12–15) that leaders who drove Israel into idolatry were to be put to the sword. Idola-

---

4. Annie Dillard, *Teaching a Stone to Talk* (New York: Harper & Row, 1982), 40–41.

trous leaders posed the greatest spiritual danger to the people of God. If the Israelites were to stop wavering between two religious opinions, they needed to put Baal worship to death once and for all and prostrate themselves before God and God alone.

The Lord has not placed the same sword into our hands. Our weapons and our warfare are spiritual, not physical. But we must put our own sins to death. Frankly, most Christians do not know how to do this very well. We are not ruthless enough with our sins. This is why we waver between two opinions, and why we do not have a proper appreciation of the weightiness of God in our worship.

Do not waver between two opinions any longer! Instead, acknowledge the lordship of Jesus the way that Thomas did when the risen Christ appeared to him and Thomas said, "My Lord and my God!" (John 20:28). We are called to take the false gods that are hiding in our hearts and put them to death. To that end, we should remember that "our old self was crucified with him in order that the body of sin might be brought to nothing, so that we would no longer be enslaved to sin" (Rom. 6:6). Then we should lie prostrate before the Lord in every area of life—offering him our work, leisure, relationships, and families. As we prostrate ourselves before him, our lives will say, "The LORD, he is God; the LORD, he is God."

40

GOD'S FIREKEEPER

1 Kings 18:36–45

And Elijah went up to the top of Mount Carmel. And he bowed
himself down on the earth and put his face between his knees.
(1 Kings 18:42)

Elijah was like the firekeeper in the longhouse. For Native American Indians of the Northeast—like the Iroquois—the longhouse was the center of tribal life. Extended families would live, sleep, eat, work, and play in a long wooden building called the "longhouse." One member of the tribe was chosen to be the firekeeper. It was his job to make sure that the flame in the longhouse was never extinguished. When the others would go off to gather, to hunt, or to fight, the firekeeper would stay at the longhouse and keep the home fires burning.

The prophet Elijah was like the firekeeper in the longhouse. When the tribes of Israel wandered in the spiritual wilderness, Elijah stayed at home and blew on the embers of biblical faith. When the prophets of Baal tried to stamp out worship of the one true God, Elijah did not allow faith in the Lord God to be extinguished. He was the keeper of the flame for the people of Israel. So when the people returned from their spiritual wanderings and

504

gathered at Mount Carmel, it was Elijah's ready spark that God used to reignite his people and turn their hearts back to him.

ONLY THROUGH PRAYER

How did Elijah do it? How did he keep the home fire burning? Elijah tended the flame through prayer. The interpretation that the apostle James offers of the life and ministry of the prophet Elijah cannot be escaped (see James 5:16–18). We keep coming back to it again and again: first and foremost, Elijah was a man of prayer.

Let us be honest, though: prayer does not sound very exciting to us. We are ready to go up the mountain with Elijah, ready to confront the people of Israel, ready to mock the prophets of Baal, ready to see the fire of God, and ready to fall on our faces and worship God. Perhaps we are even ready to put sin to death. But are we ready to pray?

Most of us find prayer to be such difficult labor that it does not excite us. Prayer is an intensely spiritual activity that cuts against the grain of our natural inclinations. For proof, consider what happens in a typical prayer meeting, where people spend plenty of time enjoying fellowship, sharing requests, discussing life's problems, and doing anything and everything except praying. Prayer is always the first thing to go. It is the first thing to go during a busy week, the first thing we leave out of our morning routine, the first thing we abandon when we go on vacation. Prayer is raw spirituality, and most of us are not very spiritual.

Yet there is no other way to receive the blessings of God except through prayer. All the spiritual blessings that God has to give come through a life of petition and intercession. If we want the good things that God loves to give, we must pray for them. Wisdom for life's decisions comes through prayer. So does the awesome presence of God in worship. Conversions to faith in Christ, the revival fire of the Holy Spirit, the reformation of a culture—it all comes through prayer.

When we look behind any great movement of the Spirit of God, we will always find prayer. Consider the Moravian revival of 1727. It began in a prayer meeting: "So overwhelmed were the people with the Presence of God, they were convicted to pray 24 hours a day, 7 days a week—and this lasted over 100 years, with astounding results around the world."[1] Or consider the ministry of William Carey, the father of modern missions and soul-winning evangelist to India. The secret of his success? Carey's supporters included a paralyzed, bedridden sister who prayed incessantly for him for fifty years.[2]

Spiritual blessings come from God through prayer. There is no way around it. There is no other way to receive spiritual blessings but to pray for them. We cannot have a demonstration of the power of God in our lives, our worship, our evangelism, our families, our church, or our nation without prevailing in prayer.

Frankly, this comes as a disappointment to many Christians. Elijah was able to get a whole nation to the top of a high mountain to see a bullfight. But imagine what would have happened if he had called it a prayer meeting instead. It really *was* a prayer meeting, of course, but the people in marketing would never let Elijah advertise it that way. No one would show up!

Except the firekeepers, that is. The firekeepers would be there, tending the flame, praying to God, and waiting for his Spirit to descend with fire. The spiritual firekeepers would gather in the longhouse for prayer, kindling their heart-fires and blowing on the coals of biblical faith.

We can become firekeepers like Elijah. We must become firekeepers, because prayer is the only way to stay warm with God. Cold days are coming for the church. We need to know how to keep the flame of faith in Jesus Christ alive in the longhouse so that other people can gather next to us and get warm.

First Things First

Elijah's example teaches at least seven valuable lessons about firekeeping for the man or woman of prayer. This is how to tend the flame: first, *pray on the basis of a sacrifice for sin*. Elijah did not dare to come into the presence of God without offering atonement for his sins.

Notice something curious about Elijah's prayer. He prayed, "The God who answers by fire, he is God" (1 Kings 18:24). But why did the prophet pray for fire? Fire would seem to be the last thing that the people of Israel

1. Henry T. Blackaby, "Revival Scenes," *Revival Commentary* 1, 1 (1996): 6–7.
2. Kent and Barbara Hughes, *Liberating Ministry from the Success Syndrome* (Wheaton, IL: Tyndale, 1987), 74.

needed. What they really needed was rain. Remember, it had not rained upon the land for three and a half years. Things were so bad that even poor King Ahab had been wandering in the desert, trying to find a little grass for his donkeys.

Given the drought in Israel, one can imagine someone at Mount Carmel listening to Elijah's challenge and saying, "Say, Elijah, couldn't we make that rain instead of fire? How about, 'The god who answers by *rain*—he is God'?" After all, rain is what God had promised to send: "After many days the word of the LORD came to Elijah, in the third year, saying, 'Go, show yourself to Ahab, and I will send rain upon the earth'" (1 Kings 18:1). If God promised rain, why did Elijah pray for fire?

Elijah prayed for fire because before the people could receive any other blessing from God, they needed to receive atonement for their sins. They needed to get right with God before they could get any rain from God. Remember that the reason there had been no rain in the land was that the people had sinned against God. Drought was God's particular punishment for idolatry: "Take care lest your heart be deceived, and you turn aside and serve other gods and worship them; then the anger of the LORD will be kindled against you, and he will shut up the heavens, so that there will be no rain, and the land will yield no fruit, and you will perish quickly off the good land that the LORD is giving you" (Deut. 11:16–17).

The reason Elijah took a bull up the mountain, rebuilt an altar out of twelve stones, arranged the wood, and cut the bull into pieces was to offer a sacrifice for the sins of the people of Israel. Only then could God's judgment be removed. It was first things first: first the repentance and then the forgiveness. First the removal of the curse and then the bestowal of the blessing. First the sacrifice for sin and then the showers of rain.

Elijah knew something about the holiness of God. He knew that God's people cannot come into his holy presence (and live) without a sacrifice for sin. He knew that there was no sense asking for rain before they received the fire to consume their sacrifice. Only then could he pray on the basis of a sacrifice for sin.

People who know Jesus Christ bring a sacrifice every time they pray. When Christians get to the end of their prayers they often say, "In Jesus' name, Amen." This is not merely a customary conclusion, like saying, "And they lived happily ever after. The End" at the end of a story. Rather, it is a solemn recognition that the only reason we can even pray to God is that Jesus has died for our sins. We do not offer a new sacrifice when we pray, but present the once-for-all atonement of Jesus Christ as the basis for our coming before the throne of God's grace.

If prayer is to be offered in the name of Jesus Christ, this may explain why some prayers go unanswered. Everybody prays. Even hardened atheists pray when their lives hang in the balance. They cannot help but pray. But they do not always get the answers they are hoping for, and when they don't, they usually blame God. They say, "I prayed that God would do thus and so for me, and he never did. In fact, I said that I would give my whole life to God if he would just answer that one prayer, and he never answered it."

Here is the question, though: was that prayer offered sincerely in the name of Jesus Christ? When we prayed, did we confess our sins and trust in the sacrifice of Jesus Christ on the cross to pay for them? If not, then we have no reason to blame God for not answering our prayers. We owe God payment for our sins; God does not owe us anything. Of course, out of his great mercy, God does sometimes hear and answer prayers that are not offered in and through Jesus Christ. But first things first. If we want the rain from God, we have to get right with God by bringing a sacrifice for our sins.

What's in a Name?

Here is a second lesson for firekeepers: *pray in the revealed name of God.* The Scripture says that "Elijah the prophet came near and said, 'O Lord, God of Abraham, Isaac, and Israel'" (1 Kings 18:36). In other words, Elijah prayed to the right God. Indeed, this was the whole point of the confrontation at Mount Carmel. Elijah did not pray in the name of Baal because it was too hard to get Baal out of bed. Indeed, there is no such god as Baal at all. The prophet prayed instead to the living and true God. He prayed to the God who never slumbers or sleeps, who hears and answers prayer. He prayed to the God who bound himself in covenant to Abraham, Isaac, and Israel.

How wonderful it is that God has given us his name! He has given us his name so that we may know him and call upon him whenever we need him. Parents learn the power of a name when their children begin to call them by their first names. "Hey, Dad! Daddy! Dad, you're not listening!" I am oblivious to the pleading of my son. "Hey, Phil!" he says, trying a new approach. Now he has my *full* attention!

God has our full attention whenever we call him by name. He has given us dozens of names to use. Any of the names or titles that God uses for himself in Scripture are appropriate for us to use in prayer: Yahweh, I Am, Almighty God, the Lord. We can pray to the God of Abraham, the God of Moses, and the God of Elijah. Or we can pray the way Jesus prayed, simply calling God "Father" (e.g., Mark 14:36). God has given us his name so that we can call upon him in prayer.

To God Be the Glory

Consider a third lesson for firekeepers: *pray for the glory of God to be revealed.* Elijah prayed: "O Lord, God of Abraham, Isaac and Israel, let it be known today that you are God in Israel" (1 Kings 18:36). With these words, Elijah was praying that God would be known to be God. He was praying that God would glorify himself. He was praying that God would reveal the glory of his deity to the whole nation. The goal of his prayer was the goal of all goals: *soli Deo gloria,* or "to God alone be the glory." According to the opening answer of the Westminster Shorter Catechism, "man's chief end is to glory God and to enjoy him forever." But on Mount Carmel, Elijah prayed toward the chief end of *God,* which is to glorify himself and to enjoy himself forever.

This kind of prayer may be termed "kingdom prayer." Kingdom prayer is directed toward the greater glory of God. It is prayer for the unhindered expansion and unlimited extension of the rule of God. It is the kind of prayer that John Piper writes about in his book on the missionary work of the church:

> Prayer proves the supremacy of God. . . . This is why God has ordained prayer to have such a crucial place in the mission of the church. The purpose of prayer is to make clear to all the participants in this war that the victory belongs to the Lord. Prayer is God's appointed means of bringing grace to us and glory to himself.[3]

3. John Piper, *Let the Nations Be Glad! The Supremacy of God in Missions* (Grand Rapids: Baker, 1993), 55.

Kingdom prayer is the kind of prayer that Jesus taught his disciples to pray: "Our Father in heaven, hallowed be your name. Your kingdom come, your will be done, on earth as it is in heaven" (Matt. 6:9–10). True disciples pray for the coming of God's kingdom, for the glorious rule of the Lord Jesus Christ to spread throughout the whole universe.

We spend too little of our time in kingdom prayer. Most of our prayer is emergency prayer. It has to do with what is happening to us right now. We thank God for his goodness to us, we pray for the sick, we pray for our own immediate needs, and that is about it. There is nothing wrong with such prayers, of course, but prayer can be so much more. Here is how J. C. Ryle commends the practice of selfless prayer:

> I commend to you the importance of intercession in our prayers. We are all selfish by nature, and our selfishness is very apt to stick to us, even when we are converted. There is a tendency in us to think only of our own souls, our own spiritual conflicts, our own progress in religion, and to forget others. Against this tendency we all have need to watch and strive, and not least in our prayers. We should study to be of a public spirit. We should stir ourselves up to name other names besides our own before the throne of grace. . . . This is the highest charity. He loves me best who loves me in his prayers. This is for our soul's health. It enlarges our sympathies and expands our hearts. This is for the benefit of the church. The wheels of all machinery for extending the gospel are moved by prayer.[4]

We need to expand our prayers to include kingdom prayer for the extension of the rule of Jesus Christ. At least some of our petitions must be devoted to praying for the glory of God to be revealed in mighty acts throughout every corner of the universe. Kingdom prayer is prayer for conversions, for missions, for churches, for cities, for nations. It is the kind of prayer offered at the end of a letter I once received: "My prayer is that God will be glorified and His Name exalted at Tenth Presbyterian Church and in the whole city of Philadelphia."

God loves to answer kingdom prayer. There is something so pure about the desire for God alone to be glorified that kingdom prayer is uniquely efficacious. F. B. Meyer writes: "Whenever we so lose ourselves in prayer as to

---

4. J. C. Ryle, *Practical Religion* (Grand Rapids: Baker, 1977).

forget personal interest, and to plead for the glory of God, we have reached a vantage ground from which we can win anything from Him."[5] But do not just take F. B. Meyer's word for it; listen to the extravagant promise of Jesus Christ: "Whatever you ask in my name, this I will do, that the Father may be glorified in the Son. If you ask me anything in my name, I will do it" (John 14:13–14). If we fail to understand this promise, it is because we do not realize that Jesus is talking about offering kingdom prayer rather than about asking to satisfy our own desires. When Jesus promises to do whatever we ask, he is talking about prayer offered for the glorification of God.

VINDICATION

Here is a fourth lesson for firekeepers: *pray for the vindication of the ministry of God's Word.* Not only did Elijah pray that God would be known to be God, but he also prayed that he himself would be known as God's servant: "Let it be known this day . . . that I am your servant, and that I have done all these things at your word" (1 Kings 18:36).

With its use of the first person, this prayer may make us a little uncomfortable. After praying for the glory of God, is Elijah now praying for his own glory? No, he is simply praying that God would vindicate his prophetic ministry of God's word.

Admittedly, some of the things that Elijah did seemed a little strange. It was strange for him to oppose the religious leaders of his day, strange to mock the religious establishment, and strange to pour water all over a sacrifice. But because the prophet did these things in obedience to God, he rightly asked God to vindicate his ministry. Elijah prayed that it would be widely known that however unpopular his ministry may have been, he himself was a faithful prophet of the Lord God.

In following Elijah's example, it is right and good for us to pray for the vindication of the ministry of the church. The success of a ministry is not measured by its size or popularity, but by its faithfulness to the Word of God. So churches rightly pray that they would be known to be faithful servants of God's Word. The pastoral staff at Philadelphia's Tenth Presbyterian Church was deeply gratified to hear the story told by a couple of visitors from out of

---

5. F. B. Meyer, *Elijah* (Fort Washington, PA: Christian Literature Crusade, 1992), 87.

town. Wanting to attend a worship service, but unfamiliar with the city, they asked a homeless man if he knew where any good churches were. He pointed to a nearby church building, but when they hesitated, he said, "Oh, you must be looking for a church that preaches the *Word*; the church you're looking for is Tenth Presbyterian Church!" This is the kind of on-street recommendation that every church should pray for: may we be known as teachers of God's Word!

The success of the preaching of the Word of God in any particular place depends on the prayers of the people of God. We should pray, therefore, as if our pastor's ministry depended on it, which in fact it does. By and large, when it comes to a preaching ministry, congregations get what they pray for.

The great London preacher Charles Spurgeon was asked why he had such a successful preaching ministry. His answer was to take guests down to the basement of his church where hundreds of parishioners would gather before the Sunday services to pray that the Word of God would be vindicated among them. Behind every faithful preacher there is a praying congregation.[6]

Prayer for Evangelism

Lesson number five is very simple: *pray for conversions*. Notice how Elijah ended his prayer: "Answer me, O Lord, answer me, that this people may know that you, O Lord, are God, and that you have turned their hearts back" (1 Kings 18:37).

We can sense Elijah's fervency from the way he repeated himself: "Answer me, O Lord, answer me." The reason the prophet was so urgent was that he was praying for conversions. He was praying that God would turn the hearts of the people back again, which is exactly what happens whenever someone becomes a Christian. The Holy Spirit takes the heart of a sinner who has wandered away and turns it back to God. A firekeeper prays for such conversions. He or she not only tends the flame, but also wants to spread the flame. A firekeeper is not content with private spiritual growth but wants to see the love of Jesus Christ burst into flame in the hearts of other people.

Typically, a congregation that is weak in evangelism is weak in evangelistic prayer, which is one kind of kingdom prayer. When we pray for someone's

6. Warren W. Wiersbe, *The Wiersbe Bible Commentary: The Complete New Testament* (Colorado Springs: David C. Cook, 2007), 694.

conversion to faith in Jesus Christ, we are really praying that God would rule in that person's heart. We are praying for the kingdom of God to come into the life of a particular person and take control.

Hudson Taylor, the pioneer missionary to China, was mystified by the numbers of souls being won to Christ at a particular mission station. He was mystified, that is, until he met a man back in England at the end of one of his public addresses. The man was so thoroughly conversant with that particular work that Taylor asked him how he knew so much about it. "Oh!" he replied, "the missionary there and I are old collegemates; for years we have regularly corresponded; he has sent me the names of inquirers and converts, and these I have daily taken to God in prayer."[7] This was the secret: a man praying daily and definitely for specific conversions.

One good way to remember to pray for conversions is to keep a list of the souls for whom we are seeking salvation. This was the regular practice of C. S. Lewis, who once wrote to a friend: "I have two lists of names in my prayers, those for whose conversion I pray and those for whose conversion I give thanks. The little trickle of transferences from List A to List B is a great comfort."[8] Every small-group Bible study should devote some portion of its weekly prayer time to praying by name for the salvation of people who do not know Christ. God will answer our prayers—as he answered Elijah's prayer—by sending the fire of the Holy Spirit to turn sinners' hearts back to himself.

Pray within the Promises

Lesson six: *pray within the promises of God.* This lesson comes from the end of the story, where the Scripture says: "So Ahab went up to eat and to drink. And Elijah went up to the top of Mount Carmel. And he bowed himself down on the earth and put his face between his knees" (1 Kings 18:42). Elijah was praying, of course. We know this because he was in a proper posture for prayer, bent all the way to the ground. He was in the same position that all Israel had been in only a little while before, when "they fell on

---

7. E. M. Bounds, *The Purpose in Prayer* (Grand Rapids: Christian Classics Ethereal Library, 2001), http://www.ccel.org/ccel/bounds/purpose.html, 53.

8. C. S. Lewis, Letter to Dom Bede Griffiths, June 27, 1949, in the Marion E. Wade Center at Wheaton College in Illinois.

their faces and said, 'The LORD, he is God; the LORD, he is God'" (1 Kings 18:39). Now it was Elijah's turn to put his face down in the dust and pray to the Lord God. Although the Bible does not command any particular posture for prayer, Elijah gives us one good example to follow. Prayer is prostration before the true and living God.

What the Bible does command is that we pray within the promises of God. It may hardly have seemed necessary for Elijah to pray for rain. After all, God had already promised to send rain upon the land. In fact, Elijah could hear it coming. "Go up, eat and drink," he said to Ahab, "for there is a sound of the rushing of rain" (1 Kings 18:41). Although Elijah could not yet see the rain, he could hear it with the ears of faith.

Nevertheless, Elijah prayed. He prayed diligently and persistently until the promise was fulfilled. For Elijah, the promise of God did not make prayer unnecessary; it made it mandatory. The prophet understood the implications of God's sovereignty for the ministry of intercession. It is the very promises of God that teach us what to pray. It was just because God had promised rain that Elijah prayed for rain. A. W. Pink explains: "as far from God's promises being designed to exempt us from making application to the throne of grace for the blessings guaranteed, they are designed to instruct us what things to ask for, and to encourage us to ask for them believingly, that we may have their fulfillment to ourselves."[9] F. B. Meyer wrote to similar effect: "Though the Bible be crowded with golden promises from board to board, yet will they be inoperative, until we turn them into prayer."[10] Thus we are called to learn the promises of God from the Word of God and then turn them into prayer.

KEEP THE FIRE BURNING

Finally, the last lesson for firekeepers is to *keep on praying*. Elijah did not give up, but persisted in prayer until God answered: "And he said to his servant, 'Go up now, look toward the sea.' And he went up and looked and said, 'There is nothing.' And he said, 'Go again,' seven times. And at the seventh time he said, 'Behold, a little cloud like a man's hand is rising from the sea.' And he said, 'Go up, say to Ahab, "Prepare your chariot and go down, lest the rain stop you"'" (1 Kings 18:43–44).

9. A. W. Pink, *The Life of Elijah* (Edinburgh: Banner of Truth, 1956), 184.
10. Meyer, *Elijah*, 93.

Six times Elijah's servant went and looked toward the sea. Six times he came back with bad news. "There is nothing," he said. There was not the slightest wisp of a cloud in the whole sky. It was blue sky from the top of Mount Carmel all the way out over the Mediterranean Sea. But Elijah did not despair. He did not abandon his trust in the promises of God. He watched and prayed right through until God answered: "And in a little while the heavens grew black with clouds and wind, and there was a great rain" (1 Kings 18:45).

How many times have we prayed and prayed without receiving an answer? Perhaps we have prayed six times and are still waiting to see the small cloud rising from the sea with the rain of God's blessing. We have prayed for the salvation of a wayward child, for example, and are still waiting. We have prayed for a good job, or for the Lord to reveal his will for our lives, and we are still waiting. We have prayed for the Lord to deliver us from some particular sin, or to heal a sickness, and we are still waiting. We have prayed for the Lord to give us a spouse or a child, and we are still waiting. We have prayed and prayed, yet we continue to receive the bad news Elijah received: "There is nothing."

Do not stop praying! Pray without ceasing (1 Thess. 5:17). If we have prayed six times, we should pray a seventh time. Indeed, we should pray seventy times seven times. We should not let our prayers come to an end, but persist in prayer until God answers. Elijah's prayers were powerful and effective because he kept praying until they were answered. "He prayed fervently," the Scripture says (James 5:17), and fervent prayer is persistent prayer. Edward Payson has this sound advice for firekeepers: "Prayer is the first thing, the second thing, the third thing necessary to minister. Pray, therefore, my dear brother, pray, pray, pray."[11] For the servants of God who live in the longhouse of faith, being a firekeeper is a full-time job.

11. This quotation of Edward Payson is from E. M. Bounds, *Power through Prayer* (Grand Rapids: Zondervan, 1982), 28.

41

I HAVE HAD ENOUGH, LORD

1 Kings 18:46—19:8

Then he was afraid, and he arose and ran for his life and came to
Beersheba, which belongs to Judah, and left his servant there. But
he himself went a day's journey into the wilderness and came and
sat down under a broom tree. And he asked that he might die,
saying, "It is enough; now, O Lord, take away my life, for I am no
better than my fathers." (1 Kings 19:3–4)

 lijah has had enough. In Felix Mendelssohn's oratorio based
on the life of the prophet, his words sound plaintive and
bitter:

It is enough, O Lord; now take away my life, for I am not better than my fathers!
I desire to live no longer: now let me die, for my days are but vanity! I have been
very jealous for the Lord God of hosts; for the children of Israel have broken
Thy covenant, thrown down Thine altars, and slain Thy prophets with the
sword: and I, even I only, am left; and they seek my life to take it away.

It is not well with Elijah's soul. The prophet has descended into the black-
ness of spiritual despair. We have been to the mountaintop with Elijah to see

the fire of the presence of God. Now we go with him into the wilderness, where he sits alone under a solitary tree and says, "It is enough; now, O LORD, take away my life, for I am no better than my fathers" (1 Kings 19:4).

THE MAN OF GOD

As Elijah fades to spiritual black, it is worth pausing a moment to remember the spiritual accomplishments of this great man of God. Elijah was the firekeeper in the longhouse: a burning and shining light for the people of God. He was bold before the king of Israel. He marched down from Gilead to Samaria—going from the boondocks to the big city—to tell King Ahab that as a punishment for idolatry, there would be no rain in the land (1 Kings 17:1).

The prophet Elijah had faith in the providence of God. He obeyed God's command to go and hide in the Cherith Ravine, where he was fed by ravens (1 Kings 17:2–6). He trusted God for daily bread in Zarephath, where the jar of flour was not used up and the jug of oil did not run dry (1 Kings 17:7–16). Elijah also had faith in the resurrection. He took the widow's dead son, stretched himself out over the boy's body, and prayed for his life to return (1 Kings 17:17–24).

Elijah was a man of zeal. He displayed courage in the face of sin. He identified Ahab as the real troublemaker in Israel (1 Kings 18:16–18) and challenged the people of God not to waver between two opinions any longer (1 Kings 18:21). Elijah had a passion for biblical worship. He offered the proper sacrifice, on a proper altar, at the proper time of day, to the proper God (1 Kings 18:30–36). The prophet also promoted God's holy righteousness by mocking the prophets of Baal and then putting them to death at the Kishon River (1 Kings 18:22–29, 40).

Most of all, Elijah was a man of prayer. For three and a half years he prayed that God would shut the rain up in the heavens (James 5:17). He prayed kingdom prayer, pleading for the glory of God to be revealed and the hearts of God's people to be turned back to their God (1 Kings 18:36–37). He persisted in prayer, praying seven times for rain to fall on Israel (1 Kings 18:42–44).

Elijah was a man of God. He was among the greatest of prophets. Little wonder that when Jesus Christ was transfigured on the mountain, Elijah was there with Moses to talk with the Messiah (Matt. 17:1–13). And little wonder that on that glorious occasion Peter wanted to give honor to Elijah, perhaps even to worship him (Matt. 17:4). Elijah was a spiritual giant. Our own spirituality does not even begin to measure up to his stature. We have rarely (if ever) seen such godliness, and we have scarcely dreamed of becoming such valiant believers ourselves.

Last of all, consider Elijah's humility. We might expect a spiritual giant to be at least a little bit proud of his kingdom accomplishments. But 1 Kings 18 ends with a striking demonstration of Elijah's humility:

> And he said, "Go up, say to Ahab, 'Prepare your chariot and go down, lest the rain stop you.'" And in a little while the heavens grew black with clouds and wind, and there was a great rain. And Ahab rode and went to Jezreel. And the hand of the Lord was on Elijah, and he gathered up his garment and ran before Ahab to the entrance of Jezreel. (1 Kings 18:44–46)

In answer to prayer, God had sent Elijah his rain. The storm clouds had gathered over the Mediterranean Sea. While the big, black thunderheads billowed above Mount Carmel, Elijah received the power of the Holy Spirit, hitched up his robes, and ran eighteen miles to Jezreel, ahead of a horse and chariot.

The point of this story is not that Elijah was a great all-around athlete, although perhaps he was. Nor is the main point of this story that Elijah was endowed with the Holy Spirit, although certainly he was. The point is not even that Elijah got to Jezreel first, as if the prophet and the king were in some sort of race. No, for Elijah to run ahead of Ahab was to identify himself as one of Ahab's servants. Elijah ran ahead as one of the king's footmen, or heralds.

In the ancient Near East, kings were almost always preceded by a company of foot servants to herald their approach. To run ahead of a royal person, therefore, was to be subservient to him. According to the book of Esther, for example, Mordecai was led about the streets of Susa on a royal horse, wearing a royal crest. Prince Haman was compelled to lead Mordecai, "proclaiming before him, 'Thus shall it be done to the man whom the king delights to honor'" (Esth. 6:11). This was a humiliation for Haman because the one who goes ahead is in the place of subservience. In the same way, Elijah submitted himself to the governing authority of King Ahab by running ahead of him to Jezreel. His zeal for the King of kings demanded respect for the king of Israel. This shows that for all his boldness, Elijah was a man of deep humility.

Indeed, these two virtues are closely related: only the person who is humble before God has the courage to stand up for God in a hostile world.

SUICIDAL THOUGHTS

Now fade to black and see what has become of this humble man of God. Having showed us Elijah at his best, the Bible also shows the prophet at his worst, when he went out alone in the wilderness and sat under a broom tree. Elijah ran away from Jezebel, away from the people of God, away from his prophetic calling, away from it all.

Here is how it happened. When they all arrived at Jezreel, "Ahab told Jezebel all that Elijah had done, and how he had killed all the prophets with the sword" (1 Kings 19:1). Notice how blind the king was. Ahab had been on Mount Carmel, but apparently he had not been paying very careful spiritual attention. He ought to have been telling Jezebel everything *God* had done, not everything Elijah had done. Yet the report he gave to the queen focused on human rather than divine action.

King Ahab was the consummate politician. He was a chameleon, or perhaps a spineless jellyfish. When he was up on the mountain, he was ready to believe in the God of Israel and let Elijah do whatever God wanted with the prophets of Baal. But when he went back home he had Jezebel to deal with, and we know who drove the chariot in that family! Because Ahab was afraid of his wife, he was careful to pin the blame for the death of her prophets on Elijah.

The queen responded swiftly and decisively: "Then Jezebel sent a messenger to Elijah, saying, 'So may the gods do to me and more also, if I do not make your life as the life of one of them by this time tomorrow'" (1 Kings 19:2). In other words, "Get out of town by sundown, Elijah, or you are a dead man!" It is not entirely clear why Jezebel did not have the prophet killed right then and there. Perhaps she was shrewd enough to sense his popularity, or cunning enough to realize that the best way to turn Elijah's victory into a defeat—and to destroy God's credibility in the bargain—was to scare Elijah off.

If this was Jezebel's strategy, then it worked even better than she hoped. After everything else we have seen Elijah say and do, we are hardly prepared for what he did next: "Then he was afraid, and he arose and ran for his life and came to Beersheba, which belongs to Judah, and left his servant there" (1 Kings 19:3). Apparently Elijah was as afraid of Queen Jezebel as Ahab was.

519

So he played right into her hands, running away from Jezreel even faster than he had run toward it.

"Shall we praise [Elijah] for this?" asks Matthew Henry, the Puritan commentator.

> We praise him not. Where was the courage with which he had lately confronted Ahab and all the prophets of Baal? Nay, which kept him by his sacrifice when the fire of God fell upon it? He that stood undaunted in the midst of the terrors both of heaven and earth trembles at the impotent menaces of a proud passionate woman. . . . Great faith is not always alike strong.[1]

Elijah's great faith had been chased out by sudden fear. The Scripture says that the prophet "ran for his life." A man can run a long way when he is running for his life, and Elijah ran ninety miles, all the way to Beersheba (1 Kings 19:3). Then the prophet went another day's journey into the desert (1 Kings 19:4). He was running all the way out of Jezebel's kingdom, almost running himself to death.

Elijah ran and ran, and then he threw himself down under a tree: "But he himself went a day's journey into the wilderness and came and sat down under a broom tree" (1 Kings 19:4). Then he prayed. After all, Elijah was a man of prayer. So how is this for a prayer? "It is enough; now, O LORD, take away my life, for I am no better than my fathers" (1 Kings 19:4).

Elijah's prayer under the broom tree was not exactly kingdom prayer. Yet even at the point of absolute desperation, Elijah did manage to pray. "I have had enough, LORD," he said. He "*asked* that he might die" (1 Kings 19:4), putting his desire to end it all in the form of a petition. Elijah did not take his own life, but acknowledged that because God is the Lord of life, only he has the right to take a life. As G. K. Chesterton once observed, "Not only is suicide a sin, it is *the* sin. It is the ultimate and absolute evil, the refusal to take an interest in existence; the refusal to take the oath of loyalty to life. The man who kills a man, kills a man. The man who kills himself, kills all men; as far as he is concerned he wipes out the world."[2]

Men of God should never kill themselves. But on occasion even a great prophet has been known to pray for death. Moses asked God to put him to death right on the spot (Num. 11:15). Job wished that he had never been

---

1. Matthew Henry, *Matthew Henry's Commentary*, 6 vols. (New York: Fleming Revell, n.d.), in loc.
2. G. K. Chesterton, *Orthodoxy* (New York: Doubleday, 1990), 72.

born (Job 10:18–19). Jeremiah cursed the day of his birth (Jer. 20:14). Jonah asked God to take away his life because it was better for him to die than to live (Jonah 4:3). So men of God do sometimes long for death; yet they do not kill themselves. Instead, they take their despair to the place where God rules and pray to the Lord of life.

When Elijah prayed, he told God that he had had enough. The prophet was suicidal. His cry sounds like the cry of despair heard in the 1996 British film *Trainspotting. Trainspotting* became a cult classic among Generation Xers in America because it offered a raw view of the meaninglessness of life. Listen to the lead character's philosophy of life (edited for profanity):

> Choose life. Choose a job. Choose a career. Choose a family. Choose a big television. . . . Choose sitting on that couch watching mind-numbing, spirit-crushing game shows. . . . Choose rotting away at the end of it all . . . in a miserable home, nothing more than an embarrassment to the selfish . . . brats that you've spawned to replace yourselves. . . . But why would I want to do a thing like that? I chose not to choose life. I chose somethin' else. And the reasons? There are no reasons. Who needs reasons when you've got heroin?

This is more or less how Elijah felt. He never watched TV game shows or did heroin, but that is basically how he felt. He was choosing not to choose life. He was choosing something else, and there were no reasons. Elijah had once been the firekeeper in the longhouse, tending the hearth fires of faith for the people of God. But sometimes firekeepers go down in flames. Sometimes firekeepers get burned out. Sometimes firekeepers have had enough.

Elijah's experience of despair challenges us not to get the wrong idea about Christianity. Many people still have the idea that if they trust in Jesus, all their troubles will be over. If they really trust in Jesus, he will give them a big car, or take care of their weight problem, or remove the temptation to homosexual sin, or help them find a mate. People have these wrong ideas about Christianity in part because the American church gets big, unhealthy doses of the health-and-wealth gospel, which goes something like this:

> Name it and claim it, that's what faith's all about!
> You can have what you want if you just have no doubt.
> So make out your "wish list" and keep on believin'
> And you will find yourself perpetually receivin'.

521

If this sounds like the gospel, then we need a heavy dose of reality: salvation in Jesus Christ does not bring an end to life's troubles. In fact, sometimes the trouble is just starting. Sometimes Christians have problems or get hurt. Sometimes they get discouraged and depressed. Sometimes they are afraid and run for their lives. Sometimes they quit in the middle of their jobs or abandon their callings. Sometimes Christians are suicidal, and not just run-of-the-mill Christians, either. Sometimes spiritual leaders get afraid, quit, run away, and think about ending it all. In this respect, as in so many others, what James said really is true: "Elijah was a man just like us" (5:17 NIV).

When we see Elijah under the broom tree, we see what a man of God amounts to in his own strength. With the power of the Lord, Elijah was the best and bravest of men. He was like the apostle Paul, who said, "I can do all things through him who strengthens me" (Phil. 4:13). But without the power of the Lord, Elijah was power*less*; he was a complete coward. As Jesus said to his disciples, "apart from me you can do nothing" (John 15:5). Or to paraphrase from yet another New Testament text, Elijah had his treasure in a jar of clay to show that his all-surpassing power was from God and not from himself (see 2 Cor. 4:7).

SPIRITUAL DEPRESSION: ITS CAUSES

It is not hard to come up with some plausible explanations for Elijah's depression. There were probably at least a dozen good reasons for him to be suicidal.

First, *fatigue*. Elijah was exhausted. King Ahab went to Carmel to eat and to drink (1 Kings 17:41–42), but not Elijah. God's prophet spent his time on the mountain in prayer. Then he ran 18 miles to Jezreel. After that, he ran for his life, some 90 miles down to Beersheba in the south. By the time he had run to Mount Horeb (1 Kings 19:8), he had run 300 miles in all (!), which is more or less equivalent to running from Philadelphia to Pittsburgh in August. Great athlete though he may have been, Elijah was on the verge of complete physical collapse, and a tired believer is a vulnerable believer. As Winston Churchill famously said, fatigue makes cowards of us all.

Second, *isolation*. No Christian can thrive or survive without the communion of the saints. Yet Elijah had been virtually alone for three years. He had very little human contact at all, let alone intimate fellowship with like-minded believers. Furthermore, by leaving his servant behind in Beersheba (1 Kings 19:3), Elijah deliberately cut himself off from godly companionship. Depression is not only caused by the absence of community; it also perpetuates it.[3]

Next, *spiritual opposition*. Elijah had stood against all the prophets of Baal. But even when he had overcome them, he was opposed by Jezebel, that mistress of Satan. Thus Elijah had been under direct spiritual attack. Relentless spiritual opposition is bound to bring a believer to the point of discouragement.

Here is another explanation for Elijah's depression: *the normal rhythms of human emotion*. Elijah had just experienced a spiritual high, the ultimate mountaintop experience. He had witnessed the mighty acts of God in fire and rain on Mount Carmel. He came back down to earth, hard, and thus it is no surprise that he became a blue believer. No one can live a godly life on sheer emotion.

Add to Elijah's emotional fragility *the feeling of emptiness that often follows ministering in the name of God*. When Elijah was up on the mountain, the strength of the Lord surged through every fiber of his being. Now the vessel was empty. There is always something draining about serving as a conduit for the word of God. Perhaps preachers understand Elijah's depression best of all. Often a pastor who gives everything he has to the Word of God on Sunday is running on empty on Monday.

What about *dashed expectations*? Very likely Elijah went to Jezreel in full confidence that the Lord God had won the day and that Israel would turn back to God. But meeting Queen Jezebel was like a slap in the face. Although Elijah had won the battle, he had not yet won the war—a discouraging reality.

Along with Elijah's shattered expectations went the very natural response of *fear*. The wording of verse 3 is striking: "Then he was afraid, and he arose and ran for his life." More accurately, "Elijah *saw* and ran for his life." In that moment, when he was gripped with fear and his life passed before his very eyes, Elijah's gaze was taken off the Lord and fixed squarely on his own troubles.

Then, on top of everything else, the prophet was dealing with his *guilt*. Elijah was a traitor to the Lord's cause. Having run off in his own direction,

---

3. I am indebted to Iain Duguid for this insight, and for many others.

he was absent without leave. He had deserted his post in the middle of the battle. He had abandoned his divine calling at the crucial moment when the spiritual destiny of the whole nation was still hanging in the balance. Thus Elijah had failed in the one area of his life that was his greatest spiritual strength: bold faith. The prophet's self-condemnation was just: "I am no better than my fathers" (1 Kings 19:4).

These words suggest another root cause for Elijah's depression, namely, *pride*. Apparently, Elijah hoped or expected to surpass his fathers in the faith—a proud ambition.

No wonder Elijah had had enough! Many factors contributed to his spiritual depression. There are simple remedies for most of them. If we are struggling with spiritual depression, we should identify its causes as clearly as we can and apply the obvious practical remedy. If we are tired, we should take some vigorous exercise and then get some rest. If our body is breaking down, we should start eating balanced meals. If we are isolated, we should go to church and talk to a Christian friend. If we are under spiritual attack, we should get others to join us in praying for spiritual protection. If we are obsessed with our troubles, we should lift our gaze to the right hand of God and fix our eyes on Jesus. If we are guilty, we should confess our sins to God.

Messiah Complex

Yet Elijah had a deeper problem that went beyond these simple remedies. There is another reason for Elijah's depression. Although it is a reason that most commentators have overlooked, it may be more important than all the other reasons put together: Elijah was suicidal because he needed a Savior.

Imagine for a moment that the Bible went up only to 1 Kings 18. If we had only the first five hundred pages or so of the Bible—which is about what Elijah had—what would we conclude about the prophet's identity? Where would we place Elijah in the history of redemption? It would be easy to guess that Elijah might be the promised Servant, God's chosen Prophet. God had promised to send a second Moses to the people of God: "I will raise up for them a prophet like you from among their brothers. And I will put my words in his mouth, and he shall speak to them all that I command him" (Deut. 18:18).

Elijah must have seemed like an excellent candidate to fulfill the promised role. He could shut up the rain in the heavens and bring manna to people without bread. He could raise the dead. He could pray down the glorious fire of God's presence. He could turn the hearts of God's people back to their God. Could it be that Elijah was the prophet like Moses? Could it be that he was the Savior God promised, who would save his people from their sins?

No, Elijah was not *the* Prophet. He was not the Messiah who was sent to save his people from their sins. His depression amounted to an admission of his failure to be that Savior: "It is enough; now, O Lord, take away my life, for I am no better than my fathers" (1 Kings 19:4). When he referred to his "fathers," Elijah was not speaking about his natural father and grandfather. Rather, he was referring to his spiritual fathers among the prophets of Israel. Elijah was no better than any of the rest of the prophets. Like every last one of them, he was a sinner.

The reason Elijah was depressed about being no better than his fathers was that he knew that what the people of God needed more than anything else—and what he himself needed—was a Prophet who *was* better than his fathers. This is what the people of God always need: a Savior who will not sin, a Savior who will never desert us or abandon his calling, a Savior who will not flinch in the face of death. But the depressing reality for Elijah was that he was no better than his fathers. He was no better than Moses or any of the other prophets. Like all the rest, he was a sinner in need of a Savior, and his suicidal depression was a desperate plea for the Savior that God had promised.

Spiritual Depression: Its Cure

One day Elijah would meet the Savior. He would meet the Prophet who was and is better than his fathers, the Savior who would save his people from their sins. Elijah would meet Jesus Christ on the Mount of Transfiguration (Matt. 17:1–13).

But long before that day came, while Elijah was sitting under the broom tree, he received God's grace: "And he lay down and slept under a broom tree. And behold, an angel touched him and said to him, 'Arise and eat'" (1 Kings 19:5). The man may have been suicidal, but God still loved him:

[God's] eye followed with tender pity every step of [Elijah's] flight across the hills of Samaria. He did not love him less than when he stood, elated with victory, hard by the burning sacrifice. And His love assumed, if possible, a tenderer, gentler aspect, as He stooped over him, whilst he slept. As a shepherd tracks the wandering sheep, from the fold to the wild mountain pass, where eagles, sailing in narrowing circles, watch its faltering steps—so did the love of God come upon Elijah, as, worn in body by long fatigue, and in spirit by the fierce war of passion, he lay and slept under the juniper tree.[4]

When Elijah had had enough, he discovered that God's grace is more than enough. In his grace, God sent an angel to minister to his prophet. When Elijah was strong in faith and prayer, it was enough for him to receive bread and meat from the beaks of ravens. But when he was alone and afraid, he needed more than enough. So in the prophet's season of depression and discouragement, God sent an angel to caress him with a physical touch and speak to him in an audible voice. God has countless means to care for our needs, but his usual practice is to give us what we need in the way we need it most.

In his grace God also gave Elijah the rest that he needed. God left his prophet to sleep under the broom tree, and then after he ate, to sleep again. This was one fulfillment of the psalmist's promise: "[The Lord] gives to his beloved sleep" (Ps. 127:2). Elijah's nap also anticipated the promise of Isaiah: "They who wait upon the LORD shall renew their strength; they shall mount up with wings like eagles; they shall run and not be weary; they shall walk and not faint" (Isa. 40:31).

Furthermore, it was God's grace to give Elijah his daily bread. How is this for room service? "And he looked, and behold, there was at his head a cake baked on hot stones and a jar of water. And he ate and drank and lay down again" (1 Kings 19:6). Even though the prophet had failed to show much sign of a positive response after his first helping, the angel of the Lord came back to bring Elijah seconds: "And the angel of the LORD came again a second time and touched him and said, 'Arise and eat, for the journey is too great for you.' And he arose and ate and drank" (1 Kings 19:7).

Best of all, it was God's grace to give Elijah all these things and not to rebuke him. God treated Elijah with mercy rather than justice. Once Elijah

4. F. B. Meyer, *Elijah* (Fort Washington, PA: Christian Literature Crusade, 1992), 111.

had run away from his calling, he could not use his personal merit to make any further claim on the mercy of God. Yet there is not one word of rebuke in this passage. Later, when Elijah reaches Mount Horeb, God will straighten him out about a few things. But not yet. Under the broom tree Elijah raged against the dispensations of God and held an egotistical little pity party. He prayed the most offensive prayer that a human being can pray to the Lord and giver of life: the prayer for his life to be taken away. Elijah did all this, yet God continued to summon the prophet to service: "Arise and eat, for the journey is too great for you" (1 Kings 19:7). This was God's grace for Elijah.

God's grace to Elijah stands as a good example for teachers and parents in dealing with the spiritual immaturity of children, or for other spiritual leaders who have the responsibility to care for people who are prone to self-pity. But what it shows us most of all is the pattern of God's grace for us in Christ. In Jesus Christ we find rest for our souls. Jesus says, "Come to me, all who labor and are heavy laden, and I will give you rest. Take my yoke upon you, and learn from me, for I am gentle and lowly in heart, and you will find rest for your souls" (Matt. 11:28–29). In Jesus Christ we receive living bread and living water. Jesus says, "I am the bread of life; whoever comes to me shall not hunger, and whoever believes in me shall never thirst" (John 6:35). In Jesus Christ we find forgiveness for our sins, without any rebuke, for "there is therefore now no condemnation for those who are in Christ Jesus" (Rom. 8:1).

When we have had enough, Jesus Christ is more than enough. He has the same grace for us that God had for Elijah under the broom tree. He hears our prayers. He knows our discouragement and depression. Yet he still loves us and is reaching out to touch us. He offers rest for our souls and forgiveness for our sins. He does not condemn us, but promises to be more than enough for us, forever.

Jesus offers this grace to us through his own sufferings and death on the cross. In a sermon on this passage—a sermon that may well have influenced Mendelssohn's *Elijah*—the old German preacher F. W. Krummacher compared Elijah's broom tree (or juniper bush) to the cross. His words bring this episode in the prophet's life to a gospel conclusion:

> But listen. As often as it will seem to you as if it were enough, as if the burden
> of life is no longer to be borne, do as Elijah did. Flee you, too, to the silence of

solitude, and I will show you a juniper bush, and there you will cast yourself down. It is the cross. Yes, a juniper, covered with thorns and barbs that pierce the soul, girded about with points and nails that wound the heart and cause old nature [Eph. 4:22] pain and suffering. But this juniper also has a scent that refreshes the soul, and a perfume through which we become the Lord's sweet-smelling sacrifice. . . . In the presence of the cross you no longer think of complaining about the greatness of your sufferings. For here you see a suffering against which your own is as nothing; and a righteous man suffers it for the sake of you unrighteous man. In the presence of the cross you will quickly be forced to forget your distress, for the love of God in Jesus Christ for you poor sinner will soon draw all your thoughts and reflections away from everything else, and into it alone. Under the cross you are safe from the thought that what you experience in your unhappiness is something strange. . . . Under the cross you are preserved from impatience. . . . Under the cross your complaining will soon be absorbed in the peace of the Lord.[5]

5. F. W. Krummacher in R. Larry Todd, ed., *Mendelssohn and His World* (Princeton, NJ: Princeton University Press, 1991), 129.

42

THE STILL SMALL VOICE

1 Kings 19:9—18

And he said, "Go out and stand on the mount before the LORD."
And behold, the LORD passed by, and a great and strong wind
tore the mountains and broke in pieces the rocks before the LORD,
but the LORD was not in the wind. And after the wind an earth-
quake, but the LORD was not in the earthquake. And after the
earthquake a fire, but the LORD was not in the fire. And after
the fire the sound of a low whisper. (1 Kings 19:11–12)

I could preach with fervor and power, I could share Christ with enthusiasm and success. I would counsel with meaningful insight and socialize with sheer delight. But without warning, any or all of these positive and delightful emotions would suddenly be forced to give way to feelings of gloom and periods of weakness. I would withdraw, and a form of paranoia would settle in. I would suddenly be overwhelmed with feelings of inadequacy and inferiority. On occasion I toyed with thoughts of self-destruction. . . . The struggle reached its inevitable climax when I found myself too weary to minister, too filled with hostility to love, and too frightened to preach.[1]

1. Don Baker, with Emery Nester, *Depression: Finding Hope and Meaning in Life's Darkest Shadow* (Portland, OR: Multnomah, 1983), 16.

These words come from the Reverend Don Baker in his book *Depression: Finding Hope and Meaning in Life's Darkest Shadow*. But they could just as well have come from the prophet Elijah, for he, too, experienced feelings of gloom, inadequacy, self-destruction, and fear.

STILL DEPRESSED?

When Elijah arrived at Horeb, he was still depressed. He had been depressed in the desert, and he was still depressed up on the mountain. He had been depressed under the broom tree, and he was still depressed in the cave.

As we have seen, God dealt graciously with Elijah when he first entertained thoughts of suicide. Strangely enough, although Elijah prayed to die, he was the one prophet who never died at all, but was taken up to heaven (see 2 Kings 2:11). This is because when Elijah had had enough, God proved to be more than enough. God did not rebuke his prophet but touched him, fed him, and satisfied him with fresh water.

We might have expected Elijah to be refreshed by his experience of God's grace in the wilderness, and thus to have recovered the joy of his salvation. But that is *not* what happened. Rather than being refreshed, Elijah was still depressed. Forty days later the prophet was still down in the dumps. The bitter aria in Mendelssohn's *Elijah* closes with the words of 1 Kings 19:10, and in it we can practically taste the bile in Elijah's throat: "I have been very jealous for the Lord God of hosts; for the children of Israel have broken Thy covenant, thrown down Thine altars, and slain Thy prophets with the sword: and I, even I only, am left; and they seek my life to take it away."

Is it surprising to find that this great man of God was still depressed? It shouldn't be. Spiritual depression is hard to shake. It is not a twenty-four-hour virus. Getting over it takes more than a pastor saying, "Take two Bible verses and call me in the morning." Even the godliest of the godly can become so discouraged that it takes months or even years to return to useful service for the Lord.

This in itself can be an encouragement. On Mount Horeb we find the greatest of saints reduced to the blackest of moods. Yet he is not condemned for his depression. On the contrary, he is called back into active service for God. And if God's grace was sufficient for Elijah, it will be sufficient for us whenever we are disheartened, discouraged, and depressed by the trials of life and sufferings we face in ministry.

Half-Truths

Why was Elijah so discouraged? As we have seen, depression can have a variety of causes, including physical and social ones. But the heart of the matter is often spiritual, and for Elijah, spiritual depression was the result of believing too many half-truths.

After Elijah ate and drank in the wilderness, he "went in the strength of that food forty days and forty nights to Horeb, the mount of God. There he came to a cave and lodged in it" (1 Kings 19:8–9). Evidently Elijah spent those forty days and forty nights mentally rehearsing the angry speech he would give to God the next time he had the chance. Over and over again he practiced in his mind what he would say about all the ways the Lord had let him down.

By the time he arrived at Horeb, Elijah had told himself so many half-truths, he was starting to believe them. He had his little speech down pat in verse 10. Then he gave exactly the same speech in verse 14, word for word. Even after Elijah had witnessed a theophany—a visible demonstration of the presence of God—he was singing the same old tune. Whenever God pressed the prophet's "play" button and asked, "What are you doing here, Elijah?" (1 Kings 19:9, 13), he heard the same reply: "I have been very jealous for the Lord, the God of hosts. For the people of Israel have forsaken your covenant, thrown down your altars, and killed your prophets with the sword, and I, even I only, am left, and they seek my life, to take it away" (1 Kings 19:10, 14).

All these statements are half-truths. The trouble with half-truths, of course, is that they are also half-falsehoods. Elijah was feeding himself a steady diet of the kinds of lies that lead to spiritual depression, which typically feeds on the wrong things that we keep telling ourselves. The prophet was preaching to himself the half-truths of self-righteousness, self-pity, and self-importance.

First, he was insisting on his own *self-righteousness*. Elijah said, "I have been very zealous for the Lord, the God of hosts" (1 Kings 19:10, 14). There was a time when the prophet (almost) could have gotten away with saying this. After all, who had been more zealous for God than Elijah? "Zealous" is

531

just the word for the man. He shut the rain up in the heavens through prayer. He pronounced God's judgment upon Ahab's kingdom. He entrusted himself to God's ravens. He raised a widow's son from the dead. He taunted Baal and put his prophets to the sword. No one had been more zealous for the Lord God Almighty than the prophet Elijah.

Sadly, Elijah was no longer as zealous as he had been. Now his purported zeal was only a half-truth. What had Elijah done for God lately? Not much. He had panicked under the threats of Queen Jezebel. He had run away from his calling. He had prayed to God for death. So Elijah really had nothing to boast about. If he was zealous about anything at this point in his ministry, it was saving his own neck (notice the irony here: the same man who prayed for death was desperate to save his life). So when Elijah claimed that he was very zealous for the Lord, he was being self-righteous. He was so full of himself that he had an exaggerated view of his personal godliness.

Self-righteousness is a constant temptation for any believer. It happens like this. First, we experience some work of God's grace in our hearts. Then, as we look back at how far we have come in the Christian life, we feel encouraged by our spiritual progress. But at the same time that other sins start to shrivel and die, our spiritual pride grows like kudzu and we become smug about our spiritual accomplishments.

Elijah thought he was zealous, but he was zealous only by half. One clear sign that the prophet was not quite as zealous as he thought he was comes at the end of verse 9, where God asks, "What are you doing here, Elijah?" There is a strong rebuke in this question, for if God Almighty ever has occasion to ask us why we are where we are, then we must not be where we ought to be! At the end of this encounter the Lord will say to Elijah, "Go, return on your way" (1 Kings 19:15). After walking with God for so many years, Elijah had decided to step out on his own, which means that he will have some backtracking to do before he gets back on course.

Have you ever run away from God? Sometimes the Lord has the same question for us that he had for Elijah: "What are you doing here?" To be more specific: "Why do I find you trapped in this sin? Why are you still caught up in this unhealthy relationship? Why have you refused to follow my calling for your life?" If God needs to tell us to go back the way we came, we had better start heading in the opposite direction from the one we are heading!

By mentioning his zeal to the Lord, Elijah was asking for special treatment. Apparently, he thought that God owed him something for his service. He thought he deserved better. Sometimes we are tempted to have the same attitude, insisting that we ought to be exempt from the flu, or car trouble, or corporate downsizing, or whatever other troubles we may have. Self-righteousness feeds spiritual depression by making claims on God that will only add to our bitterness when he fails to meet our outrageous demands.

Another half-truth that feeds spiritual depression is *self-pity*. Listen again to Elijah's complaint: "For the people of Israel have forsaken your covenant, thrown down your altars, and killed your prophets with the sword, and I, even I only, am left, and they seek my life, to take it away" (1 Kings 19:10).

There is some truth in these statements. They may even be more than half true, since each of Elijah's claims finds some legitimate basis in chapter 18. The Israelites had indeed rejected God's covenant. Elijah told Ahab, "You have abandoned the commandments of the LORD" (1 Kings 18:18). The Israelites had also broken down God's altars. When Elijah went up on Mount Carmel to offer a sacrifice to the living God, "he repaired the altar of the LORD that had been thrown down" (1 Kings 18:30). Furthermore, the Israelites had put God's prophets to death with the sword: "Jezebel cut off the prophets of the LORD" (1 Kings 18:4).

All these things were true, but they were not true any longer. Once again Elijah was guilty of selective memory. In effect, he was claiming to be the last student from the last graduating class of the last orthodox seminary in Israel. But in saying this, he was forgetting that Obadiah had rescued a hundred prophets (see 1 Kings 18:4). He was also forgetting that the Israelites had their hearts turned back to God. When the fire fell from heaven to consume Elijah's sacrifice, they had put their faces in the dust and returned to covenant worship, shouting, "The LORD, he is God; the LORD, he is God" (1 Kings 18:39). The altar had been rebuilt, at least at Carmel. Instead of putting God's own prophets to death with the sword, the Israelites had seized the prophets of Baal and slaughtered them in the Kishon Valley (1 Kings 18:40). So what Elijah said was no longer true. Conveniently, he failed to recognize that God had been at work. As a result, he was telling himself that things were worse than they actually were. In short, he was feeling sorry for himself.

Elijah's self-pity comes out perhaps most clearly in the last line of his speech: "They seek my life, to take it away" (1 Kings 19:10). Is it not true that people were trying to put the prophet to death? After all, this chapter began with a nasty message from Queen Jezebel: "So may the gods do to me and more also, if I do not make your life as the life of one of them by this time tomorrow" (1 Kings 19:2).

True? Only half true. Notice the pronoun that Elijah uses: "*they* seek my life, to take it away." Jezebel was the one trying to kill him, not the whole nation of Israel. Elijah had turned "she" into "they." By turning a queen into an entire kingdom, the prophet was magnifying his troubles, nursing his sense of self-pity.

Spiritual depression often includes an element of self-pity. We exaggerate our troubles, seeing them as bigger than they really are. We insist that the problems of life are so overwhelming that they cannot be solved. Rather than looking to God and seeing his superior strength and mighty grace, we imagine that our troubles are beyond any remedy. By making our problems seem bigger than they really are and by making God smaller than he actually is, we convince ourselves that our situation is pitiful.

The third half-truth that Elijah preached to himself was *self-importance*: "I, even I only, am left" (1 Kings 19:10). By now we can see that Elijah was holding an egotistical little pity party. No guests were invited to this party, of course, because the prophet's whole point was that he had no one to invite! "I am the only one," Elijah said. "No one understands me. No one has ever gone through what I am going through. No one can possibly help me."

It is true that Elijah was left, but he was *not* the only one. God quickly set the record straight: "I will leave seven thousand in Israel, all the knees that have not bowed to Baal, and every mouth that has not kissed him" (1 Kings 19:18). Elijah was more than a little off in his calculations! In terms of raw numbers, he had underestimated the strength of God's people by 6,999. To express the same error in different terms, he had miscalculated by a factor of seven thousand. What he was saying to God was not a half-truth, therefore, but a one-seven-thousandth truth.

In saying that he was the only one left, Elijah was exaggerating his own importance. He was trying to do everything himself, as if the destiny of God's people depended entirely on him. He had forgotten that all of God's servants are expendable, that there is always someone else who can do the Lord's work in our place.

In his commentary on this passage, the medieval scholar Moses Maimonides paraphrased the dialogue that took place between God and Elijah:

Elijah: The Israelites have broken God's covenant.

God: Is it then your covenant?

Elijah: They have torn down Your altars.

God: But were they *your* altars?

Elijah: They have put Your prophets to the sword.

God: But you are alive.

Elijah: I alone am left.

God: Instead of hurling accusations against Israel, should you not have pleaded their cause?[2]

This dialogue, as Maimonides imagines it, captures well the attitude of the prophet. No wonder Elijah was still discouraged! He had been feeding himself a steady diet of half-truths. He was claiming that he was too godly and too important to suffer. His example thus reminds us how selfish depression can be. When we struggle with spiritual depression, it is wise to figure out what we have been preaching to ourselves. Very likely we have been telling ourselves things like this: "I deserve better than this." "I can't take it anymore." "My problems can't be solved." "Nobody understands me." "Nobody loves me." "Nobody cares about me." "I am the only one." If this is what we have been telling ourselves, then it is no wonder that we are discouraged!

Spiritual depression is a vampire that feeds upon the lies in all the half-truths we preach to ourselves. This is one of the reasons why we need to preach the gospel to ourselves every day. To avoid spiritual depression, we need to fill our minds with thoughts like these: "I am a very great sinner, but Christ is an even greater Savior." "My troubles are more than I can bear, but Jesus is strong enough to carry them." "God understands me." "Jesus loves me with an everlasting love." "The Holy Spirit comforts me." "I am not the only one." "Jesus will be with me to the very end."

FAITHFUL IN THE PAST

If spiritual depression is full of self, then the way out is through the grace of God. At the lowest point in the prophet's life, God gave Elijah at least three great truths about himself—not half-truths, but whole truths with a capital *T*. Refusing to join the prophet's pity party, God showed

2. Quoted in Jonathan Sacks, "To Be a Prophet for the People," *First Things*, January 1996, 29.

himself to Elijah as faithful in the past, sovereign over the future, and gentle in the present.

As we have seen, Elijah "arose and ate and drank, and went in the strength of that food forty days and forty nights to Horeb, the mount of God" (1 Kings 19:8). This verse plainly echoes an incident from Exodus, when Moses led his flock "and came to Horeb, the mountain of God" (Ex. 3:1). Horeb is where Moses met God in the fire of the burning bush. On the same mountain—covered with lightning and smoke and trembling from earthquakes (see Ex. 19:16–18)—Moses received the commandments of the covenant. For forty days and forty nights Moses was with God on the mountain (see Ex. 34:28).

It was on the same mountain—also known as Mount Sinai—that Moses indirectly encountered the glory of God (see Ex. 33:12–23). The prophet had asked to see the glory of God. He was not allowed to do this directly because no one can see the face of God, and live. But God put Moses in a cleft in the rock and covered him with his divine hand until he had passed by; then at the last moment he removed his hand to allow Moses to see the back of his glory.

When Elijah went up Mount Horeb, therefore—for his own forty days and forty nights—he was in a place that held many reminders of the faithfulness of God. In effect, Elijah became a second Moses. He went to the mountain where God established his covenant, spoke to his prophets, and revealed his presence—a place where God had been faithful in the past.

Up on Mount Horeb the Lord told Elijah what he had once told Moses: "Go out and stand on the mount before the LORD" (1 Kings 19:11). Back in verse 9, the Scripture literally says that Elijah came to "the cave"—not just any old cave, but *the* cave. We may well wonder whether Elijah hid in the very cleft in the rock where Moses once hid from the glory of God. In any case, by telling Elijah to stand on the mountain, God was reminding his prophet of his faithfulness to Moses in the past. By doing this, he was giving Elijah a re-call. God was calling his prophet out of his self-imposed retirement and recommissioning him for kingdom service. Like Moses before him, Elijah was called to be a prophet for God.

Whenever we are spiritually depressed, or trying to help others who are disheartened and discouraged, we need to remember God's faithfulness in the past. This includes recounting the many ways that God has protected us and preserved us. It also includes reading our Bibles. We may be tempted to say, "But I don't *feel* like reading my Bible." Refusing to feed on biblical truth is like a sick person refusing to drink fluids until he or she is healthy. If we have a cold, we do not wait until we feel better to drink our juice or eat our chicken soup; we eat and drink in order to get better. In the same way, the Christian who is struggling with spiritual depression must not wait for a hunger for God's Word to return, but continue to read the Bible and hear it preached in order to be reminded of God's faithfulness in the past.

Sovereign over the Future

Another precious truth for times of discouragement is that God is sovereign over the future. The instructions God gave to Elijah clearly showed that he was still in charge.

God was in control of the nations. He proved this by telling Elijah, "Go, return on your way to the wilderness of Damascus. And when you arrive, you shall anoint Hazael to be king over Syria" (1 Kings 19:15). God sets rulers upon their thrones, so it was right and good for his prophet to anoint the next king of that pagan land (cf. 2 Kings 8:7–15; 10:32–33). God also had a king (and a prophet) in mind for his own people, so he told Elijah: "And Jehu the son of Nimshi you shall anoint to be king over Israel, and Elisha the son of Shaphat of Abel-meholah you shall anoint to be prophet in your place. And the one who escapes from the sword of Hazael shall Jehu put to death, and the one who escapes from the sword of Jehu shall Elisha put to death" (1 Kings 19:16–17; cf. 2 Kings 9–10). The political situation in the ancient Near East may have seemed like a complete mess, but God had not lost control. He was still working his plan, as he always does.

God was also sovereign over the spiritual destiny of his people. He already had a successor in mind for Elijah himself, which is why he told him to anoint Elisha as prophet (see 1 Kings 19:16). Furthermore, God had reserved seven thousand righteous souls in Israel: "Yet I will leave seven thousand in Israel, all the knees that have not bowed to Baal, and every mouth that has not kissed him" (1 Kings 19:18). This promise is an example of the doctrine of the perseverance of the saints. God always preserves a remnant for salvation, even down to the present day. As Paul testified to the Romans, "God has not rejected his people whom he foreknew. Do you not know what the Scripture says of Elijah . . . ? 'I have kept for myself seven thousand men who have not bowed the knee to Baal.' So too at the present time there is a remnant, chosen by grace" (Rom. 11:2, 4–5).

One by one, the half-truths of Elijah's depression were being replaced by the total truths of God's grace. The God who had been faithful in the past was still sovereign over the nations, for the sake of his people. By the time God was finished giving these reminders and instructions, Elijah was back on his feet and starting to serve the Lord (see 1 Kings 19:19). His depression had been replaced by faithful hope.

The same grace is available to us. We may draw strength from God's faithfulness in the past and hope from God's sovereignty over the future. Things are not as hopeless as they may seem. God is still in charge. There is plenty of work for us to do, and God will give us plenty of help in doing it. As we pursue God's mission to the world, we will find purpose in doing what God has called us to do.

Gentle in the Present

Finally, we are invited to rest in God's gentleness in the present. God may not always seem gentle, of course. He certainly did not seem gentle when Elijah was given a spectacular demonstration of his power:

> And behold, the LORD passed by, and a great and strong wind tore the mountains and broke in pieces the rocks before the LORD, but the LORD was not in the wind. And after the wind an earthquake, but the LORD was not in the earthquake. And after the earthquake a fire, but the LORD was not in the fire. (1 Kings 19:11–12)

Sometimes Elijah is depicted on Mount Horeb standing with his face exposed to the elements and his beard flapping in the wind. This is the wrong picture altogether. When the Lord told the prophet to "go out and stand on the mount before the LORD" (1 Kings 19:11), Elijah declined the invitation— a sign of his ongoing spiritual struggle. When God revealed his glorious presence, Elijah was shaking in his sandals, hiding as far back in the cave as he could get. The prophet was willing to play hide-and-seek with God, but not peek-a-boo! It was only after God passed by that Elijah "wrapped his face in his cloak and went out and stood at the entrance of the cave" (1 Kings

19:13). Even then, he did not even dare to venture one step outside the cave, but stood trembling in the shadows.

What is ironic about Elijah's fear is that the prophet had often boasted about boldly standing before the Lord. When the prophet told King Ahab that he served the Lord, he referred to him as "the Lord . . . before whom I stand" (1 Kings 17:1). Later Elijah said the same thing to Obadiah (see 1 Kings 18:15). Yet in the event he was not quite as comfortable standing before the Lord as he had led Ahab and Obadiah to believe! This is a reminder for us to be careful how we speak about the closeness of our relationship with the Lord. When Jesus Christ comes in all his glory, he will put our idle boasts to the test!

As Elijah stood trembling in the shadow of the cave, he had his cloak pulled over his face. So when he performed his pitiable, self-righteous speech for the second time (see 1 Kings 19:14), it must have been a little muffled. It is a pathetic picture: one of the greatest prophets who ever lived was cowering in the shadow of a cave, with his cloak thrown over his head like a monk. Even after receiving, Moses-like, a demonstration of God's mighty power, Elijah reiterated his self-centered complaint verbatim.

In his weakness, anything more than a gentle God would have been too much for Elijah to bear. After all, he is the God of wind, earthquake, and fire. Sometimes God's Spirit is in the wind, rushing and blowing about the earth. Sometimes God is in the earthquake, shaking the earth to show his power. Sometimes he is in the fire, as he was at Mount Carmel, when lightning fell from heaven to consume Elijah's sacrifice. But there are times when the glory of God is too much for any human being to take. His power is a terrible reality, and sometimes we simply want to know that he is our friend. This is what God revealed to Elijah: "And after the fire the sound of a low whisper" (1 Kings 19:12).

Here the King James Version employs a beautiful phrase: "a still small voice." After earth, wind, and fire, God spoke to Elijah in a still small voice. Admittedly, the commentators cannot agree what this familiar phrase means.[3] The Scripture simply gives the story without an interpretation. To some the voice speaks of revelation: God is revealed not only in nature, but also by his word. To others it testifies to God's work: the kingdom of God does not advance by signs and wonders, ordinarily, but in quiet obedience. Sometimes

---

3. Meredith Kline argues that it was not a still small voice at all, but the roaring, rushing sound of a full-scale theophany; see *Images of the Spirit* (Eugene, OR: Wipf and Stock Publishers, 1980), 99.

God reveals himself as dramatically as he did on Mount Carmel; usually he speaks as quietly as he spoke to Elijah at Mount Horeb. Maybe most of all, the still small voice means that we can have an intimate friendship with God. God is so glorious that one glance would obliterate us. He is so mighty in wind and fire that his mere presence sends us to the back of the cave. But then he speaks to us—in a still small voice—and we have the courage to come to the mouth of the cave, where he whispers to us as a friend with a friend.

Do you know the God of the still small voice? Don Baker—whose struggle with spiritual depression was mentioned at the beginning of this chapter—writes about the restoration of his intimacy with God: "Like Elijah I felt that I had been exceptionally zealous for the Lord. I had worked diligently at tearing down the 'false altars' to the 'false gods.' I was accustomed to the 'great and strong winds' and the 'rending of the mountains' and the 'fire' and the 'earthquakes,' but a total stranger to the 'still small voice.'"[4] In his grace, the God of Elijah reacquainted Don Baker with the still small voice. When the minister was in the depths of spiritual depression, God came to him in all his gentleness and grace, calling him again and again to serve.

God will come to us the same way. Perhaps we need to get reacquainted with the God of the still small voice. Perhaps we need to be restored to sweet intimacy with the God of earth, wind, and fire. Our God is a gentle God. If we want to see his gentleness, we need only to look in the face of Jesus Christ. Jesus was gentle in the manger, lying on a bed of straw. He was gentle with the sick, touching their wounds to heal. He was gentle with the grieving, weeping with those who wept. He was gentle with little children, gathering them up in his arms. He was gentle with women caught in adultery, forgiving their sins. He was gentle on the donkey, riding into Jerusalem with kingly humility. He was gentle with his disciples, restoring them to fellowship after they had denied and forsaken him.

Jesus Christ will be gentle with us as well. He will be gentle with the wounds of our souls and the sins of our hearts. He will even be gentle with us in our spiritual depression. Listen to the still small voice of gentle Jesus, who says to everyone: "Come to me, all who labor and are heavy laden, and I will give you rest . . . for I am gentle and lowly in heart, and you will find rest for your souls" (Matt. 11:28–29).

4. Baker, *Depression*, 67–68.

43

No Turning Back

1 Kings 19:19–21

*And [Elisha] returned from following him and took the yoke of
oxen and sacrificed them and boiled their flesh with the yokes of
the oxen and gave it to the people, and they ate. Then he arose
and went after Elijah and assisted him. (1 Kings 19:21)*

fterward, Elisha must have associated his decision to follow
God with the smell of roast beef, because when the prophet
Elijah came and placed his mantle on Elisha's shoulders,
"he returned from following him and took the yoke of oxen and sacrificed
them and boiled their flesh with the yokes of the oxen and gave it to the
people, and they ate" (1 Kings 19:21). There had been a great barbecue on
Mount Carmel when God sent fire from heaven to obliterate Elijah's sacrifice. There was another barbecue when Elisha decided to follow the living
God—burgers and steaks for everyone!

After this there could be no turning back—not after Elisha's livelihood has
gone up in smoke. By the time his oxen were medium-well done, Elisha was
out of a job, and by the time his family and friends had wiped the last juicy
dribbles of barbecue from their chins, he had nowhere to go but forward.

We can almost imagine Elisha waking up the following morning and planning his day: "Let's see, I have some plowing to do today. I need to get up and feed the oxen and . . . Now, wait a second. I feel like I'm forgetting something important: Oh, yes, the oxen!" By then it was too late for Elisha to have any second thoughts. From then on, his memories of the aroma of oxen slowly roasting over a burning plow would remind him of the calling he had left behind. Elisha had decided to follow the living God—no turning back.

Elisha's cookout is a powerful picture of what it means to be totally devoted to God. When a sinner first decides to follow Jesus, there can be no turning back. Likewise, when a Christian hears the call to leave a secular job and enter Christian ministry, there can be no turning back.

To Call Is Divine

The first lesson for us to learn from Elisha's decision to follow God is that *God calls every Christian into life and ministry*. Elisha's life as a disciple and his ministry as a prophet began with a divine calling. The man did not call himself; he was called by God.

Elisha's call began with what the Lord said to Elijah: "Elisha the son of Shaphat of Abel-meholah you shall anoint to be prophet in your place" (1 Kings 19:16). Elijah was in the depths of spiritual depression when God gave him these instructions. Thinking that God's work was all up to him, he was too discouraged to carry on. But God restored his prophet to active ministry by giving him some assistance. Having seen the down side of kingdom work (1 Kings 19:1–8) and been on the back side of kingdom work (1 Kings 19:9–14), Elijah was ready to experience the renewed side of kingdom work.[1]

So God told Elijah to anoint Hazael king over Aram and Jehu king over Israel and to anoint Elisha to be prophet in Israel. It was almost as if it took three men to do the job of one Elijah. Still, God was teaching Elijah that none of his servants is ever indispensable. There is always someone else who can do the Lord's work (especially when a servant develops the kind of negative attitude that Elijah displayed after he came down from Mount Carmel).

Elijah did as he was told. He went down from Horeb, found Elisha, "passed by him and cast his cloak upon him" (1 Kings 19:19). This was a symbolic

---

1. This outline is borrowed from the Reverend Paul Chaya, who serves as senior pastor of Windsor Baptist Church in Coatesville, Pennsylvania.

gesture. In fact, the expression "wearing someone's mantle" comes from this passage. By casting his mantle over Elisha, Elijah was designating the younger man as his successor. The mantle invested Elisha with all the spiritual authority that went with the office of prophet.

Anointing Elisha was God's idea. Elijah did not choose his successor; God chose him. Elisha's calling did not come from men, therefore, but from God. He still had to answer God's call, of course, but the calling itself came from heaven. God called Elisha into life and ministry.

The same is true for every Christian. We see this in the ministry of Jesus Christ. Jesus was walking beside the Sea of Galilee when he saw two brothers fishing. Jesus called to Simon and Andrew and said, "Come, follow me" (Matt. 4:19 NIV). The same thing happened to Matthew, who was sitting in his toll booth and collecting taxes when Jesus came and said, "Follow me" (Matt. 9:9). We see the same thing all the way through the New Testament: God calling people to follow him. Peter stood up at Pentecost and preached to the nations, "The promise is for . . . everyone whom the Lord our God calls to himself" (Acts 2:39). Paul wrote to Timothy, "[He] saved us and called us to a holy calling, not because of our works but because of his own purpose and grace" (2 Tim. 1:9). He wrote the same thing to the Thessalonians: "God chose you as the firstfruits to be saved . . . He called you through our gospel" (2 Thess. 2:13–14). We do not come to God on our own initiative, but are called by God into Christian life and ministry.

Theologians call this divine summons "effectual calling." Effectual calling simply means that the call of God is effective in the lives of his chosen people. There is a general call to repentance and faith that goes out to all humanity, but God graciously makes that call effectual for some, so that when he calls them to salvation, they come. This is the work of God the Holy Spirit. By convincing us that we are miserable sinners and by enlightening our minds to understand the good news, the Holy Spirit persuades us to embrace Jesus Christ as he is offered to us in the gospel. When God calls a sinner to salvation, he does not simply mail a leaflet with a general invitation to stop by heaven sometime. Instead, as God's messengers hand-deliver a summons to salvation, the Holy Spirit takes sinners by the hand and leads them to eternal life.

A divine summons is being delivered at this very moment. In the name of Jesus Christ, the words on this page are calling you to return to God with all your heart. Leave your sins behind, come to God in Christ, and do not turn back. Jesus Christ died on the cross, was buried in the tomb, and rose again from the dead. As you open your heart to him, he will save you from your sins and give you eternal life. The Spirit of God calls sinners into the Christian life by taking this general call and making it effectual for their salvation, granting them the gifts of faith and repentance.

God also calls his people into ministry. Elisha did not choose his calling; God chose it for him. The same is true when it comes to Christian ministry. No one chooses his or her own service to God. The call to Christian service—for everything from working in the church nursery to preaching from the pulpit—comes from God. God calls us to a particular form of service for him in the church and in the world.

Although the call to ministry comes from God, it usually comes *through* other believers. The Puritan preacher William Perkins posed this question: "How can you know for yourself whether God wants you to go [into some ministry] or not?" This is a question that many people would like to be able to answer. "How do I know what God wants me to do with my life?" Perkins answered: "You must ask both your own conscience and the church. . . . Your conscience must judge of your willingness and the church of your ability."[2] So it was for Elisha. He may or may not have had a strong inclination to become a prophet, but his calling came through another believer when Elijah threw him his cloak. Ultimately, the call came from God, of course, yet it was confirmed by God's people.

If we want to know how the Lord wants us to serve him, we seek to discern what desires the Lord has given us. More importantly, we step forward when we are asked to serve. But we also seek the counsel of the church. If we are truly called to some particular ministry, other believers in spiritual leadership will confirm our calling.

This is especially true when it comes to serving as a pastor or elder in the church. No one decides on his own to become a pastor. When Elisha was called to the prophetic office, his call came through the hands of another prophet. The same thing happens in the church. When a man is ordained to the office of teaching or ruling elder, the elders of the church come forward to lay their hands upon him in prayer. In effect, they are casting their

---

2. William Perkins, "The Calling of the Ministry," in *The Art of Prophesying* (Edinburgh: Banner of Truth, 1996), 189.

mantle on him. This symbolic act shows that the call to ministry comes from God, through the church.

LEAVING IT ALL BEHIND

Elisha's answer to God's call teaches us a second lesson about following God and not turning back: *To answer God's call is to leave everything else behind.*

Elisha's response to the call of God was immediate. He leaped at the chance to follow Elijah: "He left the oxen and ran after Elijah" (1 Kings 19:20). This seems to be a picture of perfect discipleship. But then things get a little confusing, as Elisha says: "Let me kiss my father and my mother, and then I will follow you" (1 Kings 19:20). Is Elisha turning back after all? Is he trying in some way to delay his decision for discipleship?

Elijah's response is equally puzzling: "And he said to him, 'Go back again, for what have I done to you?'" (1 Kings 19:20). But what does this mean? Possibly Elijah was still having negative thoughts about living the prophetic life. More likely, he was saying something like this: "Go ahead. I have not done anything to stop you from turning back." The New English Bible puts it like this: "Go back. What have I done to prevent you?"

This verse is especially hard to understand if we know the Gospel of Luke, where a man comes up to Jesus and says, "I will follow you, Lord, but let me first say farewell to those at my home" (Luke 9:61). The man seems to be making the same request that Elisha made, but Jesus gives him a very different answer: "No one who puts his hand to the plow and looks back is fit for the kingdom of God" (Luke 9:62).

By mentioning the plow, Jesus clearly reminds us of Elisha. Did Jesus think it was wrong, therefore, for Elisha to bid farewell to his parents? Not at all. How then can we explain the apparent discrepancy between Luke and Kings?

Possibly Jesus wanted to show that his kingdom comes with the demand of absolute discipleship. By alluding to Elisha, and by demanding immediate obedience, he was letting everyone know that he was greater than all the Old Testament prophets. Roger Ellsworth offers a different explanation, however. He writes:

> The answer has to lie within the hearts of the two men. Elijah knew Elisha's
> request came from a heart that was eager to follow, while Jesus knew this other

man's request came from a heart which was reluctant to follow. To go home and bid farewell was for Elisha the way to show he was making a radical break with his old life and giving himself his new task. That is why, in the process of bidding farewell, he actually slaughtered a team of oxen and barbecued them on a bonfire. . . . The man with whom Jesus was dealing, however, . . . [wanted] . . . to discuss and deliberate with his family over whether he was doing the right thing. He had obviously not yet been seized by the same spirit which gripped Elisha—the spirit of willingness to sacrifice for the sake of the call.[3]

In other words, the man whom Jesus met was trying to bargain for time. He wanted to put off God's call to discipleship, to delay the day of decision. If we ourselves have been putting God off, then we would be wise to heed the warning that Jesus gave the man. We cannot keep God waiting forever.

Instead of putting off the decision to follow Jesus, we should do what Elisha did. When he went back to kiss his father and mother good-bye, the new prophet made a powerful public demonstration of his decision to follow God. He was really saying, "Let me kiss my father and mother good-bye *so that* I may come with you." For Elisha, going back was not a way of delaying, therefore, but a way of following.

This is where the roast beef comes in. If Elisha wanted to follow God, he would have to leave his livestock behind: "And he returned from following him and took the yoke of oxen and sacrificed them and boiled their flesh with the yokes of the oxen and gave it to the people, and they ate" (1 Kings 19:21). Elisha's decision to follow God was an occasion for feasting. The prophet was so joyful that he killed not one but *two* fatted calves. He took everything that belonged to his old way of life and cooked it.

Disciples often leave everything behind when they follow God. Jesus' disciples certainly did. Jesus called Simon and Andrew while they were fishing, and "immediately they left their nets and followed him" (Matt. 4:20). The same is said of James and John: "And going on from there he saw two other brothers, James the son of Zebedee and John his brother, in the boat with Zebedee their father, mending their nets, and he called them. Immediately they left the boat and their father and followed him" (Matt. 4:21–22). Similarly, Matthew got up, left his toll booth, and followed Jesus (Matt. 9:9). If

---

3. Roger Ellsworth, *Standing for God: The Story of Elijah* (Edinburgh: Banner of Truth, 1994), 101.

Jesus is Lord, then becoming his disciple means surrendering our whole lives to him in absolute submission to his sovereignty. And sometimes this means leaving it all behind.

When people asked Jesus what they had to do to become his disciples, he told them that they had to leave everything behind. Everything? Yes, everything: "The kingdom of heaven is like treasure hidden in a field, which a man found and covered up. Then in his joy he goes and sells all that he has and buys that field" (Matt. 13:44). On another occasion, Jesus said, "Any one of you who does not renounce all that he has cannot be my disciple" (Luke 14:33).

Elisha had plenty of "everything" to leave behind. At the very least, he owned a yoke of oxen and a farm implement. But the Scripture says that he was "plowing with twelve yoke of oxen in front of him, and he was with the twelfth" (1 Kings 19:19). The implication is that all these oxen belonged to Elisha, or perhaps to his father. Needless to say, a farmer who needs a dozen tractors has a big piece of land. At the very least, Elisha was a wealthy man. He was set for life, with twenty-four oxen in the family stables and eleven servants to help drive them. Elisha was more than a farmhand; he was heir to a country estate.

It is not easy to leave behind such great wealth to follow God. One rich man asked Jesus what he had to do to inherit eternal life. Jesus said, "You lack one thing: go, sell all that you have and give to the poor, and you will have treasure in heaven; and come, follow me" (Mark 10:21). Jesus was telling the man to do exactly what Elisha did when he cooked everything he had, gave it to the poor, and followed God. But the rich man lowered his gaze from Jesus and walked away sadly, for he had many possessions. Jesus remarked, "How difficult it will be for those who have wealth to enter the kingdom of God!" (Mark 10:23).

What are we willing to leave behind to follow Jesus? Are we willing to sell our home? Leave our families? Quit our jobs? Give all our possessions to the poor? God may not ask us to do any of these things when we decide to follow Jesus. In fact, the Lord often calls us to serve him right where we are. But God did ask Elisha to give up everything. His calling to serve God superseded all other callings, even his calling as a son.

The story of Elisha's call is an example for all of us. Every Christian is *always* prepared to leave *everything* behind to follow Jesus. If we say in our hearts, "I am willing to give up everything . . . except this, and that, and the other thing," then we are in danger of turning back. A true disciple is ready at any moment to break his plow into kindling and sacrifice the fat oxen of personal prosperity in order to follow Christ.

THE PROPHET'S APPRENTICE

The last sentence of the chapter says that Elisha "arose and went after Elijah and assisted him" (1 Kings 19:21). This teaches us a third lesson about following God and not turning back: *Disciples learn how to follow Christ from older and wiser Christians.*

Elisha served as an apprentice to a prophet. To put this in contemporary terms, he was starting an internship in ministry. For him to follow in the prophet's footsteps was to be tutored in the art of prophecy. Elisha became Elijah's attendant, which meant that Elijah became Elisha's mentor.

The intimacy of the relationship between these two men is revealed in 2 Kings 2:12, where Elisha calls Elijah his "father." A good word to describe Elisha's calling is "servant." In 2 Kings 3:11 he will be introduced to the king of Israel as the one "who poured water on the hands of Elijah." The two men were not equals. Elisha ministered to Elijah in menial ways, even to the point of washing the prophet's hands.

Another way to describe their relationship is to say that Elijah was "discipling" Elisha. A disciple is simply a follower. So to be "discipled" is to be taught how to follow Christ and not turn back. Becoming a Christian involves much more than simply going forward at a revival meeting or praying the "sinner's prayer"; it means following Jesus with one's whole life. One of the best ways to learn how to do this is to follow in the footsteps of older and wiser Christians, which is exactly what Elisha did: "Then he arose and went after Elijah and assisted him" (1 Kings 19:21).

This is God's ordinary pattern for Christian life and ministry. One generation of believers disciples the next, over and over again. A good example from the Bible is the relationship between Moses and Joshua, who learned to follow God by following Israel's great prophet. Scripture says that Joshua was Moses' "assistant" (e.g., Ex. 24:13), which makes him sound something like an executive secretary for a businessperson or the offensive coordinator for a football team. A better translation is "servant." Joshua served

Moses, and by doing so he was well prepared when it came time to become Moses' successor.

A good example of a similar relationship in the history of the church comes from the life and ministry of John Knox. Knox is usually styled the father of the Scottish Reformation, but before John Knox there was a Reformer named George Wishart. Wishart traveled around Scotland preaching repentance and faith in Jesus Christ, especially from the book of Romans. John Knox served as his bodyguard, carrying a huge sword to protect him from the enemies of the gospel. In other words, Knox attended Wishart the way Elisha attended Elijah. So when Wishart was burned at the stake, Knox was ready to take his place as a minister. He had listened to Wishart preach so many times that along the way he had learned how to preach himself.

Jesus modeled this kind of mentorship by spending time with his disciples in conversation, ministry, table fellowship, and prayer. Robert Coleman writes:

> Having called his men, Jesus made a practice of being with them. This was the essence of his training program—just letting his disciples follow him. When one stops to think of it, this was an incredibly simple way of doing it. Jesus had no formal school, no seminaries, no outlined course of study, no periodic membership classes in which he enrolled his followers. None of these highly organized procedures considered so necessary today entered into his ministry. Amazing as it may seem, all Jesus did to teach these men his way was to draw them close to himself. He was his own school and curriculum.[4]

Now Christ has commanded his church to go out to the nations and make disciples (see Matt. 28:18–20). Disciple-making is God's pattern for growth in Christian life and ministry. To that end, those who are young in the faith learn how to follow Christ from those who are mature. Beginners in ministry learn from veterans. Behind every great leader of the Christian church there are one or more older and wiser believers.

Typically, discipleship turns out to be a two-way street. Obviously, it is a great blessing to the disciple to learn by example how to grow in grace. But

4. Robert E. Coleman, *The Master Plan of Evangelism*, rev. ed. (Grand Rapids: Revell, 1993), 41.

discipleship also strengthens the discipler. Every Christian has something to teach every other Christian, which means that even the newest believer can encourage an older disciple.

This was true for Elijah. When Elijah threw his cloak to Elisha, it was the beginning of the end of his ministry. His ministry was not over yet because God still had more prophetic work for him to do. But from this point on Elijah would recede and Elisha would grow from strength to strength. The old prophet had grown weary of serving the Lord, but the call of the young prophet would reinvigorate him. God had anointed Elisha to help Elijah do the Lord's work. A. W. Pink observes, "It has ever been a great consolation to godly ministers and their flocks to think that God will never lack instruments to conduct His work, that when *they* are removed *others* will be brought forward to carry on."[5]

When a young man once asked me to recommend someone to disciple him, I suggested the name of a mature Christian man who might have the time, the gifts, and the willingness to disciple him. Some months later the older man thanked me for helping to start their discipling relationship. They had been meeting weekly to talk about spiritual things and to pray together. "This has been such a blessing to me," the older man said. For his part, the younger man told me that their meetings were the highlight of his week. A discipling relationship had become a mutual blessing.

There is more to discipleship than one-on-one relationships, of course. Everything that happens in the church is part of our learning how to follow Jesus and not turn back. But there is an important place in the Christian life for discipleship through personal relationships.

The church needs more of these friendships. Young men often approach me about their need for regular discipleship from a mature man in Christ. They have a deep desire to learn how to follow Jesus. They are looking for godly men to take an interest in them, to counsel them, and to pray with them. Many young women also feel the need to receive spiritual counsel from women who are mature in Christ. Although some older men and women step forward to volunteer for discipleship, there always seem to be more people who need discipleship than there are people who are ready to give it.

5. A. W. Pink, *The Life of Elijah*, rev. ed. (Edinburgh: Banner of Truth, 1963), 246.

Discipleship ought to be happening throughout the whole church. Everyone who exercises a ministry ought to be a discipler. Sunday school teachers should help their assistants learn how to teach. Grandmothers should help young mothers learn how to mother. Deacons should help others learn how to serve. Everyone who is becoming mature in Christ should become an Elijah to some young Elisha.

I Have Decided to Follow Jesus

Some may ask whether following Christ and not turning back is really worth it. I asked myself the same question when I was about to enter pastoral ministry. At the time, I was considering the possibility of going to Romania, where an evangelical seminary wanted to establish a chair of Reformation and Puritan Theology. Eventually it became clear that the Lord was calling me to serve him at the Tenth Presbyterian Church in Philadelphia instead, but at the time my wife and I asked ourselves what we were willing to give up to follow Jesus Christ.

It seemed like we would have to leave everything behind: family, friends, home, basketball, tacos, chocolate chips . . . *everything*. I was reminded at the time of a question that Peter once asked Jesus—a question so poignant that we can almost feel the lump in Peter's throat when he asked it: "See, we have left everything and followed you. What then will we have?" (Matt. 19:27). Sometimes disciples get nervous. They remember how comfortable life was before they slaughtered their oxen, and they worry about what lies ahead. What will God have for us after we choose to follow him?

Well, what *will* God have for those who leave everything behind to follow Christ? I wrote out the answer Jesus gave to Peter and posted it in our kitchen:

Truly, I say to you, in the new world, when the Son of Man will sit on his glorious throne, you who have followed me will also sit on twelve thrones, judging the twelve tribes of Israel. And everyone who has left houses or brothers or sisters or father or mother or children or lands, for my name's sake, will receive a hundredfold and will inherit eternal life. (Matt. 19:28–29)

551

If this is what lies ahead for those who follow Jesus and never turn back, then I will join the chorus to sing the old spiritual that my father taught me when I was a little boy:

I have decided to follow Jesus,
I have decided to follow Jesus,
I have decided to follow Jesus,
No turning back, no turning back.

The world behind me, the cross before me,
The world behind me, the cross before me,
The world behind me, the cross before me,
No turning back, no turning back.

Though none go with me, I still will follow,
Though none go with me, I still will follow,
Though none go with me, I still will follow,
No turning back, no turning back.

As I sing this chorus, I remember the Savior that God has called me to follow. When Jesus knew that his calling included the cross, he did not turn back, but followed his Father's will all the way to Calvary. Now I am called to follow Jesus all the way and never turn back.

What about you? Will you turn back or follow on?

44

GOD UNLIMITED

1 Kings 20:1—43

And a man of God came near and said to the king of Israel,
"Thus says the LORD, 'Because the Syrians have said, "The LORD
is a god of the hills but he is not a god of the valleys," therefore I
will give all this great multitude into your hand, and you shall
know that I am the LORD.'" (1 Kings 20:28)

First Kings 20 is the story of two battles between Aram, led by King Ben-hadad, and Israel, led by King Ahab. The more things change, the more they stay the same, because Aram is the biblical name for Syria, and the Syrians and the Israelis have been perennial rivals since the dawn of their history.

AHAB VS. BEN-HADAD

Verses 1 through 12 describe the threats and taunts that led up to the war. From the beginning, Ben-hadad held the upper hand because he had the bigger army: "Ben-hadad the king of Syria gathered all his army together. Thirty-two kings were with him, and horses and chariots. And he went up and closed in on Samaria and fought against it" (1 Kings 20:1). Ben-hadad could sense that the battle was his to win, so he sent messengers to Israel's King Ahab with an ultimatum: "Thus says Ben-hadad, 'Your silver and your gold are mine; your best wives and children also are mine'" (1 Kings 20:2–3).

Not surprisingly, given his native timidity, Ahab capitulated: "As you say, my lord, O king, I am yours, and all that I have" (1 Kings 20:4). Spoken like a true coward! Ahab was not even the master of his own household; if he could not stand up to Queen Jezebel, how could he stand up to King Ben-hadad? Thus King Ahab was willing to become a lapdog to the Arameans.

Unfortunately, Ahab met Ben-hadad's demands so quickly that the Aramean decided to up the ante. His messengers returned to Israel with a fresh set of demands: "I sent to you, saying, 'Deliver to me your silver and your gold, your wives and your children.' Nevertheless I will send my servants to you tomorrow about this time, and they shall search your house and the houses of your servants and lay hands on whatever pleases you and take it away" (1 Kings 20:5–6). In making these demands, Ben-hadad was picking a fight with Ahab. Iain Provan describes his updated instructions as more extensive, more intrusive, and more immediate.[1] This time Ben-hadad was threatening to ransack Ahab's palace from room to room. He would confiscate his goods and take his family hostage, within the next twenty-four hours.

Such extortion was more than Ahab could bear. Coward though he was, he still had at least some shred of kingly dignity. First Ahab took counsel with his advisers: "Then the king of Israel called all the elders of the land and said, 'Mark, now, and see how this man is seeking trouble, for he sent to me for my wives and my children, and for my silver and my gold, and I did not refuse him.' And all the elders and all the people said to him, 'Do not listen or consent'" (1 Kings 20:7–8). On the basis of this advice, Ahab sent word to Ben-hadad, "Tell my lord the king, 'All that you first demanded of your servant I will do, but this thing I cannot do'" (1 Kings 20:9).

The king of Aram was a bully, and bullies always get mad when they do not get their way. So Ben-hadad responded with one of the great military boasts of the Old Testament. It sounds almost like something one of the brutes from the World Wrestling Federation might say: "The gods do so to me and more also, if the dust of Samaria shall suffice for handfuls for all the people who follow me" (1 Kings 20:10). In other words, Ben-hadad had

1. Iain W. Provan, *1 and 2 Kings*, New International Biblical Commentary (Peabody, MA: Hendrickson, 1995), 151–52.

so many soldiers and his victory would be so complete that there would not even be enough dust left to give each of his soldiers a souvenir from the Holy Land!

King Ahab knew how to wage psychological warfare, too. So he sent Ben-hadad a taunt of his own: "Let not him who straps on his armor boast himself like he who takes it off" (1 Kings 20:11). This is the ancient military version of "Don't count your chickens until they hatch." To give a contemporary analogy, it is one thing to boast when one is putting on his helmet and shoulder pads in the locker room, but another thing to give a postgame interview after scoring the winning touchdown in the fourth quarter.

Ben-hadad received Ahab's scornful message while he was having a few beers in his tent with his buddies. It made him so angry that there was nothing left to do but to settle things on the battlefield: "When Ben-hadad heard this message as he was drinking with the kings in the booths, he said to his men, 'Take your positions.' And they took their positions against the city" (1 Kings 20:12).

ON THE BATTLEFIELD

Verses 13 to 21 describe the battle of Samaria, which began with a promise that Ahab would be victorious: "And behold, a prophet came near to Ahab king of Israel and said, 'Thus says the LORD, Have you seen all this great multitude? Behold, I will give it into your hand this day, and you shall know that I am the LORD'" (1 Kings 20:13).

With these words, God promised that he would win the battle. This explains why Ahab used such unusual tactics. The prophet of the Lord told him to let his raw recruits lead his army into battle: "And Ahab said, 'By whom?' He said, 'Thus says the LORD, By the servants of the governors of the districts'" (1 Kings 20:14). Once these enlisted men had engaged the enemy, Ahab's only job would be to finish the battle. The English Standard Version has him asking, "Who shall begin the battle?" (1 Kings 20:14), but the word he uses ('sar) probably refers to mopping things up on the battlefield.[2]

This sounds for all the world like a losing military strategy. The prophet was telling Ahab to throw his most inexperienced soldiers into the heat of

2. Ibid., 155.

battle, holding his veterans back until the very end. The Lord commanded this to show that the victory belongs to God, and God alone.

God did win this battle. The Israelites caught Ben-hadad and his kings while they were still carousing in their tents: "Then [Ahab] mustered the servants of the governors of the districts, and they were 232. And after them he mustered all the people of Israel, seven thousand. And they went out at noon, while Ben-hadad was drinking himself drunk in the booths, he and the thirty-two kings who helped him" (1 Kings 20:15–16). While Ahab was taking counsel from the Lord, Ben-hadad was taking courage from strong drink. Apparently, the way that the lesser kings in his army "helped" him was to keep on handing him drinks until he was totally wasted.

Not surprisingly, when the king spoke he sounded more than a little drunk: "And Ben-hadad sent out scouts, and they reported to him, 'Men are coming out from Samaria.' He said, 'If they have come out for peace, take them alive. Or if they have come out for war, take them alive'" (1 Kings 20:17–18). One suspects that what he really intended to say was, "If they have come out for war, take them any way you can, dead or alive." After all, it is not easy to take an entire army of armed soldiers alive in battle! But in any case, the Arameans suffered heavy losses and were forced to flee: "So these went out of the city, the servants of the governors of the districts and the army that followed them. And each struck down his man. The Syrians fled, and Israel pursued them, but Ben-hadad king of Syria escaped on a horse with horsemen. And the king of Israel went out and struck the horses and chariots, and struck the Syrians with a great blow" (1 Kings 20:19–21). Thus Ahab was proved right: "Let not him who straps on his armor boast himself like he who takes it off" (1 Kings 20:11).

So much for round one. The only problem was that somehow Ben-hadad managed to escape on horseback. Israel's prophet warned Ahab that as a result there would be more trouble: "Come, strengthen yourself, and consider well what you have to do, for in the spring the king of Syria will come up against you" (1 Kings 20:22). For his own part, Ben-hadad did what most football coaches do when the season ends with a bitter defeat: he met with his coaching staff during the off-season to look for his opponents' weaknesses. His assistants thought they had found the soft spot in Israel's defenses:

Their gods are gods of the hills, and so they were stronger than we. But let us fight against them in the plain, and surely we shall be stronger than they. And do this: remove the kings, each from his post, and put commanders in their places, and muster an army like the army that you have lost, horse for horse, and chariot for chariot. Then we will fight against them in the plain, and surely we shall be stronger than they. (1 Kings 20:23–25)

This scouting report was based on what appeared to be good military strategy. The Arameans had more chariots and more soldiers, but this did not help them much up on the mountains. They needed to fight down in the valley where their men and machinery would have the home-field advantage. Yet the advice of Ben-hadad's officials also had spiritual implications. The Arameans did not believe in the living God, and thus they claimed that he had his limitations. The God of Israel was a God of the hills, they believed, but not of the plains. In other words, he was good for this but not for that; he could do this but he could not do that. Their attitude is aptly expressed in the title of a famous book by J. B. Phillips: *Your God Is Too Small*.[3] The Arameans believed that the God of Israel was everything that anyone ever wanted in a god, only less.

Our own culture is also dominated by belief in a limited deity. We too have become children of a lesser god. Some people limit God by saying that he is only a God of prosperity. Their god works for the good times, but not for the bad times. He is a god of the ups, but not the downs; a god of the victorious life, but not the cross. He seems close at hand in the day of joy, but vanishes in the day of suffering.

Others limit God by saying that he is only a God of love. Their god is a god of mercy, but not wrath. He is a god who forgives sins, but never punishes them. He offers compassion without justice.

Still others limit God by saying that religion is a private matter. Their god is for Sundays, but not for Mondays through Fridays, let alone Saturdays. He is a god to worship in the pew, but not to serve in the office. He is a god who lives in their hearts, supposedly, but not a god who rules the world.

Then there are those who limit God by saying that he is only a God for the life to come. They begin the Christian life by trusting in Christ for eternal salvation, but then they continue the Christian life in their own strength.

3. J. B. Phillips, *Your God Is Too Small* (New York: Macmillan, 1961).

They may be saved by grace, but they do not live by grace. They are like the friend who said to me, "I know how to trust God for eternity; I just don't know how to trust him for my day."

These are some of the limited deities of our times. They are gods of the hills, so to speak, but not gods of the valleys. If we follow any of these deities, we are children of a lesser god.

GOD VS. THE ARAMEANS

The point of making these contemporary comparisons is to show that 1 Kings 20 is not merely a story of ancient battles; it is really an experiment with the idea of a limited God. The Arameans show us what happens when someone takes a limited view of God out into battle and then encounters God face-to-face.

Ben-hadad listened to his advisers, and in the spring he "mustered the Syrians and went up to Aphek to fight against Israel" (1 Kings 20:26). Things did not look promising for the Israelites. They were heavy underdogs, like a local high school football team playing the Philadelphia Eagles: "And the people of Israel were mustered and were provisioned and went against them. The people of Israel encamped before them like two little flocks of goats, but the Syrians filled the country" (1 Kings 20:27).

The people of God were certainly outnumbered and probably overmatched. But they did have one thing going for them: they served the true and living God. They were not children of a lesser god, but served a deity who is unlimited in power. This was the theological basis for the encouragement that a man of God brought to the king of Israel: "Thus says the LORD, 'Because the Syrians have said, "The LORD is a god of the hills but he is not a god of the valleys," therefore I will give all this great multitude into your hand, and you shall know that I am the LORD'" (1 Kings 20:28).

The great spiritual lesson from 1 Kings 20 is that God is unlimited. He is not restricted by geography. He is God of the valleys as well as the hills. Nor is he limited in his power to save his people or destroy his enemies. He would deliver the vast army of the Arameans into the hands of his people, and then they would *know* that he is God.

The people of God should have known this already, of course. Everyone who lived in Israel during the days of Elijah knew from personal experience that the God of Israel is God of the hills. They had ascended the heights of Mount Carmel to see the prophet of God confront the prophets of Baal. There they had seen fire come from heaven to consume Elijah's sacrifice. They had knelt face-first on the mountainside to testify that "the LORD, he is God; the LORD, he is God" (1 Kings 18:39).

If the Israelites had listened carefully to Elijah, they would have also learned that the God of Israel is God of the valleys. At the beginning of 1 Kings 17, Elijah went to hide in the Cherith Ravine. God was there in that low-lying place. He gave Elijah food and water because he is God of the valleys as well as the hills. Afterward, he provided for his prophet in the town of Zarephath, because he is the God of Sidon as well as Israel.

The God of Elijah has no limitations. He is God unlimited. The true and living God is a God for this *and* for that. He is God of the hills *and* God of the valleys.

One Saturday morning during Christmas vacation in Colorado I lay sick in bed, violently ill with the stomach flu. As I was wondering how I would find the strength to preach the following morning, I feebly got out of bed, opened the shutters, and collapsed back into bed. Then, as I gazed out on the foothills of the Rocky Mountains, I remembered the words of the psalmist:

> I will lift up mine eyes unto the hills, from whence cometh my help.
> My help cometh from the LORD,
> > which made heaven and earth. (Ps. 121:1–2 KJV)

As I rejoiced in God as the Lord of the hills, I tried to remember whether the psalmist had anything to say about his rule over life's valleys. Then I recalled the words of Psalm 23:

> Yea, though I walk
> > through the valley of the shadow of death,
> I will fear no evil:
> > for thou art with me. (Ps. 23:4 KJV)

Every soldier in the Lord's army knows that God is unlimited. Over hill, over dale, God is with us on the trail.

The Arameans learned this, too, to their own dismay. They discovered firsthand that the God of Israel is God of the valleys: "And they encamped opposite one another seven days. Then on the seventh day the battle was joined. And the people of Israel struck down of the Syrians 100,000 foot soldiers in one day. And the rest fled into the city of Aphek, and the wall fell upon 27,000 men who were left" (1 Kings 20:29–30).

What terror it must have been for the Arameans to serve a lesser god, only to discover—too late!—that the living God is unlimited. In the end, anyone who denies the power of God, and then tries to defy him, will be destroyed.

GOD VS. YOUR PROBLEMS

For anyone who knows Jesus Christ in a personal way, the unlimited power of God gives hope for all the impossibilities of life.

An unlimited God gives hope for the work of missions. Other world religions seem like Ben-hadad and his thirty-two kings to us. How will the gospel ever penetrate the lands that lie under Islam? How will the good news about Jesus Christ ever reach the Hindus and Buddhists of Asia? How will salvation ever come to the skeptics of Europe and the hedonists of North America? These things could never happen if God had his limitations. But God is unlimited. He is the God of the valleys as well as the hills, of the East as well as the West, of the Arab as well as the Jew.

In 1996 a group of Christians began a two-thousand-mile, three-year trek from Europe to Jerusalem, by way of Turkey.[4] They called it the "Reconciliation Walk." The purpose of these pilgrims was to retrace the steps of the Crusaders and repent for the sins of the medieval church. Their declaration stated that the Crusaders "betrayed the name of Christ by conducting themselves in a manner contrary to his wishes and character." It went on to say that by lifting the cross as a symbol of warfare, the Crusaders "corrupted its true meaning of reconciliation, forgiveness, and selfless love."

The Reconciliation Walk received a warm response in the Muslim world. One leading imam in Europe received the letter of Christian repentance and forwarded copies to six hundred mosques under his jurisdiction. Some

4. *Christianity Today*, October 7, 1996, 90.

Muslims began to examine their own attitudes against Christians and Jews. As Christians we can pray that Muslims everywhere will go further and take their sins all the way to the cross of Christ. We pray that a new day for the gospel will dawn in the spiritual darkness of Islam. We pray that entire mosques will turn to faith in Christ. We offer these prayers in faith because we serve an unlimited God.

The unlimited power of God gives hope for victory over sin. At times we may feel defeated by the power of sin, either in our own lives or in the lives of people we love. Some people are in bondage to alcohol or some other drug. Others are in the grip of sexual sin. Still others are enslaved by an eating disorder or some other secret sin. Sometimes we feel defeated by sin and may even begin to doubt the victory of Jesus Christ. But God is God of the valleys as well as the hills. He is a God for sinners as well as saints. He is unlimited in his ability to break the power of reigning sin. We need only to admit our total inability to live a life of perfect purity in the sight of God and confess that we are sinners through and through. Then we need to throw ourselves upon the grace of the Holy Spirit and believe in the unlimited power of God, testifying that although apart from Christ we can do nothing (see John 15:5), we can do all things through him who strengthens us (Phil. 4:13).

The unlimited power of God gives hope for healing broken relationships. Sometimes a marriage or a parent-child relationship reaches the Humpty-Dumpty stage, when it seems like "all the king's horses and all the king's men couldn't put Humpty together again." But if we know Jesus Christ in a personal and saving way, then we are not dealing with all the king's horses and all the king's men; we are dealing with the King himself! He is unlimited—the King of the valley as well as the King of the hill. He is the God of the cross and the empty tomb, the God of resurrection life. Therefore, he is unlimited in his power to restore intimacy between a husband and wife or fellowship between a parent and child.

Once I received a letter from a woman describing how God was rebuilding her marriage. Some time before, I had heard that her marriage had reached Humpty-Dumpty status. This was a grief to me because of the suffering it had caused and also because it seemed like such a blow to the cause of Christ. But this letter was full of hope. The couple had realized their limitations. They had recognized that their own efforts to mend their own marriage on their own terms were bound to fail. They had begun to discover the unlimited power of God, who is Lord of the broken marriage as well as the perfect marriage.

The unlimited power of God gives hope for all the impossibilities of life. No matter how high the hill, God rules on that hill. No matter how deep the valley, God rules in that valley. He is God unlimited.

GOD VS. AHAB

God is also unlimited in his justice, which brings us to the surprise ending of 1 Kings 20. In the aftermath of the battle, Ben-hadad escaped from the Israelites and hid in an inner room in Aphek (1 Kings 20:30). The king feared for his very life, but his advisers said, "Behold now, we have heard that the kings of the house of Israel are merciful kings. Let us put sackcloth around our waists and ropes on our heads and go out to the king of Israel. Perhaps he will spare your life" (1 Kings 20:31).

Plans A and B had both failed, so Ben-hadad had no choice but to try plan C. His officials went to Ahab in all humility to plead for the life of their king: "So they tied sackcloth around their waists and put ropes on their heads and went to the king of Israel and said, 'Your servant Ben-hadad says, "Please, let me live"'" (1 Kings 20:32). When Ahab heard their request, he could hardly believe it: "Does he still live? He is my brother" (1 Kings 20:32). The Arameans were shrewd diplomats, so they knew how to use Ahab's choice of words to their own advantage: "Now the men were watching for a sign, and they quickly took it up from him and said, 'Yes, your *brother* Ben-hadad'" (1 Kings 20:33).

King Ahab had pity on Ben-hadad and made a deal with him: "Then Ben-hadad came out to him, and he caused him to come up into the chariot. And Ben-hadad said to him, 'The cities that my father took from your father I will restore, and you may establish bazaars for yourself in Damascus, as my father did in Samaria.' And Ahab said, 'I will let you go on these terms.' So he made a covenant with him and let him go" (1 Kings 20:33–34). Thus the two kings established a treaty for the return of the cities that the Syrians had taken from Israel and negotiated a favorable trade policy for Israelite goods in Damascus.

These were strokes of diplomatic genius. Ahab was shrewd to restore Israel's old cities and expand his kingdom. He was astute to open a Jewish bazaar in Syria. He was magnanimous to spare his enemy's life. Yet what he did failed to please the Lord.

Ben-hadad's life was forfeit because he had attacked God's people and mocked God's power. Ahab should not have spared him, therefore, but put him to the sword. Because God won the victory, this war was holy (see Deut. 20:16–18). The battle was supposed to be like Jericho, where all the plunder from battle was to be devoted to the Lord. But Ahab tried to turn God's blessing to his own advantage. He sacrificed a covenant principle for personal gain, treating the victory as his own achievement. Like Achan, who hid the spoils of battle under his tent (see Josh. 7), Ahab brought disgrace upon all Israel.

The story of how God exposed Ahab's sin and promised to judge it sends a tingle up one's spine:

> And a certain man of the sons of the prophets said to his fellow at the command of the LORD, "Strike me, please." But the man refused to strike him. Then he said to him, "Because you have not obeyed the voice of the LORD, behold, as soon as you have gone from me, a lion shall strike you down." And as soon as he had departed from him, a lion met him and struck him down. Then he found another man and said, "Strike me, please." And the man struck him— struck him and wounded him. So the prophet departed and waited for the king by the way, disguising himself with a bandage over his eyes. And as the king passed, he cried to the king and said, "Your servant went out into the midst of the battle, and behold, a soldier turned and brought a man to me and said, 'Guard this man; if by any means he is missing, your life shall be for his life, or else you shall pay a talent of silver.' And as your servant was busy here and there, he was gone." The king of Israel said to him, "So shall your judgment be; you yourself have decided it." Then he hurried to take the bandage away from his eyes, and the king of Israel recognized him as one of the prophets. And he said to him, "Thus says the LORD, 'Because you have let go out of your hand the man whom I had devoted to destruction, therefore your life shall be for his life, and your people for his people.'" And the king of Israel went to his house vexed and sullen and came to Samaria. (1 Kings 20:35–43)

The point of this strange story is that the law of God is to be followed to the letter. In the ancient Near East, prison guards were responsible for their prisoners, to the death. If a prisoner escaped, his guard had to pay with his own life. So it was with King Ahab. The Lord had handed Ben-hadad over to Ahab as a prisoner for judgment, but Ahab allowed him to escape, and thus his own life became forfeit. We may question the mysterious justice of God, but who can deny God's right to put his sworn enemies to death?

It is important to understand the theological error that led to Ahab's moral mistake: the king tried to limit God. His God was too small. Ahab did not understand that God is a God of justice as well as a God of mercy. Thus he took it upon himself to extend mercy where God intended to administer justice.

If the ending of this story catches us by surprise, perhaps this is because we believe in a limited deity ourselves. But the true and living God is unlimited. He is God of the valleys as well as the hills. This gives hope to all his friends for all the impossibilities of life. It also strikes fear into the hearts of all his enemies. As the Arameans discovered, and as Ahab learned to his own dismay, an unlimited God is not to be trifled with. But he is to be worshiped and obeyed!

45

SOUR GRAPES

1 Kings 21:1–29

And Ahab went into his house vexed and sullen because of what Naboth the Jezreelite had said to him, for he had said, "I will not give you the inheritance of my fathers." And he lay down on his bed and turned away his face and would eat no food.
(1 Kings 21:4)

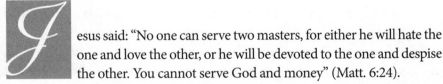esus said: "No one can serve two masters, for either he will hate the one and love the other, or he will be devoted to the one and despise the other. You cannot serve God and money" (Matt. 6:24).

When it came to God and money, King Ahab had made his choice. He had decided to make money his master. Since he loved money the most, he was devoted to serving it. The story told in 1 Kings 21 shows what happened as a result of this foolish choice.

"HE LAY ON HIS BED SULKING"

It began as nothing more than a whim. Ahab noticed that Naboth owned a nice piece of property: "Now Naboth the Jezreelite had a vineyard in Jezreel, beside the palace of Ahab king of Samaria" (1 Kings 21:1). The more Ahab thought about the property, the more he wanted it. To him it seemed like a vineyard fit for a king. So he started thinking about how he would develop the land if it belonged to him. However nice it was as a vineyard, it would be even nicer as a vegetable garden—especially a royal vegetable garden.

Eventually King Ahab made Naboth a business proposition: "Give me your vineyard, that I may have it for a vegetable garden, because it is near my house, and I will give you a better vineyard for it; or, if it seems good to you, I will give you its value in money" (1 Kings 21:2). It seemed like a fair offer, if not overly generous. In exchange for the vineyard near the palace, Ahab would give Naboth a better vineyard. Or, if Naboth wanted to get out of the grape business altogether, Ahab would pay him whatever the land was worth.

Naboth refused because he had decided to serve God rather than money: "But Naboth said to Ahab, 'The LORD forbid that I should give you the inheritance of my fathers'" (1 Kings 21:3). Naboth's refusal shows how well he knew his Bible. He knew that the children of Israel were not permitted to sell land to one another because their property belonged to the Lord. "The land shall not be sold in perpetuity," it said in the Law of Moses, "for the land is mine. For you are strangers and sojourners with me" (Lev. 25:23). Or again: "The inheritance of the people of Israel shall not be transferred from one tribe to another, for every one of the people of Israel shall hold on to the inheritance of the tribe of his fathers" (Num. 36:7).

Apparently, Naboth was one of the seven thousand men in Israel who had not bowed down to Baal (see 1 Kings 19:18). He did not fear the king, but served the King of kings. Thus he shows us how to serve God rather than money. Naboth invited the Lord to witness his business dealings. He refused to dishonor his ancestors by selling the family farm. He would not violate the law of God, even if it would be to his financial advantage. What was merely a luxury to Ahab was life itself to Naboth. God forbid that he should part with the inheritance of his fathers, a vineyard belonging to the Lord!

Naboth paid a heavy price for his obedience: he was put to death. Yet he received his true reward because he was not storing up treasure for himself on earth. Jesus said, "Where your treasure is, there your heart will be also" (Matt. 6:21). Naboth's treasure was in heaven, and so was his heart.

Ahab, on the other hand, *was* looking for earthly treasure. So he was desperately unhappy when his real estate venture began to slip through his fingers. The king just *had* to have that vineyard. When he did not get his way, he did what any two-year-old would do and went home to pout: "And Ahab went into his house vexed and sullen because of what Naboth the Jezreelite had said to him, for he had said, 'I will not give you the inheritance of my fathers.' And he lay down on his bed and turned away his face and would eat no food" (1 Kings 21:4).

Poor Ahab! He was in "one of his moods" again—the same mood he was in when God told him he had to pay for the life of Ben-hadad (1 Kings 20:43). On that occasion the king was sullen and angry with God; this time he was sulking about his fellow man. Then it was self-righteous indignation; now it was just sour grapes. F. B. Meyer treats Ahab with delicious sarcasm:

> In a room of the palace, Ahab, King of Israel, lies upon his couch, his face towards the wall, refusing to eat. What has taken place? Has disaster befallen the royal arms? Have the priests of Baal been again massacred? Is his royal consort dead? No; the soldiers are still flushed with their recent victories over Syria. The worship of Baal has quite recovered after the terrible disaster of Carmel; Jezebel—resolute, crafty, cruel, and beautiful—is now standing by his side, anxiously seeking the cause of this sadness.[1]

Even Queen Jezebel could tell that something was wrong, maybe because Ahab's sulking was worse than usual. The king would not even come to the dinner table. So Jezebel came and asked him what his problem was: "Why is your spirit so vexed that you eat no food?" (1 Kings 21:5).

Ahab's reply made it clear that he was a money-server. First, he told the queen what a juicy offer he had made. Then he conveniently (mis)quoted Naboth's refusal. He explained his actions by saying to Jezebel, "Because I spoke to Naboth the Jezreelite and said to him, 'Give me your vineyard for money, or else, if it please you, I will give you another vineyard for it.' And he answered, 'I will not give you *my* vineyard'" (1 Kings 21:6). Actually, this is not what Naboth said at all! In fact, his whole point was that the vineyard was not his to sell because it was *not* his to own. But Ahab missed the point entirely. His mistake is repeated whenever this episode is referred to as "the story of Naboth's vineyard." Because the vineyard was part of

---

1. F. B. Meyer, *Elijah* (Fort Washington, PA: Christian Literature Crusade, 1992), 135.

Naboth's inheritance in the Promised Land, it is more properly styled "the story of Naboth and God's vineyard."

Whatever we call it, the story shows what happens when a servant of money has dealings with a servant of God. It is impossible for someone like Ahab to understand the true motives of a man who serves the living God. People who love Jesus Christ often make decisions that are not based on physical comfort or financial gain, but simply on a deep trust in God. Sometimes our friends and family members will think that we are out of our minds. Of course they will! Our priorities will not make sense to them because we serve a different Master.

"She Wrote Letters in Ahab's Name"

If anyone knew how to serve money, it was Queen Jezebel, who would have made a formidable king in her own right: "Do you now govern Israel?" she asked her husband (1 Kings 21:7). In other words, "You weakling! Are you or are you not the king?" While Ahab was lying on his couch, Jezebel seized his leadership in the marriage and his authority over the kingdom. Immediately, she started issuing her orders: "Arise and eat bread and let your heart be cheerful; I will give you the vineyard of Naboth the Jezreelite" (1 Kings 21:7).

Jezebel was a more effective despot than Ahab. She was more decisive, more clever, more unscrupulous, and more deadly. First, she committed a forgery: "So she wrote letters in Ahab's name and sealed them with his seal, and she sent the letters to the elders and the leaders who lived with Naboth in his city" (1 Kings 21:8). Then the queen told a hypocritical lie: "And she wrote in the letters, 'Proclaim a fast, and set Naboth at the head of the people'" (1 Kings 21:9). Normally such a fast was called for the purpose of repentance, but Jezebel was no penitent. Finally, she committed perjury: "And set two worthless men opposite him, and let them bring a charge against him, saying, 'You have cursed God and the king.' Then take him out and stone him to death" (1 Kings 21:10). Forgery, hypocrisy, perjury . . . it all added up to murder.

Everything went according to Jezebel's conspiracy. The elders and nobles did the queen's dirty work for her: "And the men of his city, the elders and the leaders who lived in his city, did as Jezebel had sent word to them. As it was written in the letters that she had sent to them, they proclaimed a fast and set Naboth at the head of the people" (1 Kings 21:11–12). The conspirators also rounded up a couple of reprobates. These men had to be false witnesses because Naboth himself was true; there needed to be a pair of them because the law of God required two witnesses to establish the truth of an accusation.

On the day of the fast, as Naboth was seated in a place of honor, the lying scoundrels accused him of both blasphemy and treason: "And the two worthless men came in and sat opposite him. And the worthless men brought a charge against Naboth in the presence of the people, saying, 'Naboth cursed God and the king'" (1 Kings 21:13). Then, in keeping with the law of God for blasphemy (Deut. 13:10–11), "they took him outside the city and stoned him to death with stones. Then they sent to Jezebel, saying, 'Naboth has been stoned; he is dead'" (1 Kings 21:13–14). Even more heinously, Naboth's sons were also put to death (see 2 Kings 9:26). In this way, righteous Naboth was murdered by a ruthless queen—a small farmer crushed by a tyrant.

Naboth's murder is a warning against two great spiritual dangers. The first is the danger of coveting. According to the last of the Ten Commandments that God gave his people at Mount Sinai: "You shall not covet your neighbor's house; you shall not covet your neighbor's wife, or his male servant, or his female servant, or his ox, or his donkey, or anything that is your neighbor's" (Ex. 20:17). To which we might add, "You shall not covet your neighbor's vineyard."

Some people consider coveting to be a lesser sin. "Sure, it's in the Ten Commandments," they say, "but it's a lot less serious than theft. Or murder." Yet Ahab and Jezebel teach by their negative example that coveting is very wicked, especially since one sin usually leads to another. This Scripture says that "those who desire to be rich fall into temptation, into a snare, into many senseless and harmful desires that plunge people into ruin and destruction. For the love of money is a root of all kinds of evils" (1 Tim. 6:9–10). Coveting gives way to bitterness. Bitterness gives way to deception. Deception may give way to murder. Thus, what starts out as sour grapes sometimes ends in homicide.

Indeed, murder is the logical conclusion of coveting. If I cannot get what I want by any other means, I can always kill to get it. This is the logic worked out in the life of Ahab, just as it was worked out in the life of David. King

569

David coveted Bathsheba, and when all else failed, he was willing to kill Uriah to get her (see 2 Sam. 11–12).

Know that coveting is a very great sin. Child of God, living in this prosperous age, guard your heart against the love of money! Examine your heart and repent for any and every covetous desire.

Naboth's murder also warns of the danger of an ungodly marriage. Ahab made many bad decisions in his life, but possibly the worst choice he ever made was to make Jezebel his queen. Marriage does not leave us where we are, but moves us in a spiritual direction. Husbands and wives either make one another more godly or else make one another more worldly. By choosing to marry an ungodly woman, therefore, Ahab was choosing to become an ungodly man. From the day of their wedding, Jezebel always pushed him in the wrong spiritual direction. So we read that "there was none who sold himself to do what was evil in the sight of the LORD like Ahab, whom Jezebel his wife incited. He acted very abominably in going after idols, as the Amorites had done, whom the LORD cast out before the people of Israel" (1 Kings 21:25–26). The queen not only sinned herself, but also helped Ahab to sin.

What would a godly woman have done if she had found herself in Jezebel's stilettos? What would she have said to her husband? Perhaps she would have reminded him of the spiritual responsibilities of his calling. If she wanted him to behave like a king, then she should have read to him from the book of Deuteronomy, where God commanded his king "that his heart may not be lifted up above his brothers, and that he may not turn aside from the commandment, either to the right hand or to the left" (Deut. 17:20).

Or perhaps Jezebel could have warned her husband of the dangers of being discontent. A godly woman would have taught Ahab "the secret of facing plenty and hunger, abundance and need" (Phil. 4:12). She would have reminded him that "there is great gain in godliness with contentment" (1 Tim. 6:6). She would have said, "My dearest husband, don't you know that if you are not content with what you have already, you will never be content with what you think you want?"

Or perhaps Jezebel could have taken Ahab on a grand tour of his palace, showing him all the wealth in his treasury. She could have walked him through his kitchens to let him taste the fresh foods that were already his to eat. She could have taken him out into the gardens and suggested a better location for his precious vegetables. Then she could have said, "Don't you see, my beloved? We have more than everything we need!"

A godly queen would have found some way to turn her king's heart away from sin. She would have embraced her calling to serve as a means of sanctification in the life of her husband. Through prayer, through the Word of God, through her own godly example—but not through nagging—she would have encouraged her husband to serve God rather than money. This is the calling of every godly wife, and also every godly husband. Through prayer, through the Word of God, through his own godly example—but not through harsh criticism—he encourages his wife to serve God rather than money.

The royal couple of Samaria thus serves to warn us of the danger of an unspiritual marriage. If we are married, we are called to sanctify our spouse. This is true even if he or she is not yet a Christian. Love him, love her with the love of Christ and at the same time pray for his or her salvation.

If we are single, we should never court or marry an unbeliever, lest we end up like poor Ahab. Instead, we are called to seek out sanctifying friendships that are centered on Christ and blessed with the presence of the Holy Spirit. It is not enough simply to go to church on the Lord's Day and then to go about our business the rest of the week. If we are wise, we will nurture strong relationships and commit ourselves to intimate friendships with our brothers and sisters in Christ. This is one of many reasons why: so that when we are tempted to serve money, we will have a friend who loves us enough to talk some biblical sense into us.

"He Went Down to Take Possession"

Ahab did not have such a friend, or such a wife. As soon as Jezebel heard the news about Naboth's death, she ordered Ahab, "Arise, take possession of the vineyard of Naboth the Jezreelite, which he refused to give you for money, for Naboth is not alive, but dead" (1 Kings 21:15).

The king knew better than to ask any embarrassing questions about how Naboth died. Immediately, he went to confiscate Naboth's vineyard: "And as soon as Ahab heard that Naboth was dead, Ahab arose to go down to the vineyard of Naboth the Jezreelite, to take possession of it" (1 Kings 21:16). Two of his commanders rode with him in their chariots (see 2 Kings 9:25). Perhaps Ahab wanted some protection, or maybe he wanted to show off his hot new property to some of his friends. In any case, like a spoiled child on Christmas morning, Ahab finally had what he wanted. Everything had come full circle, and the story thus ends where it began: in the vineyard.

We can imagine King Ahab touring his vineyard, looking over the grape-vines and making plans for his new vegetable garden. "The beans will go in this plot," he might have said. "I will put the melons right here, and then a row of onions, and a few lentils . . ."

But before Ahab could eat his first grape or plant his first vegetable, he saw God's man Elijah standing among the vines. For while the king was claiming his new property,

> the word of the LORD came to Elijah the Tishbite, saying, "Arise, go down to meet Ahab king of Israel, who is in Samaria; behold, he is in the vineyard of Naboth, where he has gone to take possession. And you shall say to him, 'Thus says the LORD, "Have you killed and also taken possession?"' And you shall say to him, 'Thus says the LORD: "In the place where dogs licked up the blood of Naboth shall dogs lick your own blood."'" (1 Kings 21:17–19)

Truly, "the exulting of the wicked is short, and the joy of the godless but for a moment" (Job 20:5). Try to imagine the look of shock on Ahab's face when he saw Elijah. The king knew *exactly* why Elijah was there. His words betray the burden of a guilty conscience: "Have you found me, O my enemy?" (1 Kings 21:20). If God's prophet had become Ahab's enemy, it was only because Ahab had not made God his master.

With terrifying precision, God cut through all of Ahab's defenses. The legal system never would have been able to touch him. "Not guilty," he would say; "my seal may be on the letters, but the whole thing was a forgery." "Not guilty," he would say. "Jezebel made all the arrangements. She wrote the letters and directed the nobles. I have no knowledge of any wrongdoing." "Not guilty," he would say; "those two scoundrels in Jezreel were the ones who made the false accusations."

But God judges every deed that is done, whether open or secret. The condemnation his prophet gave to the king was just: "I have found you, because you have sold yourself to do what is evil in the sight of the LORD" (1 Kings 21:20). Here God used the second-person singular to hold Ahab personally responsible—not only for coveting, but also for murder. Naboth's blood was on his hands. God also used just the right verb ("sold") to describe

Ahab's ultimate allegiance. When Ahab made money his master, he was selling his soul.

Ahab's condemnation is a reminder to be scrupulously honest in all our business, and not simply to follow the guidelines of our employers and the letter of the law of the land. God's standards are much higher than the standards of our professions or the requirements of the government. We must not only do what is expected or what is legal; we must do what is *right*. This means being perfectly honest in all our motives, intentions, and transactions.

If we have not lived up to God's standards in business or finance, we are resting on a shaky foundation. We have made our money and turned our profit. And yet, like Ahab, even as we enjoy our possessions we are waiting for our sins to find us out.

God certainly found Ahab. He knew exactly where the king was and exactly what he was doing. So he sent Elijah to prophesy that the dogs would lick his blood, and also to pronounce this deadly curse:

> Behold, I will bring disaster upon you. I will utterly burn you up, and will cut off from Ahab every male, bond or free, in Israel. And I will make your house like the house of Jeroboam the son of Nebat, and like the house of Baasha the son of Ahijah, for the anger to which you have provoked me, and because you have made Israel to sin. . . . Anyone belonging to Ahab who dies in the city the dogs shall eat, and anyone of his who dies in the open country the birds of the heavens shall eat. (1 Kings 21:21–22, 24)

Ahab's ill-gotten vineyard turned out to be sour grapes, for in the end they cost him his entire kingdom. God also had something in store for Ahab's queen: "The dogs shall eat Jezebel within the walls of Jezreel" (1 Kings 21:23). Jezebel thought she was getting Ahab something for nothing, but in the end she would end up paying for Naboth's vineyard with her own life's blood.

All these prophecies were fulfilled. Jehu set out to kill every last member of Ahab's family. When Jezebel heard about it, she put on her mascara, fixed her hair, and waited by a window in the palace at Jezreel (see 2 Kings 9:30). She was dressed to kill, for when Jehu arrived he had Jezebel thrown from the window and trampled by horses. After eating a victory meal, he said:

> "See now to this cursed woman and bury her, for she is a king's daughter." But when they went to bury her, they found no more of her than the skull and

the feet and the palms of her hands. When they came back and told him, he said, "This is the word of the LORD, which he spoke by his servant Elijah the Tishbite, 'In the territory of Jezreel the dogs shall eat the flesh of Jezebel, and the corpse of Jezebel shall be as dung on the face of the field in the territory of Jezreel, so that no one can say, This is Jezebel.'" (2 Kings 9:34–37)

The queen did not even receive the honor of a decent burial, for God despised the head that plotted Naboth's death and the hands that signed his death warrant. Her death stands as a permanent warning to everyone who murders, covets, lies, cheats, or steals. It is a warning to everyone who serves money rather than God. God will judge people for these sins!

"HE WENT AROUND MEEKLY"

God's curse was so vivid and so harsh that even Ahab heeded its warning. Standing in Naboth's vineyard, he finally understood that when God says he will punish sin, he means it: "And when Ahab heard those words, he tore his clothes and put sackcloth on his flesh and fasted and lay in sackcloth and went about dejectedly" (1 Kings 21:27). Once again, the king refused to eat. But this time it was not because he was serving money. Almost unbelievably, it was because he had decided to serve God.

Ahab, repenting? It seems hard to believe. In fact, God himself could hardly believe it: "And the word of the LORD came to Elijah the Tishbite, saying, 'Have you seen how Ahab has humbled himself before me? Because he has humbled himself before me, I will not bring the disaster in his days; but in his son's days I will bring the disaster upon his house'" (1 Kings 21:28–29).

Many commentators have trouble believing that Ahab truly repented. They deny that the king really was sorry for his sins. They observe that he was making only the outward gestures of repentance. They point out that the king often went around meekly, but only because he was he easy to lead. They argue that if Ahab really wanted to repent, he needed to return the vineyard. Furthermore, in the very next chapter Ahab follows false prophets instead of seeking God's will. Thus, his actions amount to only a "Phony Repentance."[2]

Yet it is possible that Ahab really did repent of his sins. Maybe his penitent deeds came from a penitent heart. Perhaps Paul House has it right when he

2. Roger Ellsworth, *Standing for God: The Story of Elijah* (Edinburgh: Banner of Truth, 1994), 17.

concludes, "This time penitence overwhelms petulance, and [Ahab] does the right thing."[3]

What is the evidence for the genuineness of Ahab's repentance? First, God himself says (not once, but twice) that Ahab "humbled himself" (1 Kings 21:29). Furthermore, God granted Ahab a stay of execution. The proof of Ahab's repentance comes in God's mercy. Eventually Ahab died, of course. He was killed by a random arrow in the battle of Ramoth-gilead (1 Kings 22:34–35), and the dogs licked up his blood, just as Elijah prophesied (1 Kings 21:38). But Ahab's queen and Ahab's sons were not destroyed until after he died, as God also promised. The Lord had mercy on King Ahab because he repented of his sins.

Who can explain the mercy that God showed to Ahab? We can understand why God had mercy on Moses when he struck the rock in anger: he needed a man like Moses to lead his people out of Egypt. We can also understand why God had mercy on David when he slept with Bathsheba and murdered Uriah: he needed a man like David to establish the kingdom of Israel.

Turning to the New Testament, we can understand why God had mercy on Peter after he denied the Christ: he needed a man like Peter to establish his church. We can even understand why God had mercy on Paul when he persecuted the church of Jesus Christ: he needed a man like Paul to preach the gospel to the Gentiles.

But who can explain why God had mercy on Ahab? After all, Ahab "acted very abominably in going after idols" (1 Kings 21:26). He had no strengths to make up for his weaknesses, no virtues to outweigh his vices. Ahab was weak, gullible, and greedy. He was neither a great king, nor a powerful preacher, nor a stalwart missionary. Why should God have mercy on Ahab?

We cannot understand this any more than we can understand the mercy that God has shown to us in Jesus Christ, sending his only Son to die for our sins on the cross.

The mercy of God cannot be explained. But it can be received. King Ahab received free grace because he was a needy sinner. If we are sinners too—serving the wrong master, waiting in the vineyard for our sins to find us out—it is not too late for us to repent. It was not too late for Ahab, and if it was not too late for him, it is never too late for anyone!

---

3. Paul R. House, *1, 2 Kings*, New American Commentary (Nashville: Broadman & Holman, 1995), 233.

46

THY WORD IS TRUTH

1 Kings 22:1–53

And when he had come to the king, the king said to him,
"Micaiah, shall we go to Ramoth-gilead to battle, or shall we
refrain?" And he answered him, "Go up and triumph; the LORD
will give it into the hand of the king." But the king said to him,
"How many times shall I make you swear that you speak to me
nothing but the truth in the name of the LORD?" And he said, "I
saw all Israel scattered on the mountains, as sheep that have no
shepherd. And the LORD said, 'These have no master; let each
return to his home in peace.'" (1 Kings 22:15–17)

Sometimes a man's sins come back to haunt him. This always
seemed to happen to King Ahab. On one occasion, the Lord
God delivered Ben-hadad king of Syria into Ahab's hands to
be put to death (1 Kings 20:42). Ben-hadad deserved to die because he was
a sworn enemy of the God of Israel. But Ahab let him go free. In pursuit of
national security and economic prosperity, Ahab spared Ben-hadad's life
and made a treaty with Syria.

Eventually the day came when Ahab had to pay for his bargain with evil,
for when it comes to wicked kings, it is either kill or be killed. First Kings 22

tells the story of Ben-hadad's return, and we discover (surprise, surprise) that he has reneged on his deal. Ben-hadad had agreed to return all the cities he captured from the Israelites, but three years later he still had not forked over Ramoth-gilead, the disputed territory south of the Golan Heights.

Ahab was in his chambers, complaining to his officials, appealing to their patriotism: "For three years Syria and Israel continued without war. But in the third year Jehoshaphat the king of Judah came down to the king of Israel. And the king of Israel said to his servants, 'Do you know that Ramoth-gilead belongs to us, and we keep quiet and do not take it out of the hand of the king of Syria?'" (1 Kings 22:1–3). King Ahab was losing his bargain, and his sins were coming back to haunt him. So now he had a decision to make. What should he do about Ramoth-gilead? Should he recapture the city from the Arameans or let them keep it? Ahab wanted to know God's will for his life.

A MAN WHO SEEKS GOD'S COUNSEL

As the story unfolds, we witness three very different responses to God's will: Jehoshaphat seeks God's counsel; Ahab rejects God's word; Micaiah suffers for God's truth.

Jehoshaphat, the king of Judah, had come down from Jerusalem to Ahab's palace in Samaria for a summit meeting (1 Kings 22:2). The two kings were allies, so when Ahab asked, "Will you go with me to battle at Ramoth-gilead?" Jehoshaphat was willing to go. He said, "I am as you are, my people as your people, my horses as your horses" (1 Kings 22:4).

Then Jehoshaphat revealed the golden quality of his character as a man of God: "And Jehoshaphat said to the king of Israel, 'Inquire first for the word of the LORD'" (1 Kings 22:5). Jehoshaphat was brave enough to go into battle and loyal enough to help his brothers regain their land. But first things first: he wanted to know God's will.

Jehoshaphat's primary concern was to know and obey the word of God. This explains why he was not impressed when Ahab brought out four hundred prophets who said, "Go up, for the Lord will give it into the hand of the king" (1 Kings 22:6). Jehoshaphat knew better than to trust anyone other than a true prophet of God. So he asked for a second opinion. "Is there not here another prophet of the LORD of whom we may inquire?" (1 Kings 22:7).

Before he made any major decision, Jehoshaphat wanted to know what God had to say. Indeed, this was Jehoshaphat's usual practice. Whenever the king found himself at his wits' end, he sought God's wisdom. Later he would go with King Joram of Israel to fight against Moab: "And when they had made a circuitous march of seven days, there was no water for the army or for the animals that followed them" (2 Kings 3:9). The two nations were in dire straits, and the strain was beginning to take its toll on Ahab's son, Joram. Like father, like son: when things did not go Joram's way, he pouted, saying, "Alas! The LORD has called these three kings to give them into the hand of Moab" (2 Kings 3:10). But Jehoshaphat did not lose his cool, even when there was no water for his men or horses. He was a man of God, and a man of God first seeks the counsel of God. So Jehoshaphat said, "Is there no prophet of the LORD here, through whom we may inquire of the LORD?" (2 Kings 3:11).

These two episodes tell us almost everything we need to know about Jehoshaphat, who was a good and godly king. The epitaph the Bible gives him was well deserved:

> Jehoshaphat the son of Asa began to reign over Judah in the fourth year of Ahab king of Israel. Jehoshaphat was thirty-five years old when he began to reign, and he reigned twenty-five years in Jerusalem. His mother's name was Azubah the daughter of Shilhi. He walked in all the way of Asa his father. He did not turn aside from it, doing what was right in the sight of the LORD. Yet the high places were not taken away, and the people still sacrificed and made offerings on the high places. Jehoshaphat also made peace with the king of Israel.
>
> Now the rest of the acts of Jehoshaphat, and his might that he showed, and how he warred, are they not written in the Book of the Chronicles of the Kings of Judah? And from the land he exterminated the remnant of the male cult prostitutes who remained in the days of his father Asa.
>
> There was no king in Edom; a deputy was king. Jehoshaphat made ships of Tarshish to go to Ophir for gold, but they did not go, for the ships were wrecked at Ezion-geber. Then Ahaziah the son of Ahab said to Jehoshaphat, "Let my servants go with your servants in the ships," but Jehoshaphat was not willing. And Jehoshaphat slept with his fathers and was buried with his fathers in the city of David his father, and Jehoram his son reigned in his place. (1 Kings 22:41–50)

Jehoshaphat was not perfect. In fact, some of his failures are recorded in the Bible. But he walked with God and lived at peace with his brothers. He stood against sexual immorality and refused to compromise with other sinful practices. He proved to be a godly king because he sought God's counsel.

Every Christian should strive to become a son or a daughter of Jehoshaphat. A man like Jehoshaphat makes an excellent leader in society. He seeks God's wisdom for all his business. He makes an excellent husband and father. When he is faced with difficult domestic decisions about whom to marry, where to live, or how to raise his children, he says, "First, we will seek the counsel of the Lord." He does not rely on his own instincts, but rests on God's counsel.

A man like Jehoshaphat also makes an excellent leader in the church. When he is faced with difficult decisions about how to carry out ministry, spend the Lord's money, or confront sin, he asks, "What does God say about this in his Word?" He is the first man on a committee or in a Bible study to say, "Let's spend some time praying about this."

A woman who seeks God's counsel is a daughter of Jehoshaphat. She is a wise and godly woman. If she is single, she will know how to manage her personal affairs and make a major contribution to kingdom work. If she is married, she will know how to love her husband and care for her children. If she works outside the home, she will know how to work with her colleagues. If she serves in the church, she is a wise teacher or counselor. She knows the right Bible verse to apply to a difficult situation. She is often seen huddling with a friend in prayer after a worship service. She always seeks the counsel of the Lord.

How, specifically, do we seek God's counsel? Today we cannot consult the Lord's prophet in quite the way that Jehoshaphat did. God does not need any new prophets because he has already said everything that he needs to say through Jesus Christ (see Heb. 1:2). So where *do* we find God's will for our lives?

First and foremost, we learn God's will in the Bible. The Word of God gives principles for godly living. Indeed, the Scriptures of the Old and New Testaments teach us everything we need to know for life and godliness. Second, we receive guidance from Christian friends. One way God shows us his will is through the counsel of friends who know us and know the Scriptures. Finally, we discover God's will through prayer. Wisdom for life is part of the mysterious work of the Holy Spirit in the Christian's heart and mind.

Whenever we come to a major life decision, we should ask God for help. If necessary, we may need to keep on praying for wisdom about the same decision day after day and night after night. But seeking God's counsel through prayer is not limited to life's big decisions. Many Christians do not pray often enough about the little things of life. If prayer is our communication line to God, then too many of our message systems lie silent throughout the week. We pray at meals, and maybe at Bible study, but that is about all, when in fact we ought to be sending short messages to God all day long. One of our high privileges is to offer prayers every time we need God's help.

One fall I took my three-year-old son to a University of Pennsylvania football game at Philadelphia's Franklin Field. We were just about to catch a bus home after the game when suddenly I realized that his favorite baseball hat was missing. I was tempted to run back into the stadium before the hat disappeared forever. But as the tears were welling up in my son's eyes, we stopped by the gate and offered a short prayer that the Lord would help us find the hat. No doubt Jehoshaphat would have done the same thing and asked the Lord for help before he did anything else. In the event, our prayers were answered and we found the hat where it had fallen in the bleachers. Anyone who seeks God's help receives it—even for something as small as a baseball hat.

A MAN WHO REJECTS GOD'S WORD

Unfortunately, Ahab had his own way of making decisions, and it did not involve seeking God's counsel at all. Despite the fact that his former victories over the Syrians came through prophecy (see 1 Kings 20:13–14, 28), the king did not seek God's will for Ramoth-gilead. Worse still, when he finally did hear God's word, he rejected it. First Kings 22 is the sad, sad tale of a man who rejected God's word.

Because he always liked to get his own way, Ahab had surrounded himself with yes-men who would tell him whatever he wanted to hear. The Bible does not tell us who these prophets were. Perhaps they were prophets of Baal, although that seems unlikely because Elijah had eliminated so many of Baal's prophets at the Kishon River (1 Kings 18:40). Perhaps, then, they were prophets who had wandered away from God, men who had a form of godliness but denied its power (cf. 2 Tim. 3:5).

Whoever they were, Ahab's prophets were not servants of the Lord. So after they had said their piece, Jehoshaphat looked around impatiently and asked, "Is there not here another prophet of the LORD of whom we may inquire?" (1 Kings 22:7). Ahab's answer revealed his attitude about the word of God: "There is yet one man by whom we may inquire of the LORD, Micaiah the son of Imlah, but I hate him, for he never prophesies good concerning me, but evil" (1 Kings 22:8).

Shockingly, Ahab refused to hear what God had to say. He hated God's prophet because he hated bad news, even when it was the truth. What a fool! Ahab did not know that it is better to hear one painful truth from God's own mouth than a thousand cheerful lies from the lips of his enemies.

If only Ahab had heeded Jehoshaphat's quiet warning: "Let not the king say so." Instead, he tried to prove that Micaiah was out to get him. Ahab was more interested in proving that he was right than actually doing what was right. So "the king of Israel summoned an officer and said, 'Bring quickly Micaiah the son of Imlah'" (1 Kings 22:9).

When Micaiah arrived (more on this in a moment), he spoke with delicious sarcasm, mimicking the other prophets. Ahab asked, "Micaiah, shall we go to Ramoth-gilead to battle, or shall we refrain?" To which Micaiah replied, "Go up and triumph; the LORD will give it into the hand of the king" (1 Kings 22:15). Yet Ahab knew instinctively that this could not be the real message. Impatiently he asked, "How many times shall I make you swear that you speak to me nothing but the truth in the name of the LORD?" (1 Kings 22:16). If Ahab wanted the truth, well, here it was: "I saw all Israel scattered on the mountains, as sheep that have no shepherd. And the LORD said, 'These have no master; let each return to his home in peace'" (1 Kings 22:17). According to the word of God, Ahab would be killed in battle and his people would be left without a ruler, although they would return home in peace.

"I told you so!" Ahab said to Jehoshaphat. "See, I was right: Micaiah never has anything good to say!" As the Bible puts it, "Did I not tell you that he would not prophesy good concerning me, but evil?" (1 Kings 22:18).

Micaiah had a very good reason to prophesy something bad about Ahab; it was because *God* had something bad to say about him. There was also a reason why Ahab's prophets had prophesied something good about the king. It was because God himself had put "a lying spirit in the mouth of all his prophets" (1 Kings 22:22). Although God is not the author of deceit, he is sovereign over the false prophets as well as the true.

By this point Ahab had heard enough out of Micaiah. Although the prophet had spoken the word of God, the king rejected it. As far as he was concerned, majority rules, especially when the majority is in his favor by four hundred to one. So "the king of Israel said, 'Seize Micaiah, and take him back to Amon the governor of the city and to Joash the king's son.'" Then he issued the following royal decree: "Put this fellow in prison and feed him meager rations of bread and water, until I come in peace" (1 Kings 22:26–27). Ahab discovered the will of God for his life and then went out and did precisely what he wanted to do.

The last thing Micaiah said to Ahab as the king rode off to battle was, "If you return in peace, the LORD has not spoken by me." For the benefit of any bystanders, Micaiah also said, "Hear, all you peoples!" (1 Kings 22:28). As Ahab drew near to Ramoth-gilead, he began to feel a little uneasy about Micaiah's prophecy. Maybe God's word really was truth after all. Ahab knew that ancient warfare was like a game of chess: the main objective was to kill the king. This turned out to be Ben-hadad's strategy exactly, for he told his charioteers: "Fight with neither small nor great, but only with the king of Israel" (1 Kings 22:31). The more Ahab thought about all those Arameans hunting him down, the less he liked the idea of going to battle wearing his robe and crown. So he came up with a clever plan, or so it seemed: "So the king of Israel and Jehoshaphat the king of Judah went up to Ramoth-gilead. And the king of Israel said to Jehoshaphat, 'I will disguise myself and go into battle, but you wear your robes.' And the king of Israel disguised himself and went into battle" (1 Kings 22:29–30). It is not clear why King Jehoshaphat consented to this plan, but consent to it he did.

At first Ahab's plan worked to perfection. The Arameans mistook Jehoshaphat for Ahab. But right as they were about to kill him, Jehoshaphat cried out and they realized they had the wrong man: "And when the captains of the chariots saw Jehoshaphat, they said, 'It is surely the king of Israel.' So they turned to fight against him. And Jehoshaphat cried out. And when the captains of the chariots saw that it was not the king of Israel, they turned back from pursuing him" (1 Kings 22:32–33).

Nobody had a clue where Ahab was. Nevertheless, even in the fog of war, the word of God's judgment came true:

> But a certain man drew his bow at random and struck the king of Israel
> between the scale armor and the breastplate. Therefore he said to the driver of

his chariot, "Turn around and carry me out of the battle, for I am wounded." And the battle continued that day, and the king was propped up in his chariot facing the Syrians, until at evening he died. And the blood of the wound flowed into the bottom of the chariot. And about sunset a cry went through the army, "Every man to his city, and every man to his country!"

So the king died, and was brought to Samaria. And they buried the king in Samaria. And they washed the chariot by the pool of Samaria, and the dogs licked up his blood, and the prostitutes washed themselves in it, according to the word of the LORD that he had spoken. Now the rest of the acts of Ahab and all that he did, and the ivory house that he built and all the cities that he built, are they not written in the Book of the Chronicles of the Kings of Israel? So Ahab slept with his fathers, and Ahaziah his son reigned in his place. (1 Kings 22:34–40)

This is what happens to someone who rejects God's word and follows his own plans instead, in contradiction to God's will. Notice the sovereignty (and the irony) of God's justice! In Syria they called it a lucky shot, but in Israel people knew better. Ahab was able to fool the Arameans, but he was not able to fool God. The bow drawn at random was released according to divine providence. Once God had determined that Ahab would die, he might as well have ridden into battle with a huge target painted on his chest. The arrow of divine judgment always finds its mark!

Ahab's unlucky death (as it must have seemed to the king himself) vindicated the word of God. The Lord truly had spoken through his prophet when he promised that it would be Ahab's life for Ben-hadad's (see 1 Kings 20:42). The Lord truly had spoken through the prophet Elijah when he promised that the dogs would lick up Ahab's blood (1 Kings 21:19). The Lord truly had spoken through the prophet Micaiah when he promised that Ahab would not return home safely from battle (1 Kings 22:28). Just as Micaiah promised (see 1 Kings 22:17), the sheep of Israel were left without a shepherd: "And about sunset a cry went through the army, 'Every man to his city, and every man to his country!'" (1 Kings 22:36).

Ahab's son did not fare much better, for he too rejected God's word and failed to serve as a faithful shepherd. His epitaph confirms the sad legacy of Ahab's apostasy:

Ahaziah the son of Ahab began to reign over Israel in Samaria in the seventeenth year of Jehoshaphat king of Judah, and he reigned two years over

Israel. He did what was evil in the sight of the LORD and walked in the way of his father and in the way of his mother and in the way of Jeroboam the son of Nebat, who made Israel to sin. He served Baal and worshiped him and provoked the LORD, the God of Israel, to anger in every way that his father had done. (1 Kings 22:51–53)

The lesson is easily drawn: do not reject the Word of God; do not resist his will. The Scripture says that we need to confess our sins and believe in Jesus Christ. If we know this, we should not delay, but ask Jesus to be our Savior and our Lord. If we do know Christ, we should not continue to sin against our better judgment. Having a sexual relationship outside of marriage, carrying a grudge, and speaking falsehood are sins against the holiness of God. If we know that these things are contrary to the will of God, then we should not continue to have immoral sex, or carry that grudge, or live a lie. We should not allow ourselves even a small lust or petty resentment. If we know the will of God about such things and then do as we please, we are as foolish as Ahab!

We must be careful not to let Ahab's epitaph become our own! Paul House offers an apt summary of the reason for the king's demise: "Ultimately, he is judged as a man who heard from God yet did not act on the revelation he received."[1] By the grace of God, may it not be said of us that we heard from God but did not believe in him or live for him.

A MAN WHO SUFFERS FOR GOD'S TRUTH

We are called instead to become men and women like the prophet Micaiah. When Micaiah heard the word of God, he believed it and obeyed it. He refused to do anything else except to trust in the word of God. He was even bold enough to suffer for its truth.

When Micaiah first was brought before Ahab's court, it was a grand spectacle: "Now the king of Israel and Jehoshaphat the king of Judah were sitting on their thrones, arrayed in their robes, at the threshing floor at the entrance of the gate of Samaria, and all the prophets were prophesying before them" (1 Kings 22:10).

The whole scene must have been very impressive. The kings were there in all their regalia, and the false prophets with all their predictions. In fact,

---

1. Paul R. House, *1, 2 Kings*, New American Commentary (Nashville: Broadman & Holman, 1995), 240.

one of the prophets had even prepared some visual aids: "And Zedekiah the son of Chenaanah made for himself horns of iron and said, 'Thus says the LORD, "With these you shall push the Syrians until they are destroyed"'" (1 Kings 22:11). It is easy to imagine Zedekiah prancing about, putting the horns on his head and punctuating his prophecy by playfully jabbing at the other prophets. All of them were flattering Ahab with the same prediction: "Go up to Ramoth-gilead and triumph; the LORD will give it into the hand of the king" (1 Kings 22:12).

Micaiah hardly stood a chance. In fact, his escort felt so sorry for him that he quietly tried to give the prophet a little friendly inside information: "Behold, the words of the prophets with one accord are favorable to the king. Let your word be like the word of one of them, and speak favorably" (1 Kings 22:13). But Micaiah was not interested in the scuttlebutt from the palace. He was not impressed by the finery of the kings or intimidated by the babbling of false prophets, no matter how many of them there were. All he cared about was faithfully communicating what God wanted him to say: "As the LORD lives, what the LORD says to me, that I will speak" (1 Kings 22:14).

Micaiah was convinced that God's word is truth because he had spoken with God for himself. He was not overawed by King Ahab's court because he had already visited the throne room of the King of kings: "I saw the LORD sitting on his throne, and all the host of heaven standing beside him on his right hand and on his left" (1 Kings 22:19). What a wonder it must have been for Micaiah to behold the majestic splendor of Almighty God! But this was the unique privilege of God's true prophet: he had a personal audience with the Most High God. The prophet Isaiah saw the same thing that Micaiah saw:

In the year that King Uzziah died I saw the Lord sitting upon a throne, high and lifted up; and the train of his robe filled the temple. Above him stood the seraphim. Each had six wings: with two he covered his face, and with two he covered his feet, and with two he flew. And one called to another and said:

"Holy, holy, holy is the LORD of hosts;
the whole earth is full of his glory!"

And the foundations of the thresholds shook at the voice of him who called, and the house was filled with smoke. (Isa. 6:1–4)

The prophets who witnessed such wonders did not have any doubts about the truth of God's word. When Ahab commanded Micaiah to speak "nothing but the truth in the name of the LORD" (1 Kings 22:16), he could do no other. Micaiah had truth to give—truth from God's own lips. Here is what he said that he had witnessed in the throne room of God:

> The LORD said, "Who will entice Ahab, that he may go up and fall at Ramoth-gilead?" And one said one thing, and another said another. Then a spirit came forward and stood before the LORD, saying, "I will entice him." And the LORD said to him, "By what means?" And he said, "I will go out, and will be a lying spirit in the mouth of all his prophets." And he said, "You are to entice him, and you shall succeed; go out and do so." Now therefore behold, the LORD has put a lying spirit in the mouth of all these your prophets; the LORD has declared disaster for you. (1 Kings 22:20–23)

What Micaiah saw in heaven may seem strange to us as people who have never witnessed such wonders. But the important thing is that he testified to the truth of what he witnessed. The prophet suffered greatly for his proclamation of God's truth. He was imprisoned by the king and given nothing but prison rations. He was also abused by the king's prophets: "Then Zedekiah the son of Chenaanah came near and struck Micaiah on the cheek and said, 'How did the Spirit of the LORD go from me to speak to you?'" (1 Kings 22:24).

Yet even when he was provoked, Micaiah did not retaliate or defend his ministry. Knowing the truth of God's word, he was able to rest in that truth and wait for God to vindicate him. Micaiah knew that the only way to tell the true prophet from the false is to wait and see what happens (see Deut. 19:21–22). God's word always proves to be true in the end. So he said to Zedekiah, "Behold, you shall see on that day when you go into an inner chamber to hide yourself" (1 Kings 22:25). In other words, Zedekiah would know that Micaiah had spoken the truth on the day of God's judgment, when he would have to hide in a closet from his enemies, for fear of his very life.

By suffering for God's truth, Micaiah gives us a clear glimpse of the salvation that God provided for us in Jesus Christ. The sufferings of the Old Testament prophets always teach us something about the sufferings of the great Prophet, Jesus Christ. When Stephen preached to the Jews on the day of his martyrdom, he asked, "Which of the prophets did your fathers not persecute? And they killed those who announced beforehand the coming of the Righteous One, whom you have now betrayed and murdered, you who received the law as delivered by angels and did not keep it" (Acts 7:52–53).

Like Micaiah and the other true prophets of God, Jesus was opposed by the false prophets of Israel. Like Micaiah, he insisted on saying only what God the Father told him to say: "The words that I say to you I do not speak on my own authority, but the Father who dwells in me does his works" (John 14:10). Like Micaiah, Jesus was accused of being a false prophet and then falsely imprisoned. Like Micaiah, he was also slapped across the face. Indeed, when Zedekiah struck Micaiah, this foreshadowed what the Messiah would suffer for God's truth. On the night of his arrest, "the men who were holding Jesus in custody were mocking him as they beat him. They also blindfolded him and kept asking him, 'Prophesy! Who is it that struck you?' And they said many other things against him, blaspheming him" (Luke 22:63–65).

People abused Jesus the way they abused Micaiah, mocking his ability to prophesy. But like Micaiah, Jesus did not retaliate or defend his ministry. He simply rested in the truth of God's word. He was willing to suffer for God's truth, so that he could accomplish the salvation of his people by dying on the cross for our sins.

Now we are called to stand for God's truth. Are we also willing to suffer for it? The apostle Paul was. When he was brought before the religious leaders of his day, Paul looked them straight in the eye and said, "Brothers, I have lived my life before God in all good conscience up to this day." But Paul suffered for this testimony, because "the high priest Ananias commanded those who stood by him to strike him on the mouth" (Acts 23:1–2).

God's children are willing to suffer such insults and injuries for the sake of God's Word, even unto death. We can only say what the Lord tells us to say and do what the Lord tells us to do, for we know that God's Word is truth.

INDEX OF SCRIPTURE

Index of Subjects and Names

DATE DUE

MY 2 1 '12			
MY 2 9 '14			
MAR 1 8 2020			